BALTIC SEA

Vistula

Oder

Elbe

TRIBUTARY SLAVIC STATES

OSTMARK

Danube

CARPATHIAN MOUNTAINS

Dniester

Dnieper

AVARS

Drave

I A

FRIULI

ice

nna

PAL
ATES

APENNINES

SPOLETO

Monte Cassino

aples

BENEVENTO

APULIA

CALABRIA

BYZANTINE

CILY

ADRIATIC SEA

Danube

BALKAN MOUNTAINS

Constantinople

BLACK SEA

AEGEAN SEA

EMPIRE

SEA

CRETE

CYPRUS

EUROPE c. 814

*EUROPE
IN THE
MIDDLE
AGES*

EUROPE IN THE MIDDLE AGES

SECOND EDITION

ROBERT S. HOYT
UNIVERSITY OF MINNESOTA

HARCOURT, BRACE & WORLD, INC.

NEW YORK   CHICAGO   SAN FRANCISCO   ATLANTA

Library of Congress Catalog Card Number: 66–16060

Printed in the United States of America

Maps by Jean Paul Tremblay.

To STUART, JANE, AND MARTHA

Preface

Any author of a volume of such large scope as this one must feel immensely indebted to scores of other writers. Their more specialized essays and monographs provide most of the content and suggest many of the leading ideas that are incorporated into a general work of this sort. One of the reasons that writing a general history of the Middle Ages, or making an extensive study of the Middle Ages, is so enjoyable is that the great majority of these more specialized works are so interesting and rewarding. If my introductory survey of the whole period will encourage the reader of this volume to read further, and to make the literature both of and about the Middle Ages a permanent interest, then my purpose in writing this book will have been achieved.

The basic organization of this book is provided by a narrative of political events. For so long and varied a period of history no other organization of a survey has seemed more valuable. However, to the extent that all books on the same subject are inevitably different, this one differs from other surveys of medieval history in devoting relatively more space to medieval civilization and culture. Many names and factual details—important or interesting for a more intensive study of one or another aspect of the Middle Ages—have been jettisoned in favor of a more extensive treatment of the major features and characteristics of the origin, growth, culmination, and decline of a distinctive civilization, a civilization on which our modern Western civilization is directly based. Illustrations and maps have been selected and drawn for the specific purpose of illustrating remarks in the text, and hence the maps are intended to show only the location of place names, geographical areas, or territories actually referred to in the text. The Guide to Further Reading, at the end of this volume, is necessarily brief. Many fine volumes have been omitted for lack of space or because equally good books are available which provide more complete bibliographical guidance; lack of space has also imposed the necessity of omitting reference to the great number of interesting and useful articles published in the several learned journals that are devoted to, or devote space to, medieval history. To these articles in learned journals the historian today is almost as much indebted as he is to works that appear in book form.

More specifically I would like to record my grateful indebtedness to the teachers of medieval history who introduced me to the subject and who led me into the special fields in which they are truly masters: Professors George La Piana, Charles H. McIlwain, and Charles H. Taylor. It would be an impossible task to distinguish just which or how many of my views of the Middle Ages owe their origin to these three scholars, as they were expressed in lecture or in conversation over a period of eighteen years.

Still more specifically, I would like to thank and here record my gratitude to Professor Joseph R. Strayer of Princeton University, who has read and given me the benefit of his criticism of the whole manuscript on which this book is based. My cordial thanks are extended to Father Robert J. Welch, Professor of the School of Religion, the State University of Iowa, for having read the sections on ecclesiastical and cultural history, and to Professor Herbert Heaton, Chairman of the Department of History, University of Minnesota, for having read the sections on economic history in manuscript. To each I am indebted for helpful suggestions and useful criticism. My thanks are also due to the staffs of the libraries of the State University of Iowa and of the University of Minnesota for their cooperation and occasional forbearance, and to Miss Louise P. Olsen, secretary of the Department of History, University of Minnesota, for her assistance in retyping parts of the manuscript during a late stage of that work.

It is my final and pleasant duty to record here the help received from my wife and children in writing this book. My wife has read and reread the entire manuscript, with many a change and improvement resulting therefrom; both she and my son, Stuart, and my daughter, Jane, have proofread the whole; and my wife has done the major work on the index.

R. S. H.

St. Paul, February, 1957.

*   *   *   *   *   *   *

The second edition incorporates a number of changes throughout the book, rather than any major reorganization, notably in the sections on the coronation of Charlemagne, Roman law and canon law, military tactics and warfare, the Sicilian Vespers, the papacy at Avignon, and the beginning of the Great Schism. In addition, various passages have been rewritten, and some nonessential names and details have been omitted.

For helpful criticism of the text I am indebted to far more people than could be mentioned by name in a preface—colleagues and students to whom it is a pleasure to express my gratitude. For more detailed and extensive suggestions I am especially in debt to four colleagues, to each of whom my grateful thanks: Professors C. Warren Hollister of The University of California, Santa Barbara; Stephan Kuttner of Yale University; Leslie J. MacFarlane of The University of Aberdeen; and Charles T. Wood of Dartmouth College. Finally, I am grateful to my wife and to my daughter, Martha, for their help in the work of revision and reading proofs.

R. S. H.

St. Paul, January, 1966.

Contents

PART THREE

POLITICAL, ECONOMIC, AND CULTURAL REVIVAL
OF THE TWELFTH CENTURY

PART FOUR

THE HIGH MIDDLE AGES: MEDIEVAL CULTURE

PART FIVE

THE RISE OF THE WESTERN MONARCHIES AND THE DECLINE OF THE MEDIEVAL PAPACY AND EMPIRE

PART SIX

THE DECLINE OF MEDIEVAL CIVILIZATION

Maps

EUROPE
IN THE
MIDDLE
AGES

Introduction

1 THE MIDDLE AGES IN THE HISTORY OF WESTERN CIVILIZATION

The term "Middle Ages" is used to designate the period of history following antiquity and preceding modern times. The expression is purely conventional, because historians cannot agree when the Middle Ages began and ended, or else they are agreed that the beginning and end of the period cannot be assigned to specific dates. The beginning of the Middle Ages has been placed as early as the death of the Roman emperor Marcus Aurelius in 180 A.D. or the proclamation of Diocletian as emperor in 284, and as late as the coronation of Charlemagne in 800 or even the eleventh century. The end of the Middle Ages has been placed as early as the mid-thirteenth century and as late as the arbitrary and uneventful year of 1500. The only century unanimously accepted as being medieval is the twelfth. This is appropriate enough, for the twelfth century was the age in which medieval civilization displayed its most impressive and creative achievements. It was an age when antiquity was no longer a shadow cast upon centuries of decline but rather a heritage finally assimilated as a basis on which to build, and it was also an age in which institutions, ideas, and values that appear full grown only in modern times had not yet taken definite shape.

In the very medieval twelfth century educated men were divided, as they are today, in their views of the past. Of course all men thought of themselves as living in "modern times," but only a few sensed any contrast between antiquity and their own age. In religious terms this was sometimes expressed as the difference between "the darkness of error" in pagan antiquity and "the dawn of true light" that ushered in the Christian era. The contrast was also expressed, occasionally, in terms of the superiority of the ancients. This view is illustrated by the famous phrase of the popular teacher Bernard of Chartres, who characterized the men of his own time as "like dwarfs seated on the shoulders of [the] giants" of antiquity. The majority, however, thought of their own world as being essentially similar to, or continuous with, Roman antiquity. Literature in the twelfth century reveals little awareness of any difference between past and present. In contemporary romances concerned with "the matter of Troy," for example, Achilles and Hector behave just like valiant feudal vassals. Historians normally treated the period from the Incarnation to their own times as a single age, although they might divide the larger whole into parts beginning or terminating with epoch-making events like the conversion of Constantine or the coronation of Charlemagne.

In the twelfth century the idea that history could be divided into distinct periods was a commonplace of historical thought. It was inherited from the Fathers of the Church who had, in turn, adapted for Christian purposes the earlier idea of endlessly repeating cycles corresponding either with ages called golden, silver, bronze, and iron, or with ages represented by the four universal monarchies. This pattern of history had to be modified because it was impossible to fit into its cyclical scheme the great and unique events of the Christian faith, especially the Incarnation which was central to the nature of the universe and the destiny of man. Christian thinkers like Jerome and Augustine straightened out the cyclical view of history into a unilinear pattern of successive ages, and provided medieval historians with their basic patterns of periodization. Jerome, whose work on chronology was important, divided all history into ages corresponding with the predominance of the four universal monarchies, which in the Middle Ages were understood to be Assyria, Persia, Greece, and Rome. Augustine, the most influential philosopher of history in all Christian thought, divided history into six ages beginning with Adam, the Flood, Abraham, David, the Exile, and the birth of Christ. Since Rome was considered to have begun its predominance with Augustus, neither of these systems of periodization made any real distinction between antiquity and the Middle Ages. For the medieval mind, all the centuries following the Incarnation constituted a single major period of history.

The Italian humanists were the first to be aware that there was a meaningful break between antiquity and the period which followed. In the fourteenth century, Petrarch contrasted what he called "ancient histories" and "modern histories," and drew the line between them at the conversion of Constantine. In his admiration for the belles-lettres and political virtue of ancient Rome, he characterized "modern history," which extended down to his own days, as an age of "darkness" in which the grandeur that was Rome had been debilitated and debased by barbarians. Another humanist, Flavio Biondo, in the fifteenth century drew a sharp line between antiquity and the succeeding age, which he contended had begun with the sack of Rome in 410. Other early humanists were aware that in the arts and letters there had been a rebirth of the standards and values of antiquity, but none of them applied to general history this idea of a renaissance (which implies three periods in history—greatness, decline, and revival). They looked upon their political development as essentially the achievement of liberty, and they thought of this as a struggle which began several centuries after antiquity and an equally long time before the rebirth of arts and letters.

Protestant historians in the sixteenth century widened the concept of a renaissance by portraying the ascendancy of the papacy, in the period following Constantine's conversion, as part of the decline of the Roman Empire. This decline, they contended, did not end until the restoration of the primitive evangelical Church by Luther. Thus, both humanists and Protestant writers implied, although neither actually stated, a threefold division of history of whose second stage they did not approve.

The concept of a tripartite periodization was first applied to general history by historians in the second half of the seventeenth century. The Renaissance and Reformation lay far enough in the past so that three distinct periods of time could be distinguished. No longer was the intermediate period simply the era separating themselves from antiquity; it was a period which itself had ended in the past. The term Middle Ages, as applied to general history in this sense of one of three definite periods of time, derives from the title of a textbook published in 1688 by a Dutch teacher of history, Cellarius (Christoph Keller), entitled *History of the Middle Age from the Times of Constantine the Great to the Capture of Constantinople by the Turks*. He had already published a textbook on ancient history, and his work on the Middle Ages was followed by a textbook on modern history (*historia nova*). Although the term Middle Ages soon became universally accepted, Cellarius' chronological limits (c.330–1453) were not invariably followed, even by himself, in later works.

This idea that modern times were separated from antiquity by the Middle Ages, which were a period of darkness intellectually and culturally and a period of barbarism politically and socially, was strongly reinforced by the historians of the eighteenth century. The greatest of them all, Edward Gibbon, summed up the Middle Ages as "the greatest, perhaps, and most awful scene in the history of mankind." What made the period great and awful for Gibbon and others was its catastrophic effect upon the progress of civilization which they conceived of as beginning in antiquity and, after the Middle Ages, resuming in modern times. History, for the eighteenth-century historian, was a grand spectacle replete with dramatic conflicts, successes, and failures which recorded the inevitable triumph of reason. This oversimplified and biased view was counteracted early in the nineteenth century by a romantic reaction which, for the first time since the age of humanism, assigned to the Middle Ages a positive and constructive role in the formation of European civilization. This reaction was owing partly to the advance of historical scholarship and related disciplines such as linguistics and philology; partly to the growth of modern nationalism, which discovered that the origins of the modern national state could be traced back only as far as the Middle Ages; and partly to disillusionment with the preceding age of reason, which provided no nourishment for man's natural interest in his past.

Since the middle of the nineteenth century historical scholarship has steadily become more objective and critical—by some historians called "scientific." Rarely today can any scholarly historical work be classified as part of the traditional rationalist condemnation of, or the romantic adulation of, the Middle Ages. Neither Voltaire, who despised the Middle Ages, nor Sir Walter Scott, whose novels romanticized them with bold knights and fair ladies, has any disciples today. And yet, in the popular view—as depicted in newspaper editorials and best-selling "historical novels"—medieval civilization remains so much the object of ignorance that Hitler could be characterized as a "feudal dictator," which is simply a contradiction in terms. This misunderstanding of the Middle Ages is regrettable, but it is the concern of educators rather than historians.

For historical scholarship today a more vital and basic problem is the validity of the conventional tripartite pattern of periods of history. The ancient, medieval, and modern scheme may well appear unrealistic to the historian, who can easily show that there are more significant differences between the twentieth century and the sixteenth than there are between the seventeenth and fifteenth centuries. But to the medieval historian the main point is that the Middle Ages was a distinctive period, marked off from antiquity as it was from the age that followed. Between the Renaissance and the French Revolution a variety of institutions and leading ideas developed, similar to those of antiquity but radically different from those of the Middle Ages. German historians have coined the term "antique-modern" to characterize such concepts as sovereignty, the state, or public law as distinct from private law, all of which were lacking in medieval thought, as they were partially absent from the institutional organization of medieval society. Other antique-modern ideas or values come readily to mind, such as the canons of artistic and literary taste which we call classical. These canons were not unknown in the Middle Ages, nor wholly rejected; but the medieval artist's indifference toward classical models was the reason for the humanist epithet "Gothic," meaning barbarous, as applied to medieval architecture and decorative arts. Perhaps the most familiar contrast between the antique-modern and medieval civilizations is summed up in the famous phrase of the nineteenth-century Swiss historian Burckhardt: "the discovery of the world and of man." Burckhardt knew that "at the height of the Middle Ages, a genuine, hearty enjoyment of the external world" existed, and that there was a developed interest in human nature as well as in the supernatural. Later popularizers of Burckhardt's ideas exaggerated his suggested contrast to the point where the medieval mind has been portrayed as totally oblivious to the beauty of nature and the mundane activities of man, in its absorption with religious and ascetic values. Hence arises the kind of nonsense about the Renaissance "freeing the human spirit" or "breaking the shackles" which allegedly constricted human endeavor in the Middle Ages.

The tendency of historical scholarship in the past fifty years has been to push back into the Middle Ages the signs of "awakening" which were once thought to characterize the Renaissance, and to emphasize the continuity of medieval institutions and values well down into modern times. The whole concept of a "renaissance" has even been called in question. On the other hand, we may reject the interpretation of the Renaissance as a sharp break with the past and still conclude that there was a significant distinction between medieval and early modern Europe. The distinction is not wholly arbitrary, nor is it perpetuated merely for pedagogical convenience.

Antiquity bears a different relationship to the history of Western civilization from that of the Middle Ages. The ancient world was a unity centering around the Mediterranean. It included the peoples and cultures of North Africa and the modern Near East. Both of these areas developed civilizations which were in contact with Western civilization but were not part of its historical evolution. During the early Middle Ages the unity of the Mediterranean world was permanently broken: the sea which had been the center of a civilization, a channel of communication, now became a frontier to be crossed for commerce or for war. The influence of the Byzantine and Arab civilizations of the Middle Ages on the West was important, but that influence was from without, not within. Only those Byzantine and Arab influences have become part of Western culture which were borrowed, assimilated, and re-expressed in Western language, institutions, or ideas.

Antiquity was both more and less than the beginning of Western civilization. It was more because it was just as much the beginning of two other civilizations. It was less because some fundamental elements of Western civilization, as it developed from the early Middle Ages, were either absent from or antagonistic to the culture of antiquity when Rome gave peace to the civilized Mediterranean world. All three of the civilizations which replaced or grew out of antiquity share two fundamental characteristics. They were all inspired by a new religion (Christianity, in its Roman

Catholic and Greek Orthodox versions, in the West and the Byzantine world; and Islam in the Arab world), and they all expanded beyond the geographical limits of the Roman Empire and assimilated new peoples and new cultures into their common inheritance of antique culture.

This book deals with the medieval foundations of Western civilization, rather than with the medieval history of the Mediterranean world. The emphasis is on the Latin West, even in the early period when both Byzantium and Islam were far in advance of Western culture. This emphasis does not reflect the relative importance of the Western and Eastern parts of the early medieval world. A treatment of Islam and of Byzantine civilization on the same scale would double the length of this book without adding significantly to an understanding of the origins and development of Western civilization.

Historians have differed in their interpretation of the essential characteristics of the Middle Ages as a stage in Western civilization. If one thinks of Western history as beginning with the glory that was Greece and the grandeur that was Rome, one sees the Middle Ages as Gibbon did, as a long period of decline. But if one considers the ancient world as an independent civilization, though related to its successors, perhaps the most important single fact about the glory and grandeur of antiquity is that its civilization was a colossal failure. So far as the West was concerned, this failure was already final and complete before the fusion of the Roman heritage, Christianity, and the barbarian Germanic element inaugurated the Middle Ages. While this fusion was slowly taking place, there was a gradual process of separation of the West from the Greek East and an abrupt breaking off from the African and Near Eastern parts of the antique Mediterranean world which resulted from the sudden rise of Islam. The heritage of antiquity dazzled the survivors of its ruins, but the important historical fact is that these survivors did indeed build upon ruins. What they built, and how it was built, is the subject of the following pages: the medieval foundations of Western civilization.

PART ONE

THE TRANSITION FROM ANCIENT TO MEDIEVAL CIVILIZATION, c.400-750

PART ONE, illustration:
Emperor Justinian and Courtiers. Detail of mosaic
in San Vitale, Ravenna (sixth century). PHOTO: ALINARI

The Decline of the Roman Empire

On no subject have historians written more and agreed less than on the causes of what is called, after the title of Gibbon's famous book, the "decline and fall" of the Roman Empire. The problem has fascinated men's minds for over fifteen hundred years, beginning with Augustine's treatise *The City of God,* which he began in 413 as a reply to pagan charges that the difficulties besetting the Empire resulted from neglect of the pagan gods in favor of Christ. Since then, almost everything has been alleged as *the* cause of the decline—from malaria to Christianity, and from slavery to a palace revolution which in 476 deposed the last emperor in the West, Romulus Augustulus.

Much of this disagreement is simply due to different ways of defining the problem. Historians who have been interested primarily in political history have emphasized political or military events as causes. Historians who have defined the problem in the broadest terms of political, economic, social, and cultural decline have been chary of singling out any one cause but have emphasized the interrelationships between various causes. A hundred years ago it was fashionable to explain the "fall of Rome" by an interpretation which might be called "the catastrophic and abysmal theory." According to this view, the decline was sudden and the fall was to a very low depth of destruction and disintegration whose main, or only, cause was the invasions of the Empire by Germanic barbarians. One historian wrote, in 1860, "Confusion, corruption, despair, and death were everywhere; social dismemberment seemed complete. Authority, morals, arts, sciences, religion itself, might have been supposed condemned to irremediable ruin." Today most historians would consider this view exaggerated, and would interpret the decline of the ancient world as being a complex and slow process which neither began at so high a level of civilization nor ended at so low a point or so complete a chaos. Furthermore, they would distinguish, today, between the more rapid decline in the West and the slower onset of difficulties in the East, where the Byzantine world actually recovered from its difficulties in the fourth century and the vigor of the Roman Empire was prolonged well down into the eleventh century.

This chapter deals primarily with the decline of the Roman Empire in the West. The next two chapters will treat the other two major elements whose fusion marks the transition to medieval civilization—Christianity and the Germanic element.

2 POLITICAL ORGANIZATION AND INSTITUTIONS OF THE LATER EMPIRE

To understand the nature and historical significance of the later Roman Empire, two salient facts must be kept in mind. First, the later Empire was quite different in several fundamental respects from the Principate of Augustus. Second, these differences were in part produced by and increased by a great crisis of Empire in the third century whose main feature was a series of civil wars. The early Empire is called the Principate because Augustus, as effective ruler, was given the title of *princeps* ("first citizen"). He preserved the forms of the earlier Republic while concentrating in his own hands the substance of political power. In contrast, the later Empire is sometimes called the Dominate because the remnants of the republican tradition were by then destroyed and the emperor was an absolute monarch. The ruler was *dominus* ("master" or "lord").

The Principate of Augustus evolved into an Empire that reached its highest point of peace, prosperity, and stability during the Age of the Antonines, from 96 to 180. The civilized Mediterranean world enjoyed Pax Romana, universal peace imposed by Roman arms. The only serious threat to this peace came from the barbarians beyond the frontiers. The Roman genius for good government, just laws, and the applied sciences of engineering made the Empire a stable and contented world adorned with good roads, harbors, aqueducts, public baths, magnificent temples, and theaters. The ancient Roman formula "the Senate and the Roman People" (*Senatus Populusque Romanus*, usually abbreviated S.P.Q.R.) still had meaning. Although ultimate power was wielded by the emperor, the Senate and the citizens participated in the government of the Empire, which was still largely decentralized. The municipalities were allowed a large degree of independence from the central, imperial administration, provided they collected their taxes, supplied their quotas of recruits for the army, and maintained local order. This is why the early Roman Empire has sometimes been characterized as a "federation of city-states." The Empire flourished while its cities flourished; urban institutions were its strength. The governing body of each city was the *curia*, whose members, called *curiales*, were drawn from the local aristocracy or middle class. The jurisdiction of the *curia* extended beyond the municipality to the surrounding country region. The ancient city-state was more than a city. It might be compared with a modern American county whose courthouse and county officials are combined with the city government.

The Augustan Principate failed to solve one defect in the imperial structure and one problem of Empire which continued to plague Rome to the end. The defect was the nature of the succession to the imperial dignity. The problem was the defense of the frontiers. The Senate still theoretically elected the new emperor, but Augustus' effort to preserve the constitutional forms and provide a role for the Senate in the government was slowly undermined. The emperor's power ultimately rested on his control of the army. The title *imperator*, "emperor," was the Roman equivalent of our word "general." In a disputed succession the emperor's personal army, the pretorian guard in Rome, could intervene with decisive force. This happened occasionally in the first century; later the provincial armies learned this "secret of empire." By the third century the succession was determined by naked military force. The role of the Senate declined almost to the vanishing point as provincial armies fought civil wars aimed at placing their own candidates on the throne. The emperor at first ruled through the army. In the third century the army ruled through the emperor.

The problem of defense was linked to that of succession. Until Augustus, the Empire had everywhere been on the offensive, expanding throughout the civilized Mediterranean world. In the north, Roman legions had reached the wilderness of Germany. Here, in the battle of the Teutoberger Forest, 9 A.D., in northwestern Germany beyond the lower Rhine, the legions had met the first catastrophic defeat of Roman expansion. It was at the hands of a Roman-trained general, Arminius, sometimes called Herman the German. After this crushing blow the only significant expansion of Rome beyond the Rhine-Danube and other natural frontiers was into Britain and parts of North Africa, in the first century, and into Dacia, or modern Romania, in the second century. Everywhere the Roman armies were reorganized into more efficient defensive units, based on permanently fortified strong points. Maintenance of these armies was a drain on the wealth of the Empire; more important, politically, was the spreading of the military strength of the Roman world along the frontiers.

During the anarchy of the third century many of the legions which should have been guarding the frontiers of the Empire were used in its center to further the political aspirations of candidates for the throne. In the half-century from 235 to 285 it has been estimated that there were more than fifty claimants to the imperial power. Most of them led Roman armies into battle against the Roman armies of other claimants. The unguarded frontiers were breached on a wide scale. In the West, German tribes crossed both the Rhine and Danube in extensive marauding raids, to learn for the first time the advantages of Roman civilization. The civil wars and barbarian incursions, and the discontinuity and uncertainty in government, gave the Empire a shock from which it never fully recovered. The political chaos was aggravated by the favoritism which emperors or candidates for the purple were forced to show to the army at the expense of the rest of the population. Normal economic conditions were disrupted; trade and industry in several previously flourishing provinces were brought to a standstill. The strain was too great for certain parts of the Empire, especially in the West, where economic life was none too healthy even in peaceful times. In the general insecurity, many towns built defensive ring walls. The best example is the still-standing Wall of Aurelian which fortified Rome against barbarian raids and hostile Roman legions alike. It was Aurelian (270–275), also, who in 271 evacuated Dacia, the last province conquered and the first to be surrendered.

During the civil wars some twenty of the contenders for power succeeded in gaining recognition as emperor. Only one reigned longer than seven years. The temper of these times is suggested by the fates of the last four. Probus was lynched by his own troops in 282; Carus was killed, it was said, by a bolt of lightning "forged no doubt in a legionary armory," in 283; Numerianus, campaigning in Asia Minor, died under mysterious circumstances in 284; and Carinus was killed by his own troops during a battle with another contender for the throne, Diocletian, in 285. Then came a sudden shift in the fortunes of the Empire. Diocletian, proclaimed emperor in 284, reigned without opposition for twenty years (285–305). He died peacefully in bed in 316, after voluntarily resigning his rule eleven years earlier.

Diocletian, an Illyrian soldier, like many of his late predecessors, was a self-made man from the provinces, hardly aware of or interested in reviving the traditions of the earlier Empire. He was a practical and energetic administrator and organizer. The reforms which Diocletian inaugurated were intended to save the Empire from destruction; in the West they only succeeded in prolonging its agony, but in the East they laid the foundations for the Byzantine Empire.

Diocletian attempted to solve the problems of succession and of defense of the frontiers by dividing the imperial authority. The military problem was too great for any one emperor, so he associated Maximian with himself in the imperial dignity. Both assumed the title of Augustus. Then, to delegate further the military responsibility and to provide for

The Roman Empire at the End of the Fourth Century

the succession, he designated Constantius Chlorus and Galerius as heirs expectant, giving them the title of Caesar. The system of joint-emperors was based on precedent, but the provision for the succession was new, and Diocletian combined with it the additional innovation of a territorial division of the Empire to correspond with the fourfold division of imperial authority. Each of the four divisions was later called a prefecture. Diocletian reserved for himself the wealthiest and most important prefecture of the East, giving the prefecture of Illyricum, which included about half the Danube frontier, to his Caesar and designated successor, Galerius. These two prefectures included approximately the Greek-speaking or eastern half of the Empire. Maximian, as Augustus, ruled the prefecture of Italy, which included most of North Africa west of Egypt plus the area north and east of Italy on the Danube frontier. Constantius Chlorus, as Maximian's Caesar and successor, ruled the prefecture of Gaul, which included the Rhine frontier and the western provinces from the tip of North Africa to Britain. The plan worked well, so long as Diocletian remained in power and could supervise or influence his imperial colleagues. The frontier defenses were restored and internal order was re-established.

Diocletian began, and his successors continued, other reforms designed to consolidate his system of divided responsibility. These reforms can be grouped under three headings: military, administrative, and executive. The military reform created a more mobile defense of the frontier, by dividing the army into garrisons and reserve units. The former were posted along the borders, while the latter were provided with cavalry and stationed behind the lines, ready to rush to any threatened point. This reform reduced the total number of troops under any one commander, thus decreasing the resources which had led so many generals into rebellion during the anarchy of the third century. Under this reorganization the grand total of troops was increased from 300,000 to about half a million. Recruitment of this much larger force was made possible by an increased use of barbarians who were invited to settle, in return for military service, within the fringes of the Empire. Conscription of Roman citizens was transferred to civilian authorities who filled their quotas of "draftees" from among the least useful and productive of the population. More troops were thus raised, but the quality of the armed forces deteriorated. By the end of the fourth century this system had led, on some fronts, to a general barbarization of the Roman army.

A second group of reforms concerned the administration of the Empire under the four co-rulers. Military and civilian authorities were separated at every level below the two Augusti and the two Caesars. Commanders of troops had no control over civil jurisdiction and taxation; civilian officials who collected taxes and headed local governments possessed no military power. This reform was aimed, again, at decreasing the resources of army officers and governmental officials who might be tempted into rebellion. The separation of civilian from military authority resulted in a dual hierarchy and a greatly enlarged civil service. The administration was further increased by doubling the number of provinces, each with its own military and civilian hierarchy. This reform diminished the powers of provincial governors by decreasing their resources, but it also diminished the number and magnitude of problems in each province while it made possible a stricter control of the municipalities under each provincial governor. For more effective supervision and uniformity of administration, the provinces (which eventually numbered about 120) were grouped into dioceses, each administered by an official called a vicar. The dioceses were distributed among the four prefectures, whose civilian head was called a pretorian prefect. Thus, in Constantius Chlorus' division of the Empire, the prefecture of Gaul consisted of the dioceses of Spain, Gaul, and Britain, and contained, respectively, seven, fourteen, and five provinces. In provinces where troops were stationed, the military command was exercised by an army officer with the rank of duke or count who, like the civilian pretorian prefect, was directly subordinate to the Augustus or Caesar.

The executive reforms of Diocletian and his successors transformed the Empire into an absolute state. The office and the person of the emperor took on all the unlimited power and splendor of oriental despotism. To dazzle and awe their subjects, the emperors cultivated an elaborate ceremonial which raised them above the level of mere mortality. They required their subjects to hail them as "god, here with us in the flesh" (*praesens et corporalis deus*). At the imperial palace in Nicomedia, just across the Bosporus in Asia Minor, a department of the imperial court was officially denominated as "sacred." The official who would correspond with the Secretary of the Treasury was called "Count of the Sacred Largesses" (*Comes Sacrarum Largitionum*). The emperor's council was renamed *Consistorium* because its members were all required to rise together in the presence of the emperor.

The reform of the executive, however, went beyond adopting the trappings of absolutism. The central government increased its control of local administration, and the emperor appointed or dismissed at will all officials from top to bottom of either civilian or military hierarchy. This was the final blow at the declining political power of the Senate, which hitherto had still participated in the government of the Empire through its control of certain provinces. All pretense of partnership was abandoned. The Senate became only the *curia* (municipal government) of the city of Rome. Finally, the New Order of Diocletian and his successors took on the character of a police state. A special imperial bureau of investigation, whose members were cryptically styled "agents for affairs" (*agentes in rebus*), had the duty of spying on the imperial administration itself so that disloyalty, inefficiency, or corruption could be detected and eradicated.

A general estimate of all these reforms is difficult to make. In the

East they were astonishingly successful and enduring. In the West their historical importance transcends their failure. They provided the model, although debased by barbarian usages, of the Germanic kingdoms which succeeded the provincial governments of the western Empire. The political and military reforms were aimed at preserving the imperial government and keeping the frontiers intact at all cost. The fundamental criticism of Diocletian and his successors is that they failed to appreciate the relationship between the imperial superstructure (army, bureaucracy, and court) and the welfare of the total society. By the fiat of an autocrat, the resources, the institutions, and the whole political and social organization of the Empire were forced to serve the one great purpose of sustaining the government. The military and political machinery of the government was all contrived to enhance and stabilize the emperor's absolute authority. The imperial bureaucracy served the emperor and itself, not the people.

Under Diocletian the reforms provided peace and security, but within a year after his retirement in 305 the crucial feature of his system— an orderly succession to the four imperial offices—broke down because of the ambitions of the new Augusti and Caesars. From the ensuing round of new civil wars, Constantine, son of Constantius Chlorus, emerged as sole emperor (324–337). Like Diocletian before him, he recognized that the center of gravity was in the East, where population and wealth were greater, society was more stable, and where the military threat of the new Sassanid monarchy of Persia was more serious than the danger of German barbarians along the Rhine-Danube frontiers. Constantine moved the capital from Rome—near which, in 312, he had won his most memorable victory at the Battle of the Milvian Bridge—to Byzantium, on the northern shore of the Bosporus. Constantinople, as the "New Rome" was named after its re-founder, was dedicated as the capital of the Empire in 330. The removal from Rome was not a great innovation. Even in the West, Milan had replaced Rome as the normal headquarters of the emperors, largely because of Milan's military advantage in being nearer to the frontier.

After the anarchy of the third century and the reigns of Diocletian and Constantine, the political developments of the remainder of the fourth century seem uneventful. Constantine's three sons divided the Empire and alternately defended it from barbarians and usurpers or fought each other for a greater share of power. The surviving son ruled alone for eleven years until 361, when he left an undivided Empire to his cousin and designated successor, Julian (361–363). Julian's brief reign was mainly spent in campaigns against both the Germans and the Persians, but he is best known for his effort to revive the worship of the ancient pagan deities. For this Christian writers excoriated him as "the Apostate." Valentinian I (364–375) was put on the throne by his troops. He delegated the East to his brother Valens (364–378) as co-emperor, and designated his son Gratian, a brilliant young military commander, as co-emperor in the West. The reason for this new division of imperial authority and responsibility was that the internal and external problems of the Empire were once more far too great for the energies of a single ruler.

3   THE ECONOMIC, SOCIAL, AND CULTURAL DECAY OF ANTIQUITY

The civil wars and barbarian incursions of the third century aggravated several basic economic weaknesses which the success of Roman arms obscured. The earlier expansion of the Empire brought initial benefits in the form of conquered wealth and the economic development of conquered territories, but these benefits were not permanent. In some parts of the Mediterranean world, especially in the east, each new province conquered added to the resources of Rome what may be called the "capital of conquest": booty and confiscated property; the antique equivalent of machinery (slaves); and new subjects to be exploited through taxation. Conquests in the west added to the Empire relatively backward provinces, and their economic development at first profited both the new provinces and the older parts of the Empire through trade and the growth of local industries. But the limits of profitable expansion were reached by the first century A.D. It was a wise and necessary decision, on the part of Augustus and his immediate successors, to round off the limits of the Empire at the periphery of Mediterranean civilization. No windfalls of taxable wealth would accrue from pushing farther south into the African desert or into the wilderness beyond the Rhine and Danube, while the areas farther east in Asia were controlled by the powerful though economically retarded Persian monarchy. The economic development of the western provinces, which at first stimulated trade throughout the Empire, had by the third century made them a self-sufficient region for all basic needs, both agricultural and industrial. The later Empire was politically unified, but economically it was divided into regions that were no longer interdependent except for a few high-priced commodities. With no more productive areas to be conquered, Rome was thrown back upon her own resources. Although these were considerable, they were not sufficient to maintain and defend an Empire beset by both internal strife and external pressure upon the frontiers.

Slavery was the basis of antique economy. When the Empire ceased to expand, the supply of slaves, most of whom were captives of war, was greatly diminished. There was a further restriction of supply when the later emperors adopted the policy of settling captured barbarians on the frontier as self-supporting garrison troops. Also, barbarian slaves were neither trained nor accustomed to do more than the rudimentary tasks of

unskilled labor. Cheap slave labor in the earlier period had made technological improvement unnecessary. The Roman achievement in engineering
(as exemplified by bridges, aqueducts, great vaulted buildings, etc.) produced little that was economically productive. The slave-owning class was
indifferent to the use of machinery that would replace or augment human
labor. To own slaves gave status; to own machines did not. Under this
value system, human labor was held in low regard and no premium was
placed on lightening the burden of physical labor. When the number of
slaves declined there were no machines to keep up production. For example, although the water mill was known to antiquity it was never used
on a large scale because it was considered cheaper to use slave-operated
hand mills.

Another basic weakness of the economy of the later Empire was an
insufficient gold and silver coinage to sustain either prices or commerce.
The high costs of transportation militated against extensive commerce in
any but the most expensive goods. Luxuries such as jewelry, silks, spices,
fine arts, and higher-priced clothing were bought from the Near and Far
East, often from beyond the limits of the Empire. Since no products of
Western industry were in great demand in the East, this meant a drain of
gold and silver eastward. During Roman expansion this drain was not a
serious handicap, because the confiscations of conquest kept replenishing
Roman supplies of precious metals. But from the middle of the second
century the supply of money in the Empire steadily decreased. The general
insecurity of the times, and the absence of large-scale industry or commerce in which to invest, encouraged the hoarding of money and invest-
ment in land. Great landowners increased their holdings, while the middle
classes of the towns suffered from the gradual stagnation of trade and industry, caused partly by the diminishing supply of money and a consequent deflation of prices.

The government tried to counteract deflation through debasing the
coinage, but this fiscal policy was ruinous in the end. Without an adequate
coinage system, payments in kind or in services increased during the last
two centuries of the later Empire, especially in the West. Even the government accepted payment of taxes in kind (the *annona,* consisting of grain
or other produce) or in labor services (called "liturgies," i.e., work performed on maintenance of roads, construction of public works, etc.). This
substitution of payments in goods or in labor services for payments in
money is sometimes called "natural" economy. But the transition to natural
economy was never complete; even at the lowest ebb of economic activity
in the early Middle Ages, money never completely ceased to be used as a
medium of exchange.

Another economic weakness of the Empire is more difficult to measure. People who engaged in trade or industry were considered to be only
a little above the class of menial laborers. No aristocrat would soil his

hands by directly participating in productive work, either industrial or commercial. The merchants and industrialists who did make fortunes used their wealth to purchase landed estates and thus rise into the aristocracy, rather than investing it in more business ventures. These social values meant that the Roman world lacked enterprise capital to build a higher standard of living through increasing production.

When the economic and social legislation of Diocletian, Constantine, and their successors is viewed in terms of these basic weaknesses, the failure of imperialistic paternalism seems inevitable. The disturbances of the third century had already dealt a fatal blow to the economy. The fourth-century emperors tried to legislate prosperity but succeeded only in accelerating economic collapse. Taxation in the later Empire was not very heavy, but it was arbitrary and not related to ability to pay. Diocletian reformed the tax system by introducing two new units of assessment, the *jugum* as a measure of land value and the *caput* (or poll tax) as the unit of taxable manpower. Theoretically, this was equitable because all citizens were to pay according to their possession of *jugera* or *capita* of wealth; but the government met insuperable obstacles in attempting to enforce the system. The wealthy, who could afford to bribe officials, were able to corrupt the tax collectors and avoid paying their share of taxes. Thus the poorer classes suffered a heavier burden of taxation than they could survive. The failure was not, therefore, owing to bad policy but rather to the low level of public morality among the upper classes. The government recognized the situation by granting exemption from various taxes to aristocrats who would, in any event, have escaped paying them.

In the later Empire, most members of the aristocracy deserted the impoverished towns and devoted themselves to the rural life of country gentlemen. Their estates, called *latifundia*, sometimes contained thousands of acres and hundreds of dependent free or servile tenants. Partly because of the lack of trade, and partly because it was fashionable, these great landowners organized their *latifundia* into almost self-sufficient communities, the prototype of the medieval manor. Most of the wealthy landowners belonged to what was called the "senatorial" class—not by virtue of being members of the Senate of Rome or the New Rome, but because they possessed the privileges of this class, the *clarissimi* ("most distinguished"). Successful civil servants in the imperial bureaucracy were often rewarded by appointment to this class, and officials of the rank of provincial governor automatically received the privileges of *clarissimi*. From this rank, promotion in the imperial bureaucracy could lead to membership in two higher orders recognized by law to have even more valuable privileges and exemptions. Above the *clarissimi* were the class of *spectabiles* ("notables"), which included vicars of dioceses and military commanders with the rank of duke or count; and the highest rank of *viri illustres* ("illustrious men"), which included pretorian prefects in charge of the four prefectures and the highest officials of the palace, such as the Count of the Sacred Largesses. Above the *viri illustres* stood only the nobles who had gained the honor of being consuls for a year, those who by being relatives of the emperor or by imperial favor were granted the rank of *patricius* ("patrician"), and the emperor himself.

The caste system extended downward as well as upward, but the legal provisions concerned with the non-noble classes dealt with obligations rather than with privileges. Members of the upper middle class in the towns who were officials of the municipal government, or *curia*, were designated as *curiales* and burdened with a personal responsibility for the collection of all taxes in their towns. This meant that the *curiales* had to make good from their own pockets whatever they could not collect from delinquent taxpayers. No more lethal blow could have been struck at the heart of the Empire than this. When many of the *curiales* deserted their positions and fled from their cities, the government responded with compulsion. All *curiales* were by law required to remain in their status, and the status was made hereditary. Other occupations, such as that of the millers of grain and that of sailors, which were necessary for the survival of the state were made hereditary castes. The government strove to maintain the *status quo* and to legislate economic stability. In their desperate efforts to collect taxes the *curiales* adopted the same methods of compulsion, so that eventually the government had to intervene to protect the population against the *curiales*. In each oppressed municipality an official called the *defensor civitatis* ("defender of the city") was appointed to adjudicate disputes concerning taxation. But this reform only complicated matters, for the defenders were open to bribery and there was no official to protect the cities against their "defenders." The total result of the government's policy was to cripple the initiative of the middle class, deprive the lower classes of any incentive to rise into the middle class, and transform a once-fluid society into a rigid caste system of hereditary occupations. It was as if the later emperors, confronted with desertion from the ranks and malingering in duty, tried to impose military discipline on the whole population. Regulatory laws were multiplied, the imperial bureaucracy grew larger, and the cities continued to decay.

A parallel evolution was taking place in the rural districts. From the middle of the third century, there were more and more neglected fields. In vain the emperors issued edicts requiring the rural population to bring back into cultivation all lands which had ever been tilled. The later Empire suffered a continuing agricultural depression. Population was decreasing, which diminished markets for food; taxes were more efficiently collected so that the small free proprietors could not escape; the civil wars and barbarian incursions created havoc and wrought destruction; and in many parts of the Empire soil exhaustion, after centuries of poor agricultural methods, was slowly decreasing the yield of crops. Under such conditions, the small free farmers could not survive. Some of them moved to the large cities, like Rome or Constantinople, to swell the ranks of the indolent proletariat that was fed and amused by a paternalistic government. Many free farmers sought security by putting themselves under the protection of great land-owners, that is, by transferring the ownership of their land to a neighboring noble and receiving it back as a tenant for life.

The landowning aristocracy welcomed this method of enlarging their *latifundia* and increasing their labor supply. Most of the tenants of the *latifundia* were classified as *coloni*. These were originally a free class, but during the later Empire the government cooperated with the aristocracy in transforming them into a semiservile tenantry. The *coloni* were for-bidden by law to leave the estate on which they were born. Though they retained certain rights, such as ownership of personal property, they were no longer full citizens. Between them and the state stood their great land-lords who paid their poll tax, based on the assessment of *capita*. The *coloni* owed to their landlords the obedience, and many of the obligations, which fully free people owed to the state. In return the *coloni* were guaran-teed security of tenure. Their services could not be increased at the land-lord's will, nor could they be evicted from their tenements. In the institution of the colonate of the later Empire can be seen the essential features of medieval serfdom. The *colonus* already occupied the ambigu-ous position of a serf, halfway between the status of a slave and the status of a free peasant.

This brief survey of the economic and social institutions of the later Empire reveals the hardening of a once-flourishing and growing society: social regimentation and the growth of a caste system, declining produc-tivity and decaying commerce, the search for security and stability on all social levels, the abandonment of freedom, and the disappearance of op-portunity. What Ammianus Marcellinus, the fourth-century Roman historian, said of the city of Rome may be said of the Empire as a whole: "it was declining into senescence." Contemporaries could explain the phe-nomenon no better than historians today, for the process was infinitely complex. Most people then, even as today, blamed the government or pub-lic and private morals for all the ills of society. Salvian, a Christian critic of his age, asked, "Why are these disorders seen now, when peace and security have vanished from the whole Empire? Only the vices remain." Another Christian contemporary, Lactantius, complained of the extortions of the bureaucracy: "Revenue officers are everywhere. Every clod of a field is measured, as well as the number of feet in a vineyard, the number of trees is recorded, each kind of animal inventoried, and men are counted by heads."

Whatever the explanation of the decline of the Roman Empire, one fact is certain: there was a failure of nerve and an atrophy of public spirit. The imperial government's effort to meet the difficulties succeeded only in perpetuating a crisis. Fewer and fewer inhabitants of the civilized Roman world identified themselves and their interests with the survival of the Empire. By enforcing obedience, the government lost the loyalty of many of its subjects. The policy of subordinating the welfare of the people to the preservation of the government ended in alienating large groups who could see no difference between the exploitation of the Empire and the barbarism of Germanic conquerors. In the economically backward West, the system broke down and the Empire came to an end; in the more advanced East the Roman world was able to survive and to endure for another thousand years. Perhaps the answer is quite simple, after all: the more balanced and productive East could support autocracy, and even the regimentation of the later Empire could work if based on a sound economic life.

The same elements of decay and transformation which characterized social and economic life were evident in the cultural activities of the later Empire. In arts and letters, in education, and in the intellectual life of the educated classes there was little creative achievement—except, that is, among the Christian authors. But the Christian element in antique culture was alien to the traditions of classical thought and letters, and will be considered later. For the classical culture of pagan antiquity, the later Empire was an age of archaism. The literary standards and esthetic values of the past were accepted without question, but imitated without merit. In literature and learning the fourth and fifth centuries produced compendia, condensations, and compilations from the "great books" of the past, rather than original writings. In the field of legal thought, however, the greatest age of Roman jurisprudence did not close until the mid-third century, and the codification and organization of Roman law continued on into the fifth century. One of the finest cultural monuments of later antiquity was the Theodosian Code (issued c.438) which influenced profoundly the earliest legislative efforts of the Germanic barbarians.

In the arts only architecture retained some vitality, but building was confined largely to public works or imperial palaces. Municipalities no longer could afford to adorn themselves with temple and forum as in the past. Late Roman architecture at its best—or biggest—is typified by the Baths of Diocletian in Rome, where the effort to achieve monumental grandeur was fully realized. Sculpture deteriorated from the intense naturalism and animation of the second and early third centuries, until portraiture, the great field of Roman achievement, had become stylized and stereotyped. This may have resulted partly from a decline in technique. But in official portraiture at least, it was also partly owing to a desire to portray the subject as endowed with timeless and transcendent qualities, as befitted an emperor whose person was sacred if not actually divine.

Latin literature enjoyed an Indian summer during the later Empire, although almost all of it was imitative and overloaded with conventional rhetoric. The poets excelled prose writers, and in the best poetry there emerges one final expression of "the image of Rome's Eternity," which along with the idea of the unity of the Empire was passed on to the Middle Ages as a fundamental concept. Perhaps the best of the later Latin poets was the Alexandrian Greek, Claudian, whose level was reached in the West only by Ausonius and Rutilius Namatianus. All three wrote in the late fourth or early fifth centuries. All three were typical provincials, more Roman than the Romans. From Rutilius we have one of the last pagan tributes to Rome:

> Queen of a world that you have made your home,
> Amid the sky of stars, come hear me, Rome. . . .
> You brought the nations one great fatherland,
> You raised the savage with your taming hand,
> Broke him, but gave him laws to be his aid.
> One City of the scattered Earth you made.[1]

But already in Rutilius' time the "one great fatherland" was no longer the unity which he felt and expressed with such noble sentiment. Culturally, as well as politically and economically, the Mediterranean world was breaking apart. The Empire did not produce a Roman nation; it remained to the last a federation of nationalities under Roman rule. Tendencies toward provincial cultures, which will clearly emerge in the early Middle Ages, were already apparent in the schools of the later Empire, of which those in Gaul achieved some prominence. After the third century there were few educated men in the West who could speak or read Greek; the Roman world was no longer bilingual. Education centered around the study of rhetoric, in which content was subordinated to verbal niceties and an understanding of philosophy was considered less important than elegant self-expression. Late Roman education has been criticized for its neglect of the natural and social sciences. This was largely owing to ignorance of Greek literature in the West, for the greatest works in antiquity on science, politics, and philosophy were written in Greek.

---

[1] Jack Lindsay, *Song of a Falling World* (London, 1948), p. 161, reprinted by permission of the translator, Jack Lindsay, and the publisher, Andrew Dakers, Ltd.

Latin Christianity

The most important single element in the history of Western civilization is Christianity. From obscure origins, in a remote eastern province of the Roman Empire, Christianity slowly grew until it had achieved two triumphs which no other religion of the Mediterranean world came near to equaling. The first great triumph was the recognition of Christianity as the one official, state-supported religion of the ancient world. The second was the survival of Christianity not only as an important heritage of antiquity but as the most vital force in the barbarian West. Originating as a religious system profoundly antagonistic to many of the values and entrenched interests of antiquity, the historic role of Christianity in its first seven centuries was to absorb many of the best elements of antique civilization and to transmit them to the Middle Ages. There is no more important or fascinating problem for the student of history than to explain how and why these two great triumphs were achieved.

Various explanations have been offered, including the belief that the progress of the Church Militant was foreordained by Providence. Whether this is true or not is a question of greater interest to students of theology than to students of history, who must be primarily concerned with how, as well as why, these developments took place. An historical explanation of the role of Christianity in Western civilization must deal primarily with the Church in the West, that is, with Latin Christianity (influenced, as it was, so profoundly by the Church in the East). Such an historical explanation neither denies nor depends upon a belief in the providential view of history. Nor does it deny or depend upon the varying doctrinal beliefs found in the Christian world today.

The most important historical developments were the organization of the Church; the vigorous and creative intellectual leadership of the Fathers of the Church; and the rise of the papacy. In each development may be seen a different aspect of the growing influence of the Church and therefore of Christianity as a religion. From this point of view, the end of antiquity and the beginning of the Middle Ages may be summed up as the failure of secular leadership and the rise of ecclesiastical leadership.

4   THE ORIGINS, GROWTH, AND ORGANIZATION OF CHRISTIANITY

Christianity was born into a world of religious ferment. Part of its success may be explained very simply. The Greco-Roman pantheon of gods and the ethical teachings of the Hellenistic philosophical systems, such as Stoicism or Epicureanism, no longer satisfied men's religious impulses. The official religion was essentially a civic function in which the individual felt no personal contact with the deities whose worship was provided for by the state. The appeal of Stoicism, or of other currently fashionable philosophies, was beyond the grasp of the great majority. Rational counsels of resignation, or of subordination of self to the Law of Nature, were unintelligible and uninspiring to ordinary people.

This waning influence of the traditional religion and philosophy coincided with an increasing religious interest in the Roman world which has been attributed to the decline of political and economic life and opportunity. As success and happiness became more difficult to attain in the everyday life of this world, people became more responsive to the message of religions which taught that true happiness consisted in the fulfillment of human aspirations in an eternal life beyond this world. These religions were the mystery cults. Some of them originated in Greece (such as the Eleusinian mysteries) and some in the East (such as Mithraism or the cult of the Egyptian deity, Isis). These Greco-Oriental mystery cults compensated for several defects, mentioned above, in the official religion of the Roman Empire and in the philosophies which largely took the place of religion for the educated upper classes. They appealed to all, including the educated, although initially they proved especially popular among the lower classes and with people who were dissatisfied with their conditions of life.

The mystery cults emphasized individual religious experience and a personal, emotional, and intimate contact with the deity. They were exclusive. The participant had to be initiated into their rites. Their main rewards were twofold: communion with the deity during this life through participation in worship, and eternal salvation or union with the deity after this life. Specific characteristics found in one or more of the mystery cults included the following: a man-god savior whose intercession on behalf of the faithful guaranteed salvation; sacraments such as initiatory rites (baptism) or religious ceremonies intended to cleanse and purify the worshiper preparing for communion with the deity; an explanation of the mysteries of life in terms of a divine hero who in dying conquered death, and whose life was a pattern for the faithful to follow in the hope of attaining immortality; miracle-working by this divine hero and by those who were priests of the cult, as an attestation of the truth of their worship and of the power of the divine hero; and a highly developed sense of exclusive membership or brotherhood among the elect which kept their teachings secret and unprofaned.

Many people probably became interested in Christianity at first because it offered many of the things that any of the Greco-Oriental mystery cults could offer. But in addition it emphasized the Stoic concept of the brotherhood of man under the fatherhood of God, a teaching given new force by the distinctly Christian concept of love or charity. Christianity was far more than a mystery cult; it taught a positive social ideal to be followed in this life, as well as a doctrine to be fulfilled after this life. In the words of the apostle Paul, "Though I have the gift of prophecy and understand all mysteries, and all knowledge; and though I have all faith, so that I could remove mountains, and have not charity, I am nothing."

Three special characteristics of Christianity further help account for its growth and its strength during the first three centuries. Early or primitive Christianity inherited from its Judaic origins a sense of exclusiveness (and, its enemies charged, self-righteous and disdainful superiority) which helped keep Christians aloof from religious influences surrounding them, despite the similarities between Christianity and the mystery cults. Most mystery cults accepted the existence and divine nature of other gods, but for Christians the God of the New Testament was the same jealous God of the Old. Worshipping their God not just as a preferred or special deity, but rather as the one and only true God, early Christians behaved as they were described by the apostle Peter: "Ye are a chosen generation, a royal priesthood, an holy nation, a peculiar people." If this attitude made Christians unpopular, it also served to bind them together in a close-knit and self-conscious community.

A second characteristic which helped the growth of Christianity was its explicit recognition of the rights of the state. Paul laid the basis for all Christian political thought in teaching that "there is no power but of God: the powers that be are ordained of God. Whosoever therefore resisteth the power, resisteth the ordinance of God: and they that resist shall receive to themselves damnation." Christians never attacked or tried to supplant the Empire. Their Kingdom was not of this world, in which they thought of themselves as merely pilgrims passing on to a higher state. On the whole, the Roman government was lenient toward Christians because there was no open threat to the state in their teachings. No concerted effort was made to exterminate the religion before the troubles of the Empire began in the third century.

Finally, a third characteristic which strengthened Christianity was that although the early Church would not attack the state, neither would it yield to all the demands of the state. Antagonism between Christianity and the pagan Empire arose from the injunction to "render unto Caesar the things which be Caesar's; and unto God the things which be God's": an injunction which could be fully acceptable only to a Christian ruler. The specific issue between the early Church and the Empire was the refusal by Christians to participate in emperor-worship, an act which the government construed as an acknowledgment of political loyalty but which Christians could only view as blasphemy.

The Church, under Roman law, was considered an illicit society suspected of subversive tendencies. These suspicions were strengthened by scandalous reports about secret meetings and "love feasts" at which Christians were commonly thought to engage in immoral practices. For these reasons the government occasionally sanctioned minor and local persecutions of Christians on the technically legal ground that they withheld allegiance to the emperor. Actually such persecutions were more often in response to antagonistic local public opinion, or to find a scapegoat for such misfortunes as the great fire in Rome under Nero. Sporadic and ineffectual persecution made heroes of its victims. That "the blood of the martyrs is the seed of the Church" was true. There were enough martyrs to provide numerous examples of self-sacrifice for the faith, and yet not enough to exterminate the faithful. Some pagans viewed this Christian enthusiasm for martyrdom as the fanaticism of religious extremists; others were profoundly impressed by the heroism of people who would give up life itself before they would relinquish their faith. The Church gained a truly heroic tradition, carefully preserved, which attracted potential converts who might otherwise have continued to scorn Christianity as merely another mystery cult.

Perhaps the most striking difference between Christianity and other religions in the Roman world was the fact that the early Christians formed not only a collection of the faithful but an *ecclesia*, a Church with a definite (though at first rudimentary) organization whose bonds were only strengthened by hostile public opinion and occasional persecution. By the second century this organization had already taken on the hierarchical form which characterized its later development. The highest official was the bishop or leader of the local community of Christians. His authority was centered in the urban district in which almost all the local churches had been founded. The area of the bishop's jurisdiction or spiritual leadership corresponded from the beginning with the administrative unit of the Roman government, the *civitas*. From a very early date we hear of various other officials or specially distinguished members of the original Christian communities. These were the presbyters (or priests, who had spiritual authority), deacons (who were assistants to the bishop, exercising non-spiritual functions such as maintenance of places of worship or distribution of charity), exorcists, readers, and other lesser officials. As a whole, they constituted the clergy as distinguished from the rest of the faithful, who were the laity. This distinction, and the hierarchically arranged functions or dignities of the clergy, provided a nucleus of leadership and a framework of organization which took on the character of a state existing alongside of, and within, the Empire.

The survival and growth of the local churches depended largely on the personal ability of the bishops, whose position was further enhanced by a theoretical justification of episcopal authority. This was the theory of apostolic succession, first enunciated by Irenaeus of Lyons (c.180). It was commonly held as a tenet of faith that the ancient Hebrew Scriptures and the apostolic writings subsequent to the Incarnation contained the authoritative statement of Christianity. And yet questions might arise concerning the correct interpretation of doubtful points in the Scriptures. Irenaeus set forth the view that a true interpretation could only come from the spiritual heirs of the Apostles: the bishops. All bishoprics had been established by the Apostles or representatives of the Apostles, who had conferred upon the first leaders of local Churches their spiritual authority. This authority had been handed down in an unbroken chain of transference from bishop to bishop, Irenaeus declared, because even though a new bishop was designated normally by election of the local community he received his spiritual authority, or consecration as bishop, at the hands of other bishops.

The supremacy of the bishop over the Christian community of the *civitas*, or the ecclesiastical diocese, was thus recognized in the unique episcopal power to confer spiritual authority on priests within his diocese or upon bishops-elect of other dioceses. Theoretically, it might be argued, each bishop was the equal of every other bishop because all derived authority from the Apostles. But two facts tended toward the elaboration of an episcopal hierarchy in which the superiority of some bishops over others gradually came to be recognized. First, some of the bishoprics had been founded by the Apostles themselves; second, the bishoprics of important cities in the Empire were wealthier and more influential than later and lesser foundations. Both facts tended to enhance the prestige of the bishops of such cities as Jerusalem, Antioch, Alexandria, and Rome. The bishops of these apostolic sees and of the larger cities often took the lead in combating divisive tendencies within the early Church and in resisting sporadic local persecution.

The first large-scale persecution was launched in 250 by the emperor

Decius, who sought to strengthen the government by eliminating all dissident elements within the Empire. Diocletian and his associates renewed the persecution. But all such attempts failed: the survival of the Church was in large part owing to the strength of its organization under episcopal leadership. Then a sudden reversal of fortune brought the new religion from its darkest hour of persecution under Diocletian to the status of an officially recognized religion under Constantine.

Constantine's motives will never be fully known. It is clear that personal conversion played an important role at some time between his victory at the Milvian Bridge (312) and his death-bed baptism (337). It is less certain whether this conversion caused or resulted from the pro-Christian policy which he adopted in his struggle for power and in his later effort to consolidate his rule. Constantine's main claim to statesmanship was his recognition that the Church could add strength to the Empire far beyond the number of its members. In no part of the Empire were Christians in the majority. In the East they averaged about ten per cent of the population, and in the West about five per cent, but they were concentrated largely in the cities and their organization made them the most cohesive religious group in the Empire. At one stroke Constantine converted the opposition of a persecuted sect into the most effective new source of loyalty and support which any emperor had gained. This was accomplished by an agreement with Licinius, the eastern Augustus, which is usually referred to as the Edict of Milan (313). By its terms Christianity was officially tolerated, property confiscated during the recent persecution was returned to the Church, and the Christian clergy were accorded the same privileges and exemptions from public duties enjoyed by the priesthood of the official pagan cults.

Christianity had by this time largely overcome or held its own against all its external enemies, such as official paganism, competing mystery cults, the Hellenistic philosophies, and the persecutions of the Roman government. A far more dangerous obstacle to Christian growth came from within the Church. Christianity, like all religious movements, had to meet the problem of divisive tendencies, or the development of antagonistic interpretations of doctrine. For Christians, doctrine was found in or based upon authoritative Scriptures, a divinely inspired revelation of the truth. Discordant or divergent doctrines, held by minority groups who claimed to give a true interpretation, were looked upon as heresies by the great majority of Christians. Most of these heresies arose from the early spread of Christianity among educated people in the Greek-speaking East who attempted to adapt the new religion to older philosophical systems.

The two most important heresies confronting the Church in the West after the Edict of Milan were Donatism and Arianism. The Donatists were, mainly, survivors of the persecutions in North Africa. They believed that priests who had deserted the Church during persecution should not be allowed to return to their pastoral positions. They went further to declare that the sacraments administered by any unworthy priests were invalid. Although this is primarily a disciplinary rather than doctrinal question, the efficacy of the sacraments—especially baptism and the Eucharist, which were widely considered indispensable for salvation—was a fundamental problem with doctrinal implications. The Donatists claimed that their views were essential to the maintenance of purity and catholicity in the Church; extremists went so far as to exclude from membership all who had committed mortal sin, both clergy and laity. Later reformers, both in the Middle Ages and in the Reformation, tended toward or accepted the Donatist position in their criticism of sinful clergy and their concept of the Church as a communion of saints. Inevitably such a Church could not be catholic (universal, all-embracing). In Africa the bitter and sometimes violent schism was intensified by the fact that Donatus, who claimed to be the true bishop of Carthage and who became the leader of the heresy, was supported by native Africans who resented Roman rule, while his opponent and actual occupant of the see of Carthage was supported mainly by Roman provincials and others loyal to the Empire. Constantine intervened in the quarrel on the orthodox, or Catholic, side. But more important than the emperor's orthodoxy was his determination to preserve the unity of the organization on which he relied for support. His policy of favoring Christianity led to active intervention in the affairs of the Church. The question of Donatism he referred to two synods of western bishops at Rome and Arles, in 313–314, and he attempted to enforce by governmental decree the decisions of those synods, that the efficacy of the sacraments was independent of the personal character of the priest. By implication, the emperor, who was not yet even a member of the Church, had exercised ecclesiastical leadership over the bishops and had assumed responsibility, as Constantine later wrote, for "a common harmony of sentiment among all the servants of God." The orthodox view prevailed, but common harmony did not. Donatism survived in North Africa as an underground movement until the Moslem conquests of the seventh century.

Even more emphatic was Constantine's next intervention in Church affairs. This concerned the heresy of Arianism, which had spread from Alexandria throughout much of the eastern half of the Empire. Arianism arose from a dispute between Alexander, bishop of Alexandria, and his priest Arius, concerning the divinity of Christ and the relation between God the Father and God the Son. Arius' view demeaned the Son to a subordinate position: he admitted that Christ was the Word of God incarnate in human flesh, and was thus divine, but he denied that the Son had the same nature as that of the Father. Alexander insisted that Christ was of the very same nature and substance of God, since salvation depended upon being one with the Son, and this oneness would not avail unless Christ's nature was the same as that of the Father. The arguments on either side were very complicated and were altered slightly as the dispute continued, but essentially Arius' view was an effort to adapt Christian theology to philosophical distinctions, while Alexander's arguments represented the traditional Christian view expressed in philosophical language. The controversy reached a crisis when Arius was exiled and his numerous supporters came to his defense.

At this point Constantine intervened by summoning on his own authority a council of over three hundred bishops representing the entire Church, the first ecumenical council, which met at Nicaea in 325. Sitting in his presence and probably influenced by the emperor to reach a unanimous decision, the bishops condemned Arianism as heresy. The council promulgated other canons which were to be binding upon the whole Church, and formulated articles of faith which became the basis of the orthodox doctrine of the Trinity as found in the Nicene Creed (which was actually enunciated by the Council of Constantinople in 381). As we shall see, the problem of Arianism was by no means settled in 325. The heresy spread to the East German peoples who began to enter the Empire in the fourth century. The original problem which Arius had debated was widened to include the nature of the Trinity and other doctrinal problems which continued to plague the eastern Church with heresy and schism for centuries.

The Council of Nicaea set two important precedents for the development of the Church. First, an ecumenical council of all the bishops was recognized as the supreme authority on doctrinal and disciplinary matters; second, the initiative and leadership of the emperor were tacitly accepted. So long as the emperor was orthodox, no objection to his implied supremacy over the Church was voiced. But Constantine's immediate successors were as often Arian as they were orthodox, or even pagan (as Julian the Apostate), so that the danger of imperial control became obvious to the orthodox bishops. Recognition and support by the state had brought to Christianity difficulties as well as benefits. Persecution by the state now became a weapon used by Arians and Catholics against each other, depending upon the persuasion of the emperor in power.

By the end of the fourth century the problem of the relation between spiritual and temporal authority had become acute. It is not quite accurate to speak of this as a struggle between Church and state. The emperors thought of themselves as properly playing a leading role in the Church, and the bishops had begun to take an active part in civil affairs. The bishops' influence may be seen in the imperial laws of the age, which incorporated into civil legislation much of the social teachings of the Church. The jurisdiction of the bishops' courts, originally informal tribunals for settling disputes among the clergy and Christian laity, was gradually extended to include purely civil suits. The judgments of episcopal courts were as binding as those of the ordinary courts of Roman law.

Thus, "Church and state" does not explain the real nature of the conflict between spiritual and temporal authority. As the bishops saw it, the great danger was that the spiritual and ecclesiastical affairs of the Church might be controlled by the emperor.

The determination of the bishops to be independent of imperial or secular control was dramatized by an incident which made a profound impression on contemporaries. Theodosius I, the last great emperor, had, in 390, put down a minor revolt in the city of Thessalonica by ordering the massacre of some seven thousand citizens who were trapped by imperial troops in the local circus. For this atrocious deed, St. Ambrose, the bishop of Milan, forced the emperor to do penance in his cathedral, declaring roundly that "the emperor is within the Church, not above it; in matters of faith and morals bishops judge emperors." This public humiliation of Theodosius did not solve the problem of the relation of temporal and spiritual authority—the problem has never been permanently solved in Western civilization—but it graphically emphasized the attitude of a large majority of the bishops, especially in the Latin West, that in the organization of the Church the emperor was not to be supreme.

5   THE AGE OF THE FATHERS: AMBROSE, JEROME, AND AUGUSTINE

The growth of the Church was paralleled by the growing ascendancy of Christian over pagan thought and letters. Christianity attracted the best minds and the best-educated men of the later Empire because it provided a challenge and an opportunity to deal with new issues that were alive and important for contemporaries. The decline of pagan classical culture coincided with the Age of the Fathers, an age of creative achievement in literature, theology, and philosophy. The classical tradition continued to provide the form, and Christianity the substance, of much of the intellectual life of the dying Empire. The educational methods, the literary standards, the canons of taste in poetry and in art, and the corpus of scientific knowledge and philosophical ideas of classical antiquity were never wholly lost. In general, they were consciously preserved and were accepted as models to emulate or to improve upon by adapting them to Christianity.

Christians agreed with their pagan opponents, in the third, fourth, and fifth centuries, that the achievements of the past were greater than anything being accomplished in the same fields by contemporaries. Where Christian disagreed with pagan was in the belief that Christianity was totally superior to any pagan religious or philosophical pursuit of Truth. In this attitude toward the pagan classics, Christians recognized a dilemma: either the Christian should shun pagan letters, and remain uneducated because education was completely pagan from the beginner's textbook on grammar up to the highest level of philosophy; or else the Christian seeking knowledge must run the risk of losing his faith through exposure to the blandishments and beauties of pagan literature. Some, like Tertullian (d. 222), counseled against reading the errors of the pagans, claiming that the Christian could obtain all knowledge from Scripture. Most Christian thinkers, however, agreed with the greatest of the Greek Fathers, Origen (d.254), that Christians must be equipped not only to understand the mysteries of the faith but also to refute the pagan philosophers in their own terms and on their own intellectual level. While recognizing the dangers involved, men like Jerome and Augustine advocated the study of the best pagan philosophers because, in the words of the biblical injunction, it was praiseworthy to "spoil the Egyptians," that is, to take from the pagans whatever intellectual weapons might be turned against them in defense of Christianity and whatever knowledge might be useful in understanding Christian revelation. The triumph of this view is not surprising because many of the Fathers were educated pagans before they were converted to Christianity. If this view had not triumphed, the thought and teachings of the Church might have remained at the level of some of Tertullian's writings. He explained the Resurrection as follows: "That the Son died may be believed because it is absurd; that He rose from the dead is certain because it is impossible!"

Later antiquity was a great age of schoolbooks in which the learning and literature of the past were condensed and simplified for educational purposes. From these schoolbooks most Christians gained their knowledge of the errors of pagan philosophy and enjoyed the dangerous pleasures of pagan literature. Most popular of all the grammar books were two fourth-century treatises by Donatus, the *Ars Minor* and *Ars Maior* (elementary and advanced) which for over twelve centuries were standard textbooks in their field. They treated the parts of speech and syntax, illustrating them by literary extracts. In the Middle Ages the next most popular textbook was Priscian's *Institutes of Grammar* (c.500), a more advanced treatise containing a disorganized storehouse of quotations from ancient literature. In the pursuit of what we today call a "liberal education," grammar (including literature as well as language) was the first discipline or art to be mastered. There were six others: rhetoric, dialectic, arithmetic, music, geometry, and astronomy. These were the seven "liberal arts" which became the standard medieval curriculum. By the end of the fourth century this classification had been established. Early in the fifth century Martianus Capella, a pagan, composed an encyclopedic treatise on the seven liberal arts entitled *The Nuptials of Mercury and Philology.* Couched in allegory, totally unoriginal, and compiled from earlier compilations, the style is ornate, inflated, and pretentious. In the judgment of one modern historian, "possibly some good Christian of the time could have composed

a worse book," but that is hard to believe. And yet for all its stylistic deficiencies the book did preserve the basic instruction of antiquity.

Considering the low educational level of the times and the fact that
by the end of the fourth century a knowledge of Greek was a mark of very
high erudition in the West, the attainments of the Latin Fathers of the
Church are truly remarkable. The greatest in influence upon the future
were the Four Doctors: St. Ambrose, St. Jerome, and St. Augustine, who
were contemporaries, and St. Gregory the Great, who was pope two centuries later. All four typify Western thought, as contrasted with the intellectual interests of the East, in that they were attracted more by practical
than by theoretical problems, by how to achieve salvation rather than by
metaphysical distinctions about the Persons of the Trinity. But Ambrose,
Jerome, and Augustine were well read in pagan philosophy as well as in the
Christian theology of the Greek Fathers. The general significance of the
Latin Fathers for medieval thought was twofold: they mastered pagan
philosophy (notably Neo-Platonism and Stoicism) and incorporated it into
their exposition of Christian doctrine and the teaching of the Church, and
they also were transmitters and interpreters to the Latin West of the
subtleties and profundities of Eastern Christian dogmatic speculation. The
Greek Fathers excelled in dialectical sophistication and hair-splitting pre-
cision—they also distinguished themselves by controversy, eccentricity, and
even heresy. Western patristic thought, under the influence of the Four
Doctors, was superior in the intellectual and emotional qualities that were
distinctively Roman and Latin, that is, an emphasis on ethics, a juristic
insistence on clarity and simplicity in theological discussion, and a more
profound psychological insight into human nature. The Latin Fathers
were more interested in the brotherhood of man and in man's relationship
to God; the Greek Fathers were more interested in the fatherhood of God
and in God's relationship to man.

Ambrose (c.340–397) was born into an aristocratic Roman family
and, after an excellent education, advanced rapidly in the civil service to
the rank of provincial governor. When the death of the bishop of Milan led
to a dispute between the Arian and orthodox factions, over the election of
a successor, he intervened to maintain the peace. According to a story
which circulated shortly after his death, when he was called upon to ad-
dress a riotous multitude during the local controversy, a child's voice was
heard crying out, "Let Ambrose be bishop!" With one accord the whole
city pressed the episcopal office upon the reluctant governor, who was not
yet even a baptized Christian. This deficiency was made good, and within
a week he was advanced from minor orders to priesthood and consecrated
bishop. Ambrose now turned to the study of theology and to the administration of his diocese. His greatest influence on the future was his uncompromising assertion of the independence of the Church and of the
superiority of the spiritual authority over the secular in matters concerning

faith and morals. His most dramatic statement of these principles, during his contest with Theodosius I over the Thessalonican massacre, has already been noted. Ambrose was a distinguished preacher. His sermons were the basis for his most important contributions to biblical exegesis: the *Hexaemeron*, dealing with the Creation, and a shorter commentary on the Gospel of St. Luke. In these and other theological treatises, Ambrose introduced the leading ideas of Stoic ethics as expounded in the works of Cicero, especially the concept of duty, although he made clear that the first object of the Christian's duty is no longer the state but God.

Ambrose and Hilary, bishop of Poitiers (d.367), were the first Latin Fathers to expound the Scriptures on as high an intellectual level as that of the Greek theologians. In doing so they incorporated the leading Eastern ideas and methods in their work, especially the use of the allegorical method of interpretation (i.e., setting forth the hidden meaning behind words whose literal sense implies a higher, but veiled, truth). Hilary was equally interested in the literal, or straightforward, meaning of the Bible; Ambrose was equally interested in expounding Christian ethics. Both were thus typically Western and Latin in balancing the Eastern influence with a common-sense interest in the practical and the useful, in terms of a Christian aspiration for salvation. Finally, Hilary and Ambrose were the two earliest important writers of a new form of poetry set to music and used in the liturgy of the Church. Hymns were the most original Christian contribution to Latin poetry. Rarely surpassed for beauty and religious feeling, Ambrose's hymns were written for antiphonal singing, "after the manner of the eastern churches," that is, in short stanzas to be sung alternately as a response by choir and congregation, which accounts for their extreme simplicity. At least four of Ambrose's hymns whose authenticity is beyond question are still sung and enjoyed today. One of these, *Veni Redemptor Gentium*, inspired the great hymn by Martin Luther, "Now Come, the Heathen's Saviour."

Jerome (c.340–419) was born a Christian into a well-to-do provincial family. He completed his early education in Rome, probably under the grammarian Donatus, and later devoted himself to theological studies in Gaul and northern Italy. Endowed with an eager intellectual curiosity and a rather contentious nature, Jerome dedicated himself to two goals: the elevation of Christian scholarship and the propagation of the monastic way of life. Jerome was a reformer. His zeal for scholarship and monasticism was a personal reaction against what he considered to be the low intellectual level and the worldliness of the Church in the Latin West. This attitude, his forceful personality, and rather more than normal vanity gave him the reputation of being a troublemaker. These traits also made him the best-educated and one of the most influential of the Fathers.

Jerome's ardor for asceticism led him to translate the rule of Pachomius and thus make available to the Latin West the basic formula of the

Eastern form of monasticism. His theological treatises and commentaries were distinguished by two characteristics found in all his writings: first, an interest in textual criticism; and second, a constant use of the best pagan writings to elucidate Christian revelation. His great love of the classics gave him a guilty conscience. In a dream which came to him during an illness, a voice from heaven accused him, "Thou art a Ciceronian, not a Christian, for where thy treasure is, there shall thy heart be." Fortunately for Christian scholarship, Jerome was unable to keep the vow he then took, never again to read a pagan book. But the experience was decisive in his life, for it turned him to a study of biblical exegesis and the writings of the Greek Fathers which he pursued in Constantinople under the greatest of contemporary Eastern scholars, St. Gregory of Nazianzus. During this period he also learned Hebrew, thus becoming one of the very few men of his day who knew three languages.

In 382 he accepted the invitation of Pope Damasus to come to Rome. It was during the next three years that some of Jerome's most caustic criticism was leveled at the fashionable and indulgent pseudo-Christians who corrupted the Church of his day. Of course this made him more enemies than friends. He inveighed against the "luxuries of Rome," and against false widows "who remain widows from necessity, not inclination," and whose carefully made-up faces would make one think "they had not lost husbands but were on the hunt for them." He poked fun especially at the wealthy Roman matrons, pampered by flattering priests (with hands extended not to give benediction but to receive gratuities), who "after a seven-course dinner dream of the Apostles" (a barb adapted from Terence), and who "when they give alms blow a full blast on the trumpet, and when they go to mass hire the town crier."

Pope Damasus was able to harness and direct the inexhaustible intellectual energies of Jerome, turning him to the monumental task of retranslating the Bible into Latin. Since Rome was uncongenial for this scholarly task, Jerome retired to Palestine where he founded a monastery at Bethlehem and spent the rest of his life (385–419). He could not resist one final (and, we might say, ecumenical) thrust at Christians whose fervor exceeded their intelligence, observing that "only doctors practice medicine and only carpenters build houses, but searching the meaning of Scripture is the one art that everybody is sure that he possesses; it is bad enough to teach what you do not know, but worse not even to be aware of what you do not know." Jerome knew, as some modern translators of the Bible into English have learned, how strong was the force of religious conservatism against changing, even if change meant making more accurate, the traditional and familiar translation of Scripture. The final result of Jerome's prolonged study, based upon the previous textual criticism of Origen but going beyond it, was a text of both the Old and New Testaments translated accurately from the best Hebrew (or Aramaic) and Greek manuscripts then accessible. This translation used the freer idiom and more expressive figures of speech of fourth-century Latin rather than the more formal Latinity of Cicero or Virgil. The final version, the Vulgate Bible, did not gain universal acceptance in the West until the end of the seventh century, but its scholarly accuracy and faithfulness to the spirit of the original texts plus sponsorship by the papacy made its ultimate triumph inevitable.

The greatest of all the Latin Fathers was Augustine (354–430), one of the most fascinating personalities in all history as he was one of the most influential. Although his mother was Christian he attended the pagan schools of his native North Africa and at Rome. The first step in his spiritual odyssey came at the age of nineteen when he read Cicero's introductory treatise on philosophy, the *Hortensius*, which led him to investigate pagan philosophy, especially Manichaeism and Neo-Platonism. During this period, first as a student and then as a teacher of rhetoric, Augustine lived what later seemed to him a life of vice and wantonness. He was a dilettante rather than a serious student—he never mastered Greek and depended on Latin translations for his later reading of the Eastern theologians. His purpose grew more serious with time, and when his teaching career took him to Milan he came under the influence of Ambrose, whose great sermons finally clarified for him what he had been seeking and the path by which to attain it: the understanding that "all knowledge should direct itself toward knowing God."

Augustine, now intellectually convinced, was enrolled as a catechumen eagerly studying the Christian faith. His real conversion, his attainment of faith, came through an experience which he could only recognize as the operation of divine grace: "instantly, by a light as it were infused into my heart, all darkness of doubt vanished away." Shortly afterwards he was baptized by Ambrose, and then returned to North Africa where he was later ordained a priest and then became bishop of Hippo. He died during the siege of his city by Vandals in 430. During the busy years of his episcopate he found time to write on almost all the important issues of Christian doctrine. His theological treatises and his controversial writings against the heresies of his day constitute the greatest patristic achievement and the most profound influence on Western religious thought exercised by one mind. His influence dominated medieval philosophy and theology and lives on not only in modern Catholic thought but also, mainly through Calvin and Luther, in Protestant thought as well.

Augustine's earlier interest in pagan philosophies is apparent throughout his works. Many of these were undertaken to refute pagan errors and Christian heresies. In his treatises against Manichaeism, Augustine dealt with the problem of evil. The Manichaeans had argued in their dualistic system that good and evil were two irreconcilable principles, the one spiritual and the other material. For Augustine the created material world could not in itself be evil nor could evil be anything positive; evil was simply the absence of good, or the turning away from God, the Supreme Good. Neo-Platonic metaphysics helped him define good as whatever serves or tends toward God, to the degree that it achieves union with God. Intimately connected with this view was Augustine's concept of free will in human nature. Pelagius, a wandering monk from the British Isles, had been teaching in the schools of Spain and Italy that men did not inherit original sin and that human free will was sufficient to attain salvation, thus rendering divine grace and the sacraments of the Church superfluous. The naïve optimism of Pelagius did not appeal to a man like Augustine, who had suffered the torments of a will which sought but could not find Truth without grace. For Augustine human will was free to turn toward or away from God, but will was defective; free will must be fortified by divine grace because original sin turned man from God. Psychologically Augustine was on sounder ground. But his enthusiasm in refuting Pelagianism led him to emphasize so strongly the omnipotence of God and the insignificance of human good works that he also seemed to imply, logically, that the sacraments (the normal means of receiving grace, according to the teaching of the Church) were superfluous. In its extreme form this position was simply a belief in predestination. On this point the teaching of the medieval Church did not follow Augustine, taking rather a middle position between him and Pelagius, and emphasizing both the necessity of grace and the necessity of good works for the Christian life that leads to salvation.

Augustine's two best known works are the *Confessions*, an intimately personal revelation of his own spiritual quest and final attainment of faith, and *The City of God*, the greatest apologetic (i.e., defense of the faith) in all Christian literature. *The City of God* was written to answer the pagan accusation that Christianity was responsible for the misfortunes of the Empire, specifically the sack of Rome in 410. Its twenty-two books were published separately as he wrote them from 413 to 426. The work as a whole was never revised, so that it strikes the reader as repetitious and poorly organized. Nonetheless, it is still the most challenging and all-embracing statement of a Christian philosophy of history, an interpretation on the grandest scale of the ultimate meaning of human existence in terms of Christian theology. Briefly, Augustine's argument is that human history accords with a divine plan whose central theme is the continuing struggle between the City of God (*civitas Dei*, the commonwealth or community of the elect) whose triumph is assured and the Earthly City (the community of those who reject God). The two "cities" thus represent good and evil; but Augustine is careful not to confuse them with the Church and the Empire of his own age—as later and lesser minds have often done. All human history is thus a preparation for the final event, the Last Judgment, when citizens of the eternal City of God will find salvation. Those of the Earthly City, including nominal Christians who turn away from God though they are members of the Church, will be damned.

The work of Ambrose, Jerome, Augustine and the other Latin Fathers of the Church led to two general results. First, the thought of the West was finally brought up to the level of Eastern Christian thought. Many of the doctrinal and philosophical ideas of the Greek Fathers were brought permanently within the range of Western intellectual life, to form part of the heritage of Christian antiquity on which medieval culture could be built. Second, the intellectual opposition of a waning paganism had not only been met but many of its philosophical concepts, especially Stoic ethics and Neo-Platonic metaphysics, had been assimilated into Christian thought. The Church was heir to Rome not only in ecclesiastical organization; the Fathers of the Church incorporated the intellectual heritage of Rome into Christian thought.

6 THE RISE OF THE PAPACY: GREGORY THE GREAT

The fourth century was the great age of the episcopate. Recognition by the imperial government increased the responsibilities and added to the duties of the bishops. There was a great influx of converts into the Church, many of whom were less drawn by the faith than moved by a sense of expediency. Instruction and confirmation, the building of new churches, and the ordination of new priests to care for the growing number of Christians were the immediate concern of each bishop. The Church now enjoyed the right to hold property and to receive gifts. As the Church grew wealthy from pious donations, the bishops had to devote more time to maintaining and exploiting large holdings of real property and to distributing the income properly among the various activities or services which they could now extend to the great majority of the people in their dioceses. They built hospitals, maintained orphanages, dispensed charity to the poor, provided inexpensive and equitable justice in their courts, supported the clergy of their cathedrals, preached regularly to their own congregations, visited the churches under their jurisdiction, and provided the moral leadership to meet local disasters or difficulties, such as plague, fire and flood, or barbarian invasions. Because he was elected by the clergy and people of his diocese (which in practice meant the clergy of his own cathedral and the populace of the city), the bishop represented local interests and was concerned for civic welfare. The bishop, rather than any civil magistrate, was the most important person in the *civitas*.

The bishops' extensive powers, their preeminence within their dioceses, and their independence from outside authority justify the phrase "monarchical bishops" to characterize the episcopate of the third and fourth centuries. A higher dignity or prestige was accorded to the bishops of more ancient foundations, of more important cities, and especially of the apostolic sees. The hierarchical organization which had long been established within each diocese began to appear clearly in the episcopate. Recognition of Christianity by the state and the other factors which caused the growing importance of all bishops tended to increase the wealth, influence, and power of the bishops of the greater cities even more rapidly. The earlier moral preeminence or prestige came to be recognized as an ecclesiastical superiority over the other bishops of their province. Such bishops were called metropolitan bishops (equivalent to the later archbishops), and in the East their provinces corresponded with the civil provinces of the Empire. Finally, among the metropolitans the same distinctions of rank grew up, and the bishops of the most important cities acquired a recognized superiority over the other metropolitans within the orbit of their influence. These were the patriarchs of Antioch, Alexandria, Rome, and—because of its political importance—Constantinople. In the fifth century Jerusalem was also recognized as a patriarchate.

Thus the organization of the Church above the level of the diocese had become, in the fourth century, roughly parallel to the hierarchical organization of the Empire. In 381 the Council of Constantinople affirmed the superiority of the bishop of Constantinople over the bishops of Antioch and Alexandria and recognized the primacy of the bishop of Rome over the whole Church. But the patriarch at Constantinople refused to accept a subordinate position and, with support from the emperor, persuaded the Council of Chalcedon in 451 to recognize Constantinople as equal in rank with Rome and supreme over the churches of the East. The bishop of Rome, who was now usually accorded the title of pope, would not accept this equality, nor would the patriarch retreat from the claim unless forced by the emperor. Claims and counterclaims varied during the next several centuries, often in response to political exigencies in the eastern imperial court, but generally the pope was everywhere recognized as supreme in the West and was always ready to assert his supremacy over the universal Church. In the East the patriarch of Constantinople was actually supreme, and the pope was willing to recognize his eastern supremacy if the patriarch would exercise it as a bishop subordinate to the papacy.

The rise of the papacy to this supreme position in the West had its beginning much earlier than the recognition of Christianity by the Empire in the fourth century. Already in the middle of the third century some African bishops were objecting to the claims of Rome; but the greatest of them, Cyprian, bishop of Carthage, provided one of the doctrinal bases on which the supremacy of Rome was established. In his treatise *On the Unity of the Church* (c.258) Cyprian affirmed that the Church was not only a mystical union of the faithful—a spiritual commonwealth ("the bride of Christ"), whose unity is not of this world—but also that the Church was visible, catholic (i.e., universal), and one. For Cyprian it was enough to assert the unity of the Church in this world without bothering about the institutional implications. But the majority of Christians, in the West at least, agreed with the bishops of Rome that the unity of the Church could not be realized without a single supreme head who could symbolize this unity and direct the one Church.

The qualifications of the bishops of Rome for this supremacy were numerous and unequaled. Rome was the first city of the Empire, her glory and prestige unmatched even by Constantinople, as indicated by the usage of the term "New Rome" to designate the new capital. The church at Rome was the oldest and wealthiest in the West. Its founder was believed to have been the apostle Peter, and its traditions included the martyrdom of both Peter and Paul. The absence of the imperial government from Rome was an advantage because it helped to keep the bishop free from the intrigues of the imperial court and from the immediate influence of the emperors. These factors were enough to make Rome a leading church whose bishops enjoyed great influence. In addition the personal ability of the Roman bishops was impressive. They were, with few exceptions, remarkably conservative and orthodox on doctrinal matters. The fact that no heresy originated in Rome, or even in Italy, contributed to the position of the bishop as a logical mediator in doctrinal disputes between other bishops. Finally, in the ecumenical councils of the fourth and fifth centuries (which the popes did not attend personally but through delegates), the influence of Rome was staunchly on the side which ultimately became accepted as orthodox, and was firmly committed against interference in ecclesiastical affairs by the imperial government.

All these considerations help explain historically the rise of the papacy, but the bishops of Rome by no means relied upon these historical developments as the basis of their claims. This basis was a theoretical justification of papal supremacy known as the Petrine theory. The first complete and formal enunciation of the Petrine theory came from Leo the Great in his refutation of the arguments for the equality conferred upon the patriarch of Constantinople by the Council of Chalcedon in 451. But the theory was generally acknowledged in the West at least a half-century earlier, and there is evidence for its existence as early as the beginning of the third century. Leo believed that the theory had been held by the church in Rome since its foundation.

The Petrine theory is based upon the words of Christ as found in the Gospel of St. Matthew:

> Thou art Peter, and upon this rock I will build my church; and the gates of hell shall not prevail against it. And I will give to thee the keys of the kingdom of heaven: and whatsoever thou shalt bind on earth shall be bound in heaven: and whatsoever thou shalt loose on earth shall be loosed in heaven.

According to the Petrine theory these words of Christ made Peter the chief apostle, the ruler of the Church, possessed of unlimited spiritual powers. By apostolic succession, these powers descended to the successors of Peter, who was the first bishop of Rome. Hence, as successor of Peter the bishop of Rome was supreme over the universal Church.

Later, this theory became a doctrine. Opposition to it has usually taken one or more of three lines: first, a different interpretation of the text, for example, to construe "rock" figuratively as Peter's confession of faith rather than as referring to Peter personally; second, a denial of the tradition that Peter founded the church in Rome (on this point the evidence is late, and the problem is to decide how much weight can be given to early tradition); and third, a denial of the theory of apostolic succession, on which the Petrine theory is dependent.

Whatever might be the merits of the arguments for or against the Petrine theory, the rise of the bishop of Rome is clearly recorded in the historical evidence of the fourth and fifth centuries. Several milestones in this rise of the papacy illustrate the ways in which the pope was recognized as the supreme head of Latin Christianity. The Council of Sardica in 344, attended mainly by western bishops, ruled that a bishop who had been deposed by a local or provincial council might appeal his case for final decision to the bishop of Rome. This canon was never accepted in the East, but it was acted upon frequently in the West. It was during the pontificate of Damasus (336–384), the first bishop of Rome to define formally his superiority over all other bishops, that Jerome's retranslation of the Scriptures was begun under papal auspices. The result was the Vulgate Bible (from *vulgatus,* meaning spread abroad or generally known). It became the authoritative text of the Latin Bible in the Middle Ages. The next pope, Siricius (384–399), issued the first surviving authentic decretal (385), an authoritative decision in response to questions concerning matters of discipline submitted to him by Spanish bishops. From this time on, the decretals of the popes became important sources of the canon law, supplementing the canons of the church councils, as regulations binding upon the whole Latin Church in the West. Leo I (440–461), the first of three popes to be called "the Great," brought both the prestige and the power of the papacy to a new height. We have already noted his reaction to the Council of Chalcedon, and we shall note later the leadership he exercised—in default of the emperor or other civil magistrate—in the defense of Rome against the barbarian Huns (452) and Vandals (455). Another of his achievements was to secure from Valentinian III the issuance of an edict (445) recognizing in civil law the superior jurisdiction of the pope over all western bishops and directing imperial officials to enforce this obedience to Rome.

During the next century and a half only Gelasius I (492–496) made a significant contribution to the tradition of papal leadership, in his statement of the dualism of authority in this world, sometimes referred to as the Gelasian theory of the two powers. According to this theory, the spiritual and the temporal powers are entrusted to two different orders, each drawing its authority from God, each supreme in its own sphere and independent within its own sphere of the other. The two powers are closely interrelated, but secular rulers are subordinate to the spiritual authority within the latter's sphere, and vice versa. However, the authority of the spiritual power is ultimately superior because "even for rulers of men priests will have to give account in the divine judgment." This statement was a theoretical expression of the position already taken a century earlier by Ambrose. It was also a development of the teaching of the New Testament concerning the Christian attitude toward secular authority. The Gelasian theory became a fundamental premise in medieval political thought.

Most of the popes during the century and a half after Leo the Great found it difficult enough to preserve the prestige already won, without trying to add to papal power. After Leo the only unity left in the West was that of the Church, and that unity was precarious. The disorders of the barbarian invasions were climaxed in Italy by the settlement of the Ostrogoths under their Arian king Theodoric at the end of the fifth century. Although Theodoric favored religious toleration, he did not scruple to influence papal elections and papal policy. The Byzantine reconquest of Italy in the sixth century did little to improve the position of the papacy, for Justinian firmly controlled the Church. He and his successors enforced the rule that no new pope was to be consecrated without the emperor's consent. On more than one occasion a pope found himself exiled or driven to take refuge from his Ostrogothic or Byzantine opponents. During the turbulent period of the Gothic wars and the Lombard invasion, in the second half of the sixth century, papal authority over the Church in the West was rarely exercised. The popes were too absorbed in local problems of survival. However, while the popes' universal power over the Church waned during the sixth century the basis was being laid for the later temporal authority of the papacy in Rome. More and more local political power was either assumed by the popes or delegated to them by the eastern emperors, until the popes became more important in the government of Rome than the imperial officials. Elsewhere in Italy the local Byzantine governors had assumed a semihereditary and semi-independent status. The eastern government left them to their own devices so long as they acknowledged the sovereignty of the emperor and paid taxes occasionally. The only difference in Rome was that it was the pope who moved into this position of semi-independence under Byzantine sovereignty.

The decline of the see of St. Peter was now arrested by the greatest of the early medieval popes, Gregory I the Great (590–604), who consolidated the local authority of the papacy and vigorously reasserted papal supremacy over Latin Christianity. For these reasons, for his contribution to early medieval culture, and for his constructive reforms as bishop of the church in Rome, Gregory has justly been called the "Father of the Medieval Papacy." Born into an ancient senatorial family of great wealth, as a young man Gregory rose rapidly in the civil administration of Rome, reaching the highest rank, that of city prefect, in 573. His true interests were revealed two years later when, on the death of his father, he dedicated his inheritance of landed property to the foundation of six monasteries in Sicily and one in Rome, and entered the latter as a monk. His retirement from the world, which he later described as the happiest years of his life, ended with his appointment as deacon of one of the seven "regions" into which the bishopric of Rome was divided for administrative purposes. In 579 he was appointed papal envoy to the court at Constantinople, where he spent the next several years broadening his experience in both secular and ecclesiastical affairs. On his return to Rome he spent three years as abbot of his monastery. When Pope Pelagius was carried off by the plague, Gregory was elected pope.

Several developments are associated with Gregory for which he was not, perhaps, originally responsible, but they appear clearly for the first time during his pontificate and they were to have an important influence on the medieval Church. The liturgy of the Roman church (the form and order of worship including the use of vocal music called "Gregorian chant"), the organization of the diocese, and the administration and expenditure of the revenues of the endowment of landed estates of the apostolic see were all improved by Gregory. Gregory launched the Roman Ordinal (containing the daily services in the Church for the entire year) upon its eventful career by sending it with missionaries to England, from where it later spread throughout the West. The Ordinal supplanted while absorbing elements from the Gallic, the Visigothic, the Ambrosian (north Italian), and other western rites which had grown up semi-independently. The richness and variety of Christian worship, reflecting the varying temper and spiritual needs of the diversity of peoples embraced within the Church, was never in the Middle Ages crushed beneath any rigid insistence upon liturgical uniformity. But there was always a latent danger that differences in liturgical usages might lead to disunity in the Church—for ritual is a symbolic expression of the substance of faith. The historical significance, then, of the Roman rite is that liturgical differences in the West would be variations of one universally accepted rite, rather than fundamentally different rites.

As bishop of Rome Gregory is best known for his administration of the landed estates of his see, the so-called Patrimony of St. Peter, consisting of properties located in almost every part of Italy, in the Mediterranean islands, in Gaul, Africa, and the Balkans. The surviving correspondence of Gregory reveals the efficiency of a humane exploitation of papal lands.

Their revenues supported the Roman church, most of the normal functions of the imperial administration in Rome, such as poor relief, support of garrison troops, and maintenance of fortifications, as well as orphanages, schools, and hospitals. In this work Gregory relied upon the clergy of his diocese, headed by the deacons of the seven regions of Rome and by the so-called cardinal priests (i.e., the most important priests in the twenty-five, later twenty-eight, "titles" or parishes into which the city was divided). Finally, Gregory as bishop was a noted preacher. His pontificate was begun during a plague, and nearly every year thereafter was marked by some disaster, famine, or pestilence which set the atmosphere for a series of moving sermons on the theme of the Day of Judgment. The horrors of hellfire and damnation, the eternal bliss of paradise for those who are saved, the rapidly approaching end of the world in which most of his listeners stoutly believed —these subjects were not original with Gregory, but he did much to make them the stock-in-trade of medieval preaching. His graphic descriptions of demons and angels contributed to the general atmosphere of living halfway in the supernatural world which characterized later religious thought on the popular level.

As primate of the West, Gregory resuscitated the prestige of the papacy and raised it higher than ever by intervening in the doctrinal disputes and ecclesiastical affairs of every western kingdom. In Africa he continued the fight against the Donatists and encouraged appeals from local synods to Rome. The churches of Frankish Gaul were so far under royal influence that there was little hope of immediate supervision of their affairs, but by frequent correspondence with the bishops and kings he was influential in some affairs and kept alive the contact with Rome which later became an important source of power for the Frankish kings. In Spain he promoted the conversion of the Visigoths, who were Arian Christians, to Catholicism. Far more important for the future, he initiated the conversion of the Anglo-Saxons in England. By establishing this precedent Gregory was responsible for the traditional role of papal leadership in the conversion of heathen peoples in later centuries. Finally, as supreme head of the Church in the West and claimant of supremacy over the Church universal, Gregory firmly but politely rejected the claim of John the Faster, patriarch of Constantinople, to be styled "universal patriarch," pointing out that this sort of talk was more suggestive of Antichrist than of Christian humility. For himself, he preferred to use the style *servus servorum Dei* ("servant of the servants of God"), a perfect expression of the Benedictine spirit of humility, which has been, since his pontificate, the title by which popes have referred to themselves in decretals and official correspondence.

As temporal ruler of Rome, Gregory like his predecessors simply did what had to be done to meet the recurring emergencies of the Lombard invasion. Since the hard-pressed Byzantine emperor was not able to spare enough troops to garrison Rome adequately, Gregory himself raised and provisioned a local militia, supervised the defenses of Rome, conducted negotiations with the Lombard king, and worked out a separate peace— much to the indignation of the emperor—whereby Rome was saved from further attack. Technically this was insubordination or even treason, but the necessities of the case justified Gregory's action. The Byzantine government was unable to give assistance and unwilling to recognize the Lombard conquests. To the people of Rome, Gregory was a hero and a statesman who had brought peace.

Gregory's work as a theologian and writer will be discussed later, together with other cultural developments of this period. It remains only to add that, of all the many interests and achievements which Gregory the Great packed into a single career, the interest nearest to his heart and the activity which he sought most to promote was the monastic way of life according to the rule of St. Benedict. For Gregory as pope represented not only the traditions of imperial Rome united with the vigorous episcopal traditions of Christianity, he also represented a new and vital element in the Christian world of the future: the monastic ideal. In his person, "monasticism ascended the papal throne."

The Foundation of
the Germanic Kingdoms

During the fifth century the internal decay of the Roman Empire and the barbarian pressure on her frontiers culminated in the foundation of Germanic kingdoms throughout the West. The disintegration of Roman rule in the West was not sudden, nor was there a sudden collapse of the defenses of the frontier. Barbarian penetration into the Empire had been going on steadily for several centuries, and it was not entirely the result of conflict or warfare between Germans and Romans. Peaceful infiltration of individuals or small groups of barbarians dates back to before the Christian era. The "invasions" were in many cases so unmilitary in nature as to deserve the German historians' term, *Völkerwanderung* ("the wandering of the peoples"). Large numbers of barbarians were constantly on the move during the third, fourth, and fifth centuries. The later emperors, as we have seen, often settled them within the Empire to cultivate abandoned farm lands and to defend the frontier against other wandering barbarians. By the end of the fourth century, more than half of the Roman army was actually barbarian, and many Germans occupied the highest positions of command.

Even the German kings who invaded the western Empire with armies came to conquer and rule, but not to destroy. Most of them sought and many gained recognition from the emperors so that their rule might be buttressed by legitimacy. This is why, even in the West, it is impossible to fix a date for the end of the Empire. The German kings in fact ruled independently; in theory they were ruling in the name of the emperor and by his appointment. This theory was expressed in the Roman titles by which they were distinguished. Theodoric, king of the Ostrogoths, bore the dignity and rank of *patricius*; the Merovingian kings styled themselves *viri illustres*. But none of the Germanic kings dared assume the title of emperor. This fact is a striking illustration of the spell which Rome, the idea of universal sovereignty over the civilized world, cast upon men's minds. The barbarian king might rule a mixed Romano-Germanic population; he might even possess Roman citizenship and the highest Roman dignity; but he remained a barbarian, dependent for power on his control of barbarian troops and deriving his original authority from tribal leadership. He did not aspire to the purple.

7   THE BARBARIANS AND ROME

Little is known of the origins and early history of the German barbarians. It is not until the end of the first century that a Roman writer, Tacitus, provides a systematic description of the early Germans in his treatise entitled *Germania*. Perhaps there will never be complete agreement as to how far Tacitus can be trusted or as to what was his purpose in writing. For a proper understanding of Tacitus' *Germania*, two extremes should be avoided: first, the view of some nineteenth-century historians that Tacitus' opinions confirm their own romantic and idealized conception of an almost wholly virtuous "fresh, young, and vigorous" society possessing its own culture and ready to reinvigorate an effete and decadent Roman civilization; and second, the more recent tendency to reject almost all of Tacitus' opinions as artful praise of the "noble savage," veiling his criticism of the morals and politics of the Empire. The first tendency reads too much into Tacitus, and the second rejects more than is necessary. In his description of the geography and customs of a people in whom his contemporaries were interested, the author, like the modern journalist, enlivened his treatise by passing a few judgments and emphasizing features of the unfamiliar German way of life which might increase his readers' interest. Inevitably Tacitus' own point of view occasionally emerges: the view of a man who, at the end of the first century, was out of sympathy with his times. Politically, he was at heart a republican who regretted the passing of the simpler virtues of an earlier age.

With these preliminary cautions in mind, the most striking general impression derived from the *Germania* is that of a primitive society in which class distinctions existed but had not hardened, in which, despite the existence of kings, political authority was not concentrated, and in which the values and customs of daily life were rude and simple. The sanctity of hearth and home; skill and courage in warfare; and honorable dealings in personal affairs—these were the primary virtues of Germanic life. Some of Tacitus' statements imply criticism of Roman morals more than they portray those of the Germans: he roundly affirms that "German women live in chastity that is impregnable, uncorrupted by the temptations of public shows or the excitement of banquets. Adultery in that populous nation is extremely rare. . . . No one in Germany finds vice amusing, or calls it 'up-to-date' to debauch and be debauched." Tacitus adds, "Good morality is more effective in Germany than good laws in some places we know."[1]

But Tacitus was by no means blind to the shortcomings of the Germans and the land they inhabited. "Who would leave Asia, Africa, or Italy to visit Germany," he asks, "with its unlovely scenery, its bitter climate, its general dreariness to sense and eye, unless it were his home?" Physically, the Germans are distasteful and inferior, according to Roman standards. They have "wild, blue eyes, reddish hair and huge frames that excel only in violent effort. They have no power to endure hard work and exertion, and little capacity to bear thirst and heat; but their climate and soil have taught them to bear cold and hunger." Despite their virtues in battle, their wanton addiction to endless strife makes no appeal to the civilized Roman. Agriculture and the other arts of peace are neglected; "when not engaged in warfare, they spend some little time in hunting, but more in idling, abandoned to sleep and gluttony. All the heroes and grim warriors dawdle their time away, while the care of house, hearth, and fields is left to the women, old men, and the weaklings of the family. The warriors . . . love indolence, but they hate peace." They live not in cities but scattered about in villages, with an open space around each house, "perhaps as a precaution against the risk of fire, perhaps because they are such inexpert builders." Their buildings are not of stone or tile, but of "ugly timber, both unimpressive and unattractive." In short, the physical conditions of early German life were simple and severe, relieved in times of peace only by hunting, gambling with dice, dancing with swords and spears, and drinking a winelike beverage made from fermented barley juice. Like some American Indians, eighteen hundred years later, the Germans, according to Tacitus, "show no self-control in drinking—you have only to indulge their intemperance by supplying all that they crave, and you will gain as easy a victory through their vices as through your own arms."

The religion, government, and customs of the people were primitive but complex. Tacitus mentions three gods, to whom he gives the Roman names of Mercury, Hercules, and Mars, and says that the Germans "did

---

[1] These and the following quotations from Tacitus are taken from *Tacitus on Britain and Germany, A New Translation* by H. Mattingly (West Drayton, Middlesex, 1948), pp. 102, 104, 108ff., 112ff., 116f., and 120, reprinted by permission of the publisher, Penguin Books Ltd. (Copyright by Penguin Books Ltd.)

not represent them with anything like human features," but rather "call by the name of god that hidden presence which is seen only by the eye of reverence." The Germans had no temples; their places of worship were sacred groves of trees (the remote origins of our modern Christmas tree and Maypole). Human sacrifice was reserved to the chief god, Tacitus' "Mercury" (in whom we may recognize Woden, from whose name Wednesday derives), while beasts were offered to "Hercules" (Thor—whence our Thursday) and "Mars" (Tiu—Tuesday). Divine foreknowledge of human events, the Germans believed, could be gained by taking auspices. Like the Romans, they observed the flight and interpreted the sounds of birds; more elaborate was their practice of casting lots to determine divine favor or disfavor toward a particular undertaking. Through their sacred horses, maintained at public expense in the sacred groves, the deities communicated with the faithful. Yoked to a chariot and driven by the high priest or king, these "confidants of the gods" by their neighing (properly interpreted) provided the surest of omens. Finally, a military forecast could be obtained by capturing one of the enemy and pitting him at single combat with a champion of the tribe, each armed in native style.

The day-by-day government was left to each family and clan organization. Public affairs, or decisions involving the whole tribe, were determined by the "chiefs" or prominent men, if such affairs were more or less routine. If extraordinary decisions were impending, the chiefs prepared agenda for submission to a general assembly of the men of military age. "Then such hearing," Tacitus reports, "is given to the king or chief as age, rank, military distinction, or eloquence can secure. . . . If a proposal displeases them, the people roar out their dissent; if they approve, they clash their spears." Most major decisions concerned the declaring of war—other public business being relatively unimportant. The role of the warriors was restricted to simple acclamation of or opposition to a decision reached beforehand by the tribal leaders. The primitive Germanic political system was hardly democratic. It involved collective response to chiefs' decisions rather than any participation in government or the decision-making process.

The public assembly was also a judicial body for the highest crimes; and the assembly designated the chiefs who dispensed justice in the local districts or villages. Of law Tacitus has little to say. From later evidence it is clear that immemorial custom, preserved by oral tradition, constituted the legal code. From Tacitus we learn that punishment was made to fit the crime, on the principle that "deeds of violence should be paid for in the full glare of publicity, but deeds of shame should be suppressed." The traitor or deserter in time of war and "the unnaturally vicious" could expect the death penalty; all other crimes were punished by pecuniary fines proportionate to the offense. The injured party or the relatives (in case of homicide) received the major portion of the fine, while the remainder was paid to the king.

The king's share in such fines was as near to the concept of a "state," as distinct from the community of families and clans, as the Germanic tribes had attained. The primitive king was not so much a political head of the state as he was the leading dignitary of the most noble tribal family, more nearly a high priest than a monarch. The real leaders of the community were the military chieftains whose power derived from their valor as leaders in battle, and whose position in the community depended upon a following (*comitatus*) of "companions" or youths who served the person, not the office, of their leader. This element of personal attachment is the essence of early Germanic social organization. In a classic passage, Tacitus sums up the blending of valor and loyalty which is the fundamental Germanic contribution to the social values of medieval Europe:

> On the field of battle it is a disgrace to the chief to be surpassed in valor by his companions, to the companions not to come up to the valor of their chief. As for leaving a battle alive after your chief has fallen, that means lifelong infamy and shame. To defend and protect him, to put down one's own acts of heroism to his credit—that is what they really mean by "allegiance." The chiefs fight for victory, the companions for their chief.

No other passage in Tacitus is so important for our understanding of the Germanic element in the Middle Ages. In Tacitus' "chief" and his "companions" may be recognized the prototype of the feudal lord and his vassals, whose mutual bonds of personal loyalty and service were the principles on which a new European order was finally established.

The picture Tacitus draws at the end of the first century A.D. was in many respects out-of-date when the barbarians of the fourth and fifth centuries broke into the Empire. Some of the changes in Germanic society accompanied the evolution from a pastoral to an agricultural economy. Other changes were owing to contacts between the barbarians and Rome. Roman influence penetrated into the north through commercial relations; and even before the conversion of the Germanic peoples to Christianity there had been some reception of religious ideas from the Mediterranean world. Other contacts were military, bringing the barbarians under the influence of perhaps the most potent civilizing force of antiquity, the Roman army. The Roman army not only taught the barbarians how to improve their warmaking—a lesson learned at the cost of many defeats—but it educated them, first by example and later by using them as auxiliary troops, in the art of military and political organization. The Germans slowly learned to combine their forces into confederations of tribes under the rule of kings whose function was no longer religious but political and military. Often these tribes settled on the confines of the Empire in the status of *foederati* (allied or confederate troops) to serve as permanent garrisons for frontier defense. This was the most important way in which the peaceful infiltration of the Roman Empire by Germanic peoples took place. Other ways in which they were slowly absorbed into Roman society were the practice of enslaving barbarian captives of war and the practice of taking hostages from the German leaders. These well-born hostages were well treated and often entered the service of the emperors. By the fourth century some of them, like some of the German commanders of the *foederati* stationed along the frontiers, had become generals in the Roman army.

It would be grossly unhistorical to believe, then, that there existed any deep-rooted or inherent antagonism between the German and the Roman, the Teutonic and the Latin peoples. The Germans who found their way into the Empire peacefully, and especially those who rose to high station in its service, sought to make a place for themselves within, and thus to help preserve, the civilization of the Mediterranean world. The German attitude toward Rome was a compound of envy and awe. Rome— her Empire, her higher standard of living, her more civilized culture—exerted a profound influence on the barbarians. They coveted the easier life and the political power which were the prizes of acceptance within her frontiers. They set out not to destroy a civilization which to them seemed as important as it did to the Romans, but to gain acceptance either peacefully or by force. In the end, the Germans were partly romanized and Rome was partly barbarized.

On the eve of the German invasions, Rome was at the considerable disadvantage of maintaining a longer line of defense than any modern state has been required to do. She had to divide her available forces between two fronts. The later emperors had no alternative to stripping the western defenses in favor of protecting the wealthier eastern half of the Empire, threatened by the greater menace of Persian arms. Roman policy assumed that the loss of a western province might be made good, but recovery against Persia might be impossible. Another factor was the decline of civic spirit in the West. The average Roman, who was witnessing a struggle for power between Germanized Roman and Romanized German armies, cared little for the outcome. Victory for either side could hardly make his lot worse. The Roman government could not count on popular hatred of the foreigner. There was no guerrilla warfare, no "underground resistance," and conversely, there was a great deal of collaboration with the invader.

To offset these handicaps there were some real assets. The Roman army, despite deterioration from earlier days of greater glory, was still a better organization than the armies it was called on to fight. Its discipline and training were superior, and unlike barbarian armies which bogged down for lack of transport, food, and supplies, the Roman army could rely upon a rudimentary commissariat. More important was the superiority of Roman diplomacy, which had a long tradition of divide and rule. By shifting alliances and stirring up one German tribe against another, the Roman government was able to fight one tribe at a time or to induce two potential enemies to destroy each other.

On the German side also there were both liabilities and assets. The invasions were not motivated by any ideology or moral force. If the population of a conquered province was not particularly hostile, neither did it welcome the invaders as liberators, nor could the Germans count on any material assistance. On the other hand, the German population was large and it was growing. German armies were often outfought, but rarely outnumbered. They possessed the military advantage of the initiative, which enabled them to concentrate their forces, while Roman troops were scattered in innumerable defensive assignments. Settlement within the Empire did offer a positive, tangible goal, which to the barbarian mind went far to supply adequate motivation. Finally, the German leaders often had training or experience in Roman methods of government and military science.

During the last quarter of the fourth century conditions in the West deteriorated rapidly. Gratian (375–383), son of, and since 367 co-emperor with, Valentinian I, kept the frontier defenses intact, but it augured ill for the future when, on his father's death in 375 Gratian accepted his half brother, Valentinian II (383–392), as junior co-emperor. Valentinian II was a pawn in the court intrigues and the politics of the Empire. These were reminiscent of the third century before Diocletian: Gratian was assassinated by agents of a Spanish usurper and a struggle for power ensued between several barbarian generals of the Roman army. Arbogast the Frank emerged supreme. When Valentinian II made the mistake of trying to rule and reign, Arbogast had him strangled and set up a puppet emperor, Eugenius.

In the West, these political conditions were not essentially new. In the East, the successors of Constantine were confronted with an unprecedented crisis, precipitated by the movements of the German tribes. Deflected from the Empire by the Rhine-Danube frontier, one group of Germans had, at an early date, moved south and southeastward. These were the Goths, whose prehistoric origins were in the southern part of Scandinavia. Impelled by overpopulation, wars, or hunger, they wandered into the plains of southern Russia, where they split into two branches. In the fourth century, the Ostrogoths built a kingdom in the fertile region north of the Black Sea, while the Visigoths occupied the region extending westward to Dacia, just north of the lower Danube. About 375, the Goths were struck by the sudden impact of the Asiatic Huns. The appearance of the Huns in Europe was the end result of obscure movements of Ural-Altaian tribes in central Asia whose original impulse was a combination of overpopulation, the effect of climatic changes on an essentially pastoral existence, and the endless struggle for power among the nomadic tribes north of the Himalaya mountains. The plains of southern Russia were ideally suited to the military tactics of these horse-riding nomads, and the Ostrogoths were crushed and dispersed.

The terrified Visigoths, whose turn was next, begged permission to settle within the Empire in the depopulated province of Moesia just south of the natural barrier of the lower Danube. The eastern emperor Valens (364–378) allowed them to cross the Danube on the condition that they become *foederati* responsible for the defense of the frontier in return for provisions supplied by Roman officials. The provisions were not forthcoming, however, and the Visigoths suffered indignities and oppression which provoked them to abandon the frontier, renounce their alliance with the Empire, and begin a systematic plundering of the province of Thrace. To Valens this was desertion of duty and treason. As the Visigoths moved southward, threatening Constantinople itself, the emperor met them in a pitched battle near Adrianople, in 378. Here the hitherto supreme Roman infantry was decisively defeated by the heavy-armed cavalry of the Goths who were equipped with the stirrups and spurs introduced by the Goths' Sarmatian allies. Valens was killed and his army dispersed, but the Goths had no program or goal and spent the next year aimlessly pillaging Greece and the provinces to the north.

To meet this crisis, Gratian appointed as co-emperor in the East Theodosius I (379–395), a Spanish general who had been retired in disgrace only a few years earlier. Skillfully combining force and diplomacy Theodosius settled the Visigoths once more in Moesia as *foederati*. Meanwhile, the remnants of the shattered Ostrogoths drifted westward and were settled with the same status in the province of Pannonia, farther up the Danube. During this arduous work of restoration, Theodosius had spared the time and resources to dethrone the puppet emperor Eugenius and destroy his creator, the Frankish general Arbogast. For the last five months of his reign (394–395), Theodosius I ruled alone, the last to unite both East and West under one emperor. For these achievements in the service of the Empire and of Christianity (both Arbogast and Eugenius were pagans) his contemporaries and later admirers dubbed Theodosius "the Great."

Far more significant than these achievements themselves was Theodosius' accomplishment of all this by diplomacy and by the skillful use of barbarian generals for his own ends. The "Roman" army which defeated Arbogast included Visigothic forces commanded by Alaric, a contingent under Stilicho the Vandal, and even an auxiliary troop of Huns. When Theodosius died and was succeeded by two sons, one a mere youth and the other a child, the tables were turned: barbarian generals used the emperors for their ends as Theodosius had used them for his. Theodosius was the last of the Roman emperors to be appointed on the basis of ability and experience. Thereafter the dynastic principle triumphed at the expense of the Empire. The successors of Theodosius in the West were either incompetents whose claims to the throne were based on heredity, or else puppets set up and pulled down by the barbarian generals of the Roman army to whom real power had now passed.

8   THE INVASIONS: ALARIC, THEODORIC, AND CLOVIS

The recovery under Theodosius was short-lived. Within a half-century the western frontiers had been permanently breached and the various German tribes, confederacies, and "nations" had begun to establish barbarian kingdoms on Roman soil. The Germanic peoples at this time may be distinguished as East Germans and West Germans. The East Germans (whose origins were east of the Elbe river) were more migratory; they experienced earlier and more intimate contact with the civilized world; they adopted Christianity earlier; and they established their kingdoms in Roman provinces which touched the Mediterranean. The most important East German tribes were the Visigoths, Ostrogoths, Vandals, and Burgundians. The Visigoths were the first to play an important role within the Empire, but the Ostrogoths and lesser East German tribes like the Alans had even earlier pushed their raids as far as the Caucasus and into Asia Minor.

It was during such a Gothic marauding expedition that a Roman provincial family of Greek-speaking Christians was carried off as captives from their home in Cappadocia. Two generations later, a child from this family—doubtless part Gothic by now—was sent as a hostage to Constantinople. This was Ulfilas (c.310–383), who was consecrated a bishop there in 341, and who became the apostle to the Goths. Unfortunately for the Germans, he was an Arian Christian. Thus the romanizing influence of his missionary efforts among the Visigoths, and through them among all the East German peoples, created for these conquerors their most difficult single problem when they later forced their rule upon the Roman and orthodox population of the western provinces. Within twenty years of Ulfilas' death, all the East Germans were at least formally Arian Christian. The rapidity of their conversion is partly explained by Ulfilas' translation of the Bible into Gothic (for which he adapted and expanded the Greek alphabet), the earliest surviving monument of a Germanic language.

After the death of Theodosius, the Visigoths had become restive once more. Their new king, the ambitious Alaric, saw the opportunity to expand his rule. The phlegmatic Arcadius (395–408) reigned in Constantinople and was himself ruled by whatever faction was currently supreme in the endless rounds of court intrigue. The western throne was occupied by the mentally retarded child Honorius (395–423), whose early years were dominated by the able Vandal general Stilicho, a former lieutenant of Theodosius. The eastern court and Stilicho maneuvered for control of western North Africa (on which Rome and Italy depended for food) and of Illyricum (roughly, modern Yugoslavia and northwestern Greece) which Theodosius had, with faulty prevision, split between the eastern and west-

Ulfilas' Bible. Page from a manuscript written c.500.
UNIVERSITETSBIBLIOTEKET
UPPSALA.

ern halves of the Empire. Alaric, occupying the province of Moesia (in northern Illyricum), played off one side against the other.

Alaric's policy did not succeed. He ravaged the southern Balkan peninsula and Greece, but he could not conquer the fortified towns. As long as Stilicho lived, Alaric was unable to penetrate into Italy with more than temporary success. To defend Italy, Stilicho withdrew the Roman garrisons along the Rhine, leaving its defense to Frankish *foederati* who conspicuously failed to hold the line. He practically ignored an insubordinate general who crossed the Channel into Gaul in 407 with the bulk of the Roman troops stationed in Britain, leaving that province to its own defense against the raids of both Celts and Germans. What ultimate ambition Stilicho harbored will never be known, but its nature is suggested by two facts. First, he could have destroyed Alaric and his army, but instead he came to terms and courted the support of the Visigoths. Second, shortly after the death of Arcadius, Stilicho's enemies accused him of seeking the eastern throne for his son. Stilicho was arrested and executed for treason with the connivance of Honorius, whose jealousy of the barbarian was the only passion that could rouse his energy.

The execution of Stilicho in 408 was the beginning of the debacle in the West. Alaric moved into Italy with all his forces. Negotiations with Honorius were abortive—the emperor, safe with his court in impregnable Ravenna, hardly wished to replace the Vandal Stilicho with the Visigoth Alaric. For two years the barbarians ravaged the peninsula. The climax of this Italian campaign came when Alaric took Rome in 410. The fall of the Eternal City shocked contemporaries from one end of the civilized world to the other. The physical destruction was negligible, but the incident made a more memorable impression than any other event of the decline of the Empire. In his cell in distant Bethlehem, St. Jerome exclaimed, "All humanity is included in her ruins," a sentiment with which pagan and Christian alike could agree.

Alaric's next move reveals the weakness, as it does the motivation, of the Visigothic invaders. Alaric sought not the splendor of empire, nor the luxury of Rome, but food. The decay of the West had proceeded so far that Italy, the heart of Roman antiquity, could not feed his people. After three days of pillaging Rome, Alaric marched south to collect ships in southern Italy to transport the Visigoths to North Africa, the granary of the late antique world. These plans were ruined by a storm which destroyed the fleet and by the death of Alaric shortly thereafter. The first great German king to invade the Empire was buried with barbaric pomp in the bed of a temporarily diverted river in Calabria. The slaves who did the work were killed so that "no man knoweth his sepulcher unto this day."

Alaric's successor, Ataulf, led his people northward out of Italy and into southern Gaul. Meanwhile the Vandals, with the lesser tribes of Alans and Suevi, had plundered their way across Gaul and into Spain, and the general confusion was worse confounded by dissension and conflict among three Roman generals, each of whom sought the help of barbarian tribes in furthering his own ambitions. One of these generals was Constantius, successor to Stilicho as the power behind Honorius' throne. The western provinces were all but reduced to chaos. Ataulf's Visigoths found that they could not live off the ravaged country. Their newly revived status of *foederati* could not be honored by the imperial government because it depended upon delivery of African food which rebellion in that quarter, too, had now cut off.

The exasperated Ataulf now played his trump card. By a stroke of luck, Alaric had captured and passed on to his successor a precious spoil of victory: Galla Placidia, daughter of Theodosius I, half-sister of Honorius and Arcadius, and nearest in hereditary line of succession to the throne in the West. We are told that during the years of her captivity and travels in the wagon train of the Visigothic army Placidia was honorably treated, and that she and Ataulf fell in love. This is not inconceivable, and it was during this period that Ataulf (according to a story carried to Palestine during these years by a Christian pilgrim) renounced his earlier ambition to displace Rome by a Gothic empire and declared, "the unbridled barbarism of the Goths is incompatible with law, and without law there can be no state. Therefore, since I cannot supplant her, I hope to be known to posterity as the restorer of Rome." Whether or not this was related to a tender passion for Placidia, Ataulf showed every sign of wanting to imitate Stilicho, who had strengthened his position by marrying a niece of the earlier emperor Theodosius. In 414 Ataulf, attired in the garb of a Roman senator, married his imperial hostage. Constantius, who coveted (and later won) the hand of Placidia for himself as a means to succeed the childless Honorius as emperor, then drove the Visigoths out of Gaul into Spain, where Ataulf was assassinated shortly thereafter.

The new Visigothic king, Wallia, finally achieved for his people by diplomacy what his predecessors had failed to obtain by force: political autonomy within the Empire and settlement in Aquitaine (southern Gaul) with the status of *foederati*. The price for this was the return of Galla Placidia, for whom Honorius also agreed to pay the flattering ransom of nineteen thousand quarters of grain to the hungry Visigoths. The hand of Constantius can be seen in this final settlement, for he married Placidia in 417 and was appointed co-emperor in the West in 421, the same year in which he died. A better future was in store for Wallia and his successors. The Visigothic kingdom in southern Gaul was consolidated and expanded during the fifth century until it reached its height under Euric (466–484), who also began the new Visigothic expansion into Spain.

Meanwhile, Honorius dawdled out the last years of his reign and died in 423. He was succeeded briefly by a usurper whom the eastern emperor, Theodosius II (408–450), displaced with Valentinian III (425–455), the child of Placidia and Constantius. Real power was exercised by Placidia, who was given the title Augusta, and by the general Aëtius, "the last of the Romans." The greatest strength of Aëtius lay in his influence over the Huns settled on the upper Danube, whom he used as *foederati* against the German enemies of the Empire. Placidia and Aëtius cooperated in a policy of containment and stabilization, yielding territory where the Germanic pressure was too great, but repulsing the barbarians where they could assemble enough Huns and other loyal troops. Although Aëtius won several victories, success did not on the whole attend either his military or diplomatic efforts.

During the reign of Valentinian III the West lost most of its provinces outside of Italy. The Vandals in Spain crossed over to North Africa in 429, under their king, Gaiseric (428–477), the ablest general of his age. The establishment of a powerful Vandal kingdom in Africa was a double blow to the Empire. It cut off the most important grain supply for the West (or gave the Vandal king a priceless diplomatic weapon), and it also accelerated the declining security of commerce and travel on the Mediterranean. In Spain the departure of the Vandals did not restore much territory to Roman rule. The country was torn by peasant revolts, and the relatively weak tribe of the Suevi gained possession of about half of the peninsula. Britain, stripped of troops, was thrown back on her own resources to ward off the growing barbarian raids of the Picts and Scots. After a vain appeal to Aëtius in 446—the so-called "Groans of the Britons"

—the province was invaded from a new quarter. The Angles, Saxons, and Jutes arrived from northern Germany c.450.

In Gaul Aëtius was more successful. The Visigoths were prevented from enlarging their kingdom; Frankish incursions along the lower Rhine were thrown back; peasant revolts were suppressed, and Britons who had fled their ravaged province to settle in the district later known as Brittany were kept from expanding. The Burgundians did no better than the Britons. As *foederati* they had settled west of the middle Rhine and had begun to push southward when in 436 catastrophe almost obliterated the tribe. This was the work of Aëtius' allies, the Huns. The tragedy gave rise to the legends enshrined in later German epics, such as the *Nibelungenlied*. A second Burgundian kingdom was established by the survivors in the area around Lake Geneva. This kingdom slowly expanded southward along the Rhone River until it included (for a few years) Provence on the Mediterranean, reaching both its greatest extent and its height of Romano-barbaric culture under the legislator-king Gundobad (474–516).

Between their first appearance in southern Russia, when they shattered the Ostrogoths (c.375), and the near-annihilation of the Burgundians, the Huns had slowly built up a loose-knit empire of Germans and Slavs stretching from the Rhine to the Caspian. Their Asiatic ferocity had almost wholly been expended against barbarians outside the Empire, except when Roman rulers like Theodosius or Aëtius had used them inside the frontiers as *foederati*. In the fifth century the center of their power was in the plains of modern Hungary. Their loose confederation of clans gave way to centralized royal power. Kingship reached its zenith under Attila (433–453), the rude splendor of whose savage court made a profound impression on envoys sent from Rome and Constantinople. In their capacity as *foederati* the Huns had been in the pay of both eastern and western emperors; when Attila chose to look upon this arrangement as simply another tribute exacted from a dependent people, relations between the Empire and the Huns became strained. When Attila demanded more tribute, a plot to assassinate him was hatched at the court of Constantinople, but it was forestalled at the last moment. Attila referred contemptuously to "his slave, Theodosius [II], who paid him tribute but dared to plot the murder of his master."

Attila had already turned his Hunnish hordes from the subjugation of Germanic and Slavic barbarians to the plundering of the civilized Empire. He had nothing more constructive in mind than the usual conquest, slaughter, and rapine which had characterized the earlier rise of the Huns. The wealthier East attracted him first, and he pillaged the Balkans as far as Constantinople. But Constantinople held out and the Huns turned to the West. By this time Attila had earned his title, "the scourge of God" (i.e., the punishment visited by God's wrath upon a sinful people). The terror struck into the hearts of his intended victims by this sort of propaganda was a potent secret weapon. Attila gathered together all his forces, including a motley array of subject German tribes, and swept through Gaul. Aëtius hurriedly assembled a coalition of Roman provincials and armies of the Germanic kingdoms of the West. Attila avoided a pitched battle as long as he could since speed and terror rather than tactical skill were his main strength, but he was finally caught early in 451 retreating eastward from Gaul, on the Catalaunian Plains in the vicinity of Châlons (the engagement is sometimes called the battle of Châlons). Here a "battle of the nations" took place. Attila's army included, in addition to his Hunnish cavalry, such German auxiliaries as the Gepids, Ostrogoths, Thuringians, Rugians, Sciri, Heruli, northern Burgundians, and Ripuarian Franks. Aëtius' allied forces included Gallo-Roman provincials, Visigoths, Alans, Armoricans, southern Burgundians, and Salian Franks. Aëtius' generalship and the stubborn valor of the Visigoths (whose king was slain) brought the daylong struggle to a bloody close with the western forces undefeated if not victorious. The Huns withdrew eastward, never to recover from the carnage.

Attila, denied the plunder of Gaul, next turned to Italy. In 452 he sacked Aquileia, whose refugees fled to the swamps at the head of the Adriatic and founded what later grew into the city of Venice, and he pillaged Milan and Pavia. But famine and pestilence, Italy's best defense, decimated the Hunnish army. At this critical moment, an embassy from Rome, headed by Pope Leo I the Great, arrived in Attila's camp. As the result of negotiations of which we have no record, Attila decided to withdraw his forces to Hungary. Popular credulity ascribed the Huns' withdrawal to divine intervention summoned by the successor of St. Peter. Whether this can be believed or not, the important result of the interview was an enormous enhancement of the prestige of the papacy in the secular affairs of the West. There is some reason to believe that Attila was a sick man at this time. Within a few months he died of a broken blood vessel which he suffered on the night of his wedding to the German princess Kriemhild, as she is called in the *Nibelungenlied*. The empire of Attila rapidly disintegrated after his death.

Aëtius did not long survive the Hunnish collapse. Like Stilicho with the Visigoths a half-century earlier, Aëtius had nothing to gain from the destruction of an enemy whose existence had guaranteed him supremacy in the Empire's defense. His position was further weakened by the death of his long-time collaborator Galla Placidia, in 450. To compensate for this loss of influence, Aëtius forced Valentinian III to betroth a daughter to his son, but this indignity roused the sluggish emperor to have Aëtius assassinated, in 454. In the next year Valentinian in turn was murdered. In the confusion that followed these events, Gaiseric with his Vandals seized the opportunity to descend upon Rome from the sea and to plunder the city of its movable wealth, sparing only the Christian churches and works of art which could not be readily sold for money. In addition, selected hostages were carried off, including the late emperor's widow and children. By a curious distortion of this well-planned, almost systematic stripping of the city's wealth, the word "vandalism" has come to mean the wanton destruction of both movable and real property—a gross injustice to Gaiseric and his hardy adventurers.

After Valentinian III's thirty-year reign, the next twenty-one years saw nine men raised to the purple in the West, most of them puppets set up by the German general Ricimer, who controlled the army in Italy. Beyond the Alps imperial authority almost completely lapsed during this period (455–476). Roman generals in Gaul and elsewhere ignored the emperors who ruled momentarily in the court at Ravenna. Syagrius, the last Roman governor in Gaul who could claim an imperial mandate for his power, was in fact simply the ruler of an autonomous district, the evanescent "kingdom of Soissons." After Ricimer's death, another general of the mercenary troops in Italy, Orestes, deposed the emperor and set up his young son, Romulus Augustulus (475–476), as heir of the founders of Rome and the Empire. Orestes was then overthrown by a new revolt of the mercenary troops led by Odoacer, who did not bother to set up an emperor. Odoacer had been elected king by his German mercenaries, and now he petitioned the eastern emperor, Zeno, for appointment as patrician with authority to rule in the emperor's name. To gain time, since nothing could be done about the situation at the moment, Zeno granted his request. Thus the forms of imperial rule were maintained. The date 476 has been traditionally assigned to the "end of the Roman Empire of the West." In theory, however, it would be more accurate to say that 476 marked the restoration of the unity of the Empire under one emperor, for the legal basis of Odoacer's rule was explicit recognition by Zeno. Like the other Germanic kings, Odoacer was desirous of legitimizing his actual autonomy with an imperial delegation of authority.

The weakness of Odoacer's position was that what had been granted could be revoked. In a few years it became obvious to the emperor that the solution of one of his most vexing problems, the revival of Ostrogothic power, lay in making a new arrangement for Italy. Now settled on the southern bank of the middle Danube, the Ostrogoths had begun to ravage the Balkan peninsula. Their king, Theodoric, had spent several years as a hostage in Constantinople where he had acquired some knowledge of Roman government and a high respect for Roman culture. Zeno bought off the Ostrogoths from further ravaging in the East by granting Theodoric the title of patrician and delegating to him the rule of Italy. In 489 Theodoric led his people into Italy. After four years of fierce resistance Odoacer finally submitted on terms, only to be treacherously murdered at a banquet given by Theodoric himself.

The Ostrogothic kingdom of Theodoric (493–526) was in many ways the most brilliant and successful of all the barbarian realms in the

West. Theodoric was a Roman citizen, and had even held the office of consul in the East. The essence of his policy was to preserve the civilization of Rome. He achieved a revival of prosperity and of culture, in striking contrast with the continuing decline and barbarization of the other western kingdoms. After a century of turbulence, Theodoric brought peace to Italy. Even his Arian Christian faith proved no great obstacle to a stable reign, so long as his orthodox subjects were estranged from eastern emperors who supported heretical creeds. His religious policy was official toleration, and his patronage of arts and letters benefited Arian and Catholic alike. Public works were subsidized, bringing employment to town-dwelling artisans; agriculture prospered under a new security enforced by Ostrogothic arms. A new barbarian "foreign policy" may also be seen, although Theodoric's policy was new in its scale rather than without precedent. Once settled in

Germanic "Successor States" in the West, c.525

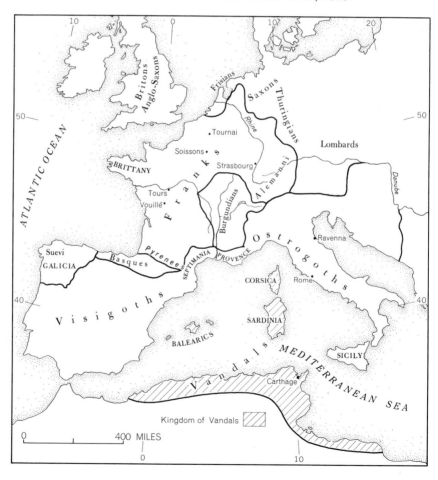

Italy, the Ostrogoths launched no further wars of conquest (although Provence, in southeastern France, was occupied for strategic reasons). Instead, Theodoric spread his influence throughout the Germanic kingdoms of the West by a system of marriage alliances. His purpose was to preserve peace by uniting the interests of the ruling houses. He himself was married to a Frankish princess; he married his sister to the king of the Vandals; his two daughters to the Visigothic and Burgundian kings; and a niece to a Thuringian king.

The conquest of Italy by the Ostrogoths was the last invasion of the Empire by an East German people. The kingdoms founded by East German tribes were all relatively short-lived, although their achievements were in many ways impressive. In contrast, the West Germans achieved less at first, but their kingdoms were more enduring. They did not migrate but rather expanded without losing contact with their homelands; they were less romanized, in some cases remaining almost wholly beyond the influence of Mediterranean civilization; and they became Christian much later, usually as Catholics rather than Arians. The most important West German peoples were confederations of lesser tribes, such as the Franks, the Alemanni (from whose name eventually arose the French word for Germany, *l'Allemagne*), the Frisians, the three other north German tribes of Angles, Saxons, and Jutes, and finally, the Lombards. The Lombards and Frisians had no significant contact with lands of the western Empire before the sixth century. The Angles, Saxons, and Jutes were hardly beyond the stage of hit-and-run raids on the derelict province of Britain. Only the Franks invaded the Empire and established a kingdom before the close of the fifth century.

The Franks appear first during the chaotic mid-third century, when they penetrated into Gaul and as far as northeastern Spain on extensive plundering raids. During the fourth century they were always a potential danger but were kept back beyond the frontier. Constantine won his spurs against them, on the Rhine, before he was proclaimed emperor. After Stilicho recalled the Roman garrisons from the Rhine, the Franks were given the status of *foederati* with the duty of holding the line. Instead, they occupied most of northern Gaul while Vandals, Alans, and Suevi swept across the frontier. As a loose-knit confederation, the Franks were vulnerable to internal dissension, and at the time of Attila's invasion two main groups (Salians and Ripuarians) were actually at war with each other and fought on opposing sides. Each group of Franks was itself split into several tribes, each with its own king.

One center of Frankish strength in northern Gaul was at Tournai (near the border of modern France and Belgium), where, five years after Romulus Augustulus was deposed and eight years before Theodoric invaded Italy, a youth of fifteen succeeded to the throne. This was Chlodovech, better known as Clovis (481–511), whose career of conquest culminated in the establishment of the Frankish kingdom of Merovingian Gaul, so called after Meroveg, the half-mythical founder of the Frankish royal house. Clovis' success was the slowly won result of years of fighting, but three military victories may be singled out as important stages in Frankish expansion. The last stronghold of Gallo-Roman rule in northern Gaul, Syagrius' "kingdom of Soissons," was destroyed in 486. The Alemanni were annihilated in a great battle near Strasbourg, in 496. This allowed the Franks to expand eastward back into Germany and ensured that the Frankish kingdom, of all the barbarian kingdoms on Roman soil, would be the most Germanic in character and would be best able to replenish its manpower among Germanic peoples. The third and crowning victory of Clovis' career was the defeat of the Visigoths at Vouillé in 507 (in west-central France, near Poitiers), which led to the conquest of all of southern Gaul to the Pyrenees. The only reverse suffered by Frankish arms was at the hands of Theodoric, who prevented Clovis from reaching the Mediterranean by occupying Provence and by helping the Visigoths to retain Septimania (a coastal province stretching from Provence to the Pyrenees).

Clovis' success cannot be explained on military grounds alone. Although motivated primarily by mere lust for power, Clovis displayed a consistency of attitude and an ability beyond simple shrewdness sufficient to warrant our considering him, with Theodoric, as capable of statesmanship, even though on the barbarian level of his age, in which calculated self-interest, brutality, and a rough sense of justice were about equal ingredients. His grasp of political realities was unsurpassed by any western ruler before Charlemagne. Toward the conquered Gallo-Romans he could afford to be lenient, since most of his Frankish followers could be settled in depopulated districts in the north, without need to expropriate landowners. Consequently the Gallo-Roman people offered no resistance; the Frankish expansion into Gaul was an invasion only in the sense of a military campaign against the armies, not the people, of its previous rulers. Finally Clovis' authority was given an aura of legitimacy. After his defeat of the Visigoths, the eastern emperor bestowed upon him the insignia of an honorary consul, although Clovis never became, like most of the East German kings, an actual official of the Empire bearing the title of patrician.

Far more important was Clovis' policy toward the Church in Gaul. He had an inestimable advantage of being, with the rest of the Franks, merely a heathen rather than a hated Arian heretic. The bishops conceived the hope, which Clovis was careful not to abate, that he might be converted to the Catholic faith and thus become the champion of orthodoxy. The Catholic bishops of Gaul formed the most powerful single political group in the country. They were allied with the Gallo-Roman nobility from whose ranks most of them were chosen; they controlled the greatest concentration of wealth; and they exercised the greatest influence over the population. The support of the bishops, and thus of the bulk of the population, was strong enough reason for a barbarian king who contemplated conversion to turn to the Catholic faith. But we do not know whether such realistic considerations motivated Clovis. Perhaps it was the persuasion of the Burgundian princess Clotilda, whom he married in 493 (a Catholic, though her people were still Arian), or the miracles which he is said to have witnessed at the tomb of St. Martin of Tours. Or was it the vow, which according to later tradition he made in the heat of battle against the Alemanni, that he would adopt his wife's faith if Christ would give him victory? It seems probable that it was a combination of realistic politics and personal inclination that prompted him to be baptized along with three thousand other Franks. The conversion of Clovis was a decisive moment in the history of the West: he became the only Catholic ruler among the barbarian kings. At a single stroke he called into being an effective "fifth column," the episcopate, within any territory on which he had designs. Further expansion took on the character of a religious war to extirpate heresy: "It grieves me," he told his troops on the eve of the campaign against the Visigoths, "that Arians should hold any part of Gaul."

Toward his Frankish followers, Clovis' policy was simple and effective. On the one hand, he provided the opportunity for fighting which appealed to their bellicose nature, together with the rewards of conquest in booty, land, and participation in the government of the conquered. On the other hand, he pursued a remorseless policy of unification of the several Frankish tribes. From being simply a Frankish king, he became king of the Franks, by methodically liquidating all other chieftains or kings who were potential competitors for the supremacy which he had won. He employed all the techniques of treachery and assassination known in the violent world of heathen barbarians. Some of his rivals (and blood relatives) he caused to be murdered by hired assassins, others he tricked into an unarmed meeting and laid low with his own battle-ax. "Thus did God daily deliver the enemies of Clovis into his hand," wrote Gregory, bishop of Tours, toward the end of the sixth century, "because he walked before Him with an upright heart, and did what was pleasing in His eyes."

9   THE GERMANIC "SUCCESSOR STATES" IN THE WEST

The Frankish kingdom of Merovingian Gaul was the last of the "successor states" to be founded on the ruins of the Empire in the West. Clovis had begun his career of conquest as a petty kinglet in 481 and ended it as the most powerful Germanic king ruling the largest territory. On his death in 511, the kingdom was divided between his four sons in accordance with the Germanic custom of treating kingship as personal property—or, more exactly, as a result of the Germanic incapacity to distinguish between private and public rights. The sons of Clovis were able to cooperate against external enemies, so that the Frankish kingdoms continued to expand. Burgundy was conquered in 534. Two years later Provence was occupied, bringing the Franks for the first time to the Mediterranean and into direct contact with the eastern Empire. One of Clovis' sons even invaded Italy, as an ally of Justinian who was then fighting the Ostrogoths, but the expedition gained nothing for the Merovingians. East of the Rhine the Franks fought their way farther into central Germany, conquering the Thuringians in 531.

Within Gaul, the sons of Clovis showed no such cooperation. Each coveted the others' shares of the kingdom, and when not conquering foreign soil they spent their time fighting each other, using the techniques of treachery and subversion which Clovis had taught them. By 558 all but one of the brothers and their heirs had been eliminated, most of them by violent deaths. The survivor, Chlotar I, briefly reunited the kingdom (558–561). On his death the Merovingian realm was again divided among his four sons, and the civil wars were resumed on an even more savage and violent scale. The degeneracy, faithlessness, and congenital criminality of the sons of Chlotar I and of their queens and concubines are all vividly portrayed by Gregory, bishop of Tours, in his contemporary *History of the Franks*. This generation had almost exterminated itself when the sole survivor, Chlotar II, was put upon the throne of a united kingdom, in 613, through machinations and murders by a group of nobles and bishops.

The only significance of the single rule of Chlotar II is that his reign marks the definitive shift of power from the Frankish monarchy to the landed aristocracy. By an edict of 614 Chlotar gave up certain royal rights over the Church and extended privileges to both the ecclesiastical and the lay nobility. Under Dagobert (629–639), "the Merovingian monarchy shone for the last time, but with a false splendor." The revival was brief, and Dagobert also made concessions to the local interests of the landed aristocracy. After Dagobert, the Merovingian kingdom owed nothing to the policy or the efforts of its kings.

And yet the future lay with the Franks. The seeming decadence of the Merovingian kingdom arises only from the misleading habit of identifying the history of a kingdom with its kings. The Merovingian realm as a whole was in a healthy if turbulent condition, when compared with the other barbarian states of the West. We have already seen that the kingdom of Burgundy was conquered by the Merovingians. It became—with Austrasia, Neustria, and Aquitaine—one of the four main constituent parts of the Merovingian kingdom. The Vandal kingdom of North Africa and the western Mediterranean islands declined after the death of Gaiseric, in 477, losing territory to Moorish tribes south of the coastal area. The weaknesses of the Vandal state were insuperable. Religious differences between Arian Vandals and Catholic provincials led to persecution by the kings and estrangement of their subjects. The Vandal conquerors failed to become assimilated economically or socially with the provincial population. They simply confiscated the property of the Roman nobility and like that nobility exploited the bulk of the people.

Meanwhile, the eastern emperor Justinian (527–565) sent an expeditionary force under the ablest general of the sixth century, Belisarius, to reconquer North Africa. Several reasons lay behind Justinian's western policy of reconquest, of which the recovery of the Vandal kingdom was only the first step. North Africa was still an important food-producing area. Vandal control of the western Mediterranean was a handicap to trade with the West. The disaffected population of the Vandal kingdom seemed to be a potential source of manpower for the Byzantine army. Finally, North Africa and Sicily could provide advance bases for further reconquest of the other lost provinces in the West. Belisarius arrived in North Africa in 533, and broke the main resistance by taking the Vandal capital at Carthage the same year. Insurrections and raids by the Moors were not quelled until 548, when the former Vandal kingdom, with its Mediterranean islands, was reincorporated into the Empire.

Having achieved command of the Mediterranean, Belisarius turned to Ostrogothic Italy. Here the situation after the death of Theodoric in 526 seemed even more ripe for easy reconquest. Already during the last years of his reign disaffection had begun among the Catholic population. The advent of an orthodox emperor (Justin) in Constantinople was sufficient to produce plots and rumors of plots against the Arian Theodoric, whose policy of religious toleration was not appreciated by his less enlightened Italian subjects. Theodoric struck back at all whom he suspected of treason with the same fury which had inaugurated his reign. Among the victims were several nobles of ancient senatorial families, including Boethius, the leading intellect of his age. After Theodoric's death, a minor heir, the regency of Theodoric's daughter, and the conflicting interests of the nobles all combined to weaken the Ostrogothic state. Belisarius took Sicily in 535 and within the next year had occupied Rome. Then the Goths swept away all hereditary claimants to Theodoric's throne and elected a military leader, Witigis, as king.

Witigis launched a bitter war of resistance which continued under him and his successor, the popular Totila, for more than twenty years. In the Gothic wars the population suffered more from plundering, pestilence, and famine than during any previous generation. Italy never fully recovered from the devastation, which was mainly the work of imperial mercenaries brought in from the East. The Ostrogoths, having some stake in the country, generally spared captured cities from loss of life and property and thereby gained substantial popular support. Thus the reconquest was not, as the orthodox Justinian had hoped, welcomed as a liberation from the Arian Ostrogoths. But by 556 all Italy, except for isolated Gothic strongholds, was ruled again from Ravenna where the viceroy, or exarch, attempted without much success to raise taxes and troops for the Byzantine armies fighting on the Persian frontier. The Exarchate of Ravenna, as the imperial government in Italy was called, endured for another two hundred years, and Byzantine control of parts of southern Italy was not extinguished until the eleventh century. But a reunited Byzantine Italy lasted only a dozen years.

The last German people to invade the Empire—for such, once more, Italy must now be considered—were the Lombards, who make their first appearance, typically, as *foederati* in the Byzantine armies fighting against the Ostrogoths, c.552. Of all the East German barbarians who entered the Mediterranean world, they were the least touched by any civilizing influence, although by the sixth century their religion was formally Arian Christian. In 568 the Lombards returned to Italy as conquerors. The impoverished country offered little resistance outside the fortified cities where imperial garrisons sometimes held out. Under their king, Alboin, the early stages of the Lombard invasion were successful. Some northern cities fell, including Pavia, which became the Lombard capital. But after Alboin's death in 572 (when his wife had him assassinated for making her drink out of her late father's skull), the Lombard dukes refused to elect a new king and the conquest of Italy proceeded piecemeal. Each of the thirty dukes captured various towns or districts and established small principalities. The most important of these were the duchies of Spoleto in central Italy and Benevento in the south.

Most of Italy was thus overrun when, in 584, the Byzantine emperor sent in troops and enlisted the aid of the Catholic Merovingians against the Arian Lombards, an effort sufficient to reunite the Lombard dukes, who elected a king in order to meet the threat. The situation was finally stabilized, and the Lombard monarchy firmly established, under Agilulf (591–616), who completed most of the conquest which the Lombards were to make in Italy. The most important districts still in Byzantine hands were Ravenna and the surrounding countryside (including Venice); Apulia and Calabria (the "heel" and "toe" of the peninsula); Sicily; Naples and Rome, with the surrounding countryside; and Genoa and its hinterland. Even in these nominally Byzantine areas, however, imperial control was not always effective. In the "duchy of Rome," for example, the popes acknowledged the sovereignty of the Empire but exercised almost complete control of the local government.

The Visigoths, as we have already seen, were pushed south of the Pyrenees by Clovis (507), except for the coastal province of Septimania which Theodoric's intervention had saved for them. Their kingdom included the whole Iberian peninsula except the northwestern corner (Galicia, occupied by the Suevi) and part of the Pyrenees (held by the Basques). The Visigothic kings had difficulty maintaining order. The

Catholic population would neither cooperate when their Arian rulers were
lenient nor were they made submissive by persecution. The remnants of
the Hispano-Roman nobility were periodically rebellious, the Visigothic
aristocracy was jealous of royal power, and the Franks menaced Septimania. After the Byzantine reconquest of Italy, Justinian's troops found
it easy to win back southern Spain for the Empire. But royal power was
restored—perhaps more dramatically than effectively—by Recared I (586–
601), who became a Catholic and under whose aegis a national council of
bishops and nobles at Toledo in 589 proclaimed Catholicism the official
and only faith to be recognized. This ensured Recared the support of the
Catholic hierarchy and of the majority of his subjects. Ecclesiastical support of the monarchy was graphically emphasized in a ceremony which

Germanic "Successor States" and Byzantine Areas in the West, c.575

became a precedent for all western Europe, the solemn anointing and consecration of Recared as king. This was a religious sanction for his rule reminiscent of the sacred character of kingship in the Old Testament.

In the former Roman province of Britain, developments took a radi-
cally different course from those which we have surveyed in Gaul, Africa,
Italy, and Spain. The least romanized of the provinces of the Empire,
Britain was the hardest hit by the political and economic disturbances of
the fourth century, and by the opening of the fifth was a derelict province
not even protected by Roman troops. Barbarian raids from the north by
Picts and Scots had already begun, when Britain was invaded by several
German tribes, notably the Angles, Saxons, Frisians, and Jutes; these tribes
were among the least affected by contact with Roman civilization. They
came at first in small war bands, perhaps like the *comitatus* described by
Tacitus; some of the earliest bands probably came as *foederati* to aid the
Romano-British in defense against other barbarians. Later, more numerous
groups, including women and children, migrated into the districts already
won, expanding and coalescing but still divided by forest and fen from
other groups. By the end of the sixth century several tribal kingdoms had
been established. In the southeast was the Jutish kingdom of the Cantwara,
or Kent, with its capital at Canterbury. The Saxons formed several petty
kingdoms in southern Britain: the South Saxons in Sussex; the East Saxons
in Essex; and the West Saxons in the region farther west along the Thames
and along the southern coast which, with its hinterland, became the later
Wessex. In the Midlands and in the region north of the Humber river
other districts were settled under tribal kings by the Angles: Mercia, a
frontier region in the Midlands; Deira, centered at York; and Bernicia
farther north. Other Angles had won the area known as East Anglia, divided into a northern and a southern kingdom, Norfolk and Suffolk.

Compared with Merovingian Gaul, Visigothic Spain, or Ostrogothic
Italy, none of these Anglo-Saxon kingdoms was important. None of their
kings was able to unite the tribes settled in Britain. The nearest to political
unity which any king achieved was a vague recognition, under the title of
Bretwalda, of personal supremacy over the other kings and kinglets. The
conquest of Britain was in several ways unique. It was achieved piecemeal
by many small groups; no single leader dominated the movement; the
primitive culture of the conquerors obliterated the decayed culture of the
conquered province; and the conquered people were so completely submerged that few traces of Roman occupation remained. And yet, beginning about the end of the fifth century, the Britons mounted a stout but
ultimately unsuccessful defense of their Celtic-Christian civilization. A
great victory (c.500) over the heathen Anglo-Saxons was won by a sub-
Roman provincial leader whose name was perhaps Artorius, the historical
personage lying behind the later King Arthur legends. This bitter resistance, together with the wars of aggression among the Anglo-Saxons, led to

the strengthening of tribal kingship and the consolidation of several tribes into larger political units. Deira and Bernicia were united into one kingdom of Northumbria by Ethelfrith (593–617), who drove a wedge between the northern and southern Britons by expanding westward all the way to the Irish Sea. In the south Ethelbert of Kent (560–616) established a hegemony over the Saxon kingdoms similar to the predominance of Northumbria in the north. This period brings to a close the heathen and heroic age of Anglo-Saxon conquest and inaugurates a second stage whose two main features characterize the rest of the seventh century: the struggle between kingdoms for predominance and the conversion of the Anglo-Saxons to Christianity.

Throughout the barbarian West, conquest enhanced and transformed the nature of Germanic kingship. Christianity had all but eliminated the priestly character of the earlier heathen kings. Now the king was primarily a military commander. Each success in war increased his power over both the conquered and his own people. The power of the successful king replaced the *imperium* once wielded by provincial governors in the western provinces of the Empire. The abstract Roman *imperium* (authority of the state) might still be recognized in theory: kings might adorn themselves with Roman titles or call their people *foederati* of the Empire. But the realities had changed. Supreme authority in the barbarian "successor states" was neither greater nor less than the personal power of the king, based upon the military strength of his army. And yet it was everywhere the policy of the kings to preserve the Roman civilization which they found in their conquered kingdoms, except in Anglo-Saxon England where there was little left to preserve. The barbarian rulers still thought of the territory subject to them as part of a larger whole, *Romania* (the Roman world).

There was no great social upheaval, nor was there any abrupt economic change. In some kingdoms, as in Vandal Africa, the barbarians replaced the provincial aristocracy by confiscating and redistributing among themselves the great estates. In other kingdoms the barbarians shared in the revenues without expropriating the Roman nobility. In others, as in parts of Gaul, there was even less dislocation of the provincial landowners. The great majority of the population hardly felt the change: their status as small peasant proprietors or as *coloni* on the great *latifundia* was unaltered, regardless of who collected their rents and supervised their labor services. There was no change in agricultural methods, and the tendency toward local economic self-sufficiency continued. In the towns, where few Germans were inclined to settle because of their preference for rural life, the provincial urban populations were relatively undisturbed except when they suffered from the ravages of war. Everywhere in the fifth and sixth centuries, the social and economic conditions of *Romania* in the West continued the decline and decay which had already appeared in the third and fourth centuries.

So it was, also, with government and administration. The barbarian rulers did not consciously destroy the Roman system; rather, they did not know how to keep it going. They tried to maintain the Roman taxes on land and commerce; but economic decline and local resistance, by gradually reducing the importance of these taxes as revenues, led ultimately to their disappearance. The Roman *civitas* (a city or town with its surrounding countryside) continued to be the unit of administration. It was governed by a barbarian count or duke appointed by the king and theoretically removable at the king's will. The count or duke exercised almost all the powers of government within the area of his jurisdiction. He collected taxes, led the local contingent of the army, presided in person or by deputy over the courts, kept roads in repair, and maintained some semblance of peace and order. Local government was far more important to the people than was the authority of the central government. The local counts and dukes were in a position to work together among themselves and, with the provincial Roman or Germanic nobility, against the interests of the royal government. In Merovingian Gaul and Lombard Italy the counties and duchies were more important and enduring political units than the kingdom as a whole. The tendency was toward political as well as economic localism.

The kings relied less upon the total resources of their kingdoms than upon the lands which they confiscated from the imperial Roman fisc. These lands had been "public domain." Their revenues had supported the Roman government. The Merovingian kings granted away large sections of the royal fisc in Gaul to the Church, in the form of pious gifts, and to the nobility in return for support during the many civil wars. This further weakened the resources of the central government and accelerated the tendency toward localism.

The effort of the Germanic rulers to preserve *Romania* and the problems that policy involved are both illustrated by the legal system of the barbarian kingdoms. The Germanic concept of law is best expressed in the phrase, "personality of law." Law was conceived as applying to people of the same tribe, a common heritage of persons bound together by kinship no matter where they might be settled. In contrast, the Roman concept of law is summed up in the phrase, "territoriality of law," or law conceived as the regulations enforced and sanctioned by a state and applying to all inhabitants within the geographical territory of that state. Germanic law was the custom of the people passed down from generation to generation, custom which the ruler could not make or change but which it was his duty to enforce. Roman law was legislated or made by the state and subject to change at the will of the government. These basic legal concepts were antagonistic, and Roman law survived only by becoming a customary code. The Germanic rulers governed their Roman subjects by a debased and simplified form of Roman law because it was the custom of that part of the people under their power.

To facilitate the work of the law courts of barbarian counts unfamiliar with Roman law, and in order to clarify the legal provisions applying in disputes between two parties of different races (thus involving both Roman law and Germanic custom), the barbarian kings issued codes of law. These codes were not exhaustive or complete statements of all the laws in force. They were official and binding instructions to judges, or clarifications of doubtful points which probably arose from particular cases in the courts and were referred to the king for final decision. The barbarian codes of Roman law (*leges romanae*) were based on the Theodosian Code (c.438) and on various legal writings of the later Roman jurists. These commentaries on the edicts and laws were accepted by the courts as authoritative interpretations of the application of laws to particular cases. The codes of Germanic customary law (*leges barbarorum*) were statements of custom governing relations between the barbarians and between barbarian and Roman peoples. The attempt to preserve each legal system as distinct ultimately led to the assimilation of the two systems. The barbarian codes were written in Latin (except in England where they were in the Anglo-Saxon vernacular, our earliest surviving monuments of the English language). The necessity of expressing in Latin the legal concepts of the Teutonic world romanized the primitive jurisprudence, or basic legal concepts, of barbarian law even though the specific legal provisions remained customary and Germanic. Equally important was the influence of the teachings of the Church, which also tended to civilize and thus romanize Germanic custom. This was true even of the vernacular Anglo-Saxon codes.

The most important codes issued by the barbarian kings were compiled in the late fifth and early sixth centuries. The earliest was the *Lex Visigothorum* issued by the Visigothic king Euric about 483. His successor, Alaric II, issued a Roman law code, the so-called *Breviarium Alaricianum*, in 506, on the eve of the attack upon the Visigoths by Clovis. It was a last minute effort to win over, or neutralize the antagonism of, his Gallo-Roman and Catholic subjects. In Burgundy the *Lex Burgundionum* or *Lex Gundobada* was promulgated by Gundobad shortly after 484. Both he and his successor Sigismund (516–524) made later additions. Gundobad also approved a code for his Roman subjects, the *Lex Romana Burgundionum*. After the Frankish conquest of Burgundy in 534 this was displaced by the *Breviarium Alaricianum*, which by its Frankish sponsorship throughout the Merovingian kingdoms became a kind of sub-Roman common law for all non-Germanic peoples under Frankish rule. This benefited the Church and the Gallo-Roman population because Alaric's "Breviary" contained concessions intended to appease his hostile subjects.

The gradual assimilation of German and Roman cultures is best illustrated in the field of law, where the Roman influence on Germanic custom and the barbarization of Roman law are recorded in surviving codes. The influence of Roman civilization and the results of conquest were effective in transforming other aspects of the barbarian way of life. The basic principle of early German social organization was kinship and the obligations and rights of kinsmen. So long as the Germans were migratory, the clan was the unit of society. Local or territorial interests and associations were subordinate to the ties which bound together a people moving about through a generally hostile environment. But when the Germans settled down within the provinces of the western Empire and intermarried with the local nobility, they took on more and more of the interests and activities of the conquered people. By the seventh and eighth centuries there was little to distinguish between the descendants of the German conquerors and Roman conquered.

The Germans preserved much of their own culture and influenced the Roman civilization as much as the Roman culture influenced theirs. Later medieval society was built on a Germanic as well as on a barbarized Roman foundation. Examples may be seen in the transformation of the ancient tribal assemblies mentioned by Tacitus into assemblies of the nobility and free people of territorial areas. The importance of the lordship of a war leader over the companions of his *comitatus* (as Tacitus described it) did not disappear after the conquests. It was rather transformed into a more stable relationship between lord and dependent which was in some cases associated with the tenure of land, or with nonmilitary service.

The one great obstacle to assimilation, and the greatest political problem for the barbarian kings, was the religious antagonism between the Arian Germans (except the heathen Anglo-Saxons and the Catholic Franks) and their orthodox or Catholic Roman subjects. This antagonism was an element of weakness at crucial points in the history of the kingdoms of the Vandals, Visigoths, Ostrogoths, Burgundians, and Lombards. Arianism in the Germanic kingdoms was a divisive force, but as a significant element it was finally eliminated by the end of the seventh century.

Thus in religion, law, and government, as well as in social, political, and economic institutions, the period of the establishment of the Germanic kingdoms in the West (c.450–700) was one of both gradual transformation and gradual assimilation of diverse elements, a process that led to and helped produce the basic unity of medieval society. The same may be said of intellectual, literary, and artistic developments in the period, but with the significant difference that the Germanic element was far less prominent in the process of assimilation. The Christian contribution to the transformation from late antique to early medieval culture was the controlling force that dominated the assimilation of the Germanic, classical, and distinctively Christian elements.

CHAPTER   *IV*

The Emergence of
Early Medieval Culture

In the cultural transition from antiquity to the early Middle Ages there was a general decline in thought and letters from the creative achievement of the Age of the Fathers. The unity of the Mediterranean world, already precarious, was definitely broken by the middle of the eighth century. In the East the decline was slower and it was arrested at a higher level than the depths from which the Latin West had to rebuild its cultural life. In the West the steady decline was characterized by efforts to preserve for the future both the patristic achievement and the elements of pagan antique culture which were considered indispensable in terms of Christian values. Little was produced that could be called original or profound. The intellectual level of the Fathers was not regained until the twelfth century.

But all was not darkness during the "Dark Ages" in the West. The expansion of Christianity continued in the rural areas of the Mediterranean world and, even more impressively, among the northern peoples. The conversion of the North for the first time extended the Christian-antique culture of the Mediterranean beyond the limits of the Roman Empire. With that extension came the assimilation of barbarian elements presaging the development of medieval culture, together with the loss of the North African and Spanish provinces to Latin Christendom. Both the expansion of Christianity and the culture of the period owed much to monasticism. The monks not only spread the faith; their monasteries were strongholds of civilization in a turbulent world. Neither missionary work nor cultural activity was part of the original impulse or purpose of the monastic movement, but such was its historic role. It is not an exaggeration to say that monasticism was the institutional basis of early medieval culture.

The seventh and eighth centuries were characterized by the brief but symptomatic appearance of intellectual and literary activity in regions which were either remote from the Mediterranean center of classical culture or in regions which had made no significant contribution to the cultural life of antiquity. The few gleams of light in the Dark Ages illuminate separate provinces or kingdoms at different periods. There were pronounced regional differences, in contrast with the more nearly common level of culture in antiquity. In the cultural transition to the early Middle Ages the predominant role was played by the Church, and the predominance of Christian ideas, values, and interests provides some unity for the period.

10   THE EXPANSION OF LATIN CHRISTIANITY AND BENEDICTINE MONASTICISM

The expansion of Christianity throughout the Mediterranean world brought important changes in its nature and character. Development of the full implications of the originally simple doctrines of the religion provided Christianity with a rich, and especially in the East a controversial, theology able to meet the criticism of pagan philosophers in their own terms. Doctrinal controversies led to heresy and schism. The unity of the Church was broken, but such controversial discussion was clear evidence of a healthy and growing interest among Christians in the ultimate meaning of all they believed. Other changes, equally far reaching but on a lower intellectual level, resulted from contact between Christianity and the popular religious customs and beliefs of the people who were converted in large numbers during the fourth century and later. New ideas and practices were incorporated which certainly enriched the spirit and the forms of worship of the religion, although conservative Christians of the time complained that there was danger of altering its substance.

Formal conversion did not always mean, for ordinary people, the complete abandonment of older and familiar religious ideas. The bishops who were directly responsible for the early expansion of Christianity found that some adaptation of Christian practices to the polytheism of the Roman official religion and to the multitude of local cults speeded their work of conversion. Augustine, for example, described how his predecessors in Africa had of course forbidden the often ribald celebration of festivals in honor of local deities, but as a "temporary concession" had allowed festivals

in honor of the holy martyrs of the Christian Church in Africa to be celebrated on the same occasions and with the same revelry. How enduring
such temporary concessions might be is illustrated by the revelry still associated with Christmas and Halloween (the evening before the festival
of All Saints), both of which festivals originated in pre-Christian pagan
rites. By the time of Gregory the Great it had become an official policy, in
his words, "not to interfere with any traditional belief or religious observance of the heathen which can be harmonized with Christianity."

The essential problem created by this policy was to preserve the distinction between the deity to whom worship was due and the less-than-
divine angels or human heroes of the faith (the Virgin Mary, saints,
martyrs, and confessors) to whom veneration only was to be accorded.
Educated Christians did not find the distinction difficult, but the ordinary
convert tended to confuse the Christian heavenly hierarchy with the
multiplicity of greater and lesser gods of the hierarchical pagan pantheon.
Furthermore, the religious atmosphere of later pagan antiquity was full
of portents, supernatural forces, and miraculous events—elements which
the early Christians by no means denied, but which they attributed to
demons working for the devil—and the popular credulity of the times was
not altered by the expansion of Christianity.

This expansion continued steadily, spreading out from the cities into
rural areas where paganism was strongly entrenched. (Our word "pagan"
comes from the Latin *pagani,* meaning "dwellers in the country.") The
struggle of Christianity against local cults, against survivals of pagan mythology, and against sheer superstitious ignorance in the rural districts of
the Empire was a far longer and more arduous struggle than was the conflict with pagan philosophies, the officially supported Roman pantheon, or
the Greco-Oriental mystery cults whose devotees were educated city-dwell-
ing people. By the end of the fourth century imperial law banned all these
competing religions. The government persecuted their followers just as it
had persecuted Christians a century earlier. But the Mediterranean world
was still far from being Christianized outside of the cities where the
churches were strongest and the government's support was effective. Laws
and persecution could not reach the ignorant masses of country-dwelling
peasants. The formal conversion of the rustic lower classes had to be followed up by the almost endless work of traveling missionaries or local
priests. Even as late as the eleventh and twelfth centuries the Church was
still trying to destroy the remnants of underground paganism—the superstitions associated with local and minor deities who guarded the fertility of
fields, and with the sprites, fairies, nymphs, and other supernatural beings
who dwelt in forest, stream, meadow, and marsh. This side of the expansion of Christianity is almost unrecorded, but it was a truly heroic, as it
was the longest, struggle of Christianity in the Western world.

In the fourth century contemporaries were fully aware of these problems, but they were more concerned with the growing corruption and worldliness among both clergy and laity, a danger which hardly existed in earlier times when Christianity was a proscribed religion attracting only those who were willing to risk losing the rewards of this world to gain the kingdom of heaven. Christianity had become in the fourth century something of a fashion and had begun to attract people who entered the Church simply because it offered a road to preferment and wealth. Devout Christians, like St. Jerome, inveighed against the worldliness of priests who behaved more like dandies than ministers of the Gospel or who pursued wealthy widows in the hope of obtaining pious gifts or legacies for their own use. Women were especially drawn to the new religion because, unlike pagan worship or the mystery cults, Christianity recognized the dignity and equality before God of both sexes. Many of the earliest martyrs had been women whose gentler virtues were for Christians as important as those of men. But after the triumph of Christianity we begin to hear criticism of Christian women who were more interested in coiffures and cosmetics than in true religion.

Many leaders of the Church thought the general decline of spiritual values a heavy price to pay for official recognition. They saw one solution to this problem in a movement which had recently originated in the East. This was monasticism, the organized and disciplined way of life which provided systematically for the spiritual needs of the individual Christian. Monasticism was not peculiar to Christianity, but was an expression of the ascetic tendencies which are to be found in every religion. Some men have always and everywhere believed they could attain a higher ideal of moral and spiritual excellence by the self-denial of bodily pleasures and by the cultivation of a contemplative life. The earliest Christian ascetics engaged in such practices as prolonged fasting, a simple diet and little sleep, the wearing of rough and irritating clothes, a deliberate avoidance of personal cleanliness (they associated bathing with the immoralities of the public Roman baths), and of course celibacy. It was believed that the individual could achieve purity of soul and could strengthen his hope for salvation by conquering the sins of the flesh and by fortifying his faith through contemplation of the sublime.

The earliest movement within Christianity toward this way of life was spontaneous and without encouragement from the Church. In the mid-third century certain devout Christians fled from the temptations of the world to the more congenial solitude of the desert in Egypt. Perhaps the climate and the economic difficulties which afflicted this area encouraged some of them. The persecutions in Egypt during the period drove others to leave their cities and escape to the desert. Here they lived in caves or huts, assembling occasionally for worship. The leading figure among these "desert fathers" was St. Anthony (c.300), who gave them a common discipline and whose personal sanctity and austerity attracted many followers. These monks were hermits. Each monk lived alone without any formal organization to regulate his religious life, even though he might have several hermits as neighbors. The relaxation of discipline and the vagaries of these hermit monks led one of St. Anthony's disciples to formulate a common way of life. This was Pachomius (fl.318), the founder of cenobitic monasticism (i.e., life in a *cenobium* or community, as opposed to eremitic monasticism or the monastic life as practised by a hermit or recluse). He drew up the first rule (in Latin *regula,* whence the phrase "regular clergy" to refer to monks) for a monastic community. Pachomius' chief concern was to provide common worship, thus combining asceticism with the sacramental system of the Church. This could only be realized by bringing the monastic community under the supervision of the local bishop who could ordain priests to care for the souls of monks. Episcopal control was thus a feature of the earliest cenobitic form of monasticism.

In the East the Basilian rule finally became the most popular monastic rule. St. Basil (329–379) provided a balanced and carefully prescribed regimen of worship and work for his monks. To the accepted monastic virtues of poverty and chastity, he added obedience to the abbot ("father") in charge of the community. The three virtues became special vows which new monks took before they were accepted permanently in the monastery. A rigorous but not excessive asceticism was Basil's ideal. His main concern was to avoid the wayward individualism and extreme austerities of the desert fathers of Egypt and the self-torturing mortification of the flesh of the spiritual athletes of Syria, whose greatest hero, St. Simeon Stylites (395–461) lived on top of a pillar for thirty years with a monthly diet, we are told, of a handful of millet seeds.

The ascetic life spread throughout the West during the fourth and fifth centuries. Among the earlier proponents of the cenobitic form of monasticism were Athanasius, patriarch of Alexandria, during his exile in Italy (c.340), and St. Martin, the soldier who became one of the earliest western monks and who, as bishop of Tours, later founded near his city a monastic community of the Pachomian type (c.360). The most important early western monastery was established on the island of Lerins, near Marseilles, before the end of the fourth century. From this center monasticism of the eastern type was taken by monks to other parts of western Europe, notably the British Isles.

Monasticism and missionary work had already been combined by St. Martin and his followers, whose efforts had been directed primarily toward converting the rural pagans within the Empire. The first tentative steps in building the new Europe whose unity would be that of Latin Christendom rather than that of the Pax Romana—a new Europe extending into the northern world which Roman arms could not conquer—were taken by missionaries to the British Isles. These were monks like St. Ninian who began the conversion of the Picts of Galloway in southwestern Scotland (c.397) and St. Patrick who reinvigorated the anemic Christianity that had filtered into Ireland and thus became the true founder of the Irish church (c.440–461). Ninian prepared for his work at Rome and at Tours, while Patrick spent several years at Lerins before returning to convert the heathen Irish who had taken him captive many years earlier during a raid on the British. The Romano-British church had survived in western Britain (especially in Wales), but it was decadent and isolated from continental developments. The extreme asceticism of eastern monasticism was congenial to the Celtic temperament of the newly converted Irish. Within the new Celtic Christian world generally it was the monastery under the abbot, rather than the bishop's diocese, that was the unit of ecclesiastical organization. Each monastery served the spiritual needs of a single tribe. The abbot was a tribal leader. The bishop was a subordinate official in the monastery, whose duties were wholly spiritual. Celtic monasticism was

Early Monastic Centers and Cultural Outposts
in Western Europe

the expression of a tribal society, just as the diocese was the ecclesiastical outgrowth of civilized society based on the *civitas*.

The vigor of Celtic Christianity was best displayed in its combination of monasticism and missionary work. By 565 St. Columba, an Irish monk, had established his monastery at Iona, from which the conversion of the Picts in northern Scotland and of the Angles of Northumbria was begun. The leaders and heroes of this movement equaled the ascetic extremes of the desert fathers. Typical of their self-mortification was the practice of standing for long periods immersed to the head in an icy stream. The missionary zeal of the Irish carried them over to the continent. St. Columbanus (585–615) introduced new life into the decadent Merovingian church and founded the monasteries of Luxeuil (in Gaul), St. Gall (in Switzerland), and Bobbio (in northern Italy). The great age of Celtic monasticism lasted from c.550 to c.650. It was not an enduring element in Western Christianity, nor was the Pachomian rule on which it was ultimately based. Both represented ideals and practices which were not adaptable to the harsher climate and the less exalted temperament of the majority of western Europeans. A thirty days' fast was easier in the Egyptian desert than in the forests of northern Europe.

Except for the work of the Celtic missionaries, monasticism in the West was declining by the middle of the fifth century. Its success was partly the cause. The early leaders were so popular, and they made the monastic life so attractive, that many men and women who had no real calling for discipline and self-denial joined the movement. Also, initial success was made possible partly by donations from the laity which financed the building of monasteries and supported the monks and nuns, thus attracting people who looked to a life of ease rather than one of devotion and service. Worldliness and corruption were already creeping into the monastic movement in the time of St. Jerome, who was particularly critical of wandering monks who moved about from monastery to monastery under no supervision or ecclesiastical discipline.

The solution to the problem of monastic decadence was provided by St. Benedict of Nursia (c.480–543). He did not consider himself a reformer or leader, except for his own community of monks, and he had no program for other monasteries to follow. He thought of his own rule as "the least of beginnings" to help the monk get started on the ascetic life. The ideal which he himself held was the life of the hermit or of the desert fathers of Egypt. However, the rule which he wrote for his monks at Monte Cassino (founded c.520) became the model for all later monastic life in the West. Benedict has justly been called "the Father of Western Monasticism."

The central feature of the Benedictine rule, like all other monastic rules, was the *opus Dei* ("work of God," i.e., worship by the monks in common at set intervals throughout the day), but the success of the rule was

St. Benedict Presents His Rule to His Monks. Manuscript illustration (eighth century). THE PIERPONT MORGAN LIBRARY, NEW YORK.

owing to four new elements which Benedict introduced. First, his rule was a constitution consisting of general regulations rather than a set of minute and specific by-laws, so that it was supremely adaptable to local conditions. Earlier rules had prescribed too much of the monk's daily life in too great detail. Relaxation of the rule had too frequently become a simple necessity which led to a general laxity. In the second place, Benedict enhanced the authority of the abbot, who was to appoint all officials of the monastery, control monastic finances, and exercise wide discretionary powers over the organization and discipline of the community. Although the abbot was elected by vote of the community, he was to be installed by the bishop of his diocese. Thus episcopal control was provided for in the rule itself. Third, in addition to the usual vows of poverty, chastity, and obedience to the abbot, a fourth was added, the vow of "stability." This was a promise not to leave the monastery except at the command of the abbot. It enhanced the abbot's disciplinary control of the community, as it increased the sense of solidarity among the monks. Finally, the Benedictine rule introduced an almost revolutionary element into monasticism by providing that all able-bodied monks share in the manual work of the community, thus enhancing the dignity of labor and also making the monastery self-sufficient.

The general character of Benedictine monasticism reflects the ascetic ideal without going beyond human frailties. Its quality of moderation has justified the Benedictine motto, *mens sana in corpore sano* ("a sound mind in a sound body"). Benedict made no specific provision for intellectual activity beyond public and private reading of the Scriptures and the works of the Fathers, and he referred only casually to the instruments of writing. Benedictine monasteries, however, normally included a school for novices, a library, and a scriptorium (writing room), and they therefore were ideally suited for the preservation of the pagan and Christian culture of antiquity. This was ultimately the greatest contribution of Benedictine monasticism, but its immediate results were an extensive reform of the monastic movement and the further expansion of Christianity into heathen lands which had never been within the orbit of the civilized Roman world.

The expansion of Benedictine monasticism and its use in missionary work were largely the achievement of Gregory the Great, who wrote the earliest Life of St. Benedict and gave to the Benedictine rule the prestige of papal support. Gregory sent a group of Benedictine monks, headed by Augustine (the first archbishop of Canterbury, not to be confused with the greater Bishop of Hippo two centuries earlier), to begin the conversion of the Anglo-Saxons in southern England (597). The ultimate triumph of the Roman mission in England, after a long struggle against both heathen barbarians and the competing Celtic missionaries (whose usages, especially their calculation of the date of Easter, were at variance with the rest of Christendom), was an epoch in the expansion of Latin Christianity, as it was in the establishment of unity under the papacy. An important stage of this triumph was reached at the Synod of Whitby in 663, where both Celtic and Anglo-Saxon leaders of the Northumbrian church agreed to accept Roman usages; within a century papal supremacy was recognized throughout the British Isles.

The ties between England and Rome remained especially close. When the conversion of the heathens in Germany began in the opening years of the eighth century it was an English monk, Boniface, who led the work under papal patronage and with the rank of archbishop and legate conferred upon him by the pope. Wherever he went in Germany, Boniface established Benedictine monasteries. The foundation at Fulda was in later years the most important German center both of learning and of missionary work. The missionary efforts of Boniface in Germany were supported also by the government of the Merovingian kingdom. This connection between Boniface and the Franks brought to the papacy an influence in Gaul which was to have important results in the future.

11   ART AND LITERATURE TO THE END OF THE SIXTH CENTURY: CASSIODORUS, BOETHIUS, AND GREGORY THE GREAT

In the fourth and early fifth centuries, developments in architecture and the other arts were neither so impressive as the achievement of the Fathers nor was the decline thereafter so noticeable. The sixth century witnessed a provincial renaissance in Italy which, in both art and thought, may be considered the last important influence of Greek cilivization on the West until the high Middle Ages.

In architecture, the earliest Christian churches were simply an adaptation of the public building, the basilica, in use by the Roman government. The early Christian basilica was a rectangular building with the altar at one end and the entrance at the other. The exterior was unadorned, but the interior was often decorated elaborately with mosaics and colored marble on the floors, walls, and the semidome over the apse (the projecting end of the building where the altar was located). The interior space of the larger basilicas is broken into three main parts, the central nave and two aisles separated from the nave by a row of columns supporting arches which in turn bear the weight of the central roof. The effect is to produce a nave arcade whose horizontal rhythms converge upon the focal point of the structure, the altar. The largest basilicas, such as Old St. Peter's (built 324–336 and demolished in the sixteenth century) or St. Paul's Outside the Walls, sometimes have two aisles on either side of the nave and also

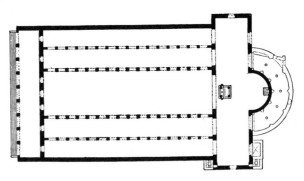

Floor Plan of Basilica

two other features which were lacking in the ordinary church: an atrium or open courtyard in front of the church, surrounded by covered galleries and serving to seclude the church proper from the noise and distractions of the street; and an interior space called the transept, whose axis is at right angles to the rest of the basilica and which separates the apse from the nave and

St. Paul's Outside the Walls, Rome: façade and nave (fourth century, much restored).

Sant' Apollinare in Classe, Ravenna: nave (sixth century). PHOTO: ALINARI

aisles. The transept sometimes projects beyond the walls of the aisles; enlargement of the transept and extension of the apse, in later centuries, produced the conventional cruciform ground plan of the medieval church. The bishop's *cathedra*, or throne, was placed in the apse behind the altar (hence a bishop's church is called a cathedral). The straight lines and wooden construction of the ceiling and the sloping roofs over nave and aisles set practical limits to the size of the basilica, as well as handicapping basilica churches with a built-in fire hazard. These were two difficulties confronting medieval architects when they began to improve upon the basilica.

In northern Italy during the sixth century, both under Theodoric and during the Byzantine occupation, an architectural revival took place. Examples at Ravenna are the church of Sant' Apollinare in Classe, a basilica with highly ornate Byzantine interior decoration, and San Vitale which introduced to the West the new Byzantine type of floor plan and construction. San Vitale is a central-space church, octagonal in shape, whose walls support a dome covering the interior. The effect is static and the vertical dimension is emphasized, compared with the horizontal movement suggested by the nave arcade of the basilica. This type of church is Syrian in origin. Its construction is a development of the arch, vault, and dome system common in Roman architecture.

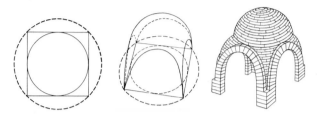

Dome on Pendentives

A vault is simply an arch extended for the desired length in a third dimension; two vaults of the same size intersecting at right angles will enclose a square space if the length of each vault is equal to the width. But the resulting structure will not be strong in relation to its weight, and its height is limited by the width of each vault. A dome is simply an arch rotated in a complete circle; its height is limited by its diameter and it cannot enclose a square space. In order to enclose a square space and achieve greater height, the Byzantine architects, in effect, mounted one dome on top of another "dome." The first dome is constructed so that its circumference touches the four corners of the square space to be enclosed, and then the portions of the dome projecting beyond the square are cut off vertically; then the top of this dome is cut off horizontally just above the top of the four arches formed by the previous vertical trimming. The resulting horizontal circle is then used as the base for the second true dome which is thus raised to a greater height than would be possible by intersecting vaults. The total result is called a dome on pendentives (pendentives are the masonry left from the first "dome": the triangular sections of a hemisphere whose diameter is equal to the diagonal of a square inscribed within its largest section). If all this is clear, the reader will appreciate the engineering problem and its greatest architectural solution, Justinian's great church, St. Sophia, in Constantinople, whose dome soars 180 feet above the interior pavement and covers (together with two half-domes built up on opposite sides) an interior space of 100 feet by 250 feet. Because the lateral thrust is so great in such a structure, buttresses of such size had to be added that the exterior appearance resembles a massive pile of masonry. The interior effect was what interested the architects. They introduced enough light and provided the spherical interior surfaces with such colorful

San Vitale, Ravenna: exterior and
interior (sixth century).
PHOTO: ALINARI

St. Sophia, Constantinople: exterior and interior (sixth century). The minarets and interior Arabic inscriptions were added after 1453. PHOTO: TURKISH INFORMATION SERVICE.

decoration as to overawe and astonish all who saw it before 1453, when the Moslems whitewashed (and thus, fortunately, preserved for the modern archeologist to restore) the beautiful mosaics. This Byzantine architectural achievement was so much greater than anything accomplished by contemporaries in the West that it affords a parallel to the relative wealth of East and West. The principles involved were introduced in the West in the church of San Vitale in Ravenna, and we shall see that some of these principles underlie future medieval architectural development, although the central-space church was to play a minor role.

In painting, sculpture, and the decorative arts, early Christian art developed from pagan prototypes in style and even in subject matter. Thus in the fourth century a Christian bridal casket is decorated with representations of Venus and cherubs, or a sarcophagus (stone coffin) in the catacombs is adorned with pagan nymphs, tritons, and mermaids. The entry of Jesus into Jerusalem is portrayed after the manner of an emperor's triumphal entry into Rome. The earliest representations of Christ (third century) show Him clean-shaven and modeled on figures of Apollo, while in the fourth century Christ is portrayed as an austere and bearded figure resembling pagan representations of Jupiter or the ancient philosophers who, artistically, symbolized Wisdom. The pagan art which was thus taken over by Christian artists was already, by classical or Hellenic standards, "degenerate": the stiffness in form, lack of proportion, and especially the unnatural facial expression betray a loss of the classical spirit. But if we divorce ourselves from classical or Hellenic standards, it is historically more accurate to say that Christianity adopted the artistic style which, in the later Empire, was "modern." Itself of provincial origin, Christianity took over the art forms and style which had been developing in the provinces as a reaction against the "official" Greco-Roman style as illustrated in the realistic portraiture of the early Empire, or in the slavish Roman copies of Greek naturalistic art of the Hellenistic period.

This provincial reaction led to the transformation of classical style into a transcendental and abstract style. The provincial pagan artists who rejected the traditional realism and naturalism of Roman art were not interested in lifelike, three-dimensional, "photographic" reproduction of nature or the outside world. Rather, they were interested in portraying a reality which transcended sense experience, a higher reality (as they conceived it) beyond time and space, and therefore to be represented as an expression of spirit rather than of material form. Thus individuality gives way to abstraction. Realistic details, which portray the merely physical and therefore changing exterior, are subordinated to a portrayal of the inner essence of the subject. For example, a typically Roman portrait-bust suggests the flesh-and-blood reality of an individual human being whose existence has been caught and reproduced at a particular moment. The "modern art" of the later Empire would instead portray the subject's soul by exaggerating the eyes and one or two details of the facial expression, all else being reduced to ornamental or abstract treatment. The Roman bust lives here and now; the provincial style represents the eternal and unchanging essence of the subject.

It was this provincial art of the borderlands, the oriental and barbarian frontiers of the Empire, which Christians found most congenial for the artistic representation of the teachings of the Church, whose main emphasis was on the eternity beyond this world, the greater reality of the infinite and spiritual than the finite and material. Understood as a positive shift in values and standards, Christian art of the later Empire cannot be considered part of a decline of antique culture in the fourth and fifth centuries, but rather as the early development of a transcendental style which reaches its height in the Romanesque period of the Middle Ages.

In popular literature, as contrasted with patristic theology and philosophy or pagan belles-lettres, there was an analogous development of new values and standards in the transition from ancient to early medieval culture. The pagan literature of entertainment was the Greek romance or a Latin version of it, such as the *Golden Ass* of Apuleius or the *Satyricon* of Petronius, often full of classical mythology and ribald episodes which were not considered fit for good Christians to read. To replace these worldly adventure stories a Christian popular literature of spiritual adventure grew up whose heroes were the martyrs or saints who had renounced the world and its vices. The earliest accounts of these heroes concerned the desert fathers of Egypt. From these were developed the later *Vitae Sanctorum* (Lives of the Saints), semibiographical stories about hermits and monks who were, pre-eminently, the models after whom the good Christian should pattern his life.

The compelling purpose behind the writing of *Vitae Sanctorum* was edification of the faithful, the inculcation of Christian ideals and conduct among simple folk who could neither read nor understand the metaphysical or mystical writings of the Fathers. Many of these "lives" grew directly out of sermons preached on the festival days of the various saints. To attract and hold attention, to emphasize the virtue of the saint, and to exemplify various points of Christian ethics, the *Vitae Sanctorum* were replete with tense situations, hairbreadth escapes, miraculous events (i.e., inexplicable in terms of ordinary human experience), and happy endings, just like some popular modern short stories. In this literature for popular consumption there rapidly grew up a huge number of legends, some of them taken over from Greco-Roman mythology and some of them attached to more than one saint. A new Christian mythology replaced the old pagan mythology. Historians can reconstruct Christian thought on the highest level from the serious writings of the Fathers; our only glimpse of the mind of the common man of the early Middle Ages is afforded by the Lives of the Saints.

In the West, the outstanding early life of a saint was Sulpicius

Severus' *Life of St. Martin of Tours* (c.400), on which many later authors (or compilers) of saints' lives based their accounts. Hagiographical literature, like the modern detective story, is dominated by conventions, and Sulpicius Severus was responsible for many of the conventions which reappear in saints' lives for the next eight centuries. The typical saint is born amid miraculous events. As an infant he performs some prodigy such as uttering a prediction at the age of two or three days, and as a child he confounds his elders with his precocious wisdom. Late childhood and adolescence are usually treated very briefly or left unrecorded, but the saint's mature years are full of miracles which he performs as proof of his virtue (virtue being conceived primarily in terms of supernatural power). After an ascetic life of renunciation and humility, his death is attended by appropriately miraculous events (such as being seen by eye-witnesses to ascend into heaven in the company of angels, or up a ladder). The resemblance between the conventional pattern of a saint's life and the life of Christ according to the Gospels is obvious. But this similarity did not surprise contemporaries who believed that a holy man should naturally model his life on the life of the Lord.

The popularity of the *Vitae Sanctorum* and the fashionable cult of saints in the West were intimately connected, the one reinforcing the other; both were intimately associated with the monastic life which produced so many saints. In addition to Scripture, novices in the monasteries were encouraged to read the Lives of the Saints in preparation for later study of the more difficult patristic literature. The Benedictine rule specifically recommended the reading of sacred literature including the writings and lives of the Fathers. The self-sufficient Benedictine monastery thus required a library together with a scriptorium where copies of books could be made and new books occasionally written. Enough education to teach all monks to read and the further education of one or two monks preparing for ordination to the priesthood were a normal part of monastic life. In such an environment the natural intellectual curiosity of human nature often led to the cultivation of reading and study far beyond the minimum requirements. Without the monastic scriptoria of the early Middle Ages the physical preservation of pagan and patristic classical literature would not have been possible.

Benedict's attitude toward learning, with true Benedictine moderation, was tolerant and permissive; his service to Western culture was incidental to his main purpose. In contrast, Benedict's younger contemporary Cassiodorus (c.490–580) was a man with a program. He rose high in the government of the Ostrogothic kingdom, in which he rendered valuable service to Theodoric and his successors as the author of their official correspondence. Cassiodorus made a collection of these letters and state papers, the *Variae*, a fascinating record of Ostrogothic policy, of contemporary interests and values, and of the deteriorated intellectual level of his age. Cassiodorus' original intention had been to found a Christian school at Rome, perhaps on the model of the pagan Academy at Athens which Justinian closed in 529. But these plans came to nothing because of the Byzantine reconquest of Italy. Cassiodorus' dubious political loyalties changed back and forth for a few years. Then he fled to Constantinople, c.540, from which he returned to his ancestral estate at Squillace, in southern Italy. Here he founded a monastery dedicated to combining his educational plans with the monastic life.

In his most important work, *An Introduction to Divine and Human Readings,* Cassiodorus outlined for his monks a curriculum of study and also his educational philosophy, which can be briefly stated in his words as "using the methods of the liberal arts to aid the study of sacred works." This involved a conscious effort to preserve and to master all the literature of antiquity for the service of Christian education. He also provided his monks with a reading list of the best books in each field, together with instruction on textual emendation, copying, and binding of manuscripts. Cassiodorus' work is an illustration of the cultural revival of Ostrogothic and Byzantine Italy in the sixth century. The *Divine and Human Readings* was a popular handbook or guide to literature, surviving in an impressive number of manuscripts.

Equally representative of sixth-century Italy, Boethius (c.480–524) was also an important official in Theodoric's government, but his interest was in theology and philosophy rather than higher education. Also, unlike Cassiodorus, Boethius was not successful enough as a politician to escape being implicated in a treasonable plot, late in Theodoric's reign, for which he suffered capital punishment after languishing in prison for a year. Boethius was the last Western scholar before the twelfth century to be thoroughly conversant with the philosophical works of Aristotle in the original Greek. His original plan was to make both Plato and Aristotle available to the Latin West in translation. Unfortunately, he got no further than the logical treatises of Aristotle, and translations of only two elementary treatises survived (plus a translation of, and commentary upon, Porphyry's *Isagoge,* an introduction to Aristotle's logic). Limited as it was, Boethius' work provided the West with its technical philosophical vocabulary and its only knowledge of Greek logic until the twelfth century. Boethius also wrote five important theological *Tractates,* all of them staunchly orthodox. One of them was a systematic application of Aristotelian logic to a problem of Christian theology—an anticipation of later achievements which has earned Boethius the title, "First of the Scholastics." As he himself put it, in a letter to a friend, his purpose was to "reconcile faith and reason."

When imprisonment cut short his brilliant career under the Arian Theodoric, Boethius found it inexpedient to continue writing on theological subjects. Separation from his books precluded further philosophical studies. Instead he wrote the literary work for which he has always been best known, *The Consolation of Philosophy,* a dialogue half in verse and half in prose between himself and Philosophia, who gently leads him from black despair over his lot to "that true contentment which reason allied with virtue alone can give." The *Consolation* is one of the great masterpieces of prison-literature. Into it Boethius poured his love of classical learning and his noblest thoughts on Christian virtue, although Christ is not mentioned and the Bible is not cited. Despite its immense popularity (over four hundred manuscripts of the work have survived), there is nothing philosophically profound or original in it.

Both Cassiodorus and Boethius were dedicated to preserving the cultural heritage of antiquity; intellectually they lived in the past, a greater age, as they were acutely aware, than their own. In striking contrast was the attitude of Gregory the Great (540–604), the last important representative of the sixth-century cultural revival in Italy and last of the Four Doctors of the Latin Church. Gregory was "modern" in that the classical heritage did not interest him; like some modern educators, he had "a vigorous desire to have done with the follies of the past, and to build on what is sound, useful, and contemporary." For Gregory the beauties of good style were irrelevant and might even divert the reader from seeking Christian truth. He once wrote that it is "unseemly to fetter the words of the Heavenly Oracle to the rules of Donatus." Gregory himself was well educated—the letter containing this statement, for example, is written in impeccable Latin according to the rules of Donatus. His style, however, is another matter, and the quality of his attainment reveals a marked decline not only from the age of Augustine but also from that of Boethius. Gregory had a great influence upon the future, for all that he wrote was both interesting and intelligible to men in the next five centuries.

The importance of Gregory's sermons and of his correspondence (over eight hundred letters have survived) has already been noted in connection with his pontificate. As a theologian he was thoroughly Augustinian but without either the depth or discipline of Augustine. In his longest work, the *Moralia in Job,* Gregory allows the freedom of his allegorical interpretation to lapse into intellectual license, as when he interprets the seven sons of Job to stand for the clergy because the parts of seven (four and three), when multiplied, give twelve which indicate the twelve Apostles who represent the clergy! The *Moralia* has fittingly been described as a "vast superstructure raised on narrow foundations." Whatever the shortcomings, Gregory's purpose in commenting upon the Book of Job was a useful and practical one, extracting good moral teaching (not doctrine) from the Bible. The same utilitarian purpose underlies his *Pastoral Rule,* in which he discusses the character, qualifications, and work of the good bishop. This treatise was immensely popular throughout the Middle Ages as a kind of standard reference book on how to perform episcopal duties. It was drawn more from Gregory's own experience than from previous writings, so it has the greatest interest for modern readers. Finally, the work which Gregory himself probably enjoyed most in writing was the *Dialogues*, in four books, of which the second was a Life of St. Benedict. The *Dialogues* did much to popularize monasticism as well as to encourage the cult of saints, veneration of relics, and popular beliefs about demons, angels, and supernatural phenomena.

12 CULTURAL OUTPOSTS IN WESTERN EUROPE: SPAIN, IRELAND, AND THE NORTHUMBRIA OF BEDE

Italy after the death of Gregory the Great suffered a cultural decline, and leadership passed to other areas more remote from the center of Roman civilization. Only two developments in Italy need be noted. First, there was an influx of Greek refugees fleeing from difficulties in the East. This immigration had no noticeable effect upon the decline, though some of the refugees were well-educated and able men, such as Theodore of Tarsus, who was sent by the pope to reorganize the English church as archbishop of Canterbury (668–690). Second, the monasteries of Bobbio in the north and Monte Cassino in the south replaced Ravenna and Rome as centers of what little learning and literary activity there was. As an indication of shifting interests, it was during this period that manuscripts of classical authors were erased so that the costly parchment could be used for copying the Bible and sacred literature. Some of these copies, known as palimpsests, have preserved pagan classical texts which can still be deciphered and which otherwise would not have survived.

In North Africa, which had produced such great men as Tertullian, Cyprian, and Augustine, a decline set in after the completion of the historical work of Orosius, the disciple of Augustine. Orosius' *Seven Books of Histories Against the Pagans* was as much an apologetic as an objective history, for he set out to prove (in support of the general thesis of his master's great *City of God*) that the miseries and disasters suffered by pagan Rome were far greater than the difficulties encountered after the establishment of Christianity. The work was the most widely read history in the Middle Ages, and many later chronicles were continuations of it. The Byzantine reconquest of North Africa did not stimulate a real revival. Within another century North Africa was permanently removed from the orbit of Western civilization by the Moslem conquest.

Sixth-century Merovingian Gaul saw the disappearance of what had been excellent provincial schools of rhetoric during the later Empire. Conditions were too turbulent for cultural activity, although one of the Merovingian kings, Chilperic (561–584), fancied himself to be a patron of arts and letters. Fortunatus (535–605), the best poet of the sixth century, wandered about Gaul visiting courts and monasteries, exchanging his pleasant, lightweight verses for room and board. The fact that his poetry should be appreciated is surprising, but it is far more surprising that Fortunatus was able to compose two really good Christian hymns, *Pange Lingua Gloriosi* and *Vexilla Regis Prodeunt*. The first stanza of the latter follows:

> *Vexilla regis prodeunt,*
> *Fulget crucis mysterium,*
> *Quo carne carnis conditor*
> *Suspensus est patibulo.*
> [The King's advancing banners wave!
> The Cross gleams out its Mystery
> Where He that made the body gave
> His body to the gallows-tree.][1]

The most important writer in Merovingian Gaul was Fortunatus' friend and occasional benefactor Gregory, bishop of Tours (538–594), a member of the Gallo-Roman aristocracy. Gregory's contribution to hagiographical literature is next in importance only to that of Sulpicius Severus and to that of his namesake and contemporary, Gregory the Great. What makes Gregory of Tours unique in his age is his remarkable *History of the Franks*, which for the period of his own episcopate (after 573) is a detailed, dramatic, and generally accurate narrative. Gregory was not particularly well educated; the classical authors (except for Virgil) he probably knew only through Martianus Capella's textbook. He reveals all the prejudices and predilections of his age (antagonism toward heretics and an unquestioning acceptance of miracles, which he loves to enlarge upon), and his viewpoint is strictly that of the high churchman, betraying no dislike of the Frankish barbarians on racial or cultural grounds but judging them solely on the basis of their attitude toward the Church. His language and style are vigorously uncouth, but they make a better medium for his vivid portrayal of barbarian life than the bombastic and artificial affectations of contemporary rhetorical usage.

After the death of Gregory of Tours, the Frankish kingdoms produced nothing of intellectual interest. As in Italy, the seventh and the first half of the eighth centuries constitute a dark age; in Gaul there are only a few wretchedly inadequate annals, the "grammatical" works of an author who assumed the name of Virgilius Maro and the geographical lore collected by a certain Aethicus the Cosmographer. Their efforts often read more like elaborate practical jokes than anything to be taken seriously.

---

[1] Jack Lindsay, *Song of a Falling World* (London, 1948), p. 271, reprinted by permission of the translator, Jack Lindsay, and the publisher, Andrew Dakers, Ltd.

Spain under the Visigoths resembled Merovingian Gaul in its turbulence and in its cultural decline from later antiquity—except that there was no counterpart among the Hispano-Roman aristocracy of Gregory of Tours. The conversion of Spain to Catholicism under Recared I (586–601) stimulated some controversial writings against Arianism, and the synods which supervised the work of conversion provided a forum for the discussion of doctrinal and disciplinary issues.

The highest point reached by Visigothic and Catholic culture in Spain is represented by Isidore, bishop of Seville (c.570–636), the most learned man in continental Europe during the seventh century. Isidore was a man of universal education, but he knew very little about almost everything—no mean achievement, however, for this dark age. In all his writings there is not a trace of originality or profundity. And yet Isidore achieved success of a kind unknown to any other early medieval writer, for he was the compiler of the standard encyclopedia of all knowledge for the Middle Ages, the *Etymologies*. The whole range of human knowledge then available was organized, in this work, according to the unifying principle of the origin and meaning of words. It is fashionable to poke fun at the fanciful explanations which Isidore drew from chance similarity of spelling or sound rather than from real linguistic knowledge. For example, a friend is one whose main concern is for the soul's welfare, because, according to Isidore, *amicus* is derived from *animi custos*, "guardian of the soul"; or again, a man cries more easily when kneeling in prayer because the knees and eyes of an unborn infant are close together in the womb. But the absurdities of Isidore's "etymological" method should not be allowed to obscure his substantial achievement in accumulating so huge a body of organized knowledge—most of it quite accurate either by the standards of his own age or by those of classical antiquity. The *Etymologies* was a kind of ultimate epitome to end all further epitomes, but it was much more than a mere storehouse of facts. In typically medieval fashion Isidore applied the allegorical method to all of human knowledge. He thus sought the hidden meaning which lies behind objective facts and tried to relate knowledge of the material world to knowledge of an intellectual, moral, or spiritual order. The *Etymologies* is full of symbolism by which Isidore strove to reduce all knowledge ultimately to unity.

Isidore was the author of other treatises, on doctrine, ecclesiastical law, history, and cosmology, whose significance lies not in their quality so much as in the fact that they were known, as was the *Etymologies*, in other parts of Europe at a very early date. None of Isidore's successors in the Visigothic church reached even the modest level of these minor treatises. When Spain once more, in the eighth century, became a cultural center, it was a Moslem culture cut off from the rest of western Europe.

Ireland was never part of the Roman Empire and the continuity of classical civilization was almost completely broken in Britain. A debased, sub-Roman, and Christian culture was pushed westward by the Anglo-Saxon invasions into Wales and southwestern England. Its expiring gasps are recorded in the little work of moral exhortation by Gildas (c.500–570), ineptly entitled *On the Annihilation and Conquest of Britain,* in which the tantalizingly scanty historical information is overwhelmed by tedious moralizing about the dreary times, and in the weird collection of anonymous schoolboy verses called *Hisperica Famina,* which read like the work of a conscientious idiot, although some critics have found in them "artistic feeling" and a commendable "directness and freedom in expression." In translation, some of the verses may even suggest the mode and feeling of some twentieth-century poetry, as in the lines:

> Roaring Westwind downbows
> > oaks with strong-cherishing boughs
> old knotty holmoaks harrows
> > flat to the furrows
> stoutly snorting harms
> > crested thatch of farms
> cracks
> > topmost tiles on the chimney-stacks
> raves
> > thrashing earth with blue waves
> and carries high
> > foamdrops on the starry sky.[2]

One of the most fascinating problems of European history is to explain how the flourishing of arts and letters in Ireland and England came about in the seventh century, when continental Europe had reached its lowest level. A cultural flourishing in the British Isles could not take the form of a revival of classical culture, because in Ireland there was none to revive and in western England the British church, cut off from Europe by the barbarians, lacked the educational resources or intellectual traditions to survive the post-Roman collapse. British Christians, moreover, were conspicuous failures in the work of converting the heathen Irish and Anglo-Saxons. When Christianity was reintroduced from the continent, by the mission of St. Patrick to Ireland and the later arrival of St. Augustine of Canterbury in Kent, it came as a new movement with the enthusiasm and dedication characteristic of evangelical work. Conversion established contact in the fifth century between Ireland and southern and southwestern Gaul, where some of the best provincial schools of the later Empire were located and where the earliest missionaries had received their training. Thus, the explanation seems to be that conversion provided the initial motivation, and contact with the surviving classical culture in southern

---

[2] Jack Lindsay, *Song of a Falling World* (London, 1948), p. 260, reprinted by permission of the translator, Jack Lindsay, and publisher, Andrew Dakers, Ltd.

Gaul provided the materials for the cultivation of arts and letters in Ireland. The monasteries which dominated the Celtic church became sheltered centers in the barbaric northern world for the study of both sacred and secular learning, and the later competition between Irish missionary monks and the Benedictines of the Roman mission during the conversion of the Anglo-Saxons stimulated debate over theological issues in the seventh century. Further nourishment of both Irish and Anglo-Saxon cultural development came from Visigothic Spain, for the works of Isidore of Seville (d. 636) and other Spanish writers were known in Ireland and England before the end of the seventh century.

In England the initial cultural stimulus of conversion was as modest as Augustine's limited success in his missionary efforts among the Anglo-Saxons. But a beginning was made, and it produced a fascinating by-product whose consequences were significant for the future. The Anglo-Saxons were the first people in the early Middle Ages to feel the full impact of the spell of Rome, the Eternal City, the symbol of man's highest achievements. Leaders of the Celtic church found in Roman Christianity an alien if not hostile spirit. Contemporary Romans could see only a collapsing world about them, "a straitened age . . . a failing world," as Pope John III referred to his own times. In contrast, the many Anglo-Saxons who made pilgrimages to Rome were profoundly impressed with the superiority of Mediterranean civilization to their own, rather than with the decay of antiquity felt by Mediterranean people for whom there was still a sense of continuity with the past. Thus what depressed the Roman, by comparison with a past with which he had never wholly lost touch, elated and stimulated the Anglo-Saxon whose only comparison was with his own barbaric culture. Pilgrims from England eagerly collected the books, jewels and objects of art, and the knowledge of architecture with which they might adorn and improve their own material and intellectual life.

Irish monasteries were already centers of learning in the sixth century, but from this early period only a penitential and some hymns survive as examples of creative work rather than the assimilation of Latin culture. In the seventh century, the most interesting and original treatise on a secular subject produced in all of Europe was the work of an anonymous Irish author. Entitled *On the Twelve Abuses of the Age* (c.660–700), it is a lively critique of contemporary social, political, intellectual, and religious life. The author was obviously well educated, wrote excellent Latin, drew on a wide range of patristic literature, and was capable of independent and original thinking. Typically Irish in genius and temper is the contentious spirit pervading the treatise, as well as the specific injunction to kings "to give no countenance to the superstitions of wizards, soothsayers, and witches."

The most distinguished representative of Irish religious culture in the seventh century was Adamnan, abbot of Iona (679–704), whose best-known works are the *Life of St. Columba* (founder of the monastery), a commentary on Virgil, and a descriptive essay *On Holy Places*. The last work was drawn from an oral account of the Holy Land by a contemporary Frankish bishop who had recently returned from a pilgrimage to Jerusalem, then under Moslem control. The far-flung cultural interconnections illustrated by this treatise (embracing Moslem Palestine, Byzantine and Orthodox Constantinople, Merovingian and Catholic Gaul, and a Celtic monastery off the northwestern coast of Anglo-Saxon England) emphasize how inaccurate it is to think of the Dark Ages as a period of isolated provincialism.

The entrance of England into the cultural life of western Europe resulted from the interaction between Irish learning (emanating from the monastery of Lindisfarne in the north, founded c.634) and the classical tradition of the Mediterranean world brought to England by Theodore of Tarsus, archbishop of Canterbury (668–690), and his companion, Hadrian. Theodore and Hadrian established a school at Canterbury (c.670), from which the Roman influence spread northward to such centers as the monasteries of Wearmouth and Jarrow in Northumbria, founded in 674 and 682 by Benedict Biscop, who was one of the most assiduous book collectors of the age. Canterbury was the only school north of the Alps in the early Middle Ages where students could learn Greek and study Roman law as well as pursue the several disciplines of the liberal arts.

The Irish and Roman traditions were combined in the West Saxon Aldhelm, abbot of Malmesbury (675–709), of whom it has been said that "no country in western Europe during the seventh century could show his equal in intellectual achievement." His early training was at Malmesbury, the only important monastery in southern England founded by Celtic missionaries; later he studied at Canterbury under Theodore and Hadrian; and, like so many of his Anglo-Saxon contemporaries, he made a pilgrimage to Rome. Few men before the twelfth century had read as much— and, it must be added, to so little purpose. He wrote poems, a tract in praise of virginity, and some letters which are valuable evidence for the cultural interests of his period. Like his Irish contemporary Adamnan, he loved the artificial language and esoteric style of Celtic scholarship; it has been questioned whether Aldhelm was capable of writing a readily intelligible sentence. But the mannerisms of his Latinity must be recognized as a cultivated art sanctioned by the fashions of his age rather than inability to compose more straightforward prose.

Northumbria, the battleground between Celtic and Roman Christianity (c.634–663), produced the greatest scholar and literary figure of the early Middle Ages. Bede (c.672–735) was brought up at Jarrow, where Benedict Biscop had assembled a magnificent library, the product of his book-collecting travels in Gaul and Italy over many years. No writer before the twelfth century was more widely read, nor to better purpose.

Lindisfarne Gospels. England (c.700); two pages showing decoration and figure drawings. BRITISH MUSEUM.

Several Irish and Anglo-Saxon scholars were acquainted with Greek in the seventh and eighth centuries, but Bede alone was able to apply his knowledge to a useful end. He drew at first hand on the work of some of the Greek Fathers, and he corrected some errors of translation in St. Jerome's Vulgate. In scholarship, if not in profundity of thought, Bede was the intellectual equal of the Latin Fathers. His own age knew and valued him primarily as a teacher and writer of didactic treatises on the Old and New Testaments and on astronomy and chronology. Bede introduced into the West the dating system of Dionysius Exiguus, that is, the modern reckoning of dates in terms of the birth of Christ (B.C. and A.D.), which later became standard. His most important work was the *Ecclesiastical History of the English People,* written in a style and language unsurpassed since the age of Augustine and for the period from 597 to 731 (when it ends), a work of sustained interest and remarkable accuracy. Even in the *History* Bede was primarily a teacher. He believed that the value of history lay in its lessons for posterity, a view shared by ancient and patristic writers. He grasped the significance of early English history as being a part of the larger whole of western Europe and of the expansion of Christianity and civilization among barbaric peoples.

Anglo-Saxon art, like learning and literature, developed under a twofold Roman and Celtic influence. The Irish influence dominated handwriting so completely that it is impossible to tell whether many of the manuscripts of the seventh and early eighth centuries were written in Ireland or England. Manuscript illustrations, especially figure drawing, were derived from the classical models introduced from the Mediterranean. To this period can be referred the Lindisfarne Gospels (c.700), "whose unique importance is due to the beauty and astonishing intricacy of its decoration." At about the same time the oldest surviving complete manuscript of the Vulgate Bible of St. Jerome, the *Codex Amiatinus* (c.689–716), was written at Wearmouth—a beautiful presentation copy sent to the pope as a gift.

C H A P T E R V

The Byzantine Empire, Islam, and the West

From the accession of Constantine at the beginning of the fourth century until the death of Leo the Isaurian in the middle of the eighth, the East and the West steadily drifted apart, until the unity of both the antique world and Christianity was broken. This was in part the result of economic, social, and linguistic differences which had made the Latin West and the Greek East difficult to unite and hold together even at the height of the Roman Empire. The separation of East and West was in greater part a result of developments during the period now under consideration. These developments were religious, political, and military: growing antagonism between Latin (Catholic) and Greek (Orthodox) Christianity under their respective leaders, the pope at Rome and the patriarch of Constantinople; the failure of Byzantine efforts to reconquer the lost western provinces of the Empire, now securely under independent Germanic rulers; and, above all, the dramatic rise of a new world power, Islam.

The expansion of Islam in the seventh and early eighth centuries marked the end of the transition from the unified world of antiquity to an enlarged medieval world in which three separate, yet interrelated, civilizations had become disentangled. In the West, Latin Christendom had lost the North African and Spanish provinces of the Roman Empire, had broken away from the East, and was expanding northward and to the northeast. In the East, the Byzantine Empire had contracted before the assaults of the Arabs and, later, was to begin the expansion of its culture and religion northward and to the northeast, so that Russia and the Slavic world eventually became the heirs of Rome in the East. Finally, Islam had extended throughout the length of the old Roman Empire from Spain, along the northern shores of Africa (including the Mediterranean islands), through Syria and beyond into Persia and India. For the Mediterranean world, the rise of Islam was the final triumph of growing oriental antagonism toward Greco-Roman domination: "Mohammed was the answer of the East to the challenge of Alexander."

13   THE BYZANTINE EMPIRE FROM CONSTANTINE TO LEO THE ISAURIAN

Byzantium was an old Greek trading city on the European side of the Bosporus. It was here that Constantine moved his capital, which soon after his death was given the name Constantinople. He and his successors saw in this move no legal change; they continued to be and to style themselves Roman emperors, with all the titles to which that dignity gave rise. Rome—the Rome of the kings, of the patricians and the plebs, of the Senate and the People, of Cicero, Caesar, and Augustus, and of the Antonines—lived on with unbroken continuity in the New Rome, the capital of what is called, for convenience, the Eastern Roman Empire or the Byzantine Empire. Only after the vicissitudes of two millennia did Rome cease to be a political entity in the civilized world, when Constantinople fell before the Ottoman Turks in 1453.

Despite this unbroken continuity of the New with the Old Rome, Byzantine civilization rapidly developed characteristics which distinguished it from the West. Culturally, Byzantium never lost contact with the heritage of the Hellenic past. Ninety per cent of our manuscripts containing the literary, philosophical, and scientific achievements of the Golden Age and later were preserved at Constantinople or in her provincial cities. Most of this material was unknown in the West during the early Middle Ages. Another element in Byzantine civilization which left the West relatively unaffected was the Hellenistic heritage of the Greater Greece of Alexander the Great and his successors, including the oriental influences associated in western minds with the term, "Byzantine." The specifically Roman heritage of laws and government the Byzantine Empire shared with the West, but again with a crucial difference. In the East the laws and institutions of Rome were preserved and adapted to changing conditions. In the West they were submerged under the culture of barbarians, whose efforts to preserve the institutions of Rome were so largely futile that one of the great achievements of the Western renaissance in the twelfth century was the rediscovery of Roman law. Finally, the specifically Christian heritage of antiquity, shared by East and West, led to a growing religious divergence. The main differences that distinguish eastern Christianity in this period were three: a different monastic system, as already discussed; an absorption in the subtleties of speculative theology which led to many eastern sects or separatist churches, most of them heretical by western standards; and the peculiar relationship between the emperor and the patriarch of Constantinople, who was ultimately recognized as supreme in the eastern Orthodox Church. Because the emperor normally dominated the patriarch, both as head of the ecclesiastical organization and with respect to the pronouncements on theology which continuing dissension required, this relationship has been called "caesaro-papism."

The most striking difference—the one which most impressed contemporaries and which accounts for the long life of the Byzantine Empire despite its many crises and catastrophes—was the wealth of the East. Economically the eastern Mediterranean had always surpassed the Western world. Agriculture flourished, but more important, agriculture was balanced with a lively trade and a productive industry. Constantinople was situated on the crossroads of Europe and Asia; the provincial cities retained a healthy urban life based upon the products of their skilled labor and the profits of their merchants. The imperial government at Constantinople, the hub of this flourishing economic activity, fostered this wealth of empire as its first goal of policy. Trade routes by land and sea were kept open and, so far as possible, under Byzantine control or influence. Byzantine fleets dominated the Mediterranean and Black Seas; Byzantine armies and Byzantine gold protected overland routes to the farther east through military campaigns, garrisoned fortresses, and diplomatic alliances. The government strictly controlled the internal economy by a system of price and wage controls and by state monopolies on key industries like silk production and the mines. The "state socialism" of the twentieth century was anticipated and successfully maintained by the bureaucracy of the Byzantine Empire.

The cities and the hinterland of Egypt, Syria, and Asia Minor were the real bases of the Empire. Because of them the Empire was able to take advantage of difficulties confronting Persia in the fifth century to effect a substantial internal recovery from the decline which had set in after Theodosius I. Zeno (474–491) deflected the threat from the German barbarians by sending them westward to fight other Germans. Instead of employing unreliable Goths as mercenaries he introduced Isaurian barbarians from Asia Minor as the core of his army. Under Anastasius (491–518), an able administrator in the Roman tradition, the Isaurian influence at Constantinople was removed. Reforms in coinage, taxation, and the sale of offices produced stability in the government. A new threat from the north, the arrival of the Bulgarians on the Danube frontier, was held off. However, both Zeno and Anastasius were handicapped by their religious leaning toward the heretical doctrine of Monophysitism, the view that Christ had only one divine nature, not the divine and human natures attributed to Him by orthodox doctrine. Heresy in the East was usually an expression of political separatism. The favor Zeno and Anastasius showed the Monophysite doctrine was in part an effort to maintain the allegiance of Egypt and Syria where Monophysitism was especially strong. Such a policy alienated the strongly orthodox provinces of Asia Minor and the Balkans.

Anastasius was succeeded by the orthodox Justin I (518–527), whose policies as ruler were influenced by his nephew and equally orthodox successor, Justinian the Great (527–565). Justinian employed all his energies and squandered the resources of the Empire in trying to realize the two great goals, as he conceived them, of a Roman and Christian emperor. As heir of the Roman Caesars he sought to restore the territorial boundaries of the Empire as they had been at their greatest extent. As a Christian ruler he considered it his duty to establish religious uniformity throughout the Empire. The two goals were connected, for Justinian's championing of orthodoxy against the German Arians gave to his partially successful reconquest of the western provinces the character of a crusade to liberate the oppressed orthodox population from their Arian masters. The ultimate failure of his reconquest was partly responsible for Justinian's failure to achieve religious uniformity. Unable to regain full control of the resources and manpower of the West, he was forced to rely upon the wealthier and more populous eastern provinces which were also the stronghold of Monophysite doctrines. Thus he was forced by events to conciliate religious opposition although his goal had been to destroy it. Ultimately, Justinian's policies were ruinous to the Empire, because his wars were so expensive and the results of his victories in Africa, Italy, and Spain were so meager. Furthermore, the western orientation of his military operations stripped the defenses of the eastern and northern frontiers. The Empire suffered reverses from Persian aggression and periodic devastation from barbarian raids across the Danube by both Slavs and Bulgarians, who now make their first appearance in the Mediterranean world.

Justinian owed much—at one critical moment in his reign he even owed his throne—to his wife, Theodora, one of the most fascinating women of history. The daughter of a bear-keeper in the amphitheater at Constantinople, Theodora was orphaned at an early age and embarked upon the career of a performer in what would correspond with modern burlesque. She distinguished herself, according to a contemporary and unfriendly writer, by "acts of extreme indecency both on and off the stage." Determined to escape from the poverty and squalor of her origins, she exploited all the opportunities open to a woman of her talents. Her native wit, beauty, and charm enabled her to grant her favors successively to more

Empress Theodora and Attendants. Detail of mosaic in San Vitale, Ravenna (sixth century). PHOTO: ALINARI.

and more important men. After several years' experience and travel throughout the eastern provinces in the company of high officials she returned to Constantinople to become the favorite, and later the wife, of Justinian. Utterly lacking in formal education, Theodora possessed in ample measure the knowledge and practical wisdom that can be gained from intimate association with people of all social levels and of many different areas. Her knowledge of conditions in the provinces probably accounts for her Monophysite sympathies and for her desire to avoid alienating the strongest part of the Empire (especially Syria and Egypt).

Her strength of character made Theodora a redoubtable empress, as Justinian and his court learned, with gratitude, during the Nika uprising of 532. In that year a riot involving two factions of the mob which followed the chariot races at the circus, but which also took a keen interest in politics, grew into a revolt of the greater part of the city against the government. When Justinian was ready to flee the capital and admit defeat, it was Theodora who finally saved the day by organizing a successful resistance. While the court was besieged in the imperial palace and government officials were discussing a means of escape, she rallied her defeatist husband by scorning flight and reminding him that "exile is intolerable for one who has reigned; for myself, the purple is a fair winding sheet."

The most enduring influence of the reign of Justinian was the product of the emperor's legislative work known as the *Corpus Juris Civilis*. The problem confronting Justinian and his legal advisers was twofold: the enormous mass of unrepealed Roman law made it almost impossible for judges and officials to master the whole of the law which they administered; and there were contradictions and uncertainties in the enacted law and in the commentaries of the jurists whose writings were authoritative guides for the law courts. Earlier collections, such as the Theodosian Code, had only partially solved the problem because they were incomplete, omitting the juridical literature. Also, they were now growing obsolete because of the imperial enactments issued since their publication. With his love of order and uniformity, Justinian directed his advisers to reorganize and revise the whole body of Roman law in one official compilation, eliminating contradictions and obsolete laws and reducing the bulk to manageable proportions. In 529 the Code was issued, a compilation of imperial statutes and decisions of the emperor which were given the force of a statute. In 534 a second edition, which supplanted the first, was issued. Laws not contained in the Code were considered repealed. In 533 the Digest was published, an authoritative condensation of the writings of the jurists: commentaries, responses and opinions on cases, and treatises and manuals on selected subjects. In this monumental task over 3,000,000 lines of juristic literature were condensed into 150,000 lines and reorganized into fifty books and 432 separate titles or subjects. The Digest was the most important part of the whole *Corpus*. It preserved the accumulated authoritative jurisprudence of the classical period (i.e., before 300) which was, in its edited form, given the force of imperial law. Most of the individual works of the jurists have been lost, and it was only in the Digest of the autocrat Justinian that the jurisprudence of the period of the Republic and of the Principate was to survive. The legal systems of all the modern national states of Western Europe are either based upon, or were in their evolution influenced by, the Digest of Justinian. The third product of the legislative work of the reign was an official textbook for beginners, the Institutes (533), on which legal education was henceforth to be based and which also had the force of law. Under Justinian's scheme of legal education the student covered the Institutes in the first year and proceeded to master the Digest and the Code in four more years. Finally, the new laws enacted by Justinian, called the Novels, were privately collected and published at the end of the reign.

The *Corpus Juris Civilis* was briefly in force in Italy during the Byzantine occupation, and an abbreviated Latin version of the Novels circulated in the West during the early Middle Ages. Otherwise, Justinian's *Corpus* did not influence Western legal development until late in the eleventh century when the study of Roman law was revived. The revival was facilitated by the fact that the Code, the Digest, and the Institutes were written in Latin, the language of Western learning. The Novels (new laws to meet changed conditions in the East), which were in Greek, had little influence in the West. Thus the Roman law which influenced Western legal development was the law of the late classical period, a law whose fundamental juridical concepts were not congenial with the later absolutist tendencies of the Byzantine state. The decay of Latin in the East made necessary not only the issuance of new laws in Greek but also the publication of Greek commentaries on the Latin text of the *Corpus*. These commentaries tended to keep Byzantine Roman law responsive to the changing conditions of the Empire, and so to diverge eventually from the Latin Roman law of the later Western revival.

Justinian's reign was superficially brilliant. He was at least officially a great conqueror, and in the best Roman tradition styled himself "Alamannicus, Gothicus, Francicus, Germanicus, Anticus, Alanicus, Vandalicus, Africanus" to commemorate the victories in the West for which he took credit. He was lavish in his expenditure of imperial revenue for the foundation of new churches and monasteries and in adorning Constantinople with new buildings. His reign was the first Golden Age of Byzantine art. In architecture his crowning achievement was the "Great Church" of St. Sophia, whose splendor and massiveness so impressed contemporaries and later pilgrims that there grew up a legend which told of its construction in terms of miracles.

The reigns of Justinian's immediate successors revealed the defects and mistakes of the great emperor's policies. The period from 565 to 610 was so deplorable that contemporaries wondered whether the end of the world was at hand. Actually, it was a period of transition from which the Empire, suffering from the burdens imposed upon its resources by Justinian, finally emerged as a Greek Empire oriented eastward and no longer seriously concerned with the Western world. The war with Persia was renewed, the barbarian Slavs and a new Asiatic people, the Avars, not only ravaged but began to settle in the Balkans and in Greece. Byzantine control of the western provinces waned before the Lombard occupation of Italy and Berber raids in North Africa. In the face of these difficulties the emperors accelerated administrative reforms already begun by Justinian: the exercise of civil authority by military commanders of local areas and the consolidation of several smaller provinces into larger administrative regions such as the Exarchate of Ravenna in Italy and the Exarchate of Carthage in Africa. The exarchates were distinguished by the almost unlimited delegation of imperial authority to the exarch and by the dominance of the military over the civil authority. During the seventh century, the whole Empire was reorganized into similar districts called themes, by which the Byzantine Empire was gradually put on a permanent war footing to meet the growing military crisis on all frontiers.

The danger from Persia reached its height in the reign of Heraclius

(610–641), when Persian armies occupied Syria and Palestine, overran Egypt, and encamped on the Bosporus opposite Constantinople. All other frontiers were stripped to meet the crisis: consequently, Byzantine Spain was now reconquered by the Visigoths (c.624), while Avars and Slavs crossed the Danube almost at will and even breached the walls of Constantinople during their raids in the southern Balkan peninsula. From this nadir in the fortunes of the Empire, Heraclius led what was perhaps the most brilliant recovery of a great power before modern times. Within six years Byzantine arms were triumphant on all fronts against Persia. Constantinople successfully withstood a combined Slav-Avar-Persian siege (626), and Persian military strength was permanently broken, thus making possible the incredibly swift Arab conquest of Persia a generation later. The Empire suffered almost as much. The provinces where Monophysite opposition to the orthodox emperors had been strongest (Egypt, Palestine, and Syria) were devastated and their inhabitants were restive. Before the Empire could recover from the strain of Heraclius' great effort against the Persians, the provinces which he had won back were lost permanently to the new power whose sudden rise took all the East by surprise: the Arab empire. In the centuries-long struggle between the Roman Empire and Persia the ultimate victor was Islam.

After Heraclius, the rulers of the dynasty which he had founded struggled unsuccessfully to arrest the decline that had already begun in the last years of his reign. The Heraclian dynasty lasted until 711. The period was marked by the steady expansion of the Arabs, the increasing settlement of Slavs within the Empire in the southern Balkans and in

*The Byzantine Empire on the Eve of
the Rise of the Arab Empire, c.630*

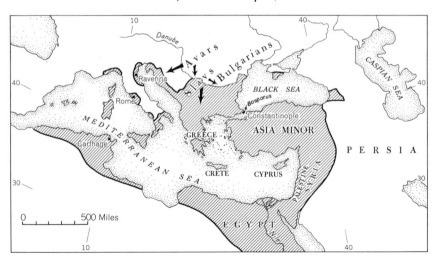

Greece, and the establishment of a Bulgarian kingdom just north of the Danube. Byzantine control of the seas was successfully challenged by the Arabs, and Constantinople was repeatedly brought under direct attack (c.669–677). The mighty fortress stood firm—mainly because of superior Byzantine defensive tactics and the use of "Greek fire," a chemical compound whose naval use roughly corresponds with the modern flamethrower or napalm bomb. Although the southern and eastern provinces were lost to Islam, Asia Minor and the other predominantly Greek areas of the Empire remained. Thus the decline in territorial extent was partially offset by an increasing homogeneity in language and culture.

The last fifteen years of the Heraclian dynasty were troubled by palace revolutions of execptional ferocity, culminating in the deposition and murder of the emperor in 711. The next six years of anarchy were brought to an end by the successful bid for power by an Anatolian general, Leo, founder of the Isaurian dynasty (717–802) under which the Empire was restored once more to a flourishing condition. The accession of Leo III the Isaurian (717–741) came at one of the most critical moments in Byzantine history, the great siege of Constantinople by the Arabs in 717–718, on both land and sea. By using "Greek fire" and employing a great underwater chain to bar the entrance into the Golden Horn (the harbor of Constantinople), and by gaining the timely alliance of Bulgarians who attacked the Arabs on land, Leo successfully defended the capital. He was the hero of the Empire, the savior of Constantinople. Leo followed up this victory by a series of campaigns in Asia Minor which halted the first stage of Arab expansion (c.630–730) at the expense of Byzantine territory.

Equally significant, Leo represented in the internal politics of the Empire the triumph of the landed aristocracy of Asia Minor over the imperial court and bureaucracy, whose interests were represented by the last rulers of the Heraclian dynasty. From this time on, a constant factor in Byzantine history is the antagonism between the court and the aristocracy, the former usually supported by the Church and the latter by the army. Although he has been given credit for more than he actually accomplished, Leo the Isaurian was responsible for the most important legal and administrative reforms since the age of Justinian. Several new codes in Greek are usually associated with Leo. The most important was the *Ecloga* (which means "selection"), issued c.726, an official condensation in Greek of the Latin Code, Digest, and Institutes of Justinian together with suitable amendments to bring the law as found therein and in the Greek Novels up to date. The *Ecloga* supplanted Justinian's *Corpus* and the unofficial Greek commentaries on the law of Justinian which in practice had replaced the no longer intelligible Latin texts. In governmental reform, Leo and his successors regularized the system of themes as the administrative units of the militarized Empire. The most important change was the reduction of the size of the themes, a salutary precaution against provincial revolt and an aid to centralized control of the defense of the Empire.

None of these developments impressed contemporaries so much as the new religious policy of Leo the Isaurian, which will be discussed later in connection with the rise of Islam and relations between the Byzantine Empire and the Latin West. Here it is enough to notice that this policy, iconoclasm, broke radically with the efforts of almost all the emperors during the preceding centuries to achieve religious harmony by endless compromise and concession.

From the end of the fifth to the middle of the eighth century, no state in the civilized East or in the barbarian world, either East or West, achieved more against greater odds or preserved its own heritage (including the highest standard of living to be found anywhere) more tenaciously and successfully than did the Byzantine Empire. Nor, it must be added, was any state less appreciated for what it was or what it accomplished. Byzantium was in fact a bastion of defense against the westward expansion of the Avars, Persia, and Islam. But to the barbarian kingdoms of the West the eastern Empire was an aggressor state that had tried under Justinian, but had failed, to reconquer the lost Roman provinces of the western Mediterranean. This failure was the beginning of the end of Byzantine political influence in the West, a beginning marked by the Lombard invasion of Italy. But the end took almost five more centuries to be finally consummated. Throughout this long period of declining influence the Byzantine Empire continued to be a factor, as we shall see, in the fortunes of the papacy, the Carolingian monarchy, and the medieval Empire of the Otto's and their successors.

The more permanent contribution to the development of the West came after the Byzantine Empire no longer played a significant political role. Only after Western expansion had overrun provinces in the Holy Land that had once been Byzantine—and had later even made Constantinople itself the capital of a short-lived Latin state—did the full economic and cultural influence of Byzantium on the West begin. Italian cities thrived on commercial contact with the Levant; but such contact took place only after the Western economy had recovered from almost complete collapse and began to pull abreast of the economic level of the eastern Mediterranean world. In the cultural sphere a parallel can be seen. The heritage of classical Greek philosophy, science, and literature was almost wholly lost in the West and played no significant part in stimulating the cultural revival of Latin Christendom. In the East there was no significant cultural advance beyond the achievement of classical antiquity. Byzantine culture for centuries was captive to the heritage which Byzantine conservatism faithfully preserved—but preserved above all to venerate and thus be condemned to do little more than imitate. When the Western cultural revival finally took place, Latin Christendom slowly absorbed the Greek heritage (beginning in the high Middle Ages and continuing into the seventeenth century). For the West it was a rediscovery in a culturally dynamic situation; the Greek heritage became a stimulus to further cultural development because it was not something long preserved and well known but essentially a new and exciting ingredient in the Western cultural revival.

14   MOHAMMED AND THE RISE OF THE ARAB EMPIRE

Mohammed was born c.570 in the city of Mecca. Of humble origin, he was orphaned at an early age, and his prospects in life seemed dim indeed. He secured the modest job of driving camels in the caravans of a wealthy widow, but it is doubtful that he would have prospered in such a career: he was not strong physically and was of a brooding, sensitive nature. But he was not without some talents, for after a short time he was able to dispense with working for a living by marrying the wealthy widow who had employed him. He could now devote himself wholly to his only real interest, religion. Arabia provided a variety of religious beliefs, no one of which was strong enough to predominate. In the deserts through which he had driven his camels, Mohammed had come in contact with the bewildering number and variety of local deities worshiped by the nomadic Bedouins. Their religious ideas hardly rose above the level of crude fetish worship: stones, springs, wells, stars, and other sacred objects. The Bedouins were wild tribesmen who eked out a subsistence living from their herds and spent much of their time pursuing tribal feuds which arose on the slightest provocation. The essential elements in the relations between their tribes have been characterized as animosity and arrogance. While the majority of Arabs lived in the desert, there were several cities along the caravan routes where Mohammed became acquainted with the higher religions, especially Judaism (which was strong in the city later called Medina) and a corrupted form of Christianity. The religious capital of Arabia was Mecca, where there was a special sanctuary, the Kaaba, enclosing a huge black stone (a meteorite) that according to tradition had been sent down from heaven in the time of Abraham. The merchants of Mecca encouraged pilgrimage to their shrine, and timed the greatest religious festival to coincide with their annual fair. It is probable that the materialistic motives of the Meccans offended Mohammed's religious instincts, as he was also offended by the polytheistic hodgepodge of the desert tribesmen.

Mohammed spent much time in religious contemplation, both on his desert trips and also in walks about the outskirts of Mecca. During these trips and walks he was visited by the angel Gabriel or received revelations from God. A personal inclination toward the ascetic life of fasting, solitary meditation, and deprivation of material pleasures increased the number of his visions and encouraged him to believe that God had appointed him to bring the true faith to his people. At first he spoke of these things only within his family, but gradually he widened the circle of his listeners to include a small following among the lower classes of Mecca. When his influence grew to embrace some of the more important citizens, the leading merchants and tribal leaders in Mecca recognized the danger to the established religious festivals of the holy city. They brought such pressure on him to desist from his religious teachings that Mohammed finally decided to leave Mecca and accept the invitation of the leading men of Medina to make that city his headquarters. This removal, or migration, of Mohammed and his companions to Medina was a crucial stage in the growth of the new religion. It was the Hegira (sometimes inaccurately called the "flight"), whose date, Friday, July 16, 622, in the Christian era, marks the beginning of the first year of the Moslem era. The Hegira made possible the full development of Mohammed's religious ideas, for the predominantly Jewish community of Medina welcomed him as their religious, and later political, leader.

The essence of Mohammed's religious teaching is the realization by man of his utter dependence upon God, and therefore man's need to submit totally to the will of God. The religion is thus called Islam (meaning, literally, submission to God). The follower of Islam is called a Moslem, regardless of his national or racial origins—whether Arab, Saracen, Moor, Berber, Pakistani, or Turk. The central tenet in Mohammed's teaching was an uncompromising insistence upon monotheism, expressed in the statement, "There is only one God and Mohammed is His Prophet." Other prophets there had been. Islam venerates as especially great prophets Abraham, Moses, and Jesus Christ, but the greatest and last Prophet, in whom the final revelation of God's will is made known, was Mohammed. Likewise, much of God's will is revealed in such scriptures as the Old and New Testaments but the final and complete revelation is contained in the Koran, the verbatim record of God's words to His Prophet. In addition to the Koran, the majority of Moslems accept a collection of the sayings or injunctions of Mohammed as preserving his teaching on points not covered in the divinely inspired Koran.

Mohammed's teaching may be divided for convenience into two parts, the doctrinal and the social or ethical. The tenets of faith and the obligations imposed upon the faithful were extremely simple and only five in number; much of the success of Islam as a religion has been due to its straightforward and easily intelligible doctrine. First, the Moslem must profess belief in only one God, Allah, and in Mohammed as His Prophet. Second, he must pray regularly, according to a simple ritual (later such prayer was prescribed at set intervals, five times a day, kneeling and facing toward Mecca). Third, the faithful must give charity to the poor of the

Moslem community. Fourth, the holy month of Ramadan must be observed by fasting and a prohibition of all pleasures between sunrise and sundown. Fifth, the Moslem must, if at all possible, make at least one pilgrimage to the Kaaba at Mecca, which was cleansed of its desecration by the return of Mohammed in 630.

The ethical teaching of Mohammed, while it embodies the highest moral principles, is even more impressive in its simplicity and utter lack of originality. Essentially, Mohammed preached peace, love of one's fellow men, and self-control. The Prophet's goal was to elevate his people's barbaric notions of right and wrong, to substitute forgiveness for vengeance, and to abolish certain primitive customs which degraded the dignity and worth of human life. Thus, infanticide (by burying alive) was prohibited, the number of wives legally allowed to a man was reduced to four (Mohammed allowed an exception to the rule in his own case), and dietary provisions prohibited the eating of pork and the drinking of fermented liquors. The central tendency of Mohammed's religious and ethical teaching was against the polytheism and materialism of the Arab world. By achieving a higher spiritual life and obeying Mohammed's injunctions, the Moslem was promised an eternal paradise which would bring all the materialistic pleasures that the believer was asked to forego in this life. Although this concept of heaven was quite different from the Christian, the idea of hell was similar, and the celestial hierarchy of angels and demons (genii) was common to both religions. Part of the success of Islam was the similarity between many of its tenets or teachings and those of Christianity and Judaism.

Mohammed had no sooner settled in Medina than he established a theocratic city-state. There was no distinction between civil and religious law, since both were to be found in the revelations preserved in the Koran. Historians disagree on whether Mohammed himself intended either to spread his religion beyond the Arabs or to conquer and rule all of Arabia or the whole world. There is no question that Mohammed meant to return to Mecca and to force the Meccans to allow his faithful to make their pilgrimages to the Kaaba. This involved Mohammed in warfare not only with Mecca but also with the Bedouin tribes allied with the holy city. Wherever Mohammed conquered in these early years, conversion to the new faith followed. By the time of his death in 632, about one third of Arabia was Moslem. Also, Mohammed had either instigated or at least approved raids by his followers upon the border provinces of the Byzantine Empire and Persia. But it is impossible to determine whether these raids constituted a deliberate policy of propagating the faith by force (the jihad, or holy war) or were merely plundering expeditions in the time-honored Arab fashion. The earliest Arab raids under Moslem leaders were undertaken by mixed groups of Bedouin tribes, whose members were Moslem, pagan, and Christian. One of the first forays against Syria succeeded only when some non-

Moslem Arabs, serving as allies in the Byzantine forces, deserted to the Moslem Arab side. The nationalist element thus seems as important as the religious in these earliest conflicts. Also, there were wholly materialistic motives that help account for Arab expansion. A growing population in the Arabian peninsula and a very natural desire by the nomadic tribes to escape from their "hot prison of the desert" into the civilized world played at least as strong a role, in the beginning, as any religious motivation.

The most important period of Arab expansion came in the thirty years following the death of Mohammed, the age of the Orthodox caliphs (632–661). No provision had been made for carrying on the work of Mohammed or for continuing the position of leadership which he had built for himself as founder of Islam. The crisis caused by his unexpected death was met by the election of one of the Prophet's intimate circle of earliest converts as his "caliph" (representative or vicar). This was Abu Bakr, whose caliphate (632–634) was spent largely in retaining the precarious allegiance of Bedouin tribes and preserving the movement intact. The fighting of this period was directed almost entirely against dissident Moslems or non-Moslem Arabs. At the end of Abu Bakr's brief reign all Arabia had been at least nominally subjugated to Islam. From these campaigns in the desert there emerged one of the great generals of the early Middle Ages, Khalid, "the Sword of God."

The next caliph, Omar (634–644), and Khalid agreed that the best solution of the problem of internal unity was foreign war as an outlet for Arab energies. Within the ten years of Omar's caliphate, all of Palestine, Syria, and the Persian Empire had been conquered, except for mopping-up

Islam and the West, c.750

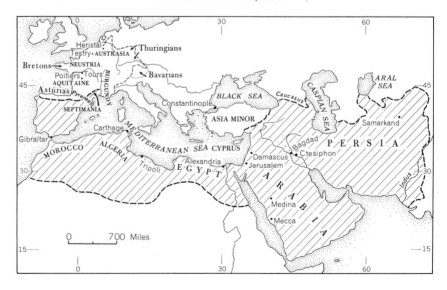

operations in the interior. Damascus fell in 635. Jerusalem was taken in 638 at the end of a long siege and after the patriarch of the city secured a promise from the Arabs to respect Christian churches and worship. Jerusalem became (with Mecca and Medina) the third holy city of the Moslems. In 637 the Persian capital, Ctesiphon, had fallen. The Arabs sent border raids into India by 643. On the western front, Egypt was quickly reduced (640–642), although the Byzantine naval base at Alexandria was not permanently in Arab possession until 646. Arab columns pushed farther westward through the desert into the Byzantine North African provinces as far as Tripoli. Meanwhile, from the coastal cities of Syria and from Alexandria, the Arabs began to challenge Byzantine naval supremacy. By the middle of the seventh century they had defeated an imperial fleet off the coast of Asia Minor and occupied the island of Cyprus.

After the middle of the century Arab expansion slowed down almost to a complete halt. Internal dissension among the Arabs had broken out over the administration and exploitation of the conquered provinces and over the succession to the caliphate. A brief civil war, 656–661, ended with the murder of the last Orthodox caliph, Ali, nephew and son-in-law of the Prophet. His successor, Muawiyah (661–680), abolished the elective principle of succession to the caliphate and founded the Omayyad dynasty, moving the capital of Islam to Damascus. The Omayyad caliphate (661–750) represented the triumph of the imperialistic Arab aristocracy, who were more interested in conquest than in religion, over the traditions of Mohammed's theocracy of Medina as represented by the Orthodox caliphate. It was also a triumph over the disorderly desert Arabs who had participated in the expansion primarily for booty and were impatient of restraint or organization from a central government. Another reason for the slowing down of Arab expansion after c.650 was that on all fronts the Arabs began to meet real resistance. The phenomenal rapidity of the first conquests was owing less to Arab military ability than to the exhaustion of Byzantine and Persian military resources, the collapse of the Persian monarchy before internal dissension, and the general disaffection of the conquered peoples for their Byzantine and Persian rulers. In Syria and in Egypt the Monophysite Christians welcomed the Arabs, whose simple and rigid monotheism was more congenial than the persecutions of the Orthodox (and trinitarian) Christians. Further, the Byzantine provincials were everywhere oppressed by efficient taxation and in Palestine and Syria they felt a closer cultural and ethnic affinity to the Semitic Arabs than they did to their Greek rulers. The predominantly Greek and Orthodox provinces of Asia Minor, on the other hand, put up a stiff resistance, and in western North Africa the Berbers were a non-Semitic people who stoutly contested control of the Byzantine provinces with the Arabs.

Under the Omayyad caliphate expansion was resumed but at a slower pace. Notable successes were achieved at sea, where Arab fleets secured naval supremacy in the eastern Mediterranean by the end of the seventh century. In the east, Moslem armies crossed the Indus river, pushed north as far as Samarkand, and reached the Caucasus mountains from the Black to the Caspian Sea. Slight progress was made on the Asia Minor front, and repeated attacks by sea on Constantinople (c.669–677) failed by a narrow margin. The most important effects of these developments on the Byzantine Empire were to cut off most of the trade routes to the Far East and to imperil communications by sea between Constantinople and the West. Byzantine commerce suffered and Byzantine control of the western provinces of Italy and North Africa was in jeopardy.

After a generation of fighting in western North Africa, Carthage finally fell in 698, when victory at sea over an imperial fleet bringing reinforcements finally broke the Byzantine resistance. Meanwhile the campaign against the Berbers slowly turned in favor of the Arabs, who gained not only the territories of Algeria and Morocco but also the military assistance of the conquered Berbers, whose conversion to the new faith brought a religious fanaticism previously unknown in the Moslem expansion. It was a Berber raid, led by Tarik, which crossed the straits between Africa and Spain and landed upon the great rock bearing the leader's name (*gib-al-Tarik* or Gibraltar), that began the Moslem conquest of the Visigothic kingdom in Spain in 711. The internal divisions of the Visigoths and a disaffected subject population made easy the rapid conquest of all the peninsula except the mountainous northwestern corner. Here the Christian principality of the Asturias maintained a precarious independence. In 720 the Moslems crossed the Pyrenees, occupied Septimania, and pushed tentatively into Merovingian Aquitaine where resistance put an end to further advance. These successes were the measure of Visigothic and Merovingian weakness rather than Moslem strength. Actually there was dissension among the Moslems in Spain not only among Arab factions but also between the Arabs and Berbers. This internal disunity continued, in varying degrees, throughout the Moorish occupation of medieval Spain.

The Omayyad caliphate provided the Arab empire with its basic governmental structure. The speed of the earlier expansion and the backwardness of the Arabs had made advisable at first the continuation of Byzantine or Persian administration and collection of taxes, under Arab control. By c.700 Arabs themselves were beginning to replace the non-Moslem personnel in the provincial governments. Arabic became the official language of law and government, and new Arabic coinage (in gold, silver, and copper) was in circulation. At first all Moslems had been exempt from the land taxes paid by the conquered provincials, but when conversion to Islam steadily diminished these revenues, exemption of the faithful from land taxes was abolished and a new poll tax was instituted from which Moslems were exempt. In addition to these political developments, the Moslems began to absorb elements of Byzantine and Persian culture. This laid the foundations for great achievements by later Moslem scholars, but in the Omayyad period little was accomplished except in architecture, of which several fine examples survive in Damascus and Jerusalem.

The Omayyad caliphate fell in 750 when a revolution established the new dynasty of the Abbasids. The success of this insurrection was owing to several weaknesses from which the Omayyad caliphs suffered after the last great ruler of the line, Walid I (705–715). The Omayyads represented the secular or political traditions of the western Arabs, whose strength lay in Syria, as against the religious interests of the eastern Arabs whose strength lay in Persia. Also, the Omayyads represented Arab racial supremacy over non-Arabs, whether Moslem or non-Moslem; and this deprived them of the support of the strongest new force in Islam, the enthusiasm and fanaticism of new converts. The future of Islam was in its universalism, embracing men of all races equally in the service of the faith. The perfunctory religious leadership of the Omayyad caliphs was as unsympathetic with the religious aspirations of Moslem Arab minority groups as it was hostile to the political aspirations of the growing numbers of non-Arab Moslems. Thus the Omayyads lacked support when these elements of opposition united in revolt.

15 THE CRISIS OF THE MID-EIGHTH CENTURY

While these developments were taking place in the Arab empire and the Byzantine Empire, momentous events were preparing in the West. The crisis to which they led profoundly altered the course of European history, shifting the political center of gravity northward and reorienting western Europe away from the Mediterranean and from the historic connection with the East. Contact with Byzantium and Islam was never wholly broken, and yet such contact and the trade and cultural intercourse it gave were not to be determining factors in the period when the feudal foundations of Europe were being built in the West. Western Europe was thrown back upon its own resources; when influences from the East once more became important, it was to be on the initiative of the West.

To understand this crisis of the mid-eighth century, it is necessary to turn to developments in Gaul, where the last Merovingian kings were rapidly losing their power and prestige. The dynasty founded by Clovis was degenerating in the members of its last generations. Chroniclers of the period often exaggerated the profligacy of rulers who did not support the Church, and we may discount the moral strictures they leveled against the descendants of Dagobert (629–639). But whether the license of their barbaric courts was responsible or not, it remains true that few of the later Merovingian kings had the physical strength to survive into manhood. Dagobert himself lived to a respectable old age of thirty-eight, but his two sons died at eighteen and twenty. The next king lived out a full span of thirty-eight years, but his sons reached only thirteen and eighteen. Under such circumstances it is remarkable that the royal race of the Merovingians was able to continue supplying kings at all. Obviously these kings were ineffective rulers. French historians have called them *rois fainéants,* "do-nothing kings." Ascending their thrones as children or striplings, they were little more than figureheads in whose names their officials ruled.

In the seventh century the real power behind the throne was exercised by an official whose title was mayor of the palace (as it is usual to translate *major domus*). The mayor was originally a household official of the early Germanic kings. Through control of the household in an age of personal and primitive government, when there was hardly a distinction between private property and public office, the mayor of the Merovingian palace gained control of the royal treasury, taxes, the royal domains, and the grants of land and immunities by which the government tried in vain to appease overmighty nobles and prelates. Thus, the mayor emerged as the most important dispenser of patronage and power in a period when civil wars and revolts were the normal means by which nobles and royal officials struggled to gain or retain political control.

The two most important kingdoms were Neustria (in northern and western Gaul) and Austrasia (in northeastern Gaul and the Rhineland). The mayors of these kingdoms aspired to rule the whole of the Frankish territories as had the earlier Merovingian kings. The climax of this struggle between the mayors was the battle of Testry, in 687, in which the mayor of Austrasia, Pepin of Heristal, great-grandfather of Charlemagne, defeated the Neustrian mayor and united the two kingdoms under his control. Pepin then turned his energies to the task of restoring the central authority over the aristocracy and over outlying lands which were once ruled by the kings but were now only nominally subject to Frankish power. Aquitaine in the southwest, Burgundy in the southeast, the Thuringians and Bavarians to the east, and the Bretons in the northwest were all ruled by local nobles who paid little attention to the central authority. After slow but note-worthy progress in combating the decentralizing tendencies in the Frankish kingdom, Pepin died in 714 and was succeeded as mayor by his illegitimate son, Charles Martel (714–741). Charles completed the re-establishment of the central authority in a series of campaigns against the rebellious aristoc-racy, a struggle in which he had the support of most of the Church in Gaul. In his alliance with the Church, which he strengthened by supporting the missionary efforts of Boniface in Germany, Charles had two goals in view: first, the extension of his power eastward, where military conquest would be consolidated by conversion to the conquerors' faith; and, second, the sup-port of the Church in meeting a new menace which had appeared in the south.

The Moslem state in Spain had pushed north of the Pyrenees into

Septimania, on the Mediterranean coast, and Gascony, on the Atlantic. In 733 the Moslems showed signs of further expansion northward when an armed reconnaissance in force penetrated into the region between Poitiers and Tours. Charles met and defeated them in a battle whose significance lies not so much in any check to Moslem expansion (actually it simply inaugurated a series of campaigns whose final outcome was not certain until the end of the century), but rather in the effect it may have had upon Frankish military policy. At the battle of Poitiers the Franks fought on foot, while the Moslems probably were mounted. After the day-long fighting, the invaders were able to withdraw unnoticed during the night and Charles failed to renew contact after the Moslems' flight was discovered the next morning. Most historians have concluded that the outcome of this battle taught Charles the value of having his own cavalry arm—a lesson whose immediate military results were to have profound consequences, ultimately, for the social structure of Western Europe. It is possible that Charles had begun to develop an elite force of mounted troops even before the battle of Poitiers, but in any case his policy becomes clear in the years following 733. Cavalry troops are more expensive than infantry. Ordinary free men could not afford horses, harness and equipment, and the more elaborate cavalry weapons, nor could they afford the time necessary to train themselves in their effective tactical use. To pay for this more costly kind of warfare Charles turned to the only source of wealth ready to hand, the lands of the Church. He forced the abbeys and bishoprics to give up the use of most of the income (though they retained title) of enough of their vast landed estates to distribute among his mounted retainers for their support. To some churhmen this was a shocking and illegal seizure of property. But the protests of expropriated ecclesiastics were overbalanced by the approval or toleration of Boniface and his party, who were willing to pay this price for Charles' support of their missionary efforts and their program of reform for the Merovingian church, a program in large part aimed at the laxity and worldliness of the wealthy bishops and abbots. The reforming party correctly saw that the reconquest of the lost southern provinces would mean the restoration of the Church and of its property in the south, and that it was fair enough for the Church to bear part of the expense.

Charles now turned to the task of beating back the Moslems in the south, and it was from this effort that he earned from later chroniclers his nickname of Martel ("Hammer"). In 739, while these campaigns were in progress, Pope Gregory III made an appeal to Charles Martel for aid against the revived threat of the Lombards in Italy, but Charles refused because he was at that time allied with Liutprand, king of the Lombards, in a joint effort to throw the Moslems out of the Rhone valley. Two years later the great mayor of the palace died.

We must now turn to the position of the papacy in Italy, and the background for Gregory III's appeal to Charles Martel. For centuries the popes had considered themselves subjects of the Roman Empire. After the collapse of the Empire in the West, they continued to recognize the emperor at Constantinople as the legitimate sovereign of the Roman Empire of which Rome and much of Italy continued to be part. The historic and natural ties of the papacy were with the East, and these ties continued to be strong despite the hazards and upheavals of the sixth and seventh centuries. In some ways these ties grew closer. After the year 550 official papal documents were dated in the name and regnal year of the emperor; beginning with the reign of Justinian, imperial ratification of a papal election was necessary before the consecration of a new pope; in some instances this imperial control had gone so far as direct appointment of a new pope by the emperor. Such direct intervention in papal affairs ceased after the reign of Heraclius (610–641), but the Byzantine influence in Rome grew even stronger toward the end of the seventh century. For example, between 678 and 752 only two of the thirteen popes were Roman by birth—the others were Syrian, Greek, or Sicilian. This did not reflect subservience to the emperor, but rather the fact that the most influential clerical and lay leaders in Rome were Greek-speaking and these people influenced papal elections. (An illustration of this fact comes from the disgruntled report of an Anglo-Saxon monk, at Rome in 704 to appeal his case to the papal *curia*, who complained that members of the pope's council, "smiling covertly and talking among themselves," spoke Greek so as to conceal from the northerners what they were saying.) Many of these clergy and people were refugees from the Moslem conquest of the eastern provinces of the Empire.

Officially and superficially, relations between the pope and the emperor during the sixth and seventh centuries might be illustrated by a pleasant exchange of correspondence between Gregory the Great and the emperor Phocas. The emperor addressed the pope as "the head of all the Churches," and the pope assured Phocas (a usurper who assassinated his way to the throne) that the Eastern emperors were rulers of free men, while the barbarian kings of the West were lords of slaves. Actually, however, relations between the two were often strained or ruptured, and the popes had slowly been growing more independent of the emperors since the pontificate of Gregory the Great.

The Byzantine Empire was never able to spare the troops necessary for the complete pacification and control of Italy. This was the responsibility of the exarch of Ravenna, but since he was never given adequate resources, the popes had to play an active role in the military defense of Rome against the Lombards and in the political alignments by which a precarious peace was maintained during most of the seventh century. When the Arab conquests of the eastern provinces began, after 634, Italy was stripped of her Byzantine garrisons. The disunited Lombards presented no immediate danger, but in the early eighth century Liutprand (712–744) strengthened the Lombard monarchy and initiated a policy of conquest both of the Byzantine areas in Italy and of the semi-independent and un-cooperative Lombard duchies. Rome was, of course, the great prize. In these circumstances the pope appealed to the emperor for aid—but in vain.

Another reason for the estrangement of the papacy from the imperial government grew out of the categorical and unyielding resistance of Italy, led by the pope, to the religious policy of Leo III the Isaurian. In 725 Leo issued a decree against images and precipitated the Iconoclastic Schism. Iconoclasm (image- or icon-breaking) was a policy with mixed religious and political motives. Leo came from the eastern part of the Empire, in Asia Minor near the Moslem frontier. In this region Christians shared, as they were perhaps influenced by, the strong Moslem and Jewish loathing for idols and idol worship. During this period the growth of superstition in the Christian East had reached alarming proportions. Theologians might teach that it was the saint who was invoked and venerated, not the image whose purpose was merely to teach through pictures or to stimulate piety. But for the ignorant masses such a distinction was too fine. Images themselves were venerated, or even worshiped as idols; and the supernatural power of Christ, the Virgin, or the saints was attributed to the image itself. Wonder-working icons were so fashionable that religion, in the opinion of the iconoclasts, was degenerating into idolatry and thaumaturgy. Leo saw the only solution in abolishing images altogether.

In the West image worship was not a serious problem. The teaching of the Church had generally succeeded in following the injunction of Gregory the Great: "To adore a picture is wrong; to learn through the picture what is to be adored is praiseworthy." Iconoclasm was stoutly opposed, both as theologically unacceptable and also as an intolerable invasion of the religious sphere by a secular ruler. When Leo informed Gregory II (715–731), "I am emperor and priest," compromise was out of the question. At a synod in Rome in 731 the new pope, Gregory III (731–741), denounced iconoclasm and excommunicated the subservient patriarch of Constantinople who had approved Leo's decree against images. The papal position had now become almost untenable. Either the pope must continue to recognize the sovereignty of an emperor with whom religious agreement was impossible, or else he must accept the breach with Constantinople as permanent and submit to domination by the Lombards. Faced with this unpleasant dilemma, Gregory III avoided committing himself irrevocably to either alternative. The emperor made it difficult to continue the Byzantine connection: in retaliation against the pope, Leo ordered the transfer of all the dioceses of Illyria, southern Italy, and Sicily to the jurisdiction of the patriarch of Constantinople, together with the expropriation of the Patrimony of St. Peter situated in those dioceses. This heavy blow at the resources and jurisdiction of the papacy helps explain why, during this critical period, Gregory III made his appeal for help to Charles Martel in 739 and supported so strongly the missionary efforts of Boniface in Germany:

the expansion of Christianity under papal auspices north of the Alps made up, in part, for papal losses in the Mediterranean.

The breaking point had almost been reached. The pope foresaw that it would come as soon as the Lombards were ready to resume their aggression. The Byzantine emperor, whose historic and proper role was that of ruler and protector of the Christian Empire, in the eyes of the papacy had not only failed to protect Italy against aggression but had become a heretic who persecuted the supreme spiritual authority. On Gregory III's death the new pope, Zacharias (741–752), did not bother to obtain imperial ratification of his election from the new emperor, Constantine V, who was a fanatical iconoclast. In Italy there was a temporary respite from the Lombard peril following Liutprand's death in 744, when a struggle began among the Lombard dukes for succession to the monarchy.

Meanwhile, in the Frankish kingdom Charles Martel was succeeded as mayor in 741 by his two sons, Pepin the Short and Carloman, who were favorably disposed toward the Church and particularly the missionary and reforming work of the papal representative, Boniface. They devoted the first several years to suppressing revolts of the nobility and the efforts of Aquitaine, Bavaria, and other outlying areas to assert their independence. Part of the brothers' program for consolidating their power was to sponsor provincial Church councils—the first to be held for many years—in which Boniface, under the aegis of both the pope and the mayors, began the work of reforming the Church in the Frankish realm. This was advantageous to Pepin and Carloman because many of the unreformed clergy were their political enemies. It was advantageous to the pope because it was at his call that the first general council in Gaul for over a century was convened in 745, and the prestige of the papacy in the West was thus brought back to the position from which it had declined since Gregory the Great. Even more important was the fact that Boniface's reforms brought the rulers of Frankish Gaul into contact once more with the pope.

Charles Martel had governed for the last four years of his life with the throne left vacant, because the existence of a puppet king had been the excuse for a revolt by some nobles who claimed to be fighting for the king against the mayor. When Pepin and Carloman became mayors, the same nobles rebelled again, alleging that they were fighting for a royalist restoration. So the brothers decided to legitimize their rule by setting up another puppet king in whose name they could rule. A search throughout the kingdom had to be made before a distant relative of the last Merovingian king could be found, and in 743 he was installed upon the throne as Childeric III, the last of his family to wear the Frankish crown. By 747 the work of consolidating their power was complete, and while Pepin continued to rule, Carloman retired to the monastery of Monte Cassino—one of several instances when an early medieval ruler retired from the world for no apparent purpose other than a sincere preference for the contemplative life.

An unaccustomed peace settled upon the Frankish realm in the next several years. It was at this time that Pepin the Short initiated negotiations which brought an end to the Merovingian dynasty and placed himself upon the throne. Pepin possessed, *de facto*, the hereditary rule of the Franks. The pope, he knew, had asked his father for aid. Why not, therefore, appeal to the highest spiritual authority for the sanction that would legitimize his accession to the crown, and secure that accession by a religious blessing which no Merovingian had ever enjoyed? The appeal was made, and the revolution was accomplished with little fanfare: contemporaries seem not to have been especially impressed, for the chroniclers recorded the whole transaction in a matter of fact way. "In the year 751 from the incarnation of our Lord," writes one, "Pepin sent ambassadors to Pope Zacharias to ask concerning the kings of the Franks, whether it were good that those who were of the royal race and were called kings, but had no power in the kingdom, should continue to be called kings." Zacharias' answer was a foregone conclusion, especially in view of the revival of the Lombard threat under the new king, Aistulf (749–756). In the same year that Pepin's ambassadors arrived in Rome, the Lombards captured Ravenna, destroying the Exarchate and Byzantine control of northern and central Italy.

Before an assembly of the Frankish nobility, the ambassadors gave Zacharias' reply to the famous question: "By his apostolic authority Zacharias answered that it seemed better that he should be called and should be the king who has the power in the kingdom, and not he who was falsely called king." Pepin was duly acclaimed king and consecrated to the royal power by Boniface as papal representative. Pepin the Short thus founded the Carolingian dynasty of Frankish kings whose authority, unlike that of the Merovingians, had the religious sanction of consecration: he was king by recognition of the supreme spiritual authority as well as by the acclamation of his subjects. He could justly claim that his power was, in St. Paul's words, "ordained of God." The final chapter of the secular Merovingian monarchy was closed when Childeric III, shorn of his long royal locks, was packed off to a monastery.

Three years later the alliance between the Franks and the papacy was sealed. The new pope, Stephen II (752–757), found the Lombard army of Aistulf besieging Rome when he ascended the papal throne. As if by habit, or perhaps to justify the appeal to Frankish arms which was now inevitable, Stephen II made a last, futile request for protection from the emperor. Then he set forth across the Alps in the winter of 753–54 as Aistulf's army waited for spring to renew the campaign, and implored Pepin to save Rome and Italy from the Lombards. Pepin was hardly in a position to refuse; moreover, he promised to restore the Lombard conquests not to the rightful sovereign, the Byzantine emperor, but to the pope himself. In return, Stephen consecrated Pepin king of the Franks once more and by his apostolic authority prohibited the Franks, on penalty of excommunication, from ever choosing a king who was not descended from Pepin. Finally, as if to underline his own usurpation of a sovereignty which the emperor was no longer able to exercise in Italy, Stephen conferred upon Pepin and his two sons the title of *Patricius Romanorum*, the traditional title of the exarch of Ravenna, which was, of course, only in the power of the emperor to confer.

The whole course of Western history was to be shaped by this alliance between the Frankish monarchy and the papacy. From the alliance both the Carolingians and the papacy were to draw strength in the future; because of the alliance political power in the West shifted to north of the Alps, where it was to remain. The crisis of the mid-eighth century broke the last important tie still binding East and West, the bond between the papacy and the Byzantine Empire.

PART TWO

THE EMERGENCE
OF FEUDAL EUROPE,
c.750-1050

PART TWO, illustration:
Coronation of Charlemagne. Manuscript illustration
(fourteenth century). THE PIERPONT MORGAN LIBRARY, NEW YORK.

IV

The Carolingian Empire

Christmas day, 800, is one of the great dates, like 476, 1066, and 1492. An event which has fired the imaginations of later historians took place on that day. The extreme view, which emphasizes the critical and revolutionary importance of the event, may be paraphrased from the words of the eminent Victorian, James Bryce, as follows:

> The Frankish host entered Rome, where Charlemagne remained for some weeks. On Christmas Day, A.D. 800, he heard mass in the basilica of St. Peter. On the spot which tradition had hallowed as that of the Apostles' martyrdom, Constantine the Great had erected the oldest and stateliest temple of Christian Rome. In its plan and decorations, the spacious sunny hall, the long row of Corinthian columns, in its brightness, sternness, and simplicity, it was a perfect expression of Roman character. The high altar was underneath and just beyond the great arch, the arch of triumph as it was called: behind in the semicircular apse sat the clergy, rising tier above tier around its walls; in their midst, high above the rest, was the bishop's cathedra, itself the curule chair of some forgotten Roman magistrate. From that chair the pope rose as the reading of the Gospel ended, advanced to where Charlemagne—who had exchanged his simple Frankish dress for the sandals and the chlamys of a Roman patrician—knelt in prayer before the high altar, and as in the sight of all he placed upon the brow of the barbarian chieftain the diadem of the Caesars, then bent in obeisance before him, the basilica rang to the shout of the multitude, again free, again the center of the world: *"Carolo Au-*

gusto a Deo coronato, magno et pacifico imperatori, vita et victoria!"
("Life and victory to Charles Augustus crowned of God, great and peace-
bringing emperor!") In that shout was pronounced the union of the
Roman and the Teuton, of the civilization of the South and the fresh
energy of the North, and from that moment modern history begins.

Today, this estimate is considered extravagant. The real significance
of the imperial coronation of Charlemagne emerges from a review of the
events of the last half of the eighth century. In such a perspective, the
coronation marks no sudden break; nor does it mark the beginning of a
new era which can be sharply set off from a preceding age. It was another
important milestone in the development of the Frankish and papal policies
which we have already traced from the days of Pepin of Heristal (680–714),
the first great Carolingian mayor of the palace, and of Gregory III (731–
741), the first pope to appeal for aid to a Western secular ruler.

16   CHARLEMAGNE

The central theme of the history of Western Europe after the coronation of Pepin as king of the Franks in 751 was the revival of the power of
the Frankish monarchy. Pepin's successor, Charlemagne, extended this
power beyond the old limits of the Merovingian kingdom into Italy, farther
eastward into Germany, and south of the Pyrenees into Spain. The Carolingian empire was the largest political unit in the West since the age of
Theodosius the Great, and its internal government was the most stable
since the age of Constantine.

This culmination of Carolingian power could hardly have been foreseen in 751. The position of Pepin the Short (741–768) was by no means
secure even after 754 when he became the first king to be consecrated by
a pope. The Frankish nobles were divided in support of the new dynasty,
and many of them opposed the intervention in Italy to which Pepin was
committed. Pepin was able to gain lukewarm approval for a campaign
across the Alps on behalf of the papacy, but only in case his negotiations
with the Lombard king, Aistulf, failed to effect the cession of the Exarchate
of Ravenna (conquered by the Lombards in 751) to the pope.

It is difficult to understand all these developments—the legal justification for Stephen II's coronation of Pepin, the claims of the pope to the
Byzantine Exarchate, and Pepin's apparent confidence that he could negotiate its transference from the Lombard conquerors to the pope—without
taking account of the most famous forgery of all time, the *Donation of
Constantine.* This document may have made its appearance as early as the
pontificate of either Zacharias (741–752) or Stephen II (752–757), and
thus may be directly related to contemporary events, or it may have been
produced later as an *ex post facto* justification of events under both Pepin

and Charlemagne. In any case, judged by later medieval standards of forgery, the document was a clumsy effort. Although widely accepted, its validity had been questioned before the end of the ninth century, and no pope is known to have made an explicit appeal to its provisions before the middle of the eleventh century. It was probably manufactured in the papal *curia* or by an ardent supporter of papal policy who had knowledge of the way contemporary imperial documents should be drafted. According to this *Donation*, Constantine granted to the pope, Sylvester I (314–335), primacy over the whole Church and political authority over Italy and all the western provinces of the Empire. The *Donation* was thus tailor-made to provide a juridical basis for papal policy in the mid-eighth century, including the coronation of Pepin, the acquisition of the Exarchate of Ravenna, and the exercise of political and secular authority wherever possible.

After futile negotiations with Aistulf, in 756 Pepin invaded Italy and defeated the Lombards. Ignoring the protests of Byzantine envoys, he gave most of the former Byzantine Exarchate to the papacy in fulfillment of promises made to Stephen II just before his second coronation. By this so-called Donation of Pepin, the revolution begun in 751 was completed, and the Papal States were founded. For over a century the popes had been temporal rulers of the duchy of Rome, in the name of the Byzantine emperor. For eleven more centuries the papacy continued to exercise temporal authority over territory which had never been part of the duchy.

For himself, Pepin sought no territorial gains in Italy because he was fully occupied in the southwestern regions of his kingdom. By 759 he had reconquered Septimania and pushed the Moslems south of the Pyrenees. Then, during the years 760–768, he reduced the semi-independent duchy of Aquitaine to obedience. In these campaigns he continued the work of his father, Charles Martel, whereas his Italian intervention inaugurated a policy which was left to his son, Charlemagne, to continue and bring to a successful conclusion. The reign of Pepin the Short was an epoch in Western European history. Unfortunately for his own fame, he was succeeded by a son whose achievements eclipsed the substantial and revolutionary accomplishments of his father.

On the death of Pepin, the kingdom was divided according to Frankish custom between his two sons, Charles (768–814) and a younger brother, Carloman, who died in 771. Charles then ruled alone, excluding his two young nephews from any share in the government. The judgment of posterity awarded Charles the epithet "the Great" (*Carolus Magnus*), so that he is best known by the French form of his name, Charlemagne. His greatness, in the eyes of contemporaries, was based upon his success in a series of wars by which he enlarged the kingdom through substantial additions of territory in Italy, Germany, and Spain.

Charlemagne's first concern was Italy, where the new Lombard king, Desiderius (756–774), owed his throne to the pope, who had supported him as the weakest candidate in a disputed succession. Once on the throne, however, Desiderius resumed the traditional Lombard policy of encroaching on lands not yet within his realm, especially the territories newly acquired by the papacy, while at the same time he conciliated the Franks. The Frankish nobility preferred to stay out of Italy, since to them an alliance with the Lombards seemed better than the papal connection which profited only the Carolingian kings. This view was shared by Bertrada, Pepin's widow. Bertrada and Desiderius even arranged a marriage between Desiderius' daughter and Charlemagne, a marriage which the pope, Stephen III (768–771), castigated as "the invention of the devil, a mere illicit union . . . a folly by which the illustrious Frankish blood would be defiled by the stinking, faithless race of the Lombards, from whom the race of lepers is well known to have sprung." Whether Charlemagne agreed with the pope or not, the royal nuptials were hardly consummated when he sent his Lombard bride back to Italy and broke relations with Desiderius. If personal repugnance was not the primary consideration, it is probable that the papal alliance was necessary in order to retain the support of the Frankish church. Charlemagne had just quelled another revolt in Aquitaine, where papal influence over the clergy was far more potent than the good will of a Lombard king whose power did not reach beyond Italy. Desiderius was incensed by the personal affront. While trying to split the Franks by promoting the claims of Carloman's sons to a share in the Carolingian government, he renewed his attacks upon the Papal States.

To the inevitable appeal from the pope for assistance, Charlemagne responded quickly. In a decisive campaign, 773–774, he defeated the Lombards, confirmed the Donation of Pepin, and restored Desiderius' recent encroachments on papal territory. Then he permanently solved the Lombard problem by assuming himself the title of king of the Lombards, thus incorporating northern Italy in a personal union with the Frankish kingdom. As king of the Lombards Charlemagne adopted many of the aims of the earlier Lombard rulers. Like them, he tried to unite all of Italy under his rule, but also like them he was able to subdue neither the independent Lombard duchy of Benevento nor the Byzantine provinces in Sicily and Naples. Carolingian control of northern and central Italy was strengthened by the substitution of new counties under Frankish counts for the older Lombard duchies, and by political and administrative supervision over the Papal States, which were ruled directly by the pope. The pope's temporal rule now differed only in two respects from the earlier situation: first, the area under his immediate control was much larger than the old duchy of Rome; and second, instead of a distant and ineffectual Byzantine emperor for suzerain he enjoyed the protection but was under the effective supervision of Charlemagne, as *Patricius Romanorum*.

By far the longest and most arduous of Charlemagne's wars was the series of almost annual campaigns against the Saxons, lasting thirty-two years (772–804). Settled on the northeastern frontier of the Carolingian kingdom, the Saxons were fiercely heathen, independent, and predatory. Their continual raids into the Rhineland posed a threat whose only solution was conquest, conversion, and annexation. Charlemagne drained the manpower and exhausted the wealth of his realm in breaking their stubborn resistance. The most notorious event of the long war was Charlemagne's massacre of forty-five hundred unarmed Saxon captives. Only by such brutal methods was Saxony subdued and organized into counties under loyal counts and dioceses under Frankish bishops. Forced conversion was backed up by capital punishment for heathen worship and for offenses against the clergy and church property. Final success was achieved, however, only by mass deportation of Saxons into other areas of Germany and the settlement of Franks and other Germans in Saxony. With the conquest of Saxony, no important German tribe remained independent of Carolingian authority.

On the southwestern frontier, Charlemagne followed up his father's

*The Carolingian Empire, c.814: The Territories
Conquered by Charlemagne and the Tributary Slavic States*

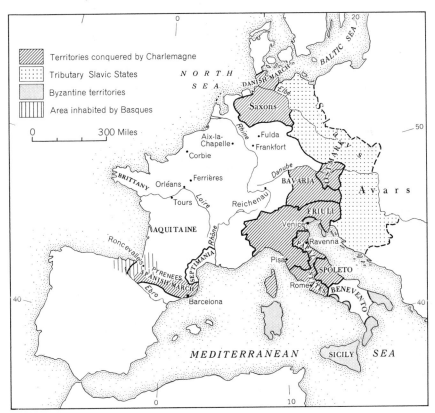

work by penetrating south of the Pyrenees. Because of his commitments in Saxony and elsewhere, it is doubtful that Charlemagne ever intended to conquer Spain. The main problem was to protect southern Gaul against marauding raids by the Moslems. The strategy of his several campaigns, between 778 and 801, was primarily defensive, and the result was the establishment of a military district, the Spanish March, centered on Barcelona. An incident of these campaigns later gave rise to the first and greatest of French epic poems, the *Song of Roland*. In it is preserved the memory of the annihilation of a Frankish rear guard at the hands of Christian Basques, as the Carolingian army returned across the Pyrenees from a season's fighting in northern Spain. Popular imagination later transformed the incident into a heroic struggle between Christian Franks and Spanish infidels. Charlemagne thus became, anachronistically, a hero of the age of the Crusades. All that history knows of Roland is that he was warden of the Breton March (the military frontier district on the border of Brittany) and that he died at the battle of Roncevalles (778) which the poem commemorates.

On the eastern frontier, an abortive revolt in the tributary duchy of Bavaria was crushed in 787, and the duke was deposed in favor of several Frankish counts. In the eastern half of Bavaria a march was organized (the Ostmark, later called Austria) against the barbarian Slavs who were then attempting to expand westward. Charlemagne forced their submission and recognized their kingdoms as tributary states, but he made no effort to convert them to Christianity or to absorb them into the Frankish realm as he had the Germanic Saxons and Bavarians. A far more serious menace than the Slavs were the Asiatic Avars who had settled on the banks of the upper Danube, from which they raided as far west and south as central Germany and Friuli, in northeastern Italy. Between 791 and 795 Charlemagne sent armies against them, and the Avars were so completely crushed that the survivors were absorbed into their previously subject Slavic population. Removal of the Avar threat opened the upper Danubian regions to German colonization, the earliest instance of a movement which was later to become a major theme in German history, the *Drang nach Osten* or eastward movement.

By the year 800, contemporaries recognized that no king had ruled so wide an area in the West since the Roman emperors of the fourth century. From the Elbe in the northeast to the Ebro in the southwest, and from the North Sea to the marches of Benevento, Charlemagne united under his authority as king of the Franks, as king of the Lombards, and as *Patricius Romanorum* or protector of the Papal States, all the western provinces of the Roman Empire which were then Christian, except Anglo-Saxon England and the southern half of Italy still under Byzantine or independent Lombard control. He had extended Christianity and Frankish rule into the heart of Germany, and he exercised a protectorate over the tributary Slavic states on the eastern frontiers. His advisers spoke of Charlemagne's authority as equal to that of the emperors of antiquity, but they were not entirely agreed on the nature of Charlemagne's *de facto* "imperial" authority. To some, Charlemagne's supreme political power was essentially similar to that of his father, Pepin the Short, except that it was even greater and was exercised over a larger territory. Pepin, mayor of the palace but in fact ruler of the Franks, had become king of the Franks; Charlemagne, king of the Franks but also ruler of other peoples and territories as well—including the ancient centers of imperial authority in the West: Rome, Milan, Aix-la-Chapelle—should be acknowledged as emperor, the highest title and dignity, corresponding with his actual power.

Another group of advisers, consisting mainly of ecclesiastical leaders, agreed but went further: Charlemagne's supreme power was greater than his father's not only in degree but also in kind. They expressed a new concept of political authority. Charlemagne was essentially the "leader of the Christian people" and "defender of the churches of Christ." In Charlemagne's rule there was a new theocratic element that was alien to that of the secular Merovingian monarchy and absent from that of his father. Even before 800 the vast multi-national territories subject to Charlemagne's rule were called a "Christian empire" (*imperium christianum*), and he was "governor of the Christian people" (*rector populi christiani*). His subjects were not all Franks, but they were all Christians. The force of these concepts can be grasped only if it is also recalled that Frankish churchmen were doubtful (even suspicious) of the orthodoxy of Byzantine Christians (especially iconoclastic emperors). Compared with Byzantine rulers, Charlemagne was thus held to be the true and proper heir of the Christian emperors of the fourth century.

Charlemagne's own attitude is by no means clear. Urged by advisers to accept the imperial dignity as befitted the protector of the Church, guardian of the faith, and ruler of most of Latin Christendom, he vigorously put into action a political role that could be described by contemporaries as "imperial" in fact if not in legal theory. And yet he seems not to have been eager to adopt the title of emperor. To some of his advisers the fact that the Byzantine throne was now occupied by a woman and usurper, Irene (797–802), meant that the Christian world had no legitimate supreme ruler. But Charlemagne had reservations about this argument—and when he did become emperor the Byzantine situation was not in fact an immediate cause of the event. Charlemagne was not opposed to being recognized as emperor, but he knew that the acquisition of a more exalted title would not increase the power he actually wielded, while it might jeopardize his power so far as friendly relations with Byzantium were concerned.

All the factors we have considered so far explain why, in the closing years of the eighth century, the coronation of Charlemagne as emperor could or probably would take place. Why, then, did it take place on

Charlemagne. Bronze
statuette (probably
ninth century).
PHOTO: GIRAUDON.

Christmas Day, 800? For the answer we must turn to developments and personalities in Rome. For half a century and more the papacy had sought and, in moments of crisis, had received protection and support from the Frankish kings, on whom they had in turn bestowed the title of *Patricius Romanorum.* But there was a flaw in papal policy. Legally, only the Byzantine (i.e., Roman) emperor could bestow such a title, even though the emperor was incapable of providing the protection of Rome and the papacy implied by the title. From this dilemma the popes could escape first by dissociating the papacy and the Latin Church from the Byzantine Empire and, second, by creating a divinely sanctioned legitimacy for Frankish protection to supersede the legitimacy of Byzantine authority sanctioned by Roman law (by this time, so far as the papacy was concerned, little more than legal fiction). We have already seen how the *Donation of Constantine* was produced in this period as a major ideological justification for papal policy.

Other steps were taken toward the same goal. For example, as soon as he became pope, Adrian I (772–795) omitted the usual reference to the year of the emperor's reign (required by Roman law) from official papal documents, and from the year 781 he dated documents by the year of his own pontificate. When Leo III (795–816) became pope he not only did not request permission from the Byzantine emperor to be consecrated (as had become customary), he waited until after his consecration as pope and then notified Charlemagne of that fact, ignoring the emperor entirely. Then, in 798, Leo began to date papal documents by the year of Charlemagne's rule in Italy, again ignoring the regnal year of the Byzantine ruler, who was then the empress, Irene. Finally, when Charlemagne came to Rome in the year 800, Leo went out to meet him, not the mile or two that by custom was a courtesy extended to the *Patricius Romanorum,* but a full twelve miles outside the walls of Rome, which contemporary protocol required as the proper distance from a city to receive a Byzantine emperor. Each one of these steps—small in itself but symbolically important—was a denial of Byzantine sovereignty and an affirmation of the supremacy of Charlemagne, even to the extent of giving the Frankish ruler honors that could only be described as imperial.

We must now consider what brought Charlemagne to Rome in 800. In contrast with Adrian, Leo had been elected pope against the opposition of the Roman aristocracy, whose hostility Leo was unable either to placate or to suppress. In April, 799, a faction of Roman nobles (led by two relatives of the late pope, Adrian) seized the person of the pope, assaulted and kidnaped him, and held him prisoner in a monastery. But Leo was able to escape; in the company of a Carolingian official he made his way north of the Alps to Charlemagne, who was engaged in a campaign against the Saxons. Leo appealed for protection from his enemies, whom he denounced as traitors; at the same time, letters arrived from Rome accusing Leo of a variety of crimes, including perjury and adultery. Leo was sent back to Rome with the security of a Frankish guard; Charlemagne himself was not free to go to Rome to settle the charges against Leo until late in the year 800. Meanwhile some advisers urged him as ruler of "the Christian empire" to sit in judgment of the pope. Others roundly condemned such a plan, arguing that the pope was not subject to the jurisdiction of anyone, least of all a layman, and that Charlemagne as protector of the Church was obligated to protect the pope, not judge him. As it turned out, Charlemagne presided over a council summoned to hear the charges against Leo— charges which none of Leo's enemies now had the temerity to put formally before the council, a circumstance which prompted some members of the council to deny that the council had jurisdiction to put a pope on trial in any case.

At this point, Leo seized the initiative. In recognition of Charlemagne's concern for the welfare of the Church and to regain Charlemagne's support, Leo volunteered to take an oath that he was innocent. The voluntary form of the oath meant that the pope was not actually on trial, and yet it was sufficient to establish that his enemies were guilty of false accusations and therefore should be punished as traitors. In Leo's view the only problem that remained was that his enemies, in strict law, were traitors

Pope Leo III and King Charlemagne, as equals, receive the symbols of authority (pallium and lance) from St. Peter. Detail of mosaic executed for Leo III in St. John Lateran, Rome (after 795 but before coronation of 800). PHOTO: ALINARI.

against Charlemagne only in the latter's capacity as *Patricius Romanorum,* i.e., an official of the Roman or Byzantine government from whom judicial appeal lay to the court of the Byzantine emperor. Leo thus could not be wholly secure unless the supreme jurisdiction of Byzantium were replaced by that of Charlemagne.

Two days after the pope took his oath, while Charlemagne was worshiping in St. Peter's on Christmas Day, 800, as the Frankish king rose from prayer Leo suddenly placed a crown upon his head, then prostrated himself before the newly-crowned ruler in accordance with Byzantine protocol due to an emperor. The assembled clergy and nobles filled the basilica with their acclamation of the new emperor. The papal *coup* was complete: Charlemagne was created emperor by the pope and by that creation was committed to protect the papacy against its enemies, whether local factions in Rome or external powers such as the Lombards of recent years. Also the "dreams of empire" indulged in by many of Charlemagne's advisers were now consummated.

And yet Charlemagne, we are told, "never would have gone to mass that day, even though it was Christmas, had he known what the pope intended to do." One reason for his reaction, as noted above, was his concern to maintain good relations with Constantinople—he would have preferred to assure the legitimacy of his title by being crowned emperor with the prior approval, or at least acceptance, of the Byzantine court rather than present it with a *fait accompli* and be considered a usurper. Far more important, however, Charlemagne resented the implications of Leo's act. That a pope crowned him implied that the pope made him emperor, and this, in turn, implied that a pope could take away what had been granted. In Charlemagne's view the imperial dignity which he accepted recognized, but did not create, the position of paramount power which he had won; coronation by the pope was a public expression of the claims to supremacy embodied in the *Donation of Constantine*, claims which Leo III had dramatically made good to the immediate advantage of the papacy. What Charlemagne thought of the *coup* may be indicated by the fact that he never returned to the city of Rome during the rest of his reign.

17   CAROLINGIAN POLITICAL INSTITUTIONS

Although its dignity was enhanced, the substance of Carolingian monarchical power was not greatly affected by Charlemagne's assumption of the title of emperor. Already as king of the Franks Charlemagne was a theocratic ruler. His power reflected the sacrosanct character imparted to the king by consecration and anointment. He exercised effective control not only over the secular affairs of the state but also over the spiritual welfare of the Christian people committed to his care. The duties of the Christian ruler, as conceived by Charlemagne, were vastly enlarged beyond any Western precedent and may be compared only with the caesaropapism of the Byzantine emperors.

The traditional theory, fostered by the Church, of the independence and equality of the spiritual and secular authorities, the theory which Ambrose dramatically vindicated at the expense of Theodosius and which Gelasius I formulated in more refined terms to assert the superiority of the spiritual authority (*auctoritas*) over the secular power (*potestas*) when the two were in conflict, was hardly congenial to Charlemagne. While he never explicitly denied or opposed what is called "Gelasian dualism," his actions and attitudes would hardly have pleased Gelasius. He considered himself responsible only to God for the spiritual and material welfare of his people, both clergy and laity. He was "successor of the Caesars, heir to the power of David and Solomon, anointed of God." As such, he considered himself to be the ruler of both Church and state; actually, the distinction blurred in his mind, and he often treated his Frankish kingdom or, after 800, his

"Christian empire" as if it were one great Church of which the clergy were but one part and the pope was his personal chaplain.

When he intervened in the affairs of the Church, his decision was final, whether it were a matter of appointment to high ecclesiastical office, discipline of the clergy, education, ritual, organization, or even doctrine. The record of one of the great synods of his reign begins with the statement: "This council was called by the grace of God, the authority of the pope, and the power of the king." But the rest of the record makes clear that God's grace and papal *auctoritas* played a role distinctly secondary to Charlemagne's *potestas* in what took place at the synod. When Leo III notified him that he had been consecrated pope (795), Charlemagne replied in clear and unambiguous language:

> It pertains to me, with the aid of divine piety, to defend in all places the holy Church of Christ with arms against the invasions of heathens and the devastations of infidels from without, and to strengthen it within with knowledge of the Catholic faith. It pertains to you, most holy father, to lift up your hands to God, like Moses, to aid us by your prayers for the success of our arms. . . . Let your life in every way be an example of holiness, let only pious exhortations come forth from your mouth. . . .

The theocratic paternalism of Charlemagne's rule is well brought out in the new oath which all free subjects above the age of twelve years were required to take in 802:

> . . . not merely, as many have thought hitherto, fidelity to the lord emperor . . . but also that each one shall strive voluntarily, in accordance with his knowledge and ability, to live fully in the holy service of God in accordance with the precept of God . . . and that none shall presume to rob or do any injury fraudulently to the churches of God or widows or orphans or pilgrims, for the lord emperor himself, after God and His saints, has constituted himself their protector and defender.

Despite this rather grandiose conception of the nature of his authority, Charlemagne in most ways continued to treat the practical problems of the monarchy much as did his Merovingian predecessors. The monarchy was still considered to be a family inheritance, descending to the sons of the ruler in accordance with Frankish custom. In 806 Charlemagne drew up a plan for the succession which ignored the imperial title completely and provided for the usual division among his three living sons. A more revealing clue to Charlemagne's attitude was the coronation of Louis, his only surviving son, in 813: he named his son co-emperor and excluded the pope from any role in the ceremony. The precedent of 800, when Leo placed the crown on the emperor's head, contained implications of papal superiority which Charlemagne could not accept. The coronation of Louis climaxed a long series of negotiations with the Byzantine emperor, Michael, which finally led to recognition of Charlemagne's imperial title, and the coronation ceremony of 813 followed Byzantine forms which subordinated the role of the Church.

The central government continued, under the Carolingians, with little institutional change from that of the Merovingians. The government was personal and primitive. In its several functions and powers, in most of its routine acts, and in all important acts, it reflected the policy and will of the ruler himself. There was no distinction between the personal servants of the monarch and the public officials of the monarchy. The highest officials were members of the household or palace who held their offices at the pleasure of the ruler. There was no capital at any one place; rather, the capital was wherever the king or emperor happened to be with his household. In his later years, Charlemagne lived a more settled life and spent much time at his favorite residence at Aix-la-Chapelle, or Aachen, but this town was in no sense a permanent capital. Of the more important officials, there were two or more counts of the palace to whom were delegated certain judicial and administrative powers of the crown. However, they were not allowed to exercise any of the financial powers which had made the old mayor of the palace (an office which was discontinued by the Carolingians) so powerful, and so dangerous to the Merovingian monarchy. Other officials were the chamberlain, whose duties were mainly concerned with public finance and the royal treasury; the seneschal, responsible for the management of the crown lands and revenues arising therefrom; the marshal or constable (count of the stable), whose duties were primarily military; and the chaplain, whose sphere included both the divine service of the household chapel and also the secretarial and legal work necessary in issuing official letters and documents. The Merovingian kings, following the example of the provincial Roman government which they succeeded, had employed laymen to prepare and preserve documents. The quality of their work, as shown by the very few surviving Merovingian documents, faithfully reflects the decline of education in their age. The Carolingian chaplain probably took over these duties because of the scarcity of suitable and literate laymen. The chaplain of the palace was thus the ancestor of the later chancellor, who was destined to become the most important official in many medieval governments. The Carolingian scriptorium of the palace evolved into the later medieval chancery.

These officials discharged the routine of day-to-day government, but for matters requiring careful discussion and leading to important decisions Charlemagne consulted with the nobles and high ecclesiastical officials. Such consultation could take place at any time on the summons of the monarch, but it was customary to hold a general assembly of the great men of the realm once a year in the spring, the so-called May Field, when

Charlemagne could discuss all problems on which he desired advice. These assemblies in no sense limited the powers of the government, and possessed, in themselves, no legislative authority. They were important as a means of securing agreement to and support of Charlemagne's plans, especially his military plans which could not succeed without the full cooperation of his nobility. Thus the general assemblies were essentially a device by which the great men were committed to decisions which the government had already reached, subject to whatever modification might seem expedient in view of the attitude of the nobility.

In the Carolingian government there was a fusion of the powers or "branches" which we distinguished today as the legislative, executive, and judicial. Partly this was the result of the extreme simplicity of the government and the small range of its activities. Besides waging war, it had little to do except maintain a system of local courts for the administration of justice, collect a few tolls, and oversee the maintenance of roads and such "public works" as fortifications and bridges. Another reason for the lack of differentiation between the functions of the Carolingian government was the almost total absence of legislation in the modern sense: the making, changing, or abrogating of laws. The Germanic concept of the personality of law, the notion that the laws by which men live are passed down unchanged from generation to generation as a tribal heritage, provided no basis for legislation as a function of government. Not even Charlemagne as emperor could legislate, because law was conceived as being beyond the reach of any human agency. And yet Charlemagne promulgated many important enactments. These were called capitularies because their contents were divided into *capitula* or chapters. They were legally binding upon all subjects. The capitularies were miscellaneous and unsystematic, very unlike a modern code of laws, being composed of specific instructions or ordinances dealing with all sorts of particular problems as they arose. Most of the capitularies were simply administrative regulations concerning the duties of governmental officials or the functions of local institutions. Others dealt extensively with such matters as organization of royal estates, regulations for the clergy, or recruitment of the army. Only rarely did the capitularies affect the legal rights of subjects, and then usually by adding certain provisions to existing laws in order to meet new conditions not covered by tribal customs.

It will be apparent from this brief review of the central government that the success of the monarchy was to a large degree dependent upon the personal ability of the individual ruler. There was no tradition of bureaucratic control, no concept of the state as an entity necessarily involving governmental functions, an entity to which men owed allegiance as distinct from the person of the ruler. The essential expression of the authority that the ruler personally embodied was his power to require obedience from all who owed him allegiance. His subjects were under the ruler's *bannum,* his command that something should or should not be done (to prohibit something is to "ban" it). The *bannum* represented the highest coercive power of the Carolingian ruler: disobedience was construed as disloyalty, and disloyalty was severely punished in accordance with contemporary notions of the sanctity and binding nature of the personal relations between subordinate and superior. This is a typically Germanic concept of political authority. It was only in this personalized and attenuated form that the idea of the state—given its most enduring classical expression in the abstract Roman *imperium*—was passed on to the Middle Ages. As for the actual political institutions of the Carolingian central government, their historical significance was that they afforded the model for later governments all over western Europe. The crucial importance of the individual ruler, the personal relationship between officials and the ruler, and the fusion of legislative, judicial, and executive powers all constituted the basis on which the medieval governments of the later feudal monarchies were built.

Carolingian local government, like central government, was largely a continuation of the Merovingian system. The empire was divided into about three hundred counties. Except in Germany, which was beyond the limits of Roman occupation, each county roughly corresponded with an ancient *civitas*. Each was governed by a count under whom were his deputies, the viscounts, and officials called *centenarii*, who were in charge of the several local districts into which the county was divided. These local officials were appointed by the count and were removable by him at will, just as the counts were appointed by the king and held office only at his pleasure. The work of the count and his subordinates consisted primarily of maintaining the peace, administering justice in local courts, and raising and leading troops in war. This county government was limited by the authority of the bishop whose diocese included the county and by the privileges and exemptions of ecclesiastical and lay nobles who had been granted immunity from all interference by royal officials. The possessors of immunities exercised the same delegated powers in their own private lands as did the count in the rest of the county.

Under the Merovingians, the counts, bishops, and ecclesiastical and lay nobles who had immunity tended to develop into local semi-independent rulers. One of the great accomplishments of Charles Martel and Pepin the Short had been to arrest this tendency toward localism. Their achievement, however, was a reflection of their personal power, and the primitive nature of Carolingian administrative machinery meant that central control of local government depended upon the personal ability of the ruler. Charlemagne realized the danger and inaugurated several reforms intended to correct the situation. One reform was the establishment of groups of permanent professional judges, called *scabini*, whose appointment by the count was to be approved by the central government and whose function was to travel around the county to give judgments at the courts presided over by the count and his officials. By cutting down the count's participation in the administration of justice to a merely formal role, Charlemagne hoped to decrease the count's influence and thus make him more amenable to central control.

A second and more important reform was the establishment of the *missi dominici*, or royal envoys, who traveled around the empire in specified circuits investigating local conditions, holding courts, enforcing royal commands, and redressing grievances of the inhabitants against local officials. The jurisdiction of the *missi dominici* was undifferentiated, like that of the central government, and they were competent to represent Charlemagne in any duty assigned to them, whether it concerned the Church or purely secular affairs. For this reason the *missi dominici* usually traveled in pairs, one an ecclesiastic and the other a lay noble. In order to ensure that they would be above taking bribes, Charlemagne appointed only the greatest men to these positions, and to ensure that they would represent the central government rather than local interests he prescribed that no *missi dominici* should operate in a circuit which included counties where they held property. Under Charlemagne this system worked well, but under later and less powerful rulers the device was unequal to the task of defeating tendencies toward localism.

On the frontiers, the unit of local government was the march, an essentially military district where greater powers were entrusted to the local representative of Charlemagne than those exercised by the count of an ordinary county. The march was under the command of a duke or a margrave (count, or *graf*, of the march). Marches were organized all along the eastern frontiers from the march of Friuli in northeastern Italy up to the march organized against the Danes, which later gave its name to Denmark.

In the marches were garrisoned the only troops who served throughout the year. For the almost annual campaigns fought during the summer, the Carolingian army like that of the Merovingians was based upon the universal obligation of all free subjects to answer the king's *heer-ban*, or summons, to serve with the army. Poorer free men suffered from being away from their fields during the summer months. Many preferred to give up their freedom and become dependent peasants of neighboring lords in order to escape the burden of military service. To prevent such an increase in the local powers of the nobility and to equalize the military burden, Charlemagne provided that military service should be proportional to the amount of property, in the sense that a free man owning less than sufficient property to support one soldier in the field should contribute proportionately along with others in the same position to the support of one soldier. In practice, free men were grouped together and took turns serving in the army. If four free men each owned one fourth of the minimum property required to support one soldier, each of the four would serve in rotation once every four years. Relief from the burden of attending local courts was arranged in the same way. These reforms, a heroic effort intended to preserve the status of the free men, in effect only contributed to the decline of the poorer people, depriving them of participation in the two vital roles of fully free men in the Carolingian system of political institutions.

Universal military service was the most important support of the Carolingian goverment, measured in terms of economic value. The immediate royal income was derived from the crown lands, whose produce was collected and either sent direct to the palace for consumption by the royal household or else sold in local markets to provide a cash revenue. The old Roman land tax and personal tax had decayed, but the indirect taxes, or tolls, levied on the sale or transportation of goods, had been preserved and provided a small income for the government. The most important cash revenue arose from fines levied in the royal courts, although one third of the county court revenues was set aside for the support of the counts who presided. In addition to cash income, the government was supported by a variety of services other than universal military service. Royal officials had the right to hospitality, or bed and board, and the use of provisions and transport requisitioned from the subjects of the empire. Also, bridges, roads, and fortifications were built and maintained by direct requisition of the labor of the neighboring inhabitants. Finally, there were the "gifts" which great men were expected to bring to the ruler at the annual May Field, and which were the nearest thing to a general tax in the Carolingian system.

18   ENGLAND AND THE CONTINENT
ON THE EVE OF THE NEW INVASIONS

In the opening years of the ninth century Europe was more stable politically than at any time since the end of the fourth century. However, the peace and security which Charlemagne brought to the continent did not bring a corresponding economic revival; rather, the long decline that had continued in the West since the end of antiquity was arrested and economic conditions were, at best, stabilized at a low level. There were few impressive indications of economic growth or improvement in Carolingian society, which was ill prepared—despite the imposing might of Frankish arms—for the disorders of civil war and foreign invasions that lay ahead. In England, too, political stability was more impressive than the social and economic foundations of society.

England during the seventh and eighth centuries suffered the same turbulence that afflicted the continent before the rise of the Carolingians.

Political developments were independent of those on the continent, but England was never wholly isolated from continental events and influences. For example, the missionary Boniface was only one of many Englishmen who aided the early Carolingian policy of conversion among the tribes of Germany. The Church not only provided the most important contact between the Anglo-Saxon kingdoms and the continent, but also provided England with the first approximation of unity. Both contributions are illustrated by the career of Theodore of Tarsus, archbishop of Canterbury (669–690). In addition to his contribution to cultural developments discussed earlier, he was the main organizer of the Church in England. He was responsible for completing the Roman victory over Celtic Christianity, after the Synod of Whitby (663), and for establishing firmly the leadership if not primacy of the archbishopric of Canterbury over that of York. In 673 he held the first synod which promulgated canons to be observed throughout all of England. Such ecclesiastical activity gave the most able and educated class a concept of unity at a time when this was by no means apparent in the political developments of the several kingdoms.

For the greater part of the seventh century, Northumbria had been predominant in the north and during intervals had subordinated the kings of Mercia, in the Midlands. Mercia proved too strong, however, to be absorbed into the northern kingdom and was able not only to maintain independence but to expand at the expense of other tribal kingdoms on the south and east. In 685 the northern Picts annihilated a Northumbrian army. From that date Northumbria slowly declined as a power in English politics. In the eighth century various contenders for the throne disrupted the kingdom with periodic civil wars, but these disturbances did not prevent the flowering of Northumbrian culture during the same period.

In the south, the earlier predominance of Ethelbert of Kent passed on his death (616) to the kings of East Anglia, whose pomp and power may be inferred from the magnificent remains in the royal funeral barrow excavated at Sutton Hoo. The barrow contained a complete ship, dragged up the hill as a sepulchral memorial and filled with weapons, objects of art both gold and silver, ornately decorated utensils, chain mail armor, costly textiles, and sundry other beautifully wrought articles. The lavish splendor of Sutton Hoo—unmatched among all other English burial remains and unsurpassed in the whole northern Teutonic world—not only indicates the advanced state of the arts in England but also reveals the wealth and the extensive contacts with the outer world which an Anglo-Saxon tribal kingdom of the first half of the seventh century could achieve. The Frankish gold coins and the silver bowls of Byzantine manufacture preserved at Sutton Hoo, in a kingdom which never achieved the first rank, warn against exaggerating the isolation of England during this early period. There is nothing in these burial remains that requires us to believe that these contacts came only from the conversion to Christianity.

Sutton Hoo. Purse cover, gold, colored glass, and garnet; intricate geometrical design with stylized animal motifs typical of northern barbarian art. BRITISH MUSEUM.

In southern England during the second half of the seventh century, an uneasy balance of power was maintained between East Anglia, Mercia, and Wessex. The West Saxon king, Ine (688–726), was able to consolidate the piecemeal conquests of his predecessors and bring all of England south of the Thames under his control. After Ine, who promoted the growth of the Church in his realm and is best known for his code of West Saxon laws, power shifted back to Mercia. Wessex declined during the eighth century to the status of nothing more than a province under the Mercian king.

The supremacy of Mercia in the eighth century was as complete as that of Northumbria in the seventh. Although Northumbria was able to preserve a tenuous independence under a succession of shadow-kings, the northern kingdom had almost dissolved into anarchy and weakness before the coming of the Northmen. As a presage of things to come, Lindisfarne, the original center of Northumbrian Christianity, was sacked by raiders from Scandinavia in 793. But this decline of northern power was not reflected in the Midlands or in the kingdoms subject to Mercia. The height of Mercian power was reached during the reign of Offa (757–796), who, in addition to ruling his midland kingdom, was overlord of all the southern kings. The extent of his claims to power is suggested by the title he assumed, "king of all the land of the English."

Offa was the first English king to foster trade with the continent, and he was the first to pursue what might be called a continental policy in his relations with Charlemagne and the pope. Charlemagne proposed the marriage of one of his sons with a daughter of Offa. In the diplomatic protocol of that age such a proposal implied the superior status or dignity of the Carolingian royal house. Offa, whose royal family was far more ancient than Charlemagne's, declined the overture unless his son were married with a daughter of Charlemagne—thus preserving the equality of status between the two dynasties. Charlemagne indignantly broke off the negotiations, and in retaliation closed all ports under Carolingian control to English traders. This is interesting evidence of the importance of commercial relations between England and the continent. When the quarrel was patched up in 796, the proposed marriage alliance was dropped, and Charlemagne and Offa entered into the earliest known trade treaty in European history. Each monarch allowed merchants from the other country free access to the markets of his own realm and protection by royal officials. In his relations with the pope, Offa received the first mission of papal legates to England since the days of Augustine of Canterbury. Offa's purpose was to obtain papal consent to the division of the province of Canterbury and the establishment of an archbishopric to correspond with his kingdom of Mercia. In this he succeeded, but his new archbishopric did not long outlast his reign.

The most enduring and impressive monument of the reign is the great earthwork, called Offa's Dyke, which extends over approximately seventy miles of difficult terrain to mark the English boundary on the Welsh frontier. It is notable both for the scale of the work and also for the skill with which the line it follows was made to command the Welsh lands to the west. In addition, Offa's reign was distinguished by the promulgation of a code of laws and the improvement of the coinage in support of foreign trade. After Offa, the kingdom of Mercia entered a long period of decline similar to that of Northumbria, leaving the West Saxons free to shake off Mercian domination and to continue their westward expansion into Devon and Cornwall.

By the middle of the ninth century, of the many earlier petty tribal kingdoms only Northumbria, Mercia, East Anglia, and Wessex remained. The kings of Wessex had permanently annexed the southeast (Kent, Surrey, and Sussex), they were recognized as overlords of East Anglia and Northumbria, and for a few years they annexed Mercia to their kingdom. It was the weakness and exhaustion of the other kingdoms, rather than the strength of Wessex, that transferred to the West Saxon kings a supremacy foreshadowing the political unity of all of England. With the reign of Ethelwulf (839–858), the age of the tribal kingdoms was in its last phase. Without achieving much himself, Ethelwulf was conciliatory toward other kingdoms, generous toward the Church, and mild toward his own subjects. He set an example and bequeathed ideals of kingship which were to guide the greatest Anglo-Saxon king in meeting the cruelest ordeal of the Dark Ages, the coming of the Vikings. That Anglo-Saxon England was about to enter a new phase in history is illustrated by two events in the reign of Ethelwulf. He was the first ruler in western Europe to defeat in full battle a Viking army (851), and he was the last of the tribal kings to go on a pilgrimage to Rome (855), from which, accompanied by his young son Alfred, he made a leisurely return through the more civilized Carolingian realm.

Politically, both England and the Carolingian empire on the continent were better prepared to meet the invasions than they had been during any period before the opening years of the ninth century. From Charlemagne's assumption of the Lombard crown until his death (774–814) continental Europe was relatively untroubled by civil wars or strife between nations located within the boundaries of Western Christendom. Although the tendencies toward localism were not wholly arrested, the central government was stronger during Charlemagne's reign than for centuries either before or after. In England, the wars of aggression between petty kingdoms, the monotonous theme of political history during the seventh and eighth centuries, diminished in the first half of the ninth as the ancient royal dynasties died out and the number of tribal kingdoms was slowly reduced from about two dozen to only four. Although Anglo-Saxon England had not achieved political unity, a new element in English politics can be seen in the great councils held during the period of Mercian supremacy. Under the auspices of the king of Mercia, these councils, composed of the great ecclesiastical and lay nobility of all of England, dealt with both ecclesiastical and secular affairs.

On the other hand, while political stability had been largely achieved in Europe, the economic structure and social organization of Anglo-Saxon England and the Carolingian empire in the early ninth century were not in a healthy condition to meet the strains and stresses soon to be imposed by new barbarian invasions. Most historians agree today that the economic and social decay that had begun on the continent during the later Roman Empire continued unabated during the whole Merovingian and into the early Carolingian period. In England the Anglo-Saxons inherited a Roman world that had collapsed rather than decayed, but the social and economic characteristics and tendencies in England and the Carolingian empire were in many respects similar. The main difference was that England had a less adequate central government, although her cultural development equaled that of the empire.

The greatest single element in the decay of antiquity had been the decline of the prosperity of the cities upon which Greco-Roman civilization had been built. This decline was already at an advanced stage when the rise of Moslem power in the Mediterranean during the eighth century increased the isolation of most of Western Europe from the more advanced East. Actually, trade with the East was no longer an important factor. So far as sea-borne trade was concerned, the Moslems moved into a commercial vacuum in the western Mediterranean. They used the sea for their own trade but had little to do with Christian ports. The West produced almost nothing that would interest eastern merchants. The Carolingian empire was a land power. For lack of shipping the Franks were cut off from eastern markets and were unable to conquer the fortified Byzantine outposts in western Europe which, because of Byzantine naval power, could maintain a tenuous connection with the East. The seaport towns of southern Italy remained under the suzerainty of the eastern emperor. Semi-independent Venice had slowly grown into an Adriatic power strong enough to survive attacks from the Carolingians and to keep open a trade route along the coast to Constantinople, the most important route connecting East and West until the eleventh century. Although Venice was legally a duchy of the Byzantine Empire, her doges (dukes) were elected by her people, and no Byzantine emperor was able to secure more than a token allegiance from the tiny island-republic.

With the absence of large-scale trade in the Carolingian period, the Roman cities of the West had become mere shells, city walls that contained very little inside. Their main purpose was to provide a center for ecclesiastical or secular administration of the surrounding territory. The decay of town life reached the point where the dwellings and buildings of an earlier age were cleared away and the vacant areas were devoted to agriculture by the few remaining inhabitants. Thus, the main distinction between cities and the great estates or small villages, where people of the surrounding countryside lived, was that within the crumbling walls of the decayed cities could be found a bishop's cathedral and household or the residence of a count and his officials and retainers. The bishop and count sometimes shared and sometimes disputed control of the city, but they exercised the same kind of lordship which the greater nobility of the rural areas possessed over their subordinate population.

The great majority of the people of the Carolingian period lived in the country and were supported by agriculture. This rural society was sharply divided between the nobility and the peasants. Among the peasantry there were several grades of status, ranging from pure slaves up to completely free proprietors. The tendency in most parts of western Europe was for the free peasants to be depressed to a status of economic and legal dependence upon the local nobility, and for slavery as an institution to die out because it was unprofitable when there was no large-scale export of the agricultural commodities produced. This meant that the only growing social class in Carolingian Europe was that of the semifree but economically dependent peasants who were exploited and oppressed by the more powerful local nobles. Although a strong ruler like Charlemagne could hold such tendencies in check, it was inevitable that before long the great mass of the population—just like the great mass of citizens in the later Roman Empire—lost any interest in, or the capacity to defend and maintain, the general welfare of the Carolingian empire. The capitularies of the early ninth century more and more frequently refer to "the oppression of poor freemen by more powerful persons" and to "poor men who are despoiled of their property" and who are, by such oppression, unable to perform their military service.

The effect of these tendencies upon the population of the Carolingian empire as a whole should not, however, be exaggerated. The trend in this direction had begun much earlier, and at least the Carolingian rulers tried to do something about it. Conditions under Charlemagne were better for the common man than before, and if there was less freedom there was more security. Although there is no evidence of significant economic advance in the Carolingian period, there was some growth of population, which could not have occurred in calamitous times. An Italian guest at Charlemagne's court wrote that "peace made the people multiply like ears of corn." This contemporary comment is a good summary of European conditions on the eve of the new invasions. Charlemagne had brought peace and security within Christendom, and although economic production did not increase, the people enjoyed some respite from the destruction of property and of life which characterized the turbulence of an earlier age. They were still not full participants in the direction of their society, but at least they did not welcome the invaders as had the inhabitants of the earlier Empire.

The Carolingian Renaissance

The vast political structure that was the Carolingian empire did not survive its founder by more than two generations. In contrast, the cultural achievement of the age of Charlemagne did not begin to decline until late in the ninth century. Even then the intellectual, literary, and artistic activities which the Carolingian court promoted survived in an attenuated form until, reinvigorated under more auspicious circumstances, they became the basis for the brilliant and complex civilization of the high Middle Ages.

Some modern historians have objected to the term "Carolingian renaissance" because they have considered Carolingian achievements to be mediocre compared with those of antiquity or of the twelfth and thirteenth centuries. Also, the cultural activities of the Carolingian period had a narrow base, being confined to the court and to certain monastic centers rather than spreading throughout Carolingian society as a whole. There are, however, several good reasons for calling the cultural activities of the period as a whole a "renaissance." This term means rebirth or revival. It does not emphasize creativity so much as it implies recapturing the content and forms of the literature and learning of the past, together with a new expression of these on a level higher than that which immediately preceding periods had achieved. Within this meaning of the term, there definitely was a Carolingian renaissance.

Any cultural flourishing in the early Middle Ages had, of necessity, to be some kind of a renaissance, because men of those times looked backward for the criteria of truth, for the canons of literary and artistic taste, and for the ideas and knowledge which they considered important. In the field of religious truth this is obvious. Revelation was contained in the Bible, a heritage of the past; the most important historical event, which provided the key to man's destiny throughout historical time, was the Incarnation which was part of the past. This attitude was reinforced by Christian eschatology (the doctrine of last things, the Judgment) which taught that the world was degenerating, if not soon coming to an end, and that the future was apocalyptic and full of catastrophe rather than a "brave new world." Finally, it did not surpass the intelligence of contemporaries to recognize that the achievement of both pagan and patristic antiquity was in all phases of cultural activity superior to the modest achievement of their own age.

The Carolingian renaissance, therefore, was an effort to assimilate and master the thought and modes of expression, both literary and artistic, of the past. Two conditions made this movement possible: the encouragement and sponsorship of Charlemagne and his successors; and the relative security and stability of the age, which made possible the movement of people and the communication of interests and ideas.

19   THE REFORM OF EDUCATION:
THE PALACE SCHOOL

The immediate motivation for the Carolingian renaissance was Charlemagne's desire to provide a better-educated clergy as part of his concern for the general welfare of the Church. He was not well educated himself, in fact he was not even literate, for if he could read—which is open to question—he certainly could not write. But he had an excellent mind and an insatiable curiosity. He recognized the dangers and difficulties of an illiterate clergy, especially in their role of bringing Christianity and civilization eastward into Germany. The Carolingian renaissance is intimately connected with the earlier efforts of Boniface and his disciples in the conversion of the German peoples. Thus the renaissance not only brought a renewed interest in pagan antiquity but even more in the patristic achievement of late antiquity. This Christian element in the Carolingian renaissance is not, however, the distinguishing characteristic of the movement when compared, for example, with *the* Renaissance which is conventionally considered to be the beginning of modern history. The humanism of the fifteenth and sixteenth centuries was, especially in northern Europe, a Christian humanism; in Italy the earlier humanistic movement was inaugurated by scholars whose interests were equally divided between Christian and pagan authors.

The Carolingian renaissance is unique when compared with all other periods of cultural flourishing to which the term "renaissance" has been applied because in its inception it was largely the result of the interest and driving force of one man, the ruler. Charlemagne's court was the original center of learning. Although the movement later spread to monastic centers throughout the empire, it remained dependent upon the patronage which the court of the later emperors provided. In contrast, the bases of cultural activity during the renaissance of the twelfth century were spread throughout medieval Europe, and no one political center played so important a role as did the court of the Carolingian monarchs in the eighth and ninth centuries. Again, in contrast with the earlier cultural flourishings in Italy, Spain, Ireland, and England, each of which has been termed a "renaissance," the Carolingian movement was not provincial in the sense of being dependent upon only one part of western Europe. Its focus was the Carolingian court, but its participants were drawn from every quarter of the Latin West.

Charlemagne did not legislate into existence a general or uniform system of education, but he did encourage both cathedrals and monasteries to improve and expand their facilities for the training of secular and regular clergy in scriptural study, liturgy, and religious music. The goal of Carolingian education was originally utilitarian. Education in the cathedral schools tended to be practical or vocational, restricted to the training of future parish priests or cathedral clergy whose work was in the world. Monastic education, in contrast, had a more spiritual purpose. It was intended for monks who had forsaken the world, and because of their indifference to immediate or practical results the monastery schools became centers of higher learning and of the preservation of knowledge.

Preparation for higher studies was grounded in the seven liberal arts as expounded in the textbooks of later antiquity. During the Carolingian period the seven liberal arts were divided into the two curricula which became standard for the Middle Ages, the *trivium* and *quadrivium*. The *trivium* comprised grammar, rhetoric, and dialectic; the *quadrivium* consisted of arithmetic, geometry, astronomy, and music. The former thus corresponded roughly with what we call the humanities; the latter were thought of as sciences. Music was a science because it was studied as a branch of mathematics, involving the relationships between tones. Of the *trivium*, grammar continued to be the most important discipline, as it had been in antiquity, and it continued to embrace both the parts of speech and literature in general. Of the *quadrivium*, astronomy was important because under that heading was included the calculation of dates and the making of calendars, while music was a central study for those preparing for the priesthood.

Charlemagne's grandfather, Charles Martel, and his father, Pepin the Short, had both maintained a school in connection with the central court where the sons of the nobility as well as their own offspring might be taught the rudiments of learning and what passed, in that age, for polite behavior. Charlemagne transformed the palace school into a serious educational enterprise, and from it there emanated throughout the empire new standards of education and of scholarly interest. What made possible this new influence of the palace school under Charlemagne was his determination to bring to his court the best teachers of Latin Christendom, wherever they might be found. A truly international group of the intellectual elite was assembled. Most important and influential of the scholars invited to Charlemagne's court was Alcuin of York (d.804), who was educated at the best academic center of England, the cathedral school at York where his schoolmaster had been a pupil of Bede.

Alcuin was a prolific writer. His main contribution was as a teacher and as a composer of didactic works in which little originality or profundity of thought may be discerned. But his achievement in the field of literary and theological scholarship provided the solid basis on which later Carolingian writers were to build. Late in life, Alcuin became abbot of the great monastery of St. Martin of Tours, where he devoted his last years to activities typical of the cultural interests of the Carolingian period as a whole. He wrote commentaries on the Bible, dogmatic treatises, and controversial theological tractates; he collected and directed the copying of manuscripts, adding many volumes to the monastic library; and of course he supervised the monastic school. The abbacy of this monastery was one of the most important in the Frankish realm. It was Alcuin's fitting reward for the services he rendered to Charlemagne in the years since his arrival from England in 782.

From an intellectual point of view Alcuin found his new position more burdensome than rewarding, for he had to turn to the task of elevating the cultural level of the monks in what he called his "daily battle with the rusticity of Tours." One by-product of this struggle was a reform in handwriting whose lasting influence is illustrated by the print which you are now reading. At Tours there was developed the style of handwriting called Caroline minuscule, using both small and capital letters, a system which was more easily legible than the earlier Merovingian cursive scrawl, the more elegant script of Anglo-Irish scribes, or the southern Italian hand then employed at the papal *curia*. The great majority of the important surviving works of classical antiquity were copied during this period in Caroline minuscule. After the invention of printing, in the fifteenth century, the early printers who published the works of classical authors found that the best and most ancient manuscripts of these works were the Carolingian copies written in Caroline minuscule, and in imitation of this remarkably legible writing they designed types which would reproduce as nearly as possible the appearance of the Carolingian manuscripts. This is called roman type, to distinguish it from other styles such as italics or

Merovingian cursive and Caroline minuscule. Extracts from a royal diploma of Theuderic III (c.680) and from a manuscript of Carolingian capitularies (c.825). The cursive illustrates Merovingian handwriting at its lowest stage of degeneration and is thus an extreme example; the minuscule is an average or typical example of Carolingian handwriting in the early ninth century. ARCHIVES NATIONALES, PARIS; ST. GALLEN STIFTSBIBLIOTHEK.

Transcriptions of the first two lines of each text:

Theudericus rex francorum uir inluster cum (ante dies) in nostri uel procerum nostrorum presencia conpendio in palacio nostro

Item eiusdem ut si quis sacerdotum contra constituta decretalia pre-

Gothic (black letter), and in the roman type of the modern printing press may be seen daily the modern descendant of the Caroline minuscule.

Perhaps the most characteristic and widespread work of the period was that of copying manuscripts. The purpose was to increase the number of books available for the education of the clergy, and in this work Alcuin was a representative leader of his age. It has been estimated that ninety percent of the Latin literary works of classical antiquity now extant owe their survival to having been copied in Carolingian scriptoria and preserved in Carolingian cathedral and monastery libraries. If the Carolingian renaissance had achieved nothing else than this, it would still mark a great epoch in the cultural history of Western civilization. One reason for this achievement was fortuitous, so far as Carolingian scholars themselves were concerned. By the eighth century, locally produced parchment had generally superseded papyrus, which had become too expensive to import into the economically backward western countries. Parchment manuscripts could survive the cold and damp climate of Europe far more readily than those written on papyrus, the great majority of which were preserved in Egypt.

Another important achievement of the period, in which Alcuin played a prominent role as Charlemagne's adviser on educational and religious matters, was the emendation and revision of the texts of the Bible. Jerome's Vulgate was by that time the standard version, but its universal acceptance had come slowly, and as education declined in the sixth and seventh centuries copyists made frequent mistakes which were perpetuated and multiplied by other copyists. Moreover, the provincial pre-Vulgate texts of the Bible influenced copyists in various regions so that different versions of the Vulgate began to appear. The textual tradition of the Anglo-Irish Bibles, for example, was different at many points from the Italian version of the Vulgate at that time. Alcuin led the joint efforts of a group of scholars who carefully collated the oldest available manuscripts, correcting many errors and eliminating many discrepancies. A completely uniform text of the Bible was not attained, but the so-called Alcuinian recension of the Scriptures which resulted from these labors called a halt to further scribal corruption, and in some ways it even improved upon the Vulgate as Jerome had left it.

Of the many scholars attracted to Charlemagne's court Alcuin, although not brilliant, was the most productive. Representing the final phase of Northumbrian scholarship, he helped to inaugurate the first phase of the Carolingian renaissance. Among others who accepted the patronage of Charlemagne, the most distinguished were Paul the Deacon and Peter of Pisa, both from Italy; Theodulf, from Christian Spain, who became bishop of Orléans; and Einhard and Angilbert, who were both Franks from the eastern part of the empire. In the period when the revival was under Charlemagne's direct sponsorship, Theodulf was the ablest poet and Paul the Deacon's *History of the Lombards* was the outstanding historical work. Except for Einhard, whose contribution will be discussed later, the others were active in educational rather than in scholarly or creative activity.

These men formed the nucleus of the palace school, an inner circle of the intellectuals with whom Charlemagne loved to surround himself. They spent much of their spare time engaged in discussions ranging all the way from the gravest issues of theology to amusing but trivial nonsense. The reports we have of these discussions portray a group of self-conscious dilettantes striving to imitate, or recreate what they conceived to be, the intellectual atmosphere of antiquity. Thus each took a biblical or classical nickname. Charlemagne was called David, as befitted his royal dignity, while Alcuin, who prided himself on his abundant but uninspired versification, chose the name Flaccus, after the Roman poet Horace (Quintus Horatius Flaccus). Theodulf has left an often quoted description in verse of the lighter side of the activities of this inner circle which gives us a glimpse of the personalities of the court:[1]

> And father Alcuin would sit, surrounded by youth
>   and clad in authority and years,
> Ever about to utter pious words, while freely
>   eating his fill of food with hand and mouth. . . .
> In the midst of all presides David, scepter
>   in hand,
> Dispensing huge portions to all, in order un-
>   perturbed. . . .
> And the large-limbed hero, Wibod, summoned to
>   the royal presence,
> Approaches with trembling knees, his swollen belly
>   marching afore his chest.

Such was the first generation of Carolingian scholars, those whom Charlemagne patronized and promoted. Their substantial achievement was to reform and reinvigorate education, arrest the decline of letters, preserve the literature of antiquity, and withal, enjoy themselves immensely.

20 CAROLINGIAN THOUGHT AND LETTERS

After the death of Charlemagne in 814, the patronage of the imperial court no longer played so important a role in the cultural development of western Europe. The ninth century was characterized by three main tendencies. First, there was a growing effort to understand, assimilate, and re-express the pagan and Christian heritage of antiquity. Appreciation and preservation of that heritage had been the more modest goal of the first generation of the Carolingian renaissance. Second, the most significant cultural activity shifted toward the eastern half of the empire, a shift which heralds the entrance of Germany into the main stream of Western Latin culture. And third, as the Carolingian world grew more unstable and insecure, the cathedral schools declined and the monasteries emerged as the preeminent centers of Carolingian thought and letters.

The most important field of intellectual interest, measured by contemporary standards, was theology, and the study of patristic literature was stimulated by doctrinal controversies which had already arisen during

---

[1] M. L. W. Laistner, *Thought and Letters in Western Europe* A.D. 500–900 (London, 1931), p. 329, reprinted by permission of the publisher, Methuen & Co., Ltd.

the reign of Charlemagne. Events in the East had stirred up the old issue of iconoclasm, with a new twist. Irene, then ruling as Byzantine regent for her son, had convened a council at Nicaea in 787 which obediently sanctioned an extreme iconodule statement in favor of the worship of images. The pope, Adrian I (772–795), welcomed this attack upon iconoclasm, but Charlemagne was offended by the claim of the council to be ecumenical, when the Frankish church was not represented, and also by the idolatrous doctrine that images were legitimate objects for worship. At his instigation a group of scholars composed the Carolingian answer in the *Libri Carolini*, reaffirming the position of Gregory the Great and taking the traditional middle course between the extreme iconoclasts and the extreme iconodules. Adrian was constrained, unwillingly, to accept the doctrine of the *Libri Carolini*, which therefore became the definitive orthodox statement for the Latin West: veneration of saints was approved, but not worship which was to be reserved for God alone; images of saints were appropriate in churches to remind the faithful of the holy lives and virtue of the saints and to make places of worship more attractive.

Another instance in which Charlemagne asserted his leadership of the Western Church in doctrinal matters was the endorsement by a synod, held in 808 at Aix-la-Chapelle, of the doctrine, defined a few years earlier by Alcuin, concerning the relations between the Holy Spirit and the First and Second Persons of the Trinity. According to Byzantine theologians, the Holy Spirit should be understood to proceed "from the Father *through* the Son," a concept repugnant to theologians who agreed with Alcuin's statement of the traditional Western definition of the Holy Spirit as proceeding "from the Father *and* the Son." From the crucial words of the Latin formula, this dispute is known as the *filioque* ("and the Son") controversy. The popes did not oppose the Carolingian view, which was derived from both Augustine and Gregory I, an expression that minimized any distinction between the Father and the Son in theology. But they were reluctant to press so fine a distinction at the risk of further alienating the eastern from the western half of Christendom. However, under pressure from the Carolingian theologians, supported by Charlemagne and his successors, the Frankish definition was allowed as an acceptable addition to the Creed, and in the twelfth century it was incorporated into the orthodox Latin statement of the Creed.

One other important theological controversy during Charlemagne's reign arose from the reconquered portion of Spain, where the last vestiges of Visigothic Arianism found expression in the heresy of Adoptionism. According to this view, Christ was the Son of God, in His human nature, only by divine grace or adoption. Charlemagne's theologians roundly condemned the doctrine, as did the synod held at Frankfort in 794, where the monarch presided and engaged in the debates.

Apart from their religious interest, these theological disputes have a significance for general cultural history in showing the mastery of the Latin Fathers attained by the first generation of Carolingian scholars. They restored patristic studies to the level achieved by Bede. During the reign of Charles the Bald (840–877) further advances were made. The earliest formal treatises on the problem of the Real Presence in the Eucharist were written by Ratramnus and Radbertus, two monks of the abbey of Corbie, in northern Gaul. Although both based their arguments on the writings of Augustine, each came to an irreconcilably different conclusion. It is usual to emphasize that no controversy ensued on this abstruse subject, the implication being that settlement of the dispute was beyond the intellectual reach of contemporaries. From another point of view, it is just as important that for the first time since Augustine a mystery of the faith was being treated in philosophical terms and with some originality.

Essentially metaphysical problems did not interest Western theologians so much as questions bearing directly upon Christian ethics and salvation. Thus the problem of predestination and human free will, which was revived from the new mastery of Augustine's writings, stirred up the greatest number of controversial treatises of the whole period, although this problem is no less difficult philosophically or intellectually than the Eucharistic question. The leading figure in this controversy was a Saxon, Gottschalk (d.869), the first man to apprehend the full logical consequences of Augustine's writings on grace, free will, and predestination. Gottschalk's treatises on these subjects included several views which were unorthodox and some statements which had been explicitly rejected by earlier Church councils. His most extreme doctrine was that of a twofold predestination (i.e., that God not only predestines the good to salvation but also the evil to damnation). It follows, according to Gottschalk, that the sacraments of the Church cannot save the wicked, that Christ did not die for all men but only for those predestined to salvation, and that human free will is totally inadequate even to assist in attaining salvation. Most of Gottschalk's opponents concentrated on vindicating the efficacy of free will and of the sacraments. Others launched a bitter persecution of Gottschalk, whose independent temper and rather strident personality had involved him in breaches of clerical discipline.

The theological interests of the Carolingian age were not exhausted by doctrinal controversies. Less well known but equally constructive were the continuing efforts to provide adequate commentaries on the books of the Bible, a work in which Bede and Alcuin at the beginning and end of the eighth century had excelled. A culmination of this kind of literature was reached in the compilations of two German scholars, Hrabanus Maurus (d.856), abbot of the great monastery at Fulda, and Walafrid Strabo (d.849), his pupil and abbot of Reichenau. Walafrid's *Glossa Ordinaria*, an abridgment of all patristic commentaries, became the standard reference work in the field for the whole Middle Ages.

The greatest thinker of the ninth century was an Irish refugee who enjoyed the patronage of the emperor Charles the Bald. This was John Scotus Erigena (d.877). John took part in the controversy over predestination, although contemporaries understood just enough of what he wrote to condemn it as unorthodox and to dismiss his contribution as "Scot's porridge." He was acquainted with pagan philosophy and his knowledge of Greek was sufficient to enable him to translate the treatise attributed to Dionysius the Areopagite, *On the Celestial Hierarchy.* The work was actually a late fifth-century effort by an anonymous writer to harmonize Neo-Platonic metaphysics and Christian theology. The influence of Neo-Platonism, as well as of both the Greek and Latin Fathers, is evident in John's most ambitious work, a philosophical discourse entitled *On the Division of the Universe.* John's learning, his preference for reason over authority, his effort to combine theology and philosophy, and the degree of originality he attained have made him the most interesting personality of the Carolingian period to modern historians. More important in terms of the cultural development of western Europe is the fact that no thinker of equal ability had less influence upon contemporaries or upon the future, partly because few people could understand him and partly because there was little interest at that time in speculative philosophy. When later philosophers turned to his work it was not difficult to see the pantheistic tendencies of his treatise, and it was condemned as heretical in 1225.

Even John Scotus Erigena was not wholly exempt from the dependence upon tradition and authority which characterized Carolingian thought and letters as a whole. In education, theology, and philosophy the sources of knowledge, the criteria of truth, and the range of intellectual interests were all dictated by the past. Where some independence or originality was achieved, it was usually accomplished only in the sense of applying the heritage of the past to new conditions or problems. In poetry this was especially true. The great bulk of Carolingian poetry was imitative, conforming monotonously with the models of Christian and pagan antiquity. Only when dealing with completely new conditions did some originality appear, as in Theodulf's account (already quoted) in verse of the inner circle of Charlemagne's court.

The same is true of correspondence. The personal letters which have survived from the period reveal the same imitative character, based on earlier models. But of necessity they dealt with contemporary events and interests and are therefore more interesting than most of the other writing. More than one hundred letters are extant from the pen of Lupus of Ferrières (d.862), the greatest classical scholar of the period. From these and other letters we learn much about the eager search for manuscripts, the care in copying and preserving them, the emendation and correction of texts, and the other activities of ninth-century humanists.

The most significant advance was made in textual criticism. Lupus was not content simply with accurate copies of literary works, but by collating (systematically comparing, word for word) all the available manuscripts of the same work he sought to improve the existing texts. Part of this work included systematic glossing of the texts by insertion, between the lines or in the margin, of words or brief notes to explain the meaning of difficult terms and phrases. A glossary is thus a collection of such terms and phrases with explanatory notes, extracted from the text and arranged alphabetically. Lupus' classical studies did not absorb all his energies. He was a theologian of the first rank, abbot of his monastery at Ferrières, an active adviser and emissary of Charles the Bald, and he even found time to accompany the army on more than one campaign. Despite these heavy drains on his time, his knowledge of classical literature and his literary style were unsurpassed in the whole period from the death of Bede until the twelfth century.

In the writing of history, the Carolingian period made a notable advance. The classical influence is evident in such works as Einhard's *Life of Charlemagne,* which is closely modeled on the biographies of Suetonius, even to the extent of using the same words in portraying Charlemagne as Suetonius employed in describing Augustus. Carolingian annals do not betray any significant classical influence, beyond being written in much more grammatical Latin than their immediate predecessors. In content they are a vast improvement over the miserable annals of the Merovingian age. The two outstanding works by individual historians were Paul the

Charlemagne's Palace Church at Aix-la-Chapelle: interior (ninth century). PHOTO: DR. HAROLD BUSCH.

Deacon's *History of the Lombards,* already mentioned, and the *History of the Sons of Louis the Pious,* by Nithard. While Paul wrote about the Lombard past, Nithard's narrative is a detailed account of his own age. Written in an unassuming style, Nithard's *History* combines the interest in dramatic events reminiscent of Gregory of Tours with the clear prose and remarkable accuracy associated with Bede. It is to Nithard that we owe the preservation of "the oldest extant specimen of a Romance language," the version of the Strasbourg Oath (842) which he copied down in the *lingua Romana* of his day. In the following extract the original Strasbourg Oath in Romance is is on the left and a modern French translation on the right:

Pro Deo amur et pro christian poblo et nostro commun salvament, d'ist di in avant, in quant Deus savir et podir me dunat, si salvarai eo cist meon fradre Karlo et in aiudha et in cadhuna cosa, si cum om per dreit son fradra salvar dift. . . .	*Pour l'amour de Dieu et pour le peuple chrétien et notre salut commun, à partir d'aujourd'hui, en tant que Dieu me donnera savoir et pouvoir, je secourrai ce mien frère Charles par mon aide et en toute chose, comme on doit secourir son frère, selon l'équité. . . .*

Carolingian interest in the Germanic past is illustrated by Charlemagne's unsuccessful effort to preserve in writing the old Teutonic myths and by his order that the customary laws of the Germanic tribes within his empire be written down. If this project was ever completed, the results have not survived, but the Salic Law of the Franks was re-edited and published in an official version at this time.

Carolingian art displays such a rich diversity of traditions and influences whose interrelations are so complex that generalizations are hazardous. Celtic motifs, the abstract styles of the North, Mediterranean models and the late Roman naturalistic style, contemporary Byzantine neo-Hellenistic narrative representation, and Greco-Oriental ornamentalism are all the intermixed ingredients of Carolingian manuscript illustration and decorative arts such as ivory carvings, jewelry, and bas-relief miniatures. Perhaps it is not too much of an oversimplification to say that Carolingian art differs from that of the preceding period mainly in a greater mastery of the models of late antique Mediterranean plastic art, without losing the animation and abstract quality of the earlier northern traditions. In architecture, monumental sculpture, wall paintings, and mosaics, nothing of interest or value was accomplished in the period. Charlemagne's palace church at Aix-la-Chapelle, the only surviving architectural monument, is a slavish copy of the Byzantine central-space church of San Vitale, in Ravenna. The Carolingian builders were not only dependent upon San Vitale for their design; they even had to bring the columns and mosaics adorning the walls of the church at Aix-la-Chapelle all the way from Italy.

VIII

Disintegration and Recovery in the West

Within a century of Charlemagne's death, the superficial unity which he imposed upon continental western Europe had disintegrated. The causes usually assigned for this collapse are the civil wars which disrupted and weakened the empire during the course of the ninth century, and the new barbarian invasions which threatened or pushed back the frontiers, destroyed the material wealth, and decimated the population of Latin Christendom. Both of these internal and external causes certainly contributed to the collapse, but they do not fully explain it. The new invasions would not have been so devastating, and they might even have been repulsed, if the empire had not already been sapped by civil strife and dissension. The civil wars would not have destroyed the political fabric of the empire if Charlemagne's regime had not already been suffering from basic weaknesses which were fatal to the system as soon as a severe strain was placed upon it. The new invasions were thus as much a result of the initial internal collapse as they were a contributing cause of the final disintegration of the Carolingian empire.

The basic weaknesses of the empire were its vast geographical extent, its economic backwardness, and the tendencies toward localism inherent in its political and social structure. Communications and transport, the rudimentary administrative machinery, and the military organization were all inferior to those of the Roman Empire and unequal to the task of binding together such far-flung territories. It was the greatness of Charlemagne, as an individual personality, that kept his empire intact as long as he lived; it was the fatal flaw of his system that only such a personality could preserve it.

Tendencies toward localism were accelerated by the events of the ninth century. Political and military control was dispersed among the counts and dukes, who exercised in their areas not only the powers of the former Carolingian local officials but also, more and more frequently, the powers formerly wielded by the central government. When the civil wars subsided and the invasions had finally been checked, the security and stability of western Europe were re-established, during the tenth century, on the basis of political and military decentralization. No one attempted to abolish the imperial title and dignity, but the successive partitions of the Frankish territories finally reached the point where, by the end of the ninth century, the rulers of the duchy of Spoleto and the march of Friuli, in Italy, alternately contested for the title of emperor with each other or strove to keep it from the king of Provence and the king of the East Franks. The imperial crown had become little more than the prize of warring factions among the Italian nobility.

21 THE COLLAPSE OF THE CAROLINGIAN EMPIRE: CIVIL WARS AND THE NEW INVASIONS

Except for three years before the death of Charlemagne's brother, Carloman, in 771, supreme authority in the Carolingian realm was vested in one ruler during three generations, from 751 to 840. This unity was the fortuitous result of unforseen circumstances, for succession continued to be controlled by the ancient Frankish principle of equal division among the sons of the late ruler. The problem of succession afflicted the Carolingians just as it had plagued the Roman Empire, but in the ninth century this problem was more serious to the degree that the governmental system was more primitive and personal. Disputes over the succession, and quarrels between the Carolingian kings among whom the empire was divided, led to weakening internal wars that laid western Europe open to invasion from outside.

Louis the Pious (814–840) succeeded alone because his two older brothers predeceased Charlemagne. Like his father before him, Louis assigned kingdoms within the empire to be under the nominal rule of each of his three sons. Unlike Charlemagne's plan of 806, however, Louis also provided, in 817, for the succession to the imperial dignity. He associated with himself his oldest son, Lothair, as junior co-augustus and designated heir to the title of emperor. When he became emperor, according to this plan, Lothair was to exercise superior authority over the other two brothers in matters of peace and war and on all questions affecting the whole empire. The plan of 817 was thus a compromise between Frankish custom and a new ideal of imperial unity growing up in the ecclesiastical atmosphere of Louis' court.

It is doubtful that even Charlemagne could have enforced such a scheme; under Louis it proved unworkable within a few years. Louis was intelligent, well educated, and zealous for the religious and secular welfare of his empire, but compared with his father he was weak and too often influenced by others. In many ways he was an exemplary monarch, especially in the piety which earned him his sobriquet. It was characteristic of him that one of his first acts was to banish those of his father's officials whose licentious living had given the imperial court its reputation for loose morals, though these officials had only been following the notorious example set by Charlemagne. Under the influence of ecclesiastical advisers, Louis promoted reforms in the discipline of monastic and cathedral clergy, restoring the Benedictine rule for the former and introducing a quasi-monastic life for the latter.

These constructive reforms were in the best tradition of his father's leadership over both Church and state, but Louis failed to maintain Charlemagne's ascendancy over the papacy. Although the papacy had been excluded from any role in the imperial coronation of Louis in 813, he allowed himself to be crowned and anointed again by the pope in 817. This act revived the theory which Leo III had hoped to establish and which Charlemagne had refused to countenance, that the papacy had the right to bestow the imperial crown and must therefore be superior to the imperial authority. The theory was strengthened when Louis permitted the pope to recrown his son Lothair in 823. From that date until the end of the Middle Ages, according to legal theory, "no one was emperor who had not received the crown in Rome at the pope's hand."

The rest of the reign was dominated by a struggle for power between Louis's sons. The struggle was complicated by the early death of Louis' first wife, his remarriage, and his efforts to revise the division of 817 to provide for his son by this second marriage by taking territory from his three half brothers. Each of the four sons built up a party by granting lands and privileges to likely supporters, thus weakening the central authority by strengthening the local power of the nobility. Civil war among these sons and their supporters was chronic during the last decade of the reign, as each attempted to increase his power and extend his territory. Louis occasionally took sides, but he was little more than a pawn of the rival ambitions of his children. When he died in 840, one son was already dead, but the remaining three inherited a realm confused by almost twenty years of shifting alliances, revolts, and betrayals.

Lothair (840–855) succeeded without opposition to the title of emperor, but here agreement among the surviving sons ended. Lothair's goal was to relegate his brothers to the subordinate position intended in the settlement of 817. He was supported by most of the magnates of Austrasia, Burgundy, and Italy, and also by the papacy and the ecclesiastical lords who adhered to the ideal of imperial unity. His brother, Louis the German (840–876), was king of the East Franks; his half brother, Charles the Bald (840–877), was king of the West Franks. They combined forces to reduce Lothair to an equality in fact which would leave him only the superior titular dignity of emperor, while they sought full independence for their respective kingdoms. Louis the German and Charles the Bald stood for the ancient Frankish principle of equal succession of all the sons.

Another round of warfare was inevitable. In a bloody but inconclusive slaughter known as the battle of Fontenay, 841, Lothair's ambitions were checked. Charles the Bald and Louis the German met at Strasbourg in the following year. Here their alliance was sealed by the famous Strasbourg Oath, whose significance in cultural history was noted in Chapter 7. Charles took the oath of alliance in the contemporary German vernacular so that his half brother's troops might understand him, while Louis for the same reason swore his oath in the Romance tongue then spoken by the western Franks.

Confronted by this alliance, Lothair submitted. By the treaty of Verdun, 843, the Carolingian empire was divided into three independent kingdoms, while Lothair retained the imperial dignity. Historians have sometimes referred to this partition as the remote origin of modern France and Germany. In a very elementary, geographical sense this is partly true, i.e., most of the lands of Charles the Bald's kingdom have been, in modern times, part of France, and most of the lands assigned to Louis the German have been part of (or claimed by) modern Germany. But it would be a mistake to assume that the three brothers were motivated by protonationalistic considerations. The boundaries drawn in 843 ignored linguistic, natural, or strategic frontiers (and, of course, there were no cultural or economic differences that could be distinguished by a line on a map). The strangely zigzagging boundaries were drawn, primarily, so that each brother would receive an approximately equal share of the Carolingian crown lands (the resources at the immediate disposal of each ruler), but also with some regard to including the bishoprics and the landed estates of the ecclesiastical and lay nobles who supported each of the three brothers. Of the three realms, Lothair's middle kingdom exhibited the greatest diversity of language, culture, and economic life; from a military point of view it was the least defensible. The significance of the partition of Verdun can be summed up as the final disappearance of the actual political unity of Western Christendom, although the ideal of unity survived as a basic concept in the political ideology of the West.

The next stage in the disintegration of the Carolingian empire followed the death of Lothair, who as emperor had championed the principle of unity. In 855 his middle kingdom was divided equally between his three sons. Louis, his eldest son, took Italy and the imperial title. Charles reigned but hardly could be said to have ruled in the kingdom of Provence (between the Alps on the east and the Rhone on the west, from Arles in the south to Basel in the north). Lothair II received the northern third, "Lothair's Kingdom" or Lotharingia (*Lotharii regnum*), as it was called, comprising the modern Lorraine and the Netherlands. After Lothair II died, Lotharingia was split between Charles the Bald and Louis the German by the partition of Mersen, in 870. Their successors were not content with this division of Lorraine and wasted their resources in wars intended to reunite Lothair's kingdom under either West Frankish or East Frankish rule.

By the last quarter of the ninth century the same disintegration was in fact taking place within the kingdoms of Charles the Bald and Louis the German, although each maintained a façade of formal unity in contrast

The Partitions of 843, 855, and 870

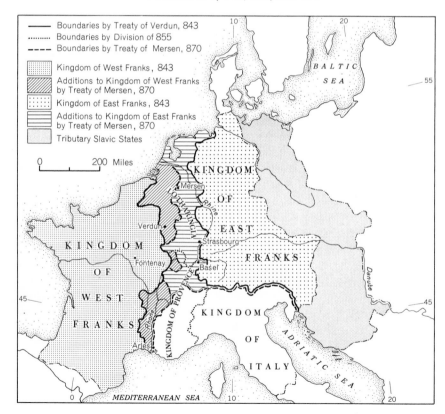

with the partition of Lothair's middle kingdom. The later Carolingian rulers all exhibited a curious, unrealistic ambition to increase the territories under their formal rule and to acquire the title of emperor, when actually they could not enforce their authority in the several regions within their realms, and the imperial dignity had become almost meaningless in terms of political power. After Louis of Italy died, in 875, for example, his uncles contested the imperial succession, thus diverting their military resources from far more important problems in their own realms. Charles the Bald was successful, and for the last two years of his life, 875–877, he was recognized as emperor. But it took an expedition to Italy to gain the empty honor, and his absence from the West Frankish kingdom encouraged the local nobility to take more of the effective power into their own hands.

Several years later only one adult Carolingian was left, Charles the Fat, son of Louis the German, who for three years (884–887) was recognized as emperor. The failure of Carolingian leadership was underlined by his pitiful ineptitude, and he was deposed by disgusted magnates of both the West Frankish and East Frankish kingdoms. The later Carolingians, known to history by their brutally accurate sobriquets—"the Stammerer," "the Fat," "the Child," "the Simple"—continued to dream of empire, to grant away their crown lands to treacherous supporters, and to squander their few remaining resources in ceaseless wars to increase their territories. Meanwhile the hard realities of contemporary politics passed them by, and the nobles who were able to meet the new problems of an age of crisis steadily gained more power over the local regions in which their landed interests lay.

The most serious problem was defense against the new invasions which began in the second quarter of the ninth century and reached a crisis about the time when Charles the Bald and Louis the German were dividing their brother's inheritance by the treaty of Mersen (870). Barbarian and heathen invaders from Scandinavia, the Vikings or Northmen, had first appeared in western Europe during the eighth century, sometimes as traders and sometimes as plunderers, as occasion might allow. Both Charlemagne and Louis the Pious were aware of the danger, and both rulers were careful to maintain cordial relations with the strongest northern kings, playing off one against another by a diplomacy calculated to neutralize their strength. Their raids were no great problem for the Carolingian empire until the quarrels between the sons of Louis the Pious had weakened the central government and diverted military resources into wasteful civil wars. The year 834 marks the beginning of incessant raids by the Vikings on the continent, and this date corresponds with the breakdown of central authority in the empire.

Other factors than Carolingian weakness were responsible for the sudden increase of raids from the north, because the continuing raids on England and Ireland began in 835, and the Scandinavian penetration east-

ward and southward into Russia reached Kiev by 839. The causes of this
Scandinavian expansion were complex, but the most important reason
was political. In Denmark especially, and to a smaller degree in Norway
and Sweden, kings were beginning to consolidate larger territories under
their rule and to maintain firmer control over a traditionally free and free-
booting population of subsistence farmers and fishermen. Petty tribal kings
and rebellious subjects were forced into exile. With greater security at
home the population grew beyond the limitations of the meager natural
resources of the land and sea. It was, therefore, a combination of population pressure and of political consolidation which provided the manpower
and the leaders for the Viking raids. The Viking chiefs were ambitious and
unruly members of the reigning or ousted dynasties who were unable to
find a place in the larger kingdoms of Scandinavia.

The New Invasions:
Vikings, Moslems, and Magyars

Viking ship (tenth century, much restored). UNIVERSITETETS OLDSAKSAMLING, OSLO.

At first the Vikings contented themselves with hit-and-run raids, striking swiftly against undefended ports or penetrating up rivers to pillage monasteries and towns. By c.850 they were plundering the coasts of southwestern France and Spain and the shores of the Mediterranean where they struck at both southern France and Moslem North Africa. Their greatest asset was surprise. They appeared without warning in swift, low-slung, oar-propelled ships, sacked a town, and departed before the slow-moving local defenses could be concentrated against them. During the second half of the ninth century, the Northmen grew bolder. Having landed on the banks of one of the greater rivers, like the Rhine, the Seine, or the Loire, they would first seize all the horses in the area and then build a semipermanent camp. From this base they would engage in an extensive and systematic devastation of the surrounding countryside. These expeditions sometimes lasted for several months, sometimes for a year or two. Such important towns as Aix-la-Chapelle, Rouen, Paris, Tours, and Bordeaux suffered "the fury of the Northmen." The Carolingians won a few local victories, but more often they bought off the Northmen with tribute.

The Moslem raids from the south, though usually on a smaller scale, were just as harrowing as those of the Northmen. The earliest attack came in 827 on Byzantine Sicily, which the Moslems conquered piecemeal and from which they launched raids upon the coastal towns of southern Italy. In 840 the Saracens captured the strategic port of Bari, and in 846 they raided Rome. Unable to breach the Wall of Aurelian, they pillaged the suburbs, including the basilicas of St. Paul's Outside the Walls and St. Peter's (also, at that time, outside the perimeter of the walls of Rome). Two years later, Leo IV (847–855) strengthened the defense of his city by repairing the main walls and enlarging fifteen towers as strong-points. Finally, he enclosed the Vatican suburb (which included St. Peter's) with a new wall, thus adding the so-called "Leonine city" to the fortified city of Rome. Meanwhile the Saracens had launched attacks on southern France, plundering Marseilles in 848. At about this time they began to occupy coastal strips permanently, either as Moslem principalities or simply as bases for more extended pillage. Of the latter the two most important strongholds were Fraxinetum, on the coast of Provence between Marseilles and Nice, and a fortress on the Garigliano river on the west coast of Italy between Rome and Naples. From the former base the Saracen "mountain goats," as they were called, ranged inland into the Alpine passes, plundering traders and travelers, and pillaging as far north as southern Germany. From their base on the Garigliano, the Moslems destroyed the monastery of Monte Cassino, in 881, and plundered the Papal States. The most effective check on these Moslem raiders was their own division by internal strife. Their leaders were often rebels against the North African rulers and were thus cut off from reinforcements. This was fortunate for Italy and southern Europe, whose Christian defenders were no less divided against themselves than were the Moslems.

Before the close of the ninth century a third wave of invasions had begun, this time from the east. The Magyars arrived in the plains of the upper Danube, taking over the area formerly controlled by the Avars, the modern Hungary. In 899 they poured into northern Italy and left Lombardy in a shambles. In the following year they began a series of almost annual raids into Germany.

22 THE FOUNDATION OF THE MEDIEVAL EMPIRE

The East Frankish kingdom was more stable than any other part of the Carolingian empire in the late ninth century. Germany had suffered less because there was less wealth to attract raiders; the nobility was powerful locally but there were fewer immunities and privileges excluding the central power; and finally, the local tribal districts were kept under Carolingian control by assigning them to sons of the monarch. Thus, on the death of Louis the German in 876, one son succeeded as king of Bavaria, another as king of Saxony, and a third son, Charles the Fat, as king of Swabia. By 882 the older sons were dead and for five years Charles reunited the whole East Frankish kingdom. This generation of Carolingians was not very prolific. Only one of the three brothers had a son who survived to manhood, and his birth was illegitimate. This was Arnulf, who was given the duchy of Carinthia in the southeast and assigned the task of defending the frontier against the Slavs. For lack of sons or nephews Charles the Fat had no other recourse than to allow the several tribal districts to revert to their previous status as duchies ruled by dukes appointed by the king.

These dukes were great magnates who represented local landed interests as much as the central government. The growth of localism in Germany centered around five great duchies: Saxony in the north, Franconia in the center, Swabia in the south, Bavaria in the southeast, and Lorraine west of the Rhine. In political and social development, Lorraine resembled the West Frankish realm where feudalism was developing as the basis for a new organization of society. The slower growth of feudalism in the other four duchies, where a tribal society persisted, has given rise to the expression "stem duchies" (Stamm or tribal duchies), but tribal unity was not so important in determining the policy of their dukes as the simple dynastic ambition to acquire power and convert the office of duke into a hereditary family possession. The German dukes of the late ninth and tenth centuries behaved much like the dukes of Aquitaine and of Bavaria during the reigns of Pepin the Short and Charlemagne, and their greater success in achieving local predominance is the measure of the decline of Carolingian central authority.

When Charles the Fat's incompetence led to his deposition in 887, the German magnates ignored the claims of the grandson of Charles the Bald, a mere boy, and instead chose as king the grandson of Louis the German, Arnulf, duke of Carinthia. He was the only adult Carolingian who had some experience with German affairs and problems. Arnulf (887–899) devoted most of his time to border warfare against the Slavs on the eastern frontier. Against the Northmen he won a great victory (891) on the river Dyle in modern north-central Belgium, after which Germany was no longer troubled by invasion from that quarter. Following this and other victories, the pope called upon him for protection against the factions in Italy whose quarrels and ambitions threatened not only the Papal States but the independence of the papacy. Arnulf made two expeditions into Italy, but he was unable to enforce his authority there even after he was crowned emperor in 896.

Arnulf was succeeded by his son, Louis (899–911), a child of six, whose reign brought the central power in Germany to its nadir. The dukes, counts, and other magnates made war on each other, each seeking to increase his power at another's expense, except when they were forced to cooperate against the Magyars. In 911 Louis the Child died. The magnates were confronted with the same problem as in 887 except that now no German Carolingian survived, of either legitimate or illegitimate lineage. Once more they refused the grandson of Charles the Bald whom they had rejected as a child in 887—he was Charles the Simple, now king of the West Franks. Instead they elected as king the duke of Franconia, Conrad I (911–918), who strove valiantly but in vain to reassert royal authority over his dukes and magnates. He allowed Charles the Simple to annex the duchy of Lorraine; he lost control of upper Burgundy, and the Magyars penetrated into the Rhineland and as far as Burgundy and Lorraine on devastating raids. If Louis the Child had been too weak to try, Conrad I tried and failed to maintain the traditional leadership of the king over the German duchies.

After Conrad's death, only the nobles of Franconia and Saxony could be gathered for the election of a new king. This was the duke of Saxony, Henry I the Fowler (919–936), so called according to later legend because he ignored the electoral assembly, and when messengers brought him the news, he was found indulging his favorite pastime of hunting. Henry reversed the policy of Conrad. He forced all the dukes to recognize him as king, but then he left them almost wholly alone and concentrated on building up the strength of his own duchy of Saxony. He repulsed the northern Slavs and pushed them eastward—the beginning of a deliberate German policy of the *Drang nach Osten*, or eastward movement. To consolidate these gains he encouraged colonization by loyal Saxons and fortified the frontier towns. Against the Magyars he also built fortifications around exposed settlements and raised a force of trained cavalry with which to inflict upon the fast-moving Magyar raiders their first defeat (933). But as king he gave no support to the other duchies under attack. Instead he used his resources to reannex the duchy of Lorraine (925), binding it to Saxony by a marriage alliance. Henry the Fowler made himself the strongest duke in Germany, founded the Saxon dynasty (919–1024), and gave Germany her strongest king since Louis the German.

Henry's son, Otto I the Great (936–973), became king by what was in fact hereditary succession although a formal election was held in accordance with custom. The dukes were quite willing to accept the son of a father who had left them largely independent. Otto continued his father's efforts to strengthen his duchy of Saxony, and he pressed forward the wars against the Slavs to the east. In all other important matters, however, Otto reversed his father's policy. He intended to rule as well as reign, to enforce his authority over the dukes and magnates, and to bind his realm into a united German nation. As soon as this became clear to the dukes, the inevitable rebellions began, and Otto spent the first five years in stamping out revolts. He tried to solve the problem of the semi-autonomous duchies by placing members of his own family in control as dukes of Bavaria, Swabia, and Lorraine and by retaining control of Franconia himself. This plan failed when his own sons joined in local rebellions against the central power, so Otto turned to the only source of support that was not irrevocably bound to local interests and family ambitions, the German church.

Otto's policy of alliance with the Church was the keystone of his power, and most of his successors continued to rely upon ecclesiastical support against the lay nobility. To be effective, this policy depended upon control of the Church, especially of the appointment of archbishops and bishops. Otto successfully reasserted the old Carolingian rights over ecclesiastical lords, wresting from the dukes whatever influence over the Church they had usurped within their duchies. In frontier districts he established new bishoprics and, like Charlemagne, considered the ecclesiastical organization of newly won territory just as important as military defense. In other ways he revived the Carolingian tradition of supporting the cultural activities as well as the material interests and the missionary work of the Church. In return Otto obtained ecclesiastical support from which he derived three main advantages. First, he could employ as officials in his government men recruited from the best educated and most able class in his kingdom. Second, the rule of celibacy which was enforced among the higher clergy prevented ecclesiastical lords from building up local family interests or hereditary lordships which in time would undermine their loyalty to the monarch. And third, he could rely upon the wealth and power of the bishops not only as a counterbalance against rebellious magnates within their bishoprics, but also to provide him with the manpower necessary for a loyal army to use against both external and internal enemies. In return for numerous grants to the Church of both lands and local privileges, Otto and his successors demanded a much heavier military service from the ecclesiastical lords than from the lay nobility.

Otto the Great had become the most powerful ruler in Europe by the middle of the century. In many respects his reign was a revival of the Carolingian system, or an adaptation of the means employed by Charlemagne to secure results which, under new conditions, were not dissimilar to the goals achieved by Charlemagne. And like his Carolingian predecessors, Otto became involved in Italy. The German court had been a refuge for political exiles from Italy as early as 945. Otto's intervention could swing the balance in the confused and petty struggles for the Italian kingship. In 951 an opportunity presented itself that was too tempting to turn down. Adelaide, the widow of one of the contestants, appealed for succor from the marriage which her archenemy plotted to force upon her in order to secure the crown for himself. Otto solved her problem by invading Italy, marrying Adelaide himself, and assuming the title of king of Italy. Contemporaries were delighted; they saw in these events a romantic episode in which the hero, Otto, rescued the lady in distress from the clutches of the evil suitor. Actually, Otto had sound political reasons to respond to this opportune appeal. Only by intervening himself could he prevent the king of Burgundy and his own overmighty subjects, the dukes of Swabia and of Bavaria, from rescuing Adelaide in order to win the throne. Control of the wealth of Italy would augment his meager revenues from the German crown lands and regalian rights. And finally, Otto was already planning to revive the imperial title, which had been vacant since 924. As it turned out, a hostile pope and rebellion at home forced Otto to abandon these plans temporarily and to return to Germany.

An aftermath of the rebellion at home was a renewal of the Magyar raids into Germany. In fact, some of Otto's rebellious magnates may have appealed to the Magyars for help against their king. Otto dealt the Magyars a crushing defeat in the battle of Lechfeld, near Augsburg, in 955, after which they never again harassed Germany. Equally important, by this victory Otto secured his lines of communication with Italy and was now ready to revive his Italian plans. His second intervention south of the Alps came in response to an appeal from Pope John XII for protection against Berengar, marquis of Friuli, who had recently won general recognition as king of Italy in defiance of Otto's assumption of that title. Otto crossed the Alps in 961, put Berengar's forces to flight, and early in 962 received his promised reward by being crowned emperor by John XII.

This imperial coronation, so reminiscent of the coronation of Charle-

The Foundation of the Medieval Empire:
Central Europe, c.962

magne in return for protection of the papacy, was the real foundation of the medieval Empire. However, both in geographical extent and in the powers exercised by Otto and his successors, the revived Empire fell short of the Carolingian model. The most obvious difference was that Otto depended upon the support of the Church. Otto's control of the Church gave him power, whereas Charlemagne's power gave him control of the Church. Also, the relations between the new emperor and the pope were by no means clear in 962, as they had been in 800. To Otto, his position as protector of the papacy meant that he had the right to control the pope just as he controlled the German bishops because he was their protector. In John XII's view, the emperor was protector only in the sense of defending the Holy See and the Papal States from enemies, while the papacy should retain its independence and its jurisdiction over both Rome and the Papal States. Before the end of the year a complete breach came when Otto demanded that no future pope should be consecrated until he or his son had approved the election. John XII refused to accept this imperial domination and was driven from Rome. He was deposed by a synod presided over by Otto. Subsequently, on two occasions Otto forced the election of his own candidates, thus setting a firm precedent for imperial control of the papacy.

Until the year before his death, Otto spent most of his time in Italy consolidating his control of the north and trying unsuccessfully to extend his power over the south. He also secured recognition of his new status from the Byzantine emperor, confirmed by the marriage of his son with a Byzantine princess, Theophano. After the substantial achievements of Otto the Great, the reign of his son, Otto II (973–983), was anticlimactic. Most of his time and energy was devoted to Germany, where he was on the defensive. He was able to suppress revolts among the dukes and magnates and to repel attacks by the Danes and the French, but the Slavs recovered the northern part of the territory conquered by his father. Toward the end of his reign he was finally free to pursue his personal ambition, the conquest of southern Italy. His attempt ended in a disastrous defeat (982), and he died a year later, leaving an infant heir, Otto III (983–1002), under the regency of Theophano and Adelaide.

The succession of Otto III was unopposed in Italy. In Germany the regency was accepted only after lengthy and tortuous diplomacy, whose success was partly owing to the now youthful emperor's indifference to German affairs, and his willingness to allow the dukes and magnates a larger measure of autonomy than they had enjoyed under Otto the Great and Otto II. Toward the papacy Otto III continued the policy of his predecessors. During the last years of his reign he enjoyed the cordial cooperation of Gerbert, his former tutor, whom he appointed pope as Sylvester II (999–1003). In contrast with his father and grandfather, Otto III conceived of his imperial dignity not simply as a titular supremacy in the West reflecting the supreme power exercised by the king of Germany and of Italy, but rather as implying a real revival of the ancient Roman Empire (*Renovatio Imperii Romanorum*). He was more at home in Italy than in the barbarian north, considering Italy rather than Germany to be the center of his Empire as it had been in the ancient world. He sought to translate the Byzantine conception of empire, which he learned from his mother Theophano, into an imperial policy embracing all the Christian West. The grandiose schemes of Christian harmony under the dual leadership of himself and Sylvester II were chimerical: they dreamed of unity under joint imperial and papal, secular and spiritual, rule over the Frankish, German, Italian, and Slavic West, but there were in fact so many irreconcilable differences that these aspirations defied reality. Otto III died childless; his only heritage was an ideal. The problems confronting the revived Empire he left unsolved.

23   THE FEUDAL STATES OF EUROPE

The contrast between Germany and France in the tenth century is striking. In Germany the kings, and after 962 the emperors, re-established political order and led the defense against the Northmen, Slavs, and Magyars. Recovery followed the fortunes of the central authority. In France the power of the kings of the West Franks dwindled steadily until the end of the tenth century, and it did not begin to increase again until toward the end of the eleventh. Recovery of some measure of political stability and defense against barbarian invaders were accomplished on a local basis. The role of the king in this recovery scarcely differed from the parts played by a dozen great lords who were his nominal vassals but who in many instances were far more powerful than the occupant of the throne. In Germany the authority of Otto the Great far exceeded that of Louis the German a century earlier; in France the authority of Charles the Bald (840–877) was not equaled by any of his successors until the twelfth century.

This weakness of the central authority in France was partly owing to a contest for the throne between the Carolingians and the Robertians. The latter descended from Robert the Strong (d.866), count of the march of Neustria, which stretched across the territory roughly between the Seine and Loire rivers. After the inglorious reign of Charles the Fat and his deposition in 887, the French magnates, like the German dukes and counts, ignored the claims of the next in line of the Carolingian family. They chose instead Robert's son, Odo (887–898), because of his heroic defense of Paris when it was under siege by the Northmen in 885. During the century following the accession of Odo, three Robertians occupied the throne at different times for a total of twenty-five years, while four members of the Carolingian family were kings for a total of seventy-five years. In their efforts to retain the crown, the Carolingians weakened the central authority still further by granting away most of the crown lands and much of their jurisdiction over duchies and counties to the local lords in return for often worthless promises of support against the Robertians. The most powerful magnate of the tenth century was a grandson of Robert, Hugh the Great (d.956), who styled himself duke of *Francia* and whose son brought the crown back into the Robertian family permanently in 987. This was Hugh Capet (987–996), founder of the Capetian dynasty which lasted in the direct line for over three centuries.

The achievements of Hugh Capet and his early successors were very modest, but they kept the monarchy alive as a political force and they arrested any further decline. One reason for the success of the early Capetians was the absence in France of large-scale and concerted rebellions, such as plagued contemporary German rulers, because the French monarchy was no threat to the interests and ambitions of the great feudal lords. The weakness of the monarchy was a guarantee of its survival. Furthermore, the monarchy could hardly grow any weaker. The Capetians could not continue the Carolingian practice of granting away crown lands in the hope of gaining supporters, for there was practically none left to grant. Nor did the Capetians follow the vain policy of the later Carolingian kings who dissipated their energies in trying to assert their authority over the whole of France and to extend it over Lorraine. With few exceptions the early Capetians were realistic enough to pursue what has been called a "domainal policy." They restricted their efforts to enforcing obedience and maintaining order within the royal domain, which had shrunk until it included only the cities of Paris and Orléans and a strip of territory connecting the two. Over this area Hugh Capet, his son Robert II the Pious (996–1031), and his grandson Henry I (1031–1060) all pursued much the same policy as most other territorial magnates of the times. They contracted advantageous marriage alliances for their children; they waged endless petty wars against unruly lesser barons ensconced in hilltop forts; and they were always ready to seize a town or occupy a fief on the slightest pretext, thus adding bit by bit to the meager royal domain. So long as the early Capetians were content to behave like any other feudal lord, and made no real attempt to enforce their obedience, the greater dukes and counts were willing to give a nominal allegiance to the king.

Despite the inadequate material resources at their disposal, the Capetians were as a family well endowed with competence, tenacity, and longevity, and with a remarkable ability to produce male heirs who reached maturity. Their dynastic record has never been matched. During the first seven generations, 987–1223, the average Capetian reigned thirty-four years. And yet, in spite of the length of their reigns, most of them succeeded to the throne as adults with some experience in government. In order to avoid a disputed succession, Hugh Capet had taken the precaution to have his son, Robert II, crowned and associated with himself as co-ruler. This precedent of crowning the designated successor before the death of the father was followed until the second half of the twelfth century, when the dynasty was firmly established on a hereditary basis. The elective principle, which seemed about to triumph in the tenth century, could not survive under such circumstances.

The early Capetians inherited certain advantages which, no matter how slight was their real power, provided a basis for future growth. The monarchy gave them prestige. They were the heirs of Charlemagne, they were kings anointed of God, they were the vassals of no other lord, and their moral authority was supported by the teachings of the Church. Also, they inherited from their Carolingian predecessors certain regalian rights which no French duke or other feudal lord could assert. Most of these rights were ecclesiastical in nature and derived from Charlemagne's control of the Church. The Capetian kings could nominate new abbots and bishops in monasteries and bishoprics founded by earlier kings or which were under royal protection. They could collect revenues arising from the lands or the ecclesiastical courts of vacant abbeys and bishoprics, that is, after the death of the old and before the election of the new abbot or bishop. These, with other rights, extended over two dozen bishoprics and three dozen monasteries both within and outside the royal domain. Finally, the feudal position of the Capetians, if it weakened their power in some ways, was also a safeguard. Any attack upon them by the more powerful magnates would destroy the sanctity of the feudal bond between lord and vassal on which the magnates, in turn, had to depend for obedience from their own vassals.

The rest of France was divided into feudal principalities, ruled by lords who were for all practical purposes independent, although most of them were royal vassals. A few were the descendants of Carolingian counts who had converted their offices into hereditary titles and their counties into hereditary fiefs; others were magnates who had risen to local predominance and had gained recognition from the king and from the lesser lords of the region. All of them fulfilled the same functions in their provinces as the king in the royal domain: maintaining a precarious semblance of order, protecting their subjects and vassals from external attack, and enforcing obedience from them.

The duchy of Normandy is an exception to these generalizations. The Northmen had begun to occupy the area around Rouen, on the lower Seine, in the opening years of the tenth century. The contemporary Carolingian ruler, Charles the Simple, was powerless to drive them away, so he ceded them the region (c.911) on condition that they become Christian and protect northern France from further Viking raids. The Normans rapidly assimilated the culture of their new home. Their ruling family assumed the title of duke, French became their language, conversion proceeded apace, the duchy expanded along the Channel coast, and feudal institutions grew precociously. By the middle of the eleventh century, Normandy had become the best organized and most orderly feudal principality of western Europe. The dukes did not achieve this result, however, without much struggle against their restless vassals, an arduous task whose success was attended by the emigration—partly caused by overpopulation in the flourishing duchy—of the more adventuresome Normans into other lands to seek their fortunes.

To the west and south of Normandy was the county of Brittany, whose half-Celtic people were no less independent of the French king but were much less assimilated to the culture of Carolingian and Capetian France. East of Brittany and south of Normandy in the valley of the lower Loire river was the county of Anjou, whose counts were descended from leaders in the resistance against Viking raids. In the eleventh century they were absorbed in quelling the violence of their vassals or expanding their domain by a singular display of ferocity.

South of Anjou and stretching across much of south-central France toward the Rhone lay the former Carolingian kingdom of Aquitaine. It

Feudal States of Western Europe, c.1032

had become a duchy in 877. At first the ducal title was held by the counts of Auvergne, in the eastern part, and then it was contested between the counts of Poitiers in the north and of Toulouse in the south. By the middle of the tenth century the counts of Poitiers had won out, and within a century they had annexed the duchy of Gascony to the south. Meanwhile the counts of Toulouse pushed eastward to the Mediterranean by conquering Septimania, now known as the march of Gothia after its earlier Visigothic rulers. These southern provinces—Aquitaine, Gascony, Toulouse, and their dependent counties—differed from the north both culturally and in the slower growth of feudal institutions. Collectively they came to be distinguished as the land of the Languedoc (from *oc*, or late Latin *hoc*, for "yes") in contrast with the northern regions of the Languedoil (from *oil*, or late Latin *hoc ille*, the modern French *oui* for "yes").

East of the duchy of Aquitaine were Provence and Burgundy: the coastal region to the south, the Rhone valley, and the mountainous regions of eastern France, western Switzerland, and the border between France and Italy. Carolingian control in this area lapsed after the death of Lothair I in 855. Lothair's son Charles (d.863) tried vainly to curb the unruly and volatile local nobles, while conditions steadily deteriorated with the advent of Saracen raiders. Then one of the nobles, Boso, organized resistance in Provence and subdued the Rhone valley as far north as Lyons. During a colorful career Boso had married the daughter of the emperor, Louis II of Italy (855–875), acquired such titles as count of Vienne and duke of Lyons, and had acted briefly as regent in Italy for Charles the Bald after the latter became emperor (875–877). In 879 Boso assumed the title of king of Provence with the acquiescence of enough of the bishops and counts to be able to defy the efforts of the Carolingians to oust him. On Boso's death in 887 the southern half of his realm passed to his son as king of Provence, while in 888 an adventurer named Rudolph made good his claim to be king of Trans-Jurane Burgundy in the north. The two kingdoms of Provence and Trans-Jurane Burgundy remained separate until about the middle of the tenth century, when Otto the Great made the united kingdom of Burgundy an imperial protectorate under the rule of his protégé, Conrad, a descendant of Rudolph.

The successors of Boso in both kingdoms were able to preserve enough order at home to indulge in desperate gambles for a foothold in Italy. One of them gained the imperial title for a few years and another won a precarious recognition as king of Italy. These ventures weakened the hold of the kings upon Provence and Burgundy so that the tendency toward localism, which Boso had temporarily checked, continued. The local counts were practically autonomous. It was by their combined efforts that the Saracens were finally routed from their stronghold at Fraxinetum in 972, thus permanently freeing the Alpine passes into Italy and Germany.

We have already seen how the whole peninsula of Italy suffered from civil strife, incessant struggles for the crown, and the raids of plundering Moslems on the coasts and Magyars in the northern plains. Recovery from the worst phase of these difficulties began when, under the leadership of Pope John X (914–928), a combined force of north Italian, papal, and Byzantine troops from the south, cooperating with a Byzantine fleet, annihilated the Saracens in their stronghold on the Garigliano river (915). Moslem raids continued throughout the tenth century and the Moslem conquest of Sicily was completed in 917, but conditions in Italy never again were so hopeless as during the period c.880–915. Petty wars between rival principalities continued until intervention by Otto the Great restored some order in Lombardy and the Papal States. Otto and his successors all failed to dislodge the Lombard, Moslem, and Byzantine rulers in the south. The turning of the tide came in the opening years of the eleventh century, when two new forces in Italian history appeared. These were the rise of the sea power of the Italian ports and the arrival of Norman adventurers who found the turmoil of southern Italy ideal for their opportunistic ambitions. After defeating the Saracens twice in defensive engagements near Bari (1002) and Reggio (1005), Italian fleets went over to the offensive by occupying Sardinia, in 1016. In the following year the Normans first appeared in Italy as mercenaries supporting an Apulian rebel against Byzantine rule. With such events a new age of Mediterranean history was beginning.

The petty states and principalities into which the Carolingian empire dissolved, outside of Germany, represent the failure of the Carolingian program of unity. In another sense, however, their achievement of local order and defense against external invasions was the basis on which the larger medieval states could grow. Most of the petty states had their origins in the late ninth and tenth centuries. By the opening years of the eleventh century they had attained internal cohesion on a local basis, and by the mid-eleventh century the rulers of these states were being drawn into relations with one another out of which the larger and more stable political units of the high Middle Ages were to evolve. The pattern was not invariable, but where feudalism was well developed this evolution was most likely to take place. Before turning to later political developments, therefore, it is necessary to consider the development of feudalism.

IX

The Feudal Organization
of Medieval Society

An understanding of feudalism is essential for a just appreciation of both the Middle Ages and also many of the ideas and values, as well as institutions, of modern Western civilization. This subject is complex, and it is beset with modern misunderstanding. The following discussion presents a simplified picture intended to stress the fundamental features and to minimize the complexity of feudal society. Much of the modern misunderstanding of feudalism can be cleared away if a few basic points are grasped at the outset.

First, feudal *institutions* should not be confused with feudal *society*. Feudal institutions are specific ways in which men have solved certain personal, proprietary, and governmental problems. A feudal society is one in which these feudal institutions are so important and useful that they dominate the social and political organization of that society. Feudal institutions may appear earlier and linger on later than the society which is properly termed feudal. Some of these feudal institutions survived into modern times, when they were anachronistic and were thus properly the object of severe criticism. But in the tenth, eleventh, and twelfth centuries the growth of feudal institutions was the most convincing sign that European society was achieving stability and was capable of further development. It is grossly unhistorical to criticize medieval feudalism simply because feudal institutions which met the needs of medieval society survived as useless remnants in modern national society.

Second, there was no "feudal system" common to all Europe. Rather, there were endless diversity and variety. The most thoroughly feudalized area was northern France, but feudal institutions spread throughout all of Europe, appearing later and exercising less influence on government and society the farther away from northern France they appeared.

Third, feudal institutions (as contrasted with a whole society which we may call feudal) involved and concerned only the upper classes—the nobility, both lay and ecclesiastic. Slaves, serfs, peasants, many men who though free were poor and unimportant, and even most merchants (some of whom were wealthy and influential) had little or nothing to do with feudal institutions. Feudalism directly concerned roughly the upper tenth of the population; or, to put it another way, the feudal institutions which dominated medieval feudal society were only indirectly related to the economic activities of the manor and the town.

Finally, where feudalism was strong, as in England and France, strong and united national states emerged, but where feudalism was weak, as in Germany and Italy, particularism resulted.

24   THE ORIGINS AND GROWTH OF FEUDAL INSTITUTIONS: VASSALAGE, THE FIEF, AND PRIVATE JURISDICTION

Medieval feudalism consisted of three closely related elements—the personal, the proprietary, and the governmental. In feudal terminology these were vassalage, the fief, and "justice" or private jurisdiction. Each of these elements had a distinct and separate origin. In the Carolingian period they began to merge, and by the tenth century feudal institutions became so closely and coherently interlocking that we may properly speak of a feudal society.

For the origins of vassalage we must turn to the turbulent conditions of the sixth and seventh centuries, especially in Merovingian Gaul where the government was too weak to preserve order and was itself the prize of warring factions. In such a predatory society the strong preyed upon the weak and the weak could only seek protection from the strong. It is not surprising, then, that in the Merovingian age there were various kinds of personal dependence. The institution which Tacitus called the *comitatus*, in which the "followers" or "companions" were attached by strong ties of personal loyalty to a war leader, continued to exist throughout the Germanic world. Among the Anglo-Saxons the king or leader is sometimes called *hlaford*, whence our word "lord," and his companions were *gesiths* or in Latin *comites*, reminding us of Tacitus' *comitatus*. Merovingian kings had companions called *antrustiones* because they constituted a personal retinue or bodyguard called the *trustis*. In addition to such armed companions there were other dependent royal retainers whose service was not military. They were under the king's special protection and were maintained in his household, where they performed either honorable or menial tasks. Such dependents also swelled the households of the Frankish and other Germanic nobility. The Roman provincial aristocracy were not unfamiliar with the personal dependence of the weak upon the strong and with conditions under which the strong protected themselves by acquiring retinues. Their armed retainers were called *buccellarii*, and like the German nobles they also had dependents whose service was not military and might range from the menial tasks of the household servant to the support and assistance of a near-equal. In Roman law the relationship was recognized as patronage or clientage, whereby the client or retainer was under the protection of his patron before the law.

Most of the growing numbers of men who sought protection and security during the seventh and eighth centuries were not qualified for the status of armed companion to a king or great noble. These men had to accept a more humble relationship of dependence, neither military nor honorable in nature. This relationship of protection and of authority of lord over man was sometimes called *patrocinium* or patronage, after the Roman legal term, or it could be expressed by the Latinized Germanic word, *mundeburdis* or *mundium*. The act by which the dependent established the relationship was called commendation, another Roman legal term.

Both lord and man found commendation advantageous. The dependent preserved his free status and secured both personal maintenance, including food and clothing, and protection. The lord increased his own security and power by gaining the service of another retainer. The mutual benefits of commendation are illustrated by a legal document of the eighth century in which the man commending himself is represented as saying to his new lord, "as long as I live, I shall give you service and obedience, befitting my free status, and will not have the power to withdraw from your authority and protection." The act of commendation was in theory voluntary. It was binding upon both lord and man until one or the other died. Men who had commended themselves were described by terms reflecting their social status or the service they performed. The *fidelis* ("faithful man") was a member of the upper classes who had taken an oath of fidelity to his lord. Armed retainers of the lesser sort were variously described as *pueri* ("the boys"), *viri fortissimi* ("strong-arm men"), *satellites* ("henchmen"), or *custodes* ("guards"). The commended man of humble status, whose service was menial, might be called a *vassus* or *vassallus*.

In the eighth and ninth centuries, this term *vassus* or vassal gradually came to denote a man who served his lord in a military or honorable capacity. The Carolingian rulers, as mayors of the palace, kings, and finally emperors, were responsible for this transformation of the character of vassalage and for a tremendous increase in the number of vassals. In their rise to power the Carolingians needed a loyal and efficient army based upon heavily armed cavalry which could move swiftly to deliver a crushing blow against local rebellions or enemies upon the frontiers. They also needed a large force of reliable officials to govern their realm. They secured both by requiring their supporters to become their vassals, thus tying to their own rising fortunes men who hoped to gain new power and position for themselves. The result was twofold: vassalage was no longer degrading for the royal vassal, whose service was so important in a military or governmental capacity; and on the other hand, vassalage emphasized the personal subordination of the royal vassal and the exaltation of the ruler who was his lord.

Until well into the eighth century great men—dukes, counts, bishops, and abbots—did not willingly demean themselves by becoming vassals. If they commended themselves to the king or emperor, the act was essentially no more than a pledge of loyalty whereby they became his *fideles* or faithful men. But the Carolingians gradually broke down this attitude. In 757 Tassilo, duke of Bavaria, was caught in a net of local political intrigue which placed him in the position of being a rebel and traitor, and he was forced to commend himself to Pepin the Short as a vassal. Again in 787 Charlemagne forced Tassilo to acknowledge his status as a royal vassal. By these submissions the Carolingian rulers intended to solve a troublesome political problem, that is, forcing their overmighty subjects to recognize their superiority. Contemporaries were shocked to witness the formal commendation of a duke not as a *fidelis* but as a mere vassal. But the significance of the intended degradation of Tassilo was just the reverse. By degrading the duke to the status of a vassal, Pepin and Charlemagne gave the institution of vassalage a higher social position and respectability. If a duke could be a royal vassal, who else could shun that status?

The proprietary element in feudalism derived wholly from Roman origins, and in its association with vassalage the Carolingians again led the way. In order to support the more expensive cavalry of their new army and to attract more vassals to their forces, the Carolingian rulers granted to their mounted vassals the use, but not the ownership, of estates with which to meet their expenses. Such an estate was a benefice, a landed property held on very favorable terms or even gratuitously. The benefice was much like the earlier Roman form of tenure known as a *precaria* and it was sometimes called by that name. In Roman law a precarial grant conveyed to the grantee the use and occupation of the property granted, while ownership remained with the grantor, for a specified period of time. By the seventh century this period was normally the lifetime of the grantee. During the eighth century lords frequently used this kind of grant to provide the maintenance which they owed to their men under the terms of commendation, including men who had the status of vassals. Such an arrangement was often more convenient than maintaining vassals in the lord's household.

Not all vassals, as yet, held benefices, but the practice of bringing the two institutions together had begun. Charles Martel and Pepin the Short, as we have seen, forced churches and monasteries to grant benefices to royal vassals. Such grants were called *precariae verbo regis* (precarial grants at the king's command). The recipient of the benefice paid a nominal rent to the church or monastery but was a vassal of the king. This situation was confusing and unsatisfactory for all parties, and by the end of the ninth century most of these benefices were held either by royal vassals as benefices of the king, or else by church vassals as benefices of a church. This tendency to unite the institutions of vassalage and benefice-holding was characteristic of the period of the disintegration of the Carolingian empire. In the tenth century it was the general rule that if a vassal held a benefice he held it of the lord to whom he had commended himself.

When this point was reached, the benefice was looked upon as the reward, the *quid pro quo*, for becoming a vassal. By becoming a vassal, a man could increase his wealth. The original purpose of the benefice had come to be reversed. At first benefices were granted because vassals performed services; now services were performed by vassals because they received benefices. Men were no longer willing to become vassals unless they were granted a sufficient benefice. As the personal and proprietary elements were bound more closely together, the bargaining power of vassals increased because lords could no longer secure supporters without granting benefices. Thus the later Carolingian rulers granted away most of their crown lands in a futile effort to retain support or gain new support. Other great lords did the same. The Robertians rewarded their followers with most of their family estates throughout the march of Neustria. This is why the Capetian royal domain in 987 consisted of little more than Paris and Orléans with a connecting strip of territory. The more powerful vassals of kings and dukes, in turn, granted benefices to their vassals. By the end of the ninth century the feudal hierarchy was beginning to emerge clearly.

At about the same time the term benefice was giving way to a new term, *feudum* or the fief. From this term the whole new social and political organization is called feudalism, a fact which reflects the enduring importance of the proprietary element. Finally, the fief became hereditary. This last development gave coherence and stability to a society whose wealth was in land and it also gave the vassals who occupied fiefs a stronger hold on that wealth. Once fiefs were recognized to be hereditary, the lord could not regain the fief so long as the service due from the vassal was performed and so long as there continued to be heirs. Heritability of fiefs first appeared in northern France, being recognized officially as a widespread custom among the higher nobility in a capitulary of Charles the Bald in 877. It took almost two centuries for the hereditary principle to spread throughout the limits of feudalized Europe and to be extended down to include the lowest subvassals in the feudal hierarchy.

The third element in feudalism was "justice" or private jurisdiction, which had two roots, one going back to Roman times and producing the negative aspect of private jurisdiction, the other going back to the chaotic conditions of the disintegrating Carolingian empire and producing the positive aspect. During the later Roman Empire, estates of the imperial fisc often enjoyed a privileged condition called "immunity" which excluded the imperial government and most of its activities from the area: no taxes were collected there, imperial officials could not enter to enforce the laws, and the inhabitants were exempted from the normal duties of Roman citizens. This kind of exemption was continued under the Merovingian kings who extended the privilege to the lands owned by certain favored churches and monasteries. These grants of immunity were confirmed by the Carolingians, who occasionally made similar grants. Moreover, immunity from the government was sometimes granted directly to laymen or transferred from churches and monasteries, the original grantees, to royal vassals when they acquired benefices from church lands. The immunist exercised within his privileged lands the authority and powers normally exercised by the government. Immunity increased during the ninth century in two ways. There was a greater number of royal grants extorted by vassals as the price of their support. Also, powerful vassals often usurped for all of their lands the immunity they had been granted for a few of their estates.

The second origin of private jurisdiction went back to the collapse of the Carolingian empire. The kings tried to strengthen the loyalty of dukes and counts by making them royal vassals. Estates traditionally set aside for the support of Carolingian officials were assimilated to the benefices these officials held as vassals. Finally, the heritability of fiefs was assimilated to the heritability of offices which were now associated with those fiefs. The office of duke or count thus became itself a fief; or more accurately, the office itself, the lands associated with the office, and the benefices held as vassal rather than as official, all merged into one hereditary fief. There was no distinction between office and landed endowment. This development was not necessarily authorized, or acquiesced in, by the kings. It grew out of the brutal necessities of the times, when the local strong man rose to power on a local scale, usurping powers which under Charlemagne had been controlled by the central authority. The existence of immunity provided, in some cases, the starting point of usurpation. Conversely, usurpation of private jurisdiction was often given a specious legality by later grants of immunity or of hereditary governmental authority. The significance in either case was the growth of feudalism, in the sense that the personal, proprietary, and jurisdictional elements had begun to merge during times which, above all, required a stable and concentrated authority within the various regions into which the civilization of western Europe had disintegrated.

25   ENGLAND AND THE CONTINENT: THE POLITICAL, ECONOMIC, AND SOCIAL CONSEQUENCES OF FEUDALISM

Although feudal institutions grew more slowly in southern France, Italy, and Germany than in northern France, nevertheless by the middle of the eleventh century an essentially feudal society had emerged throughout western continental Europe. With this continental development, England before the Norman Conquest presents a great contrast. To understand the results of feudalism, it may be useful first to examine briefly what happened in a country where a feudal society failed to develop.

As in Germany, where feudalism was a late growth, in England the monarchy took the lead in defense against the new invasions, with the very important difference that the geographical scope of the English monarchy in question, Wessex, was more like that of a continental duchy or county. At first the Scandinavian invaders were even more successful in the British Isles than on the continent. By the middle of the ninth century Vikings from Norway had established colonies on the coast of Ireland, later to be absorbed by the native population. After 835, when the Danes first appeared in England, their raids grew more extensive until by 879 the greater part of the Danish forces had settled down permanently in Northumbria, East Anglia, and the eastern half of Mercia. The area under Danish occupation, later called the Danelaw, covered roughly the eastern third of England north of the Thames. Only Wessex, though harried and pillaged by raiding armies, survived intact through the heroic defense led by Alfred the Great (871–899).

The period of resistance against Danish invasions was brought to a successful close when Alfred expelled the Danes from London and occupied it with a West Saxon garrison in 886. This was the first reconquest of territory held by the Danes; it encouraged the English to hope that under Alfred's leadership recovery of the Danelaw might be possible. In the same year as the occupation of London, a contemporary chronicler wrote, "all the English people submitted to Alfred except those who were under subjection to the Danes." This recognition of Alfred marks the beginning of English political unity. He and his successors were not merely the overlords of other kings ruling confederated and semiautonomous kingdoms, as were earlier kings like Offa of Mercia or Ethelbert of Kent. Beginning with Alfred they ruled directly over all their subjects, both in

Wessex and beyond. They were leaders in a national enterprise, first of resistance against invasion and later of a slow and hard-fought reconquest of the Danelaw. When the last great Viking leader of the heroic age, Eric "Bloodaxe," was driven from his kingdom of York in 954, the grandson of Alfred could style himself, without exaggeration, "King of the English and Ruler of All Britain."

The success of the monarchy worked against the development of feudalism. The English kings never had to strengthen the allegiance of their more powerful subjects by special ties of vassalage, nor were they constrained to ensure loyalty by granting fiefs to supporters. In military tactics they relied upon piecemeal conquest consolidated by frontier fortifications much like those used by their contemporaries, Henry the Fowler and Otto the Great, in Germany. For garrisons and field armies they relied on the obligation of all free men to serve in the royal army, while lightening this burden of universal military service by requiring only half the entire force to be active at any given time. Since neither the Danes nor the Anglo-Saxons fought on horse (horses were employed only for rapid movement of infantry troops), the English kings were not dependent upon the mounted knight, the typical vassal of the continent. The rudimentary lease-

England, c.886

hold tenure, or benefice-holding, used by the Anglo-Saxons was never directly associated with the performance of military service by the tenant, as the continental fief normally was.

The strength and prestige of the monarchy were so great that grants of private jurisdiction were a rare privilege, limited almost wholly to monasteries and churches. The normal machinery of local government remained under the authority of the king, and the reconquest of the Danelaw provided the opportunity to introduce reforms that made local government more effective and more amenable to royal control. The king's local representatives, called reeves, were put in charge of new local districts into which old Wessex and the newly reconquered Danelaw were divided. Larger districts were the shires, under shire-reeves or sheriffs; the shires were composed of smaller territorial units called hundreds or, in the Danelaw, wapentakes. The novelty of this system and the need for constant vigilance over the recently conquered and potentially rebellious Danish areas led to such close royal supervision that ambitious local lords had little chance to usurp the functions of local government. Commendation and lordship were common enough in English society at this time, but this was primarily an economic and social relationship which the kings were able to keep from interfering with the subject's allegiance to the crown. The kings not only accepted lordship but found it useful as a political device by which they could enforce their subjects' appearance in court and their fulfillment of legal obligations by holding their lords responsible. Finally, the reconquest of the Danelaw extended English rule over a people whose primitive institutions were characterized by a large degree of equality and freedom, not at all congenial with the growth of feudal institutions. Most important of all, however, was the failure in England of the personal, proprietary, and jurisdictional elements—each essentially feudal in form—to combine into a coherently organized feudal society. The ordinary subject in England might be under the lordship of one person, hold his land either freely or by paying rent and performing services to a second person, and owe suit to a public court or to one in the hands of a third person. Compared with the mergence of feudal institutions on the continent, which concentrated men's interests in a close-knit set of relationships, the obligations of society in England were diffused, and the political, economic, and legal interests of one individual might easily conflict.

Under strong leadership, the Old English state could possibly have been held together, but the first disputed succession to the crown and the advent of an incompetent king, Ethelred the Unready (979–1016), revealed its weakness. Events in Denmark—consolidation of the kingdom under a strong ruler and the consequent ousting of chieftains and nobles who could seek power only in foreign adventure—led to a resumption of Danish raids in the west at about the time when Ethelred became king, and England soon proved to be the easiest prey. Because of the doubtful legality of his succession, Ethelred could not count on the loyalty of the important men and higher officials of his government. Partly for this reason, and partly owing to his own ineptitude, Ethelred was unable to coordinate the military resources of the kingdom. In a desperate move to gain time to build up his forces, he adopted the expedient that some of the later Carolingians had employed as a last resort: purchasing peace from the Danes. In 991 a treaty with the invaders provided for the huge payment of 22,000 pounds of gold and silver. To raise this sum, Ethelred levied a heavy tax on land, the Danegeld, which further alienated his subjects.

Meanwhile the character of the Danish expeditions was changing from annual raids under leaders of the second rank into a full-scale and systematic war of conquest under the direction of the king of Denmark. This was Swein, who in one great campaign in 1013 conquered England and annexed it to his Danish kingdom. Shortly thereafter, Swein was succeeded by the greatest Scandinavian ruler of the age, Cnut (or Canute), who combined the kingdoms of England, Denmark (1019), and Norway (1028) in one great northern empire. Cnut's reign (1016–1035) inaugurated the spread of Latin Christian culture into the Scandinavian world, for he allied himself with the Church in return for its support. The first king of England since Alfred to make a pilgrimage to Rome, in 1027, he was the first Viking to be "admitted into the civilized fraternity of Christian kings."

The stability of Cnut's reign in England brought a generation of peace after thirty years of war. The unity of the Old English kingdom was strengthened by the fact that as a foreign conqueror Cnut was not influenced by regional interests. His alliance with the Church strengthened the central government, which was already strong enough to assess and collect the only national tax on land being levied in western Europe at the time. The Danegeld (sometimes also called heregeld) was continued, in all essentials, as a tax for the support of Cnut's standing army of personal retainers, the housecarls. Our earliest unequivocal evidence of a royal treasury and chancery comes from this period, but it is probable that Cnut created nothing new and merely preserved the institutions of government as he found them. Cnut's conquest was an essentially military operation, not a migration of people as in the earlier colonization of the Danelaw. Old English society remained largely unchanged until its superstructure was swept aside by the Norman Conquest later in the century.

On the continent, in contrast, the growth of feudalism continued to transform society. The most notable feature of this development was the concentration of political, economic, and social power in the hands of a comparatively small nobility of lords and vassals. The most feudalized region was the land stretching north from the Loire and east to the Rhine. In this region direct local government was in the hands of the lord (seigneur, viscount, castellan, etc.) of each district. The typical seigneur was the vassal of a count, marquis, or duke, and was thus a subvassal of the king. He might have, himself, from a half-dozen to two dozen vassals. The local court, the former Carolingian public court, was now a feudal court whose suitors were the seigneur's vassals. In many cases these vassals were the descendants of the more important people in the district who, as semi-professional judges called *scabini*, had constituted the earlier public court. In the seigneur's court disputes concerning land were adjudicated and criminal law was administered. The seigneur presided, but his vassals were the judges; it was the seigneur's duty to enforce the judgment which they delivered. Vassals who were litigants before the court, of course, did not participate in the collective judgment of their co-vassals or peers. Also, this collective judgment by peers had nothing to do with the origins and nature of trial by jury; judgment by peers was essentially a feudal principle; the jury was in its origins a royal administrative device that developed much later.

The feudal court was also a meeting place for deliberation, when the lord took counsel with his vassals over questions of policy, and for ceremonial occasions such as the performance of homage to a new lord or by a new vassal. By this act the feudal bond between lord and vassal was publicly acknowledged. Attendance at the lord's court (called suit of court; those who attended were called suitors) was an obligation rather than a right. The vassals were required to attend because the lord could be sure of their loyalty only so long as they were willing to take part in the work of the court and thus bind themselves to its decisions, the most important of which concerned the waging of war. Suit of court was thus the counterpart of the most important obligation of all, military service, on which each seigneur relied not only to serve his own lord but also to promote his own ambitions.

The amount of military service owed by a vassal varied from region to region, and within the same region it would often vary in accordance with the size or value of the fief. In each individual case there was an understanding between lord and vassal as to the service due, and sometimes the terms and conditions of this service were strictly defined—including a stipulated number of days in the field, so many days spent in the garrison of the lord's castle, or the right of the lord to additional service at the lord's expense. Failure on the part of the vassal to perform the required military service was punished by forfeiture of his fief. Thus the vassal's material interests were united with his fidelity to his lord. The development of feudalism produced results that were the reverse of the original intentions of the Carolingians. They had tried to buttress their political authority as rulers by adding the personal loyalty of vassals to themselves as lords; this policy finally ended with the fidelity of vassal to local lord replacing the political allegiance of subject to ruler.

So important was the military service due from each vassal that, before fiefs became hereditary, children and women were not allowed to be vassals. Later the custom spread by which the lord acknowledged their right to inherit but resumed control of the fief during the minority of the heir or, in the case of a widow or heiress, controlled the marriage to ensure that the husband was loyal and capable of performing military service as the new vassal. Other feudal customs grew up defining the rules of inheritance, transfer of fiefs, and certain rights of the lord called the incidents of feudal tenure. These latter included the right of the lord to hospitality (or to be lodged by his vassal during his travels) and to financial aid on such occasions as the knighting of his eldest son or the marriage of his eldest daughter, or for a ransom to redeem him should he be captured in war. These customs varied in their details from region to region and from barony to barony. By the end of the tenth century feudal customs had almost everywhere replaced the older tribal laws. Feudalization was thus a reversion from the principle of personality of law to a territorialization of law; but unlike the territorial law of antiquity, feudal custom was not legislated by the state. It grew up slowly from the necessities of the everyday relations between the lords and vassals of fiefs.

Feudalism re-established political order on a local basis following the collapse of the Carolingian effort to stabilize Europe on a universal basis. And yet the "blood and iron" age of feudalism was chaotic and confused. Contemporary chronicles are filled with accounts of endless petty wars. Each lord sought to enlarge his territory and increase his power, and each vassal sought to climb higher in the feudal world by defying his lord at an opportune moment and acquiring more vassals for himself. It has been said that feudalism "would have been a very excellent device if it had been administered by archangels." In other words, theory and practice diverged, in the tenth and eleventh centuries, even as they do today. But feudal strife should not be exaggerated; armies were small, wars were local, and fighting rarely extended beyond the summer months. The feudal age knew no total war, no genocide, no mass destruction of life or property—all characteristic of a more modern civilization. In a world where violence and hardship were normal, where the danger of invasion was perennial, rather than recurring from one generation to another as in the twentieth century, feudal lords and vassals accomplished much without benefit of archangels and without being angelic themselves.

The economic results of feudalism were both beneficial and detrimental to the standard of living and to the material well-being of the total population. Economically, feudalism meant specialization of a rudimentary sort. The noble and fighting class did not produce, and the producing class for the first time since the later Roman Empire was not expected to divert its energies into making war. Because the peasants and the lower ranks of the free men constituted the overwhelming majority of the population, a much greater labor force was, under feudal conditions, available for production. But under feudalism commerce, or the movement of goods, was impeded by the numerous local tolls imposed by lords within their seigneuries and also by the insecurity of travelers and merchants whose property was frequently plundered by the more lawless feudal nobility. Merchants who needed freedom of movement had no place in feudal society. Security and social position could only be obtained in the local hierarchy of lords and vassals.

In the eyes of the feudal nobility merchants were no better than peasants, for they neither waged war nor governed people. The social values of the early feudal world were restricted wholly to the relations between lord and vassal, and they served to rationalize the relationship in terms which emphasized the lord's rights and the vassal's obligations. Loyalty was the highest social ideal. The further development of medieval civilization depended in part on the eventual triumph of this ideal over the actuality which was so often characterized by ambition, treachery, and violence. Already in the ninth century, when Carolingian vassals were bargaining away their loyalty to the highest bidder, the ideal is expressed in a letter written by a noble lady to her son: "May the madness of infidelity be ever far from you; may evil never find such a place in your heart as to render you unfaithful to your lord in any matter whatsoever." More of the future lay in such pious injunctions than in the turbulence of the early feudal world.

26   CORRUPTION AND REFORM: THE CHURCH IN FEUDAL SOCIETY

> Cities are depopulated, monasteries are in ruins and ashes, and the country is reduced to a wasteland. Every man does what pleases him, despising the laws of God and man and the ordinances of Holy Church. Some monasteries have been destroyed by the heathen, others despoiled of their lands. In those which have survived the monastic rule is no longer observed, and there are no longer any legitimate superiors, because of the domination of monasteries by lay abbots with their wives and children, and with their soldiers and dogs.

Thus the bishops and abbots of the archbishopric of Reims viewed with alarm the conditions of their own age while meeting together in a provincial synod in the year of grace 909. It was a healthy sign. When the situation had really been hopeless, in the seventh century, Church councils had ceased to meet and churchmen had ceased to criticize abuses because corruption had become the normal and accepted condition of the Church. The prelates of 909 gave an accurate analysis of contemporary difficulties. They deplored the material destruction, the violence, the encroachment on ecclesiastical lands, and secular control, which were the four greatest dangers confronting the Church during the disintegration of the Carolingian empire and the growth of feudalism.

Churches and monasteries suffered severely from the violence and destruction wrought by civil wars and barbarian invasions because they offered the greatest concentrations of booty with the least adequate defense against plundering expeditions. Where the Vikings settled down, as in Normandy and the Danelaw, Christianity was wiped out. The heathen conquerors were slowly converted during the course of the tenth century, but the organization of the Church had to be rebuilt almost entirely from the ground up. The diocesan administration of western Normandy in the mid-eleventh century still resembled that of the frontier missionary work on the eastern borders of Germany.

Far more serious was the danger from involvement in secular affairs during the period of disintegration. The higher clergy played an active role in later Carolingian politics and usually supported whoever stood for the unity of the empire or of the kingdoms into which the empire had been divided. In their espousal of the ideal of unity, the bishops and abbots who engaged in political activity were supported by the popes. One result of the break-up of the empire was the brief emergence of the papacy as the supreme representative and champion of the unity of Western Europe, a role that the secular rulers forfeited by their jealousies, civil wars, and general incapacity. Nicholas I (858–867) established important precedents for later medieval popes by successfully asserting his independence of imperial influence, his right to judge all secular rulers in matters of morality, and his universal authority over the Church.

Nicholas found it easier, however, to overawe the shadow-emperor Louis II (855–875) and to force king Lothair (855–869) to give up his mistress and take back his wife, than to control the higher clergy of the kingdoms north of the Alps. Supremacy over the Church depended upon the support of a strong emperor, but a strong emperor would subordinate the papacy to the role assigned it by Charlemagne. Nicholas saw an escape from this dilemma in an alliance with the Frankish bishops against the growing claims of the archbishops or metropolitans. These archbishops were led by Hincmar, archbishop of Reims (845–882), who stood for spiritual leadership of the weakened secular power and for metropolitan control of the episcopate. The majority of the bishops were unwilling to concede to the metropolitans any superiority beyond a higher dignity, such as the right to preside over provincial synods. The bishops' claim for substantial independence of metropolitan control had precedent on its side, but to strengthen the episcopal position an anonymous compiler produced an elaborate collection of papal decretals, the so-called "False Decretals," c.850. In the collection authentic decretals were mixed with wholly forged or interpolated ones whose general purpose was to demonstrate that bishops were subject to the papacy rather than under metropolitan authority.

Actual conditions in the late ninth century were no better suited for the survival of central authority in the spiritual than in the secular sphere. Nicholas I had little more than his personal ability and an ideological justification to support his wide claims. As the power of the emperors declined, imperial protection against the vicissitudes of local Roman politics disappeared, and the papacy became once more the prize of party strife in Rome. To survive at all, the popes had to become leaders of factions and to incur the risks of factional struggle. The turning point was the pontificate of John VIII, after whose murder in 882 fifteen popes came and went during only thirty-two years. Most of them gained the pontifical throne through crime or intrigue and vacated it by deposition, exile, or assassination.

Some stability was recovered under John X (914–928), the ablest pope of the period. A man of many talents, he distinguished himself by leading the army which drove the Saracens from their stronghold on the Garigliano river in 915. He was the only pope during the first third of the tenth century who could match the influence and circumvent the plots of the ambitious and quarrelsome local Roman nobility, chief of whom was an unscrupulous magnate named Theophylact who assumed the title of "Senator of the Romans." After Theophylact's death under doubtful circumstances, power passed to his widow, the notorious Theodora, and her daughter Marozia. Current scandal connected each of them with a half-dozen popes in the capacity of mistress, or mother, or murderess. In this period, its nadir of corruption and degradation, the papacy was little more than the spiritual puppet of the local tyrant Alberic, son of Marozia, who controlled Rome for twenty-two years (932–954). Secularization of the papacy was completed when Alberic's son and successor as tyrant became pope himself, as John XII (955–963). His misbehavior and difficulties finally led to intervention by Otto the Great in 962, with consequences that have already been noted in Chapter 8.

One of the fascinating contrasts of medieval culture is the survival and influence of the ideal of universal papal spiritual authority despite the ugly facts of nearly a century of decay and corruption in the institution itself. Closely parallel is the transcendence of the ideal over the actuality of Empire. For both the imperial and papal tradition, Rome was still the supreme symbol. This sway over men's minds and emotions is illustrated by a tenth-century pilgrim's song, written perhaps when the tyrant Alberic ruled Rome as a petty principality and treated popes as his private chaplains. It remains the noblest expression of the grandeur and dignity of the Eternal City:

> *O Roma nobilis, orbis et domina,*
> *Cunctarum urbium excellentissima,*
> *Roseo martyrum sanguine rubea,*
> *Albis et virginum liliis candida. . . .*

[Oh noble Rome, mistress of the world,
Of all earthly cities most excellent,
Resplendent in red with blood of the martyrs,
Shining lily-white with the virtue of virgins. . . .]

Throughout Latin Christendom secularization and corruption affected the Church at all levels of the hierarchy in much the same way as the papacy had been degraded. Bishops and abbots were the pawns of the local nobility; ecclesiastical property was exploited, if not confiscated, for secular ambitions. The one great difference between the papacy and Church offices north of the Alps was that the latter were drawn into the feudal reorganization of society. Local lords forced their children or vassals upon churches and monasteries as bishops and abbots; or, to assure the loyalty of ecclesiastical officials, they required bishops and abbots to become their vassals. Thus bishoprics and abbeys were treated as fiefs from which were expected the same services and obligations as lay fiefs, even including military service. Warrior bishops and fighting abbots were not uncommon, although occasionally they would employ a mace instead of a sword, in deference to the canonical prohibition against the shedding of blood by the clergy.

During a vacancy, the church office and property were resumed into the hands of the lay lord who collected the revenues therefrom just as he dealt with a fief held in wardship because of a minor heir. The successor did homage to the lord, and in the case of a bishopric he received from his lay lord the staff and ring which were the symbols of episcopal office. This lay investiture was assimilated to the ceremony by which any vassal received his fief from his lord. The feudal relief, the payment made by a new vassal to his lord when he did homage, was often exacted at the time of lay investiture of episcopal or abbatial office. Such payments were considered by feudal lords to be important and legitimate revenues, but they were in fact clear breaches of the canonical injunction against simony, so called after Simon Magus who was rebuked by Peter for attempting to purchase the power of the Holy Spirit. Simony infected the clergy everywhere; the basic reason for its existence was not feudalism but rather the degradation of ecclesiastical discipline and the great wealth of the Church which attracted covetous lay lords and ambitious prelates alike. Control of the wealth of the Church became a necessary basis of political power in every region. Feudalization of Church property went even further among the lower clergy because marriage of priests and hereditary succession to parish churches were more common than among the abbots and bishops. Under such conditions corruption of the secular clergy spread to the regular clergy until monasteries were as often centers of indolence and license as of worship and discipline.

Ecclesiastical reform began as a revival of the monastic ideal. The reform movement was not confined to any one locality, but leadership in

The Abbey Church of Cluny, c.1030 (reconstruction). DRAWING BY PROF. K. J. CONANT, REPRINTED FROM SPECULUM (JAN. 1954).

the movement was associated with a newly founded Benedictine monastery, Cluny, in French Burgundy near the borders of the kingdom of Trans-Jurane Burgundy. Cluny was established in 910 by the duke of Aquitaine whose foundation charter was designed to ensure freedom, both from feudal entanglement and from subordination to the bishop of the diocese, by exempting the monastery from all secular obligations and placing it directly under the supervision and control of the papacy. Since the far-away and corrupt papacy was at this time hardly able to influence events beyond the Alps, this freedom made reform possible. It was accomplished by the dedication of the Cluniac monks, led by a fortunate succession of distinguished and able abbots. The first six abbots ruled Cluny for a total of two hundred years. At first their only goal was to restore the Benedictine rule in the monastery at Cluny and thus provide a model of monastic discipline and religious life. The reform spread when Cluniac abbots were called upon to reform other monasteries and to found new houses. The essentially conservative character of the movement was now given a radical new development, when the Cluniac reformers introduced a "congregational system" according to which all reformed monasteries or new foundations were affiliated as priories with the mother house of Cluny. Thus the abbot of Cluny exercised absolute control over a growing number of monastic centers of reform. These ultimately reached over two hundred in number and stretched across all of Europe. The reform spread into the ranks of the secular clergy when secular rulers began to appoint Cluniac monks as bishops.

There were other reform centers in the tenth century which were not institutionally connected with Cluny. The most important were in upper Lorraine, where monastic reform was promoted by the bishops, and in England where monasticism had almost disappeared during the Danish wars. Under the patronage of the kings, English reformers founded new monasteries in the ravaged Danelaw and re-established decayed houses with new endowments. Their work was so extensive and it had so important an effect on the secular clergy that it has been characterized as "the tenth-century reformation" in England. The guiding spirit of this reform movement was Dunstan, archbishop of Canterbury (960–988), who reinvigorated the Church in England on the eve of the conquest by Cnut.

The goals of the reformers were essentially threefold: to elevate the moral standards of the clergy; to restore monastic discipline; and to abolish simony. In this program the Cluniac leaders generally received ample cooperation from secular rulers who valued the movement as an element of stability in their kingdoms and principalities. They began to rely upon the reformed Church for recruiting trained and competent administrators in the growing feudal governments. It was from the reforming impulse and from the patronage of reform by local feudal rulers that the earliest efforts grew to limit the turbulence of the feudal world. Before the tenth century had closed, in Aquitaine and Burgundy several diocesan and provincial synods had anathematized military operations on the lands of the Church and of the poor. Their decrees solemnly pronounced that noncombatants (the clergy, women, children, and peasants) should be inviolate in time of war. Such regulations, endorsed by local rulers, were collectively called the Peace of God. The movement spread, and in the early decades of the eleventh century the Peace of God was reinforced by what was called the Truce of God, according to which military operations were to cease on Sundays and other Church festivals. Ultimately, the Truce of God extended from Thursday evening until Monday morning of each week as well. The Peace of God and Truce of God did not endure beyond the eleventh century as effective checks to feudal warfare, but they did discourage irresponsible fighting when such discouragement was most needed. They also gave an excuse to greater lords to limit the feuds among their vassals and they helped nourish the fundamental idea that peace and order should be the normal condition of Christian society.

The Medieval Manor

In discussing feudalism we have been concerned with about ten percent of the total population of Europe in the tenth and eleventh centuries. Feudalism was essentially a political organization of society in terms of the personal, tenurial, and jurisdictional relationships among the important people who controlled the new feudal states of Europe and the fiefs into which they were divided. The great bulk of the population were peasants who had nothing to do with feudalism except to support the military and clerical classes by their agricultural labor. The typical peasant was a serf who worked with his hands; the typical noble was a vassal who fought as a mounted knight and, usually, was the lord of one or more manors which constituted his fief.

The village was the normal unit of medieval peasant population and of medieval agrarian economy. However, the village was by no means the only type of settlement. In the more backward and less fertile areas, which could not support a large population, scattered independent farmsteads or small hamlets were the rule.

The administrative unit of medieval agrarian economy was the manor, which may be defined as the human and other economic resources (especially the land) that were under the jurisdiction and economic control of one lord. Often the village and the manor coincided, in that the village was entirely in the hands of one lord; frequently, however, one village was divided into two or more manors, or a single manor consisted of two or more villages, hamlets, or farmsteads.

In its agricultural activity and even in its manorial organization, the medieval village was in some ways similar to the late Roman great landed estate, or *latifundium*. In the more Romanized parts of western Europe the latter evolved into the medieval village, and each could be described by the more general term, *villa*. The most important difference between the ancient and the medieval *villa* was the result of profoundly changed conditions in the world in which they existed. Agriculture in antiquity was an enterprise for profit as long as the flourishing cities provided a market for food. With the decline of trade and industry in the early Middle Ages, cities declined proportionately. The market for food practically disappeared, and the urban manufacture of goods declined. Industry and trade, and the circulation of money on which they depended, never wholly disappeared, although the medieval *villa* normally produced only enough for its own population and became almost wholly independent of outside sources for its consumption of goods. The village became for all practical purposes a self-sufficient economic unit. This situation was not altered until the revival of trade in the twelfth century fostered the growth of towns and reestablished a market for surplus production of food.

27 EARLY MEDIEVAL AGRARIAN ECONOMY: THE VILLAGE

Early medieval society was relatively far more rural and agricultural than modern American society is urban and industrial. Before the twelfth century perhaps ninety-five percent, or even more, of the population lived in the country. Trade and industry had declined until almost the only form of wealth remaining was land. The economy was therefore overwhelmingly agrarian, and a description of economic life must concern primarily the resources and activities found in the typical economic unit, the village. Villages were of various sizes, ranging from a population of less than a score of families to several hundred families. The agricultural pursuits of the peasantry varied from region to region depending upon the fertility of the soil and the natural resources available. In mountainous, forested, or marshland areas the methods of husbandry, as well as organization and size of population centers, had to be adapted to exceptional conditions. Any brief description of the medieval village must ignore these many differences and deal with what was typical or normal in the districts where the soil was rich and the population was dense.

The predominant physical feature of the typical village was the arable land surrounding the cluster of huts and cottages where the peasants lived. This land was ordinarily divided into two open fields whose size might vary from less than a hundred to more than a thousand acres. The fields were "open," that is, not fenced off into separate plots or tenements, because husbandry was necessarily a cooperative effort. No single peasant was wealthy enough to own a whole plow team of eight oxen, and few peasants owned plows, but by combining their oxen and plows the villagers could cultivate large fields jointly with greater efficiency than they could farm small plots with their individual resources.

The open fields were divided into blocks whose shape was dictated partly by the contour and drainage of the land and partly by the fact that the blocks, in turn, were divided into a number of strips. The length and breadth of the strips were determined by the requirements of plowing with a large team of oxen. Ordinarily, a strip was as long as the team could continue a sustained effort in pulling the plow without rest. This varied with the strength of the oxen and the condition of the soil. In northern Europe it averaged about 220 yards (the length of a furrow, or furlong). The width of a strip was ordinarily about sixteen and a half feet (a rod), the distance dictated by efficiency in turning the plow at the end of a furlong under the customary system of plowing successive furrows alternately on either side and outward from the center of each strip. A greater width would have required too much time and effort in turning the team to resume plowing on the other side of the strip. Four such strips made up approximately one acre: four rods in width and a furlong, or forty rods, in length. The modern acre is thus derived from the approximate area which a medieval team could plow in a normal day's work, four strips in the open fields.

The arable land of the village was divided into two fields so that fertility could be preserved by rotation. Each year the field in use was planted about half with autumn-sown winter wheat, to be harvested early in the following summer, and the other half with spring wheat, to be harvested in the fall. The other field was allowed to lie fallow after the harvesting of spring wheat in the fall until it was planted with autumn-sown winter wheat in the following year. The fallow field was plowed twice to help it recover fertility, and when not being plowed it was used as an additional pasture for animals, thus providing feed for the animals and fertilizer for the soil.

The annually recurring pattern of open-field husbandry for the majority of medieval peasants may be summarized as consisting of six operations, beginning in the fall: (1) harvest of wheat planted the previous spring in the first field, which then lies fallow; (2) autumn planting of winter wheat in half of the second field; (3) planting of spring wheat in half of the second field; (4) late-spring plowing of the first field; (5) early summer harvest of winter wheat in the second field; and (6) midsummer plowing of the first field. The following year repeats this pattern with the fields reversed, the second field being fallow after the harvest of spring wheat planted in the third operation listed above. The cycle of open-field

Heavy wheeled-plow. Manuscript illustration (thirteenth century). BIBLIOTHEQUE ROYALE DE BELGIQUE.

cultivation was broken twice each year, once during the winter when field work was impossible and once after the midsummer plowing of the fallow when all villagers turned to haymaking in the meadow, a task which was usually completed by August 1.

Under this system of two-field rotation a village with a total of 600 acres of arable land required 900 acres of plowing, as may be calculated from the foregoing summary of operations, to produce 300 acres of grain, the basic food crop. The yield was very small, whether it is measured against the amount of labor or the proportion of seed to harvested grain. Weather conditions and other variable factors caused great variations in the yield, but on the average, in northern Europe, about two bushels of seed were sown to produce approximately eight to ten bushels of wheat per acre. An average sowing of about one bushel of seed produces approximately twenty-five bushels of wheat on a modern midwestern American farm. One of the many reasons for the low yield was that the medieval peasant scattered his seed by hand. Every planting was thus a race between the soil and the birds to germinate or devour the broadcast seeds. The medieval yield was not so poor, however, when compared with that of antiquity or of early modern times. Not until the eighteenth century did the adoption of more scientific methods substantially increase the ratio of two-to-ten from seed to harvest.

There were other methods of increasing the total production of grain which did not depend on improving the yield as measured against the amount of seed planted. During the ninth, tenth, and eleventh centuries three improvements in agricultural technique appeared in northern Europe which mark a permanent advance over Roman methods of cultivation. The first was the wider use of the heavy plow (known earlier in a few regions). It was mounted on wheels and could turn the richer and heavier soils of the northern river valleys. Such soils could not be cultivated with the light Roman plow adapted to the drier Mediterranean soils. The heavy plow was later equipped with such refinements as an iron plowshare to cut into the earth and a moldboard to turn over the sod.

A second innovation appeared first in northern France and spread slowly wherever conditions permitted. This was the division of the arable land into a three-field rotation, which increased production while decreasing the amount of plowing. With three fields in rotation, one lying fallow each year, 600 acres required a total of 800 acres of plowing to produce 400 acres of crops—a gain of one third in grain production and a decrease of one ninth in plowing. The three-field system had other advantages. It permitted a shorter time for plowing of the fallow field so that the plowing and planting of the two fields in use, as well as lesser jobs like harrowing and weeding, could be spread more evenly over the year. But despite these advantages, the two-field system remained the most widspread in medieval Europe, and it was supplanted by three-field rotation only in the most fertile districts. Three-field rotation tended to exhaust all but the best soil, it afforded less grazing area on the fallow field, and it could not be used effectively in drier climates where the growing season was shorter.

The third improvement over ancient agricultural practice, the introduction of horses instead of oxen in plow teams, was closely associated with the three-field system. Horses had to be fed grain as well as the hay and fodder on which oxen lived, but horses did not need so much pasture. As draft animals their advantage was in their greater speed. Fewer teams were needed to plow the same area, and the same number of teams could plow far more rapidly so that changing weather conditions were less hazardous. Horses could not be used for plowing until three technological improvements made their appearance. In antiquity horses were harnessed as draft animals by a thick leather strap passing around the neck, an arrangement which threatened the horse with strangulation every time it tried to use its full strength. By the tenth century the modern horse collar had been adopted, by which all of the horse's power was exerted against a stiff padded collar resting well down on its shoulders. The second improvement was the use of horseshoes, thus increasing traction and permitting the use of horses on stony soil which injured the feet of oxen. The third improvement was the development of tandem harnessing so that any number of horses, one before the other, could be used to pull the plow. In antiquity horses were harnessed side by side, a method which decreased efficiency with the addition of each horse to the team. Horses never wholly supplanted oxen. They could be used economically only in conjunction with three-field rotation which produced more grain. They were not so strong as oxen and could not be used on the heavy clay soils. And they were more liable to disease.

The open fields which produced the main crop of grain were the most important single part of the village. Each peasant's holding consisted of a number of strips scattered throughout the fields in such a way as to equalize the holdings in terms of accessibility and of fertility of the soil. In addition to his strips, each peasant possessed a small plot of ground surrounding his hut from which he could supplement his basic diet with garden vegetables and where he could keep a few chickens or cultivate fruit-bearing shrubs and trees.

Keeping the plow beasts and other animals alive was essential to the survival of the human population. Every village had to have a meadow from which sufficient hay could be mowed to feed the oxen during the winter. In the spring and summer animals grazed on waste land and pasture which, like the open fields, were used in common by all the villagers. After the harvest of crops and haymaking, the fields and meadow were opened to the oxen so they could forage from stubble and scattered bits of grain. These sources of feed were not always adequate, especially during a bad year. When it appeared that because of a shortage of fodder the oxen or cows could not survive the winter and be strong enough for spring plowing, the villagers enriched their diet by slaughtering animals in the fall. The regular meat supplement for the human diet was pork obtained by slaughtering the half-wild pigs which roamed about in the woodland of the village, where they eked out a tough and stringy existence on acorns and beechnuts. If larger pastures were available, herds of sheep were kept to provide milk, cheese, and wool. Sheep were not eaten unless their survival over the winter was in doubt. The medieval peasants' meat diet of pork and occasional beef and mutton was incredibly unpalatable by modern standards. It had a strong gamy flavor and was usually too tough for complete mastication, even when smoked and salted for consumption during the winter. But it was an important source of fats in northern Europe where butter was scarce and vegetable fats, like the olive oil of the Mediterranean area, were unobtainable.

Woodland was also important as the main source of both fuel and building materials. Each villager took his proportionate share of dead wood and undergrowth, but trees were felled only for special purposes and at a rate which did not exceed normal growth unless the village were in a region of abundant forests. In that case the forest might be systematically cleared in order to add to the arable land of the village. Other assets common to most villages were a pond or stream from which fish were caught, a mill for the grinding of grain, roads and paths, and a common oven for baking bread. Grain was consumed in liquid form as ale or beer, the standard beverage except in wine-making regions. Water was considered—quite correctly, considering the lack of sanitation—to be unhealthful. Although thin and weak, medieval beer had a sufficient alcoholic content to be far safer than milk or water for human consumption.

Almost every village had a church or chapel. The parish normally coincided with the village. The church was endowed, for the use of the priest, with a holding or glebe consisting of strips scattered throughout the open fields and a share in the meadow, pasture, and woods just like any other peasant tenement. Although personally free, the priest usually participated in the husbandry of the village and was himself a peasant.

A village of any consequence would, finally, have a more substantial house set apart from the peasants' huts. This was the residence of the lord —or if more than one lord had possession of part of the village there might be more than one lord's residence. This house was called, originally, a manor. Because the village was thought of as belonging to the lord's residence and under the jurisdiction of the court held in his hall, the term manor was extended to embrace the village over which the lord had proprietary and jurisdictional rights. It then became usual to refer to the lord's residence as his manor-house or hall, and to the village as his manor.

28   ORGANIZATION AND CONTROL OF AGRARIAN EXPLOITATION: THE MANOR

The manorial organization of medieval villages was the result of a slow evolution from two quite different points of origin—the Roman *villa* and the Germanic village community—an evolution which proceeded at different rates of growth in various regions. In the ninth century the manor had already developed many of its typically medieval characteristics in parts of Italy, eastern France, the Rhineland, and southern Germany. Manorialization came much more slowly in other regions, appearing in England as a fully developed institution only after the Norman Conquest of 1066 and in Denmark later still. Some parts of north-central Germany and southwestern France were still incompletely manorialized in the later Middle Ages, and the manor never developed at all in parts of the Netherlands and Scandinavia. Even in the countries where the manor developed completely, there were marked differences between the manors of different regions. An introductory sketch of the manor, like that of the village, must ignore these differences and emphasize characteristic features commonly found in the most thoroughly manorialized parts of Europe.

The essence of the manor is the subordination of the peasantry to the lord of the manor. In the evolution of the Roman *villa* the most important development toward manorialism was the gradual disappearance of slavery and the assimilation of most dependent tenants to a status resembling that of the *coloni* of the late Roman Empire, personally free but bound to the soil as an hereditary caste of peasant laborers. Slavery was an economically unsound method of exploiting human labor when there was no large-scale export of foods. Even in antiquity slave labor was inefficient and flourished only so long as the Roman wars of conquest provided a cheap source of slaves. The great landowner of the late Roman and Merovingian periods found it to his advantage to emancipate slaves and settle them on his estate as dependent cultivators. At the same time the poorer free peasant proprietors found it advantageous, or even essential for mere survival, to put themselves under the protection of a great landowner by giving up title to their land and receiving it back as economic and legal dependents of their new lords. These dependent cultivators, whether they were themselves former slaves or formerly free—or whether descended from slaves or free men—began to be referred to as serfs in documents of the Carolingian period. The essence of a serf's condition was his personal dependence on (or subordination to) the lord of a great landed estate. The serf was thus neither a free man nor was he a slave, but he was definitely unfree.

In the evolution of the Germanic village community toward manorialism, the starting point is not the economic power of a landlord but the political authority of the local chieftain of the village whose position was recognized by the customary gifts from the free villagers. The Germanic village community was originally independent in its agricultural life, which was entirely communal and ruled by custom rather than directed by the chieftain. Although slaves and half-slave freedmen were known in Germanic society from the earliest times, the typical members of the village were free peasants. In the evolution of the community toward manorialism the most important development, beginning soon after the invasions of the fifth century and continuing into the Carolingian period, was the depression of free men to the status of dependent peasants, tied to the soil and subject to the authority of a local lord who protected them in return for their economic support.

In the ninth century the evolution of the Roman *villa* and of the Germanic village community had merged into the growth of the manor. The legal notions underlying the Roman development and the role of the peasant community in the German development had become assimilated, in greater or lesser degree from region to region, until throughout most of the central part of the Carolingian empire the manor had become the typical unit of economic administration. Then with the disintegration of central government in the ninth and tenth centuries the economic control of the manorial lord was enhanced by the addition of local jurisdiction, or political authority, exercised over the peasants of the manor. Whether this jurisdiction originated in a grant of immunity or resulted from local usurpation, by the eleventh century every lord of a manor had his court. The manorial court was the heart and core of every manor.

In the following description of a medieval manor, the economic rights of the lord will be outlined first. Then we shall consider the jurisdictional rights of the lord by which, ultimately, his lordship as well as his economic rights were made good. Despite the endless variety of manorial organization, there were certain almost universal characteristics of the medieval manor and it is with these primarily that we shall here be concerned.

The most prominent feature of every manor was the division of the open fields of the village, or of the part of the village which comprised the

Harvest Scenes. Manuscript illustration (late twelfth century). LANDESMUSEUM, BONN.

manor, between the lord's demesne and the tenements of the peasants. The lord's manorial demesne was the part reserved for himself, not occupied by the peasants but made productive by their labor. In extent this demesne of the manor averaged about one fourth to one third of the arable land, though it might vary from nothing to more than one half in exceptional cases. The demesne was usually intermixed with peasant tenements, being scattered like them in strips throughout the two or three open fields. The basic obligation of the peasants was to plow, plant, and harvest the demesne for the lord. The ordinary peasant—the serf or villein of the eleventh century—fulfilled this duty by what was called "week work" and "boon work," that is, during most of the year devoting three days a week to cultivation of the demesne, and during the harvest season giving all of his labor to the demesne before harvesting the crops from his own strips. This rule applied to all ordinary serfs or villeins who held uniform tenements in the open fields.

On many manors there were peasants who were free men although they held tenements within the manor. From these free tenants lighter services were required and in some instances no labor on the demesne was due. Other peasants possessed smaller tenements than those of the ordinary serfs and villeins, and they were lower in personal status. Such peasants can be classified into three different groups. There were slaves, still to be found on some manors, who spent all their time and labor on the lord's demesne. There was a higher peasant class of cottars or cottagers, who also held no strips in the open fields but who worked on the demesne in return for their huts and gardens. And there were peasants who held less than the ordinary tenement in the open fields—sometimes these peasants were called half-villeins when they held half the number of strips of the ordinary peasant. In return for their tenements they performed half the service of the ordinary villein on the lord's demesne. Peasants of this last group often hired out their services either to the lord or to other peasants, and with the profits of their labor were sometimes able to rise to the status of a full villein.

Except for the free tenants, none of the peasants—villeins, half-villeins, cottagers, and slaves—had any legal rights against the lord of the manor. To the modern mind it seems a reasonable question to ask why such varied classes of peasants were not all subjected to as many labor services as it might please the manorial lord to exact. The only answer supported by contemporary evidence and opinion is that the force of custom was as great as the will of the lord. In a rough-and-ready way the labor exacted from the peasantry corresponded approximately with the personal status and the size of the tenement of each peasant.

The demesne of the manor included more than merely the lord's part of the open fields. Part of the meadow, for example, was in the demesne—but not necessarily a physical part, like the lord's strips in the open fields. The demesne of the meadow usually consisted of a certain fraction of the hay produced and an equivalent proportion of the grazing rights after haymaking was finished, these rights being measured in terms of the number of the lord's animals allowed to graze. In like fashion, the demesne extended over the pasture, the woodland, the waste, the stream or pond, and other so-called "appurtenances" of the manor like the mill, the oven, and the roads. The demesne right of the lord varied from a proportionate share to full ownership, subject to the customary use of the peasants.

In return for such customary right of use, the peasants, again according to the personal status or according to the various sizes of their tenements, owed to the lord certain services or payments. They had to make hay for the lord and carry it to the lord's barn. The lord's oxen or other animals had entry to the pasture freely, but the peasants were often required to pay small sums for their use of the pasture or else provide a shepherd to keep the animals. Peasants who had use of the woodland paid an annual sum called pannage, in proportion to the number of pigs they were allowed to have forage therein. They were required to produce the lord's proportionate share of dead wood and undergrowth and to fell timber for the lord's use.

Various fees or services or proportionate shares of the product were exacted from the peasants for their use of the waste land and the stream or pond. Ordinarily, the mill and the oven of the manor were owned completely by the lord. Peasants were required to render a proportion of the flour ground and the bread baked and they were prohibited from using any other mill or oven but the lord's. In northern France, such monopolies were called banalities, a term derived from the *bannum* of the Carolingian rulers which meant a command that could not be disobeyed. This is evidence of the local assumption of public authority by the lord of the manor over his unfree peasants.

The list of peasant payments and services is not yet complete; nor is the origin of many of the additional services and dues known. For example, villeins or serfs on many manors owed a dozen eggs to the lord on Easter (the origin of our modern Easter eggs), while half-villeins paid a half-dozen eggs, and cottagers three eggs. At Christmas on some manors each peasant owed his lord one goose, on other manors some other payment in kind such as beeswax (for candles) or honey or feathers (for arrows) or cheese. In addition to such payments, the peasantry of most manors owed to their lords a variety of services like carrying or carting crops and timber when required and those called *corvées*, such as maintenance of roads, paths, and bridges and cleaning or digging of drainage ditches.

All the foregoing services and payments have a direct relationship with the lord's control of the economic activities of the manor. In addition, the lord's personal rights over the peasants as subject to his will were represented by a variety of other payments, which constituted a substantial part of his manorial revenues. The most important were the heriot, a customary fee exacted by the lord on the death of a serf or other unfree peasant, and merchet, which was a payment for permission for the daughter of a serf or villein to marry a man who was not the lord's peasant. Both payments were usually in kind, that is, in produce or cattle rather than in money. The liability for these two payments later became the crucial tests in legal actions as to whether an individual was a free tenant of the lord or an unfree peasant. On all peasants—even including the free men in many instances—fell the arbitrary manorial tax called tallage, or *taille*, which the lord theoretically could exact at will and in any amount. In practice tallage was restricted to a customary payment taken at more or less regular intervals, and assessed in proportion to the extent of the tenement or the amount of movable wealth of the individual peasant.

Since the typical lord of a manor was a vassal who spent much of his time serving his feudal lord or else hunting or otherwise amusing himself, and since many manorial lords were great men—kings, dukes, margraves, counts, viscounts—whose interests and duties hardly allowed time for attention to their manors, manorial administration and enforcement of the lord's complex and diverse rights were ordinarily entrusted to an official representing the lord and residing permanently in the manor. In Carolingian times this official was called the *villicus* or *maior* (mayor) of the manor. Later he was more commonly called the bailiff or steward. He was assisted by a subordinate official chosen from among the peasants, the provost or reeve, who supervised the agricultural activities of the peasantry.

Enforcement of the lord's jurisdiction over the peasants rested ultimately on the force which the lord, as a member of the military and feudal aristocracy, could bring to bear on his peasants. But for all ordinary disputes among peasants, questions of obligations and duties to the lord, and maintenance of the tranquility and productivity of the manor, the court held in the hall of the manor house was the normal resort. Over this court the bailiff, as representative of the lord, presided and gave judgment. But the law enforced in such a court was the custom of the manor, the local rules and regulations handed down from generation to generation within the village community. Thus the arbitrary aspect of manorial lordship was tempered by a recognition of the communal life of the peasants. The medieval manor continued to be, as it had begun, a balance between the proprietary and jurisdictional rights of the lord and the customs of the village community.

PART THREE

POLITICAL, ECONOMIC, AND CULTURAL REVIVAL OF THE TWELFTH CENTURY

PART THREE, illustration:
Norman Knights. From the Bayeux Tapestry (c.1077). THE BAYEUX TAPESTRY,
ED., SIR FRANK STENTON, PHAIDON PRESS, LONDON.

The Medieval Empire and the Rise of the Papacy

During the eleventh century the medieval Empire attained the height of its power. The emperors ruled a larger territory, had at their disposal greater resources, and were served by a more highly developed administrative system than any contemporary ruler. Developments took place in the nature and role of the Empire that seemed to justify the belief expressed by a later historian that it was "an institution divine and necessary, having its foundations in the very nature and order of things." When one recalls how Otto the Great and John XII, as very temporary allies in what was hardly more than just one more Roman brawl, founded the medieval Empire in 962, and when one scrutinizes the means of aggrandizement used by the emperors, it is tempting to take the opposite view, that the Empire was but "the product of an almost fortuitous chain of historical circumstances."

The slight foundations on which the imposing edifice of the medieval Empire was built were revealed when the emperor's control of the German and Italian church was contested by a reformed and revived papacy. By the middle of the eleventh century the ecclesiastical reform movement inaugurated by the foundation of Cluny and promoted by the majority of secular rulers, including the emperors, not only pervaded the whole Church but had been given aggressive leadership by the reformed papacy. Ironically, the emperor Henry III, under whom the Empire reached its zenith, had forced upon the Roman factions and the Roman church the very reform that ultimately led to the decline of the Empire.

The initial struggle between the Empire and the papacy, usually referred to as the "investiture struggle," lasted almost half a century (1075–1122) and left each party to the conflict weakened both in material resources and in prestige. The supreme spiritual authority and the highest secular authority in medieval Christendom had exhausted each other, and in so doing had lost their leadership in European developments. The expansion of Europe, the economic revival of towns and trade, the rise of the feudal monarchies, and the quickening of intellectual interests and cultural activities were all developments in which neither the Empire nor the papacy played a predominant or controlling role. When the contest between Empire and papacy was renewed in the second half of the twelfth century, it became a simple struggle for power. In this struggle the papacy finally triumphed because it had re-established its leadership and influence over the new conditions of the renaissance of the twelfth century.

29   THE MEDIEVAL EMPIRE AT ITS HEIGHT

The eleventh-century emperors were confronted with four continuing problems of major importance. These were the problems of succession to the crown; the need for strengthening the imperial government; the effort to achieve a territorial stabilization of the Empire; and relations with the spiritual authority in the several parts of the Empire (and later, relations with the papacy).

The first problem arose with the unexpected death in 1002 of Otto III, who was a youth of twenty-two years, without a direct heir. An election was now necessary, but the influence of the hereditary principle can be seen in the choice of the nearest kinsman of the Saxon line, the duke of Bavaria, Henry II (1002–1024). Henry's main qualification for the crown was his devotion to the reforming party in the Church. Otherwise, his Bavarian interests did not appeal to the northern Germans, and his connection with the northern house of Saxony alienated many of the southern German nobility. His first years as emperor were spent in putting down the usual rebellions among magnates who had gained substantial independence under the absentee emperor, Otto III.

The problem of succession was raised again when Henry II died without an heir. The successful candidate this time was Conrad II (1024–1039), duke of Swabia and founder of the Salian dynasty of emperors. He was supported by the antireform party within the German church. Like his predecessor, Conrad II devoted several years to stamping out rebellion and consolidating his control of Germany. Although the great lay nobles shared

Conrad's indifference or hostility to ecclesiastical reform, they were even more opposed to Conrad's effort to increase his power. The great nobles had secured for themselves a hereditary position in their offices and for their estates but had opposed the tendency toward hereditary fiefs among the lesser nobility, their vassals. Conrad became the champion of the hereditary principle and thus of the lesser nobility, as against the greater magnates who sought independence from imperial authority. Further, whenever a duchy became vacant by failure of heirs, Conrad granted it to his own son to hold by hereditary right. Every duchy except Saxony and Lorraine had come into the hands of Conrad's heir by the end of the reign. As a final precaution, Conrad within his own lifetime secured the election of his son as king of Germany. Thus the hereditary principle was once more firmly established.

Conrad's successor was Henry III (1039–1056), the first emperor to succeed to the throne without having to devote the early years of his reign to suppressing rebellion. The Salian emperors succeeded each other, from father to son, until a century after the accession of Conrad II when the line became extinct with the death of Henry V in 1125. The hereditary principle was so strongly established that it survived a regency of ten years (1056–1066) during the minority of Henry IV.

After succeeding to the crown, the next problem of the eleventh-century emperors was that of strengthening the imperial government. No satisfactory solution was ever achieved. Partly this was because the resources of the Empire were too meager to be stretched across the vast area from Lorraine to the Slavic frontier and from the Baltic to central Italy. Failure was also owing to the inconsistency of the policies of successive emperors whose efforts tended to cancel out the gains of preceding reigns. Henry II reversed the policy of his predecessors by almost ignoring Italy in favor of consolidating his position in Germany. He appointed churchmen to most of the important administrative positions. Government improved in quality, and the fact that the clergy could not pass on their offices to heirs increased imperial control of the administrative system. However, Henry's piety and his zeal for reform (which earned him canonization as Saint Henry) led him to grant away a large proportion of the resources of his government in the form of landed endowments for churches and monasteries. He was also generous with grants of various revenue-producing royal rights (*regalia*) such as market-tolls and jurisdiction over royal forests. By 1024 the crown lands had shrunk and the administrative system depended upon ecclesiastics in high office, many of whom were sincere reformers. As the successful candidate of the antireform party, Conrad II could hardly continue the policy of Henry II. Instead he recovered alienated royal domain wherever possible—both crown lands and regalian rights—and transferred control of the administration from ecclesiastics to a new bureaucracy recruited from low-born, often servile, men. These new officials, called *ministeriales*, were completely dependent upon the emperor's patronage, since they had no wealth or position other than what they gained in imperial service.

Henry III pursued both of his predecessors' policies without gaining the full advantages of either. Henry supported and used in his administration ecclesiastics of the reform party; but he alienated much of his royal domain in support of further reform. He also continued and even increased the use of *ministeriales*; but he no longer championed the lesser nobility against the greater nobles whom the *ministeriales* antagonized. Henry III's policy seemed to work well during his own lifetime. The imperial government was in fact never so strong either before or after his reign. But his success sprang not from his policy or his personal ability so much as from his impressive inheritance: all but two of the duchies plus other large fiefs; a new and well-trained corps of *ministeriales*; and a German church whose higher officials, ignored in Conrad's government, were happy to cooperate with a new ruler who would support their aspirations. His government, based upon a professional but servile civil service plus the cooperation of the clergy, antagonized both the greater and lesser lay nobility who could see no advantage for themselves in such an arrangement. Henry III's system, like that of Otto the Great, depended on the cordial cooperation between the emperor and churchmen under imperial control of both Church and Empire.

The territorial problem of the Empire had two interrelated aspects: first, the territories brought under the rule of the emperor; and second, the concept of "empire" as it was influenced by the territorial nature of the Empire. On the eastern frontiers Poland and Bohemia and the Magyar state of Hungary had, toward the end of the tenth century, been consolidated under rulers ambitious to be recognized as kings, to be wholly independent, and to recapture lands occupied by Germans east of the Elbe and in the upper Danube valley. Henry II maintained friendly relations with his royal brother-in-law, St. Stephen (997–1038), who ruled Hungary and had received his crown from Pope Sylvester II in 1001. Bohemia was torn with anarchy and presented no threat. But Boleslav the Brave (992–1025), duke of Poland, aimed at the union of all the western Slavs under his rule. Henry II fought a long series of campaigns, finally driving Boleslav out of Bohemia, but elsewhere Boleslav's conquests were so impressive that he was able to obtain the title of king in the last year of his long reign.

Conrad II was neither related to Stephen of Hungary nor sympathetic with the saintly king's religious policy. Conrad followed his peremptory demand for homage by an invasion of Hungary in 1030. Stephen successfully resisted, thus preserving the independence of his kingdom from the Empire. Then Conrad intervened in the kingdom of Poland, which after Boleslav's death had been stripped of Slovakia (by Hungary), Moravia (by Bohemia), Pomerania (by Denmark), and Ruthenia (by Russia).

This "partition of Poland" was finally ended when the Polish ruler did homage to Conrad for his kingdom in 1031–1032.

Henry III finally brought all three of the eastern states under the suzerainty of the emperor. Poland, divided by civil war, was reduced to the status of a duchy held by its ruler as an imperial fief. Bretislav I, duke of Bohemia (1034–1055), had set out to conquer the Slavic lands that would justify recognition of Bohemia as a kingdom. Henry crushed these ambitions by forcing Bretislav to give up his conquests and do homage for his duchy as an imperial fief. Hungary, after the death of Stephen, was the prize of several claimants whose struggles invited German intervention. Henry was able to place a pro-German contender on the throne, in return for which the kingdom was held as a fief of the Empire. The eastern frontier was now stabilized. The duchies of Poland and Bohemia and the kingdom of Hungary were all imperial fiefs held by rulers who had done homage to Henry III.

On the western borders of the Empire an even more impressive territorial settlement resulted in the acquisition of the kingdom of Burgundy, consisting of the older kingdoms of Provence and Trans-Jurane Burgundy now reunited under Rudolph III (993–1032). Being childless, Rudolph had provided for the inheritance of his kingdom by his nephew, the emperor Henry II, but Henry predeceased Rudolph. Conrad II then urged his own claims, both as successor to Henry II and because his wife was a niece of Rudolph. The unruly nobility preferred another nephew of Rudolph, the count of Blois and Champagne, under whom they could anticipate a mild and ineffective rule, but Conrad II took possession of the kingdom and in two years had defeated the count's bid for the succession.

The significance of the union of the kingdom of Burgundy with the Empire was twofold. By securing the western passes of the Alps, it protected Italy from French intervention, a danger brought home to Conrad in 1024, when the anti-German Italian nobles had offered the imperial crown first to Robert II, king of France, and then to the duke of Aquitaine. Second, in a more general sense the union marked the transition of the concept of "empire" from that of a dignity to that of a territorial bloc. The earliest document in which the medieval phrase "Roman Empire" occurs in a territorial sense, meaning the three kingdoms of Germany, Italy, and Burgundy, rather than in the Carolingian or Ottonian sense of the highest secular authority, is dated 1034. Hitherto, "empire" had been a word that could be dissociated from any particular territories, as exemplified by the recent appeal to the king of France and the duke of Aquitaine. Henceforth, "empire" was to be a territorial concept meaning the kingdoms that were united as one political unit under the emperor and passed as one bloc by hereditary succession to the new emperor. This territorial stabilization was given further expression when Conrad, during his own lifetime, had his son Henry consecrated "king of the Romans," a title which from then on designated the heir who, as co-ruler of the kingdoms of Germany, Italy, and Burgundy, was the emperor-elect.

Henry II and Conrad II devoted most of their time to problems north of the Alps. Henry had visited Italy briefly three times, and Conrad spent two years there climaxed by his imperial coronation on Easter Day, 1027, a memorable event attended by two royal pilgrims, King Rudolph of Burgundy and King Cnut of England and Denmark. Except for one more visit late in his reign Conrad neglected Italy, so that the Italian nobles regained much of the unruly autonomy they had enjoyed before the intervention of Otto I. During this period the papacy once more fell under the control of the Roman aristocracy. At first the Crescentii dominated Rome and installed three puppet popes in succession. Then, in 1012, the count of Tusculum seized power and gave the papacy to his able brother, Benedict VIII (1012–1024). Benedict cooperated with Henry II in ecclesiastical reforms, but his heart was rather in leading the armies against Saracens in southern Italy. He was followed by two more Tusculan popes, his brother John XIX (1024–1032) and his nephew Benedict IX (1032–1048), under whom the papacy once more declined amidst charges of scandal and corruption. In 1044 the Crescentii drove Benedict from Rome and later installed their nominee, Sylvester III (1045). But the Tusculan faction returned to power and reinstated Benedict IX. Then Benedict shocked even the disillusioned Roman populace by ceding the papacy to a wealthy archpriest whose ambition was to use his fortune in reforming the Church. He took the name of Gregory VI (1045–1046), presenting Europe with the spectacle of a pope opposing such abuses as simony, himself accused of simony. The situation became completely confused when Benedict IX reasserted his apostolic claims and returned to Rome. For several months the three rival popes occupied the city while mobs reduced the streets to anarchy with their riots in favor of one or another of them. Benedict IX held out in the Lateran palace; Gregory VI converted the basilica of Santa Maria Maggiore into a fortress; and Sylvester III held St. Peter's and the Vatican.

At this point Henry III intervened to strengthen his control of Italy and to extend to the papacy itself the reform that he had sponsored in Germany and the control he exercised over the German prelates. Most reformers welcomed the emperor's intervention. Peter Damiani, an ardent reformer, compared it with Christ driving the money-changers from the temple in an allusion to the simony of which all three rival popes were accused. In three successive councils, the most important of which was the Synod of Sutri in December, 1046, Henry prohibited simony throughout the Empire and deposed Sylvester III, Benedict IX, and Gregory VI. On Christmas Day the emperor completed his task when his own nominee, the German bishop of Bamberg, was elevated to the throne of St. Peter as

Clement II. Clement was the first of four successive German popes nominated by the emperor, dependent upon imperial support, and freed from the debilitating influence of local Roman factional strife.

30   THE HILDEBRANDINE REFORMATION
OF THE PAPACY

Henry III's triumph in reforming the papacy and freeing it from Roman factions did not satisfy all reformers. The venerable Odilo, abbot of Cluny, applauded the imperial reform program, but other reformers feared that the emperor was making the Church a department of the secular government. This was the view of a little band of dissident clerics who accompanied Gregory VI into exile. In this group was kept alive the ideal of papal supremacy over a reformed Church free from secular control. Gregory stood for all the specific reforms of the Cluniac movement, but he went beyond the Cluniac program in emphasizing reform of the entire hierarchy (not merely monastic reform) and the necessity of papal leadership. The leading spirit and soon the dominating personality among reformers who held this view was the young monk and chaplain to Gregory VI, Hildebrand of Soana. Because of the final triumph of this program, the period is called the age of Hildebrandine reform.

The success of the program was made possible by four developments. The first was the re-establishment of the ultramontane influence of the papacy, that is, influence beyond the Alps or throughout Latin Christendom, as opposed to its Italian or local influence. This was the work of Leo IX (1049–1054), who was the emperor's cousin Bruno, bishop of Toul. He was appointed pope by Henry III following the very brief pontificates of the imperial appointees Clement II (1046–1047) and Damasus II (1048). Bruno was an able and loyal bishop of the Empire, but he had scruples about an imperial appointment without canonical election in due form. He chose to go to Rome as a mere pilgrim, leaving it to the clergy and people of Rome to elect him canonically if they would have him. On his way, he stopped at Cluny briefly, where Hildebrand joined his entourage. Following his elevation to the papacy, Leo spent several years traveling through France, the Low Countries, and Germany, holding synods at which decrees against simony, clerical marriage, and other abuses were enacted under the immediate leadership of the Pope.

Leo IX was the first pope since Nicholas I in the ninth century to impress upon all Europe the force of his personality. His fearless leadership gave new energy to reform everywhere. At the Synod of Reims in 1049 he won his most striking victory by excommunicating the French bishops who had, under royal pressure, boycotted the meeting. By adjourning the most difficult cases of contested elections and alleged abuses to be heard and adjudicated later at Rome, Leo was able to avoid an open rupture with the more powerful transalpine antireform prelates, and at the same time to secure recognition once more of papal supremacy in ecclesiastical causes.

The second development underlying the Hildebrandine reform movement was the assertion of papal supremacy over the Greek Orthodox Church. In 1054 this claim resulted in the mutual excommunication of Michael Cerularius, patriarch of Constantinople, by the pope, and of Leo IX by the patriarch. The dramatic anathemas hurled at each other by the heads of the Greek and Latin Churches have led some historians to exaggerate the significance of this "affair of 1054" and to speak of it as the final and complete schism of the Greek Orthodox and Roman Catholic Churches. No contemporary thought of the breach as final. The faithful of each communion were scarcely affected or involved, and the incident actually grew out of negotiations intended to reunite the two communions. It is true that certain doctrinal differences separated the Greeks from the Latins—the old quarrel over *filioque* was still unsettled and there were animadversions concerning the use of unleavened bread in the Eucharist— but these differences were neither then nor thereafter considered insuperable. Negotiations for reunion were soon resumed, and they have continued not only throughout the Middle Ages but even down to the twentieth century. The real significance of the breach of 1054, and what has continued to be the real obstacle to reunion, was the unqualified and determined assertion by Leo IX of papal supremacy over all Christendom, an assertion from which none of his successors has retreated and which no patriarch of Constantinople has conceded.

The third development leading to the rise of the papacy was the growth of its temporal power in Italy. To be effective leaders of the universal Church, popes had to be free from domination by local Roman factions. This freedom could be gained by imperial intervention and protection, but such intervention was intermittent and unreliable, and it set limitations upon papal leadership of the universal Church. There were two possible solutions to this dilemma. One was for the papacy itself to become a strong Italian power able to protect itself from local factions. Such a policy, if successful, would eliminate the need for imperial protection but only at the cost of embroiling the papacy in Italian problems and politics. This policy appealed to Leo IX, particularly because it coincided with his desire to recover for the papacy the churches of southern Italy. These churches had been under the jurisdiction of the patriarch of Constantinople ever since the iconoclastic controversy in the eighth century. Leo, therefore, with the approval of Henry III, who even granted to the pope the duchy of Benevento, set out to accomplish what the armies of the Saxon and Salian emperors had failed to achieve, the military conquest of southern Italy. The pope had, however, badly underestimated the growing strength of a new power in the south, the Normans, who met and defeated the papal army at Civitate, in 1053. This policy of conquest was continued by Leo's successor, Victor II (1055–1057), although the time for effective military operations against the Normans had long since gone by.

The alternative solution of the papal dilemma was to abandon the hope of temporal domination of Italy by the papacy itself in favor of alliance with Italian states opposed to mutual external enemies. Such a policy, if successful, would eliminate the need for imperial protection, and it would leave the papacy relatively free from embroilment in Italian politics. The death of Henry III in 1056 and the succession of his young son under a regency provided the opportunity to pursue this policy. At this time the emperor's strongest German opponent was the duke of Lorraine; his strongest Italian opponent, and a warm supporter of the papacy, was the countess of Tuscany. Negotiations between the two led to their marriage, and the union of their anti-imperial interests culminated in the election of the duke's brother, the abbot of Monte Cassino, as Stephen IX (1057–1058). Hildebrand had played an important part in securing the appointment of Victor II and the election of Stephen IX. On the premature death of Stephen, Hildebrand's influence was decisive in combining the forces of the duke of Lorraine and those of the countess of Tuscany to secure the election of the Burgundian bishop of Florence, Gerhard, as Nicholas II (1059–1061). The papacy had found in Tuscany the power to withstand local domination, and the reforming party was now securely in control of papal policy.

One of Nicholas' first acts was to carry forward the policy of Italian alliances by recognizing the Norman Robert Guiscard, as duke of Apulia and Calabria "by grace of God and of St. Peter," and future duke of Sicily when he could win that title by military conquest. In return the Normans became both the vassals and the allies of the papacy. Henceforth, the papacy could rely upon the support of both the Norman principalities to the south and Tuscany to the north against the Roman nobility and against imperial intervention from north of the Alps. The terms of the Norman alliance—recognition of the pope as overlord of southern Italy and Sicily —set the pattern for future papal alliances in which secular rulers became the vassals of the pope.

The fourth development leading to the increased powers of the papacy was also the work of Nicholas II. This was the establishment of a more precise method of canonical election of popes. Hitherto, the "clergy and people" of Rome (as in any diocese) had been the authority by which the pope, the bishop of the see of St. Peter, was elected. As in the great majority of the episcopal sees all over Christendom, "election" by clergy and people was often simply a polite form that masked the substance of power politics dictating the actual choice. Many recent popes had been in fact appointed by emperors, although their election was considered canonical because the clergy and people of Rome were induced to accept the imperial nominees. Such election was hardly free, except in the technical sense that the clergy and people were free to acquiesce in the imperial nomination, but it conformed with a pattern that was generally accepted in Western Europe. Long after the papacy was relatively free from secular influence, a king could write to the "clergy and people" of a western diocese: "I command you to hold a free election, but, nevertheless, I forbid you to elect anyone except Richard my clerk, the archdeacon of Poitiers." Freedom of election to ecclesiastical office was an issue which had interested neither the antireform elements within the Church nor the reformers who counted on the leadership of secular rulers in promoting reform. In fact, reform had often depended upon successful intervention by secular rulers. On many occasions they had forced through the election of their own better qualified candidates, as in the case of the papacy itself. The reformed papacy entered a new and radical phase of its history when it declared its independence not only of local factions that had degraded it but also of imperial control through which it had been reformed.

This independence was achieved by the promulgation at the Lateran Synod of 1059 of a decree providing that the cardinal-bishops, cardinal-priests, and cardinal-deacons of the see of Rome were henceforth to be the official electors. Their choice of a new pope was in actual fact to be final, although provision was also made for acclamation by the other clergy and the people of Rome and for notification to be sent to the emperor *after* election took place so that he might confirm the election. Subject to minor modifications made at later dates, this system has continued to be the method by which new popes have been elected ever since 1059. The reform party led by Hildebrand was now in the ascendant. On the death of Nicholas II, the cardinals elected Anselm, bishop of Lucca and friend of Peter Damiani, as Alexander II (1061–1073). The emperor was ignored—as well he might be—since he was an eleven-year-old boy under the tutelage of regents absorbed in quarrels among themselves.

The pontificate of Alexander II was relatively uneventful. The papacy had achieved its independence, acquired allies in Italy for protection against both local and imperial influence, asserted its spiritual supremacy over all of Christendom, both Latin and Greek, and had made its influence and leadership felt throughout Western Europe. Under Alexander matters that the papacy had formerly left to local prelates or simply ignored were now, more and more frequently, dealt with by papal legates. No Christian, regardless of rank or station, was immune from the spiritual jurisdiction of the papacy. This fact was brought home vigorously to secular rulers whose private lives had in some notorious instances fallen below the moral standards of the Church. Young Henry, the boy emperor, felt the new papal authority even before his youthful intentions could become licentious deeds. At the age of fifteen he had been married to Bertha, daughter of the count of Turin, a woman several years his senior whom he had never met. When he did meet her, he found her so repulsive that he declared publicly that he would not live with her and would seek an annulment. To deal with this scandal, Peter Damiani, fresh from a victorious campaign against married clergy in northern Italy, was sent to Germany in 1069 as papal legate. Henry was compelled to yield. The grateful Bertha ultimately won the emperor's affections and became not only the mother of his four sons but his steadfast supporter and comforter in the long trials and tribulations of his reign.

The guiding spirit behind the rise of the papacy during the twenty odd years since the accession of Leo IX had been Hildebrand, archdeacon of the church of Rome. On Alexander II's death, Hildebrand became pope, taking the title Gregory VII (1073–1085), as an affirmation of the validity of the pontificate of his earliest patron, Gregory VI. Like the elevation of Gregory VI, that of Gregory VII was also irregular. The popular archdeacon was dragged (with a conventional and proper show of reluctance on Hildebrand's part) by an enthusiastic mob to St. Peter's basilica, where he was enthroned and acclaimed pope. The cardinals acquiesced in the *fait accompli* although such a procedure violated both the letter and spirit of the electoral decree of 1059. Gregory VII, with admirable forethought, waited until the emperor confirmed his election before allowing himself to be consecrated as St. Peter's successor, thus salvaging some legitimacy for what was a foregone, if irregular, conclusion.

The pontificate of Gregory VII was the dramatic climax to which the events of the preceding generation had been leading. Equaled in stature and influence only by Gregory I and Innocent III, Gregory VII stands out as the most vivid and heroic ecclesiastical personality of the whole Middle Ages. His sense of destiny and mission, the fervor of his dedication and his strength of will, his realistic and even crafty statesmanship, his willingness to employ force or guile as occasion required, and the contrast between his aggressive leadership of Christendom as pope and his profound spiritual humility as a devout Christian, fascinated and bewildered his contemporaries as they have perplexed historians who have tried to assess the significance of his career. Perhaps the best judgment of Gregory VII was that of his equally forceful contemporary, Peter Damiani, who was attracted and repelled by the complex mixture of diabolical saintliness and saintly worldliness in his friend. Peter stood in awe of the man whom he characterized as a "holy Satan."

31 THE INVESTITURE STRUGGLE

The medieval emperors usually supported reform so long as they could control the Church. But in the long run political and secular considerations meant more to them than the reformers' opposition to simony, married clergy, and uncanonical elections. The sale of ecclesiastical offices could be condoned if not justified by the emperor because this practice was an occasional source of imperial revenue. The reformers opposed the marriage of priests because marriage diverted their attention from spiritual matters to more worldly and personal concerns such as providing for their wives and families. But to the emperors loyal married priests were politically preferable to celibate clergy whose support was in doubt. Free elections were potentially dangerous because high church officials held extensive imperial fiefs and governmental offices which could not safely be allowed to fall into the hands of political enemies. The struggle between the Empire and the papacy was, then, inevitable in the sense that the independence of the Church under papal supremacy was incompatible with the survival of an Empire that was administered and supported by prelates named by the emperor. The issue that brought this incompatibility into sharpest focus was lay investiture.

Lay investiture was the practice by which secular rulers and lords invested, or delivered over spiritual offices and functions to newly elected clergy by conferring upon them the symbols of spiritual authority; for example, they invested bishops with the ring and the staff. So long as secular rulers and lords exercised this right, they could be sure of a loyal clergy and they could even support a certain degree of reform. But the reformers refused to concede that spiritual office could legitimately be conferred by a layman. The demand for investiture by the proper superior spiritual authority logically entailed the demand for freedom of election. Without such freedom spiritual investiture could only amount to a right of veto against an unworthy candidate, which in turn might result in prolonged vacancies in high offices and a cessation of the work of the Church.

But to understand the ideas that motivated Gregory VII we must go further than the specific issues of simony, celibacy, election, and investiture. Underlying his attitude toward these issues was a larger vision of the meaning of Christendom. Perhaps more than any earlier pope, Gregory was impressed with the plenitude of spiritual authority inherent in his office; or, as he put it in a letter concerning Henry IV:

> When God gave to Peter the power of binding or loosing in heaven and on earth He excepted no one. . . . If the Holy Apostolic See has jurisdiction over spiritual things, why not also over temporal? When kings and princes of this world set their own dignity and profit higher than God's righteousness and seek their own honor, you know whose members they are . . . they are members of Antichrist.

Legitimate rulers, therefore, can only be those who "prefer the things of God above those of man," and only the pope, as St. Peter's successor, could

Emperor Henry IV.
Manuscript illustration
(early twelfth century).
CORPUS CHRISTI
COLLEGE, CAMBRIDGE.

judge whether rulers served righteousness or their own earthly profit and glory.

The situation in Germany appeared to be favorable for the application of these Gregorian ideas. Until 1065 the young emperor Henry IV (1056–1106) had been under a bungling regency which was unable to prevent the deterioration of the imperial administration and the usurpation of regalian rights and revenues. When, in 1065, Henry was declared to be of age and able to govern in his own right, the young emperor's desperate efforts to strengthen the weakened government antagonized the nobility, and a serious revolt broke out in Saxony in 1073. In this struggle the support of the German church was indispensable, and until the revolt was put down Henry made every effort to appease the Hildebrandine party. He graciously confirmed the irregular election of Gregory VII, and in correspondence with the new pope he humbly acknowledged, "not only have I encroached upon the property of the Church, but I have sold churches themselves to unworthy persons poisoned with the gall of simony," admitting that "somewhat repentant and remorseful, we turn to your fatherly indulgence, accusing ourselves and trusting in you. Your direction shall be scrupulously followed . . . and I humbly beseech your fatherly support."

Gregory was too astute to take these protestations at face value, or to fail to connect the emperor's conciliatory correspondence with the revolt in Saxony. The pope responded with admonitions to Henry to continue "your efforts at self-improvement," with the assurance that he would continue "beseeching Almighty God to confirm you in your present good intentions," and hinting that he had "cause to expect still higher and better things" of Henry.

At this strategic moment, early in 1075, when Henry's difficulties in Saxony were greatest, Gregory launched his decree prohibiting lay investiture. Then the situation was suddenly altered by Henry's victory over the rebels in June, 1075. The victorious emperor, busily occupied with the settlement of the conquered duchy's affairs, was in no mood for concession. His earlier promises were ignored. He continued to appoint and invest bishops of the Empire, and he chose this time to install two favorites in vacant Italian sees. By the end of the year relations between the pope and emperor were at a breaking point. Gregory now sent a letter of stern admonition, giving Henry "apostolic benediction on the understanding that he obey the Apostolic See as becomes a Christian king." This letter was borne by legates who privately and orally threatened the emperor with excommunication as the penalty for continued disobedience.

Henry's swift reaction was to summon a synod at Worms early in 1076. Here his loyal German bishops drew up a letter to Gregory addressing him as "Brother Hildebrand" and renouncing their obedience to him as pope. The emperor sent a covering letter which began, "Henry, king not through usurpation but through the holy ordination of God, to Hildebrand at present not pope but false monk," and ending with Gregory's deposition: "I, Henry, king by grace of God, do say unto thee, together with all our bishops, descend, descend, to be damned throughout the ages."

The letters reached Rome during the Lenten Synod of 1076, which promptly excommunicated the archbishop of Mainz, chief author of the bishops' letter, and deprived of their offices all imperial bishops "who voluntarily joined his schism and still persist in their evil deeds." Gregory then deposed Henry, released his subjects from their allegiance, and excommunicated him.

This action was the signal for general rebellion in Germany. Most of the bishops were on Henry's side; most of the nobility supported the pope. Papal legates were active in Germany stirring up the nobility, bringing pressure on ecclesiastical leaders, rallying the abbots against recalcitrant bishops, and rekindling the smouldering resentment of the Saxons. Success attended these efforts when the German nobles demanded that Henry cease to exercise his royal authority. They then decided that unless he could obtain absolution from the pope at a council to be held the following February at Augsburg, where Gregory had agreed to preside, Henry was to be considered deposed and a new emperor would be elected—formally elected by the nobles, presumably, but certainly not without guidance and influence from the presiding pope. It appeared that the events of Sutri under Henry III were about to be reversed at Augsburg under Gregory VII.

This was the low point in Henry's fortunes. If the council were allowed to meet, deposition appeared inevitable. He therefore set off for Italy hoping to force a meeting with Gregory before the pope could cross the Alps. Gregory, on his way northward, had reached Canossa, a castle of the countess Matilda of Tuscany. Here, in January, 1077, occurred the dramatic episode which became for later generations a symbol of the submission of the secular to the spiritual power. Henry presented himself before the castle gate accompanied by only a few intimates, having laid aside all royal insignia in favor of a humble penitent's coarse attire. Standing three days barefooted (in the falling snow, according to later legend) he tearfully besought forgiveness and absolution—until, as Gregory later complained, "some even cried out that we were showing not the seriousness of apostolic authority, but the cruelty of a savage tyrant." The pope's reluctance is understandable but there was nothing he could do. Gregory as a priest could not deny absolution to a penitent Christian. Henry, on the surface, had submitted to a public humiliation. But to Gregory and Henry and their contemporaries, the emperor had won a resounding diplomatic victory. Gregory could claim from the incident no more than he had claimed before: the right to judge and to excommunicate any sinner, even the emperor himself. Henry had never denied the papacy that right, even while denying Gregory's authority to act as pope. Now, by recognizing Gregory as pope, Henry had prevented his own deposition by securing absolution before the scheduled council could meet at Augsburg.

Civil war continued in Germany. Despite Henry's absolution the German nobility elected a new king, and the military conflict was prolonged without decisive result. Gregory then put forth the novel claim that he as pope had the right to judge between the two rivals. It was a foregone conclusion when, in 1080, he decided against Henry's claims and, because Henry refused to recognize the papal judgment, excommunicated the emperor for a second time. By the following year, however, Henry was strong enough to defeat his rival, proclaim the deposition of Gregory once more, and arrange for the election of an antipope—Guibert, archbishop of Ravenna, formerly a friend of Hildebrand but loyal to Henry during the struggle. Henry now invaded Italy. Brushing aside the forces of Matilda of Tuscany, he took possession of Rome in 1084 and went through the forms of receiving the imperial crown at the hands of his antipope. Gregory called upon his vassal, Robert Guiscard, for help, and Henry withdrew before the superior military force of the Normans. The Normans then proceeded to subject Rome to such pillaging as the Eternal City had never before suffered. When they finally withdrew, Gregory had no choice but to seek refuge with them from the resentment of the outraged Roman populace. The pope retired to Salerno where, in 1085, he fell sick and died, bitter but not disillusioned. His last words were typical of the monk Hildebrand, true to the pope Gregory: "I have loved justice and hated iniquity; therefore I die in exile."

The tide now seemed to be turning in Henry's favor. Germany was relatively pacified and he could devote several years to subduing Italy. The antipope Guibert retired from the tumult of Rome to his archbishopric of Ravenna. Gregory's successor, Victor III (1086–1087), sought the quieter atmosphere of Monte Cassino, and Urban II (1088–1099), after a few months in Rome, also fled to a safer haven in Norman territory. In northern Italy papal fortunes slowly improved. Urban negotiated an alliance between his staunch supporter, Matilda, the able countess of Tuscany, and Henry's most dangerous German enemy, the duke of Bavaria, in a marriage uniting the pious and forceful Matilda with the duke's ineffective young son. Matilda's forces doggedly held out in her mountain castles, while her partisans in Rome battled the imperial faction for control of the city. Then the emperor's eldest son, Conrad, was persuaded to revolt, and Henry suffered reverses on both sides of the Alps until in 1097 he was forced to abandon Italy altogether, in the hope of salvaging some power in Germany. After Conrad's death, the emperor's second son, Henry, revolted in 1104. The aging and embittered emperor witnessed in his closing years the collapse of the imperial government which his minority had inaugurated. The beneficiaries of the investiture struggle were the German nobility who had permanently increased their collective strength against the German monarchy.

The antagonism between papacy and Empire continued after the death of Henry IV. His successor, Henry V (1106–1125), gave up none of the claims of his father. The new pope, Paschal II (1099–1118) sincerely desired peace, but his proposed solution was so naïve that his efforts only embittered the contending parties. His plan was to return to the secular authority all lands, jurisdiction, and privileges held by ecclesiastical officials by feudal tenure, in return for which the emperor was to give up lay investiture. In effect, the Church's temporalities were to be exchanged for complete freedom, while the emperor would acquire a vast new royal domain on which to rebuild his government. The German nobles were shocked at such imperial aggrandizement, and the German and Italian prelates were furious, especially because Paschal had made a special exception in favor of the temporal possessions and jurisdiction of the papacy. Paschal was forced to give up his visionary scheme, and Henry V extracted from him a formal statement approving lay investiture. Now the reformers were shocked, and there was talk of deposing Paschal as a heretic until he solemnly rescinded his approval of lay investiture as having been made under compulsion. These events not only discredited Paschal as leader of the Gregorian party; they demonstrated the futility of any extreme solution. The need for a compromise formula was now obvious.

After the brief pontificate of Gelasius II (1118–1119), whose only major act was to excommunicate Henry V, the cardinals elected an able ecclesiastical statesman, Calixtus II (1119–1124), the first pope since 1061 who had not been a monk. Calixtus negotiated a compromise settlement with Henry V: the Concordat of Worms, in 1122. The Concordat was based on the same principles that governed an earlier settlement of the investiture question in England in 1107. The twofold nature of the office of bishop or abbot was recognized, with due provision both for spiritual independence and for the duties and obligations of prelates as great vassals of the king or emperor. The essential provisions of the Concordat were: (1) elections were to be "canonical," that is, by the clergy in a positive sense rather than simply as a rubber-stamp approval of the choice of the emperor or lay noble; but in Germany elections were to take place in the presence of the emperor and in a disputed election the emperor's decision was to be final; (2) in Germany, the bishop- or abbot-elect was first to be invested by the emperor with the *regalia* of his office (the temporalities, or lands, jurisdiction, and privileges held of the emperor as a vassal, for which he did homage) and only then was the bishop or abbot to be consecrated and invested by his ecclesiastical superior with his *spiritualia* by the ring and staff (the spiritual authority and property of the church or abbey not held of a secular lord); and (3) in Italy and Burgundy the bishop- or abbot-elect was to be invested by his ecclesiastical superior with the ring and staff immediately, and investiture with the *regalia* by the emperor or his representative was to follow automatically within six months.

With the Concordat of Worms, the investiture struggle had ended in a realistic compromise which, though it did not satisfy extremists in either camp, recognized what had, since 1075, come to be the actual situation. The emperor's actual control of the German church was conceded, but the emperor agreed to give up lay investiture of spiritual functions and to exercise his control within the canonical regulations of the Church. Outside Germany, the pope's actual control of the Church in Burgundy and Italy was conceded by the emperor, though the temporalities were to be held as imperial vassals. If we compare the provisions of the Concordat of Worms with the old Ottonian system of domination of both Church and state by the emperor, the outcome of the investiture struggle must be considered essentially a papal victory. No longer could the emperor appoint and invest whom he pleased. The papacy had imposed canonical regulations on the form of elections and had taken from the emperor control over about half of the prelates of the Empire. As a peace treaty, the Concordat was an admirable attempt to render to Caesar the things that are Caesar's, and to God the things that are God's. As in all such attempts, spokesmen for Caesar and spokesmen for God differed in their definitions of the proper things to be rendered. The contest between Empire and papacy would no longer revolve around investiture; but the struggle for supremacy was soon to be renewed with even greater violence.

The East and the Expansion of Feudal Europe

From the middle of the eighth until the middle of the eleventh century, European history was dominated by developments taking place in the Frankish-Germanic center of western continental Europe: the rise and collapse of the Carolingian empire, the feudal reorganization of society, the evolution of a manorial economy, the Cluniac reform movement, the foundation of the medieval Empire and its culmination. All these developments are characteristic of the period in the sense that the Mediterranean world and the Iberian, Celtic, Scandinavian, and Slavic periphery of Latin Christendom did not participate fully in the main course of events. Such contact as was maintained with the Byzantine East and the Arabic world was historically insignificant.

In the eleventh century developments in areas lying beyond what had been the Carolingian empire once more became important. The rise of the papacy may, from this view, be understood as one phase of the resurgence of the Mediterranean area as a vital part of western Europe. The Christian awakening in Spain and the offensive against Saracen and Byzantine control of the western Mediterranean and southern Italy were signs of expansion into and revival of the south. In the north and on the eastern frontiers expansive tendencies are illustrated by the Norman Conquest of England, the penetration of Latin Christianity into Scandinavia and Poland, and German pressure exerted all along the Slavic frontier.

The Crusades were the most striking result of the expansion of feudal Europe. They were the military and political phase of the re-establishment of contact with the Byzantine and the Arabic East. But they were only one phase of a general expansion that was even more important in several other aspects: the economic revival, the growth of population, and the widening horizon of intellectual and cultural interests, which had all begun well before the First Crusade. Contact with the East served, in turn, to intensify and quicken some of the Western developments of the twelfth century, but the Crusades themselves were not the *cause* of any significant advance or achievement in the West.

Far more important than the minor role played by the Crusades is the fact that Western Europe in the eleventh century was no longer simply struggling for survival. Wealth, leisure, and a surplus of population were now available for enterprises that went beyond merely local needs or merely military protection against external enemies. Indicative of these changed conditions is the fact that, in each decade of the eleventh century, hundreds of peaceful pilgrims preceded the first crusading army at the end of the period.

32   THE BYZANTINE EMPIRE BEFORE THE CRUSADES

The Byzantine Empire has puzzled and fascinated historians because, although it seemed for centuries to be tottering on the brink, it would never fall. This view rests on the fallacious assumption that following antiquity there must be a decline. Actually, the Byzantine Empire was a continuation and transformation of the Roman world. There was no general decline as there was in the West. The civilization of Byzantium was far superior in every way to that of Western Europe in the whole period from the foundation of the Germanic kingdoms to the investiture struggle. In the East there was no period so dark as the seventh century in the West nor any collapse so complete as the Carolingian disintegration of the ninth century. Although there were periods of retrogression they were followed by recovery.

The fundamental reason for the difference between Eastern and Western development was the balanced economy in Byzantine lands which preserved both industry and commerce in the cities and a flourishing agriculture in the country districts. The political history of the Empire is alternately dull and dramatic, punctuated by palace revolutions and intrigues, but the vagaries of court politics were supported by a highly developed government which maintained its power through crisis and catastrophe. The imperial bureaucracy, despite its notorious venality in some periods, for a thousand years—from the fourth to the fourteenth century —served the Byzantine state more efficiently than any other government of that period. Equally impressive was the record of the army. No army, not even the Roman army of antiquity, had a finer record of victorious campaigns and of recovery from defeats in the field than the Byzantine army. It was almost always outnumbered and confronted with enemies on all sides of the Empire. The force of tradition and a sense of continuity with the past account for much of the longevity and toughness of the Empire which to its subjects was still *Romania.* Perhaps the greatest contrast between Byzantium and the West was this sense of being "at home with its past." For centuries the Byzantine Empire, as a bulwark against Eastern enemies, made possible the very survival of Western Europe, a service to Latin Christendom which was, needless to say, almost wholly unappreciated.

The imperial government was the prize of contending interests within the Empire. We have seen in Chapter 5 how the Isaurian dynasty (717–802) was based on an alliance between the landed aristocracy and the army against the court or bureaucracy and the Church. The aims of Isaurian policy were territorial expansion, protection of the frontiers, agricultural prosperity, and taxation of commerce for the support of military operations. The Isaurian dynasty came to an end with Irene (797–802), whose pathological craving for power led her to mutilate her own son, in whose name she ruled as regent, and to assume the title of empress.

The period of the Amorian emperors (802–867) began with a palace revolution against Irene, and brought the return to influence of the bureaucracy and an imperial policy of encouraging commerce and of re-establishing religious peace. The iconoclastic controversy had degenerated into a struggle for power that had weakened both Church and state. Although there were iconoclasts among the early Amorian emperors, the images were restored by a Church council in 843 and the controversy was finally closed. During the Amorian period social and economic discontent in Asia Minor led to an abortive rebellion and to the increasing subordination of the free peasantry to the landed aristocracy.

In literature, learning, and art the age of the Isaurian and Amorian dynasties was dominated by the iconoclastic controversy. The greatest theologian was John of Damascus (d.750), a staunch defender of images. The works of the iconoclasts were entirely destroyed by their enemies, and we have to reconstruct their arguments from the polemics of their opponents. Iconoclasm obviously created an uncongenial environment for religious art, but the period is characterized by a revival of Hellenistic naturalism in secular painting and sculpture. Higher education was patronized by the Amorians. The patriarch Photius (d.891) was a teacher in the imperial palace school, and during his stormy career he found time to produce the most notable literary work of the period, the *Myriobiblon* ("Thousands of Books"), an enormous compilation of extracts from and commentaries upon classical Greek authors. Another teacher was the older of the two brothers, Cyril and Methodius, "the apostles of the Slavs." For the southern Slavs they played approximately the same role as Boniface had for the Germans, a century earlier.

Missionary rivalry between the Greek and Latin Churches produced in the ninth century as much antagonism as the earlier iconoclastic schism. Eastern missionaries brought Orthodox Christianity and the culture of Byzantium into the barbarian Slavic world. Their first notable success was the conversion of the Bulgarian ruler, Boris, in 865, an event which led to sharp competition between the Orthodox and Catholic missionaries for the ecclesiastical allegiance of the western Slavs. Embittered relations between Constantinople and Rome reached the breaking point when the emperor deposed a patriarch for high treason and appointed in his place the scholar Photius. The pope at this time was Nicholas I, whose vigorous assertion of papal supremacy has already been discussed. It surprised no one when Nicholas promptly excommunicated Photius as a usurper. Photius, in turn, held a great council in 867 which condemned as heretical all points of doctrine and liturgical usage in which Latin Christianity differed from the Orthodox faith. Then the patriarch excommunicated Nicholas. This Photian schism did not last long. Photius was deprived of his patriarchate in a palace revolution, and though he regained it a few years later he was deposed once more in 886. The schism was not a cause but a symptom of the widening breach between the two communions. The real issue was papal supremacy. Only when this issue arose were the several doctrinal differences rehearsed and debated and made the basis on which the patriarch and the pope mutually excommunicated each other, as they did again in 1054.

In reality, Photius' or any other patriarch's position as against the claims of the papacy depended upon the emperor's relations with Rome. Once the Bulgarians had been won for the Byzantine sphere of influence, it was more important for the emperor to be on good terms with the pope than to promote the ambitions of his patriarch, because the emperor needed help in meeting the Moslem attack on the western Byzantine provinces. Sicily was almost wholly lost by the end of the ninth century, and the Moslems were beginning to occupy parts of Byzantine Italy. We have already seen how the pope and a Byzantine fleet cooperated against the Saracen stronghold on the Garigliano river early in the tenth century. On the eastern frontiers the Moslem danger had subsided because of internal strife after 833, but the island of Crete was lost to Saracen adventurers. A new enemy appeared in the year 860 when the Russians made a surprise attack by sea on Constantinople—the first recorded fact in Russian history. The unsuccessful attackers were probably from the newly organized principality of Kiev founded (or conquered) by Scandinavians earlier in the ninth century.

The greatest menace to Byzantine security during the period of the

Macedonian emperors (867–1057) was on the northern frontier. Here the Bulgar people had become thoroughly intermixed with native Slavs and had built up a well-organized kingdom after the Byzantine model. Under Simeon (893–927), the first ruler to assume the title "tsar" (Caesar), Bulgaria included most of the Balkan peninsula, stretching from the Adriatic to the Black Sea. The Byzantine emperor allied with the Magyars against Simeon, who countered by employing another Asiatic people, the Patzinaks, with whose help he drove the Magyars up the Danube where they later founded the kingdom of Hungary. Simeon then attacked the Byzantine Empire and forced upon the emperor the humiliation of paying an annual tribute.

Events of the tenth century proved more favorable. Border warfare against the Moslems turned slowly in favor of the Byzantines, and on the sea Nicephorus Phocas (963–969) recovered naval supremacy in the eastern Mediterranean. He reconquered Crete in 961 and Cyprus four years later. The Empire attained its greatest military strength, prosperity, and political stability under Basil II (976–1025), who employed arms and diplomacy with equal skill. Although Bulgaria had declined after the death of Simeon, a new Bulgarian dynasty of rulers renewed the war with the Empire late in the tenth century. Basil's war on the Bulgarians resembled Charlemagne's Saxon wars in length and brutality. At one point, Basil returned to the Bulgarian tsar fourteen thousand prisoners, all of them blinded except for one in every hundred to serve as guide—at the sight of whom the tsar is said to have died of shock. A few years after this incident the conquered "empire" of Bulgaria became a Byzantine province and the triumphant Basil was acclaimed by his people with the appropriate title *Bulgaroctonos* ("Slayer of the Bulgars").

During the reign of Basil II relations with Russia became important. At one critical moment, when confronted with a large-scale rebellion in Asia Minor and invasion by the Bulgarians, Basil saved the situation only with the assistance of six thousand Varangian (i.e., Scandinavian Russian) troops supplied by Prince Vladimir of Kiev. The outcome of this crisis was a treaty of alliance (c.989) by which Vladimir accepted Christianity and married a Byzantine princess. Thus began the expansion of Byzantine and Orthodox culture into an area almost as large as Latin Christendom. Peaceful relations between the courts of Constantinople and Kiev were supported by a mutually profitable commerce.

A social revolution in the tenth century weakened the Byzantine state and set the stage for decline in the eleventh century. Most of the Macedonian emperors were military men whose first concern was the strength and dependability of the army. The best troops were recruited from the free peasantry of Asia Minor, where the continuing tendency toward larger estates increased the subordination of the peasants to the great landowners. This transformation of the free peasantry into dependent cultivators undermined both the recruitment of troops—only the free owed military service—and the collection of taxes. The magnates evaded taxes, corrupted the officials, and grew more powerful at the expense of both the state and the peasantry. For most of the tenth century the government was beset with rebellions in the provinces of Asia Minor, and several of the best emperors of the period were themselves successful aristocratic rebels. But most of the Macedonian emperors waged a relentless war of legislation against the economic power of the aristocracy, a policy designed to protect and benefit the free peasant class and thus preserve the army.

Under strong rulers this paternalistic protection of the peasants was successful, but ultimately the economic power of the aristocrats won out. After Basil II there was an uneasy balance of power between the local authority of great landowners and the weakened central authority at Constantinople. The turning point came when the central government gave up the struggle to collect taxes directly. Instead, taxes were farmed to local nobles who paid into the treasury a fixed sum and then recouped themselves with all they could extort from the peasants of their districts.

The decline of the Byzantine Empire in the eleventh century did not affect cultural activities as it did political stability and social welfare. The Macedonian era was a brilliant period in arts and letters. Scholarship, building, and the decorative arts flourished under imperial patronage. There was a renewed interest in the literature of antiquity, though learning in this field tended to be arid and encyclopedic. The outstanding figure was Psellus (d.1078), a teacher of philosophy and rhetoric, whose interests were similar to those of Photius in the ninth century. Several good histories were written in the tenth and eleventh centuries, but Byzantine authors particularly excelled in writing technical monographs and treatises on political and military administration. One of the best was *On the Administration of the Empire* by Constantine VII Porphyrogenitus (913–959), who was the ablest scholar at his own court.

Under the last Macedonian emperors (1025–1057) a decline set in which was accelerated in the following "time of troubles" (1057–1081). The struggle against the Bulgarians had exhausted the Empire, the successors of Basil II were pathetically incompetent, and the aristocracy of the provinces increased its power at the expense of the central government. External enemies made inroads on Byzantine territory. In the west the Norman conquest of southern Italy had begun, and in the north the Patzinaks threatened the Danubian frontier. Far more serious, the Seljuk Turks moved into the eastern provinces of both the Byzantine Empire and the Caliphate. In 1071 at Manzikert the Byzantine army suffered its worst disaster since the battle of Adrianople. The Seljuk Turks destroyed the forces raised by Romanus IV and captured the emperor. In the same year Byzantine rule in Italy was brought to an end with the fall of Bari. Subsequently the Turks conquered most of Asia Minor, while the Serbs and Bulgarians overran most of the Balkan provinces. Palace intrigues and rebellions by ambitious generals reduced the Empire to a state of anarchy. But in her darkest hour a new military hero appeared to preserve and revive the Byzantine Empire. This was Alexius Comnenus (1081–1118), whose careful husbanding of his military resources and whose astute diplomacy put the Empire back once more on a sound though circumscribed basis.

33   SPAIN AND SICILY:
THE BEGINNING OF WESTERN EXPANSION

The expansion of feudal Europe began in Spain and southern Italy during the eleventh century. Although the First Crusade was the most dramatic and best publicized chapter in European expansion, conquest and colonization on every other medieval frontier either began earlier or produced more conclusive results than any of the Crusades. Expeditions to the Levant were essentially overseas campaigns which involved greater problems of supply, transport, and reinforcement than were met on the periphery of feudal Europe where the more enduring expansion took place.

In Spain expansion at the expense of the Moors (Spanish Moslems) did not begin in earnest until the decline of the Omayyad dynasty. As we have already seen in Chapter 5, the Moors rejected the Abbasid revolution of 750 and were ruled by an Omayyad emir, or governor, after 756. The Emirate of Cordova recognized the caliph in Bagdad in religious matters but was politically independent. For a century the Omayyad emirs spent most of their time suppressing local revolts and consolidating their authority. Part of their difficulties sprang from the diversity of their subject population. The Arab aristocracy, concentrated in towns, slowly fused with native converts to Islam, but the majority of the immigrant Berbers from Africa lived in the countryside and led a pastoral and agricultural life. Spanish Christians and Jews were protected by the tolerant Omayyads. Many of them were converted to Islam, but throughout the period Arabic-speaking Christians, the Mozarabs, continued their worship without molestation. In the middle of the ninth century the bishop of Seville, after a century and a half of Moorish rule, felt it necessary to translate the Bible into Arabic for the benefit of his flock. During the tenth century the height of Moorish civilization, measured in terms of both cultural achievement and political stability, was reached under Abd ar Rahman III (912–961), who proclaimed his complete independence of Bagdad by assuming the title of caliph in 929. The Caliphate of Cordova lasted until 1031, when Moorish Spain disintegrated into about a dozen petty principalities (1031–1086).

During the ninth and tenth centuries two Christian territories survived in the Iberian peninsula: the kingdom of the Asturias in the northwest and the county of Barcelona (the old Spanish March of Charlemagne, now independent) in the northeast. They had taken advantage of occasional periods of civil strife among the Moors to increase their size. By the end of the tenth century the Asturias had grown into the kingdom of Leon and the county of Castile, and the country of the Basques at the western end of the Pyrenees had become the kingdom of Navarre. The rulers of these petty Christian states spent most of their energies in wars of territorial conquest, sometimes against each other in alliance with Moorish principalities, sometimes in shifting alliances with each other against the Moors. No single Christian state was large enough to develop a central government which could hold together for long the territories which one or another of the rulers had won.

The collapse of the Caliphate of Cordova in 1031 coincided with political developments in the Christian states which made possible the beginning of a new period of Christian expansion. The conquests of Sancho the Great of Navarre (1000–1035), and the subsequent division of these territories among his sons, resulted in the establishment of the kingdom of Castile (1033) and its union with Leon (1037), and the establishment of the kingdom of Aragon south of the middle Pyrenees (1035). At this time each of the Christian states—the kingdom of Castile and Leon, the kingdom of Navarre, the kingdom of Aragon, and the county of Barcelona— was more powerful than any of the bordering Moorish principalities. Dynastic rivalries among the Christian rulers had become less profitable than war against the Moors. The *Reconquista*, or reconquest, became a national venture of all the Christian states. The papacy had kept in close touch with Spanish Christians and officially encouraged volunteers from Normandy, Burgundy, and other areas to join in the "perpetual crusade" against the infidel. During the eleventh century landless younger sons of feudal lords emigrated to Spain to make their fortunes in the wars. The first great expansion was a cooperative effort by Castile and Aragon, ending with the conquest of Toledo in 1085.

The fall of Toledo so alarmed the Moors that they appealed for aid to a new Berber power which had risen in North Africa, the Almoravides. The Almoravides came over to Spain and in a single year brought to a sudden halt any further Christian expansion. Then they turned to the conquest of the Moors, incorporating all of Moorish Spain into their African empire except the Emirate of Saragossa in the northeast. The last decade of the eleventh century and the early years of the twelfth were a confused period in which Castile and Leon were torn by civil wars, the Almoravides pushed the frontier northward, and Aragon slowly expanded at the expense of Saragossa. It was during this period that adventurers rose to power by exploiting the weaknesses of both Moslem and Christian rulers.

The most famous was a Castilian noble, Rodrigo Diaz de Vivar, better known in legend as the Cid, who spent thirty years fighting both for and against a half-dozen Christian and Moorish rulers. He ended his career as the ruler of Valencia, 1094–1099, withstanding the Almoravides' repeated assaults. For later generations, the Cid became a national hero and the symbol of the Christian *Reconquista;* in history he was only the most able and successful of the many opportunists on either side.

In the twelfth century the Almoravides declined, and the Christian kingdoms resumed their expansion. Aragon conquered Saragossa by 1118 and in 1140 was united with Barcelona in an enlarged kingdom whose further expansion was to be eastward into the Mediterranean islands. Castile pushed southward in the center of the peninsula. But internal struggles for power in Castile provided the opportunity for the count of Portugal to assume the title of king of Portugal in 1139, a rank which he justified by the conquest of Lisbon eight years later. This was the farthest penetration southward made by any of the Christian rulers. By the middle of the twelfth century, about one half of Spain was in Christian hands.

The expansion of Latin Christendom in the central Mediterranean area was even more impressive than in Spain. In southern Italy, the Lombard, Byzantine, and Saracen states had for more than a century jostled one another until by the opening of the eleventh century the Moslems had been expelled from the mainland and retained only the island of Sicily. The heel and toe of the peninsula, Apulia and Calabria, were wholly Byzantine. The rest of the south was split into more than a dozen petty duchies, counties, and marches under local rulers who shifted their allegiance and asserted their independence as occasion demanded or allowed.

Spain, c.1140, and Italy, c.1091

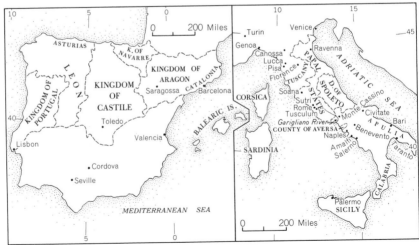

This confused and anarchic situation might have lasted indefinitely. As it turned out, political and social conditions in the far-off duchy of Normandy were ultimately responsible for introducing a new element in southern Italy which was to be decisive for the future.

Normandy at the beginning of the eleventh century suffered from a shortage of fiefs and a surplus of younger sons of feudal lords. What, for example, were the twelve sons of Tancred of Hauteville, a vassal of the middle rank in western Normandy, to do? One would inherit the Hauteville fief. Two or three others might gain preferment in the Church. But the rest could win themselves fiefs in Normandy only at the risk of the duke's stern reprisal against illicit warfare and at the even greater risk of defeat at the hands of other equally well-trained and aggressive Norman knights. The younger sons of the feudal lords of Normandy found it more profitable to emigrate to unsettled regions like Spain or Italy where their services were in demand and where, with luck and daring, they could make their fortunes.

A little band of such wandering adventurers from Normandy reached Rome in 1017, seeking employment as mercenaries. From the pope, Benedict VIII, they learned that they might be of use to a certain noble named Melo who conspired to overthrow the Byzantine provincial government in Apulia. That same year Melo and his rebel army, including the Norman mercenaries, were badly beaten in pitched battle with the Byzantines, whose troops were stiffened by a contingent of Russian mercenaries. Despite this inauspicious beginning, groups of Norman knights continued to emigrate to southern Italy and hire themselves out to local rulers, whether Lombard or Byzantine. In 1029 one of the Norman leaders was given the county of Aversa, the first Norman principality in southern Italy, as a reward for services to the duke of Naples. The prospects of such advancement attracted more Norman adventurers, including several of the sons of Tancred of Hauteville. These brothers soon joined in a new Apulian revolt against Byzantine rule, and by 1046 had carved out an independent Norman county in northern Apulia which was recognized by the western emperor, Henry III. The several Norman leaders rapidly extended their holdings, while at the same time they engaged in fierce rivalry among themselves. However, they were capable of uniting with vigor against a common enemy, as we have already seen in the case of Leo IX's ineffective intervention in the south and his defeat in the battle of Civitate, in 1053.

Meanwhile, yet another of the sons of Tancred of Hauteville had arrived from Normandy. This was Robert Guiscard (the "wary" or "cunning"), who established himself in the mountains of Calabria. He began his Italian career by preying on the cattle and sheep of Calabrian peasants and ended it as "the most gifted soldier and statesman of his age." After the death of his oldest brother in 1057, Robert Guiscard took over Apulia and forced the other Norman lords to recognize his leadership. In 1059 he secured from the pope, Nicholas II, the legitimization of his rule in return for a treaty of alliance. Henceforth Robert was recognized as duke of Apulia and Calabria, and of Sicily whenever he could reconquer it from the Saracens. In return he became the pope's vassal and held these territories as fiefs of the papacy. It took Robert twelve more years to complete the conquest of the southern mainland, ending in 1071 with the capture of Bari, the last Byzantine stronghold. Earlier, Robert had helped his brother Roger initiate the conquest of Sicily in 1061. With the fall of the main port, Palermo, in 1072, Roger was granted Sicily as a fief to be held with the title of count from his brother, Duke Robert. Roger's conquest of the island was completed in 1091.

The success of the Normans, where Charlemagne and his successors and Otto the Great and his successors had failed, is an impressive example of adaptation to a new environment. The Normans were superior fighters, as their contemporary reputation attests. But more than that, they were able to surpass the local rulers in guile, brutality, and treachery. The rise of Norman power in southern Italy and Sicily appalled even the Byzantine catapans and the Saracen emirs, who were well schooled in the arts of ambush, assassination, and betrayal. Finally, the Norman conquest of southern Italy and Sicily was made easier, if not inevitable, by the division and weakness of the enemy. The Saracens of Sicily could not unite in a common defense, and the Byzantine Empire had fallen into serious difficulties in the third quarter of the century, climaxed by the catastrophe at Manzikert in the same year that Bari fell to Robert Guiscard.

Norman success on land was matched by the growth of Italian sea power. Pisa and Genoa began the offensive against Saracen control of the sea in 1016 by an attack on Sardinia, which led to its conquest in 1022. This was followed by a series of attacks on Moslem ports of North Africa. By the end of the century the Italian seaports had contributed to the success of the First Crusade and had swept Saracen shipping from the Mediterranean. The year 1100 is a milestone in the growth of Italian maritime power. In that year a Venetian squadron attacked and defeated a Pisan fleet on its return from delivering reinforcements to Jerusalem. Having made the Mediterranean a Christian lake, maritime rivalry between the Italian towns continued for the rest of the Middle Ages.

The Normans in southern Italy and Sicily were unable at first to compete in the development of sea power. Amalfi, once the maritime rival of Genoa and Pisa, declined after it fell to the Normans in 1077. When Robert Guiscard and his son Bohemond of Taranto attempted to extend their conquests of Byzantine territory into northern Greece, the Venetian fleet cut their communications and caused the Norman campaign to collapse (1081–1083). In return for this service, the Byzantine emperor, Alexius, granted Venice such favorable trading privileges that her merchants dominated commerce in the Levant for over a century. From this unsuccessful venture Robert returned to Italy in time to deliver his lord and ally, Gregory VII, from his imperial enemies and to put Rome to the sack in 1084. A year later both Robert and Gregory were dead.

By all odds Robert Guiscard was the most brilliant political and military opportunist of the eleventh century. Only the Cid in Spain—where the situation was much like that of southern Italy—can be compared with him. After half a century of intrigues and battles, *Terror Mundi Guiscardus* ("Guiscard, terror of the world") died in bed at the age of seventy from an epidemic which struck his army while it was invading the Ionian Islands of the Byzantine Empire.

Bohemond of Taranto, born of Robert's first marriage, was passed over in the succession to the duchy of Apulia in favor of Roger Borsa (1085–1111), the eldest son of Robert's politic marriage with the sister of the last independent prince of Salerno. Robert's brother, Roger I (1061–1101), continued to hold Sicily as count and vassal of his nephew. Under this division, Sicily flourished and the duchy of Apulia with its dependent principalities declined. In 1127 Roger Borsa's son and successor, William, died, and Roger II of Sicily united the two Norman states of Apulia and Sicily. In 1130 Roger II the Great (1130–1154) assumed the title of king of Sicily.

The Norman kingdom of Sicily was an exotic compound of feudal, Byzantine, Saracen, and Lombard elements. The king maintained a harem in Moslem style; he exercised the authority of papal legate and thus controlled the Church more completely than any other ruler in Latin Christendom; and his government issued commands in Latin, Greek, and Arabic to officials who were variously styled justiciars, constables, logothetes, catapans, and emirs. The kingdom possessed the strongest political institutions of any realm in the first half of the twelfth century. Its subjects lived under feudal customs and a mixture of Roman-Byzantine-Moslem laws, but the will of the king and the justice of the royal courts overrode and consolidated the confusion of divergent local laws and customs. The king of Sicily was more nearly an autocrat than any other ruler in Latin Christendom.

The prosperity of the kingdom of Sicily grew under the enlightened and benevolent despotism of Roger II. His policy was aimed primarily at developing the sea power which his predecessors had lacked and at promoting trade and industry. Control of the western Mediterranean was ensured by conquest from the declining Almoravides of the North African ports opposite Sicily. During the last years of Roger's reign the kingdom of Sicily was the strongest maritime power in Italy, an achievement which united Genoa, Pisa, and Venice against Sicily until they had, in the second half of the century, regained mastery of the central Mediterranean.

34   ISLAM AND THE FIRST CRUSADE

In the Moslem world the period from the middle of the eighth century to the middle of the eleventh witnessed the flowering of Arabic civilization, especially in its economic and cultural aspects. Politically, however, the Moslems suffered from chronic decentralization. Lack of unity among the Moslem states made them relatively easy victims of the conquering Turks, whose expansion in the Near East set the stage for the First Crusade.

The accession to power of the Abbasid dynasty in 750 was more than a palace revolution. Three important segments of the Arab empire were discontented with Omayyad rule: the eastern Arabs, non-Arab Moslems, and a large part of the urban mercantile and industrial classes. The eastern Arabs, whose main strength lay in Persia, opposed the secular traditions of the western Arabs of Syria who supported, as they were represented by, the perfunctory religious leadership of the Omayyads. Non-Arab Moslems, including many recent converts whose enthusiasm for the new religion was high, opposed both the secularism of the Omayyads and their policy of Arab supremacy over non-Arab peoples. Merchants and artisans of the cities opposed the predominance of the Arab military aristocracy who were the main support of the Omayyad caliphate, but whose purpose and function in the empire had ceased with the end of Arab expansion. The Abbasid revolution meant that the future of Islam was in its universalism, embracing all races equally in the service of one faith, and that the unity of Islam was to be religious and economic rather than political and military.

The Abbasid caliphate (750–1055) marks the transition of the Arab empire "from a Byzantine successor state to a Middle Eastern empire" whose civilization was Oriental, cosmopolitan, and conservative. The Abbasids moved the capital eastward from Damascus in Syria to Bagdad on the Tigris, in Iraq, at the center of the far-flung trade routes. There the Abbasid caliphs assumed all the splendor and trappings of Oriental despotism. The caliph ruled by divine right, his power was absolute, he was "the Shadow of God on earth." But even Harun al Rashid (786–809), contemporary of Charlemagne and the greatest of the Abbasid caliphs, did not command the allegiance of all of Islam. Political decentralization began early, though it was neither so chaotic nor so complete as the disintegration of the Carolingian empire in the Christian West. Spain refused to recognize the new dynasty and continued to be ruled by the Omayyads after 756; Morocco was an autonomous province under a local dynasty after 788, Tunisia after 800, and Egypt after 868. Persia was divided between local dynasties during the ninth century, and by the middle of the tenth century the caliph at Bagdad in fact ruled little more than Iraq. By then, however, the caliphs had become simply figureheads dominated by the chief official of the government, the grand vizier, who was himself often merely the puppet of the palace guards. Most of the local dynasties were founded by provincial army commanders whose nominal recognition of the caliph's position took the form of occasional tribute, inscription of the caliph's name on provincial coinage, and the mention of his name during prayers on Friday.

Political decentralization did not affect the prosperity of Islam. The provincial rulers promoted industry and commerce and preferred the profits of peace to the risks of war. The honest and successful merchant occupied an esteemed position in society. In the bazaars of Bagdad and other cities commodities from China, the East Indies, India and Ceylon, central Asia, Russia, Scandinavia, east-central Africa, and Spain were bought and sold. Not all of this commerce was in Moslem hands. Moslem coins have been found in Sweden, for example, but they were brought back by Swedish traders who had sold in Islam such exports from the Baltic area as furs, wax, birch bark, arrows, fish glue, horsehides, honey, nuts, falcons, cattle, and—most expensive of all—slaves and amber. The trade with China, on the other hand, was handled by Moslem shipping as early as the eighth century. Imports from China were primarily high-priced luxury goods, such as spices, silks, paper, gold and silver utensils, drugs, and jewelry. From Africa the most valuable imports were gold and slaves. A large part of Moslem commerce distributed the products of Islam, both agricultural and industrial. The most important Moslem industry was in textiles, especially cotton goods (originally imported from India), silks, and carpets. Manufacture of paper was introduced in the reign of Harun al Rashid and had spread throughout Islam by the tenth century. Such a flourishing economy was just as important as a universal religion and a universal language in uniting Islam in one cosmopolitan civilization.

Bagdad, the fabulous city of the *Arabian Nights*, was the capital and center of Moslem culture, as it was of commerce, long after its political significance had disappeared. The cultural achievements of the Abbasid period were more impressive and more enduring than anything attained in the West before the twelfth century. Like Western culture, Moslem learning, literature, and art were largely built upon the heritage of antiquity. But the Moslems exploited Greek and Persian rather than Latin sources, and Moslem interests were primarily scientific in contrast with the contemporary Byzantine revival of classical literature. Men from all parts of Islam contributed to intellectual and cultural activities through Arabic, the language common to all educated people.

Arabic scholars excelled particularly in the fields of mathematics, medicine, and geography. Our "Arabic" numerals were known in the middle of the eighth century by Moslem mathematicians who called them "Hindu" numerals after the country from which they borrowed them. With these numerals and with the addition of the zero, Moslems developed the science of algebra (*al-jabr*) a century later. Arabic physicians studied diseases empirically and were especially successful in the diagnosis of rare maladies and of those whose symptoms were superficially similar to other ailments. But Arabic medicine was clinical rather than experimental. For theory it was dependent upon classical Greek medical works. An advanced system of hospitals aided the practice of medicine, but religious injunctions prohibited dissection and thus prevented any advance in surgery. Arabic geography was descriptive and highly practical; its main contribution was a great accumulation of new facts based on travelers' reports and commercial contacts beyond the boundaries of Islam. Finally, ancient Greek philosophical treatises were an important interest of Arabic scholars. The earlier work consisted of translations into Arabic. Later scholars wrote elaborate commentaries on Aristotle and other Greek philosophers, in which the main effort was to reconcile Greek philosophy with Moslem religion.

Cultural contacts between Islam and the West became increasingly important after the eleventh century. In a later chapter we shall consider the specific influence of Arabic philosophical and scientific thought on the intellectual revival of Latin Christendom. Compared with Byzantine culture, Arabic intellectual interests were more varied and original and also more influential upon the West. This influence was transmitted by individual scholars and patrons of learning, not by crusaders and merchants who generally lacked both the learning and curiosity to take advantage of the cultural achievements of Islam.

Islam under the Abbasid caliphate was, economically and culturally, a unified and brilliant civilization, but its political and military decentralization made it fall rapidly before the assaults of the Seljuk Turks. Appearing first in the tenth century in the region around Samarkand, this Asiatic tribe adopted the Mohammedan faith and with the zeal of new converts swept westward to restore religious orthodoxy and political unity in the greater part of Islam. By 1055 they had captured Bagdad and the person of the caliph, in whose name the Seljuk leader ruled with the title of sultan. At its height following the great victory over a Byzantine army at Manzikert in 1071, the Seljuk empire included Persia, Iraq, Syria, and most of Asia Minor. The center of Seljuk power was in Persia, and the sultan relied upon a Persian bureaucracy to hold together the several conquered provinces. After 1094, however, the same decentralization that had afflicted the Abbasid caliphate set in throughout the Seljuk dominions.

When the Byzantine emperor, Alexius I Comnenus (1081–1118), turned to the task of reconquering the provinces lost to the Turks, it was no longer a united Seljuk empire that he faced but rather the semi-independent Seljuk state which the Turks called Rum (i.e., *Romania*, consisting of the former Byzantine provinces of Asia Minor). But Alexius lacked manpower. The historic role of Asia Minor in the Byzantine Empire had been to provide fighting men for the imperial army. Alexius' predecessors had recognized the problem, and already within a year or two after Manzikert they had entered into fruitless negotiations with the Normans of southern Italy and with Pope Gregory VII to raise an army of western mercenary troops. Alexius renewed these efforts to gain western allies. In 1090 and again in 1095 he appealed both to lay rulers like the count of Flanders and to the pope, who was now Urban II. At the same time, negotiations were resumed between representatives of the patriarch and those of the pope with a view toward healing the schism of 1054 between the Latin and Greek communions.

A later Greek chronicler, who had access to information now lost, summed up the situation as follows:[1]

> Considering it impossible to defeat the Turks alone, Alexius saw that he would have to call in the Italians as allies, which he did with cunning, adroitness, and deep-laid planning. Realizing that westerners found unbearable the domination of Jerusalem by the Turks, he managed by dispatching ambassadors to the bishop of Old Rome and to kings and rulers of the western parts, by the use of appropriate arguments, to prevail over not a few of them to leave their own countries, and he succeeded in directing them to the task which he had in mind.

The "appropriate arguments" by which the emperor secured military help are unknown. Most historians agree today that Alexius proposed to Urban II that the Orthodox and Catholic branches of Christendom be reunited under the supremacy of the pope in return for papal sponsorship of an army to help Alexius reconquer the lost provinces of the Byzantine Empire. The times were propitious for such a proposal. Urban, with a broader vision of the world situation than Alexius could have appreciated, saw in the emperor's appeal an opportunity to realize several of the objectives of the Hildebrandine reform program.

Alexius had asked for some mercenary troops; what Urban II gave him was the First Crusade. The Crusade was preached by Urban at the Council of Clermont, in 1095, in one of the greatest orations of all time. This council was another of the reforming synods called under papal auspices to combat simony, clerical laxity, and other targets of the reforming party in the Church. Urban confirmed papal leadership in this reform program and tied it in with the grand new project of marshaling the forces of Latin Christendom to succor the oriental Christians from Seljuk oppression and to recapture Jerusalem and the Holy Sepulcher from the infidel. The Crusade would divert the restless military energies of the West to the service of the Church, thus giving the papacy universal leadership in maintain-

---

[1] Abridged and paraphrased from Peter Charanis, "A Greek Source on the Origin of the First Crusade," *Speculum*, XXIV (1949), 93, reprinted by permission of the Editor of *Speculum*.

ing peace at home (the Peace of God) and in directing a counterassault upon Islam which would reunite "the churches of God in the eastern parts" with the Western Church under papal supremacy. Prospects for the success of this grand project appeared more favorable than for many years because the struggle with Henry IV was turning definitely against the emperor. In preaching the First Crusade Urban II gave to Europe an ideology of expansion, and to feudalism a new moral purpose. From now on the highest ideal of knighthood was to be service to the Church; the expression of this service was to be war against the infidel.

Public opinion was prepared for this idealistic appeal to arms. The nobles and clergy assembled at Clermont responded to Urban with a zeal approaching frenzy. Shouting *"Deus volt"* ("God wills it"), hundreds of Urban's listeners took the cross. In the ensuing months preachers traversed western Europe enlisting men from all social classes in the Crusade. The most effective response came from the lesser nobility among whom the crusading spirit consisted in equal parts of religious zeal, zest for fighting, and materialistic ambitions—"younger sons in search of principalities and sinners in search of profitable penance." No king responded to the call. The military commanders included great nobles like Raymond, count of Toulouse; Godfrey of Bouillon, duke of Lorraine, and his brother, Baldwin; and Bohemond of Taranto, son of Robert Guiscard. Bishop Adhemar of Le Puy, the papal legate on the Crusade, was the nominal leader. He was charged with guiding the crusaders' efforts toward the goals outlined by Urban at Clermont while at the same time respecting the agreement, confirmed on oath by the lay leaders of the Crusade when they had reached Constantinople, to return to Byzantine rule the provinces that had formerly belonged to the eastern Empire.

Alexius was dismayed at the motley throngs that constituted the crusading army—the answer to his appeal for disciplined mercenary troops to bolster the imperial army. Almost immediately, the western leaders quarreled with him and fell to bickering among themselves. From Alexius' point of view the only constructive achievement of the Crusade was the capture of Nicaea, across the straits from Constantinople, and its return to the Empire in 1097. After this victory the crusading armies struck southeastward toward the Holy Land, leaving Alexius to attempt the reconquest of Asia Minor alone. Before the crusaders reached Jerusalem, however, Baldwin detached his own troops from the main body and seized Edessa in 1098, thus establishing the first of the Latin "crusader states" of Syria. Under Baldwin and his successors, the county of Edessa was a strategic salient thrust into Moslem territory protecting the northern flank of the Christian states in Palestine. This military advantage was counterbalanced by the fact that Alexius was alienated by what he considered to be an illegal seizure of former Byzantine territory. Eventually, Byzantine antagonism was as great a threat to the crusaders as Moslem enmity.

While Baldwin was conquering Edessa, the crusaders besieged Antioch, whose capture would open Syria to invasion. After a prolonged struggle, the city fell in 1098. By that time the leaders of the Crusade were bitterly divided over who should rule there. Some favored returning the city to Alexius, while Bohemond of Taranto and Raymond of Toulouse vied with each other to follow the example of Baldwin in Edessa. Finally Bohemond, who had played the major role in its conquest, was recognized as lord of Antioch by his fellow crusaders. By now all the leaders were more interested in capturing principalities than in completing the Crusade. Bishop Adhemar of Le Puy had died recently, Alexius' claims to the return of reconquered provinces were forgotten, and the First Crusade was about to degenerate into a series of petty land-grabbing expeditions, when Godfrey of Bouillon emerged as the leader and spokesman for the rank and file who demanded that the army press on to the Holy Sepulcher without further delay.

Under Godfrey's lead the crusaders reached Jerusalem in June, 1099, and after a month's siege the Holy City fell. Then the Christian conquerors got out of hand. Although leaders like Godfrey of Bouillon and Raymond of Toulouse spared the defenders who surrendered to them personally, almost the whole of the population—soldiers, noncombatants, the aged, women, and children—were indiscriminately slaughtered. After this brutal

*Islam, the Byzantine Empire,
and the First Crusade, c.1100*

carnage, a Moslem army tried to reconquer the city, but in August, 1099, the crusaders decisively defeated the Moslems at the battle of Ascalon, near Jerusalem.

The First Crusade was now completed, and the organization of the conquered territory began. Godfrey of Bouillon, who had the fewest personal enemies among the strife-ridden leaders, was elected king of Jerusalem, but the pious Godfrey declined that title (refusing to wear a royal diadem where the Lord had worn a crown of thorns); instead, he became ruler of Jerusalem and the surrounding country with the title Defender of the Holy Sepulcher. The implication was that his secular authority was subordinate to that of the new Latin patriarch of Jerusalem, whose obedience was to Rome rather than Constantinople. But before a year had passed, Godfrey died and was replaced by his brother, Baldwin of Edessa, who had no such pious scruples. Baldwin took the title of king and with his accession in 1100 the Latin kingdom of Jerusalem was established.

Baldwin and his successors were competent, but the problems and perils confronting the crusaders' kingdom were greater than they could overcome permanently. The initial problem, survival in a hostile world, was solved partly by the establishment of two military orders whose members took religious vows and were dedicated to protecting pilgrims and fighting the infidel: the Knights of the Hospital of St. John of Jerusalem (c.1099), and the Poor Knights of Christ and of the Temple of Solomon (c.1119). These orders, the Hospitallers and the Knights Templars, recruited membership and received economic support throughout western Europe. Their history, as we shall see, became entangled with the growth of the western monarchies long after their service in the Holy Land had become only nominal.

Economic Revival

THE BOURGEOISIE AND PEASANTRY

In the ninth century a Carolingian bishop wrote that society was divided into three classes, "those who pray, those who fight, and those who labor"—the clergy, the feudal nobles, and the peasantry. This analysis was accurate for his times, but by the end of the eleventh century it was no longer an adequate description of Western society. A fourth class had emerged: the bourgeoisie who dwelt in towns rather than in the countryside. The appearance of the bourgeoisie was part of a profound transformation of the conditions affecting all social classes in the eleventh and twelfth centuries.

The basic causes of this transformation were a marked increase in agricultural production and a corresponding increase in population. More food meant that more people could live longer, more people were stronger physically so that they could survive diseases or accidents, and—the most important factor—mothers were stronger and thus better able to nourish their offspring through the critical period of infancy. In a primitive economy the birth rate, sanitation, and the level of medical care are constant and unaffected by the food supply; therefore these factors cannot account for a substantial change in population. The infant mortality rate will also be high, but in an economy in which there are no canned or bottled formulas or baby foods, if more mothers have more food, then more children will survive infancy to add to the population and—with more food available—will be better able to survive diseases and accidents.

The food supply was increased by an improved agricultural technology and by bringing new land under cultivation. Peasants did not undertake this back-breaking effort in order that, as a result of their labor, they might increase the population. They did so because there were more mouths to feed: a growing population in both rural areas and in the new urban centers. More food produced a larger population; but a growing population called forth the production of more food. The effect had a reciprocal influence on its cause. Finally, both the growing population and the increasing agricultural production were promoted by the greater political and social stability achieved in the tenth and eleventh centuries.

Towns and the bourgeoisie were dependent upon commerce. Commerce largely depended upon a market for surplus agricultural commodities. The bourgeoisie provided part of the market, while part was provided by the growing rural population. Trade was further stimulated when manorial lords began to specialize, selling a surplus of one crop and purchasing supplies no longer produced locally from areas where they were more cheaply grown. This rudimentary specialization, accompanied by increased production at a lower cost per unit, resulted in the accumulation of greater wealth among the landowning nobility as well as among the merchants. This wealth in turn stimulated a greater demand for manufactured articles obtained either locally or in long-distance trade.

The increase in population which underlay the growth of towns and helped to provide the knights who conquered Spain, southern Italy, and the Holy Land as part of the political expansion of feudal Europe, also provided the basic pressure for an internal expansion within Europe. Great tracts of forest, swamps, and marshland were cleared, drained, and ditched to relieve the land-hunger of a growing population. The tremendous amount of labor expended in this internal expansion is one of the great economic facts of European history, comparable only with the American westward movement of the nineteenth century.

35   THE GROWTH OF TOWNS AND TRADE

The period from the beginning of the fifth to the end of the tenth century was the golden age of the great estate, the almost wholly self-sufficient village organized and administered at the end of the period as the medieval manor. For six centuries large-scale commerce was a negligible factor in the production, distribution, and consumption of goods. And yet throughout the period neither local nor long-distance trade wholly ceased. Money, the indispensable medium of exchange and the lifeblood of commerce, continued to be coined at a diminished rate; markets continued to be held although the stream of products bought and sold became a mere trickle; and for every century of the early Middle Ages there is scattered evidence of the occasional movement of commodities, both luxury goods and the necessities of life, from regions of greater production and supply to regions of dearth and demand. Trade did not disappear completely, but it became so unimportant that there was no longer a significant social class of wholesale and retail merchants, and the decayed towns were no longer important centers of commerce.

Most of the once flourishing Roman cities had declined until they had become little more than the administrative centers from which the bishop or, infrequently, a count or other secular official ruled his diocese, county, or bailiwick. Under such conditions there was no truly urban life. The Paris which Count Odo defended against the Vikings in 885 was the seat of a diocese and a strategic military strongpoint, but it was not yet a focus of important trade routes nor a concentration of population and wealth.

Trade in the early Middle Ages did not affect many people. The higher clergy, the royal courts, and some of the wealthier nobility were supplied with silks and other costly textiles of Byzantine and Moslem manufacture, with furs imported from the Baltic region, and with oriental spices. Spices were used by the few who could afford them. They smothered the taste of the semiputrefied food served up from the typical medieval kitchen. Or, on death, one could be "embalmed in spices instead of being rudely preserved in salt." This restricted commerce in luxuries barely affected the total economy. The small class of professional merchants, many of them Jews and Syrians from the eastern Mediterranean, had little or no influence in society. Payments from the West were usually made in gold. This caused a drain of that metal eastward, and from the eighth century until much later in the Middle Ages the silver penny was the standard circulating medium of exchange in Western Europe. The West also paid for imported luxury goods by exporting such basic raw materials as timber and iron, scarce in Moslem lands, and the more expensive slaves who were captured in wars either within or on the frontiers of Latin Christendom.

Local trade within the West declined even more than long-distance trade; but at no time did local markets completely disappear, nor did peddlers cease to hawk a few goods from village to village. The commodities sold in this local trade were mainly necessities which could not be produced in every locality: salt, fish, wine, linen textiles, and cattle. Few merchants were at first engaged in this local trade. Peasants brought their own small surplus, or the goods of their lords, to markets that were usually held on only a single day at two- or three-week intervals. Some of the greater lords, especially the abbots of larger monasteries, employed special agents called "negotiators" to travel about purchasing necessities and a few luxuries in larger quantities at various markets. These negotiators occasionally indulged in a little private trading, and they were therefore the earliest discernible class of professional merchants in the West who were not engaged in long-distance luxury trade.

The general decline of trade after the fifth century removed the incentive to keep the ancient system of Roman roads in repair. Lords who had jurisdiction over roads through their territories found it less profitable to keep them repaired and collect tolls from commerce passing over them than to use their peasant's labor in agricultural production. The few merchants and peddlers who transported goods from market to market had no means of their own to keep up the roads, so they turned to the many rivers, lakes, and coastal waterways where transportation was cheap. Overland transport was limited largely to commodities of higher price and smaller bulk which could be carried by pack animals, especially horses and mules which were able to travel faster and, with their shoes, over rougher terrain than could slow-moving carts drawn by oxen.

A basic cause of the revival of trade in the eleventh century was the growth of population. But the growth of population would not necessarily have stimulated trade if agricultural production had kept pace steadily and in all regions with that growth. Medieval agriculture was more vulnerable to the vicissitudes of weather and disease than modern agriculture. In a good season a surplus of grain was usually produced. Bad weather or pestilence, striking either crops or cattle, almost inevitably brought famine. The earliest significant revival of trade in the West resulted from the sale at high prices in famine-struck areas of basic necessities such as grain and cattle bought at low prices in regions where harvests had been plentiful. Economic revival was thus not the effect of a reopening of the Mediterranean routes to the East, but was rather the cause of that reopening. Long-distance trade on the Mediterranean involved a high proportion of expensive luxury goods for which the demand could not increase substantially until there was a greater concentration of wealth in the West. The increase in wealth providing this demand arose from greater production of essential commodities and the profits of trade in those commodities.

The earliest centers of commerce were in areas where agricultural production lagged behind the increase in population. Venice led in the southern revival of trade, and was closely followed by other Italian and southern French seaports which could not feed themselves. Cities like Venice, Pisa, and Marseilles traded salt for food and later branched into other commodities obtained by their shipping. Survival depended upon trade because these cities were not agriculturally self-sufficient. Venice had two great advantages: first, a favorable geographical location, assuring protection from enemies on the mainland and a sheltered trade route along the Adriatic coast to the Levant; and second, a favorable relationship with the Byzantine Empire—a semiautonomous position which allowed freedom of enterprise and gave her trading privileges within the Empire. In the eleventh century other Italian seaports made aggressive efforts to wrest trading privileges in Byzantine and Moslem lands. Sometimes by peaceful negotiation, and sometimes by a show of armed force, Genoa, Pisa, Amalfi, and Gaeta won favorable treatment in various North African and Levantine commercial centers. In the twelfth century Venetian supremacy in trade with the East was no longer secure. Mediterranean commerce came to be dominated by several Italian cities, all intermediaries between the economically advanced Levant and the western European markets.

In the north, commercial revival also began in areas where agricultural resources were insufficient to support a growing population. Such a region was Flanders, at the center of potential trade routes radiating by land and sea toward the Baltic area, the Rhineland, northern France, and the British Isles. Flemish soil was not suited to grain growing but it was suited for raising sheep. The earliest industrial enterprise north of the Alps that grew beyond the stage of handicraft output for local consumption was the Flemish woolen textile industry. Flemish cloth was exported in the eleventh century, as a cheaper product of higher quality, in exchange for the food of nearby regions of richer soil or for the lumber, furs, and metals of more distant northern regions. Lesser centers of commercial revival in the north were the Rhineland, the Île-de-France (the region surrounding Paris), and the ports of the North and Baltic Seas.

The luxury trade played only a small role in the north, compared with Mediterranean commerce, but contact with the East was maintained through the hazardous route from the Gulf of Finland down the Dnieper to the Black Sea or the Caspian Sea. Toward the end of the eleventh century Italian merchants began to cross the Alps with commodities from the Levant. One transalpine route crossed the western Alps into the Rhone Valley, whence goods were carried northward into the populous river valleys of the Loire, Seine, Meuse, and Moselle with their tributaries. Another transalpine route lay over the eastern passes and into the upper Danube and Rhine valleys, from which commodities were transported to western and central Germany by way of the lower Rhine, the Main, and the Elbe rivers and their tributaries.

The revival of commerce was the direct cause of the revival of towns. The early merchants were the first settlers in what came to be urban communities in the Middle Ages. Although merchants never constituted a majority of the population of any town, their settlement drew to a town the small shopkeepers, drivers, carters, artisans, and laborers whose livelihood depended upon the existence of large-scale trade. Merchants needed three conditions for success: first, a base of operations strategically located along trade routes, near local markets, and favorably situated for warehousing and the transportation or transshipment of goods; second, security in the form of protection by a strong local power against the dangers of war or violent seizure of property by lawless elements in the feudal world; and third, freedom of movement and freedom from the restrictions and routine of the manorial peasantry. Wherever merchants found these three prerequisites for successful commercial activity—favorable location, security, and freedom—towns grew and flourished.

Some of the important new medieval towns, such as London, Paris, or Cologne, had been cities under the Roman Empire, and were now revived after centuries-long decline. Other towns grew up where a ruler or great feudal lord had built a castle or fortified strong point, such as those of Alfred and his successors in England, called *burhs*, or those of the tenth-century kings in Germany, called *burgen*. In France the same word, *bourg*, appears with the same meaning. Originally, the inhabitants of these fortifications were members of a permanent garrison, but the revival of trade transformed the life of some of the "boroughs" from that of an essentially military installation into that of an essentially business and urban society. Almost without exception, former Roman cities and tenth-century boroughs that remained merely military forts were not located along important trade routes. And almost without exception, those which were favorably located did grow into towns whose inhabitants—the burgesses of England, the burghers of Germany, and the bourgeoisie of France—lived by trade and industry rather than by husbandry and bearing arms.

The earliest mercantile settlements were not within the fortified area, or inside the walls of the borough, but adjacent thereto. The origins of medieval towns are, paradoxically, to be sought in the suburbs, the *faubourgs*, which were clusters of houses and buildings outside the original walled enclosure. During the eleventh and twelfth centuries the growing towns built new walls to surround these enlarged areas. The same pattern of growth is characteristic of towns which had their origin in a mercantile settlement next to a great monastery or a royal manor. The protection afforded by the abbot or king, plus favorable location, provided the incentive for settlement, and as the nascent town grew up it eventually enveloped the original monastic or manorial center. This happened most frequently where the king or abbot or other lord was enlightened enough to see that encouragement of trade was more profitable than plunder, and where lords were willing to grant freedom to the urban inhabitants from the labor services and burdens of the peasantry.

The original impulse for bourgeois freedom came from the needs and demands of the merchants who associated themselves in organizations called gilds. The merchant gild grew naturally out of the efforts of the earliest merchants to survive in a hostile feudal world. Individually they were unable to protect themselves from robbery on the highways and waterways or to withstand the exactions levied by feudal lords as tolls and customs charged on their goods whenever they crossed a bridge, or passed a boundary, under the jurisdiction of a different lord. Collectively, however, the merchants discovered that they could resist these losses and exactions either by paying for security or by controlling the movement and sale of goods so that uncooperative feudal lords would lose the profits of tolls and customs. Thus the liberties or franchises enjoyed in greater or lesser degree by every lord were first extended to a part of the non-noble population of Europe as a result of the economic pressure which merchants, associated together in gilds, could bring to bear on feudal lords. The liberties obtained by these merchant gilds consisted of specific and particular privileges and exemptions, rather than any general or abstract freedom. Merchants, in other words, were like peasants: both unfree and ignoble except for specified privileges. They never became the social or legal equals of the nobility, whose freedom was qualified only by the restrictions or obligations specified by feudal custom.

The earliest bourgeois liberties were almost entirely economic and social, rather than political. Outside of Italy self-government in medieval towns was, with few exceptions, a development which came after the twelfth century. Typical of the eleventh and twelfth centuries was the recognition by charter, the legal instrument by which proprietary rights were granted in the feudal world, of certain basic rights and privileges that made possible the economic activity of the new mercantile class and its urban dependents. Although bourgeois liberties varied from region to region and within regions from town to town, according to the charters secured by the collective action of the merchants, there were certain basic liberties that were typical of urban life in the Middle Ages. Foremost was the free status of the inhabitants of the town, a condition guaranteed by the legal provision that any inhabitant who could prove residence for a year and a day within the town was accepted by the territorial lord of the region as being free in person. Any villein who could escape from his manor and "go underground" within a chartered town for a year could thus free himself from the servile obligations and the status of a serf attached to the soil.

Freedom to enter into binding contracts covering the purchase and sale of urban property and the commodities exchanged in commerce was just as important for the bourgeoisie as freedom of person and freedom of movement. The earliest charters of liberties to medieval towns therefore granted the right to buy, sell, or lease land within the town, exemption from the labor services owed by peasants, the substitution therefor of fixed money rents due to the lord of the town, and finally the right to sue and be sued only in the urban court, a court where disputes were adjudicated according to the customs of the town. The overall effect of these early town charters was to create within the feudal world jurisdictional immunities of a wholly new sort. In such privileged towns the customs and procedures of the feudal and manorial courts of the region were ignored in favor of the special needs of the bourgeoisie engaged in commerce. In the urban courts there grew up a new corpus of law, later called the *ius mercatorum* or "law merchant." This law provided speedy remedies, actions on debt and contract not covered by feudal custom, and the enforcement of rights over real property and chattels which were alienable (i.e., subject to purchase and sale) without the restrictions of feudal or manorial custom. Finally, the most typical of all bourgeois liberties was the right to hold a perpetual market, that is, the right to buy and sell goods at any time and under the terms and conditions established for such trade by the merchants of the town themselves. The resident merchants, moreover, were usually granted monopolistic control over the trade within the town and sometimes within a part or the whole of the region subject to the lord who granted the charter.

Lords who first granted these bourgeois liberties found that rights given up by charter were more than paid for by the profits accruing therefrom. The merchants paid large sums of money to induce lords to grant town charters; also, tolls and customs collected by the lord grew as a result of larger trade; and the profits of the lord's neighboring manors increased because of the growing market for agricultural products created by growing towns. In the early twelfth century the more enlightened lords, led by the kings of England and of France, founded new urban settlements with the same privileges as those granted to the merchants of older towns. Sometimes these new towns were laid out where no previous settlement had existed, as Henry I's foundation of Newcastle-on-Tyne; in other cases, a rural village was granted a charter in the hope that it would develop into a full-fledged urban and commercial center, as the little town of Lorris in northern France. Louis VI's charter to Lorris and that of Henry I to Newcastle became models according to which liberties were granted widely to both old and newly founded towns in France and England. In Germany the kings did not promote trade and urban development as effectively as the greater lords. The count of Zahringen, for example, provided his newly established town of Freiburg (in southern Germany, between the headwaters of the Danube and the upper Rhine) with the charter of liberties that became the model for urban colonization eastward. Where these new foundations or older settlements were favorably situated with respect to trade routes and local markets, they often flourished. Otherwise, the grant of privileges to artificially created mercantile settlements only stimulated the peasants of neighboring rural communities to aspire to the same degree of freedom.

36 THE IMPROVEMENT OF RURAL ECONOMIC CONDITIONS

Important as were the growth of trade and the origins of urban life, the economy of medieval Europe remained preponderantly agricultural and rural during the eleventh and twelfth centuries. For the great majority of people, the economic revival meant greater agricultural production and more efficient manorial exploitation. Although the ecclesiastical and secular lords of manors profited by the general increase in total production, by the rise in the general standard of living, and by the growing importance of money in the economy, it was the peasants who were the chief beneficiaries of improved economic conditions.

The basic and ultimate causes of rural and manorial revival were the same interrelated phenomena which have already been noted as the ultimate causes of the expansion of commerce and the rise of a commercial class, that is, the growth of population and the achievement of political and social stability by the new feudal states and principalities of Europe. In addition to these underlying causes, four more immediate causes of economic revival directly affected rural conditions. These were the influence of the towns upon rural economy and social conditions; the expansion of the total land under cultivation, both by enlarging established manorial units and by settling new land; the impact of a growing money economy upon manorial self-sufficiency; and the introduction and spread of technological improvements in agriculture.

The main economic effect of the towns upon the countryside was to provide a cash market for food. For the first time since the end of the Roman Empire, there was an incentive for maximum production of food. From the sale of surplus food in town markets, manorial lords and the peasantry derived money to purchase commodities that were either unobtainable on the manor or less expensive to buy in the towns than to manufacture locally. This early and partial specialization of production led to a slow rise in the material standard of living. The existence of a cash market made possible the accumulation of savings by the peasantry, an impossibility under the subsistence farming of the past, and with these savings villeins could now purchase from their lords concessions or even complete emancipation from their servile status. More directly, the towns were a haven of refuge for peasants who were willing to take the risk of flight from their manors. Not all migration into the towns was due to illegal flight from serfdom, however. The overpopulation of many manors led enlightened lords to permit younger sons to depart from the overcrowded villein tenements and take up residence in the towns in return for a single cash sum or for yearly payments in place of the manorial services and dues formerly owed. It was difficult for a lord to retain his rights over the descendants of such emigrants to the towns, and in this way a substantial number of peasants were able to make the transition from manorial serfdom to urban freedom. In some regions, especially in northern France, the example of the towns led the peasants of villages to combine in small federations, known as rural communes, and bring pressure on lords to grant them collectively the same kind of municipal privileges being won by the bourgeoisie. The rural communes never achieved urban status. Economically they remained agricultural, and the ownership of the soil remained with the manorial lord in contrast with the proprietary rights of the bourgeoisie over their houses and lots within towns.

Just as important as the influence of towns on peasant conditions were the results of the great expansion of the total area of land under cultivation. This expansion was a continuing process for over three centuries, beginning as a search for better land even before the rapidly increasing population in the eleventh century required the cultivation of more and more land. By about the year 1300 this movement had practically come to an end, and the cultivated area of western and central Europe was not substantially increased during the next five centuries. There were two ways in which the expansion took place: first, by the extension of existing settlements through clearing woodland or draining marshes; and second, by the establishment of new settlements through colonization of previously uninhabited stretches of forest, swamp, and wilderness—both within the general area of western Europe and on the eastern frontier of central Europe. In either case, the peasantry benefited more than did the lords who owned the land.

Plots recovered from the waste or woods of a manor were called assarts. These assarts were cleared or drained and brought under cultivation only at the expense of much human and animal labor, above and beyond the customary labor services which the peasants owed to their lord. A lord who sought to increase the acreage of his productive land found it necessary to offer his peasants especially attractive terms to induce them to undertake the effort of clearing assarts. Usually the inducement took the form of a special contract or agreement exempting the peasants from most of the services and dues normally paid to the lord, but reserving a money rental or a share in the agricultural produce. Sometimes the lord agreed to long-term leases including the right of the peasant to mortgage or sell his rights in the assart with the lord's consent. Since these peasants occupied small clearings, which did not fit into the strip system of the open fields, they were often exempt from labor on the lord's demesne and the services connected with cooperative husbandry that bound the other peasants together under the supervision of the lord's bailiff. For many practical purposes such peasants were no longer serfs, for they had escaped from many of the burdens and restrictions which serfdom entailed. Most of them remained unfree in their legal status, as villeins or serfs under the manorial jurisdiction of the lord and bound to the soil they tilled. But the general pattern of medieval villeinage was broken. In some instances such privileged villeins even gained complete personal freedom, both in their legal status and from the economic burdens of serfdom, in return for a cash rental of their lands.

Assarts involved either individuals or small groups of peasants who continued to live in the village of their ancestors. The colonization of new land involved whole communities of peasants who moved into regions of virgin soil. They built new village settlements complete with open fields divided into the usual strips and the meadows, pastures, and woods for common use. In the eleventh century the new settlers in previously unin-habited territory were often vagrant and landless peasants crowded out of overpopulated manors, "squatters" who took up occupancy uninvited and unsupervised by the lord whose forest or waste land they began to clear. In the twelfth century lords began to take the initiative in clearing new land. An enlightened lord could augment his cash income by inviting colonists to a suitable site and granting them generous terms on which they were to clear and cultivate the land in return for a rental in money. For the lord this enterprise was strictly an economic venture to increase his income; hence the new settlements almost never included a manor house or a ma-norial demesne. To induce villeins to move and to undertake the labor of clearing land, the lord had to grant personal freedom and exemption from the usual manorial services. The colonists all came from the servile class, but they left serfdom behind when they moved into the wilderness. Their only obligation to their lord was to pay rent in recognition of the lord's proprietary rights in the land they cleared. In this sense they were the lord's "invited guests," or *hôtes* as they were called in France. Many peasants—especially the more adventurous young unmarried men and other young men whose future, with a wife and growing family, on a small and servile ancestral tenement appeared bleak—fled from their lord's manor to become the *hôtes* of a new lord under more favorable conditions. This situation created a competition for labor, especially in regions where manors were not overpopulated with peasants. Lords of older manors in these regions were forced to reduce the services and payments of their peasants if they hoped to retain their labor. This competition between lords of newly cleared lands and lords of old and established manors contributed to the decline of serf-dom in many parts of Europe.

The *hôtes* enjoyed their security of tenure and status under the guar-antee of a charter, since there was no immemorial manorial custom to govern their condition. These charters of lords who founded new settle-ments—the *villes neuves* or "new towns" of northern France were typical—were the legal instruments that provided such settlements with many of the privileges of the bourgeoisie of the municipalities. They also were used as a means to attract more settlers. In some instances lords sent copies of their latest charters to be read aloud in the market places and church yards of the surrounding country, to give wide publicity to the advantages of resi-dence in their newly founded settlements. In this respect the medieval ma-norial lords set a precedent for the great landowners and railroad companies who opened up the American western frontier with a barrage of propaganda to convince potential settlers of the advantages of going west.

The third cause of improved economic conditions in the twelfth cen-tury has already been mentioned in its relation to the influence of towns and to the expansion of land under cultivation. This was the growth of a money economy. The use of money for the payment of obligations, or as a medium of exchange in trade and industry, has never completely superseded payment in kind (as in the modern form of farm tenancy called "share-cropping") or exchange by barter (the best modern examples being large-scale international transactions). After the decline of the Roman Empire and before the revival of the eleventh and twelfth centuries, money was unimportant because there was so little trade: almost all economic activity was geared to local self-sufficiency for subsistence rather than for profit. The growth of trade and the growth of production which supported trade in-creased the circulation of money and created a need for more money. The nobility supplied the initial demand for better and more expensive necessi-ties, such as food and clothing, and for more luxuries obtainable through trade with the eastern Mediterranean area. Hence, lords were willing to accept money payments from their peasants instead of the various manorial services and payments in kind. This commutation of labor services into money rents usually was effected in piecemeal fashion, the result of specific bargaining with respect to one or another of the services due to the lord from individual peasants. As the twelfth century wore on, however, it be-came more common for lords to give up the direct exploitation of the manorial demesne, leasing it instead to individual peasants or to the whole community of peasants collectively. The basic labor services—"week work" and "boon work" on the lord's demesne—were of necessity commuted for all the peasants, and sometimes this commutation covered all of the peas-ants' services and dues. Without any change in the legal and social status of the villeins of the manor, their economic condition in such a case was transformed because they retained all their profits beyond the money rental to their lord. This fact by itself introduced an incentive to higher produc-tion strong enough to break the old routine of manorial self-sufficiency.

Commutation had one other result that was even more beneficial to the peasants, although it was a slow-working force which neither lords nor peasants became aware of until the thirteenth century. The shortage of metal for coinage in the eleventh and early twelfth centuries, together with the force of custom, tended to keep prices down or to maintain the value of money at a high level. When commutation took place the labor services, considered by both lords and peasants to be immutably fixed by the custom of the manor, were commuted for the current approximate cost of hiring the equivalent of the peasants' labor. Wages and prices, and therefore money rents, were relatively low. After the middle of the twelfth century, if not earlier, there began a long-term inflationary tendency. Prices slowly rose, and with them rose wages. But the commuted rents, the money equiv-alent of unchanging and customary manorial obligations, tended to remain fixed. The peasants thus profited from an unearned increment resulting from inflation. For example, an English peasant whose labor services had been commuted in 1150 for two shillings provided his lord with a cash rent which would purchase about nine bushels of wheat; with the same income from the peasant's descendant in 1250, the descendant of the lord could purchase only four bushels. Prices rose in response to relatively free market conditions, while rents tended to remain stationary because of the force of manorial custom which they represented. The peasants received more money for the sale of their surplus food, and they paid the same amount of money of much less value for their land. This price revolution of the twelfth and thirteenth centuries was one of the most important economic factors influencing the welfare of the medieval peasantry. In the twelfth century the rise in prices generally benefited the peasants; we shall see later that in the thirteenth century manorial lords became aware of the situation and often took drastic steps to redress the economic balance in their own favor.

The conversion of property rights into cash revenue, the essential effect of commutation from the lords' point of view, was also associated with improved methods of manorial administration and exploitation. In this movement two new religious orders took the lead. These were the Knights Templars and the Cistercians. As a military order dedicated to fighting in the Holy Land, the Templars were endowed widely throughout western Europe with bequests of lands from the faithful in lieu of personal participation in the Crusades. The Templars needed revenue to finance the Holy War more than they needed the agricultural produce of their estates, and therefore on their manors commutation was more common than elsewhere. Where labor services were exacted and exploitation of the demesne continued on the Templars' estates, the manorial officials of the Order were primarily interested in selling the crops to raise revenue. The efficiency of Templar administration is illustrated by the great number of their manorial accounts of the twelfth century. These are the earliest business records which have survived in a large number.

The Cistercians were a reformed Benedictine order whose goal was to flee from the world and live up to the Benedictine ideal in all respects, including manual labor of the monks. Most of the endowments granted to the Cistercians were waste lands far from population centers and usually in areas not previously cultivated because of the poor quality of the soil. To survive at all, then, the Cistercians had to be efficient in their agricultural exploitation. They became experts in the clearing of forests and in the best methods of crop rotation and cultivation. Instead of splitting up their fields into individual tenements they farmed them in large blocks called granges where there was no distinction between demesne and peasant holdings. Some of the Cistercian lands were too poor for any crops. On these the monks and their lay brothers pioneered in the development of better sheep and cattle through advanced methods of animal husbandry, especially in cattle breeding.

The last important influence on rural economic conditions during the revival of the twelfth century was the introduction of technological innovations and the more widespread use of earlier technological improvements: three-field rotation, the heavy plow mounted on wheels, and horses in plow teams and as beasts of burden. The most striking technological advance was the introduction of the windmill in the second half of the twelfth century. The windmill may have originated in Persia, although there is no surviving evidence to tell how knowledge and use of windmills spread westward. By the end of the twelfth century the four basic sources of power known before the harnessing of steam in the eighteenth century— oxen, horses, water, and wind—were available for agricultural production and for the grinding of grain. Windmills brought power to regions where there were no streams or the waterfall was too slight to allow water mills, appearing earliest in the Netherlands, England, and northern France. Even more important for the economic revival of Europe than the appearance of windmills was the greatly increased number of water mills in use. By the end of the eleventh century there were over five thousand water mills in England alone: a figure of particular interest because there were approximately the same number of knights in the feudal army of the king of England. Not only were many more mills being built, a sure index of the growing demand for power, but the methods by which power was transmitted were improved during the eleventh and twelfth centuries. Gears were used to convert the slow motion of the waterwheel into the high-speed rotation of millstones; also, the rotary motion of the mill wheel was now for the first time converted into a reciprocal (back-and-forth, or up-and-down) motion needed in the fulling of cloth or in crushing materials such as bark for tanning leather. The main economic effect of these and dozens of other minor technological improvements did not come until much later, but the economic revival of the twelfth century was the period from which "must be dated that increasing mechanization of life and industry, based on the ever-increasing exploitation of new forms of mechanical power, which characterizes modern civilization."

The Feudal Monarchies, the Empire, and the Papacy

The political aspect of the revival of the eleventh and twelfth centuries may be divided chronologically into three major periods. The eleventh century was climaxed in the 1070's and 1080's by the investiture struggle between the Empire and the papacy, by the *Reconquista* in Spain, and by the establishment of a Norman state in southern Italy and Sicily. The century was brought to a close with the First Crusade and the foundation of the Latin kingdom of Jerusalem. In France and England during the eleventh century only one event of equal magnitude took place, the Norman Conquest of England in 1066, followed by a rapid development of the Anglo-Norman government into the strongest feudal monarchy in all of Europe except for the Norman kingdom of Sicily.

The second phase of political revival corresponds roughly with the first half of the twelfth century. It was a period marked by no great events. The contest between the popes and the emperors subsided, and the settlement at Worms in 1122 was followed, after the death of Henry V, by a disputed succession in Germany and a period of anarchy and localism on both sides of the Alps. The most important new development was the struggle for local autonomy by the communes of northern Italy. In France this was a period of political consolidation rather than expansion, under the stalwart and able Louis VI and his successor, the tenacious though less fortunate Louis VII. In England the strong rule of Henry I, last of William the Conqueror's sons, was followed by a disputed succession and a period known in English history as "the Anarchy," corresponding chronologically with the anarchy in Germany. Throughout western and central Europe the constructive energies of the feudal governments seemed to have been exhausted.

The third period began just after the middle of the twelfth century. In 1152 Frederick I Barbarossa succeeded to the imperial throne, and in 1154 Henry II became king of England. Each ruler energetically set about restoring the rights and powers of his crown, and each sought to expand and increase his control of the lands under his suzerainty. In response to these developments the papacy and the Capetian monarchy once more found the strength to defend their traditional claims. The papal revival began with the accession of Alexander III in 1159, while the French monarchy shifted from the defensive to an offensive policy against the English king with the accession of Philip II in 1180. In the second half of the twelfth century political issues had become just as clear-cut, and the development of political institutions had become just as important, as they had been during the eventful years dominated by such personalities as Gregory VII, William the Conqueror, and Robert Guiscard.

37   ANGLO-NORMAN ENGLAND AND CAPETIAN FRANCE

Cnut (1016–1035) brought peace and order, but he did not preserve the unity of the Old English kingdom. The older county system of local government was subordinated to a new Anglo-Danish system of combining several counties into a few great provincial governments under all-powerful earls, who did not at first represent any local or landed interest within their earldoms. Under Cnut the earls were effectively controlled by the king, but between his death and the Norman Conquest the kingdom was periodically disturbed by the ambitions and intrigues of four or five great provincial magnates headed by Godwin, earl of Wessex, and his sons.

Following the brief reigns of Cnut's two sons, the house of Alfred the Great was restored to the throne in the person of Edward the Confessor (1042–1066), son of Ethelred the Unready and the Norman princess, Emma, who had later become Cnut's wife. Edward grew up in Normandy, and he brought with him Norman advisers and ecclesiastical officials as a counterbalance to the powerful Anglo-Danish earls. Edward was pious and popular, but he was a mediocre king and his authority was weakened by failure to produce an heir. Conspiracies and rebellions reduced him to little more than the reluctant puppet of the powerful Earl Godwin and, later, of

Godwin's son Harold. One of the most serious crises of the reign was precipitated when Edward promised the succession to his kinsman, William, duke of Normandy. Then, during a later reaction against the Norman influence in England, the Norman archbishop of Canterbury was exiled and replaced by Stigand, the nominee of Earl Godwin. This act was regarded as uncanonical by reformers in Rome, where Stigand was excommunicated. Harold was the most powerful man in England during Edward's last years, when it became clear that both William of Normandy and Harold Hardrada, king of Norway, would claim the throne. On his death-bed, the Confessor nominated Harold of England to be his successor, a popular choice since only Harold was strong enough to defend the kingdom against invasion.

Duke William considered Harold a usurper and a traitor to himself personally. The English earl had recently sworn an oath to uphold William's claims—so the Normans argued—during an obscure incident that began with Harold's capture on the coast of Normandy and ended with his honorable entertainment at the duke's court and later release. William assembled the last and greatest feudal expedition in the eleventh-century expansion of Normandy. The Norman Conquest differed from earlier feudal adventures. It was led by the duke himself, with most of the Norman lords, his vassals, participating in the expedition. William also enlisted many of the feudal lords of Brittany, Maine, Flanders, and northern France, offering them the spoils of victory in return for military service. The times were auspicious, for the new French king was a child under the regency of William's father-in-law; the neighboring and traditionally hostile county of Anjou was neutralized by a civil war; and William obtained papal blessings for his expedition, which reformers in Rome expected to result in the deposition of the uncanonical archbishop, Stigand.

The success of the Norman Conquest was assured by events beyond William's control. The first invasion of England in 1066 struck in the north, where Harold Hardrada of Norway crushed the forces of the earls in charge of defense of the northern counties. Harold of England rushed northward with his housecarls, the specially trained bodyguard of the king. Five days after the rout of the northern earls, Harold defeated the Norwegians at the battle of Stamford Bridge. Two days later, previously unfavorable winds on the Channel shifted and the Normans were able to sail. On the news of William's landing, Harold and his housecarls immediately set off for London where the local militia was ordered to gather. Harold's courage was in the best Anglo-Scandinavian military tradition, but his decision at this point altered the course of English history. His weary housecarls had not rested after two forced marches and a great battle, all within three weeks, and the levies from the southern shires were only half-assembled, when Harold decided to push on from London in order to fight the mounted knights of the Norman host on high ground of his own

choosing. This would favor the tactics of the housecarls, the backbone of his army.

As it turned out, the battle of Hastings was almost Harold's victory. The day-long struggle was slowly turning in favor of the English, whose defense was based upon the wall of shields behind which stood the house-carls and against which the Norman cavalry charged in vain. Finally the Norman knights fell back in a disorderly retreat which seemed to augur victory for Harold but in fact sealed his defeat. Some of the English infantry broke ranks and rushed down the hill in pursuit, from the flanks of the defense line. The Normans were then able to cut to pieces the separated elements of the defending forces. The housecarls never moved from their prepared position, but now that their flanks were exposed they slowly succumbed and perished to a man, Harold with them.

The Norman Conquest was not completed until several years later, after resistance in the north and west had been put down. William as king declared the lands of those who fought at Hastings, and of those who later resisted, to be forfeited for treason. In addition, he required all bishops and abbots to hold their ecclesiastical lands by feudal tenure. In effect, William the Conqueror (1066–1087) became feudal lord of all the land of England. This introduction of feudalism was the most important result of the Conquest. Before 1066 only a small minority of the approximately two thousand landed estates in England were the possessions of men who were primarily warriors or were dependent upon the king as their personal lord. After the Conquest, these estates were consolidated into approximately two hundred major fiefs all held by military service by the king's immediate vassals, his barons or tenants-in-chief. Subinfeudation of vassals by the tenants-in-chief had become extensive by the end of the Conqueror's reign, and England soon became the most thoroughly feudalized part of Europe. Feudalism simplified the social structure and transformed the aristocracy into a tightly knit feudal nobility organized primarily for war, giving "the upper ranges of Anglo-Norman society a stability and cohesion unknown in the pre-Conquest state."

The rest of society, including the Church, was relatively less affected by the Conquest. Stigand and three other bishops were deposed, but not until 1070 and then only by a synod presided over by papal legates. Lanfranc, William's new archbishop of Canterbury, proceeded to introduce the reforms which were gaining acceptance on the continent. The most important reform was effected jointly by William, who prohibited the hearing of

The Norman Conquest. Scenes from the Bayeux Tapestry (c.1077). From top: Harold, touching two shrines, takes an oath to Duke William, enthroned. Harold, crowned and enthroned at Westminster, is acclaimed king. The Norman invasion fleet crosses the Channel. Norman cavalry charge against the English shield-wall. THE BAYEUX TAPESTRY, ED., SIR FRANK STENTON, PHAIDON PRESS, LONDON.

spiritual pleas in secular courts, and by Lanfranc under whom courts of ecclesiastical jurisdiction were established. For the bulk of the population—the peasantry—the change to Anglo-Norman rule had little influence other than to depress gradually into manorial servitude many of the numerous free peasants.

In government, the Norman settlement preserved the local institutions of the county court, the hundred court, and the borough court. The personnel who controlled these courts were now French, but the law continued to be the customary laws of the Anglo-Saxons plus such modifications in criminal law as were necessary to maintain order in the newly conquered realm. To stress the legitimacy of his succession, William confirmed the laws and customs of Edward the Confessor and vigorously asserted the rights of the Old English crown. These rights gave him powers exercised by no other feudal ruler at that time, especially the right to collect a national tax on land (the Danegeld) and the transcendent criminal jurisdiction which inhered in the English "king's peace." Under the king's peace private warfare was outlawed, and all military service by vassals and sub-vassals was performed only in the king's behalf. Feudalism, grafted onto the rights of the Old English crown, made the Anglo-Norman kings the most powerful feudal monarchs in western Europe.

William the Conqueror impressed contemporaries as a king who "excelled all the rulers of his time in wisdom and magnanimity, who was never deterred from an enterprise by toil or danger, and who could cope with adversity as he could profit from prosperity in his fortunes." Personally, he was stern and harsh of voice, but scrupulously just and properly pious. "He was temperate in eating and drinking, for he so abhorred drunkenness that he rarely drank more than thrice after a meal." In the history of Normandy and England, William's greatness lies in the ruthless energy and determination with which he enlarged and consolidated his rule as duke and king. The foundation of the Anglo-Norman state marks the political transition, in northern Europe, from the "iron age" of feudalism, an age of survival and recovery of some political order, to the greater feudal age of constructive state-building from which the modern nations of Europe have descended. The most typical act of William's career was the result of "deep speech at Gloucester" where he held his council at Christmas, 1085. It was decided to make a detailed investigation of the human and material resources of the whole kingdom. Only a powerful ruler with an efficient government could carry through the great survey of England of 1086, an administrative effort more impressive than anything since the time of Diocletian and Constantine. County by county, and fief by fief, royal officials listed all the manors of England, together with a statement of who held each manor, its assessment for Danegeld, its value, the number of plows and peasants, and other details of manorial resources. Similar information was compiled for each town or borough. The results are still preserved in

Land of the King.   In Woking Hundred.

In Guildford King William has seventy-five
houses in which one hundred and seventy-five men dwell.
In the time of King Edward it rendered eighteen pounds
and three pence. Now it is valued at thirty
pounds and nevertheless it renders thirty-two pounds.

Passage from Domesday Book. PUBLIC RECORD OFFICE, LONDON.

Domesday Book. It was "an undertaking without precedent, forced upon a reluctant country by the king's will." In its thoroughness and detail, Domesday Book is unmatched for any country until the first United States census in 1790.

William divided his dominions between Robert, his eldest son, who inherited the duchy of Normandy, and William II Rufus (1087–1100) who received the conquered kingdom of England. Henry, the youngest son, was given no land to rule but received a huge treasure in compensation. Robert could not control the Norman baronage and climaxed his weak rule by joining the First Crusade, where he could indulge his love for warfare without the responsibilities of government. William Rufus' reign was beset with rebellions and a quarrel with Anselm, the new archbishop of Canterbury, over the question of lay investiture. Henry, landless but ambitious, used his wealth to stir up trouble for both brothers. Henry may have had a hand in the "accident" from which William Rufus died while hunting. A friend of Henry's shot the arrow which killed Rufus; Henry, a member of the hunting party, immediately rode off to Winchester to seize the royal treasure and claim the crown while his brother's corpse lay rotting in the forest where he fell. Few subjects mourned the dead king, but there was considerable sentiment in favor of the elder brother, Duke Robert, who was now returning from the Crusade.

The first act of Henry I (1100–1135) was to issue a coronation charter of liberties abolishing the "evil practices with which the realm of England has been unjustly oppressed," an obvious effort to gain the support of the ecclesiastical and lay nobility. His policy was to forestall opposition or rebellion on behalf of Robert by concessions. Henry invited the archbishop, Anselm, to return from the exile into which Rufus had driven him and, having repelled an invasion by Robert, he patched up the quarrel over lay investiture in a compromise agreement in 1107. Meanwhile Henry had invaded his brother's duchy and, at the battle of Tinchebrai in 1106, defeated Robert and reunited Normandy with England.

The rest of Henry's reign was important for the development of the central government, notably the appearance in England of a specialized department of the *curia regis* (king's court) devoted to finances. This was called the Exchequer after the chequered cloth covering a large table on which accounting was done by means of counters, on the principle of the abacus (a device with which calculations are made by sliding or moving pieces along grooves or on rods). Our earliest reference to the Exchequer dates from 1110. The central government under Henry, or when he was absent on the continent under a viceroy called the chief justiciar, exerted a strict control over the sheriffs and other local officials. Henry also recruited a new class of government officials from the lesser nobility, or even from the non-noble class, who rose to prominence on their own merits and owed their positions wholly to the king.

Toward the end of the reign a reaction was developing against this increase of central power, and on Henry's death a disputed succession provided the nobility an opportunity to redress the balance. Henry's only surviving legitimate child was Matilda, widow of the emperor Henry V. While Henry lived he had been able to force his barons to recognize Matilda as his successor, but now most of the Normans and many English nobles gave their allegiance to Stephen of Blois (1135–1154) whose claim descended through his mother, a daughter of William the Conqueror. Stephen's rule was never wholly effective throughout the kingdom, and toward the end of the reign his lifelong foe, Matilda, was gaining the upper hand. When his son predeceased him, Stephen came to terms and recognized Henry, Matilda's son by her second marriage to Count Geoffrey of Anjou, as his successor. During this period of disputed succession and civil war, "the Anarchy" as it is called, central government almost collapsed. It is significant, therefore, that feudal lords strove to limit private warfare and suppress disorder within their fiefs by means of private treaties among themselves. These documents show that feudalism and anarchical conditions were incompatible. The feudal lords objected to a superior authority that had grown too powerful, but not to the orderly government which that authority had achieved.

In the period 1066–1154 there were few decisive events affecting the Capetian monarchy and France. When King Henry died in 1060, he left to his young son, Philip I (1060–1108), a royal domain scarcely larger than that of Hugh Capet. Philip's domain controlled communications through the heart of northern France, connecting the Loire with the Seine. It was a prosperous and populous area of agriculture and contained two growing towns, Paris and Orléans. But compared with his four most important neighboring vassals, the king of France had neither the wealth of the count of Flanders to the north or of the count of Champagne, whose fiefs almost surrounded the royal domain, nor the military power of the count of Anjou to the west and the duke of Normandy to the northwest. Compared with the simple royal household whose officials nominally governed the royal domain, Normandy possessed a relatively advanced administrative system firmly under the duke's control. All that Philip I could hope to do was to keep these neighboring vassals divided, concentrate his efforts on controlling the royal domain, and, when opportunity arose, attempt to encroach upon the border lands. Philip rivaled the power of the duke of Normandy and excelled that of his other vassals only in his control of Church offices and revenues. However, he was an opponent of reform and he spent several years under excommunication for moral lapses including a bigamous marital adventure with the wife of the count of Anjou.

The balance of feudal politics in northern France was upset when the duke of Normandy became king of England. Philip supported the ineffectual Robert, first aiding him in rebellion against his father and, after 1087, in war against William Rufus, in an effort to keep Normandy separated from England and under weak rule. Philip's intervention was ultimately unsuccessful; and for this failure his avarice and sloth were responsible. According to a contemporary, at one critical stage when William Rufus invaded the duchy, Philip "belching from daily excess went hiccupping off to the wars, but having accepted a bribe he returned to his feasting."

Philip's successor, Louis VI (1108–1137), inherited little from his father beyond a tendency toward corpulence. In later years he had to be hoisted onto his horse. He was called "the Bruiser," a sobriquet that suggests the bulldozer-like force with which he beat into submission the petty barons and vassals of the Île-de-France. He was the first Capetian whose authority over the royal domain was completely effective. The officials of the royal household usually held their offices by hereditary feudal tenure, which gave them a measure of independence. Louis expanded the *curia regis* to include minor ecclesiastics and bourgeois laymen who were dependent on him and in whose hands he placed the real administration. Louis was also the first Capetian to make his royal authority effectively felt in the internal affairs of distant provinces in central France.

Louis VI spent twenty-five years, with short interruptions, in actual hostilities with Henry I. The French king suffered two major reverses, but at the end of the reign the balance of power abruptly shifted when the duke of Aquitaine entrusted to Louis the marriage of his daughter and heiress, Eleanor. Eleanor of Aquitaine was promptly married to Louis VII, who had already been crowned king in accordance with Capetian policy. The Capetian monarchs became for the first time the greatest feudal lords in the realm, since Eleanor's dowry was the duchy itself, one third of the territory of medieval France.

Louis VII (1137–1180) gave France a long and weak reign, during which the fortunes of the Capetian monarchy were more than once in danger. And yet the monarchy as an institution was stronger than ever at the end of Louis' reign. His personal popularity and his protection of the Church and the bourgeoisie were partly responsible; but the growth of the monarchy was primarily the work of able clerical and lay officials of the government. The most distinguished of these civil servants was Suger (d.1151), abbot of the monastery of St. Denis, who was regent of the kingdom during the king's absence on the Second Crusade (1147–1149). This venture, Louis' least effective project among several failures, led to the annulment of his marriage with Eleanor of Aquitaine. At first happily married, the high-spirited Eleanor soon grew weary of Louis' solemn piety and dull personality. She is said to have exclaimed, "I thought I married a king, but instead I am the wife of a monk," and Louis grew exasperated with her behavior which, especially while she was accompanying him on the Crusade, gave rise to scandalous reports. Such reports were exaggerated. Eleanor was later accused of infidelity with Saladin, who was about six years old at the time. It is doubtful that Louis would have given up Eleanor and her duchy, if it had not been for the fact that after fifteen years she had borne him only two daughters who survived infancy. The prospect of a failure of heirs led Louis to secure an annulment, on grounds of consanguinity, in 1152.

With the annulment Louis lost Aquitaine. This would not have been a catastrophe except that within two months Eleanor, piqued perhaps by an injured pride, rushed into matrimony with Henry Plantagenet, count of Anjou, son of the late Count Geoffrey and of Matilda of England. By his father's recent conquest Henry was already duke of Normandy, and by his mother's perseverance he was about to become king of England. Now he became duke of Aquitaine in right of his wife, and the balance of feudal politics once more shifted in favor of the Capetians' hereditary enemy and greatest vassal. For Eleanor, also, it was quite a change. She presented to her new husband not only three daughters but also five sons. Louis gained little solace from his second wife, who bore him two more daughters. His third marriage was more successful both politically and dynastically, for it allied the powerful counts of Blois and Champagne with the Capetian house and it produced the longed-for heir, Philip II.

38   HENRY II AND THE "ANGEVIN EMPIRE"

When Henry II (1154–1189) was crowned king of England, he issued a coronation charter confirming "to God and to Holy Church, and to all my barons and vassals" the liberties and free customs granted by his grandfather Henry I. Stephen was not mentioned, and in this omission may be detected Henry's policy toward England: the restoration of the realm to the conditions existing before the Anarchy. His first task was to re-establish royal authority. Mercenary troops were expelled and the unlicensed castles which had made possible local defiance of central authority were either razed or resumed into royal control. So successful was Henry's forceful assertion of royal power that he was able, within thirteen months, to return to the continent where his real interests and his more important problems lay.

As duke of Normandy Henry was also ruler of Maine, as count of Anjou he ruled Touraine, and as duke of Aquitaine he was suzerain of the counties of Poitou and Auvergne and had claims to the overlordship of Toulouse. His territories stretched from the Scottish border to the Pyrenees, a congeries of dominions usually called the "Angevin Empire." The phrase

The "Angevin Empire" and France, c.1154

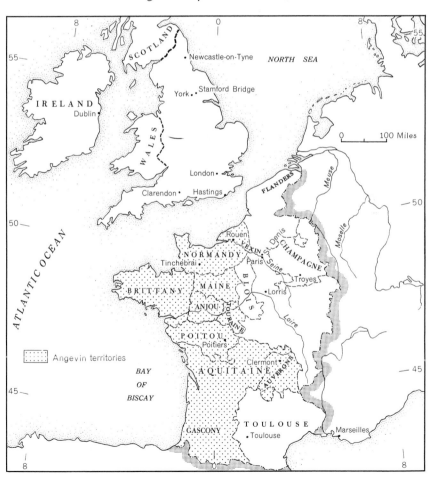

is a convenient expression because it emphasizes the essential point of view of its ruler, that of a count of Anjou, and it suggests a rough parallel with the complex of territories and rights which constituted the medieval Empire. Henry Plantagenet was above all a French feudal lord. He could not speak English, and he considered England valuable primarily for the prestige of a royal title to balance against that of his continental lord, the king of France, and because England provided revenues with which to pursue continental ambitions. Except for the emperor, Henry was the greatest feudal ruler in Europe. But the Angevin empire was bound together by only one real tie, the personal allegiance of the feudal lords of England, the two duchies, and the several counties to Henry. There was no common government, no common financial or judicial system, and no common linguistic, ethnic, or cultural tradition. It was only because of Henry's restless energy and feudal statecraft that his "empire" was held together and even enlarged.

Henry's initial effort was to make good his claim to the county of Toulouse, in 1159. Louis VII, exhibiting a rare flash of energy, rushed southward to aid the count, his brother-in-law, and entered the city just before Henry's armies could surround it. Henry did not dare to attack his own feudal lord within the walls, because he could not afford to set such an example to his vassals. The main result of his campaign was to stimulate the French king to make the most effective intervention in southern France since the later Carolingians. Henry's next objective was to annex the Norman Vexin, on the border between the royal domain and Normandy, over which kings and dukes had quarreled for two centuries. The strategic area was then held in trust by three custodians as the prospective dowry of one of Louis' daughters, who had been betrothed to Henry's four-year-old son in 1158. Thwarted at Toulouse, Henry now resorted to diplomatic sharp practice. The two infants were married in 1160, thus delivering the Vexin to Henry's control as his two-year-old daughter-in-law's dowry in spite of Louis' protests. Henry further enlarged his empire in 1171 when his son Geoffrey became count of Brittany, thus securing control of the lower Loire and protecting Henry's north-and-south communications.

Henry's grandiose plans on the continent will never fully be known because they were not allowed to mature. His influence extended beyond the Pyrenees, into Italy, and east of the Rhine, in each case through marriage alliances involving his daughters and the sons of ruling houses. His relations with the Norman kingdom of Sicily were especially close. Henry's enemies believed he was also trying to purchase the support of the northern Italian communes for some unknown scheme, perhaps for the union of Sicily with his own dominions including northern Italy, or perhaps for nothing less than the imperial crown. Louis VII and Henry's own family were responsible for the failure of his plans. Eleanor's marriages had taken her from one extreme to the other, from the monkish Louis to the profligate Henry whose only concession to his wife's feelings was to keep his infidelities relatively unpublicized. Eleanor took her revenge by stirring up discontent among their children. Young Henry, crowned king of England in 1170 in imitation of the Capetian practice, did homage to Louis for the continental possessions which he was to inherit (Normandy, Maine, and Anjou), while his brothers Richard and Geoffrey did homage for Aquitaine and Brittany, the lands assigned to them. The grievance of each was that his authority was only nominal. Eleanor and Louis encouraged them into open rebellion. If the rebellion, which began in 1173, had been well co-ordinated it would have broken the Angevin empire into its constituent parts. Henry was confronted with risings in England, Normandy, Brittany, and Aquitaine. But the Church remained loyal, as did the officials of his several governments, so that Henry was able to crush the rebels separately. The sons were forgiven and treated generously, but Henry was ruthless in destroying the private castles of lords who had supported his sons, while he repaired and strengthened the royal castles. As for Eleanor, she was kept under detention so long as Henry lived.

The collapse of the great rebellion of 1173–1174 gave Henry ten years of relative peace. Relations with Louis even grew friendly. Henry was no longer so eager to build up an empire for ungrateful heirs, and he devoted more attention to his kingdom. Before 1173 he spent only a third of his time in England; after 1174 only one year passed without a visit. Henry's purpose originally was to create a government in England which could rule effectively in the absence of the king. In a feudal age of personal rule, when the strongest political bond in society was still the homage and fealty of vassal to lord, Henry's achievement of this purpose makes him one of the great medieval statesmen. His work in England was the permanent monument of his reign.

Having re-established royal authority after twenty years of disorder, Henry restored the institutions of the central government. The Exchequer resumed its semiannual sessions. The regular revenues from the shires and from the royal courts, plus the extraordinary revenues arising from feudal incidents or special taxes, were accounted for on records called Pipe Rolls because of their cylindrical appearance when rolled up. These rolls, preserved in a continuous series from the second year of the reign, are the earliest surviving routine governmental records of any nation. In the Pipe Rolls can be traced the collection of royal revenues and improvements in financial administration. For example, scutage was the commutation of military service for a money payment. Instead of serving in person, the vassal paid a sum with which the king could hire mercenary troops called soldiers because they fought for wages (*solidi*) rather than as vassals owing military service to their lord. Another lucrative tax was royal tallage, by which the king was able to tap the growing wealth of the boroughs and the agricultural profits of his demesne manors.

Closely related to financial developments were reforms in the general administration and in the control exercised by the central government over local officials. Henry II designated one official of his *curia regis*, the chief justiciar, to act as viceroy responsible for routine administration during the king's absences from England. When a special problem arose Henry personally directed developments. One instance was an inquiry concerning the enfeoffment of knights by tenants-in-chief, the results of which are preserved in the *Cartae Baronum* of 1166. Henry had two motives: first, to obtain the allegiance of all subvassals on the eve of a prolonged stay (1166–1170) on the continent; and second, to find out which barons had enfeoffed more knights than the military service they owed the king necessitated, and to charge scutage on the total number of knights enfeoffed rather than upon the knights' service customarily due.

On his next visit to England Henry was confronted with widespread complaints about extortions and malpractices by sheriffs and their bailiffs. Also, his barons and their stewards were charged with misgovernment within their baronies, and complaints were lodged against other officials such as royal foresters and minor ecclesiastical officials. Henry suspended all the sheriffs from their offices and instituted a great inquest into these miscellaneous grievances: the Inquest of Sheriffs of 1170. As an assertion of royal authority over local government and over the affairs of his barons, this inquest went beyond even the Domesday survey of 1086. The majority of the sheriffs, many of them feudal lords of great local influence, were replaced with officials of the *curia regis*. After 1170 the monarchy relied more on professional administrators than upon local magnates in local government, and this change was one of the reasons why some English barons joined in the rebellion of 1173–1174. It is a significant measure of the strength of the government that the justiciar could quell the rebellion in England without assistance from the king. A more immediate result of the inquest of 1170 was the suppression of corrupt practices which enriched sheriffs and other officials at the expense not only of the people but also of the central government. Behind these reforms may thus be seen a financial motive.

The same is true of the judicial reforms for which Henry II is called the "founder of the common law." The common law was that part of all the laws and customs of England which was administered, according to uniform procedures, by the king's courts. Since only the king's courts had jurisdiction throughout all the realm, the procedure and the laws recognized by the royal courts became common to the whole of England. Justice administered in the king's courts was less expensive, more rapid, and more equitable than the justice obtainable from feudal courts and courts of local or private jurisdiction. Because royal justice was better justice, the common law grew and the diverse laws and customs administered by feudal and local courts declined.

The three principal means by which Henry II built the common law were the itinerant justices, the sworn inquest or jury, and royal writs. None of these was new; but the way in which Henry employed all three together was new and very effective. What had previously been only an occasional use of justices representing the king in the counties became, after 1166, regular and frequent. In that year Henry issued the Assize of Clarendon: instructions to his itinerant justices on the administration and enforcement of criminal law. The most important provision concerned the sworn inquest of lawful men of each locality who were commanded to present or state on oath to the itinerant justices whether any person in their neighborhood was suspected of having committed a crime. The jury of presentment was the ancestor of the modern grand jury which, essentially, fulfills the same function, presenting an indictment on the basis of which a trial may take place. Henry was putting to a different use the same sworn inquest used by William the Conqueror in the Domesday survey eighty years earlier.

The essence of the inquest was the oath taken by its members to speak the truth; hence, they are called a jury (having been sworn, *jurati*) and their statement is a verdict (*veredictum*, something truly said). The person presented or accused of a crime was required to stand trial. In the twelfth century this usually meant that he was put to the ordeal of cold water, a procedure by which the accused was trussed and lowered into a pool of water which had been solemnly purified by a priest. Because the consecrated water was believed to receive the pure and reject the sinful, if the accused sank he was innocent (and hauled out before drowned), but if he floated he was guilty. Henry relied less on such providential signs than he did on the verdict of a local jury; if the accused was absolved by the outcome of the ordeal he nevertheless was required to abjure the realm if he was a man of ill repute.

At about the same time Henry II decided to employ the jury in "common pleas," or civil suits between two individuals concerning property. There are occasional precedents for this use of a jury, but Henry II extended to all free men what his predecessors had infrequently granted as a favor. In this use of a jury, the connection between criminal and civil actions at law was originally very close. Medieval lawyers and judges drew a sharp distinction between *possession of* property and *right to* property. In an age of rugged individualism, self-help rather than due process of law often determined possession *de facto*, in contrast to possession *de jure* or by legal right. The king of England had a direct interest: if party A dispossessed party B of property, without the judgment of a court authorizing party A to do so, there was a presumption of violence and breach of the king's peace. To preserve peaceful possession without prejudice to either party's ultimate right to the property, Henry II issued instructions to his judges by which possession was protected through a procedure which employed the jury. These instructions, and the jury which they authorized, were each called an assize. The legal action in the court was called a possessory assize. The possessory assize enabled the plaintiff a speedy remedy by submission to a jury of a simple question whose answer had to be either yes or no, without qualification, based upon local knowledge. Was the plaintiff dispossessed of such-and-such property without judgment of a court? Was the plaintiff's father, whose heir he is, possessed of the property on the day on which the father died? Did the plaintiff, or the man whose heir he is, last nominate the incumbent of such-and-such a church or benefice? If the jury's answer was affirmative, the plaintiff was restored to possession (the property could be intangible—the right to nominate to a church office, as well as real property), and the defendant was dispossessed by judgment of the court. The possessory assizes helped maintain the king's peace by reducing self-help in a violent age, and the Exchequer profited no matter how the case ended. If the plaintiff lost, he was amerced (or fined) for a false plea; if the defendant lost, he was amerced for having broken the law.

This judicial machinery for swift and equitable justice in the royal courts was set in motion by royal writs designed for each type of litigation. A writ was simply a written command addressed by the king to one of his officials, such as a royal justice or a sheriff, directing that the plaintiff be heard and a jury assembled. Writs were standardized in their wording, they could be written quickly, and their price was nominal. Thus every free man in England could secure protection of his possession of property against illegal seizure.

Questions of right, as opposed to possession, were normally tried in the feudal courts. But the king stood behind the plaintiff or claimant even in a feudal court if it appeared that he might fail to obtain justice in a proprietary action respecting title. By the end of Henry II's reign the government was issuing the writ of right, whereby any claimant could secure a hearing in his feudal lord's court at the lord's risk of contempt of the royal command to do justice. If this failed to procure justice, another writ was available to transfer the case into a royal court. This development favored the plaintiff, initially, but it led to a legal rule which favored the defendant, that "no man is compelled to answer for any free tenement except at the command of the king." Judgment of the case always followed a trial, which in a suit involving title to property was normally the judicial combat. The two litigants or their hired champions simply fought out the issue, the victor being adjudged in the right. Judges doubted the real justice of such an appeal to skill and force, and Henry II shared this view. In 1179 he instituted the Grand Assize, by which any free man could defend his proprietary right on the evidence of a jury of knights rather than submit his case to the uncertain outcome of a duel. The Grand Assize and the possessory assizes were the origin of modern trial by jury, but the medieval jury gave a verdict based upon the local knowledge of the jurors, while the modern jury's verdict is essentially a judgment of evidence admitted in the trial.

Henry II had been planning, ever since he became king, to recover royal rights over the Church which had been allowed to lapse under Stephen. During the Anarchy the organization of the Church had been strengthened because of closer relations with the papacy and because of the growth of the canon law. The jurisdiction of the ecclesiastical courts had been enlarged to include the trial of cases which earlier had been restricted to royal courts. Henry waited until the death of the archbishop provided him the opportunity to nominate a man of his own choosing, with whom, like William the Conqueror and Lanfranc, he could cooperate. The king's choice fell upon Thomas Becket, who had been Henry's chancellor for eight years, a faithful and able servant of the crown. "Tom O'London," as his enemies derisively referred to his obscure origins, was typical of the class of non-noble professional administrators in the Angevin government. Having gained rapid preferment in the household of the late archbishop and then in the royal government, he was still only in minor orders when in 1162 he was ordained priest and consecrated archbishop on the same day. But as primate of England Becket was transformed. From the stalwart supporter of royal policy he became the ardent champion of the Church. Henry was disillusioned and furious with this turn of events. In addition to the conflict between royal and ecclesiastical interests, there was a collision between two equally forceful and antagonistic personalities.

Becket's gratuitously aggressive conduct embarrassed the pope and lost him the support of a majority of the English bishops. Henry took advantage of the situation to draw up a precise statement of the customs governing relations between the Church and the Anglo-Norman kings. This statement, the Constitutions of Clarendon (1164), was approved by all the bishops and barons, including Archbishop Thomas. But then Becket changed his mind. A bitter quarrel led to the archbishop's flight from England and protracted exile. A reconciliation of sorts took place in 1170, but the main points of dispute were unresolved. Most important was the issue over "criminous clerks," members of the clergy convicted in an ecclesiastical court for committing a crime. Henry did not claim the right to try them, for he recognized the exclusive jurisdiction of ecclesiastical courts over the clergy. But he did claim the right to punish criminous clerks after they had been degraded from their clerical status. Although learned opinion was on Henry's side, Becket refused to yield or compromise in his insistence that degradation was itself sufficient punishment and that double punishment for one crime—degradation plus punishment by the secular arm—was illegal.

Despite the reconciliation, this intransigence angered Henry. When news was brought to him that Becket's first act upon returning to Canterbury was to excommunicate his enemies, the king flew into a rage. Four of his household knights took Henry's threats literally and hastened off to Canterbury where they murdered the archbishop before the altar of his

*Murder of Archbishop
Thomas Becket.* Manuscript
illustration (thirteenth
century). THE PIERPONT
MORGAN LIBRARY, NEW YORK.

cathedral. After this martyrdom of St. Thomas of Canterbury (the archbishop was canonized within three years), Henry had to compromise all the
outstanding issues, including that of the criminous clerks. Henceforth the
jurisdiction, including punishment, of the ecclesiastical courts was final over
all who could successfully plead "benefit of clergy." The control of the king
over the Church within his realm still remained stronger than that of most
continental rulers, but on one point, far more important than criminous
clerks, Henry had to give way in order to obtain absolution from his partial
responsibility for Becket's death. This was the freedom of appeal to the
papal *curia* from English ecclesiastical courts. This concession by Henry
brought the English church back under full papal authority and within the
scope of canon law, after the temporary interruption caused by the Constitutions of Clarendon and the exile of Becket.

Henry's differences with the Church were settled by a general agreement with the pope in 1176, and the next four years were peaceful and
prosperous. In the British Isles Henry extended his influence. Scotland had
become a fief of the English crown after the Scottish king's inglorious participation in the great rebellion of 1173–1174. Henry's relations with the
most powerful of the Welsh princes were cordial. And the conquest of Ireland, inaugurated by some barons with royal approval in 1169, was now
firmly under royal control. An Irish justiciar, as viceroy of the king, ruled

the conquered area from Dublin, and in 1177 Henry created his youngest son, John, "lord of Ireland."

The last years of Henry's long reign were beset with difficulties, owing to the jealousies which divided his sons and to the ambitions which occasionally united them against their father. In 1183 young King Henry joined Geoffrey in attacking Richard, but young Henry's untimely death ended that threat. Then Geoffrey died at a tournament in 1186, removing another source of discord. Meanwhile Louis VII's successor, Philip II Augustus (1180–1223), was stirring up the sons' hatred for their father. This was not difficult when it became known that Henry was scheming to disinherit Richard and secure the succession for his favorite son, John. In 1189 Richard led a rebellion supported by Philip Augustus. The king was defeated, but he was already broken, embittered, and dying. The final humiliation of his great career came on his deathbed when he learned that even John had joined Richard and Philip against him. His last words to his son Richard were, "God grant I die not before worthily avenging myself on thee." And in his death agony the last coherent words he was heard to utter were, "Oh shame, shame, on a conquered king!"

39 FREDERICK BARBAROSSA, THE PAPACY, AND THE LOMBARD LEAGUE

When the emperor Henry V died in 1125 without a direct heir, the Empire was thrown into disorder. Some of the nobility in Germany preferred the nephew of Henry V, Frederick of Hohenstaufen, duke of Swabia, but a majority opposed him because he seemed too powerful. The reforming party within the German church also opposed a candidate who seemed likely to continue the Salian policy of control over the Church. The reformers and the nobles who wanted a weak central government combined to elect the devout and popular duke of Saxony, Lothair (1125–1137). Lothair was unable to accomplish much. A revolt by the Hohenstaufens led to intermittent civil war north of the Alps which diminished Lothair's power in Germany and restricted his attention to Italy to only two visits which gained him little more than his imperial coronation (1133).

Lothair's position was greatly strengthened when he married his daughter and only child to Henry the Proud, duke of Bavaria, who thus became heir in his wife's name to the duchy of Saxony and consequently the most powerful German noble. Lothair intended to have his son-in-law succeed him, but the nobles had no interest in increasing the power of their greatest peer. Hence the election went to the Hohenstaufen duke of Franconia, Conrad III (1138–1152), who was the younger brother of Frederick, duke of Swabia. Conrad's first act was to deprive Henry the Proud of his duchies of Bavaria and Saxony, and civil war broke out once more. In Germany the two parties were called Welfs (after Henry the Proud's Bavarian ancestors and family name) and Waiblings (after a favorite residence of the Hohenstaufens at Waiblingen). In this early period Welfs generally represented ecclesiastical independence under the papacy plus feudal particularism, while the Waiblings stood for control of the Church and a strong imperial government. The struggle in Germany had its counterpart south of the Alps, among the allies of each party, where the Italian form of the names, Guelph and Ghibelline, has become the English usage. Later, Guelph and Ghibelline were to become merely the names of opposing factions without much reference to the original principles on which the parties were built.

Under Conrad the central authority was almost extinguished in many parts of Germany and most of Italy. He was the first German king since Henry the Fowler not to make at least one visit to Italy to receive the imperial crown. The Guelphs made steady progress, marked by the restoration in 1142 of the duchy of Saxony to Henry the Proud's ten-year-old son, Henry the Lion. Conrad, like his predecessor Lothair, had some success on the eastern frontier, where he reasserted the feudal suzerainty of the German crown over Bohemia and Poland, but the eastward movement which at this time began to have important results in the north was primarily the work of local lords. Conquest of Slavic areas led to colonization by Germans and the building of commercial centers, like the town of Lübeck on the Baltic, and of new feudal states where the local autonomy of the margrave was likely to be almost complete. Conrad could not participate effectively in this work because he was tied down by incessant revolts. It was as much to escape these struggles in Germany as it was from a sense of piety or Christian duty that the king joined Louis VII and Eleanor on the Second Crusade (1147–1149), where the two monarchs failed conspicuously to accomplish anything.

Frederick I Barbarossa (1152–1190) was the candidate of the bishops and magnates who desired peace between the Guelphs and Ghibellines, even at the price of electing a more powerful ruler. Frederick was a Hohenstaufen, the nephew of Conrad; but his mother was a Welf, the sister of Henry the Proud. The new ruler was thus a compromise candidate satisfactory to all but extremists in either party.

Frederick is a controversial figure. Some German historians have criticized him for neglecting Germany in favor of unrealistic dreams of Empire and glory. Actually, Frederick did not neglect Germany; he was her strongest ruler since Henry III. Frederick was motivated by the values and goals of a twelfth-century ruler, not those of a modern patriotic historian who has the advantage of hindsight. Given his problems and the conditions of his time, the policies Frederick Barbarossa pursued were reasonable and almost inevitable. Like his contemporary, Henry II of England, Frederick sought to restore all the rights of the monarchy and to extend his rule over wider territories. He also strove to revive the imperial authority from the evil days of Lothair and Conrad.

In Germany, Frederick's first efforts were directed toward reconciliation with the Guelphs. To his cousin, Henry the Lion, Frederick confirmed the duchy of Saxony and granted the Guelph duchy of Bavaria. Within

The Medieval Empire, c.1190

these duchies and over the lands he conquered and colonized east of the Elbe, Henry exercised authority that was almost entirely independent. So long as Henry the Lion and Frederick cooperated, peace was practically assured in Germany. For twenty-five years the arrangement worked fairly well, although the Saxon nobles were restive under Henry's strict rule. Then his marriage with the daughter of Henry II of England allied Henry with a ruler who was increasingly antagonistic to Frederick's policy toward the popes. Finally, Henry refused to assist Frederick in his most difficult campaign in Italy. The emperor now resolved to crush his overmighty subject, and in 1179 he allowed charges to be brought against Henry the Lion by his discontented vassals. When the duke refused to appear in court, his fiefs were judged to be forfeited and he was condemned to three years' exile. Saxony and Bavaria were broken up and distributed to Frederick's supporters, an important stage in the development of German particularism. The fall of Henry the Lion severely weakened the power of the Guelphs in Germany, though his family continued to play an important political role for a generation after Henry's death in 1195.

Frederick was determined to restore peace after the disorders of the two preceding reigns. Shortly after his accession, he issued a proclamation of peace (*Landfriede*) in Germany, with penalties specified for its breach, and later he promulgated a Constitution of Peace for the entire Empire. Frederick was apparently trying to revive the Pax Romana of the ancient Empire, but his means of enforcement were inadequate to the task. Realizing this, he worked hard to build up a more efficient royal government. Like his predecessors in the eleventh century, he relied increasingly on the lesser nobility and the non-noble *ministeriales*. To support this government Frederick consolidated and enlarged the royal domain by purchase or exchange of lands, marriage alliances, and agreements with churches and monasteries which gave him rights and revenues in return for royal protection in their secular affairs. Frederick's German strength was based on his duchy of Swabia, the crown lands of the Rhineland, and the kingdom of Burgundy where by marrying the heiress of its most important county he was able to exercise real authority for the first time since Henry III.

Over the Church in Germany and Burgundy, and over the lay nobles, Frederick revived and enforced the regalian or feudal rights which had been allowed to lapse under Lothair and Conrad. He controlled the election of prelates and enlisted the help of bishops and abbots in royal administration. The lay magnates were required to swear fealty and do homage for all fiefs held of the crown, and the feudal incidents were rigorously exploited. But there was one fatal defect in the feudal position of the crown. In enforcing feudal rights Frederick was obliged to recognize feudal custom, and in Germany the rule had become sanctioned by custom that fiefs which had escheated or had been forfeited to the crown must be granted out to new vassals. For this reason Frederick Barbarossa was ultimately no more able to build an extensive royal domain than were his predecessors. The German nobility held a permanent endowment which could not be diminished, though its individual parts shifted from one magnate to another and tended to be split up into smaller fiefs as were Saxony and Bavaria.

The revival of the German monarchy was Frederick's first step toward his larger aim, the restoration of the Empire. Conditions in Italy had changed vastly since the days of Henry V. The main developments were the rise of the communes, a temporary decline of the papacy, and the consolidation of the Norman kingdom of Sicily. The communes were the political expression of the economic revolution in northern Italy. Merchants, taking advantage of the collapse of imperial and papal authority after the investiture struggle, combined to oust the lords of towns who represented imperial or papal authority. These lords of cities were often bishops, and the popes therefore opposed the communes. The papacy itself was the victim of a communal revolution in Rome led by Arnold of Brescia, an ardent reformer and condemned heretic who wanted to strip the Church of wealth and political authority. During the twenty years before Frederick's accession the popes were as often in exile as they were resident in Rome, and the Holy See was once more on the verge of becoming the prize of local factional struggles. To maintain even a tenuous hold on Rome, the popes had to rely on the armed force of their nominal vassal and ambitious ally Roger II, king of Sicily. Under these conditions, the towns of the Papal States established communes claiming independence of the papacy just as the larger cities in Lombardy threw off the lordship of bishops and of imperial counts or viscounts.

When Frederick Barbarossa made his first Italian expedition in 1154–1155, the situation was ripe for an unprecedented alliance between the emperor and the new pope, Adrian IV (1154–1159). Each desired the removal of Arnold of Brescia: Adrian for his attack upon the Church and Frederick for his visionary program of a renovated Senate and Roman People to replace the German monarch as medieval emperor. Also, Frederick viewed the Norman kingdom of Sicily as an infringement on his own claims to all of Italy, while Adrian found his nominal vassal so independent and antagonistic that one of his first acts was to excommunicate the new king, William I the Bad, son and successor of Roger II. Finally, both pope and emperor opposed the communes of central and northern Italy.

As it turned out, Frederick and Adrian cooperated only to the extent of consigning Arnold of Brescia to the stake as a heretic. On his progress southward through Lombardy, Frederick's brutal repression of towns that did not immediately acknowledge imperial rule alarmed the pope, who was wary of an alliance with a ruler potentially more dangerous than the Norman king to the south or the communes in the north. The old question of papal versus imperial superiority was revived in dramatic fashion when Frederick arrived and was greeted formally by Adrian at Sutri, outside Rome.

According to custom, the emperor was beholden out of courtesy to support the pope's stirrup while he alighted from his mount. Frederick would have none of it. The symbolism of such an act implied the submission of emperor to pope as groom to master. Adrian's mettle was equal to the occasion. After a protracted delay filled with last-minute negotiations, Frederick performed the customary ceremonial, muttering loudly for all to hear, "*Petrum, non Hadrianum*" ("For St. Peter, not for Adrian"). In this atmosphere Frederick was crowned emperor, and after bludgeoning the Roman mob for an attack on his troops he hastily retired north of the Alps with his then malaria-ridden army.

Relations between the emperor and the pope were further embittered at the great imperial diet of 1157 held at Besançon in Burgundy. A letter from the pope protesting the mistreatment of a Danish archbishop returning from Rome through Frederick's dominions was presented by Adrian's trusted cardinal, Roland. It was translated aloud by the imperial chancellor for the sake of the nobles who did not understand Latin. The pope reminded Barbarossa that the Roman church had "most willingly conferred upon thee the distinction of the imperial crown," and assured the emperor that he would rejoice if "thy excellency had received from our hand even greater *beneficia*." These were dangerous, because ambiguous, words. In the conservative language of formal charters, the words "confer a benefice" were a technical legal phrase meaning "grant a fief" as from a lord to his vassal; while in classical or literary Latin the term *beneficium* retained its general sense of kindness or benefit. The imperial chancellor, whose duties in the government included the issuance of charters, translated the phrase in its technical sense, thus implying the feudal lordship of pope over emperor. This threw the diet into an uproar. Violence was threatened to Cardinal Roland, who made matters even worse by asking, "From whom else, then, does the emperor hold the Empire, if not from the pope?" The pope later disavowed the legal meaning of his phrase, but it was clear that there were papal supporters who held to the theory of imperial subordination to the pope.

Frederick made his position equally clear. In the same year as the Diet of Besançon (1157), documents of the imperial chancery began to refer to the *sacrum imperium*, the Holy Empire, putting the imperial authority on the same footing as that of the *sancta ecclesia*, Holy Church. Secular authority was divinely sanctioned, and it was not bestowed upon the emperor by ceremonial coronation at the hands of the pope. When representatives of the Roman senate asked Barbarossa from whom he held the Empire, the emperor replied, "From God alone!" For this view of imperial authority, Frederick could appeal to the language of the Christian emperors of the later Roman Empire as found in the Digest and Institutes of Justinian. Frederick not only claimed theoretically all the imperial authority of antiquity, he intended to base his Italian rule on Roman law as it was being revived in the schools of northern Italy, rather than on the feudal and customary rights of his Saxon and Salian predecessors. Henceforward it is permissible to speak of the Holy Roman Empire, as it is usually referred to, although that title first appears in medieval documents in 1254.

The year after the Diet of Besançon, Frederick crossed the Alps with the greatest army ever to accompany an emperor on an Italian expedition. In 1158 he held the Diet of Roncaglia, in northern Italy. Here the emperor solemnly claimed all the *regalia* that had slipped from his predecessors' hands either through usurpation or by grants extracted from earlier rulers as the price of support. The *regalia* thus claimed were all based on Roman law: customs and tolls, control of coinage and mints, taxation, appointment of governing officials, and general jurisdiction. This program was a deathblow to the communes' aspirations for independence and self-government. Frederick appointed a governor called the *podesta* for each commune and proceeded to collect a large revenue. Most of the communes of Lombardy now put aside their disputes and prepared to resist. Milan was the leader of the anti-imperial communes. It took Frederick three years to subdue Milan; he then punished the Milanese by expelling all the citizens, tearing down the walls, and razing the city to the ground. By 1161 all resistance was broken and Frederick organized a great imperial domain in Lombardy whose revenues and manpower he could now use to conquer the rest of Italy.

Meanwhile Adrian had died and the cardinals were split into two parties, imperial and anti-imperial, the latter being the majority that elected Cardinal Roland as Alexander III (1159–1181). The minority elected an antipope, a protégé of the emperor. Frederick called a council to adjudicate the claims of the two; the council was boycotted by Alexander's supporters; and the result was schism, mutual excommunication, and resumption of the struggle between Empire and papacy. Most bishops outside Germany supported Alexander III, while the kings of England and France gave him tentative support which could be disavowed if the struggle went against the papacy. Alexander was forced to flee from Rome, but during his exile (1162–1165) in France he won over Louis VII to his side and encouraged rebellion among the Lombard communes.

Military success attended Frederick's punitive expedition to Italy in 1166–1167. He was about to launch his long-planned invasion of the kingdom of Sicily, when pestilence struck his army and he was obliged to retire north of the Alps. Alexander now openly joined the communes, which established the Lombard League, in 1168. In honor of the pope the communes gave their new town, jointly founded to control western Lombardy, the name of Alessandria. Not until 1174 was Frederick able to renew the war, and even then he had only lukewarm support from his German vassals —among whom Henry the Lion was conspicuously negligent in supporting his lord. After some fruitless siege operations, a full-scale battle was fought at Legnano in 1176, where for the first time—and for the last time also—an Italian army met and defeated in pitched battle a northern invader, without the help of non-Italian allies.

The communes were now exuberant and adamant; Frederick and Alexander III were conciliatory. Within a year the pope and emperor came to terms. Frederick disavowed his most recently created antipope, and by recognizing Alexander ended the schism which had resulted from the double election of 1159. In his moment of triumph Alexander was moderate, perhaps with an eye on the Lombard League. Nothing was said about papal supremacy or about the emperor holding his Empire from the pope. Alexander absolved Frederick from excommunication and agreed to recognize all the schismatic bishops and abbots who had supported the imperial side. Frederick was permitted to retain his control over the German church. The struggle thus terminated in a papal victory: the emperor had been defeated in war and prevented from imposing his antipope upon the Church. Frederick's failure was a blow at imperial prestige and a confirmation of papal independence of secular domination.

To mark the end of the schism and emphasize papal leadership of the Church, Alexander called a general council, the Third Lateran Council of 1179. Most of the canons it enacted concerned reform of the morals and discipline of the clergy, but one of them grew directly out of the recent schism. This was a provision that election of future popes was to be by a two-thirds majority of the cardinals, the will of this majority being valid and final against any minority and without confirmation by the emperor. This rule prevented future double elections such as had begun the schism in 1159.

The Lombard League members felt deserted by Alexander and betrayed by a "separate peace" which did not guarantee their claim to independence. The pope felt justified because the communes were hostile toward their bishops, having gained their autonomy at the expense of episcopal lords as well as by usurping imperial authority. As bishop of Rome Alexander and his successors struggled for another twenty years against the efforts of the Roman commune (or senate, as the governing body styled itself) to achieve self-government. Frederick and the Lombard League finally came to terms in the Peace of Constance of 1183. By this time it had become clear to the emperor that lenient treatment of the communes would prevent a resumption of their alliance with the papacy. The communes were granted all the essentials of self-government, including the right to elect their own officials, raise taxes, and control the judicial administration. In return the communes recognized the suzerainty of the emperor. Their magistrates took an oath of loyalty and received their offices by investiture from the emperor or his representative.

For Frederick, only the problem of Sicily remained and here, after he turned from war to diplomacy, he won his most notable Italian success.

In the Norman kingdom, William II had become involved in an ambitious scheme to conquer Constantinople and was eager for an alliance with Frederick that would aid him in that enterprise while removing the threat of invasion from the north. The alliance was effected by the marriage in 1186 of the emperor's son, Henry, who was already the crowned king of both Italy and Germany, with William II's aunt, Constance, who was heiress to the Sicilian throne because William was childless. When the betrothal was negotiated, the pope had not been particularly alarmed, for William was then only thirty-one. He would have to predecease his aunt and also die childless before Constance could inherit the kingdom. Three years after the marriage, these improbable events had occurred. The keystone of papal policy for the past century and a half was destroyed. The Empire was united with the kingdom of Sicily, the Papal States were sourrounded, and with the alienation of the communes the papacy was deprived of any secular allies in Italy.

Frederick did not live to see his plans come to fruition. In 1187 Latin Christendom was shocked by the news of the fall of Jerusalem. The emperor and three kings (of France, England, and Sicily) led the Third Crusade (1189–1192) to rescue the Holy Land. Frederick Barbarossa, at the head of the greatest crusading army ever assembled, was on the last stage of his march across Asia Minor when he drowned in a small stream. Thus ignominiously did the career of feudal Germany's greatest ruler come to an end.

Feudal Europe

INSTITUTIONS AND IDEAS

Who were the feudal nobility? How did they live, what did they think about their world, and what ideals did they hold? These and related questions can never be answered completely for a period in the past, any more than they can be fully answered with respect to a social class today. Generalizations are hazardous, because within any social group there is bound to be diversity of customs and conventions, values and ideas. The feudal aristocracy were by no means a homogeneous class. If the force of custom was strong in feudal society, it was the custom of the fief, not the custom of Christendom or Europe or a whole nation, and such local custom varied from fief to fief.

The lay nobles comprised approximately the upper ten percent of the population, a thin veneer spread across the whole of Europe. The lowliest knight in the feudal hierarchy lived quite differently from a great lord. A minor vassal who owed a fraction of one knight's military service, who held his small fief of a lord who was the vassal of a higher lord who was in turn the vassal of a count or duke, possessed resources which were more nearly comparable with those of a prosperous peasant than they were with the wealth and power of a count or duke. Yet each was a member of the feudal nobility. Even at the same level of the feudal hierarchy, as many differences as similarities characterize such contemporaries as Stephen of Blois and Roger II of Sicily, both of whom were counts before they became kings. Generalizations about "the" feudal nobility have to cover a wide range of the sorts and conditions of men, and these generalizations cannot be accurate for all of them.

Another reason why it is difficult to generalize concerning feudal institutions and ideas is that feudal society was changing steadily, if not rapidly, century by century. Too often feudalism has been depicted incorrectly as a static society. In modern times the word "feudal" has come to be an epithet meaning "reactionary," or "ultra-conservative," or simply "bad." In fact, feudalism and the feudal nobility present a different picture in each succeeding age. The description of any tenth-century feudal lord would be inaccurate for his eleventh-century successor, and it would be a mere caricature of his twelfth-century descendant. The general tendency of changes in feudal society was in the direction of greater political stability and larger political units, a rising standard of living for the nobility, and a widening range of ideas and values as the feudal world developed toward greater complexity and sophistication.

40   THE SOCIAL AND POLITICAL IDEAS OF THE FEUDAL WORLD: LORDSHIP AND KINGSHIP

The ideas of the feudal nobility about the world they lived in are difficult to recapture. The earliest treatises about feudalism deal with only one aspect of that world, its legal system. Most of them were written no earlier than the thirteenth century when feudalism was already declining, when the tenurial relations of the law had become so complex that the first problem of any legal writer was to simplify and systematize, and thus inevitably to distort, the complex realities. They are too late to be useful guides to thought in the tenth, eleventh, and twelfth centuries when feudal society was flourishing. The theoretical writers of those three centuries reflect feudal ideas to a certain extent, but theoretical treatises as well as letters or charters or chronicles were written by learned men, and the learning of the schools at that time had little to do with feudalism and much to do with theology, philosophy, Roman or canon law, and belles-lettres. The great bulk of the surviving literature of the feudal age was produced by men influenced more by their learning than by the feudal world in which they lived. The feudal nobility were, on the whole, an illiterate class. Feudal nobles were men of action, not of articulate ideas. Hence, much of what we know about the feudal nobility is told us by writers who are critical, if not actually hostile. For chroniclers and writers sympathetic with the ideas and values of the lay nobility we have to wait until the later Middle Ages. But by that time feudalism had been transformed into a system of property law and a set of chivalric and romantic ideals.

Until the end of the twelfth century feudal society remained relatively fluid. Noble families could rise or fall several levels in the feudal hierarchy within two or three generations. Where primogeniture was the rule of inheritance, and this was the general rule in feudal society, the younger sons of the lesser noble families were likely to slip down the social scale, perhaps even to become free but dependent peasants. This was one reason why so many of the Norman feudal nobility left their homes to seek their fortunes in Spain, Sicily, and England. Not all the children of noble parents could be provided for by marriage to an heiress, by enfeoffment from a different lord, or by entering the ranks of the ecclesiastical nobility.

Before the thirteenth century there was not yet a nobility of birth, and it is incorrect until then to speak of a "feudal caste." Most nobles, of course, had noble parents, but admission to the ranks of the feudal nobility did not come automatically by descent. In lay society there were two criteria of nobility: feudal tenure of property and knighthood. Each was acquired by a formal and public act: homage, and being knighted. The act of homage placed a man in his rank within the feudal hierarchy and created a relationship between superior and inferior, or lord and vassal. Initiation into knighthood placed a man within the military fraternity of the nobility. Knighthood was a bond between equals who shared the same privileges and duties, the same training, experience, and code of the mounted fighter. Feudalism was both hierarchical and equalitarian. The noble had inferiors who were his vassals (unless the noble was at the bottom of the hierarchy); he had his equals, who were his co-vassals or peers holding fiefs of the same lord or who occupied the same rank in the hierarchy; and he had his superiors, his lord (or lords) from whom he held his fief (or fiefs) and their lords. As a knight, on the other hand, the feudal noble was the equal of all other nobles, whether emperor or king or the lowliest knight who had little more than his horse and his hauberk (coat of mail).

The institution of knighthood, important as it was, did not influence political and social ideas very much. The great virtues of the knight were originally valor and prowess, brute courage in battle, and skill in fighting. These virtues were primarily individualistic rather than social in their bearing; their value lay in nourishing the spirit of fraternity, the *esprit de corps* or consciousness of kind which tended to bind together the knighthood of Europe as a military elite. By the middle of the twelfth century this class consciousness had developed into a code of behavior that conventionally governed relations between knights. Most important among these conventions was the notion that a knight did not take advantage of another knight, an idea that lay within the larger concept—honor—to which other conventions made their contribution. A knight was expected to fight fairly, not by stealth or ambush or when his opponent was not in a position to defend himself. The vanquished knight was not to be butchered like a soldier (who fought for wages rather than because he owed his lord military service); his life should be spared so that his person might be ransomed.

This growing refinement in the feudal institution of knighthood in part reflects the general transformation of European society from the brutal and violent tenth century to the more orderly and civilized twelfth century. One specific influence which helps to account for the refinement of knighthood was the teaching of the Church. In the eleventh century most religious-minded ecclesiastics looked upon knighthood with aversion and disdain, as something contaminated with the shedding of blood and the commission of sin. The official attitude of the Church toward feudal warfare was expressed in the Truce of God and the Peace of God, both of which were sponsored by provincial synods to curb the destruction of life and property. A new attitude began to develop with the investiture struggle, when the papacy and the reformers were compelled to rely upon force to defend themselves. The new attitude comes out clearly in the propaganda connected with the launching of the First Crusade: the highest purpose of knighthood is the service of God, acquitted by the good knight in protecting the poor, punishing the wicked, and defending the Church.

The influence of religion can be traced in the solemn and ceremonial act of initiation into knighthood. The earliest accounts of knighting, in the mid-eleventh century, describe a simple and secular rite by which the young noble entered the ranks of the mounted warriors. In the early twelfth century the ceremony has become more elaborate, but it is still secular. For example, just before Henry I married his daughter Matilda to Geoffrey of Anjou in 1128, the young count was made a knight by his prospective father-in-law. The ceremony took a whole day. First Geoffrey took a bath, then he was dressed in fine clothes, after which he paraded in public with companions who were to be knighted with him that day. Finally he and his companions received horses and arms and engaged in military exercises. The essence of being knighted was to receive arms, or be "girt with sword" by a noble who was already a knight. In the next generation, initiation into knighthood was beginning to take on the form familiar to modern readers of historical romances. Knighthood was becoming sanctified. The new knight was expected to confess his sins, keep an all-night vigil of fasting and prayer, lay his sword upon the altar as a symbol of his service to God, hear mass, be dubbed—that is, be given a sound but ceremonial thwack with the broadside of a sword while kneeling before the altar, and finally be girt with the sword. All this could obviously take place only in a church, and it was usually done on the day of an important festival.

By the end of the twelfth century knighthood had been Christianized and thus transformed from being merely a military fraternity into an institution whose highest purpose was service to society. But knighthood never became as important as homage and the relationships which homage established, so far as social and political ideas were concerned. Originally, homage created a relationship of total subordination of vassal to lord. The ceremonial act of homage was, and remained, wholly secular except for the

*Rite of homage (top)
and investiture
with various types of
fief.* Manuscript
illustration (fourteenth
century).

vassal's oath which necessarily implied religious sanctions. Kneeling, the vassal placed his hands within the hands of his lord and declared himself to be his man, solemnly swearing that he would be faithful to his lord "against all men" or "against all creatures that can live and die." The greatest virtue of a vassal who had done homage was loyalty, and this loyalty was understood in a very individualistic and concrete sense as the loyalty of a man to his lord. Feudal thought had little room for abstract conceptions such as the "state" or "the government." Society and politics were understood in terms of the relationships between individuals, between vassal and lord. The tenth and eleventh centuries were a golden age of rugged individualism in this sense. The public functions of government were completely merged with the private rights and duties of vassal and lord whose personal relations were created by the feudal bond of homage.

The most important forces that influenced feudal institutions fall under three heads: custom, contract, and Christianity. The feudal world, so far from being chaotic or unregulated, was organized according to definite and specific rules and regulations which arose from custom. The essential idea governing the relations between inferior and superior in the feudal hierarchy was contract. The ideals, or ultimate sanctions, serving to explain and justify the organization of feudal society were derived from the teaching of the Church; that is, the ethics as well as the doctrine of Christianity.

Custom had legal force; the law which the feudal court administered was custom. A rule that had survived "from the time whence the memory of man runneth not to the contrary" impressed feudal lords as a good rule, not simply because feudal lords were conservative by nature, which they were, but for two other reasons. A rule must be good to stand the test of time, and a custom of long standing must be well known by everyone. It was accepted by usage, and through usage it was public. No one made or legislated law; law was above human will. Theorists who knew Roman law or canon law might talk about law being something that is reasonable, or something enacted by the ruler, but the feudal mind was uncongenial with such notions. If new conditions or some crisis arose which custom did not cover, then a clarification of law might be necessary, or even some modification, but that should be done only with the consent of those who were to use the customs so affected. It follows that every lord, including the lord king (*dominus rex*), is under the law and his government is limited by law. There is no room in feudal thought for arbitrary power or absolute rule. The most important function of the feudal ruler, whether he is a petty lord or a great king, is to do justice. Judicial administration is accomplished by the judgment of the lord's court—not the judgment of the lord but of the vassals who are by duty obligated to attend the court. When Henry II forced Becket into exile, it was the legal result of a court action, a judgment rendered not by Henry but by Becket's co-vassals or peers in the *curia regis*, and the same is true of Frederick Barbarossa's treatment of Henry the Lion.

Another limitation upon the lord, which also applied to the lord king, grew out of homage. Homage created not only a relationship between inferior and superior, it also created reciprocal obligations to which both lord and vassal were bound. In the year 1020 a French bishop expressed this concept when, after describing the vassal's duties, he wrote, "the lord must also in all things do similarly to his vassal." According to Glanvill, author of the treatise *On the Laws and Customs of the Realm of England* (c.1190), the vassal owes no more to the lord, by his homage, than the lord owes to the vassal, "reverence alone excepted." Homage implied a contract. Loyalty and service by the vassal were conditional upon the lord's fulfilling his duties of protecting his vassal and providing justice. If the vassal broke the contract by failure to perform his service, or by disloyalty, the lord could not punish him without first securing the judgment of the vassal's peers in the lord's court. If the lord broke the contract by depriving the vassal of his rights, the vassal could not rebel until he had formally and publicly defied his lord; that is, withdrawn his homage and fealty by a ceremonial act called *diffidatio*. The concept that government involves a contract between the ruler and the governed, together with the corollary that the subject has an inherent right of resistance against an arbitrary ruler, is the most important feudal contribution to the political ideas of Western man.

By the eleventh century feudal relations had become more complicated by the fact that so many vassals held fiefs of more than one lord. This created a problem of plural allegiance, a particularly vexatious problem when two lords of the same vassal were at war. At first, the vassal had to choose between them at the risk of suffering the loss of the fief held of one of his lords. The solution of this problem came with the notion of liegeancy, according to which the vassal served one of his lords, his liege lord, without reservation, and gave service to his other lords only to the extent that it did not prevent him from fulfilling his duties to his liege lord. For example, if his liege lord and another of his lords were at war, the vassal might serve the former in person and send hired knights to serve his other lord. Since these relationships could become quite complicated, it became the custom in the twelfth century for a vassal with several lords to stipulate the service owed to each under various possible conditions, "saving his fealty" to his liege lord. In England the kings were powerful enough to enforce the rule that the king was the liege lord of all free men. The vassals of his barons were required to take an oath of fealty to the king, as we have already seen when Henry II made his feudal inquest of 1166. Elsewhere, except in Normandy, rulers were not powerful enough to require an oath of fealty from the vassals of their own vassals until Frederick Barbarossa tried to enforce the rule, without much success, in his effort to maintain peace in Germany.

Just as there was a Christian influence on knighthood, the social teachings of the Church influenced the feudal concept of society and of lordship and kingship. The basic idea that the created universe was a hierarchy, in which all created beings were assigned a proper rank and station, was congenial with the feudal notion of status within the feudal hierarchy, where every member had his proper rank with its attendant rights and duties. Feudal monarchy had a strong religious aura. The king was more than merely the highest secular lord. He was also the anointed vicar of God. His duty to maintain peace and to do justice implied a higher end than merely the welfare of earthly society, for peace and justice were conditions favorable to the salvation of souls. The Church enhanced kingship above all other feudal lordship by consecrating it in the rite of coronation. Religious teaching also reinforced the contractual view of feudal kingship. Before placing the crown upon the new king's head, the officiating prelate in the coronation ceremony required the ruler to swear an oath in which he promised to protect the Church, maintain peace, and do justice. The crowned king who did not fulfill his coronation oath was considered to have broken the contract between the ruler and his subjects. Finally, all feudal relationships rested upon an ultimately religious sanction because these relationships were created and confirmed by oaths. Breach of an oath was perjury; perjury was sin that endangered the salvation of the perjurer. In the twelfth century a vassal who broke his oath of fealty to his lord was considered a traitor not only to his lord but to God.

41 THE LIFE OF THE FEUDAL NOBILITY

For the feudal nobility it was literally true that a man's home was his castle. The feudal lord's castle was his home. The size, shape, and construction of a castle depended upon the resources of the lord and upon the advantages or possibilities offered by the terrain. The feudal castle of the period c.950–1150 bore only the slightest resemblance to the massive piles of masonry, complete with turrets and mechanical devices, described in almost all modern historical romances or shown in almost all motion pictures that deal with the Middle Ages. Parts of the feudal castle might, rarely, have been constructed of stone, but ordinarily it was entirely an earth-and-timber fortification.

Because of the general similarity of arrangement or plan, most of these fortifications are referred to as "motte and bailey" castles. The motte was a large mound (from one to a half-dozen acres in area) surrounded by a wooden palisade; the bailey was an adjacent courtyard or open space usually much larger in area, also enclosed by a palisade. Depending upon the terrain, either the motte or bailey or both were surrounded by a ditch, called a moat, just outside the palisade. If the location of the castle allowed, the moat was connected with a stream by which it could be kept filled with water as an additional obstacle to the entry of an attacking force. Where the land was very flat, the motte was built by using the earth excavated in digging the moat, but usually it was possible to take advantage of a rise in the ground or some natural feature such as a cliff or bank at the bend of a stream, so that little human labor was needed to build up the elevated area of the motte. An indispensable requirement was a source of water within the fortified area, and castles were often built near streams or in hilly country where natural springs were plentiful or wells could be sunk.

In the center of the motte was built the largest structure, dominating the whole castle: a wooden tower called the donjon or keep. On the ground floor of the tower, and sometimes in cellars below ground level, were storerooms for food and supplies. At this level there was no means of entry, and the thick walls were unbroken by any windows or openings. (The modern notion that a dungeon is a dark, underground prison derives from the medieval practice of keeping prisoners in one of the lower rooms of the tower or donjon.) Entrance to the tower was gained at the level of the second story, by means of a narrow and steep and thus easily defended gangway which led up to a small door. When under attack, the defenders could easily destroy this gangway and seal up the door. Other openings in the walls of the

Motte and bailey castle, Great Berkhampstead. The ruined stone walls shown here are much later than the eleventh-century wooden palisade on the earthworks surrounding the bailey and the wooden tower on the motte (right). PHOTO: AEROFILMS, LTD.

tower were rarely larger than slits through which arrows could be shot. Inside at this level were the lord's hall and residential quarters, which in a large tower might occupy two stories. Above were the battlements from which the defenders could hurl stones, boiling tar or pitch, logs, and other missiles intended to discourage attack.

Except in the largest castles, the tower was the only building within the palisade enclosing the motte. The bailey contained all the buildings necessary for the normal life of the castle: barracks for the garrison, storehouses for food and supplies, the stable, a smithy and other workshops, and a chapel or church which usually served as the parish church for the neighboring village. The castle was more than a fortified residence for the security of the lord; it also served to defend a whole district. When invasion threatened, the villagers and people from the surrounding countryside took refuge at the castle, driving their cattle and carrying their movable goods within the shelter of the bailey.

The greater proportion of military operations in the eleventh and twelfth centuries consisted of the humdrum business of siege warfare. Pitched battles involving large numbers of cavalry, such as the battle of Hastings (1066) or Legnano (1176), were infrequent although when they did occur they were often decisive. Normal warfare was on a smaller scale and consisted mainly of besieging the enemy's castles. No territory could be conquered until the castle that dominated and protected it was taken. Almost any garrison could defend its castle successfully against a frontal assault, unless overwhelmed by the greatly superior numbers of an enemy willing to accept enormous casualties. Rarely could so large an attacking force be assembled, so the more usual and economical method was to blockade the castle and starve the garrison into submission. Before the end of the twelfth century siege warfare was still an undeveloped science.

The military training of the nobility was devoted to the art of fighting on horseback rather than to the more technical and mechanical aspects of siege operations, which were considered more fitting for the non-noble mercenary soldier than for the status and dignity of the knight. The education of the noble youth consisted of little else than training for the profession of arms. The essential function of the nobility was to fight. From a materialistic point of view, the nobility preserved their position as a non-productive and exploiting class by their monopoly of force: one knight was the equal in fighting capacity of several dozen unarmed and untrained peasants. It is interesting, however, that this point of view is almost never found in contemporary records or other writings. Rather, the view is almost invariably expressed that the status of the nobility corresponds with and is justified by the obligation to defend the rest of society. It is doubtful whether many nobles pondered long about the selfish or altruistic motives that theoretically were supposed to justify their own behavior. In practice, it is clear that the chief interest and most absorbing pleasure of the feudal noble was war.

The son of a noble was customarily sent away from his own family, usually to the castle of the father's lord or of some other lord of higher station in the feudal world, to receive the training that would lead to knighthood. Most of the youth's time was spent in long hours of practice in riding and in using the sword, the lance, and the shield. In World War II, the Army of the United States trained soldiers for combat duty in the infantry in a period varying from fourteen weeks to six months. In the twelfth century the training of a knight took the greater part of a youth's time from his seventh or eighth year until he was twenty-one. Little attention was given to his intellectual development, apart from indoctrination with the knightly virtues of courage and loyalty. Knowledge and wisdom were not cultivated as part of his education; they were attained, so far as they were attained at all, through experience. All feudal nobles were, like Parzival, "brave men slowly wise."

Superbly trained for individual combat, knights were also capable of simple tactical maneuvers either as unsupported cavalry or in combined operations with supporting infantry and archers. At Hastings the Norman cavalry coordinated their attack with the covering "artillery" fire of archers. In the climax of that battle the cavalry were well enough disciplined to prevent a retreat from becoming a rout and to improvise a counterattack that turned the tide of battle in favor of the Norman host. On the other hand, crusaders in the Holy Land often suffered heavy casualties when confronted with the superior tactical ability of the Turks. Actually, the knight was at his best when man-to-man. The massed charge of one cavalry force against another, resulting in a great crash of horses, human beings, and metal, could rapidly degenerate into a multitude of individual fights—some still astride a mount, others on foot. In hand-to-hand combat, the foot soldier was at a serious disadvantage, and the development of tactics in medieval warfare is associated with the infantry rather than the cavalry. When forced to meet cavalry in the open, foot soldiers could survive only if they exploited all the possibilities of field fortifications, the element of surprise, maneuver and deployment, concealment, and fighting in small groups. One mounted knight could dispose of an endless number of foot soldiers encountered individually, but when three or four confronted the knight from different directions it was relatively easy for them to cripple the horse and then overcome the dismounted knight.

Military leaders of the feudal age understood the need for planning a campaign, but by modern standards their grasp of strategy was deficient. They paid little heed to the problem of supply, because the feudal army lived off the country through which it passed. This meant that an effective scorched earth policy could usually defeat any large-scale invasion. Feudal armies were often committed to battle with inadequate information concerning the strength, disposition, and probable intentions of the enemy. In western Europe these deficiencies were shared by both sides and the result was not fatal, but against the Moslems in Italy and in the Holy Land the results were sometimes disastrous.

Although the feudal nobility lived in a constant state of readiness for war, not all of their time could be devoted to fighting. Warfare was limited not only by the Peace of God and the Truce of God, which the Church could enforce with the fairly effective sanctions of excommunication and interdict, but also by the greater lords who could curb the ambitions and the destructive energies of the lesser lords who were their vassals. The peacetime life of the nobles, apart from the time devoted to preparing for future wars, consisted largely of either seeking diversion from the boredom of not being able to fight or of simply vegetating. So far as daily life in the castle was concerned, modern amenities and standards did not exist and therefore were not missed. There was no plumbing, and the advantages of sanitation were hardly grasped. Of one great lord (who was, in fact, a king) we know that he took a bath at least once a year—presumably whether he needed it or not—but it would be rash to generalize from that instance that lesser lords bathed as often. Cleanliness was not a virtue next to godliness. It was simply pointless, impossible to achieve in a world in which filth abounded. In the life of the castle there was no privacy, whether for sleeping, dressing, eating, or talking. The lord's immediate family and the rest of his household, including his officials, domestic servants, squires, huntsmen, and relatives, all occupied the same quarters during the day, and only lords with larger castles possessed a private chamber in which to retire for the night. Few of the inflammable wooden castles of the age had fireplaces and chimneys. The only extent to which most castles were heated in the winter months was by the bodies of their inhabitants. It was a hard, tough life, though not quite so hard as that of the peasants who, in their cottages and hovels, had less to eat and drink.

Perhaps the most striking impression a twentieth-century American would receive, were he by some means transported back to a feudal castle of the eleventh century, would be a shock to his sense of smell. A world without dentists or drugs, without laundries or bathrooms, would offend modern sensibilities. The odor of decaying food, filthy and mildewed clothing, rotting teeth and foul breath would confront such a visitor at every turn. It would require sympathy and a great deal of imagination to appreciate the feudal lord's sense of enjoying a better materialistic life than that of his peasants. The most obvious difference was that the peasant's existence was reduced almost to the same level as that of the animals with which they, literally, shared their daily lives. In the winter the animals in their huts helped keep the peasants warm. Nobles, who lived at one remove from animals, in the winter wrapped themselves in furs. In some parts of northern Europe the wearing of furs was as much a distinguishing mark of the noble as the bearing of arms.

Diversion from the monotony and restrictions of peacetime life in the castle consisted mainly of activities which provided some of the experience and pleasure of fighting. The tournament was the favorite feudal outdoor game. It resembled a small battle, the differences being that as a social event there were spectators and there was an "out-of-bounds" area for either side, where knights could don their armor or retire with safety. The participants lined up at the far ends of a field and charged at each other with lances leveled. The knight who was unhorsed and captured lost horse and arms to his captor. After the tournament, the knight who could afford it would redeem his lost equipment for a money payment. Thus the tournament was a lucrative game for the winners, and it provided practice in fighting for participants and excitement for all.

The nobles' favorite outdoor sport was hunting. Hunting larger animals could be dangerous. The wild and tusked boar was almost impossible to hit with an arrow, because of the underwood and brush which he inhabited. When brought to bay he was likely to charge into his tormentor with such speed and force that unless struck down with a single accurate blow his tusks might leave the hunter permanently maimed with a vicious wound in the leg. Killing wild boars, bears, and wolves served the practical purpose of ridding the forests of dangerous animals. Shooting deer with the crossbow provided the lord's table with venison, which was far more palatable than the scrawny beef and tough mutton that was occasionally available. Falconry was an art popular with both lords and their ladies. The falcon was trained to kill wild fowl in the air and return with the prey to its master or mistress. Most great lords employed professional foresters, huntsmen, or wardens to patrol their forests and enforce the local customs against encroachment and poaching, so that the lord's game might be preserved for his own hunting and consumption. In the eleventh and twelfth centuries, nobles, like modern Sunday-morning golfers, were sometimes criticized for indulging their passion for hunting rather than going to church. For example, we are told that Baldwin II, count of Guisnes, "harked more eagerly to the huntsman's horn than to the priest's bell."

Castle life provided little indoor diversion, apart from the infrequent great occasions of feudal life such as the marriage of the lord's oldest daughter or the knighting of his oldest son. At such times it was appropriate to invite many guests and to entertain them with a banquet, where quantity exceeded quality both in food and drink. Festivities might be prolonged for a week or more. During inclement weather and after dark the nobles had little to do. Very few of the lay nobility were literate, but they did enjoy listening to stories told by wandering minstrels or jongleurs. Another form of amusement was provided by entertainers who often accompanied the minstrels from castle to castle, where they put on acts featuring juggling and tumbling. These entertainers and other travelers were usually welcome to stay at castles, because they were a link with the outside world, the purveyors of news and gossip. Without them the daily life of the feudal noble would have been even more isolated than it was, for his castle was often many miles from the nearest other castle, and he took no part in the activities of the village community of peasants in whose midst the castle was situated.

The foregoing description, like that of feudal institutions, is necessarily schematic; it portrays the life of the nobles of perhaps a little higher than average rank. Actually, the habits of life and the resources of the nobility varied greatly. The lowliest knight in the feudal scale possessed no castle himself, but lived in the household of a great noble who might have a standard of living somewhat better than suggested by the foregoing description. Next above the household knights were the petty nobles who had been enfeoffed with a fief of no more than a manor or two. Such a noble lived in a fortified residence that was little more than a small manor house surrounded by a simple wooden stockade. The vassal who was lord of several manors spent much of his time moving about from manor to manor, since it was easier for his family and household to go to the source of supplies than it was to transport the produce of his manors to a central location. One of these manors was the lord's principal residence, where he held his feudal court. It was fortified as well as the lord's resources would allow, usually in the form of a small motte and bailey castle. The greatest feudal nobles (kings, dukes, counts, barons) possessed far-flung fiefs consisting of from a dozen to several hundred manors. Such a great lord might have several or many castles strategically located for the defense and administration of his barony. Such a castle was not so much a residence of the lord (who would visit it occasionally) as it was of his officials who held court for him and stored his revenues there.

42 THE COURTLY LITERATURE OF FEUDALISM: EPIC AND ROMANCE, AND THE DEBUT OF POLITE SOCIETY

The twelfth century marked both the apogee and the transformation of feudal society. The heroic age of feudalism that had restored order to Europe reached its culmination in the first half of the century. The new age of chivalry—a refined and civilized feudalism grafted onto the customs and conventions, ideas and ideals, inherited from the preceding age—emerged in the second half of the century. That feudal society had reached maturity is illustrated by the appearance of a literature written for an audience of feudal nobles and expressing the interests and values of the feudal nobility. In a preliterate society the earliest literature is poetic in form, epic in style, and vernacular in language. For feudal nobles, simple alliterative verse lent itself to recitation and remembrance by both the performer and listeners. Most of the unwritten literature of this early age is now lost; but the earliest surviving feudal epics reveal a developed content and form that indicate a long literary tradition. This tradition consisted of the epic poetry of the prefeudal northern world.

The Anglo-Saxon, Teutonic, and Scandinavian epics all reflect a simple but aristocratic society, a world that was basically heathen but superficially Christian, and a life that was determined by natural and supernatural forces beyond men's control. Taken as a whole, these northern tales are tragedies in which heroic men meet their assigned fate with indomitable courage. A typical scene is that of the lone warrior holding off an attacking army on a narrow bridge, doomed to perish but bravely fighting on to die a hero's death. Most northern epics portray life on a small canvas; the themes are particular incidents or specific events. If the few surviving poems are typical of the literature as a whole, and if they portray accurately the intellectual and emotional atmosphere in which the early Germanic peoples lived, then the prefeudal society of the North was somber, moody, and violent. The heroes of these epics were not very happy or cheerful as they went about performing great deeds. They lived close to nature, but the bards who sang these epics (accompanying themselves with a harp) usually depict the natural environment in a minor key, as it were, grim, unfriendly, and ominous. In *Beowulf*, to take one example, the land is "wild and lonely," ridges are "wind-swept," the stream is a "falling torrent" which plunges into "gloom and shadow" under the "darkening cliff." For the aristocratic audience that listened to these lays, life was essentially a struggle against nature, against human enemies, and against the mysterious forces and marvelous creatures of the supernatural world. The main episodes in *Beowulf* tell how that hero slays first the monster called Grendel, then the mother of Grendel (another monster), and finally a dragon.

In many ways the earliest surviving French epic poetry is similar to the epics of the earlier Teutonic world. It is possible that a Frankish tradition lies behind the feudal *chansons de geste* (songs of great deeds) parallel to the Teutonic tradition, although there is no clear evidence. The *chanson de geste*, like the northern epic, is in the vernacular and thus intended for a lay audience. It is essentially tragic in theme and simple in meter, employing assonance rather than rhyme and intended to be recited aloud rather than read. It embodies traces of historical events as preserved and distorted by oral tradition. The same basic virtues of courage and loyalty are glorified, and the central plot revolves around the remarkable feats performed by the hero. Both the Teutonic and the early feudal epic portray a masculine society whose members behave according to the conventions and values of a tightly knit group. The action is all external; the individual is submerged beneath an idealized portrayal of abstract types, such as the good lord, the faithful man, the treacherous vassal.

In addition to these similarities, the *chansons de geste* reveal marked differences from the Teutonic epic. First and obviously, they reflect feudal conditions and a more complex society in which Christianity is fully assimilated. The story is developed on a larger scale. Geographically the whole of the realm of France, or even Christendom, might be encompassed in the tale in contrast with the petty kingdoms of the northern epic. Also, the feudal *chanson* deals with a greater number of important characters, giving more attention to the interrelations of these characters, in contrast with the concentration on the central figure in the northern epic. The element of the marvelous remains, but it is not so prominent and its quality has changed. Instead of myth and monster there is Christian miracle, but in general the limits of nature are better respected just as the physical aspect of nature is less awesome. The typical heroic battle of the North is fought under lowering skies, but when feudal knights meet the paynims (Saracens), "fair was the day and bright the sun, and all their harness glistens in the light." The feudal heroes are still portrayed from the outside, but they strike the audience as more nearly human in their wider range of emotion and more developed sensibilities. Returning from the wars, at first sight of *la douce France*, the knights of Charlemagne "call to mind their own fiefs, their young maidens and gentle wives, till there is not one that does not weep for pity."

As a literary form, the *chansons de geste* had already begun to deteriorate when they began to be written down early in the twelfth century. By far the best, indeed one of the great monuments of all European literature, is the earliest surviving French epic, the *Song of Roland*. The story dates back in oral tradition at least to the mid-eleventh century (it was sung to the Norman host on the eve of the battle of Hastings), but in the form that survives, the poem was composed by an anonymous author writing some time between the years c.1100 and 1130. The story is based on an obscure incident, the ambush of Charlemagne's rear guard returning over the Pyrenees from his first Spanish campaign. This kernel of history is elaborated and embellished into a full-scale narrative of four thousand lines in which Charlemagne is the leader of Christendom against the infidel. *Roland* is the earliest of more than thirty epics developing this general subject. The influence of crusading zeal is evident, but the religious ideas are those of the feudal nobles unaffected by the reform movement within the Church. Archbishop Turpin, a prominent actor in the drama, is "a right good knight, for well he knows how to smite with lance and spear." The essence of the tale is the glory that comes to Roland and his loyal companions, despite insuperable odds. Roland as the brave and faithful vassal is the central theme, to which the treacherous vassal, Ganelon, contributes by way of contrast. Although women have their place, subordinate and in the background, there is no hint of a love interest. Roland's dying thoughts are of Durendal (his sword), the many lands he had won by his valor, "sweet France," his liege lord Charlemagne, and, at the very end, the salvation of his soul. So little did Aude the Fair, his betrothed, mean to the hero. As for Aude, she forthwith collapsed and died on receiving news of Roland's death. To the modern reader this is a bit naïve and there is good reason to believe that contemporaries felt so, too. After the *Song of Roland* other epics continued to be written—some eighty of them —but they appealed to old-fashioned people who were still stirred by the simple, if very sincere, values of primitive feudalism.

At about the same time that *Roland* was being composed in northern France, the home of feudalism, William, count of Poitou and duke of Aquitaine, dashed off a poem from which the following verses are taken:[1]

> I'll make some verses just for fun
> Not about me nor any one,
> Nor deeds that noble knights have done
>   Nor love's ado:
> I made them riding in the sun.
>   (My horse helped, too.)
> When I was born I cannot say.
> I am not sad, I am not gay,
> I am not stiff nor dégagé;
>   What can I do?

---

[1] C. W. Jones, ed., *Medieval Literature in Translation* (New York, 1950), p. 668, reprinted by permission of the translator, T. G. Bergin, and of the publisher, Longmans, Green & Co., Inc.

> Long since enchanted by a fay
>   Star-touched I grew.
> I have a lady, who or where
> I cannot tell you, but I swear
> She treats me neither ill nor fair.
>   But I'm not blue,
> Just so those Normans stay up there
>   Out of Poitou.
> I have not seen, yet I adore
> This distant love; she sets no store
> By what I think and furthermore
>   ('Tis sad but true)
> Others there are, some three or four,
>   I'm faithful to.

This poem is not typical, but as an extreme example of the new style being cultivated in southern France it serves to introduce the literary revolution that was to replace the epic, in the second half of the twelfth century. The new lyric poetry of the south and the new romance of the north (in poetry and prose) are the real beginning of modern literature. Both the lyric and the romance deal with themes that are unknown to the epic tradition and that continued to pervade if not to dominate European literature.

In contrast with the epic, the new lyric poetry of southern France dealt with intimate and personal themes. The poet felt free to express a mood, to coin a phrase, or to reveal his inmost thoughts and emotions. He was interested in analyzing the inner life of his characters, especially their emotions, rather than in describing their external actions. More often than not the lyric poet wrote about himself. The epic was a long and serious poem to be recited or chanted with dignity; the lyric was short and clever, intended to divert, flatter, or even shock the listener. When the lyric was serious, it was passionate; when in a lighter vein, it was gay and often humorous. Above all there was a premium on originality, both in versification and in content. The poets who introduced this new lyric form were called troubadours in the south (from the Provençal *trobar*, "to find" or "to invent"), and their northern imitators were called trouvères. They were not the anonymous clerks or wandering, lowborn minstrels and jongleurs who made a living by reciting epics. Most of the troubadours were of knightly station, living in the household of their lord, and a few were great nobles like William of Aquitaine (grandfather of Eleanor of Aquitaine), who was reputed to be the first troubadour.

To the earlier ideals of feudalism—courage and loyalty derived from the earlier Germanic tradition, and service to Christendom and charity toward the weak as taught by the Church—the troubadours added a new set of ideals which reflect the more sophisticated and refined feudal life of the twelfth century. These new ideals may be summed up in the word *courtoisie*, the courtly ideal of feudalism. Our English word "courtesy" conveys only part of the meaning of this new concept, being restricted in ordinary usage to the sense of politeness. *Courtoisie* in the chivalrous sense employed by the troubadours implies gallantry, gentility, generosity, and the etiquette or mannerisms conventional in the courtly life of a castle where the crudity and roughness of an earlier age have made room for refinement and delicacy.

The troubadours expressed the new courtly ideal, but obviously women—or, more accurately, feudal ladies—were behind the movement. The alliance of noble ladies and troubadours introduced a social revolution the essence of which was the new idea of courtly love. Before the twelfth century all women, including ladies, were considered to be socially useful primarily as mothers of children, as domestic laborers who produced clothes and managed households, and as the means of effecting alliances between men through marriages that united fiefs and families. Apart from a few who achieved sainthood, almost no woman played a significant role either in public affairs or in daily life. We hear occasionally of the feudal lady who defends her lord's castle during his absence, or who displays some other masculine virtue such as being able to keep up with the men in their hunting. But distinctively feminine characteristics were those which exemplified or rationalized woman's subordinate position in society.

Then in the twelfth century the idea slowly grew that the lady was, if in some ways inferior, in other ways far above the men of her social class. Many influences combined to produce this result, including a higher standard of living and more settled conditions. Both made possible more leisure, and feudal ladies found more time to devote to themselves as well as to participate in the recreational activities of the nobility. There was probably also some influence on the ideas of the southern French nobility coming from the romantic literature of Arabic Spain. In any case, the troubadours began to compose love songs in lyric form in honor of their ladies—not their wives, of course, for they had married in accordance with the dictates of feudal policy and materialistic advantages—and these lyrics portray love for the first time as a passionate emotion, both carnal and spiritual, essentially the same kind of "love" that modern motion pictures or popular novels describe, complete with moonlight and roses, sighing swains, and incredibly beautiful heroines.

Perhaps the most interesting aspect of courtly love as cultivated by the troubadours and patronized by the feudal nobility was the problem of how this new romantic concept could be fitted into the teaching of the Church concerning marriage and the relations between men and women. The modern solution of this problem, that a man and woman who are in love should for that reason be married, was rarely possible in the feudal world. A feudal lady was married off by her parents at an early age in

accordance with the advantages that her dowry might bring. Some troubadours argued, in their poems, that love between man and wife was impossible or even unnatural; others admitted the possibility and rejoiced when
an instance of conjugal love came to their notice, but added that where
there was no love each spouse was free, or even obligated, to seek love outside the bonds of matrimony. This problem absorbed the interests of the
troubadours and their audience. Noble ladies, like Eleanor of Aquitaine,
took the lead in holding courts of love after the example of feudal courts of
law. These courts were great social occasions at which troubadours performed and the grievances or petitions of lovelorn damsels or their swains
were presented for "judgment" by the "court." It was a wonderful device
for amusement and diversion, and the ladies of the castle took the lead in
festivities which probably left their husbands somewhat befuddled. Among
the "judgments" delivered by one such court of love were the following,
each "judgment" being based on a "case" presented to the assembled noble
ladies and their lords: (1) marriage is not a good excuse for rejecting love;
(2) no one can love two at once, but there is no reason why one woman
should not be loved by two men, or one man by two women; (3) it is love's
nature always to increase or to lessen; (4) love when made public does not
endure; (5) every lover turns pale or trembles in the sight of his beloved;
(6) easy conquest destroys love, difficulties in wooing make the loved one
dearer; (7) when in love one eats and sleeps little; (8) happiness for a true
lover consists in what pleases his beloved; (9) a slight fault in the lover
awakens the beloved's suspicion.

Courtly love as portrayed by the troubadours allowed no room for
promiscuity. True love was not an unregulated passion. Its essence was
absolute loyalty and self-denial, service and travail, in favor of one's lady.
Only by suffering and by the accomplishment of great deeds could the
knight-errant prove his mettle and demonstrate the unblemished quality
of his courtly love. In strict accord with the rules of this game the lady was
equally obligated to respond to her knightly lover once his deeds had proved
his faith and revealed his passion. Hedged in by such rules, it is no wonder
that feudal lords and ladies sometimes fell short of abiding by either the
teachings of the Church or the alternative conventions of courtly love.

Although the trouvères of northern France composed lyric love
poems, they excelled in composing romantic narratives in verse. These
French romances were the counterpart of the Provençal lyrics, in being concerned with courtly love; they differed in being much longer and more
imaginative. The love poem usually dealt with the author himself and his
beloved, a real person. The author of the romance did not intrude in his
story, and his characters were often invented. Some romances developed
the epic theme of Charlemagne, others were devoted to stories about
ancient Troy and King Arthur and the Knights of the Round Table. These
subjects were considered to be fundamentally historical, but the author was

free to develop both incidents and characterization with complete originality. The romance was a combination of a love story with an adventure, and
the adventure took the form of a quest or search. The object of this search
might be the Holy Grail or a lost loved one, but this object was usually a
symbol, just as the incidents and encounters which befell the knight-errant
are symbolic. The author probes the innermost sufferings and emotional
stresses of his hero, and essentially the romance becomes what today is
called a psychological novel. The theme is the search for love, for union
with the object of desire. The romance is thus concerned with experience
which is both highly individual and also universal. Such literature appealed
to more delicate and refined tastes than those of the typical feudal lord. It
is not surprising that most authors of romances were patronized by noble
ladies, as Chrétien of Troyes, the greatest of the twelfth-century writers of
romances, was patronized by Eleanor of Aquitaine.

The feudal romance did not describe literally the feudal society of
the second half of the twelfth century, but it portrayed courtly ideals of
conduct and new human experiences for which, ultimately, an audience
of women was responsible. Thus both the southern lyric poetry and the
northern romances are sure signs of the influence of women in shaping the
future development of feudal society. The courtly ideal of feudalism for
which women were primarily responsible introduced the revolutionary concept that feudal nobles should be gentlemen.

The Renaissance of the Twelfth Century

The post-Carolingian disintegration of western and central Europe undermined but did not extinguish learning and literature. In some of the monasteries, at the courts of some rulers, and in a few cathedrals of northern France, manuscripts continued to be copied, the rudiments of grammar, rhetoric, and science continued to be taught, and the writing of annals continued at a reduced pace. In England, under the patronage of Alfred the Great, the earliest beginnings of a vernacular culture can be seen in the translation of Latin works into Anglo-Saxon and in the compilation of a chronicle in the native tongue. In Germany Otto the Great encouraged a few scholars and kept alive the imperial tradition of patronage for education, the arts, and letters. But these activities were unimpressive both in quality and in quantity. The few cultural centers were relatively isolated from each other. The little that was achieved depended upon only a few individuals, and there was no continuity of interests or activities that might have grown into a more general cultural movement. Europe lapsed into cultural provincialism and decadence.

The intellectual level of the period is illustrated by contemporary opinion concerning the best-educated man of the tenth century. This was Gerbert, the friend of Otto III who died as Pope Sylvester II in 1003. Gerbert's modest knowledge of science was so far ahead of his times that he was popularly supposed to be a magician who had gained access to secret lore by being in league with the devil. Gerbert knew much more than the best-educated man of the seventh century. The post-Carolingian decline (c.875–1050) was real, but it never descended to the degraded level of arts and letters in the pre-Carolingian period (c.600–775).

With the re-establishment of some measure of political stability and economic prosperity, conditions were favorable for an intellectual and cultural revival by the middle of the eleventh century. When that revival came, the patronage of courts and the directing influence of rulers played an unimportant role, in contrast with the Carolingian period. The renaissance of the twelfth century, which developed out of the eleventh-century revival, was "international" in scope like the Carolingian renaissance. But it involved a larger Europe, it affected far more people, and it was influenced much more by intellectual interests and developments from outside Latin Christendom. The immediate impulse came from the daily ecclesiastical needs of churches and monasteries scattered all over western Europe. From communication and interchange between these many centers there developed a general cultural revival embracing all of Latin Christendom in the twelfth century.

43   INTELLECTUAL INTERESTS: ANSELM AND ABELARD

In the tenth century, learning and literature did not disappear entirely. In England, the vernacular culture inaugurated at the court of Alfred was sustained by monastic leaders like Ælfric, the author of homilies and Lives of the Saints written in Old English. In Germany, Hrotsvitha, a nun of the convent at Gandersheim, wrote some mediocre poetry and a half-dozen plays. The plays were modeled on Terence in style, but Terence's glamorous courtesans were replaced by Christian virgins whose chastity invariably emerged triumphant after various temptations. To the modern reader the most interesting works of the period are those of Liutprand, bishop of Cremona, who wrote a gossipy narrative of the chaotic history of Italy and a lively account of an embassy to Constantinople in the service of Otto I. The classical allusions that adorn the writings of authors who enjoyed imperial patronage have led historians to refer to an Ottonian "renaissance" of the tenth century, but actually there was no substantial achievement. Classical Latin literature was imperfectly understood and no lasting literary revival resulted.

Far more important was the work of Gerbert, whose great achievement was to reawaken interest in logic. It is interesting that his students were more impressed with his knowledge of arithmetic, music, and astron-

omy, and that Gerbert himself considered rhetoric the pre-eminent study
for which all others were preparatory. This priority of rhetoric Gerbert
accepted from the late classical emphasis given that subject, for he was
essentially conservative in his interests. But in reviving the knowledge of
late antiquity Gerbert was also led to study, and later to teach, the art
of dialectic or systematic logic. This was a momentous event in the cultural development of Europe. Gerbert was not satisfied with the superficial
manuals of logic used in the Carolingian schools. Instead he turned to
the treatises associated with the name of Boethius. These were Boethius'
translations of Porphyry's *Isagoge* and of Aristotle's two elementary treatises
on logic, Cicero's *Topics*, Boethius' commentaries on all four of these works,
and Boethius' own three treatises on the art of argument. This Boethian
corpus of logic—later called the "Old Logic" to distinguish it from the
advanced works of Aristotle, recovered in the second half of the twelfth
century—was the foundation for the revival of philosophy in the eleventh
century. Gerbert was the first man since Boethius to master this corpus, and
even more important, his achievement led to further advance. In the intellectual revival of Europe, the greatest need was for a means by which the
enormous mass of revealed truth, the writings of the Church Fathers, and
the knowledge inherited from antiquity could be understood and assimilated. Logic became this means. It was the most popular study in the
eleventh century, because it afforded an orderly and systematic approach
to knowledge. For this reason Boethius has justly been called "the schoolmaster of medieval Europe."

The influence of the "Old Logic" on the intellectual revival of the
eleventh century is illustrated by the controversy between Lanfranc (d.
1089), before he became archbishop of Canterbury, and Berengar of Tours
Tours (d.1088) concerning the Real Presence in the Eucharist. Berengar,
a grammarian, emphasized the necessity of rational argument. In response
to Lanfranc's reproach for introducing dialectical questions into a sacred
subject, Berengar summed up the basic position of medieval rationalism:
"Recourse to dialectic is recourse to reason, and he who does not avail
himself of reason abandons his chief honor since by virtue of reason man
was made in the image of God." Berengar did not deny the ultimate authority of revelation in matters of faith. But how, other than by reason,
could one resolve the difficulties and seeming inconsistencies to be found
in Scripture? Lanfranc was remembered later as an expert in law, but in
his own day he was renowned as a dialectician. Against the novel arguments of Berengar, who denied that the bread and wine of the sacrament
could become the Lord's body and blood, Lanfranc brought to bear the
new logical distinctions between substance and accidents, or essence and
external form. Although taking the conservative side in the controversy, in
his rebuttal Lanfranc demonstrated that the art of dialectic had now become more than merely skill in argument. From this time on, dialectic

was concerned with applying the categories and definitions of logical analysis to the increase of knowledge and to the solution of important problems.

The widening scope of logic is illustrated by the treatment given a passage in Porphyry's *Isagoge*, the most famous statement in the whole corpus of the "Old Logic":

> As to genera and species, whether they actually exist or are present merely in thought, or if existing whether they are corporeal or incorporeal, and whether they are separate from sensible objects or are really existent only in and with reference to them—I cannot answer here, in an elementary work. 'Tis a lofty topic, one that requires further investigation.

This passage is an allusion to the metaphysical problem of universals, a problem which both Porphyry and Boethius, his commentator, recognized as inappropriate for discussion in an elementary treasise on logic. This treatment did not satisfy the optimistic rationalism of men like Roscellinus of Compiègne (d.1122), who taught at several schools including the cathedral school of Tours, or Anselm (d.1109) who, like Lanfranc before him, was a noted scholar and teacher, as well as prior, at the monastery of Bec in Normandy before he became archbishop of Canterbury (1093).

The problem of universals is basically quite simple, but it leads to a multitude of complications in both philosophy and theology. Do universals have a real existence? In Porphyry's terms, do genera and species (in reference to which we use words of general signification, like "man" in contrast with "this particular man") exist in themselves, or are they merely words of convenience denoting something which the mind abstracts from the data of sense experience? And if they exist, what is their nature and what is the relationship between universals and particular things? The earliest scholars to deal with the problem tended to take an extreme position in either denying or affirming the real existence of universals. Nominalism was the philosophical doctrine, usually associated with Roscellinus, that denied the existence of universals. For example, the nominalist would argue that from sense experience we can vouch for the existence of this, that, or the other particular man, but it is only the mind's ability to observe and remember similarities between particulars that leads to the notion "man," a notion that refers to no thing-in-itself. Universals like "man" can be said to have only whatever reality we might fancy to inhere in the breath of air that occurs when their names (*nomina*) are spoken. This could lead to dangerous or even heretical beliefs, for what reality could be allowed to such general terms as "the Church" if only the particular churches which everyone can see and count have reality? Or, with reference to the nature of the deity, how could the unity of God be maintained against the reality of the three particular Persons of the Trinity? This latter belief, tritheism, was the heretical error into which Roscellinus was generally thought to have fallen, and his nominalistic doctrine was condemned by a council held at Soissons in 1092.

The opposite view maintained that universals were not only real but were possessed of a higher degree of reality than could be ascribed to particular things. This view is called extreme realism. It derived directly from Augustine, and through Augustine it was descended through Neo-Platonism from the metaphysics of Plato. Particular things cognizable through sense experience are always *not quite* what they "are." This particular dog limps, that table has a broken leg—but it is not of the true nature of dog or table to limp or have a broken leg. Particular things come and go, they begin, they change, they disappear. Real as they may be, their reality is transient and imperfect. But the idea, the general notion, or universal, of these particulars does not change, and knowledge of the universal will tell us more than knowledge of many defective particulars. The universal must therefore have a higher degree of reality. For example, a moment's reflection will convince the reader that no particular triangle is truly a triangle. It is only, and can only be, an approximation to a triangle, for even if the "lines" he sees were perfectly straight lines the mere fact that he can see them demonstrates that they are two-dimensional (and thus not really lines). Any representation of a triangle cognizable through sense experience, therefore, cannot quite be really and truly a triangle. And yet it is impossible to deny the reality of "triangle"—not only the reality but the very practical utility of the concept, since distances are measured every day by the aid of this concept.

According to realism, then, the universal is a pattern or model in accordance with which the particulars of sense experience exist and are known. There are difficulties in store for the extreme realist, just as for the nominalist. In theology, for example, the path marked out by realism could lead to the notion that all particulars are subsumed under general ideas having greater reality, so that ultimately the reality of everything in the universe depends upon the degree to which it is included in the highest reality which is God. The conclusion to which this kind of reasoning usually led was the heretical error of pantheism.

Anselm was a realist but he did not fall into this error. Like the majority of his contemporaries who were concerned with a philosophical approach to religious truth—an approach buoyed up by confidence in the right use of logic—Anselm was convinced of the priority of faith over reason. By reason alone man can know many things, but faith can guide reason to more truth than unaided reason could attain. Or, as Anselm put it, "I believe in order that I may know" (*credo ut intelligam*). What made Anselm just as much a rationalist as Berengar or Roscellinus was his conviction that faith leads to knowledge that is rationally grasped and just as firmly known as the lesser things that unaided reason can know. Nominalists overemphasized the three Persons, and might lapse into error about the unity of God; extreme realists overemphasized the transcendent reality of one God, and might lapse into error about the created universe. The solution of these difficulties, for Anselm, was the acceptance of faith as the guide to reason.

Anselm's faith in reason is best illustrated by his ontological argument by which he sought to prove that God exists. It is an *a priori* argument, that is, a chain of reasoning that proceeds from the nature of God's being to the conclusion that such a Being must exist. It has been criticized for being naïve, circular, and confusing; but it remains the greatest monument of the new rationalism of the eleventh century. The heart of the argument may be paraphrased as follows:

1. The name "God" connotes (even to the fool who would deny God's existence) "a-being-than-which-none-greater-can-be-conceived."
2. Evidently, such a being-than-which-etc. cannot exist solely in the understanding but must also exist in reality;
   a. for if it is in the understanding, it can be *thought of* as existing in reality, and this is greater;
   b. therefore, if that-than-which-none greater-can-be-conceived exists in the understanding, then that-than-which-none-greater-can-be-conceived is the very thing than which a greater *can* be conceived;
   c. but this is self-evidently impossible and self-contradictory.
3. Therefore it is indubitably true that a being-than-which-none-greater-can-be-conceived must exist both in the understanding and in reality.

This argument is grounded on the premises of metaphysical realism. For Anselm, proof of God's existence cannot proceed by deduction from the data of sense experience, because no merely logical argument can lead from the particular to the universal or the absolute. Hence, it is justifiable, even necessary, to resort to an *a priori* argument, one that begins with the nature of God's being.

The culmination of the intellectual revival, in the period preceding the recovery of the advanced works of Aristotle, is represented by Abelard (1079–1142). For the history of thought his outstanding contribution was in method, both in logical analysis and in the rational synthesis of broad fields of knowledge. In logic he supplied that "further investigation" of the problem of universals alluded to by Porphyry in his *Isagoge*. His essential achievement was to work out the position called moderate realism, a compromise between nominalism and extreme realism that salvaged the strong points of each. Abelard accomplished this by demonstrating the logical consequences of some important distinctions, such as the distinction between the word that stands for a thing, the thing itself, and the concept of the thing in the mind. Thus universals are not mere sounds or words, as nominalists held, nor are they things-in-themselves as extreme realists believed, but are concepts in the mind. As such, universals are real, although derivative from a process of mental abstraction from particulars—except, Abelard adds, for the universals that exist in God's mind as the patterns of things created. Thus the universal is not a metaphysical reality but a concept that exists and is real in the mind. It is with such concepts that it is the proper business of logic to deal.

In his intellectual interests and in much of his attitude toward knowledge, Abelard was a product of his age. He considered theology the most important discipline, in which he set his sights to excel all others. He unequivocally accepted the authority of revelation and of the Church. He was a medieval rationalist who believed reason to be more effective than experiment in seeking truth. But for Abelard reason played a different and more important role than for Anselm. He stressed the necessity of understanding what is believed; reason was to guide faith to understanding. He thus reversed Anselm's formula, saying in effect, "I understand in order that I may believe" (*intelligo ut credam*). For Abelard the role of reason was to elucidate the mysteries of the faith, mysteries which conservative religious leaders of his day preferred to leave mysterious, to be confirmed through intuition and experience. But what really antagonized others was Abelard's insistence that in Scripture and in the writings of the Fathers there were passages that were unclear, inconsistent, or even contradictory, and that by reason the truth could be ascertained. This attitude appeared to give reason priority over authority. Finally, Abelard was disputatious and encouraged a spirit of doubt. In his most famous work, *Sic et Non* ("Yes and No"), he listed one hundred and fifty-eight theological propositions and then cited authorities affirming and denying the same propositions. The work was itself not a fruitful or profound contribution to theology, especially since some of the citations were specious. Also, this sort of compilation was not wholly original with Abelard. One of the most popular kinds of manuscript in monastic libraries was the *florilegium*, a collection of extracts from various authors arranged topically. What Abelard did was to show how this method could be used for the systematic discussion of theological and philosophical problems.

In the revival of learning logic had led the way. But by the middle of the twelfth century logic was no longer the predominant discipline. Partly this was the result of the growth of other interests, in which logic had been assimilated as a necessary method of study. Partly it was the result of opposition to rationalism. For example, the most powerful man in the Church of his age, St. Bernard of Clairvaux (d.1153), was convinced that Abelard was sacrilegious and heretical, and he pursued the would-be theologian from council to council where Abelard's opinions were condemned. Bernard represented the reaction of the mystic and conservative who was emphatically certain of the priority of faith over reason. And yet it would be as much of a caricature to portray Bernard as an obscurantist as it would be to call Abelard a skeptic or a free-thinker. Bernard was alive to the intellectual tendencies of his times. He made a positive contribution to them in the support he gave to scholars, notably Peter Lombard, the greatest theologian of the century.

Another theologian of the twelfth century was Abelard's contemporary, Hugh of Saint-Victor (d.1141). Hugh is the best representative of intellectual and devotional piety as an alternative to rational inquiry in the search for truth. As a teacher he approved of dialectic and the other arts, but he believed they were merely the necessary first steps in a much grander ascent toward the end of human existence which is salvation. No one is saved by logical disputation. Or, as he put it, the path to truth is marked by three stages: cogitation (reason applied to the arts and sciences); meditation (the intellect seeking to penetrate beyond knowledge derived from sense experience); and contemplation (the attainment of truth, or knowledge of God, through the union of intellect and love reinforced by grace). Hugh is usually classified as a mystic and an Augustinian. Like most mystics and in contrast with the rationalists, he took a keen interest in physical nature. For him the whole of the created universe, in its many and complex parts, was a series of symbols of higher truth. As a thinker in the Augustinian tradition he recognized the rational character of knowledge at all levels, but insisted that man's unaided reason provided only the starting point in a quest for truth that involved emotion and intuition as well as logic. This was a view which Abelard and his followers could neither understand nor appreciate.

44 THE RISE OF THE UNIVERSITIES: BOLOGNA AND PARIS

In the tenth century the most important centers of learning and literature were, with a few exceptions, the monasteries that were least affected by the disorders of the period. Here could be found some wealth and security. The division of labor among the monks permitted a corporate life that was more than merely a struggle for survival. A minimum of cultural activity was sustained in response to the daily needs of ecclesiastical life. In the eleventh century, the more intense devotion and the fuller religious experience fostered by the Cluniac reform movement spread to widely separated monastic centers.

The cultural expression of the reform movement consisted of more elaborate liturgical texts for church services, more lives of saints written in connection with the growing number of saints' festivals, and an increasing number of psalters, gospels, hymns, antiphons, lectionaries, and other texts in support of the primary and fundamental work of the monks: the *opus Dei* ("God's work," i.e., worship and prayer). This activity provided many opportunities for original contributions in setting words to music and in composing new prose, poetry, and music. In many monasteries the monks were required to make a thorough study of one book each year, a custom that provided some demand for copying and preserving manuscripts of the writings of the Fathers of the Church, of ecclesiastical historians, and even of pagan classical authors such as Livy. On the more practical side, the administration and exploitation of monastic lands required mathematical knowledge so that bailiffs could keep their accounts and legal knowledge so that contracts and conveyances of property could be properly recorded.

From these varied needs of ecclesiastical life the monastic schools of the eleventh century occasionally developed into centers of learning where a whole program of studies in the liberal arts (the *trivium* and *quadrivium*) could be pursued. Such was the abbey of Bec, in Normandy, when Lanfranc as prior (c.1043–1063) and Anselm as prior and then abbot (1063–1093) were distinguished scholars and teachers of grammar, dialectic, and theology. Lanfranc's students included a future pope, two future archbishops, and many future bishops and abbots. There were other less distinguished monastic centers of learning like Monte Cassino, the mother house of the Benedictine Order, and Cluny, the center of the monastic reform movement. But generally the monasteries did not make a significant contribution to the advance of learning. Their role was essentially conservative, to relearn what had once been known and then to preserve that knowledge. The greatest monastic contribution to medieval culture, aside from matters of religious interest, was the writing of chronicles, an activity in which the Benedictine monasteries excelled. In the new religious orders of the later eleventh and early twelfth centuries the emphasis on faith and on the contemplative life provided an uncongenial atmosphere for intellectual inquiry.

The future of the intellectual revival lay not with the monastic schools but with the cathedral schools. Teachers and students in the cathedrals accepted the authority and truth of revelation, of the Fathers, and of the teachings of the Church, just as the monks did. But in the cathedral schools there was a less conservative attitude toward the heritage of learning and literature from the pagan and Christian past. In the words of Bernard of Chartres (d.1126), one of the best teachers at the great cathedral school of Chartres: "We are like dwarfs seated on the shoulders of giants; thus we see more things than the ancients." The giants of antiquity were greater men, but the whole point is that the modern "dwarf" can master and then go a little beyond the learning of antiquity. This was the spirit of the cathedral schools, which were less bound by routine and tradition than the monastic schools. Located in towns, at the administrative centers of dioceses, the cathedral schools were more open to new interests and influences. They were better equipped to respond to the growing demand for education that a larger population, more settled conditions, and more wealth had brought about. By the opening years of the twelfth century students were flocking to the classrooms of the more popular teachers in cathedral schools. Going to school for an education beyond mere reading and writing had become almost a fad; and it was the best road to preferment in the Church or in the secular governments of western Europe.

One or another cathedral school, in the tenth century, had enjoyed a short-lived reputation because of the work of one man. The school at Reims, for example, was famous as long as Gerbert taught there. Fulbert, chancellor and then (1006–1028) bishop of Chartres, was the first great teacher to found a school whose reputation and tradition lived on after him. Some of his students became outstanding teachers at Chartres and elsewhere, many others rose to important positions in the cathedrals and monasteries of northern France and Germany. His most distinguished pupil was none other than Berengar of Tours, who taught at the cathedral school in that city, and Berengar's most distinguished pupil—and later theological opponent—was Lanfranc. Lanfranc, in turn, taught at the cathedral school of Avranches before joining the monastery of Bec, where he taught Anselm among many others. Thus in the eleventh century a continuity of studies and of intellectual activity was re-established for the first time since the decline of the Roman Empire. This achievement was largely the work of the leading cathedral schools. These were at Chartres, Tours, Orléans, Paris, Reims, and Laon.

In Italy the situation was different in two ways. Although there were both monastic and cathedral schools, the leading centers of learning were schools that had no connection, or only a slight connection, with either cathedral or monastery. Second, the leading Italian schools were devoted to the higher studies of medicine and law, studies for which courses in some if not all of the *trivium* and *quadrivium* were preparatory. At Salerno the school of medicine was important as early as the tenth century. It was a center for the dissemination of medical knowledge based on Greek, Jewish, and Arabic sources, to which its geographical location in southern Italy gave access. In northern Italy there were several cities where Lombard (i.e., customary) law was taught and where the study of rhetoric introduced students to the art of writing letters and documents, including legal documents. At Bologna there was such a school of rhetoric in the eleventh century. Although not Italy's earliest law school, Bologna was the first school where Roman law and jurisprudence could be studied as part of the curriculum in legal rhetoric. Rhetoric and law were finally separated into two independent disciplines at Bologna by Irnerius (d.c.1125), who was first to teach systematically from the *Corpus Juris Civilis* of Justinian rather than from the meager compends or extracts from the *Etymologies* of Isidore of Seville that satisfied most teachers of rhetoric.

Irnerius' lectures on Roman law drew students to Bologna from all of Italy and from beyond the Alps. The Bolognese law students were older, and usually more serious in purpose, than the students who were still learning the arts and sciences in cathedral schools. This is one reason for the distinctive form in which the University of Bologna came to be organized. The word "university" today refers to an institution of higher learning that grants graduate degrees like the degree of master of arts (M.A.) or doctor of philosophy (Ph.D.). In the Middle Ages the word "university" (*universitas*) meant any corporate society or corporation. A gild of merchants or craftsmen, a cathedral chapter, or a community of monks might be called a *universitas*, an organized group. During the twelfth century the students at Bologna organized themselves into two groups or "universities" consisting of the Italian students (the Cismontane university, students "this side" of the Alps) and the students from north of the Alps (the Transmontane university). These two "universities" of students were actually what is called *the* University of Bologna.

The purpose of organization at Bologna was twofold: for protection against exploitation by the townspeople who charged what the market would bear for food and lodging, and for assurance that the course of legal instruction should be worth the tuition fees paid by students to their professors. Against the townspeople the students relied upon the threat of simply moving away en masse, a threat that was easy to put into effect because the university itself was simply a group of people, not a campus with buildings and grounds permanently located. The university of students thus slowly gained the right to fix prices and rents and to regulate not only student life but the relations between "town" and "gown" (i.e., the students collectively, so called because of the clerical garb worn by the great majority of students who were in minor orders). Against the professors the students relied upon the threat of boycott. Since the professors' income derived from students' fees, the organized students could dictate the nature of the curriculum and could enforce minimum standards of instruction by the simple device of not attending the courses of unsatisfactory professors. In the earliest surviving statutes of the university the professors were subjected to minute and stringent regulations. They were required to begin lecturing with the bell and finish within a minute after the next bell; they could not be absent without permission, and had to post bond for their return if they left Bologna; they were required to proceed systematically through the subject matter of the *Corpus Juris*, and not to omit or postpone difficult sections. If a professor were unable to attract at least five students to a scheduled morning lecture, he was subject to the same fine as if he were absent without leave.

The professors at Bologna had their own organization, called a "college." Admission was gained by passing an examination administered by professors who were already members. The successful candidate for admission was granted a certificate or license to teach (*licentia docendi*). The license enrolled the new teacher in the society or college of law teachers as a doctor (*juris doctor* or J.D.). When other studies were added to the curriculum at Bologna the license to teach created doctors of medicine (M.D.), theology (D.D.), and philosophy (Ph.D.). During the twelfth century Bologna became the leading center of canon law as well as Roman, or civil, law. The student who passed the examination in both became a "doctor of each law" (*doctor utriusque juris* or J.U.D.), after which he was entitled to teach either civil law or canon law. Many students took the examination for a license, not in order to teach but because the license was a certificate of competence. Thus the *licentia docendi* was the ancestor of all modern academic "degrees," and the master's or doctor's degree today still connotes both the recipient's competence in a discipline and his qualification to teach the subject. The academic assembly at which degrees are awarded, today called a "commencement," is derived from the medieval inception, where the candidate passed an examination and delivered a lecture in which he "commenced" to teach.

The development of northern universities was different in several ways from the growth of Salerno, Bologna, and other Italian institutions. In the north the universities were not only connected with but grew out of cathedral schools, and the northern universities were societies or gilds of teachers, not students. The earliest university north of the Alps grew up at Paris, where classes were held at schools connected with the cathedral of Notre Dame and with the churches of Saint-Victor and Sainte-Geneviève. The most famous of the early teachers was William of Champeaux (d.1121), a contemporary of Irnerius of Bologna. By far the most popular teacher of the whole twelfth century was Abelard, who attracted so many students to Paris that he is sometimes considered to be the founder of the university. Actually, the earliest university organization took shape in the second half of the century. This was the gild or society of masters who taught the seven liberal arts (the *trivium* and *quadrivium*), and who received their licenses to teach from the chancellor of the cathedral of Notre Dame. The chancellor also granted the *licentia docendi* to the doctors who taught theology, philosophy, and canon law. The masters of arts and the doctors of the three higher studies constituted the four faculties, each with its own elected dean. The masters of arts were so numerous that they were organized into four "nations," the French, the Norman, the Picard (including the Low Countries), and the English (including Germany and northern Europe). The four nations elected the rector (or president) of the university. This was the essential organization of the University of Paris.

It is impossible to say when each of the elements of the university's constitution first appeared. Like Bologna, the University of Paris was not founded; it just grew. By the end of the twelfth century it had achieved a corporate identity, and the masters were well organized to protect their interests against the chancellor of Notre Dame, the townspeople, and the royal government. The earliest surviving document of any university is the royal charter of 1200 in which the rights and privileges of the masters and scholars at Paris were given legal status by the French king. Typically, this charter was issued as the result of a town and gown riot involving the death of a student at the hands of an overzealous royal official. By their royal charter the masters were granted exemption from lay jurisdiction. Additional rights of self-government were secured in the thirteenth century by papal privileges, notably the bull *Parens scientiarum*, 1231, which was issued to settle a dispute arising from another town and gown riot. Before receiving this papal privilege the masters had shut down their classrooms for two years in protest against the invasion of their rights by local royal officials.

The University of Paris was the model for most of the northern universities. In some instances the migration of masters and students from Paris, during periods of strife such as the one that ended in 1231, directly influenced university development elsewhere. It influenced Oxford and Cambridge which had become recognized universities by the middle of the thirteenth century, after developing slowly from obscure origins reaching back into the twelfth. Other universities were founded at a particular date, such as the German universities of the fourteenth century. For example, Heidelberg was created by a charter in 1386 that specifically enjoined that the new university should "as a handmaid imitate Paris in every possible way." Most northern universities adopted the curriculum in the arts and higher studies as developed at Paris. This included the lecture system, examinations for the bachelor's, the master's, and the doctor's degrees, and the special privileges and exemptions enjoyed by teachers and students and recognized by secular rulers and ecclesiastical officials.

Institutionally, one feature of the organization of the University of Paris has had a more important role in English universities than in the "mother of universities." This is the college system, which dates from the twelfth century at Paris but is usually associated with the foundation of a college there by Robert de Sorbon in 1258. Originally the college was simply an endowed residence hall where needy and worthy scholars could obtain free board and lodging. The Sorbonne at Paris was the model for similar colleges at other universities. At Oxford and Cambridge, however, the colleges were so well endowed with property and revenues that they began to support teachers in residence as well as students. In England the university thus became essentially a federation of colleges, its primary educational function being limited to examination and granting degrees. This English system began in the thirteenth century with the foundation of the oldest colleges, Merton and Balliol at Oxford and Peterhouse at Cambridge.

Although the majority of medieval universities were founded in the later Middle Ages, the institution itself was the product of the renaissance of the twelfth century. Few institutions in all of Western civilization have been more long-lived; none has made a more significant contribution to the preservation of learning and the increase of knowledge.

45 THE CULTURAL REVIVAL OF THE TWELFTH CENTURY

In the intellectual development of Europe, the great achievements of the twelfth century were the recovery of knowledge lost since antiquity, the assimilation of the heritage of patristic writings of late antiquity, and the earliest successful efforts to summarize and to treat systematically large fields of knowledge. In no field was the twelfth-century revival simply a renaissance in the narrow sense of the term. Besides a rebirth or regeneration of the ancient heritage, the century produced much that was original and creative, either in the reworking of old materials newly mastered or else in fields in which there were no models from the past. In both these aspects of revival the twelfth century provided the foundation on which the mature culture of the high Middle Ages rested. Five main areas may be distinguished in which the recovery of ancient knowledge was most impressive. These were literature, science, law, theology, and philosophy, the last more especially in the discipline of logic.

We have already seen how the rationalists of the eleventh century exploited the Boethian corpus of treatises, the "Old Logic," as the most fruitful of the three disciplines that made up the *trivium*. While interest in logic by no means flagged in the twelfth century, the study of grammar and rhetoric led to a classical renaissance, a revival of interest in the belles-lettres of antiquity that marks the high point of medieval humanism. Medieval humanism was restricted to the Latin classics, except for one or two Greek works such as Plato's *Timaeus* that were accessible either in translation or through the commentaries and treatises of Latin authors. The number of authors known and the range of Latin classical literature available were almost as great in the twelfth century as today. In their own writing the humanists of the twelfth century demonstrated their wider reading, their more thorough understanding of, and their more enthusiastic devotion to the classics than can be found in any earlier period since antiquity. Their attitude tended to be undiscriminating, as between mediocre and better authors, and they lacked a scholarly or critical appreciation of classical literature as the expression of a society quite different from their own. But to their credit, the medieval humanists were able to recognize the superiority of Virgil and Ovid in poetry and of Cicero in prose.

The two most important centers of humanism in the twelfth century were the cathedral schools at Chartres and Orléans. Chartres continued the tradition of Fulbert, emphasizing a broad or "general" education based upon grammar (i.e., literature) and leading to philosophy in its widest or most literary sense. It was here that Bernard of Chartres taught. The finest alumnus of the school was John of Salisbury (c.1115–1180), who ended his long and varied career as bishop of Chartres. John, the best-educated man of the twelfth century, represented the humanistic reaction to the growing specialization and vocationalism in the schools of his day. Bright young students had a secure future in the service of secular or ecclesiastical government or in teaching in the schools. Students demanded and in many schools teachers provided short cuts through the normal liberal arts curriculum by eliminating subjects that were not "useful" or that did not have a direct bearing on training for a vocation. According to John and the humanists, this sort of education produced ignoramuses who could debate the subtleties of logic or who could use the jargon of learning but lacked the intellectual maturity and wisdom that were slowly won through assiduous study. John himself knew more logic than most of the teachers of logic, and he was better trained in ancient philosophy than any twelfth-century philosopher. What he objected to was the narrowing of these fields into pedantic and technical disciplines cut off from the totality of human experience as represented by literature and the other disciplines. Anyone familiar with the main tendencies of philosophy in the twentieth century, when philosophers usually talk only to other philosophers, can appreciate the humanistic reaction in the twelfth century.

In the classrooms the humanists fought for a losing cause, but the general influence of the classical revival is evidenced in the abundance and in the higher quality of the literature written in the twelfth century. Some of the poetry of this period, for example, imitated ancient models so well that later scholars mistook it for the work of classical poets. More important, the classics provided inspiration and new themes not only for poets who wrote in Latin but also for vernacular poets and prose writers. Twelfth-century humanists filled their works with apt quotation, mythological allusions, and metaphors familiar in classical literature. The number of commentaries on ancient authors written during the century is greater than for any other period before the fifteenth century. In style and grammatical usage the best Latin writing of the twelfth century does not measure up to the standards of Cicero, but this is because Latin was a living language. Medieval Latin has a larger vocabulary and a freer syntax than classical Latin, to express ideas and describe things unknown to antiquity. Twelfth-century prose writers were, on the whole, easily intelligible; what they lacked in grace and elegance they made up for in clarity. For this result the humanist revival was in large part responsible, because the humanists gave priority to the study of grammar and rhetoric over logic in the liberal arts.

Scientific knowledge had declined so low in late antiquity and the early Middle Ages that the recovery in this field which began in the eleventh century was revolutionary. Before this revolution took place, practically all the science known in the West could be found in the encyclopedic *Etymologies* of Isidore of Seville or in the elementary manuals of Bede, Cassiodorus, and Boethius. The earliest additions to this knowledge were made in the field of medicine at Salerno, where scholars had contact with Arabic learning. By the opening years of the twelfth century Latin scholars were coming to southern Italy, Sicily, and Spain to seek out the superior Arabic works in mathematics and natural science. Through these works in Arabic ancient Greek science was recovered, since Moslem science was based upon Arabic translations of Greek treatises. The western translators valued equally the Greek treatises and the Arabic commentaries upon them, and their translations were necessarily rather free. Many of the translators knew so little Arabic that they depended upon trilingual Jews who had Hebrew translations at hand and could explain the texts in Latin. Some of the ancient works thus reached the Latin West by a circuitous route from the original Greek through successive translations into Arabic, Hebrew, and finally Latin. A few works were translated directly from Greek into Latin in the twelfth century, but these were often neglected in favor of translations of the same works from the Arabic, because the latter usually included commentaries. The natural sciences were a living part of Arabic culture, and the treatise-with-commentary from Arabic was often more valuable because "up-to-date" than the treatise alone from the Greek.

Through the work of the translators, the first three sciences of the *quadrivium* (arithmetic, geometry, and astronomy) were transformed from rudimentary studies on the elementary level into the basic mathematical disciplines that are necessary for advanced scientific work. Adelard of Bath (c.1126) translated Euclid's *Geometry* and introduced the Western world to trigonometry from the works of the Arabic mathematician al-Khwarizmi. Robert of Chester (c.1145), another Englishman, later translated the same mathematician's basic work, *On the Restoration and Opposition of Numbers*. Arab scholars referred to it as "The Book" (*Al Gebra*), and from this reference the advanced mathematics of algebra derives its name.

In astronomy the traditional curriculum was vastly enlarged by the translation of the most exhaustive work on the subject in ancient literature. This was Ptolemy's *Almagest*, first translated by an unknown scholar direct from the Greek, c.1160, at Palermo. The Greek manuscript of the *Almagest* had been given by the Byzantine emperor to the king of Sicily. But this translation had little currency in the Middle Ages, and it led to no further exploitation of Greek scientific works preserved at Constantinople. The translation of Ptolemy made at Toledo by Gerard of Cremona (c.1175) was preferred, partly because of the prestige of Arabic science and partly because it contained Arabic corrections of Ptolemy's predictions of future locations of planets and stars.

Other fields of science were advanced or, so far as western Europe was concerned, introduced for the first time by the translators. In the twelve years (c.1175–1187) Gerard of Cremona stayed at Toledo, the chief center of this work, he translated over seventy treatises from Arabic into Latin. Many of these were Arabic translations of ancient Greek works. The most important of Gerard's translations were in medicine, including several writings of Galen and Hippocrates. He and other translators introduced the Latin West to physics, optics, mechanics, biology, meteorology, and psychology, including most of Aristotle's scientific treatises. Two other medieval sciences which no longer can be dignified by that title were also expanded by new knowledge gained from Arabic literature and from the Greeks through Arabic translations. These were astrology and alchemy, which medieval scholars thought of as "applied astronomy" and "applied physics," the first surviving into modern times as a pseudo-science and the second developing into the modern science of chemistry.

For the study of law the twelfth century witnessed a revival almost as revolutionary as the advance of scientific knowledge. As in science, legal studies owed a tremendous debt to the recovery of works lost since antiquity, but with a difference. The revival of law as an intellectual discipline depended almost wholly on the rediscovery of a single work, the Digest of Justinian, and, to a much smaller degree, of the other parts of the *Corpus Juris Civilis* that had dropped out of sight in the West about the year 600. During the early Middle Ages the Institutes, an abridged version of nine of the twelve books of the Code, and an abridged Latin version of the Novels were known in the West, though they had little influence. In the last quarter of the eleventh century the Digest was rediscovered, most of the missing parts of the Code had been recovered, and a better and more complete Latin translation of the Novels was available. The revival of legal knowledge that followed did not depend on either Arabic learning or classical Greek sources, and the revival was not, as in science, mainly a revival of substantive knowledge; it was a revival of jurisprudence as well, that is, the study of principles underlying a legal system and the development of a method of systematic study and exposition. Thus the revival of Roman law provided other legal systems, such as feudal custom and the canon law of the Church, with a method of organizing and analyzing particular legal rules so that inconsistencies and inequitable provisions could be eliminated and the rest could be revised or developed according to rational principles of justice. Every modern legal system of the Western world bears traces of this medieval influence of Roman jurisprudence.

Roman law was part of the curriculum at several schools in Italy and at a few north of the Alps, notably Montpellier. But the outstanding center was Bologna, where Irnerius and his successors were collectively known as "the Glossators" because of their characteristic method of expounding legal texts in lectures and in their writings. This method, borrowed from biblical scholars, consisted of brief explanatory comments and cross references to parallel texts, emendations to establish a more correct text, notes to clarify the meaning of technical terms, and whatever else would aid the reader (or, probably, serve as lecture notes for the professor expounding the text of the *Corpus Juris* in the classroom). Such writings, additional to but closely associated with the text, were inserted either as marginal or as interlinear glosses. In some surviving manuscripts the glosses are more bulky than the legal texts themselves.

The main task of the Glossators was textual analysis and literal explanation, together with extracting general principles from particular passages of the text. The situation confronting the jurists of the canon law was different. The development of canon law was continuous from antiquity. Instead of a single authoritative source like the *Corpus Juris*, the canonists had diverse authoritative sources. The most important were the Bible, the canons of Church councils, decretals of the popes (a decretal is a pronouncement or formal judgment, in the form of a letter, providing an official decision in a legal dispute or on a point of ecclesiastical law), the writings of the Fathers, and miscellaneous other texts (e.g., imperial Roman laws, Carolingian royal ordinances, liturgical texts, etc.). Obviously there is much more in this vast body of literature than legal material. As early as the fifth century extracts were being collected from many of these sources to make the law of the Church handily available in a single volume. None of these collections had the status of an official code, although certain collections gained general recognition and were considered almost as authoritative as the sources from which they had been compiled. In the West, the most important early collection was that of Dionysius Exiguus (c.500) in Rome; this was later known as the *Dionysio-Hadriana* because in 774 it was sent (in a modified and expanded form) by Pope Adrian I to Charlemagne in response to the king's request for a collection of canon law as approved in Rome. The other most important early collection was the seventh-century *Collectio Hispana*, originating in Spain but also widely used in the Carolingian empire. We have already noticed the so-called *False Decretals* (c.850), in which the genuine canons and decretals of the *Hispana* were cleverly interspersed with forged texts, the whole collection being attributed to Isidore of Seville (and hence also known as the Pseudo-Isidorean collection).

In the first half of the twelfth century there were about three dozen collections, of which the most important were the *Decretum* of Burchard of Worms (c.1020); a group of collections, closely related but not widely circulated, that are associated with the proponents of the Gregorian reform movement; and the *Pannormia* of Ivo of Chartres (c.1096). Ivo's work was largely a combination of the standard materials in Burchard's *Decretum* and newly discovered texts culled from the sources of the compilers interested in promoting papal reform. Ivo improved the arrangement of his materials, presenting them systematically by topic (rather than chronologically) for easier reference. His *Pannormia* set a new standard for accuracy and was remarkably free of forged or doubtful texts; also, he maintained a judicious balance between the tendencies toward enhancing the position of bishops or the authority of popes, found in other collections. Finally, Ivo's collection marked an advance in legal scholarship. Noting that his authorities occasionally disagreed, he proposed methods to be used in reconciling contradictions among the sources.

In the twelfth century canon law was added to the curriculum of higher studies at several schools. Bologna was the outstanding center, as it was already the center of the revival of Roman law. Here Gratian opened a new epoch of canonistic jurisprudence by compiling the definitive collection, the *Decretum* (c.1140) as it was usually called, which superseded all previous collections and became the authoritative statement of canon law as it then existed. Subsequent collections of decretals supplemented but did not replace the *Decretum;* they contained only the new law since Gratian's time. But Gratian did more than collect. He applied the methods of the schools to the study of canon law. His own title for his work was *Concord of Discordant Canons.* Instead of merely providing his collected extracts with commentary, Gratian wrote what was essentially a treatise, his socalled *Dicta,* into which he inserted appropriate extracts from more than 4,000 texts. The *Decretum* was both the largest collection of texts together either before or after his time by a canon lawyer, and it was also a treatise or textbook in which the meaning of the texts was expounded and general principles of law were deduced from the sources. Like Ivo before him, and also like Abelard in the field of theology, Gratian recognized that there were inconsistencies and contradictions among the authoritative statements in the sources. His main purpose was to reconcile these differences or else to show how one statement must defeat other statements among the authorities. By his work Gratian consolidated the learning of the past and organized the whole field for systematic study.

The canon law became an independent and rational system of jurisprudence, as the Roman law had been for centuries. Just as the *Corpus Juris* was the great text to be critically studied and expounded by the Glossators of the Roman law, Gratian's *Decretum* became the text to be glossed by a rising school of canon law glossators, known as Decretists.

In theology and philosophy, the twelfth-century revival follows a pattern familiar from the development of other disciplines: greater mastery of the sources available, consolidation of the learning of the past, and the organization of each field for systematic study. In biblical studies the two most important commentaries produced were the *Glossa Interlinearis* attributed to Anselm of Laon (d.1117) and the *Historia Scholastica* of Peter Comestor (d.1178), a manual of scriptural history. Each work represented an advance by providing a better commentary on Scripture, but neither took up the problem adumbrated by Abelard's *Sic et Non*, that is, how to deal with contradictions or divergent statements in the patristic authorities. Peter Lombard (d.1160) was the first to meet this problem squarely. Peter studied law at Bologna and then theology at Paris, where he became one of the best teachers. His *Four Books of Sentences,* written under the influence of Gratian and Abelard, provided a systematic summary of the faith which also included a critical analysis and harmonization of patristic theology. Peter Lombard's *Sentences* became the standard textbook in theology for the rest of the Middle Ages.

In philosophy, which was not sharply differentiated from theology, the second half of the twelfth century produced no one so original or profound as Anselm, Abelard, and Hugh of Saint-Victor in the first half. The important new fact was the translation of the philosophical works of Aristotle, including the advanced logical treatises that were destined to transform the study of logic. These advanced treatises were the *Prior Analytics,* dealing with the construction of syllogisms, the *Posterior Analytics,* dealing with logical demonstration, the *Topics,* dealing with arguments leading to logical probability, and the *Sophistical Refutations,* dealing with the refutation of false conclusions. These four works were called the "New Logic" to distinguish them from the Boethian corpus of logical treatises. For philosophy the recovery of the works of Aristotle, translated either directly from the Greek or from Arabic together with Arabic commentaries, was to have as revolutionary an effect as did the rediscovery of the *Corpus Juris Civilis* in the study of law. Humanist critics who complained that logic was driving letters out of the schools, and that dialectic had degenerated into quibbling, did not foresee that in the next century Aristotelian logic would be the basis for the greatest medieval achievements in theology and philosophy.

PART FOUR

THE HIGH MIDDLE AGES: MEDIEVAL CULTURE

The Church at Its Height

Many elements contributed to the unity of medieval civilization. Feudal society and the manorial organization of the rural population covered most of Europe, despite endless variations in social institutions from region to region. There was a high degree of economic localism but the development of commerce tied together the various regions of Europe. A common language of learning, Latin, made communication easy between educated people. In a more intangible way people were conscious of being heirs to a common tradition that reached back to the Roman Empire and through Rome to ancient Greece and Israel. But none of these elements contributed enough to the unity of medieval civilization to engage men's loyalties or provide goals for united action except on a very small scale or on a local level. Patriotic sentiment was directed toward the *patria*, the locality or region, not the kingdom or larger political area. The state as a concept barely existed in theory because it had hardly begun to be a fact.

The nearest approximation to the modern state in the Middle Ages was neither the kingdom nor the local region but rather the "international" Church. The one thing that everyone had in common was membership in one all-embracing Church under one supreme head, the pope. Theologians might speak of the Church as the mystical body of Christ, or as the City of God in preparation, or as the bride of Christ, or as the communion of all the faithful. But in addition the Church was a tangible institution which included the laity as well as the clergy. All of Latin Christendom constituted one community of the faithful to which everyone, except a small minority of Jews, belonged or should have belonged. Perhaps the most important single fact of the whole period from c.1050 to c.1300 was the growth of the Church as an organization, a "state" that embraced all other political units and gave to medieval civilization its basic unity. So far as all men agreed upon the meaning and end of human life, a code of behavior, or the standards of human relationships, this common agreement was either based on or influenced by the teachings of the Church. In the high Middle Ages the leadership and influence of the Church were more effective than ever before or afterwards.

Within this unity provided by the framework of the Church there was room for individual expression, diversity of views, and bitter disagreement over fundamental issues. The medieval Church never even reached liturgical uniformity, while the area within which divergence concerning doctrine was permissible remained larger in the Middle Ages than orthodox theologians, either Catholic or Protestant, would allow in the period after the Reformation.

46   THE ORGANIZATION OF THE MEDIEVAL CHURCH

The basic unit of ecclesiastical organization was the diocese. It varied greatly in size, from the many small Italian and southern French dioceses to the large ones in northern and eastern Europe like Lincoln in England or the great missionary bishoprics in the still half-converted Slavic lands. There was no theoretical or ideal size of a diocese, either in area or in population. The oldest usually coincided with the administrative unit of the Roman Empire, the *civitas*, and almost invariably the center of a diocese was the most important city in the region. Here the bishop had his church, called a cathedral because it contained his *cathedra* (chair or throne), from which he presided in his official capacity over the affairs of his diocese.

The chief spiritual duties of the bishop included ordination of priests, confirmation, dedication of altars, consecration of churches and chapels, and reconciliation of consecrated sites that had been polluted by bloodshed. Most episcopal duties were administrative in nature. Their twofold purpose was the spiritual welfare of the clergy and laity and the temporal management of the Church in the diocese. Supervision of the parochial clergy took much of the bishop's time. Most parish churches were considered the property of the manorial lord, who usually had the right to nominate or present the rector to the bishop for institution to the church. The bishop was expected to approve only qualified nominees and to reject the unqualified, a responsibility that involved him in endless disputes with lay patrons of his local churches. Also, the revenues attached to parish churches were divided between the rector and the patron, and like any other property these revenues could be alienated to other persons. The rector might be a nonresident priest whose actual parish work was performed by a vicar paid out of the revenues. These and other complications arising from the fiscal administration of the parish churches sometimes led to abuses or to the impoverishment of churches, thus endangering or neglecting the spiritual welfare of the local population. It was the bishop's responsibility to prevent such from happening and to protect the incumbents of churches from exploitation by their lay lords or ecclesiastical superiors.

Originally the administration of the diocese had been the responsibility of the bishop alone, assisted by the clergy attached to his cathedral. By the twelfth and thirteenth centuries part of the administration was delegated permanently to one or more officials called archdeacons. A large bishopric was divided into several archdeaconries over which the bishop exercised little direct control. As the deputy of the bishop for his area, the archdeacon was responsible for the supervision of parish priests, maintenance of the discipline and morals of both clergy and laity, building and repair of churches, and the filling of parish vacancies (i.e., seeing that local churches were provided with new priests without undue delay after death, promotion, or some other cause removed the incumbent). The archdeacon held meetings of the clergy under his charge and made visitations periodically to keep informed of local conditions. The archdeacon's court exercised a jurisdiction delegated from the bishop over minor ecclesiastical causes. Since these included both offenses by the clergy and moral lapses on the part of the laity, punishable under canon law, the archidiaconal court was almost universally detested. Some archdeacons were not above accepting bribes from suspected offenders in return for not prosecuting, or even blackmailing likely but innocent parties—lucrative malpractices that gave all archdeacons an unsavory reputation. Medieval students at the universities amused themselves by debating the mock-serious question: is it possible for an archdeacon to be saved?

The archdeaconry was subdivided into several rural deaneries or groups of parishes under the supervision of one of the parish priests who was distinguished by the title of archpriest or rural dean. The archdeacon left much of the local administration to the rural dean, but the latter did not possess very wide executive or judicial authority except by express mandate from the archdeacon.

At each level of this diocesan hierarchy, from the parish priest to the bishop, it was possible and often necessary to delegate to a deputy most of the actual functions of one or another office. The bishop, for example, was frequently absent from his diocese on ecclesiastical business or as an important adviser to a king or other secular ruler. Benefices such as a parish church or the office of archdeacon were often granted to nonresident clerks for their support while in the service of kings or great lords. Hence deputies with various titles often undertook the daily performance of the duties of many church offices. In the thirteenth century most bishops appointed an official to act in their stead and to preside over the episcopal court for all ecclesiastical causes that had not already been delegated to the jurisdiction of the archdeacons. And as mentioned above, nonresident parish priests appointed a vicar to take their place in the care of souls in the parish.

Diocesan administration was further complicated by the existence in each cathedral of a group of clergy called the chapter. Their main purpose was to provide for the liturgy, or daily service, in the cathedral church, as was done by the regular clergy in the monasteries. The chapter was usually organized as a collegiate body, sometimes consisting of monks who lived according to the Benedictine or some other monastic rule, and sometimes consisting of ordinary secular priests. But the typical cathedral chapter of the high Middle Ages was composed of canons. In contrast with monks who usually did not take orders, canons were ordained priests who also lived according to a rule. The canons had a common dormitory and refectory, and the chapter as a whole was endowed with property from which each canon was assigned a prebend, or revenue from a particular manor or other estate of the collective endowment.

The head of the chapter was the dean, who was elected by the canons and confirmed by the bishop. Other officials were the precentor (whose duties were primarily liturgical), the treasurer, the chancellor (who supervised the cathedral school), and the subdean. In the administration of the diocese, the chapter normally had charge of the other churches in the cathedral city and, in addition, had jurisdiction over certain parishes and rural deaneries. This control had been granted by earlier bishops as the proprietary right or endowment of the chapter, just as the archdeacon's jurisdiction and right to hold an ecclesiastical court had been granted by bishops to the archdeacons, who were usually selected from the canons of the cathedral chapter. The vested interests of the chapter and the archdeacons gave them a semi-independent position in their relations with the bishop. Often the bishop's interests conflicted with those of the archdeacons or of the chapter. Disputes arose frequently as to the respective spheres of their jurisdiction within the diocese.

The bishop maintained his own household of servants and diocesan officials, apart from the cathedral chapter, although some of his officials were canons who were permitted to be nonresident for that purpose. An episcopal household was staffed with chaplains and clerks, many of whom were assigned specialized duties such as drawing up documents, having custody of records, collecting and auditing revenues, helping to judge suits in the bishop's court, and advising the bishop on matters of policy. When the bishop was present in his diocese the delegated jurisdiction of his vicar-general lapsed. When the bishop visited any of the archdeaconries to investigate the condition of churches and clergy, to receive complaints, and to correct abuses, the jurisdiction of the archdeacon lapsed during the visitation. The archdeacon assisted in the visitation and many of the disputes and complaints brought to light were adjudicated in his court.

In addition to periodic visitation of his diocese, each bishop was expected to hold an annual diocesan synod to which were summoned the leading clergy of the bishopric. Here the most important ecclesiastical disputes were settled and legislation was enacted. The episcopal "constitutions" included not only local rules and regulations but also various injunctions to the clergy and a summary or restatement of the canon law. Diocesan legislation was thus an important means by which pronouncements of the popes and of the higher councils of the Church were communicated to all the clergy of each diocese. For example, the episcopal constitutions enacted by a thirteenth-century synod held by the bishop of Lincoln began by repeating the Ten Commandments, the seven deadly sins, the seven sacraments, and the Creed, and then proceeded to warn parish priests against frequenting taverns, attending entertainments, playing with dice, carrying arms, or allowing questionable women to live in their houses.

Some bishops possessed, in addition to the normal episcopal jurisdiction over their own bishoprics, a superior dignity and jurisdiction over several other dioceses. These were the archbishops. Some archbishops had few suffragan bishops under them; others had as many as a dozen or more. The archbishop of Canterbury ruled a province of eighteen dioceses, while the archbishop of York had only three. A few archbishops were effective rulers of their provinces, enforcing their jurisdiction by regular visitation of each diocese, by assuming the control of all spiritualities (administration of the sacraments and the revenues arising from pastoral duties) during episcopal vacancies, and by close supervision of their suffragans. Most archbishops, however, exercised little effective control, and were content to express their higher dignity by presiding at infrequent provincial synods of the higher clergy and by consecrating new suffragan bishops. A strong archbishop was able to make his archiepiscopal court one of appeal from the courts of his suffragans, as well as a court of first instance in certain cases for the province as a whole.

The regular (or monastic) clergy, in the high Middle Ages, did not fit completely into the diocesan and archdiocesan organization of the Church. Normally the monasteries within a diocese were subject to the bishop and his officials, but after the Hildebrandine reformation of the papacy a growing number of monasteries secured exemption from this episcopal jurisdiction, including exemption from episcopal visitation. Exemption did not make monasteries independent but rather transferred supervision to the papacy. Monks were eager to claim exemption on the ground of custom, alleging that a bishop's predecessors had never visited the monastery and that therefore their monastery was subject neither to visitation nor to the bishop's ordinary jurisdiction. Frequently the monks were in a strong position because bishops were too pressed with other duties to be able to visit their dioceses regularly or completely. In the thirteenth century, however, the papacy required the monastery to prove its claim, rather than the bishop to prove his right, before exemption from diocesan visitation was confirmed. Episcopal jurisdiction was further safeguarded by the rule that exemption for a monastery did not automatically entail exemption for its daughter-houses, each one of which must specifically be granted exemption.

Some monasteries were under archiepiscopal jurisdiction although exempt from that of the bishop. The thirteenth-century popes rejected claims to exemption by abbots unless such claims could be proved against both the bishop of the diocese and the archbishop of the province. The archbishop's relations with his bishops and abbots were determined more by historical circumstances and by the personal ability of individual archbishops than by any theoretical considerations or by the nominal position of the archbishop in the hierarchy of the Church. For example, in Italy many bishops were exempt from archiepiscopal control as a result of the efforts of the Hildebrandine popes and their successors to strengthen the papal position in the Empire. These exempt bishops and their dioceses were withdrawn from the control of archbishops who supported the emperor during the investiture struggle.

The hierarchy of the Church in the high Middle Ages was further complicated by the fact that the regular clergy were directly under the authority of the abbot of the monastery, or of a prior if the establishment were a priory dependent on a mother-house. Except for exempt monasteries, the abbot was blessed and installed by the bishop if the diocese in which the house was located. The abbot was usually elected by the monks themselves, or, if there was a disagreement, by the "greater and wiser part" (*maior et sanior pars*) of the community of monks. In a serious dispute in a nonexempt monastery the bishop could intervene to decide the election because he had the right of installation. Other duties of the bishop included surveillance of the spiritual, disciplinary, and financial state of the monastery. But in the case of a daughter-house the monks were also subject to the control of their superiors in the monastic order. Organization of the regular clergy thus often cut across the hierarchy of the secular clergy, organized into parishes, rural deaneries, archdeaconries, dioceses, and provinces.

In its territorial structure and in the administrative functions of its officials, the Church was heir to the Roman Empire, but like Rome the medieval Church was the product of historical growth. Its organization was simple in plan, but the historical development of the Church introduced conflicting interests and divergent practices that were reflected institutionally at every level. It is a mistaken notion to think of the medieval Church as a symmetrical and uniform hierarchy with authoritarian channels of command running from top to bottom. The structure did not function automatically, nor did it operate without some friction.

The work of the Church depended on the successful functioning of this vast organization, an organization in which the role of the bishop was prominent. The triumph of the Church as an institution that united and provided leadership for all of Latin Christian society in the high Middle Ages resulted from the impact of three new forces. All three began to have their effect toward the end of the eleventh century. A monastic revival infused the whole Church with new vitality; the papacy became the effective head not only of the Church but of all of Latin Christendom; and the canon law became a binding force which united the Church under the papal monarchy. All three of these developments had a profound influence upon lay society as well as upon the ecclesiastical hierarchy of the Church.

47   MONASTIC REFORM AND THE FRIARS: BERNARD, FRANCIS, AND DOMINIC

By the middle of the eleventh century the Cluniac reform movement had lost much of its initial enthusiasm and drive. Partly this was due to success; partly it followed from the participation in ecclesiastical reform by secular rulers who took the initiative for their own purposes. The Cluniac program had been essentially negative, aimed at eliminating moral and disciplinary abuses within monasteries and, later, throughout the Church. Then the Hildebrandine papacy took over these goals and converted them into a positive program of freedom of the Church from secular intervention so that the Church might be reformed under papal leadership. The essentially monastic aspect of the Cluniac revival largely succeeded, but the spirit of reform declined. Life in the Cluniac monasteries had become respectable and comfortable. Most of these houses were so richly endowed that the administration and exploitation of property consumed the energy and deadened the ardor that in earlier days had been dedicated to reform.

One of the fascinating aspects of Western monasticism in the Middle Ages was its capacity for recurrent revival. The foundation of several new orders inaugurated another wave of monastic reform that reached its height in the twelfth century. The earliest were loosely organized communities of hermits established by Romuald (d.1027) and his disciples in central Italy. Their goal was escape from the temptations of the world through a life of solitude, intense asceticism, and meditation. The hermit temper of eleventh-century Italy—extreme mortification, fierce hostility toward all things carnal, and passionate craving for salvation—was reminiscent of the desert fathers of Egypt and Syria. North of the Alps, in 1084, Bruno of Cologne resigned as head of the cathedral school of Reims and founded at La Grand

Chartreuse (*Carthusia*), in the mountainous wilderness of eastern France south of Cluny, a community somewhat similar to those of Romuald. Here the monks worshiped together in a chapel but lived in isolated cells, combining the eremitic with the cenobitic form of organization. The ideal was severance from the world and seclusion of the brethren from each other, so that they might achieve in manual labor, contemplation, and strict asceticism a higher spiritual life. About 1130 the customs and practices of the community were written down, thus forming a rule for the Carthusian Order. Later in the twelfth century the Carthusians received papal recognition and approval, but the Order remained small because its rule was too austere to attract large numbers. The Carthusians were and still are an elite group, justly proud of their unique record of having been "never reformed because never deformed" (*nunquam reformata quia nunquam deformata*).

By far the most important new order in the monastic reform movement of the twelfth century was founded in 1098 by Robert of Molesmes at Citeaux, in eastern France in the wild country north of Cluny. The purpose of the Cistercians was to restore literally and strictly the observance of St. Benedict's Rule. The Cistercian ideal was midway between the ascetic extremes of the hermit communities and the relatively lax discipline of the Cluniac houses. The early success of the monks of Citeaux led to the foundation of four daughter-houses, and eventually these five monasteries multiplied to over seven hundred. Instead of the centralized Cluniac system, in which all houses were priories subject to the abbot of Cluny, the Cistercian foundations were independent monasteries under their own abbots. Each monastery was required to observe the customs and the discipline of Citeaux. Uniformity was enforced by the rule that each abbot must visit annually the daughter-houses of his monastery. For the duration of this visitation the authority of the abbot of the daughter-house lapsed to the visiting abbot. The four "primary abbots" of the Order (those of the first four daughter-houses) jointly visited Citeaux each year, assuming abbatial authority for the duration of their visitation, to ensure that the mother-house of the Order adhered to the Benedictine Rule and Cistercian customs. Once a year all the abbots of the Order gathered at Citeaux to hold a meeting or chapter. An erring abbot who obdurately persisted in innovation or departure from the customs of the Order was subject to deposition by the abbots in chapter meeting. The Cistercian constitution was a successful combination of local autonomy with control by superior authority which still avoided centralization.

Although the Cistercians were severely austere and by preference built their monasteries in wild and remote places, to escape from worldliness, the impact of the Order on medieval life was in many ways quite worldly. Their contribution to learning and the arts was small because of the emphasis on contemplation and manual labor rather than study and because of the Cistercians' suspicion of beauty as a distraction from their dedication to the monastic life. But they became the leading agriculturists of Europe. The White Monks (they wore white to distinguish themselves from Benedictines, who wore a black habit) were usually endowed with submarginal land that had never before been tilled or used in any way, and they were thus forced to develop more efficient methods of land utilization. They exploited labor more efficiently than in the traditional open-field system; they were experts in clearing forests, draining swamps, and breeding cattle; and they pioneered in greatly increasing wool production by converting waste lands into pasture and by improving the breeds of sheep. The success of the Order brought Cistercian leaders to the attention of popes and kings who employed them in positions of responsibility. Thus Cistercian ideals and Cistercian success combined to bring the Order back into the world from which the first White Monks had fled.

In the year 1113 a young Burgundian noble persuaded several relatives and friends to join with him in entering the monastery of Citeaux. Three years later he was directed by the abbot to establish Citeaux's third daughter-house on the lands of the count of Troyes. Setting forth with

*Ecclesiastical and Cultural Centers
in the High Middle Ages*

twelve companions, he journeyed to the austere solitude of *Clara Vallis* where he built the new monastery and became its abbot. This young man was St. Bernard of Clairvaux (1090–1153), who was destined to become the dominant personality of his Order, of the Church, and of all Latin Christendom. Bernard combined the qualities of the soldier of Christ with a mystic's love of God and of man. From first to last he was the eager monk and the reluctant man of affairs. Only in his cell at Clairvaux could he find contentment and peace; only in the world could he find those battles for the Lord (as he thought) which challenged and satisfied his militant nature. To some of his contemporaries Bernard's wholehearted piety and rigid orthodoxy were irresistibly attractive. To others his aggressive self-righteousness was equally repulsive. Bernard is difficult to evaluate. He was a controversial figure in his own day, and so he has remained. Compared with his contemporaries he was obviously a great man. But how great? Bernard had the fortune or misfortune to live in an age of second-rate rulers and leaders.

As abbot, Bernard made Clairvaux a model of Cistercian asceticism. Burning with love for the monks in his charge, he subjected them to an uncompromising and severe regime for the good of their souls—whether, one is tempted to add, they liked it or not. But with a few exceptions they liked it very much. So attractive was life at Clairvaux that the monastery was always filled to capacity, with more seeking entrance. The only solution to the problem of numbers was to send out a steady stream of monks to establish daughter-houses. By the end of Bernard's life over one hundred and sixty monasteries had been founded by the monks of Clairvaux and by the monks of the daughter-houses of Clairvaux.

His success as a Cistercian abbot and the force of his personality led Bernard to play a dominant role in ecclesiastical affairs. He was prominent in Church councils. He took the lead in criticizing monastic laxity, especially in the Cluniac Order. His influence was decisive in swinging the disputed papal election of 1130 to Innocent II against the antipope Anacletus. He led the attack on what he considered Abelard's rationalistic subversion of the faith. He inspired and influenced the drafting of the original rule of the Knights Templars (1128), and he was both friend and patron of leaders of the monastic reform movement outside the Cistercian Order, notably Norbert (1080–1134), founder of the Premonstratensian Order of canons regular. Bernard's influence over the papacy reached its height when a former monk of Clairvaux was elected Pope Eugenius III (1145–1153). To religious literature Bernard made a substantial contribution in the form of several hundred sermons, over five hundred letters dealing with all phases of monastic life and contemporary issues, and several treatises on theology and liturgy. Through these writings Bernard had a profound influence on the development of mysticism, especially in his exposition of the four stages of love as an ascent toward God.

Bernard's earliest participation in secular affairs was as an adviser to the French king. The project dearest to his heart was the Second Crusade (1147–1149), to which he devoted his brilliant gifts as an orator. His success in enlisting thousands for the cause, including Louis VII of France and Conrad III of the Empire, was followed by bitter disillusionment when the Crusade failed. His last years were spent largely in rallying the opposition against Arnold of Brescia, the antipapal revolutionary who temporarily ousted the pope and re-established a "republic" in the city of Rome (1146–1155), but he did not live to see his last enemy defeated and executed by the joint efforts of the pope and emperor. There were few important movements in Latin Christendom in which Bernard did not play some role, and there were few popes or rulers for whom he was not an adviser or critic, friend or foe. His whole public career exemplified the Church Militant, just as his private life was a forceful expression of the monastic ideal.

The second half of the twelfth century witnessed a gradual decline in the relative importance of the monastic orders, and in the influence of monastic leaders in the life of both the clergy and the laity. This is not surprising because the monastic revival was remote from developments that were transforming Europe during this century. Monasticism provided an escape from the world, but the world was becoming far more interesting and important. Cistercians were out of touch with the intellectual awakening and the commercial revolution that made the center of gravity in medieval civilization shift from the manor and the monastery to the city and the cathedral. In religious life there were repercussions of this growth of the cities. While urban centers grew rapidly, their ecclesiastical organization remained almost unchanged. The building of new parish churches lagged behind the increase in population. This inadequate pastoral care of a growing flock made townsmen particularly susceptible to popular religious movements that were critical of, or even hostile toward, the Church. The marketplace was a concourse for the exchange of ideas as well as goods. Anticlericalism most often took the form of opposition to the wealth and worldliness of the secular clergy, but sometimes this criticism of the hierarchy drifted into doctrinal disagreement and heresy.

The last great medieval monastic reform movement was designed to meet these problems. If there were too few priests, then the new monks were to settle their communities within cities rather than to flee from urban temptations. If the clergy were criticized for wealth and worldliness, then the new monks were to set an example of poverty and piety. If there was danger of heresy, then the new monks were to meet it head on with stout orthodoxy and active preaching.

The first of these new orders was founded by one of the most remarkable personalities of the whole Middle Ages, St. Francis of Assisi (1181–1226). Francis was the son of a fairly prosperous merchant. After a halfheartedly wayward youth, he experienced a conversion, renounced the secure but dull life in store for him, and dedicated himself to complete poverty and service to the poor and needy. Unlike the hermits, Francis did not turn to nature as a refuge from the world but saw in each created thing an object of love because it was a sign of the glory of the Creator. For this reason he enjoyed the life of a solitary apart from human society and delighted in preaching the word of God to birds and beasts—who, according to report, found his preaching eminently worth hearing. But Francis' real calling was service to "Our Lady Poverty," a task to which he turned with the same devotion that a knight-errant gave his lady. Serving the poor took him to the towns where they abounded, and most of his life was spent preaching the Gospel while living in complete poverty among the common people.

Francis' charm, simplicity, humility, and gracious manner attracted many followers. He drew up a brief rule for them, modeled on the life of Christ. In 1210 he sought from the pope, Innocent III, approval of his work and his group. The great pope hesitated, perhaps a bit doubtful about the orthodoxy or even the sanity of his cheerful but beggarly (and filthy) petitioner, but finally allowed Francis to continue his work and to govern his followers as an authorized religious order. With typical humility, Francis called his followers the Order of Friars Minor ("Little Brothers"). Under Francis and for a few years after his death, the Franciscans were forbidden to own anything, either as individuals or as a corporate group. Because they relied upon charity for their livelihood, they were a mendicant (begging) order.

The Franciscans were immensely popular, and with their rapid growth a more elaborate organization and rule was—against Francis' own wishes—authorized by Honorius III in 1223. The history of the Friars Minor illustrates how success so often changes the aims and the character of a religious movement. By the end of the thirteenth century the Franciscans were corporately wealthy, and they were bitterly divided between the "spiritual Franciscans" who tried to emulate their founder's simplicity and the great majority of the Order. Finally, to prepare themselves better for preaching the Franciscans entered the universities and many of them became leading scholars and teachers of theology and philosophy, a development that Francis scarcely had envisaged.

The other new order was founded by Francis' contemporary, St. Dominic (1170–1221), a Spanish priest who had undertaken an unsuccessful mission to win back heretics in southern France. Convinced that the best way to fight heresy was to combat ignorance among the orthodox clergy and laity, Dominic founded an order whose special task was to study theology and preach. This purpose could not be fulfilled by retiring from the world. As Dominic told his followers, "Henceforth the world is your home: go forth into the whole world, teach and preach." In 1216 the Order was sanctioned by Honorius III and given the name of Friars Preachers. The

Dominicans were mendicant like the Franciscans, and like the latter they too relaxed the early rules against possession of property. Some Dominicans spent so much time in study and teaching that the only preaching for which they could take credit, indirectly, was through their students who went out as "hounds of the lord" (*domini canes,* a pun on the name *dominicani,* "Dominicans") to keep sheep from straying from the flock.

The constitution of the Dominicans was based on that of the Augustinian canons, but an important modification was introduced that was to influence the organization of other religious orders. This was the system of elected officials and elected representatives. Each Dominican house had an elected conventional prior. All the conventional priors of a province, plus one friar elected from each house in the province, met together annually in a provincial chapter meeting. The provincial chapter elected a provincial prior and four administrators to govern the province during the ensuing year. The master general of the whole Order was elected by a general chapter composed of the provincial priors and special representatives elected from each province.

Both of the new orders of friars had a privileged position. They were exempt from bishops and directly under papal jurisdiction. They were authorized to preach anywhere and were specially trained to preach effectively. Later, they were also authorized to hear confession, impose penance, and grant absolution. The friars thus competed with the work of the parish and diocesan clergy. When the laity diverted their offerings to mendicant friars, the revenues of the ordinary diocesan clergy suffered, and this competition grew into open antagonism. Ultimately such rivalry damaged the position of the Church in society, but the immediate effect was to stimulate the bishops to reform the local clergy and improve their own work. The friars performed the greatest of their many services in reviving the influence of the Church where it was in greatest danger, in the towns where anticlerical criticism was strongest and in areas where heresy was rife.

48   INNOCENT III AND THE PAPAL MONARCHY

Under Innocent III (1198–1216) the medieval papacy reached the height of its prestige, leadership, and power. Innocent III was the greatest pope of the Middle Ages, but without the development of the papacy as an institution during the preceding century and a half the position he occupied would have been unattainable. Ever since the days of Leo IX (1049–1054) and Gregory VII (1073–1085) the popes had pressed their claims, with varying fortunes and through many vicissitudes, to supremacy over the Church, freedom of the Church from secular intervention, and the superiority of the spiritual authority over the secular. Innocent came nearest to realizing these claims in fact. During his pontificate Latin Christendom came nearest to being united under one supreme head, and the papacy emerged as a monarchy that possessed the machinery and the moral force sufficient not only to govern the spiritual work and the organization of the Church, but also to arbitrate, intervene in, and control the affairs of secular rulers.

Innocent's first achievement was to solve a problem that had vexed almost all the twelfth-century popes: security in Rome and control of the Papal States. A pope who could not dominate the Roman nobility could hardly aspire to rule Christendom. Innocent worked out a compromise that withdrew the papacy from active participation in the strictly local affairs of city government, thus freeing the Holy See from local factional strife. The majority of Roman citizens were pleased with the arrangement. The Eternal City, as the administrative and spiritual center of the Church, attracted a steady flow of pilgrims, suitors to the papal court, and ecclesiastical officials with their retinues. It was easier for the citizens to make a profit by supplying the provisions and lodging for this "tourist trade" than it was to compete with the other Italian centers of commerce and industry. Toward the Papal States Innocent could not afford to be conciliatory. By armed force, or the threat of force, he revived the full temporal authority of the papacy over the duchy of Spoleto and the march of Ancona, which together reached northeastward from Rome to the Adriatic Sea. Control of the Papal States was especially important because of the political situation in the Empire and in the kingdom of Sicily.

Frederick Barbarossa's son, the emperor Henry VI (1190–1197), had united Sicily to the Empire by his marriage with Constance, heiress of the Sicilian throne. This turn of events deprived the papacy of its Norman allies to the south and replaced them with the Hohenstaufen enemy. To make matters worse, part of the Papal States had fallen under imperial control. Henry had isolated Rome and secured his own communications between the southern kingdom and the Empire. Then, fortunately for the pope, Henry died suddenly and a fierce struggle for the succession broke out in both Germany and Sicily. Constance appealed to Innocent for help in preserving the Sicilian throne for her three-year old son, Frederick, against the ambitions of the Norman nobility. Shortly before she died, in 1198, Constance recognized the pope as feudal lord of the kingdom and renounced the extraordinary powers over the Sicilian church formerly exercised by the king. In return, Frederick became a papal ward and was recognized as heir to the kingdom.

In Germany civil war was raging between the adherents of the late emperor's brother, Philip of Swabia, who was the Hohenstaufen candidate, and the candidate of the Guelph party, Otto of Brunswick, son of Henry the Lion. Innocent asserted his right to decide between them, basing the claim upon his duty to judge the fitness of a candidate before performing the coronation of the emperor. From Otto, his choice, Innocent obtained an almost complete renunciation of the royal control of the German church that had been secured by the Concordat of Worms (1122). However, as soon as he was crowned emperor (in 1209) Otto disregarded his promises and resumed as imperial a policy as that of any Hohenstaufen, including an invasion of southern Italy to reunite Sicily with the Empire. Innocent had no other recourse than to absolve Otto IV's vassals from their fealty, stir up rebellion in Germany, and promote the candidacy of Frederick II, king of Sicily. His young ward promised never to reunite Sicily with the Empire and confirmed all the concessions that Otto had made before being crowned emperor. Philip Augustus of France helped Innocent win over the German nobility. In retaliation Otto IV invaded France in a campaign timed to coincide with an attack by John of England, but the effort ended in a disastrous defeat for the Anglo-German alliance at the battle of Bouvines, 1214. Otto's support in Germany deteriorated rapidly, and Frederick was confirmed as emperor-elect.

In his relations with the Empire Innocent had seemingly won a resounding triumph after many tribulations. His protégé and vassal had secured the imperial throne; Sicily, a papal fief, was to be separated forever from the Empire; the German church was freed from royal control and subordinate to full papal jurisdiction; and the Papal States were once more subject to the pope's authority. As events later proved, Innocent's victory

Coronation of an Emperor. At left, Henry VI is received by Celestine III (top), is anointed (middle), and is invested and crowned by the pope (bottom). On right, Henry VI enthroned. Manuscript illustrations (late twelfth and early thirteenth centuries). BURGERBIBLIOTHEK, BERN, AND BIBLIOTHEQUE ROYALE, BRUSSELS.

was not permanent. The successes he achieved created problems for later popes. The pontificate of Innocent left the papacy firmly committed to a policy which was to keep the popes of the thirteenth century embroiled in Italian politics.

In his relations with other secular rulers Innocent was almost as successful. He negotiated a truce between Philip Augustus of France and Richard I of England. In the later quarrel between Philip and John he intervened vigorously, though unsuccessfully, to prevent war. This dispute was feudal in nature—between lord and vassal in terms of feudal law. While claiming no jurisdiction over a purely feudal matter, Innocent enunciated an important principle that canon lawyers later employed to justify the indirect power of the pope. Whenever war is threatened there is an imminent danger of commission of sin by Christians. It is the pope's duty, Innocent argued, to intervene in any temporal affair where sin is concerned (*ratione peccati*) and to pass judgment as the Vicar of Christ.

The papal claim to supreme jurisdiction over all moral, spiritual, or ecclesiastical causes led Innocent to intervene in the internal affairs of most of the kingdoms and principalities of Europe. Philip Augustus proved least tractable, but even he lost a long conflict with Innocent. Philip had made a political marriage with the Danish princess Ingeborg in 1193. For reasons that are not entirely clear, "on the very morrow of the wedding," Philip "developed a compulsive horror of his new queen," a reaction which he had shown neither to his first wife nor the lady he took as his third "wife," nor to his only other known romantic interest (a certain "damsel of Arras"), the mothers respectively of his son and heir, a daughter and son subsequently legitimized, and another son. The day after their marriage Philip put Ingeborg away and, as soon as it could be arranged, he obtained an annulment from a council of French bishops. Ingeborg resolutely appealed to the papacy, but to no avail until Innocent became pope in 1198 and supported her cause. Twenty years after their nuptials—during which Philip remarried, raised a family, suffered an interdict upon his realm decreed by Innocent, and went through the empty forms of public reconciliation that gave the lady no solace—Philip finally restored Ingeborg to her full rights as wife and queen. She was the victim of the political realities of her age, because Innocent's moderation in her case was dictated by his dependence on Philip's support in his struggles against John of England and the emperor Otto IV.

Conflict between John and Innocent arose from a disputed election to the archbishopric of Canterbury in 1206. Representatives were sent to Rome by all three contending parties, the cathedral chapter, the suffragan bishops, and the king. Innocent quashed all previous proceedings in the case and persuaded the representatives of the chapter to elect his own candidate, Stephen Langton, an English cardinal and formerly a professor of theology at Paris. John refused to recognize the election and Innocent retaliated in 1208 by putting England under an interdict. A year and a half later John was excommunicated. Innocent threatened deposition and negotiated with Philip Augustus with a view to replacing John with a Capetian. Under this pressure John finally capitulated and, in 1213, recognized the pope as his feudal lord from whom he and his successors were to hold England as a papal fief. John's submission is considered Innocent's greatest victory in his relations with the secular rulers of Europe. It is a striking example of the supreme jurisdiction, the "plenitude of power" (*plenitudo potestatis*) in the canon law phrase, which the pope claimed to wield directly in all spiritual causes and indirectly in all temporal matters.

Innocent also used the spiritual weapons of the inderdict or excommunication in his relations with the rulers of Castile, Leon, Navarre, and Norway. By the end of his pontificate Innocent was acknowledged as feudal lord of the kingdoms of Sicily, Portugal, Aragon, and England in the west, and of Bulgaria and Armenia in the east, while Hungary, Bohemia, and Poland recognized the pope's superiority and right to intervene or arbitrate in their internal affairs. It is a mistake, however, to consider Innocent's position in Europe simply the result of papal aggression. In every case the secular ruler gained as much and sometimes more from the feudal relationship. John of England, for example, was in desperate straits when he became a papal vassal and thereby gained the neutrality of the English church as well as his strongest supporter in his new lord, Innocent.

One of Innocent's most cherished goals was to organize a successful Crusade, a project that he initiated as soon as he became pope. Conditions seemed favorable, for the response among the feudal nobility was warm and no ruler was ready to compete with papal leadership. Yet the Fourth Crusade, launched in 1202, became a grotesque perversion of the crusading ideal. From the very beginning Innocent lost control. The Venetians persuaded the crusaders to conquer the Adriatic port of Zara for them, in payment for transportation provided by the Venetian fleet. Innocent excommunicated the whole army for attacking a Christian city. Nothing daunted, the Venetians and the leaders of the Crusade then concluded an alliance with a claimant to the Byzantine throne, promising to restore him in Constantinople in return for money, supplies, and troops to use against Egypt. Although the treaty looked to the eventual conquest of the Holy Land and promised the reunion of the Greek and Latin Churches under Rome, Innocent prohibited this further diversion from the Crusade. The pope's instinct was sound, for the only result of the whole venture was the conquest of Constantinople and the establishment of a Latin Empire under the French leaders. The former Byzantine Empire was irreparably weakened as the French carved it up into petty feudal principalities. Economic interests and political ambitions had distorted the Fourth Crusade into a travesty. It was Innocent's only conspicuous failure. But he did not abandon his goal; in 1215 he extracted a promise from Frederick II to lead another crusade.

Pope Innocent III. Wall painting, Subiaco (thirteenth century). PHOTO: ALINARI.

Against the heretics of southern France Innocent had greater success, though with ultimate results that he neither foresaw nor desired. When the local bishops failed to extirpate heresy in this region, papal legates were entrusted with the task. They were authorized to call on secular rulers for assistance. When they did so, a war broke out and Innocent caused a crusade to be preached in northern France against the heretics. Land-greedy feudal nobles joined in the Albigensian Crusade, which rapidly got out of hand. Until Innocent's death the situation remained fluid and confused. The pope's objective was to win back heretics; the lay leaders of the "crusade" followed their own ambitions. This mixture of religious and purely selfish motives produced extreme ferocity on both sides, from which the economy and culture of Languedoc were never fully to recover.

Over the Church Innocent exercised the papal "plenitude of power" with unqualified success. In fact, the degree of his success in directing the temporal affairs of Latin Christendom depended on his supremacy over the Church. Although the pontificate of Innocent III marks the beginning of a new era for the papal monarchy, he created little that was new either in theory or in practice. What did happen was a rapid growth and elaboration of the papal government in response to the increase of business it transacted. The papal *curia* or "court" consisted of the cardinals; officials of the pope's cathedral as bishop of Rome, St. John Lateran, and of the other four major basilicas of Rome (St. Peter's, St. Paul's Outside the Walls, S. Maria Maggiore, and S. Lorenzo); and the notaries, clerks, secretaries, auditors, scribes, and others who assisted the pope and the cardinals. Originally this *curia* was small and its functions were undifferentiated. Any member of the *curia* might be assigned to any task, whether it concerned executive, judicial, or financial business. If a decision required the promulgation of some new rule or regulation—that is, if legislation resulted from any of this activity—the pope consulted with the cardinals together with other members of the *curia* whose advice would be expedient before issuing the decretal incorporating such legislation.

As business increased this primitive *curia* began to develop specialized branches responsible for different kinds of routine business. The chancery consisted of members of the *curia* permanently assigned to the drafting of official correspondence. The drafting of a decretal required not only exactitude in expression and felicity of style but also legal training and some knowledge of affairs, so the higher officials of the chancery were advisers on policy as well as experts in writing well-phrased letters. Because papal letters carried the weight of supreme authority there was constant danger of forgery by unscrupulous partisans in some dispute or important transaction. Therefore the chancery developed a system of issuing letters whose authenticity could be recognized immediately by chancery officials. An intricate seal made of lead, called a *bulla*, was attached to each document so that it could not be removed without fracturing the lead. Official papal documents are called "bulls" from this seal. Even the counterfeiter who could reproduce the seal convincingly had a greater hurdle to surmount before he could execute a successful forgery. The papal chancery employed a method of writing known as the *cursus*, whereby key phrases or whole sentences were cast in a nonclassical meter which no one ignorant of the system could detect. The secret of the *cursus* was so well kept that only in the nineteenth century were scholars able to unravel its mysteries and thus once again able to distinguish authentic from false papal documents.

The financial bureau of the *curia* was the *camera* or chamber. Revenues were derived from many sources. The pope collected taxes and dues as temporal ruler of the Papal States, received income from the estates and other property with which the see of St. Peter was endowed, and collected revenues of various sorts as head of the Church. Among the latter were fines and fees charged in the normal course of judicial administration, revenues paid by exempt monasteries and bishops, taxes levied on the clergy in support of crusades and for other purposes, and a variety of payments from clergy and laity alike ranging from the gifts of pilgrims in Rome to extraordinary fees for special services or privileges. Although papal income grew rapidly under Innocent III and his successors, the *curia* and its expenses grew even more. The main reason for this growth was the increase of judicial business.

The pope was supreme judge (*judex ordinarius*) of all spiritual causes and—indirectly, as he claimed—of many, if not all, temporal disputes.

Although the pope heard many important cases in person, the number of suits initiated in the *curia* or appealed to Rome from lesser tribunals was so great that cardinals were delegated to hear and determine most ecclesiastical causes in the name of the pope. Each department of the *curia*, like the chancery and the *camera*, retained the original judicial authority of the whole *curia* and could bring suits to final judgment. In addition there were special tribunals to adjudicate special kinds of cases. For example, the penitentiary was a committee of cardinals and their assistants with jurisdiction over excommunications, interdicts, indulgences, absolutions, and dispensations from the canon law, plus the litigation that might arise in connection with such activities.

The basic reason for the enormous growth of the business and therefore of the size of the *curia* was the more rational and equitable justice obtainable there. Litigation was often slow, but the *curia* made few mistakes. Appeals were carefully prepared by committees of experts so that all the evidence was properly presented for judgment by the appropriate tribunal. When the auditors found evidence lacking or testimony conflicting, the suit might be sent back to the locality of origin, where special judges delegate were commissioned to receive further testimony, to try the case, and to pronounce judgment in the name of the pope. A large proportion of appeals to Rome were by this method actually determined locally by men who knew conditions best, even though the final sentence took the form of a decretal from the pope issued out of the chancery in Rome. Centralization of judicial authority in the Church was achieved without losing touch with local conditions.

Besides the hearing of appeals, both locally and at the *curia* in Rome, there were two other methods by which papal authority was extended throughout both the Church and lay society. We have already had occasion to notice the work of papal legates. Ordinary legates were, like the Carolingian *missi dominici*, representatives of central authority empowered to act or to make binding decisions in matters specified by their commissions. In addition there were plenipotentiary representatives with broad and unspecified powers, the legates *a latere*. For all practical purposes the latter could do anything the pope could do, but their delegated authority was restricted to a particular area or for a specified period of time. Most legates were cardinals or other members of the *curia* sent out from Rome, although a few were resident locally and appointed from the local clergy. The archbishop of Canterbury, for example, was *ex officio* a papal legate.

The most impressive expression of papal authority was the meeting of a general council of the whole Church. In antiquity such councils had been called by the emperors. Beginning in the mid-eleventh century the papacy took the initiative in calling councils as a means of enforcing reform. Councils whose attendance was especially large and representative of the whole Latin Church were later recognized as ecumenical, their legislation

Fourth Lateran Council, 1215. Manuscript illustration (thirteenth century). CORPUS CHRISTI COLLEGE, CAMBRIDGE.

being universally binding like the canons of the ecumenical councils of antiquity. The greatest of such medieval councils was the Fourth Lateran Council called by Innocent III to meet in November, 1215. Over four hundred bishops and eight hundred abbots and priors attended, together with proctors of prelates who were absent and representatives of the leading secular rulers. The agenda were prepared by committees of the *curia* and faithfully reflect Innocent's wide range of interests. The canons enacted may be grouped under four main headings: doctrine, discipline, reform, and political affairs.

In matters of doctrine the Council condemned certain heresies of the day, including that of the Albigensians, and pronounced the theory of transubstantiation—long debated pro and con by theologians—to be a dogma of the Church. Henceforth it was necessary for a Christian to believe that the substance (as opposed to the "accidents" or outward appearance) of the bread and wine, when consecrated in the sacrament of the Eucharist, was changed into the body and blood of Christ.

Many canons affecting discipline, both of the clergy and laity, were enacted. Of the two most important, one prescribed confession, and the performance of penance imposed, at least once each year by all Christians; the other required every Christian to partake of the sacrament of the Eucharist (communion) at least once each year.

Like all councils, the Fourth Lateran dealt at length with reform. The clergy were prohibited from wearing certain apparel and from engaging in unworthy occupations or participating in undignified games or recreational activities of the laity. Bishops were required to preach regularly or provide substitutes to do it for them, and all priests were forbidden to receive fees for administering the sacraments. The most important reform canon prohibited the participation of the clergy in ordeals, which were pronounced to be superstitious. Since the validity of the ordeal depended upon divine intercession which only a priest could be expected to call forth, this canon had a far-reaching effect on the development of secular law. In England it led to the use of trial by jury in criminal cases.

Finally, the work of the Council included much that was general or political in purpose. Innocent proclaimed and the Council approved a new Crusade which Frederick II agreed to lead. Otto IV was deposed in favor of Frederick II, and Raymond VI of Toulouse was excommunicated as a heretic and replaced by the leader of Innocent's Albigensian Crusade, Simon de Montfort. The English barons who were in rebellion against John, now a papal vassal, were condemned, while the suspension of archbishop Stephen Langton, who supported the rebels, was approved. The principle that the property of heretics was subject to confiscation by the secular ruler was confirmed, and the status of Jews in Christian society was defined.

Of all the events of the pontificate of Innocent III, the Fourth Lateran Council best illustrates the papal monarchy of the high Middle Ages in action. In the spiritual life of Europe, in the organization of the Church, in the reform of the clergy and the suppression heresy, and in the temporal affairs of the Western nations—in short, in the unity of Latin Christendom—the papal monarchy was the supreme authority and the directive force.

Medieval Christendom

It is difficult for the modern reader to grasp how immediate and pervading was the role of religion in the daily life of the high Middle Ages. There were few human activities, none of any importance, that did not have a religious aspect or that did not fall under the influence of the Church to some degree. The explanation is twofold. On the negative side, there were few competing activities or distracting interests. In a world where there were no newspapers, motion pictures, radio, television, spectator sports, or automobiles, a world where total war, the incredibly high standard of living now enjoyed, and the political and economic revolutions of our past half-century were unknown and unthinkable—in such a world the daily life of ordinary people could revolve around religious festivals and be directed by the teachings of the Church.

Religion obviously meant more, relatively speaking, in an age when alternatives to religion were either lacking or weak. On the positive side, Christianity provided, as it still does for many people, the greatest challenge and the most satisfactory explanation of human life. The Church was predominant in medieval society because it could satisfy the highest aspirations that men experienced: the search for truth, the enjoyment of beauty, and the desire for a "good life" that was *good* rather than simply filled with consumers' goods. In ways that no other institution came near approaching, the Church was a civilizing force. In its organization, its law, its authoritative revelation and tradition, the Church was a symbol of the divine order that in the Christian view underlay the confusions and complexities of both society and the whole created universe. The strongest unifying element in medieval culture was this categorical certitude which men shared as to the meaning, purpose, and final end of human existence.

What is even more difficult for the modern student to grasp is how there could be, within this larger framework of general agreement, so much diversity of religious experience. Tags and labels like "the age of faith," as applied to the Middle Ages, are misleading because they suggest a submissive and unquestioning society, accepting without doubts a monolithic world view forced upon it. Such in fact was far from the case. Within the Church there was vigorous dissent from the modes of thought and devotion of the majority. This included continuous and sometimes acrimonious theological dispute concerning doctrinal matters that had not been defined officially. Quantitatively, in terms of the amount of literature produced by the participants in these debates, the differences between orthodox writers far exceeded the differences between the defenders of orthodox doctrine and those who were considered heretical. When dissent by minority groups actually led to movements of heresy, the Church Militant reacted with determination and, occasionally, with violence.

49   THE CHRISTIAN LIFE IN THE MIDDLE AGES

Eternal salvation was the goal of temporal life. Only the worship of God was more important in the work of the Church than helping the faithful to attain this goal through the ceremonies and acts by which divine grace, necessary for salvation, might be received. These were the sacraments: the means of grace and the visible signs of invisible grace. The administration of the sacraments was the most time-consuming duty of the priest in his relationship with the laity; it was the essence of his care of souls. For centuries the various rites of the Church had in a very general sense been referred to as "sacraments," but in the twelfth century a more precise distinction arose between sacraments which actually conferred grace and those "sacramental" rites which were merely the occasion rather than the cause of grace. The sacraments which of themselves were considered to impart sanctification to the participant were seven in number. Five were for all Christians, one was reserved for the laity, and one was for priests only.

The first sacrament was baptism, which washed away all sin, including original sin, and gave to the baptized a new birth or regeneration into a life of the Spirit and a mystical union with Christ. Baptism was normally administered in infancy by the parish priest. The bishop, or priests at his delegation, administered the sacrament of confirmation: the laying on of hands to confer the Holy Spirit, which children normally received at age twelve and after instruction in the faith.

Because neither baptism nor confirmation could guarantee that man would not sin—no sacrament could do that—a third sacrament was necessary for the remission of sin committed after baptism. Man's capacity to sin was more than matched by man's capacity for repentance fortified by God's power to forgive. The contrite sinner could still hope for salvation through the sacrament of penance. On confessing his sin to the priest, the penitent received absolution. Every priest—whether he were the rector of a country parish or the pope himself—had the power and was obligated by solemn duty to absolve the contrite penitent from the guilt of his sin and from the eternal punishment (damnation) that it entailed. But the sinner did not escape punishment; he was only guaranteed that it would not be eternal. Divine justice being, ultimately, a mystery beyond human comprehension, the priest could only help the sinner to atone for his sin by assigning a temporal punishment or penance to be performed on earth. Penance might take the form of a few extra prayers or additional fasting or almsgiving, or it might be as severe as a long pilgrimage or a substantial contribution to the work of the Church. When Henry II was absolved from his share of the responsibility for the murder of Archbishop Thomas Becket, for example, the king was required to support two hundred knights for a year in the defense of Jerusalem, establish three new monasteries, allow appeals to be made freely to the papal *curia*, and make restitution to all who had suffered loss by supporting Becket. For the sins of ordinary persons priests normally assigned penances listed in the penitentials, which were statements of appropriate penances approved by the Church through custom and usage.

Connected with the notion of sin and divine justice was the doctrine of purgatory. The saint might go straight to his reward, but for the ordinary Christian there might be an intermediate state after death where further temporal punishment was imposed for sins that had not been expiated by penance performed in mortal life. The canonistic maxim, "What man does not punish, God punishes," referred to the temporal punishment in purgatory as well as to the eternal punishment of damnation. The truly penitent might obtain relief from the suffering of purgatory in accordance with a doctrine developed by theologians in the high Middle Ages. As successors of the Apostles, all bishops possessed the power of the keys. In the words of Christ: "Whatsoever thou shalt loose on earth shall be loosed in heaven." A bishop could therefore draw upon the inexhaustibly superabundant "treasury of merit," made up of the virtue of martyrs, saints, and good Christians and of the infinite merits of Jesus, and from this treasury grant an indulgence to the ordinary sinner whose penance would, for all he knew, fall short of satisfying divine justice. The theological doctrine was consistent and clear, but popular credulity sometimes confused the remission of punishment in purgatory (which an indulgence did grant) with remission of sin itself (which an indulgence could not grant).

Of all the sacraments, the Eucharist had the greatest liturgical significance because it was essential to the celebration of the Mass. The Mass, as the central rite of the Church, combined the worship of God with the quest for salvation. Both were expressed sacramentally in the Eucharist, a sacrifice which represented and repeated the sacrifice of the Cross, and which could be performed only by a priest and only at an altar. The Eucharist was completed when what had been offered and consecrated was then consumed in Holy Communion with the Lord, that is, eating the body and drinking the blood of Christ into which the bread and wine had been transubstantiated. In the thirteenth century, however, it became the common practice for the laity to receive only the bread (communion under one form) while the priest partook of both bread and wine. The Church taught that the sacrament did not work like magic, guaranteeing salvation to all participants, but rather that it conferred the grace of redemption by making the communicant one with Christ. Its efficacy depended in part upon the participant's moral attitude and condition. In the words of St. Paul, "Let a man examine himself, and so let him eat of that bread, and drink of that cup. For he that eateth and drinketh unworthily, eateth and drinketh damnation to himself."

Extreme unction, consisting of prayer and anointment with consecrated oil by a priest, was the sacrament for the dying. These last rites of the Church were normally preceded immediately by confession and absolution, since the efficacy of extreme unction was considered to depend on the recipient's being free from mortal sin. Where it was impossible to hear confession, or to determine whether the dying person was in a state of mortal sin, the sacrament was conditionally administered anyway, since it could do no harm and might help.

The sacrament of marriage was reserved for the laity alone. Virginity was considered a more nearly perfect state than marriage, but the latter was immeasurably better than a state of unmarried incontinence. Two persons could be married by a civil ceremony, and the resulting marriage was not only a binding contract in terms of local custom but a valid marriage and hence a sacrament according to canon law. But by the end of the twelfth century the Church was taking a stronger stand, insisting that while such marriages were valid they were not proper: marriages ought to be solemnized by the Church with the appropriate religious ceremony. During the Middle Ages, however, the essence of the sacrament of marriage remained the intention and free consent of the two parties concerned. For example, a marriage that had been celebrated by a priest, even with the birth of children subsequent to that marriage, would have been declared null if it were discovered that one of the parties had formed an earlier marriage based upon the mere exchange of spoken consent between himself and a third party.

Ordination to the priesthood was accomplished by the sacrament of

Holy Orders, which could be administered only by a bishop. By his ordination the priest received the spiritual power that set him apart from the
laity and the clergy in minor orders: the power to offer the sacrifice of the
Mass, to remit sins, and to administer the sacraments. This power was in-
delible. It could not deteriorate or be deficient in efficacy, nor did it depend
upon the priest's moral condition. Only by due process of law, the canon
law, could a priest be degraded, and then only by superior ecclesiastical authority. But even the process of degradation did not destroy or withdraw
the spiritual power itself; rather, the priest was suspended from the use
of the power.

The sacramental system was the heart and core of the religious life
of the regular and secular clergy, but for the great majority of the laity the
sacramental aspect of relegion was reserved for special occasions and did
not play an important role in daily life. The parish church was as much a
social center as it was a place of worship, while the church yard was often
the local market place. Except for the great feast days of the Church, like
Christmas or Easter, the importance of saints' days and other festivals
varied greatly from one locality to another. The saint to whom a local
church had been dedicated, especially if his relics were preserved there,
tended to be as important in the religious life of the people as the more
remote Persons of the Trinity. Elements of the older local paganism often
survived in the popular mind to influence or to color the meaning of such
religious festivals as when the priest and his parishioners honored local
saints, prayed for good crops, or rendered thanks for abundant harvests. To
the common man, illiterate and uneducated, it was easier to ascribe the
health of his family or the fertility of his fields to the prayers of his priest or
to the intercession by his patron saint than it was to understand the more
complex mysteries of the sacraments.

During the eleventh and twelfth centuries a gradual change was
completed, whose results might be described as the humanization of Christianity. The shifting emphasis in religion and in religious experience is
evident at all levels, from systematic theology down to popular piety and
subreligious superstition. In theology, for example, the early medieval explanation of the Incarnation and the Crucifixion assigned to human beings a
relatively unimportant role. God became Man for the purpose of battling
the devil for the souls of men. God as Man was roughly analogous to the
hero of an early medieval epic. Men, in thrall to the devil, stood by as help-
less spectators witnessing a cosmic drama, trembling in the hope that God
would win but overawed by the mystery of the Incarnation.

By the middle of the twelfth century this view had come to be considered an inadequate or incomplete account of man's Redemption. Instead of being a mystery beyond understanding, an act by which the
hero-God confronted His archenemy, the Incarnation was explained as
a supreme act of divine mercy in which God as Man confronted men. The

Incarnation and Crucifixion were thus not only incidents of cosmic drama but the historical events in human history by which Christ offered man the way to salvation. The element of mystery remained; but the humanity of Christ was now in the foreground. The incidents of the human life of Jesus—being born of a woman, nourished with her milk, suffering weariness, hunger, thirst, etc.—were the true mysteries, culminating in the ultimate mystery of His suffering on the Cross. The Son of God in this view was roughly analogous to the hero of a twelfth-century romance. Christ was no longer remote, austere, representing some power external to man's immediate experience.

It should be added that this greater emphasis on the humanity of the Saviour in the piety of the twelfth century was not a new emphasis as a theological concept. The Fathers had agreed in attributing man's Redemption to what had happened in and through the humanity of Christ. The early liturgical prayer of the Church was directed *per Christum hominem ad Christum Deum* ("through the human Christ to the Divine Christ"). The humanity of Christ as a central fact in Christian theology had been defended by the Latin Fathers in all the Christological disputes of later antiquity. In the twelfth century and for the rest of the Middle Ages, however, there was greater concentration on the humanity of Jesus and an increase in devotional practices concerned with that humanity. Compassion for Jesus, who suffered for man because of His love, was the first step by which man could turn from carnal love to love of His flesh, and through that spiritual love to salvation.

An inevitable development from this new piety was the elevation of His human Mother to a more prominent place in popular devotion. The Blessed Virgin Mary had been an object of veneration from the earliest days, but for the great mass of Christians there were two obstacles to the growth of a cult of the Virgin. First, the Virgin's body had been carried straight to heaven, and thus necessarily there were no relics of the Mother of God left behind to perform those miracles that to the popular mind were an important feature of religious experience. Second, until the earlier idea of Christ as the conquering Prince of Heaven, struggling with the devil, had given way to the greater emphasis on the suffering Son of God, the Mother of God remained as aloof and remote as her awe-inspiring Son. In the twelfth century the Virgin remained the Queen of Heaven, but a transformation took place in her cult. Collections of *Miracles of the Virgin* spread the new devotion; these tales constituted a new popular literature in which the Mother's intercession with her divine Child reflects the elements of tenderness, compassion, and love that characterize the piety of the high Middle Ages.

The change from earlier miracles to those of the Virgin is parallel to the change in secular literature from epic to romance. Older saints' lives were full of the supernatural aid given to the property or the church or the community whom the saint protected. These early medieval miracles were specific and detailed as to time and circumstance, and they were usually localized at or near the places where the saint's relics were preserved. In contrast, the Virgin's miracles were universal. They have what is called "human interest," and there is an imaginative quality that removes them from time and place. The Virgin was especially concerned with salvation, so her main appeal was to the individual. She was, above all, the protectress of the common man, the weak in spirit, the sinners and the fallen who, except for their allegiance to her, were sure to be damned. Her compassionate intercession was easy to invoke for she represented the quality of mercy in divine justice as the Mother not only of Christ but, through that Motherhood, as the spiritual Mother of all Christians.

The new tendencies of the twelfth and thirteenth centuries did not replace, but were added to, the older forms of religious life. Just as the Church as an organization was expanded and strengthened, Christianity in the high Middle Ages had become a fuller, more variegated, and above all more humanized religion. Its appeal was heightened to the same degree that it had been brought closer to human aspirations and emotions.

50 PIETY AND PROTEST: ANTICLERICALISM AND HERESY

In the words of the Fourth Lateran Council, "It frequently happens that bishops, because of their manifold occupations, bodily ailments, warlike activities, and other causes—not to mention defective knowledge and zeal—are not capable of ministering to the people the word of God." Anticlericalism was nourished by such shortcomings of the clergy as individuals. The contrast between the ideal and the actual, between Christ and His ministers, was the target for most of the criticism of the clergy, and much of this criticism came from completely pious people. The anticlerical movement was not antireligious; it was wholeheartedly devoted to true religion, as understood by the anticlerical leaders. Extreme piety often led these men to expect perfection. As perfectionists they sometimes forgot that the Kingdom of Christ was not of this world.

There were three main causes of anticlericalism. The Church was wealthy and was entangled, at all levels of the hierarchy, with feudal obligations. According to the anticlerical leaders the clergy neglected their spiritual mission for the business and distractions of the world. Second, the efforts of townspeople to secure freedom from their lords, many of whom were bishops, often led from a purely political program to an attack upon the hierarchy. What began as a struggle against the political power of the bishop would end as opposition to his ecclesiastical and spiritual claims as well. Third, the growth of towns often led to economic and social discontent which found expression in anticlericalism because the Church, as the greatest vested interest in society, was usually opposed to change. Political and economic radicalism were almost invariably linked with anticlericalism. Arnold of Brescia, for example, was primarily a political radical; as we have already noted, he was forced into an anticlerical position by the Church's resistance to his effort to revive the Roman Republic.

Anticlerical movements by their nature either tended to develop into pietistic sects within the Church, as a kind of silent protest against the worldliness of clergy and laity alike, or else they developed into heretical groups that rejected the doctrine and authority of the Church because they rejected the hierarchy as unworthy. Examples of the first sort of movement were the groups of associations in the Lombard communes of northern Italy, known collectively as the *Humiliati*. These groups made up a loosely organized lay brotherhood of pious workingmen dedicated to a simple life in common, in accordance with their understanding of the Gospel precepts. For the clergy they advocated a return to apostolic poverty. In 1201 Innocent III recognized the *Humiliati* as a religious order and confirmed their way of life. Some of the more extreme groups of the *Humiliati* broke away from the approved order and joined other "underground" pietistic sects that had heterodox tendencies, such as the Arnoldists (as Arnold of Brescia's later followers were called) and local groups known as Poor Men, who rejected the authority of the Church.

The outstanding example of an anticlerical but orthodox group that developed into a heretical movement, was that of the Waldensians. A wealthy merchant of Lyons, Peter Waldo, founded the organization when he decided (c.1173) to give his worldly goods to the poor and dedicate himself to charitable works and a life of poverty. His followers were a lay society, the Poor Men of Lyons, whose members traveled about preaching to the common people. In their effort to win back the uneducated masses to a life of apostolic simplicity, they translated parts of the New Testament into the vernacular. This activity was tentatively approved by the pope in 1179, on condition that the Poor Men obtain permission to preach from the local bishop. But the ideas of the Waldensians about apostolic poverty and a more spiritual clergy did not endear them to the bishops and their diocesan clergy. Friction rapidly developed into open hostility, and the organization was condemned by the pope in 1184, after the Poor Men had developed doctrines and practices that were clearly heretical. They preached that laymen could administer the sacraments, that the Bible alone was authoritative on religious questions, and that the Church possessed no spiritual authority. A later split in the movement brought a few of the Poor Men of Lyons back into the Church in 1205, but Waldensian doctrines continued to spread into Spain, northern France, Germany, and the Low Countries, and, in more extreme form, among the more radical "Poor Lombards" of northern Italy.

Of all the medieval heresies the least dangerous to the Church were those that arose from philosophical speculation. These were isolated and sporadic. They derived from the views of one man who at best had a few disciples rather than a mass following. We have already noted the difficulties that Abelard encountered because of his heterodox tendencies. The application of logic and philosophy to the field of theology was a fatal attraction for such intellectuals.

Like Abelard, Gilbert de la Porrée (d. 1154) was a victim of St. Bernard's impatience with those who would apply dialectic to the Trinity. At the council which tried him for heresy in 1148, Gilbert admitted that certain of his sentences, when taken out of context, might be heterodox and he willingly retracted them. But he denied that his view of the Trinity as a whole was unorthodox, and Bernard failed to prove that it was. Gilbert refused to discuss the matter further with Bernard, whom he considered too inexpert in theology, while the pope (who presided at the council) tried to keep up with the rarefied debate by pronouncing "that the essence of God should not be predicated in the sense of the ablative case only, but also of the nominative." It is doubtful that more than a handful of persons understood the points at issue, and they, like John of Salisbury, were sympathetic with Gilbert. The whole incident illustrates the nature of most philosophical heresies. All too often it was the novelty of expression rather than actual heterodoxy that called forth a charge of heresy.

With only one significant exception, all the intellectuals and theologians who were accused of heresy stoutly denied the charge. Siger de Brabant, a teacher at Paris in the thirteenth century, tried to circumvent the whole issue by the theory of double truth. The philosophical school called Averroists, of which he was the leader, accepted the whole of the philosophy of Aristotle together with the commentaries of the Arabic scholar Averroës (d.1198) as being irrefutably true, i.e., incapable of being refuted by unaided human reason. This position involved certain glaring doctrinal difficulties, for Aristotle taught and Averroës forcefully confirmed that the visible world was eternal, that the intellectual substance shared by all men was a unity, and that consequently there could be no salvation of individual souls. Admitting that these propositions were opposed to revelation, Siger argued that what was true in philosophy might not be true in theology, and vice versa. This effort to separate truth into two parts was condemned as heresy in 1277, along with the main tenets of the Averroistic school.

Far more dangerous than the philosophical or speculative heresies were movements which offered their own doctrines and incorporated Christianity, in a wholly unorthodox way, into their own religious system and ecclesiastical organization. The Albigensian heresy was of this type. Its origins may be traced back to the Manichaeism which, as we have noted, interested St. Augustine before he became a Christian. The doctrines of

Manichaeism derived from the half-Christian philosopher Mani, who flourished in Persia in the third century. His teachings, modified by other ethical
and religious views, appear in Asia Minor in late antiquity; in the Balkans
in the early Middle Ages; and, by making their way along the trade routes
from town to town, in northern Italy and southern France in the eleventh
century. The general name given to believers was *Cathari* ("the pure"). In
the Balkans they were called Bogomiles and in the West they were often
called *Bulgari* (Bulgarians). Their teachings also influenced other groups
such as the Poor Men or the Patarenes in Italy. The *Cathari* were known
most generally in the West as Albigensians, from the center of their greatest
strength, the town of Albi in Languedoc.

The Albigensian religion was thoroughly dualistic. Instead of one
God, there were two gods, a god of light (truth) and a god of darkness
(error), the former being the god of the New Testament, the latter the god
of the Old Testament. Life on earth, indeed all existence, was a struggle
between these gods and their principal forces, spirit and matter. Anything
associated with material wealth or worldliness was evil; the Church of orthodox Christians was therefore, to the Albigensians, the Synagogue of Satan.
The good life for human beings was a gradual purification from matter (i.e.,
evil). Hence, the Albigensians logically condemned marriage, procreation,
and even eating food. They abhorred war and physical violence, the veneration of relics, the use of pictorial representations (especially the cross), the
wearing of vestments, and the employment of anything material in worship,
as in the Mass. Because they refused to take oaths, they were subversive to a
society that rested upon the oath of vassal to feudal lord. They also opposed
any form of political authority as being worldly and therefore evil. All these
tenets and teachings represent the extreme doctrine, and in practice even
the Albigensians recognized the needs of human nature and human society.
A good Albigensian was not required to stop eating, but he did have to be a
vegetarian.

The Albigensians were divided into the few *perfecti* (the perfect),
who as clergy were expected to adhere to the rigid asceticism of the religion,
and the great mass of followers called *credentes* (believers). The main
duties of the *credentes* were to venerate the *perfecti* and prepare to become
perfecti themselves. This was accomplished by receiving the only sacrament
allowed, the *consolamentum* (consolation). Because the sacrament, ideally
and properly, should be administered only once for an individual, it was
often postponed until the recipient was about to die. But if doubt arose
concerning the purity of the *perfectus* who had bestowed the *consolamentum*, those under his ministry could be reconsoled by receiving the sacrament again from some other *perfectus*, just to make sure. Alternatively,
perfecti who fell from grace by backsliding from the tenets or practices of
the faith might also be reconsoled and thus re-established in their status,
though in such cases the renewed *perfecti* lost influence over the *credentes*.

Another solution of the problem was developed later. If the newly consecrated *perfectus* showed evidence of not being able to live up to the ascetic discipline of his new calling, his friends could still ensure the salvation of his soul through a ceremonial death by suffocation, called the *endura*. *Credentes* who did not receive the *consolamentum* did not worry too much, however, for they were taught that such places as purgatory and hell were false Christian myths. The only "hell" conceivable was the imprisonment of the soul in a material body, life in this world. This teaching probably underlay the Albigensians' reputation for licentiousness. After all, if living in sunny southern France was the worst that could happen, the temptation to ignore conventional standards of morality was very strong. For this reason some Albigensian leaders taught that the souls of those who were not saved transmigrated into the bodies of lower animals. After such a punishment their souls then proceeded upward from animal life to human life once more and again they had the opportunity to achieve freedom from incarnation in a material body. For Albigensians this freedom was salvation.

Southern France at the end of the twelfth century was a pleasant and prosperous land, the center of a flourishing Provençal civilization. Wealthy towns, castles and courts, and an unruly feudal nobility were prominent in this home of the troubadours. Christianity was very old in this area; but the orthodox faith had now become little more than an external form. In this tolerant and cosmopolitan society persecution was unknown, Jews and Moslems traded without hindrance, and the only real element of religious interest or fanaticism was the burgeoning Albigensian "church." The feudal nobles and the wealthy bourgeoisie were attracted to the heresy, some because of its tenets and others because they were eager to plunder the Church—the Albigensian program included the confiscation of the lands and wealth of the orthodox clergy. But few of the important lords actually joined the Albigensian movement. Most were content to tolerate or protect the heretics within their lands, without committing themselves on the religious issue.

For the general history of Europe the bloody war (1209–1229) that finally stamped out the Albigensian movement had three main results. It was the first important instance of the use of a crusade against heretics in Europe instead of against infidels abroad. After the local ecclesiastical authorities failed to win back the heretics, Innocent III granted to laymen who participated in the repression of heresy in Languedoc the privileges and exemptions of the crusaders in the Holy Land. But it was not until after the murder of a papal legate by agents of Count Raymond VI of Toulouse, the leading supporter of the Albigensians and a suspected heretic himself, that the crusade was successfully launched. This Albigensian Crusade set a precedent for using the crusade as a weapon against papal enemies in Europe, whether they were heretics or political opponents. A second main result was the annexation, first of several strategic cities and then, in 1271, of all the southern provinces to the royal domain. The French monarchy was the ultimate gainer from the long and bloody struggle that suppressed the Albigensians. Along with its independence, desolated Languedoc also lost its leading position in the economic and cultural development of the western Mediterranean region. And third, the Albigensian Crusade provided the immediate impetus for the development of the Inquisition.

51   THE THEORY AND PRACTICE OF THE INQUISITION

The problem of heresy was almost as old as Christianity. The great majority of the Fathers had favored peaceful persuasion as the means to win back heretics to the orthodox faith. Hilary of Poitiers (d.367) expressed this view neatly: "The true Church suffered persecution; it did not persecute." The Church then emerging from persecutions still represented a minority religion, officially allowed and encouraged but not yet state supported. Like most minority religions, the Church advocated toleration, and even in the fifth century, after all other religions were officially prohibited, the majority of the Fathers continued to favor toleration of heretics. The best weapons to use against dissenters were still considered to be persuasion and spiritual penalties such as excommunication.

In his earlier years Augustine (d.430) agreed with this majority view. But after he became involved in the bitter Donatist struggle, as bishop of the North African see of Hippo, Augustine modified his position. He developed a theory of "moderate persecution," according to which heretics and schismatics were to be regarded as sheep who had gone astray, whom the shepherd was obliged to bring back to the fold for their own good. Under these circumstances the use of the whip and goad might be necessary—not cruel tortures, such as the civil power might use against common criminals, but a little salutary flogging which might be justified in the same way that school teachers and parents of that age justified not "sparing the rod" when concerned for their children's welfare. The severest penalty that Augustine would allow against the heretic was a monetary fine followed by exile. He condemned the death penalty as being contrary to Christian charity.

In these views the Fathers reflected the policy and role of the Church. The coercive power of the state in religious matters was a different question. Religion and politics were inseparable in the Roman Empire, both before and after it became Christian. Constantine acted as if he had the authority of a bishop, and his successors intervened constantly in ecclesiastical and doctrinal problems. To the state schism and heresy were political crimes subject to any penalty, including death, as determined by the state in defending itself against subversion. When civil disturbances grew out of religious quarrels, the state inflicted punishment for rebellion without regard for the religious issues involved. The Fathers were divided in their opinions of the role of the state. Some favored but most deplored the secular punishment of heretics. Even when heresy led to riot and rebellion most of the Fathers refused to sanction the death penalty inflicted by the civil power. On the other hand they all agreed that the state not only had the right but was under the duty to help the Church in suppressing heresy.

No final agreement or consistent theory of coercive power against heretics, either by Church or state, was achieved by the Fathers. During the Carolingian period a new form of punishment was developed: imprisonment in a monastery. Imprisonment was unknown to classical Roman law. The early Carolingians used it for political crimes or necessities, as when Pepin the Short put Childeric III, the last Merovingian, safely away in a monastery. Imprisonment was a favorite Carolingian punishment for crimes that were also sins, such as adultery. About the same time ecclesiastical courts began to impose this penalty, at first for clergy and later for the laity. Imprisonment was considered an ideal penalty for the heretic, according to the ideas of the eighth and ninth centuries, because it prevented him from spreading false doctrine that could endanger others' souls, and it provided him with the opportunity to atone for his sin.

In the eleventh and twelfth centuries heresy once more became an important problem, and again the question of the coercive power of the Church arose. At first most churchmen agreed with the Fathers that persuasion and spiritual penalties were the appropriate weapons to use, while for the convicted obdurate heretic the most severe punishment should be imprisonment. Church leaders in the twelfth century also agreed with the Fathers in accepting and expecting the aid of the secular power. As heretical movements grew during the twelfth century, canon lawyers developed a consistent theory of the duty of secular assistance. According to this theory, excommunication should automatically entail a secular sanction. For heretics this should be banishment from the territory of the secular ruler. Later, the penalty of confiscation of the property of the heretic was added. By the end of the century canonists went even further. They claimed that an ecclesiastical court had the authority to impose both banishment and confiscation, and that it was the duty of the secular ruler to execute the sentence on pain of incurring the same excommunication suffered by the heretic. The theory underlying these penalties was expressed by Innocent III:

> Civil law punishes traitors with confiscation and with death; it is only out of mercy that the lives of their children are spared. All the more should we excommunicate and confiscate the property of traitors to the faith of Jesus Christ, for it is an infinitely greater sin to offend the Divine Majesty than to attack the majesty of the secular ruler.

The heretic was essentially a traitor to God, from whom all authority, both spiritual and secular, was derived. But Innocent III did not recommend the death penalty.

Meanwhile, the death penalty for heresy had in fact begun to be imposed once more. The revival of Roman law and its influence on canon law may have helped rationalize or justify this penalty since the legislation of the later Roman emperors was full of decrees inflicting death upon heretics. However, the revival of Roman law could not have been the cause of the development which, ultimately, made burning at the stake the extreme penalty for obdurate heretics, for the earliest known instance of burning a heretic at the stake occurred in 1022, a date far too early for any influence of the revival of Roman law. Two other factors must be considered to account for burning heretics at the stake. First, the early instances of this form of punishment are associated with popular intolerance and mob action, suggesting that this method of dispatching the heretic was the medieval equivalent of modern American "lynch law." Second, in almost every early case the heretic who was burned to death was a civil rebel, or a social revolutionary, as well as a heretic. The subversive person was in the Middle Ages assumed to be irreligious, even as today subversives are frequently called "Godless communists," to underline their threat to social order and security.

When the Fourth Lateran Council met in 1215 the official position of the Church did not go so far as to require the death penalty for heretics. But by that date there had been many instances of burning at the stake, the result of official secular action approved both by popular clamor and by jurists who accepted the authority of the secular power over heresy, as provided in the Roman law. A pope of the stature of Innocent III could withstand such a development, but after his death the papacy quickly fell in line with the theory that obdurate heretics deserved the death penalty and, specifically, burning at the stake. When the normal remedies for heresy failed, such as the preaching and the spiritual penalties for which a bishop was responsible in his own diocese, and when even specially assigned papal agents could not bring heretics back into the Church, some new remedy for the situation became necessary.

This new remedy was the Inquisition, a special tribunal instituted by Gregory IX (1227–1241). It was a permanent court under direct papal control whose jurisdiction was restricted to cases of heresy. Instead of employing local clergy the Inquisition was staffed by Dominicans and Franciscans, judges trained to detect and convert heretics. The friars were especially suited for the job because they were free from local jealousies and local circumstances that might induce prejudice or favoritism.

The main task of the Inquisition was to identify heretics by due process of law. A regular procedure was followed. When the inquisitors arrived at the locality to which they had been called or sent, they preached a sermon in the most public place, such as the square of the largest town.

At the end of the sermon a period of grace was set, during which all persons who came forward to confess their lapse from orthodoxy would be received back and treated leniently. On the expiration of the period of grace, the judges began to collect evidence consisting of the testimony of witnesses sworn to answer truly to questions put to them. From this procedure by sworn inquest the Inquisition derived its name. On the basis of this evidence all persons accused of heresy were summoned and interrogated. If the interrogation resulted in an admission of heresy and a desire for reconciliation, then the Inquisition received confession from the penitent, granted absolution, and assigned an appropriate penance. The majority of cases ended at this stage. The few persons against whom the sworn testimony of witnesses was conclusive and who, in addition, refused to admit heresy or recant heretical beliefs of which they were aware, were judged by the Inquisition to be guilty of obdurate heresy. The final act of the ecclesiastical tribunal was then to deliver such persons to the secular authority for sentence and punishment, that is, burning at the stake.

Under this procedure it was almost impossible for the accused to prove himself innocent. He was not allowed to see the testimony against him nor to learn the names of his accusers. This secrecy was necessary to protect witnesses from recrimination, but it also encouraged false accusations. The accused was not allowed counsel, nor was he allowed witnesses in his own behalf. The Inquisition did permit the accused to name his enemies, and the testimony of these known enemies was nullified. But this provision rarely helped very much, for the testimony of only two witnesses was sufficient for conviction.

During the thirteenth century the procedure of the Inquisition was refined in the interests of equity, but with unfortunate results. For example, all the written evidence was reviewed by a panel of legal experts before the court passed judgment. This review was intended to guard against bias, but as it worked out it actually made conviction even more certain. When a case was stripped of all extenuating circumstances, personalities, and motivation, and was presented in the abstract, it was a simple matter for a trained expert to detect some deviation from orthodoxy. Another refinement was intended to guard the accused from self-incrimination while under torture. All medieval criminal courts used torture, not as a punishment, but as a means of extracting information from a witness or a confession from the defendant. The canon law did not allow a forced confession, so the words uttered under torture had to be repeated later in the courtroom. Also, the popes forbade the Inquisition to employ torture for longer than a half hour at one time. A stubborn defendant who really thought he was innocent of heresy might, under these circumstances, suffer a remarkable amount of periodic torture, so long as he was willing to disown later anything he might have said while on the rack or while his feet were burned with hot coals. A favorite torture of the Inquisition was the strappado, by which the accused was allowed to fall from a height of several feet against a rope binding his wrists behind his back. If done with skill, this could be kept up for many half-hour periods of excruciating pain before the defendant's shoulders were dislocated.

Much casuistry has been expended, both in the Middle Ages and later, in an effort to absolve the Church from responsibility for the capital punishment that followed conviction of heresy and delivery to the lay power. Such efforts are misdirected. If the secular ruler to whom the heretic was delivered did not impose the death penalty he was himself excommunicated by the Inquisition, and if he were not absolved from this excommunication within one year he was regarded as incurring the guilt of heresy himself. Enlightened canonists did not worry about the Church's responsibility because they saw the role of the secular authority in this case as simply a specific example of the theory of the two swords. As expressed by St. Bernard (who, ironically, preached most vehemently against heretics but also rejected the death penalty), "Both the spiritual and temporal swords belong to the Church, the latter to be drawn for the Church, the former by the Church." Finally it should be remembered that very few convicted heretics were actually burnt at the stake. The great majority were given sentences by the Inquisition itself, punishments ranging all the way from rather light penance to life imprisonment. The primary purpose of the Inquisition was to win back heretics, not execute them. Where heretics refused to be converted, they were put where they could not endanger the salvation of others' souls. Only with obdurate heretics did this properly involve the death penalty.

The whole work of the Inquisition was justified by Thomas Aquinas in the name of Christian charity. Charity, he reasoned, has for its object the spiritual and material welfare of one's neighbor; since salvation is the highest welfare, charity must prevent heretics from contaminating the faithful. If this sometimes could be done only by imposing the death penalty, the justification remained unchanged, for the obdurate heretic's soul was already lost.

The Medieval Synthesis of Thought and Learning

I: THEOLOGY AND PHILOSOPHY

Several tendencies evident in the intellectual life of the twelfth century reached fruition in the thirteenth. In theology and philosophy three main phases may be distinguished, which correspond roughly with the chronological development of systematic thought in the high Middle Ages: the acquisition, analysis, and synthesis of knowledge.

The first phase began when scholars were no longer content with the manuals and compends of the early Middle Ages, and instead turned to the original works of classical and patristic authors. As these were being mastered, a new source of knowledge began to appear in the recovery of ancient Greek philosophy and science. As we have seen, the recovery of the knowledge of antiquity occupied much of the time and effort of the teachers and the translators of the twelfth century, and this work continued into the thirteenth century. The later translators sought better texts and made improved translations, and they also found treatises hitherto unavailable in the West.

The second phase consisted of mastering this material—the analysis of individual treatises and a systematic restatement of their content in the characteristic form of the commentary, whose purpose was to interpret and to clarify a given text. This stage represented the mastery of a body of knowledge in terms intelligible or most meaningful to the commentator and his readers. Here again important work continued into the thirteenth century. For example, the two most extensive and complete commentaries on the works of Aristotle were written by Albertus Magnus and Thomas Aquinas.

The third phase, the synthesis of knowledge, had also begun in the twelfth century and reached its culmination in the thirteenth. The reconciliation or combining and harmonizing of conflicting authorities were the great achievements of several twelfth-century authors. But their interests were limited to patristic works. In the thirteenth century the problem of reconciliation was far greater, for it included both the patristic heritage and the newly recovered corpus of Aristotelian philosophy. Between Aristotle and the Fathers there were gaps more dangerous and more challenging than Abelard or Peter Lombard had ever confronted in the works of the Fathers alone. The thirteenth century has a special interest and importance, in the history of Western thought, as the period in which the pagan and patristic traditions of classical thought were harmonized in a new synthesis of Christian thought and learning.

52   THE PATRISTIC HERITAGE AND THE RECEPTION OF ARISTOTLE

In the world of medieval learning, theology was the "queen of the sciences." All other "sciences," or fields of human knowledge, were not considered to be ends in themselves but to subserve this supreme "science" that alone dealt with truth beyond merely human reason. Philosophy was the chief handmaiden of theology, for the philosophers could reach truths concerning the nature of man, of the universe, and even of the deity that had an independent validity of their own.

In medieval thought, there was no sharp distinction between the *scientia* of philosophy and the *sacra doctrina* of theology. Philosophy proceeded by rational enquiry from first principles that could be established by unaided reason; theology might make use of all the content of philosophical knowledge, but in addition proceeded from first principles derived from revelation. The two fields overlapped so largely that in practice most medieval writers ignored the formal distinction, even though they were often interested in defining the limits claimed for each field. This is why there is so little medieval philosophy that is not also specifically a Christian, or theological, philosophy. And in the formal and technical literature of theology, as opposed to devotional or literary works, there is practically no medieval theology that is not heavily in debt to systematic philosophy.

In the university curriculum this interdependence was reflected by the fact that theology students normally spent most of their first year studying philosophy. Many of the important treatises in either subject grew directly out of classroom lectures. The interests, the content, and the method of both were so much influenced by the schools that medieval philosophy and theology are usually referred to as "scholasticism," or scholastic philosophy and theology.

Scholastic method is usually associated with the type of formal treatise called a *summa*. The *summa* was a work that treated exhaustively a given subject, whose various aspects were dealt with systematically. The reader could expect to find the distinctions and refinements necessary for a complete logical analysis of all the arguments for and against each proposition that made up the successive topics that constituted the subject. Peter Lombard's *Sentences* was an early form of the *summa*. In addition, there was another type of treatise that was equally important in the earlier development of scholastic thought. This type consisted of a discussion of several topics or problems, called the "Questions" of a particular author, as the *Questions* of Stephen Langton, who was a leading teacher of theology at Paris before he became archbishop of Canterbury. In contrast with a *summa*, a treatise of this sort dealt with whatever problems interested the author, whether they were related or not, and in each of the several discussions the purpose was to supply a convincing answer to a particular problem rather than to deal exhaustively with every aspect. Sometimes an author's *Questions* included a thoroughly logical analysis of several topics, but often the author's interest was didactic and expository, and these treatises dealt as often with problems of moral or pastoral theology as they did with systematic theology.

The Bible continued to be the foundation on which theological studies were based. Commentaries by the scholastics of the later twelfth and thirteenth centuries tended to be more minute and technical than earlier works, but the most important advance was one of textual organization. The Bible consisted of universally recognized books, but the order of these books varied according to several different traditions, and the books were either not divided into chapters or else the chapter divisions were different in the different textual traditions. Toward the end of the twelfth century Stephen Langton, recognizing the difficulty involved in lecturing to students, worked out an order of books and a division of the books into chapters that was adopted by the theological teachers at Paris. The modern Catholic and Protestant versions of the Bible are still organized according to the basic plan that Stephen introduced for the convenience of his students in following the scriptural references in his lectures on the Bible.

One difficulty for the modern reader of the philosophical and theological works of the scholastics is that their writings are filled with scriptural quotations and allusions. To appreciate their work, or even to understand it fully, it is necessary to possess an equally intimate knowledge of Scripture. In addition to the Bible, the theology of the high Middle Ages was built on the writings of the Fathers. Patristic writings did not carry the same weight of authority as that of Scripture, but where Scripture presented problems of interpretation the scholastics approached such problems in terms of what they found in the Fathers, especially in Augustine. The influence of Augustine was all-pervasive, even in the philosophical and theological works of the scholastics who were most devoted to the philosophy of Aristotle. The intellectual division among scholastics was not between followers of Augustine and those who preferred Aristotle, but rather between those who were simply Augustinian in their basic assumptions and interests and those who were, in addition to their Augustinian theology, influenced by Aristotelian philosophy as well. This latter group tended to accept the *Sentences* of Peter Lombard as a definitive restatement of patristic authorities, without going behind Lombard to his original sources. The *Sentences* became for this group the object of systematic commentaries that led to the more elaborate and exhaustive *summae* of the thirteenth century.

The full impact of the newly recovered Aristotelian philosophical and scientific works began to be felt in the opening decades of the thirteenth century. Not only was the range or content of philosophy enlarged but the techniques of the "New Logic" of Aristotle were eagerly adopted as the tools by which theology could be established as a more precise and scientific discipline. The reception of Aristotle led directly to some of the greatest monuments of medieval thought. Specifically, this ancient knowledge newly available falls under three headings. First, there were new and better translations that superseded works already available through the efforts of the twelfth-century translators. The latter, it will be recalled, usually worked from Arabic texts and thus produced translations of translations. The leading teachers at centers like the University of Paris recognized the inadequacy of these older translations and based their own study of Aristotle on new versions rendered directly from the original Greek. The conquest of Constantinople and the establishment there of a Latin Empire (1204–1261) provided the opportunity for western scholars to go to the sources. The leader of this new school of translators was William of Moerbeke (fl. c.1260), a Flemish Dominican who became bishop of Corinth and who collaborated with the Paris teachers.

Second, the new knowledge of the thirteenth century included the whole corpus of Aristotelian philosophy. In addition to the "New Logic," Aristotle's *Physics* and some of his treatises on natural science were available before 1200. About the turn of the century the *Metaphysics* was translated from the Arabic, together with Arabic commentaries; and in the thirteenth century the rest of Aristotle's writings were translated from the Greek, notably the *Ethics, Politics, Rhetoric,* and *Poetics.* Third, the whole of this Aristotelian philosophy was digested and assimilated in Western thought by the numerous and extensive commentaries of the scholastics. These commentaries, including commentaries on Arabic commentaries, were the necessary preliminary to the creative phase of scholastic thought. The *summa* was based upon the commentary.

The reception of Aristotle raised problems for the thirteenth-century scholastics that their predecessors, who were familiar only with the "Old Logic" and the "New Logic," did not have to face. Logic is neutral; metaphysics borders on, and at points is even based upon, doctrine. And the metaphysics of Aristotle was pagan. Most philosophers of the two faiths related to Christianity, like the Moslem Avicenna (d.1036) and the Jew Maimonides (d.1204), had already confronted the problem created by the differences between Aristotle and orthodoxy. Some had simply ignored, and others had explained away, the elements of Aristotelian philosophy that contradicted Jewish-Moslem-Christian revelation. Now, in the thirteenth century, Christian philosophers were confronted with the problem in an especially difficult form.

The *Metaphysics* of Aristotle arrived in Latin Christendom accompanied by the commentary by Averroës. Averroës did not have a great influence in the Moslem world, but, as we have already seen, his commentary on Aristotle was so convincing in certain Christian circles that it led to the major intellectual heresy of the thirteenth century, called Averroism, together with its corollary, Siger de Brabant's theory of double truth. The dangers of unmitigated Aristotelianism were recognized by a provincial council at Paris, in 1210, which prohibited the study of Aristotle's natural philosophy and specifically condemned Averroës' commentaries. In 1215 Aristotle's *Metaphysics* was banned, and in 1231 the pope renewed the prohibition and appointed a commission of scholars to review the works of Aristotle and of his commentators and to purge them from error. But these prohibitions and efforts at censorship came to nothing, and in fact they illustrate the degree of academic freedom enjoyed in a medieval university. What actually happened was that the professors at Paris continued to expound Aristotle, and the papal commission never got around to its work of expurgation. In 1255 the University of Paris openly prescribed the whole of Aristotle as required reading.

The problem of Aristotle was solved, not by prohibitions and censorship, but by a continuing intellectual debate. In the end it was not the Averroists who won, but the Franciscans and, especially, the Dominicans at Paris who, to sum up a long job briefly, "baptized" Aristotle and his Arabic commentators. The first scholar to make use of Aristotle's physics, metaphysics, and natural science in a systematic treatise designed to harmonize Aristotelian philosophy with Christian theology was the Englishman Alexander of Hales (d.1245). He was also the first Franciscan to be a professor of theology at Paris. Albertus Magnus (1193–1280) was even more important in the development of scholasticism, for he was the first to master the whole corpus of Aristotle. Born in Swabia of noble parentage, he became a Dominican in 1223 and taught in Dominican schools in Germany from 1228 until 1245, when he spent three years teaching at Paris. From 1248 until 1254 he taught at Cologne, after which he was successively the provincial governor of the Dominican Order in Germany and bishop of Regensburg until 1262, when he retired to the Dominican convent at Cologne. During this active and varied career he wrote twenty-one massive volumes, the bulk of which was devoted to commentaries on Aristotle's works and to theological treatises based on Aristotelian philosophy. His main interest lay in the natural philosophy of Aristotle and the problem of reconciliation between Aristotelian philosophy and Christian revelation. Above all he was the expositor and interpreter of Aristotle for the Christian West. And yet, despite his monumental achievement, Albertus Magnus is best known in the history of Western thought as the teacher of a philosopher and theologian who was even greater than himself. His pupil was Thomas Aquinas.

53   THOMAS AQUINAS

St. Thomas Aquinas (1225–1274) was born in southern Italy near Monte Cassino, where he was sent to school as a boy. After a few years at the schools in Naples, Thomas joined the Dominican Order in 1244 and went to study under Albertus Magnus at Cologne and Paris. In 1252 he was lecturing at Paris, and he later taught briefly at Rome, Bologna, and Naples. In 1268 he returned to Paris at the height of his career as a teacher and scholar; four years later he left, having been directed to establish a Dominican university at Naples. He died before he was fifty years old.

Incredible as it may seem, Thomas' written works total eighteen folio volumes. These include commentaries on most of the books of the Old and New Testaments, on the *Sentences*, and on thirteen works of Aristotle; about twenty short treatises and as many "academic disputations" on theological and philosophical topics; and a number of miscellaneous works ranging from sermons to part of a handbook for princes. The two works on which his reputation rests are the *Summa Theologica* and the *Summa contra Gentiles*. The first is the greatest monument of scholasticism. Together they represent an orderly and encyclopedic summary of Christian thought, the first based on revelation and the second designed to show how far unaided human reason could buttress the Christian faith. In each, Thomas makes use of Aristotelian logic to incorporate and harmonize Aristotelian philosophy with Christian theology and philosophy.

Thomas' method represents the ultimate scholastic refinement of the organization, analysis, and synthesis of knowledge whose earlier development is illustrated by Abelard's *Sic et Non* and Peter Lombard's *Sentences*. Thomas built a vast ideological structure concerning the nature of God, man, and the universe, a systematic exposition in which each of the broader topics is taken up in logical order, just as each statement in the detailed analysis follows logically upon the preceding statement. The *Summa Theologica* consists of three "Parts" (the second Part is actually divided into two, the *Prima Secundae* and the *Secunda Secundae*). Each of these consists of a number of "Questions" or general topics, totaling over six hundred for the whole treatise. Each Question is broken down into "Articles," or specific queries beginning with the word "Whether. . . ." For example, in the *Summa Theologica, Prima Secundae,* Question 94 is entitled "Concerning Natural Law," and the fifth Article under this Question is headed, "Whether natural law can be changed?" The bulk of the *Summa* consists of the arguments systematically marshaled *pro* and *contra* in the Articles. Taking the same example (which would be referred to briefly as *S. Theol.*, 1a 2ae, XCIV, 5), Thomas first enumerates three objections or arguments *contra*, one drawn from Scripture, another in the form of a syllogism, and the last a logical inference from a statement quoted from Isidore of Seville, all three seeming to lead to the conclusion that natural law is subject to change. The second part of the Article contains Thomas' own answer, supported both by authority and by his own argument. The third and final part of the Article consists of Thomas' refutations of the objections with which the Article began. It has been estimated that the *Summa Theologica* contains over ten thousand objections to the more than six hundred conclusions in the Articles, each objection being refuted. In the refutations Thomas frequently cites the authority of revelation, the Fathers, or Aristotle, but the main burden of the argument is invariably a logical analysis.

Even more important than his method was Thomas' attitude toward the role of reason. It is sometimes said that Thomas occupied a middle ground between the rationalistic Averroists and the traditional Augustinians. The Averroists believed that human reason could establish truth even though contradictory to faith; the Augustinians were skeptical of the usefulness of reason in comprehending the supernatural truth contained in revelation. Both Averroists and Augustinians were agreed, therefore, that reason was futile as a means of understanding the higher truths of the faith. Thomas disagreed with both. He could not admit that between faith and reason there could be any real contradiction, so long as rational inquiry was properly conducted. Where the two seemed to conflict, faith provided guidance for human reason to reject error and reach a correct conclusion. According to Thomas, human reason could not by itself comprehend the whole of the Christian universe, but when aided by revelation reason could establish more certainly what a person already accepts by faith. The basis of this Thomistic rationalism was the premise that between revelation and reason, which both come from God, accord must be necessary. If faith leads to a conclusion that defies rational explanation, the seeming incompatibility exists because of a failure of human reason.

The role of reason, then, is to make deductions from the first principles laid down by faith, as well as to acquire knowledge from the data of sense experience. Reason, for Thomas, is a connecting link between the natural and the supernatural parts of the universe, even though access to knowledge of the latter is made possible by revelation. It would be fruitless for man to attempt to prove or disprove the first principles of revelation; the undemonstrable cannot be demonstrated. But by proceeding from the articles of faith, reason can vastly enlarge the body of certain knowledge that man can rationally comprehend.

The actual content of the Articles in the *Summa Theologica* and the *Summa contra Gentiles* can be divided into two main parts. First, there are conclusions logically deduced from premises which are undemonstrable, that is, articles of faith. If the premises are accepted, the conclusions are guaranteed by the application of Aristotelian logic. For the dissenter who does not grant the premises, the necessity of these conclusions has not been demonstrated philosophically, nor can it be. But Thomas' faith in reason is sufficient for him to hold that articles of faith can be rationally proved to be not impossible. For example, it is by faith alone that man can believe that the world, created in time, is not eternal; and this belief cannot be demonstrated. But natural reason can demonstrate that this belief is logical, possible, and even probable. And objections to Christian doctrine can be shown by reason to have failed to demonstrate the contrary. Thomistic rationalism is thus a weapon in defense of faith as well as a means of deducing knowledge from premises provided by faith. Finally, these conclusions illustrate the kind of knowledge to which man would not have rational access, were it not for faith guiding reason.

The second group of Articles, in the content of the two *Summae*, contain conclusions that are based only on natural reason. These conclusions are demonstrably necessary, without regard for the premises of faith, but of course in these Articles there can be no attempt to deal with doctrine. They deal rather with the visible world of sense experience, and with some of the problems of the nature of man and of natural theology. The existence of a deity, for Thomas, would fall under the last heading; the existence or nature of the Trinity would not. Where man and nature are at the forefront of the discussion, the elements of Aristotelian physics and metaphysics predominate. Where God and the supernatural are discussed, revelation and Christian teaching predominate in the discussion.

Thomas agreed with Aristotle that the universe is orderly and rational. But for Thomas the guarantee of that rationality could only be in the divine order and in the reason in God's mind that are both reflected in the universe as comprehensible to human reason. Thus in harmonizing

Aristotle's philosophy with Christian doctrine it is the Aristotelian element that must be fitted into the Christian system, not the other way around. This is why Arisotle is never used, in the two *Summae*, in large blocks but rather in bits and snatches. Particular statements from Aristotle are taken out of context and put into a new Thomistic context. For this reason Thomas has been criticized as having failed to grasp Aristotelian philosophy as a system whose parts are interdependent. However, the commentaries on Aristotle written by Thomas show that it was not because of any intellectual failure to see Aristotle as a whole that Thomas used Aristotle in piecemeal fashion.

To summarize Thomas' view of the Christian universe, part is cognizable by unaided natural reason, and it is connected in logical probability with the second part which must, ultimately, be accepted on faith. But if revelation be granted as providing valid premises or first principles, this second part also can be shown to be no less rational than the first part. The two parts of the Thomistic universe are nature and supernature. The conclusions concerning nature can be demonstrated to be true; nature can be demonstrated to be consonant with supernature as revealed, in the sense that by arguments from natural reason no revealed truth can be demonstrated to be false and all revealed truths can be demonstrated to be not impossible. The Christian universe is thus coherent: its parts fit together logically if faith is accepted, and if faith is not accepted it still cannot be shown that the two do not fit together logically. Hence the final conclusion that the universe is one and rational.

As the reader will have noted already, it is difficult to separate Thomistic philosophy from Thomistic theology. And yet Thomas was always insistent upon the proper role of revelation. Revealed truth is never the proper object of rational inquiry; it is not to be tested by reason but accepted by faith. Where revelation and reason conflict, reason may confidently be assumed to be in error. But this does not mean that faith controls or dominates reason; rather, it indicates the area in which rational error has been made. Then it is the proper function of reason to correct its own mistakes by a further effort of reason. (No wonder, under these circumstances, that Thomas was glad to raise ten thousand objections to his own exposition of theology.)

Revelation provides those additional data concerning the total universe which unaided reason could never discover. Who, for example, could ever deduce rationally from sense experience the Triune God of Christian doctrine? Thus revelation acts as a guide for reason and a check on the results of rational speculation. On the other hand, Thomas never introduces faith into any argument leading to a conclusion he considers demonstrable by human reason alone. Philosophy and theology are equally valid, each containing knowledge equally true in its own sphere. They are neither independent nor contradictory, but are interdependent and supplementary.

The achievement of St. Thomas, who was canonized in 1323, earned him the title of "the Angelic Doctor," but in his own lifetime and immediately thereafter there was considerable opposition to his supremely confident rationalism. Traditional-minded Augustinians, the great majority of the Franciscans in the universities, and many of the secular clergy were hostile to the general plan and purpose of his work, while certain specific doctrines and philosophical arguments were condemned as being in error.

Perhaps what rankled his critics most was Thomas' adaptation of Aristotle's ethics to Christian doctrine. Man's supreme good, according to Thomas, was his salvation, his beatitude. Beatitude must be man's ultimate actuality, and hence the result of some kind of action. But this action cannot involve mere physical sensation and must therefore be the action of man's intellectual faculty. Man's intellect functions in knowing, and thus beatitude consists in knowledge of God. Hence man's supreme good is the intellectual vision of God. But, as Thomas' critics were quick to point out, this conclusion gives knowledge and understanding priority over will and love. What about the man of good will who yearns for beatitude, but who is also a bit stupid? Does defective intelligence endanger salvation? Thomas, of course, meant no such thing. When he argued that cognition of God through faith alone was imperfect, he meant that in this life, from which faith leads to salvation, actual union with God is impossible, since supreme felicity is attainable only after death. Thus "knowledge of God" for him was the same as "union with God" or salvation. This identification of knowledge with salvation was too intellectualistic (to use the technical term applied to Thomistic theology) for the great majority of his critics, who preferred to emphasize man's will—man's freedom of choice to turn toward or away from God—as the central fact in explaining salvation.

The *Summa Theologica* was the product of Thomas' last years (1267–1272), and he died leaving it still not completed. Thus he was unable to reply to the criticisms of his major work, but in the long run the reasonableness, cogency, and clarity of his thought finally triumphed. No other single work in the whole of the Middle Ages could match it as an exhaustive and orderly exposition of the faith. The only other medieval treatise that has had a comparable influence on the history of Western thought is Augustine's *City of God*.

54 MEDIEVAL MYSTICISM AND SCIENCE: BONAVENTURA AND GROSSETESTE

The alternative to Thomistic rationalism was vigorously presented by a group of Franciscan scholars whose theology was more traditional and Augustinian, and whose philosophy made a considerable advance in the natural sciences. Conservative thought of the thirteenth century was derived from Bernard in the twelfth. As against Thomas Aquinas' reconciliation of reason with faith, the Augustinians preferred to reaffirm the priority of faith over reason. A contemporary of Thomas best represents this viewpoint: John of Fidanza, better known as St. Bonaventura (1221–1274). Thomas was the son of an Italian count; Bonaventura was the son of an Italian commoner. Thomas the rationalist was so modest and retiring as to be dubbed the "dumb ox" in his student days; Bonaventura the mystic was at home in the world, something of a politico, rising to be Governor-General of the Franciscan Order and a cardinal of the Church. The two men knew each other well at Paris, where Bonaventura arrived as a student of Alexander of Hales in 1242 and taught after 1248.

Bonaventura emphatically placed man's goodness of will and love before man's intellect in the quest for union with God. It followed therefore that the total Christian universe could not be comprehended by the human mind. The natural intellect was a tool of fallen man, and only the visible world of physical nature could be the province of human reason. Supernature, or the mystery of the divine order, was cognizable only by a supernatural agency. Just as nature requires supernature to complete the Christian universe, natural reason requires supernatural aid in apprehending this universe, including God, with any certitude. Such apprehension is possible only by divine illumination, that is, knowledge implanted by divine grace, not captured by unaided reason.

"In everything," said Bonaventura, "that is perceived through sense experience, God lies concealed." The supernatural is hidden from view by the natural. While human cognition can see nature unaided, when fortified by grace it can see through nature to supernature and to God. Nature is dual. It is both literal and symbolic, in that it truly is what sense perception tells us, but it is also something more. Physical nature consists of an almost infinite variety of symbols hinting at the real meaning and full significance of the supernatural. But how is knowledge of the supernatural to be acquired? Bonaventura's answer is best given in his own words: "If you ask how these things may be known, interrogate grace and not doctrine, desire and not knowledge, the groaning of prayer and not study, God and not man—not the light of reason but the fire of yearning, all aflame and tending toward God with devotion and glowing affection."

To put this a little more simply: for Bonaventura as for all Augustinians the emotions have cognitive value. Love and intuition play a part in the search for understanding revealed truth, and faith is more useful than reason in establishing the certainty of human knowledge of the total universe. Bonaventura, like the founder of his Order, was a mystic. For him the supernatural was all-important, and finite nature was of such slight consequence that it could be consigned to mere natural reason and Aristotelian logic, or any other useful activity of the human intellect such as observation or experiment. This was not to disparage reason, but simply to recognize its proper role. Furthermore, Bonaventura's Augustinianism did not amount to an oversimple rejection of Aristotle. For example, he was able to reconcile the Augustinian theory of divine illumination with the Aristotelian theory of knowledge, according to which the mind abstracts ideas from the data of sense experience and stores them in the memory. In effect what Bonaventura did was to put one on top of the other, fitting illumination and abstraction together in man's mind. Man, standing half-way between God and created nature, uses illumination in seeking knowledge of supernature above, and abstraction when confronted with natural objects below.

This interest in philosophy gave to Bonaventura's mysticism a quality of intellectual discipline quite lacking in Bernard. In his essay *On Leading the Arts back to Theology* Bonaventura expounded the relationship between secular knowledge and revelation, showing how the former subserves understanding of the latter. With Hugh of Saint-Victor he agreed that things of the natural order are symbols of truths of the supernatural order: "The wisdom of God lies hidden in every human cognition." Bonaventura's two systematic theological treatises were his commentary on Peter Lombard's *Sentences* and his *Breviloquium*, a compendium of Christian doctrine. His best known work, and the one which best portrays his mysticism, is aptly entitled *The Itinerary of the Mind to God*. It is both a description of, and an exhortation to, the ascent toward God which is salvation. All human faculties are needed for this search for man's supreme good and final end. While the mind unaided begins the journey, and reason uplifted by grace can contemplate the divine mystery, what Bonaventura calls the final "passing over into God" is an experience of which love and yearning are the necessary but insufficient human causes and God's grace is the sufficient cause.

This brief summary cannot do justice to Bonaventura's mysticism. Mystical experience is so intensely personal that it cannot be communicated fully to another person, even at length. What made Bonaventura so attractive in his own day and has drawn people to him ever since, is that compared with other mystics he is relatively intelligible. Not that his system is simple—quite the reverse—but rather his clarity of style and succinct exposition, in many difficult passages, derive directly from a thorough training in the liberal arts and in systematic theology. Bonaventura was a teacher of both at Paris for many years.

The separation between faith and reason in Bonaventura's thought was developed by mystics of the later Middle Ages, especially the Spiritual Franciscans, into a kind of skepticism—a doubt not in faith but in the usefulness of reason, a doubt which corresponded with their disinterest both in reason and in nature. Reason, according to them, cannot be trusted in the realms of the supernatural. Therefore the Christian must rely on faith alone; any effort to harmonize Aristotle and Christian theology is a waste of time. The later mystics were convinced of the undemonstrable nature of dogma and the primacy of will over intellect in the quest for salvation.

Another group was very much interested in nature, and they developed Bonaventura's Augustinian position in the opposite direction. While they agreed that reason was not very useful in dogmatic theology, they also pointed out that doctrine was of little use in understanding nature. This was the attitude of the majority of the Franciscan scholars. Typical of this group (but not himself a Franciscan) was Bonaventura's older contemporary, Robert Grosseteste (1168–1253), who as chancellor of Oxford University and its most influential teacher founded a school of scientific thought that included such men as Roger Bacon (d.1292) and Duns Scotus (d.1308).

In his criticism of Aristotle and of Arabic scientific works, Grosseteste became the first to elaborate a systematic theory of experimental science. His essential contribution was one of method, specifically the development of an intellectual procedure by which knowledge of observed facts could lead by abstraction to a statement of the principles which explain the observed facts. This is the inductive method, working from fact to theory, as opposed to Thomas Aquinas' deductive method of working from general principles to a statement of the particular and logical consequences. Modern science is rooted in Grosseteste's assumption that it is necessary to proceed inductively from effects to causes before it is possible, with accuracy, to apply knowledge of cause to explain the nature of effects. In his own work, Grosseteste employed controlled experiments which could be observed and repeated if necessary, in order to follow his inductive method. For example, he sought to explain the nature of the rainbow by studying the properties of refraction in a glass lens. In addition to experiment, Grosseteste insisted on the application of mathematics to scientific procedure both in describing phenomena and in correlating the results of experiment and observation. The thirteenth-century scientific work at Oxford, Paris, and elsewhere, in which Franciscans were prominent and Grosseteste was the earliest leader, resulted in the first major advance beyond the science of the Greeks and the Arabs.

Like Bonaventura, Grosseteste was also a busy churchman and theologian. He was bishop of Lincoln during the last eighteen years of his life and he ardently championed episcopal rights against interference by the archbishop of Canterbury and even the papal *curia*. He was active in English politics and, although a patron of the Friars Minor, he was friend and counselor to politicians like Simon de Montfort who distrusted Franciscans as agents of the papacy. Grosseteste had little interest in systematic theology, but his commentary on the corpus of writings attributed to an anonymous fifth-century writer erroneously called Dionysius the Areopagite was a popular source of ideas for the mystics of the later Middle Ages. None of the originality or creative thought that are so evident in his scientific speculation appears in Grosseteste's religious writings.

Although the great advance in medieval science came with the new criticism of Aristotle and the Arabs, older scientific or pseudo-scientific interests continued to be pursued. Before the end of the twelfth century most scholars were preoccupied with finding the moral or symbolic meaning, or else the magical or astrological properties, in the objects and events of physical nature. Such was the motivation behind Alexander of Neckham (1157–1217), who compiled a lengthy encyclopedia of facts and fables, for the most part culled from literature but also based in part on firsthand knowledge or observation. This work, *On the Nature of Things*, contains the earliest reference to the mariner's compass. Later encyclopedias were produced by several compilers, including Albertus Magnus and his pupils. They were devoted less to drawing moral lessons from the facts of nature than to presenting an accurate description of natural phenomena. All these works were largely dependent on Arabic and Greek sources.

Vincent of Beauvais (d.1264) was the most industrious compiler. He put together three massive encyclopedias "containing," as he wrote in his introduction, "whatever has been made or done or said in the visible or invisible world from the beginning until the end, and also of things to come." The resulting work, which Vincent called the *Speculum Majus* or "Greater Mirror," was divided into a "Mirror of Nature," a "Mirror of Doctrine," and a "Mirror of History." They are uniformly derivative, mediocre, and dull. Natural philosophy and science are not included in the "Mirror of Nature," which is mainly concerned with systematic theology. Instead they form a section of the "Mirror of Doctrine." In Vincent's view, knowledge of the arts and sciences should subserve man's welfare, and because his highest welfare is salvation, all this knowledge comes under the heading of doctrine which leads man to salvation.

Far more important work than that of the encyclopedists was accomplished in particular fields of science. The thirteenth century witnessed the triumph of the Ptolemaic system of astronomy as against an effort to revive Aristotle's less accurate system. Dissatisfaction with some aspects of both systems led to the earliest independent hypotheses concerning the motion of heavenly bodies. For example, a Franciscan scholar, François de Meyronnes, raised the possibility of the earth's revolving rather than the stars being borne around the heavens on revolving spheres. Astronomical observation and calculation were improved by the use of better astrolabes, quadrants, and armillary spheres. With such instruments the correct latitude of Paris was determined in 1290 by a student of Roger Bacon. The most accurate set of calculations of the movement of planets and stars before the work of Copernicus in the sixteenth century was completed about 1270, at the order of King Alfonso X the Wise of Spain. These *Alfonsine Tables* were in general use throughout the West by the end of the century.

Biology was a chief interest of medieval scientists. Botany was important primarily for medical reasons, and zoology for providing the material from which to draw moral lessons. In the thirteenth century scholars began to treat these fields as important areas for investigation based on observation and accurate description. The best work in botany was done by Albertus Magnus and by Rufinus (c.1287), who catalogued and classified plants as well as giving their healing properties. In zoology the outstanding work was written by the emperor Frederick II (1215–1250). *The Art of Hunting with Birds* not only remains an excellent introduction to the subject of falconry but also contains extensive descriptions of the anatomy and habits of birds, based on Aristotelian and Arabic writings and on the observations of the emperor himself. Where his own experience differed from what he read, Frederick did not hesitate to brand the authors of earlier books on the subject as liars.

Knowledge of human antomy was almost wholly based on the treatises of Galen (c.200) and the Moslem Avicenna (d.1036), but it is probable that at the medical school of Salerno dissection of animal and human bodies had begun in the twelfth century. In the thirteenth century human dissection was definitely practiced at Bologna, in connection with post-mortem examination to establish the cause of death for legal purposes. The earliest surviving formal report of a post-mortem was written by Bartholomew of Varignana, c.1302.

Much of the newly recovered ancient and Arabic science and much of the recent progress in scientific knowledge began to appear in textbooks and students' manuals before the end of the thirteenth century. One of the most popular writers was John of Sacrobosco (c.1240), whose textbooks in mathematics and astronomy were widely used in the high and later Middle Ages. In his *Sphere* Sacrobosco presented a convincing empirical argument that the world must be round. If a sailor on a boat sailing out to sea watches a landmark on the coast, he will see it disappear under the horizon, but if he then climbs the mast he can see the landmark again; also, stars at night rise in the East earlier than in the West, but this could not be true if the earth were flat. Hence the world is round. In his other works he helped popularize the use of Arabic (i.e., Hindu) numerals, first introduced to the Latin West by Leonard of Pisa, a mathematician patronized by Frederick II, in his *Liber Abaci*, c.1202. The *Sphere* of Sacrobosco continued to be so popular that after the invention of printing it went through sixty-five editions before 1647.

CHAPTER XX

The Medieval Synthesis
of Thought and Learning

II: LAW AND POLITICAL THOUGHT

Law and politics were important subjects for medieval philosophers; they were also the concern of men of affairs: the lawyers, judges, officials, and rulers. Legal and political ideas in the Middle Ages exhibit two aspects, the theoretical and the practical, or the scholastic and the professional. Scholastic philosophy and theology treated the fundamental principles underlying law and the political organization of society as those principles were related to the total Christian view of the nature of man and the universe. Separate from this theoretical interest, the legal and political interests of more practical men led to the first systematic treatises on law and government to be written in the West since later antiquity, to a growing body of controversial political literature, and to the earliest handbooks and manuals for the professional training of lawyers in a non-Roman or noncanonistic legal system.

The basic propositions of medieval political thought prior to the thirteenth century were derived largely from St. Augustine, who was in turn profoundly influenced by Cicero. The highest end of the state, in the

Augustinian view, is the maintenance of justice. The political structure of society is to be understood in juristic terms, as a system of rights. A "republic" (*res publica*, by which medieval theorists meant a well-ordered monarchy) is a society united in consent to law. A true republic must conform with the principles of divine law in order to achieve human justice. Law is thus prior to the state, not the product of the state. Both Cicero and Augustine accepted the Stoic concept of the natural equality of man as a condition antedating political institutions, under which men are unequal and subject to the coercive force of secular authority. According to Augustine human institutions resulted from the Fall and had their origin in sin. Government itself is not sinful, but is rather a remedial institution divinely ordained for the benefit of fallen man.

The key to understanding these propositions is the concept of natural law. Natural law, according to Thomas Aquinas, is the part of divine law which man can know as a rational creature. It is the guide or criterion of true human law, and any legal rule that violates natural law is a violation of divine law and thus invalid. But human laws, like human institutions, are those of fallen man. Hence the basic problem of legal and political thought alike was the reconciliation of the precepts of natural law and the realities of a world conditioned by human sin.

55 ROMAN LAW, CANON LAW, AND FEUDAL LAW

Bologna continued to be the center of Roman legal studies in the twelfth and thirteenth centuries. The work of Irnerius (d.1125), founder of the school of Glossators, was continued by his disciples, notably Martinus, Bulgarus, Hugo, and Jacobus, who were known as the Four Doctors. The greatest achievement of the Glossators was to develop the analysis and exposition of Roman law as it was contained in the *Corpus Juris Civilis*. Originally the gloss was a simple explanatory note or paraphrase; later it was elaborated and refined into several different kinds of systematic textual exegesis. The purpose of these exegeses was to establish the correct text, determine the literal meaning, settle or harmonize contradictory passages, deduce legal maxims or general principles, discuss the implications of particular cases, analyze a general term or phrase into its several specific meanings or applications, distinguish the legal rules in the Novels that rescinded or altered the meaning of older rules, and collect parallel passages bearing on a given problem. All these, originating in the simple gloss, were still glosses on the text. When separated from the *Corpus Juris* and presented as an independent treatise they constituted what was the equivalent of the scholastic commentary.

In the next generation after the Four Doctors, the Glossators began to produce other literature than glosses. Placentinus (d.1192) wrote a treatise on legal procedure, the first work to present a large portion of Roman law arranged according to a given topic rather than following the order of the sources. Placentinus also wrote an abbreviated paraphrase or *summa* of the Code of Justinian. This *summa* is one of the earliest surviving modern textbooks of legal studies in the Western world. Later he wrote a *summa* of the Institutes and planned, but did not complete, a *summa* of the Digest. The most popular of the later Glossators was Azo (fl.1190–1220), whose *summae* of the Code and Institutes became the standard textbooks during the remainder of the Middle Ages. Azo's glosses were so numerous that they provided an almost complete exposition of the entire *Corpus Juris Civilis*.

Besides Placentinus and Azo there were about two dozen other known legists at Bologna and elsewhere who wrote glosses, *summae*, and other treatises. The culmination of the school of Bologna was reached in the work of Accursius (d.1260), whose *Glossa Ordinaria* was a composite commentary on the *Corpus Juris* compiled from the works of all the Glossators. It has been estimated that Accursius collected over 96,900 glosses. The *Glossa Ordinaria* quickly gained an authority in courts admitting Roman law almost as great as that which Gratian's *Decretum* enjoyed in ecclesiastical courts.

During the twelfth century the teaching of Roman law spread to other centers. The Italian Vacarius (fl.1140–1160) taught in England where he compiled the *Liber Pauperum*, a condensation of the Code of Justinian together with extensive extracts from the Digest, a book written especially for poor students who could not afford the complete texts of the *Corpus Juris*. Roman law was taught at Oxford at least as early as the last quarter of the twelfth century. Placentinus taught not only at Bologna but also at Mantua and at Montpellier, and Roman law flourished at the University of Orléans. In Germany, however, the legists made little headway in the schools until after the thirteenth century.

In estimating the influence of Roman law in the Middle Ages an important distinction must be kept in mind. The three constituent parts of any legal system are its substantive law, its procedural law, and its jurisprudence. The first consists of the legal rules governing personal and property rights, the second provides the procedure by which these rights are adjudicated in courts, and the third consists of the principles of justice or philosophy of law on which the two former are based. The influence of Roman substantive law was greatest in countries where Roman law survived in a debased form from antiquity as local custom. Thus in Italy the Four Doctors attended Frederick Barbarossa's Diet of Roncaglia (1158) to assist in determining imperial rights over towns and revenues in Lombardy. In southern France, "the land of written law," the courts gradually accepted the Code and the *Glossa Ordinaria* as authoritative where local usage was deficient or inequitable. In northern France and in countries where ancient

Roman law had never been strong, local custom was relatively untouched by the substantive Roman law. But beginning in the twelfth century the jurisprudence and the procedural rules of the civil law began to influence the development of feudal law in such countries, either directly from Roman law books or indirectly through canon law.

The growth of canon law in the high Middle Ages in some ways paralleled that of medieval Roman law. In the schools canon law was studied and expounded according to the methods of the Glossators, and in procedure ecclesiastical courts borrowed freely from the doctrines of the legists. In two important respects, however, canon law was quite different from medieval Roman law. First, canon law was a growing body of legal rules. Canon law not only grew by the legislation of popes and councils, it was also in part a "judge-made" law, growing by the successive alterations and additions made by judicial decisions in the ecclesiastical courts, especially those of the papal *curia*. The latter were incorporated into decretals that settled particular cases but also had a general application. The decretals of popes like Alexander III (1158–1181) and Innocent III (1198–1216) filled in gaps in the existing law and also modified or reversed previous decisions. Thus canon law was in large part a case law in the twelfth and thirteenth centuries. It was in the same phase of development as Roman law had been when emperors made law by deciding individual cases, before Roman law became and remained largely a closed corpus, the *Corpus Juris Civilis* of Justinian.

Second, Roman law, as a body of substantive law, was restricted to certain territorial areas. Canon law was the law of the Church universal; it applied everywhere in Latin Christendom. But it was restricted in its application to cases under the jurisdiction of the ecclesiastical courts. These fell under two headings. Ecclesiastical courts claimed jurisdiction *ratione personae* (by reason of the person involved) over all tonsured clergy, widows and orphans, and "miserable persons" who could not protect themselves, such as paupers, lepers, and the insane. The Church also claimed jurisdiction *ratione materiae* (by reason of the matter involved) over both clergy and laity on all questions of ecclesiastical organization, discipline, and administration; over the property rights of ecclesiastical bodies; over all questions touching the sacraments, marriages, wills, vows, oaths, and contracts resting on good faith; and over all matters concerned with doctrine such as heresy. These wide claims to jurisdiction often led to a collision between the ecclesiastical and secular authorities, as in the quarrel between Henry II of England and Thomas Becket.

Although Bologna was the leading center of canon law studies, it did not dominate the field so completely as it did in the study of Roman law. The canonists at Bologna and elsewhere glossed and wrote commentaries on Gratian's *Decretum*, compiled and glossed collections of decretals, and wrote manuals for students and practitioners in the ecclesiastical courts.

Many treatises and glosses were written by canonists of the French, Anglo-Norman, Rhenish, and other regional schools, while canonists from these areas came to Bologna to teach and write, making it an international center of canonistic studies. Perhaps the greatest of the commentaries on the canon law was the *Summa Aurea*, or *Summa super Titulis Decretalium*, written by Henry of Susa, cardinal bishop of Ostia, better known as Hostiensis (d.1271).

The great number and variety of decretals issued after the *Decretum* (c.1140) posed a problem in providing ecclesiastical courts with an authoritative guide to the new law of the Church after Gratian's time. An official collection of these decretals was made by the canonist Raymond de Peñafort and published in five books by authority of Gregory IX in 1234. This collection, the *Liber Extra*, contained all decretals outside (*extra*) the *Decretum* that were henceforth to be binding in the courts; no decretals omitted from Gregory IX's five books were to be held valid. In 1298 Boniface VIII published a sixth book, the *Sext*, containing decretals since 1234; in 1317 the decretals of Clement V (1305–1314), the so-called *Clementines*, were officially published; and in the fifteenth century a final collection was added, the *Extravagantes*, consisting mainly of the decretals of John XXII (1316–1334). These were the five parts of the medieval *Corpus Juris Canonici*: Gratian's *Decretum*, which contained the "ancient law" of the Church; and Gregory IX's *Liber Extra*, the *Sext*, the *Clementines*, and the *Extravagantes*, which together contained the "new law."

To the legist and the canonist, Roman law and canon law meant a body of written enactments. To the feudal lawyer, law was essentially the immemorial custom of a community understood in a territorial sense. Law was the custom of the fief, of the county, of the realm. Customs that had been held "since the time whence the memory of man runneth not to the contrary" were thought to be beyond the will of the ruler. Customs were spoken of as being defined, approved, promulgated, enforced, maintained, or strengthened by the prince or ruler, but they were not conceived as being made or changed at his will. The essential quality of feudal or customary law was the approval and usage of the community, not the enactment of a legislator. Nor was feudal law a subject for specialized and systematic study in the schools or law books until long after the revival of Roman law. In feudal society everyone had to be an amateur lawyer because of the vassal's duty to attend his lord's court and participate in judicial work by helping to "declare the custom of the fief" in a particular case and to render judgment in settling the dispute. By its nature feudal law varied from place to place, and all the nobles had to know their local unwritten customs as part of the daily business of life.

The lawyers recognized the great difference between Roman law and feudal law by their reference to the former as written law (*lex scripta*) and the latter as unwritten law or custom (*lex non scripta* or *consuetudo*).

The lawyers also recognized that where customary law was affected by the growth of royal power, bureaucratic methods of government, and the activities of royal courts, it did not remain wholly unwritten or wholly customary. The procedural and administrative provisions by which the law was enforced and administered were, themselves, part of the law, such as the possessory assizes of Henry II which were written and enacted by the ruler. To such provisions the Roman law term, *leges*, was usually applied, but such *leges* were distinguished from the fundamental legal rules which protected the property, the rights, and the status of the free man. These latter were customs, or *consuetudines*.

The literature of feudal law—aside from documents and records of a legal nature—grew out of written statements of local customs. The earliest collection of such customs is contained in the *Usages of Barcelona* (c.1068), followed early in the twelfth century by the Lombard *Libri Feudorum* in Italy and the *Leges Henrici Primi* (c.1110) in England. Even these three earliest collections do not contain "pure" feudal law; each is influenced in content or method of treatment by the nonfeudal interests of their anonymous compilers. Technical terms and expressions are occasionally introduced from the "two laws" (Roman law and canon law), and the subject matter includes topics of concern to the Church and the central government as well as to feudal lords and vassals.

The romano-canonical influence is even stronger in the first real treatises on feudal law, which begin with the work attributed to Henry II's justiciar, Glanvill, entitled *On the Laws and Customs of the Realm of England* (c.1190). The substance of the book is English law; the romanesque element is in the systematic organization and exposition of the subject. It is the earliest general treatise which can fairly be described as a textbook of feudal jurisprudence, rather than merely a compilation of customs together with some commentary. The most important law book of medieval England was written by another royal justice, Bracton. This work, bearing the similar title, *On the Laws and Customs of England* (c.1250–1258), reveals an intelligent understanding of the principles of romano-canonical jurisprudence as they were applicable to feudal law. Treatises of a similar nature began to appear on the continent during the thirteenth century, those written late in the century being both better and also under a greater debt to the jurisprudence of Roman law. The *Tres-ancien Coutumier de Normandie* (c.1200–1220) was followed by the *Grand Coutumier de Normandie* (c.1258). The best work by a French feudal jurist was Beaumanoir's *Coutumes de Beauvaisis* (c.1283). In Germany the *Sachsenspiegel* at the beginning of the century was followed by the more romanesque *Schwabenspiegel* (c.1275). The *Assizes of Jerusalem* reflect the twelfth-century feudal customs of the provinces from which the French crusaders had come.

In the second half of the thirteenth century manuals and books of precedents for the training of pleaders or the guidance of judges in royal, feudal, manorial, and other local courts began to appear, a sure sign that a true legal profession was emerging in the field of customary law. Such books were the *Brevia Placitata*, the *Casus Placitorum*, and various handbooks bearing the title *La court de baron*, which were all popular in England. Growing out of this kind of tract were the English Year Books; the earliest surviving examples date from 1292, just a century later than the oldest surviving official records of pleas in the king's court. The Year Books were specifically intended for the training of professional pleaders, the sergeants-at-law, in the royal courts.

56   MEDIEVAL POLITICAL THOUGHT

Medieval political thought was extensive, rich, and varied; it derived from many different sources. And yet there was almost unanimous agreement on a few fundamental ideas and assumptions. Some kind of monarchy was the best form of the political organization of society. The purpose and end of temporal authority included the maintenance of justice. The good ruler could not be indifferent to the claims of religion or the spiritual welfare of his subjects. The good society was necessarily a Christian commonwealth. All authority must derive ultimately from God. No human authority, either spiritual or temporal, could legitimately be unlimited. But agreement ended, and vigorously controversial views began, when more specific questions were raised. What was the nature of social and political institutions, and of political authority? What should be the relations between the spiritual and temporal authorities? To what degree and in what way was government limited? Medieval political thought consisted largely in the answers given to these questions by theologians, philosophers, jurists, and propagandists, both ecclesiastics and laymen.

John of Salisbury best represents the traditional, Augustinian view in the twelfth century. In his treatise, the *Policraticus* (1159), the divine character or sanction of kingship is emphasized. The king is exalted as vicar of God because his chief duties are to protect the Church, maintain peace, and secure justice. To fulfill these heavy duties he must have appropriately wide powers, but the end of these powers is the good of the Christian commonwealth, not the prince's good. The king exists for the sake of the people, not the people for the sake of the king. The tyrant, who rules for his own sake, is the vicar not of God but of the devil. At this point John makes his one really new contribution, his doctrine of tyrannicide. Since there are no constitutional sanctions, no legally established organs of government or judicial process to invoke against the tyrant, it is permissible and even necessary to slay the ruler who transgresses the law, for all legitimate authority can rest only upon law. John was by no means an antimonarchist. His greatest contribution to medieval political thought was to present systematically an organic theory of society, a theory that was not original with him except in the detail with which he spelled it out. The commonwealth, according to this theory, is a body endowed with life; its head is the prince, who is subject only to God and to those who represent Him on earth (i.e., the Church), even as in the human body the head is governed by the soul. John held so high a regard for the majesty and the duties of the true king that any perversion of kingship was correspondingly wicked: the remedy was tyrannicide. But there was no justification whatever for regicide.

The development of political theory at the philosophical level is best illustrated by the difference between John of Salisbury, who systematized and restated the ideas of the early Middle Ages inherited from the classical and patristic past, and Thomas Aquinas, who best represents the thirteenth-century effort to reconcile that heritage with the pagan philosophy of Aristotle. Thomas' most radical break with the Augustinian tradition concerns the nature of human institutions. Thomas accepted the Aristotelian proposition that man was by nature a social and political animal. Hence human institutions, such as government or society, are grounded in man's nature and cannot be against natural law. Without explicitly contradicting the Augustinian explanation of social and political institutions as the result of and the divine remedy for sin, Thomas did reject this as a complete or adequate account of political authority or of man's role in society. For Augustine, the state was *against* natural law because it did not exist in a state of Nature (before the Fall); for Thomas Aquinas, the state did not exist in a state of Nature, but it was *according to* natural law in the specific sense that it was necessary because it fulfilled man's nature, and not only because of sin. Thus human institutions were additions to Nature that provided for man's development in accordance with the precepts of natural law.

For Thomas, political obligation, or the subjection of men to a ruler, would have been necessary even without the Fall (or sin) because of man's natural inequality—another basic proposition which Thomas accepted from Aristotle. The essence of political obligation is the common good of the whole community. Thomas agreed with John of Salisbury that the king exists for the sake of his people. A human law was valid only if promulgated by a properly constituted ruler for the welfare of the whole community in accordance with the dictates of reason, or natural law. The ruler who degenerated into a tyrant should be deposed, but Thomas shrank from tyrannicide, believing there was a greater risk of evils in that doctrine than there was in suffering the tyranny. The proper course was for the whole community or the leading men, the nobles as spokesmen for the community, to resist the tyrannical ruler.

Perhaps the greatest achievement of medieval political thought was

the general theory, embracing political authority, property, and social relations, worked out by Egidius Romanus in his treatise *On Ecclesiastical
Power* (1301). This was the theory of *dominium*. Egidius, a doctor of both
laws and a competent Aristotelian, was the first to combine in one system
the juristic, the Aristotelian, and the Augustinian viewpoints with the feudal
concept of tenure. The theory begins with the proposition that the universe
exhibits a divinely established order. All created things are related to each
other: some are superior, others are inferior. The relationship of superior
to inferior is *dominium*, that is, the divinely ordained control by the higher
over the lower, or service of the lower to the higher. Where this relationship
is that of a person over a person, *dominium* is expressed in terms of government or authority, such as that of a ruler over a subject or a lord over a
serf. Where the relationship is that of a person over a thing, *dominium* is
expressed in terms of property, such as the proprietary rights of a lord over
his fief. A person might control persons or things by mere force and not by
right; in this case there is no true *dominium*. God exercises total *dominium*
over all the created universe; any partial *dominium* exercised by a person
over people or things must therefore be derived from God. Such derivation
of legitimate authority or property rights can come only through grace.
These propositions are the essential argument of "dominion founded in
grace." Applying this argument to political realities, Egidius drew several
inferences. Grace is conferred through the sacraments administered by the
Church. Hence legitimate authority or ownership cannot be transmitted
merely by inheritance from father to son. Being born is not so important
as being reborn through baptism within the Church, by which grace is
received. Being the natural son of one's father creates a presumptive right;
being the spiritual son of the Church completes and perfects that right
through grace. Rulers, for example, derive their authority over their realms
more through their spiritual mother, the Church, than they do from their
fathers by hereditary succession. Born of their earthly fathers in original
sin, they are estranged from God until receiving grace through baptism.

   The theory of *dominium* as expounded by Egidius Romanus was
obviously designed to lead to the final conclusion that the Church, and
within the Church the pope, was supreme over all temporal affairs. Egidius
was the first writer to assert in full detail the extreme doctrine of the later
medieval canonists, that the pope was supreme lord of the whole world in
both spiritual and temporal matters. Behind this extreme doctrine lay a
long and bitter controversy, stimulated in the high Middle Ages by the
investiture struggle. The polemical literature of that struggle was popular
and propagandistic, the opposite extreme from the scholarly and philosophical treatises of John of Salisbury, Thomas Aquinas, and Egidius
Romanus. These propaganda pamphlets were important for political
thought because their authors raised fundamental questions concerning
the origin, nature, and limitations of political authority. Both papal and

imperial supporters shared the assumption that the whole of Christendom was one society, in which the spiritual and temporal authorities were but two aspects of one Christian commonwealth. The quarrel was not between "Church" and "state" in the modern sense, as two separate institutions. Christendom, the Church, and the state were coextensive. The problem was what their proper relations should be. Neither side denied the legitimacy of the power claimed by the other: temporal authority was ordained of God, episcopal authority had a divine origin and character. The crux of the controversy was that while each side claimed independence of the other, what each side considered to be essential to its independence the other side regarded as fatal to its own. Thus arguments that began as a claim for independence ended by claiming supremacy. The papal pamphlet writers had one great advantage. Even their opponents were willing to admit that the spiritual was in some sense superior to temporal authority, in dignity if not in power, just as the soul is "higher" than the body. But this did not mean that the pope was above the emperor in secular affairs, nor even that the pope had any secular authority. Although Gregory VII used strong language in characterizing Henry IV or the Empire, he never claimed to be acting on any other ground than as the shepherd of the Christian flock, of whom Henry was a member.

Among the arguments of papal supporters were the theory of the two swords expressed by Bernard in the twelfth century and the claim by Innocent III of the right to intervene in temporal affairs where sin is involved and the salvation of souls is endangered. No pope in his official capacity before the middle of the thirteenth century made the claim, put forward by a few exceptional papal supporters, to a direct power in temporal matters. The more extreme and later view of papal power was developed by the canonists, beginning with Sinibaldo Fieschi, who became Pope Innocent IV (1243–1254). Drawing their arguments from the canon law, and using the logical methods of the schools, the canonists held that the pope possessed a divinely ordained jurisdiction or "plenitude of power" not only over all spiritual matters but also over all temporal affairs, directly and not merely by reason of sin (*ratione peccati*). The pope may delegate this jurisdiction to rulers, but rulers have no lawful power other than what the pope has delegated to them. As for the emperor, Hostiensis (d.1271) argued that he held his authority from the pope and should properly be described as the vicar of the papacy. Egidius, as noted above, provided the papal claims with a comprehensive theory of the nature of society, social relations, and political authority. With few exceptions the canonists made more extensive claims than either theologians or the popes acting in their official capacity. Thomas Aquinas, for example, was on the papal side of the great debate but he could see nothing more than an indirect power in temporal affairs arising from papal plenitude of power.

The most forceful and convincing arguments on the imperial side came from the legists. In the twelfth and thirteenth centuries, supporters of the Empire were generally on the defensive. They admitted the full scope of papal authority in spiritual matters, and most of them admitted an indirect authority in temporal matters. But they claimed complete independence of the temporal from the spiritual authority in ordinary governmental affairs. They held that both emperor and pope derived their authority directly from God, and that the former could not be subordinate to the latter. Essentially this was a restatement of the Gelasian theory of the two powers, each independent in its own sphere. During the thirteenth century some of the legists began to apply these arguments to the western monarchies, justifying the independence of royal as well as imperial authority by the legal maxim that "the king is emperor in his realm." The most able of these royalists was John of Paris, a Dominican theologian at the University of Paris and supporter of the king of France, Philip IV (1285–1314), whose *Treatise on Royal and Papal Power* (1302) was an able reply to Egidius Romanus' *On Ecclesiastical Power*.

The great bulk of the civil law codified in Justinian's *Corpus Juris* consisted of the law of the later Roman Empire, the period of absolutism. The revival of Roman law ultimately enhanced the temporal authority and provided a theoretical justification for the growth of absolutism in the later Middle Ages and in the sixteenth and seventeenth centuries. However, the Glossators of the high Middle Ages generally did not emphasize these absolutist tendencies found in the maxims and legal rules of the *Corpus Juris*. At the Diet of Roncaglia (1158) Bulgarus, one of the Four Doctors, told Frederick Barbarossa that the maxim, "all things belong to the prince," meant only that the emperor's authority extended over his subjects' property by way of jurisdiction, because it was his duty to protect his subjects' property—an interpretation that would have astounded Diocletian or Justinian. The medieval jurists were agreed that private property was beyond the authority of the ruler. It was his duty to govern in accordance with the law and the same law which made him king also protected his subjects' proprietary rights.

Another maxim of the civil law, a favorite of the later absolute monarchs, equated the prince's will with law: "What has pleased the prince has the force of law" (*quod principi placuit legis habet vigorem*). This categorical statement was explained away by both Thomas Aquinas and the feudal lawyer Bracton as a harmless affirmation of their own concept of the nature of law. For Thomas, the maxim merely means that the prince's will is controlled by reason, the essential quality of true law: otherwise the will of the prince would be iniquity, not law. For Bracton, the king as vicar of God can do nothing which is not according to law, so the maxim refers not to any rash expression of royal whim or fancy but rather to what the king duly defines with the counsel of his greater nobles. In other words, Bracton refused to construe the maxim as meaning that the prince could make law, but interpreted it instead to refer to the usual promulgation or definition of law after consultation with the feudal members of the *curia regis*.

Feudal lawyers like Bracton in England and Beaumanoir in France were familiar with the arguments of the canonists and legists, as they were with the pamphlet war between imperialist and papal writers, but on the whole they were remarkably independent in their use of concepts or arguments borrowed from those sources. We have already discussed the feudal view of the nature of lordship and kingship, in Chapter 15. In terms of the issues and interests of the writers discussed in this chapter, the contribution of the writers on feudal law to medieval political thought may be summed up as an emphatic assertion of the limitation of government by law, an emphasis on the ruler's duty to protect the rights of his vassals and subjects, and a concept of law and rights that placed both beyond the reach of the ruler's personal will.

From this brief survey of the political thought of the high Middle Ages it is clear that with very few exceptions, and despite the diversity of views and conflicting claims of the propagandists, political writers agreed on most questions that in later periods have been considered basic. The source and sanction of political authority is a question of right, not of might; the end and purpose of authority is the welfare of the governed, not of the ruler who governs; and the rights of both ruler and subject are inviolable by each party to the governmental relationship. There is practically nothing democratic, nor is there any support for modern authoritarian or absolutistic doctrines, in the political thought of the Middle Ages.

Romanesque and Gothic Art

Writing about the middle of the eleventh century, a French chronicler remarked, "The whole world seems to have shaken off her slumber, cast off her old rags, and clothed herself in a white mantle of new churches." The period marks a new era in the history of Western art because it was the beginning of an age of great building, all over Europe, and because the prevailing Romanesque style represents the first significant medieval advance beyond architectural styles of the past. In the other arts, the period is not an important turning point; rather it witnesses the continuing development of themes and techniques that have much earlier origins.

In medieval architecture and art the influence of the Church was predominant. The Church possessed the wealth and the trained organization necessary for large-scale and continuing construction, and only a strong religious motivation could have initiated the vast expenditure of labor and resources that went into cathedral building in this period. Ecclesiastical interests also dominated the representational and decorative arts such as painting, sculpture, and manuscript illustration and illumination.

Like medieval thought and learning, art was in large measure derivative from the classical and patristic past, but with a significant difference. The canons of taste and style in ancient art were not accepted as authoritative to the same degree that classical and patristic ideas were. During the humanistic revival of the twelfth century and during the thirteenth-century appropriation of ancient philosophy and science, contemporary medieval architects and artists were developing their own styles with almost complete independence from the classical models to which, ultimately, medieval art can be traced. Like feudalism and the university, Romanesque and Gothic art and architecture preserved a thread with the past but were essentially original products of the medieval genius.

Today the terms Romanesque and Gothic suggest or imply "old" or "traditional" or even "old-fashioned." Our nineteenth-century forebears, moved by romantic impulses that had nothing to do with the real and historical Middle Ages, built churches and public edifices that still adorn our towns and cities with imitation "medieval" buildings. The impression created by these neo-Romanesque and neo-Gothic structures is not truly medieval in spirit. They imitate the past. In contrast, the Romanesque and Gothic styles of architecture in the high Middle Ages were, for that period, just as new and revolutionary as the "modernistic" architecture of the twentieth century.

57   THE ROMANESQUE ACHIEVEMENT

Art in the Carolingian renaissance, under the patronage of the imperial court, had an international character. With the disintegration of the empire, provincial differences became more marked until by the tenth and eleventh centuries artists in different areas developed the Carolingian traditions into distinct "national" styles. In part these provincial differences reflected the various artistic traditions upon which the Carolingian style had been superimposed, and in part the provincial schools of post-Carolingian art reflected the varying degree in which different areas were influenced by the revival of Byzantine art. Under the Macedonian emperors of the tenth century, Byzantine art reached its second Golden Age. This period was characterized by renewed interest in classical models and a new combination of Hellenistic naturalism with oriental design and ornament. The result was a phase in which Byzantine artists produced works that were simple and monumental.

The outstanding post-Carolingian centers in the West were in England and in Germany. In England the Winchester school of manuscript painting produced illustrations of Gospel and biblical texts that create an impression of lively movement and animation. The exuberant quality of this work is heightened by the rich ornamentation derived from earlier Irish and Northumbrian manuscript illumination. The best contemporary work in Germany was done by the Reichenau school of painting, especially during the Ottonian period (c.960–1025). The Byzantine influence was strong because of the connection between the eastern and western imperial courts. German miniature painting is thus more solemn, monumental, and abstract than the English work. Realistic detail is suppressed in favor of conveying the essential message or meaning to be illustrated. Instead of English animation, the German artist concentrated on the emotional content inherent in the scene. The Winchester painter portrayed his figures in motion, their garments fluttering in the breeze, and their arrangement on the page such as to give the illusion of great activity. The German painter simplified his composition, preferred figures that were blocklike and massive, and by slight exaggeration of gesture or facial expression achieved a much greater dramatic effect. By thus combining emotion and monumentalism, the Reichenau school achieved the spiritual and the transcendental qualities that were conspicuously absent from the representational art of classical antiquity.

These qualities, first produced by the miniature painters of the tenth and eleventh centuries, received their ultimate medieval expression in Romanesque architecture. The Romanesque cathedral of the late eleventh and twelfth centuries marks a revolutionary advance from several points of view. In construction the new buildings were either wholly or preponderantly made of stone, thus eliminating the fire hazard that destroyed so many earlier churches. The cathedrals and large abbey churches were much greater in size, often reaching huge proportions, thus reflecting the dominant position of the Church in medieval society. The style was made possible by the solution of several engineering problems, notably the effective use of stone vaulting for roofs and the buttressing of the thrust created by these heavy roofs.

The greatest achievement of the Romanesque builders was esthetic. The esthetic problem that challenged the designers of these new cathedrals and churches was to relate the parts of the building to each other, to subordinate all the parts to the whole, and thus to create an organic unity. In the developed Romanesque style, no single part of the building stands by itself but contributes to the total impression conveyed by the entire structure. The most important specific problem was to link together the walls by means of vaulting. The old-fashioned basilica type of church had a flat wooden roof which provided a cover but fulfilled almost no esthetic function; the roof indicated where the walls ended and thus established the proportions of the interior, but beyond that function the roof was simply there.

The ground plan of the Romanesque church followed that of the basilica church: a cruciform plan consisting of nave with aisles on either side, a transept at right angles to the nave to form the cross, and a rounded apse extending beyond the transept. The orientation of the church was west to east, with the altar at the eastern end, just inside the apse. In some of the larger churches and cathedrals a section called the choir extended eastward from the transept before the apse was reached, so that in the largest buildings the choir and apse together were about as long as the nave. In such a building the transept formed a crossing midway be-

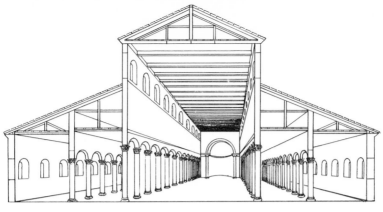

Clerestory (Basilica)

tween either end of the church. It was also common in the larger buildings to have an ambulatory, that is, a continuation of the aisles beyond the transept, going around the apse or choir-and-apse.

In the basilica type of church the roof over the nave was often raised higher than the roof over the aisles by building up two walls resting on arches thrown between the columns on either side of the nave. These walls, called the clerestory, permitted the interior of the nave to be higher than the aisles, and also permitted light to enter through windows cut into the clerestory. Romanesque builders also used the clerestory to heighten the structure and allow the entrance of light.

The round arch and the round vault were the basic structural elements of the Romanesque style. On the outside, portals and windows were enclosed by arches, the windows often being in the form of adjacent double arches so that the wall above the opening was provided with a support running up through the middle. Inside, the aisles and nave were covered by vaulting which supported a very light, sloping roof to shed rain. This vaulting continued the motif of the round arch along the longitudinal axis of the interior. The earlier churches were small enough, and the aisles and nave narrow enough, so that one continuous barrel vault could be employed. In this case the transept was formed by the intersection of another barrel vault, forming a cross vault. The weight of a barrel vault rests evenly along the whole length of the walls on which it is constructed. This meant that a barrel vault of great size would require such massive walls that no windows could be cut through them. The walls could be built higher and the nave and aisles wider, however, if the weight of the vaulting were reduced or concentrated at certain points where buttressing of the wall might contain the thrust. This was accomplished by substituting a series of cross vaults for the one barrel vault.

Cross vaults whose length and width are equal enclose a square space, and the thrust of such a cross vault is concentrated at the four corners. The nave, the aisles, and the transept could be made much larger

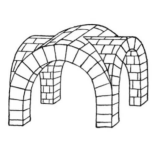

Cross Vault

and higher by covering them with a series of such cross vaults and reinforcing the walls underneath the corners of each successive vault. This reinforcement had to be strong, because the thrust of a round vault points outward as well as straight down, the resolution of forces being at a forty-five degree angle. The Romanesque interior is characterized by the same rhythmic succession of vertical lines along the axis of the structure that marks the interior of a basilica. The difference is that the columns of the smaller and lighter basilica have been replaced by the massive compound piers necessary to bear the weight of Romanesque construction. Between these piers the walls were light enough to be pierced by windows, both on the outer walls of the aisles and the clerestory wall supported by the main piers of the nave. The choir, apse, and ambulatory were treated in the same way, except that the rounded end of the church could be covered by a half dome.

The total effect of the interior of a great Romanesque cathedral or abbey church has to be experienced to be understood. Photographs provide little more than a descriptive portrayal of the proportions, lines, and surfaces. From these it is apparent that the Romanesque builders succeeded in creating an artistic unity out of many distinct parts. Each vertical line or surface is directly connected, through the arches and vaulting, with the corresponding lines and surfaces of the opposite side. More important, and more difficult to describe, is the subjective impact of the interior on the observer or worshiper. The windows are so small in proportion to the total wall area that, even though the surfaces were often whitewashed, the light admitted does little to brighten the interior. This dim atmosphere, together

St. Savin (left) and Abbaye-aux-Dames, Caen: Romanesque naves, with barrel vault (left) and ribbed cross vault (late eleventh and early twelfth centuries). PHOTOS: JEAN ROUBIER, AND UNDERWOOD AND UNDERWOOD.

with the massive piers and huge vaults, produces a monumental and transcendental effect. The Romanesque builders created a feeling of being in the presence of the Deity and in touch with eternity. In the history of architecture this was an original conception of the artist's goal: ordered mass was subordinated to a subjective impression of abstract harmony. No single part of the interior intrudes or distracts the observer from the impression created by the whole structure. This is why Romanesque churches have been described by such phrases as "colossal austerity" or "impersonal massiveness."

The exterior of the Romanesque cathedral also marks a radical break from the older basilica style of church. The older churches presented a rather bare appearance, except for the colonnaded porticoes of some of the larger basilicas. In contrast the Romanesque builders adorned their churches with decorative patterns along the outside walls, usually emphasizing horizontal lines which harmonized with the window and portal arches. The most prominent external feature of the Romanesque style was the addition of one or more towers. Sometimes a single tower was raised above the supporting arches of the transept; more often the façade or front of the structure was provided with two towers, one on either side. The façade, taken as a whole, was dominated by horizontal lines and decorative motifs so that the height of the towers was not emphasized. In the space beneath

Abbaye-aux-Dames, Caen (above), and Church of the Magdalen, Vézelay: Romanesque façades (late eleventh and early twelfth centuries).

the arches which surmounted each portal (one for the nave and one for each aisle), sculpture was employed for decorative effect.

In the Romanesque period large-scale or life-size sculpture was used for the first time since later antiquity. Esthetically this sculpture was completely in harmony with the architectural style with which it was integrated. The human figure, animals, and natural scenery were rendered in a style designed to bring out the message or symbolic significance of the subject matter. Naturalistic representation, insofar as it might detract from this significance, was avoided. Instead, all unnecessary detail was suppressed, form was exaggerated or distorted to bring out the salient features, and surfaces were often given a smooth and rounded treatment to emphasize mass. This style developed gradually out of the miniature carving and the painting of the tenth and eleventh centuries. It represents the final stage in a slow transformation of classical naturalism, influenced by northern and barbarian ornamental and geometrical abstraction, into a new style that was abstract, monumental, and—by directing the observer's attention to the spiritual or symbolic meaning of the subject matter—transcendental.

Romanesque sculpture was strictly subordinated to architecture, both in its physical location and in its purpose. The sculptured figures and scenes were fitted into the building, especially above the portals and along the façade. The elongation of the human body, characteristic of Romanesque style, served to harmonize the sculpture with ornamental col-

Romanesque Sculpture: inner portal, Church of the Magdalen, Vézelay (early twelfth century). PHOTO: FRENCH EMBASSY PRESS & INFORMATION DIVISION.

umns. Sometimes these figures took the place of the columns, standing on the same bases and supporting the same capitals that would have been used for columns. In theme or subject matter, the most common representation was the story of salvation of the blessed and damnation of the wicked, including the particular scenes and events from the Bible wherein the sufferings of Christ and His plan for redemption are set forth.

58   GOTHIC ARCHITECTURE AND THE DECORATIVE ARTS

During the twelfth century several innovations in the art of building led from the Romanesque to the Gothic style of architecture. The transition was gradual, and most of the typically Gothic methods of construction appeared first as particular features of churches that were otherwise Romanesque in style. The pointed arch is the basic structural element of Gothic architecture, as the rounded arch is basic to Romanesque style. The origin of the pointed arch is a matter of dispute. Perhaps it was first used on a small scale as a decorative device, possibly as early as when churches were still constructed with wood. It has been conjectured that the pointed arch might have been "discovered" when builders found that it was easier and safer to bend two timbers to meet at the top in a point rather than in a true semicircle. In any case, the crucial development that led to the Gothic style as a whole also involved the appearance of the pointed arch as a structural element.

This development was the use of the ribbed vault instead of the simple cross vault. A ribbed vault in its simplest form consists of six ribs, in the shape of round arches, over a square or rectangular area to be covered. Four of these arches connect the corners along the sides of the area; two connect the four corners diagonally across the space. The height of a round arch is proportional to the span it crosses; hence the two diagonal ribs will be higher than the other four, since the span is greater across the diagonal of a square than across its sides. The span, and thus the height of the arches, is even greater diagonally across a rectangular space. Romanesque builders introduced the ribbed vault in order to decrease the total weight. This was done by filling in the four triangular panels created by the diagonal ribs with very light masonry. Almost all the weight of the entire vault thus consisted of the heavy ribs.

The paneling of light masonry, however, had two defects. Esthetically, it was not satisfactory to have the surface of the panels twist from the semicircular plane of the four side arches to a new semicircular plane of the two diagonal arches, which were of greater dimension and revolved around forty-five degrees. Structurally, this sort of masonry tended to be

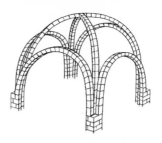

Ribbed Vault: six round arches (diagonal and on sides) enclosing square area.

weak because the direction of thrust at any one point was never the same as the thrust at any other point. An understanding of solid geometry and engineering makes this clear to the modern student; medieval builders learned by trial and error. A solution of both difficulties is achieved if the two diagonal ribs are constructed in the form of round arches and if the other four ribs are built along symmetrical curves ending in a point at the greater height of the diagonal arches. What has actually happened is that the two intersecting barrel vaults have been replaced by two vaults which are now an extension of a pointed arch rather than a round arch. Now the panel of masonry between the arches follows a uniform plane, without any change or twisting, so that both structurally and esthetically the result is satisfactory.

The system of vaulting by ribs and panels, together with the pointed arch or vault implicit in that system, was the essence of Gothic architecture. The more obvious features of the Gothic style all follow logically from this great innovation for which the Romanesque builders were originally responsible. The first large Gothic building was the abbey church of St. Denis,

Gothic Ribbed Vaulting: two round diagonal arches and four pointed side arches, enclosing square area. Mont-St.-Michel (early thirteenth century). PHOTO: FRENCH GOVERNMENT TOURIST OFFICE.

near Paris, rebuilt by the abbot Suger during the middle years of the twelfth century. By the end of the century, almost all new construction employed a system of vaulting based on the pointed arch rather than the round arch.

Many advantages, from an engineering point of view, resulted from the new style. The structure could be built higher, since the height of the pointed arch was not bound by the span it covered. The higher the pointed arch, the greater was the efficiency in buttressing, since the thrust was directed in a more nearly vertical direction as the height increased. Even more important was an innovation in buttressing developed originally by Romanesque builders and employed extensively in Gothic construction. Instead of allowing the whole thrust of the vaulting to descend upon the main piers of the nave, half-arch supports were built from the base (and from just above the base) of the rib of the nave vault outward and over the aisle to a pier located outside the structure. This was the flying buttress. It contained part of the thrust and brought it to rest where a massive support would not interfere with the walls of the church. This meant that the walls carried no weight but their own and were relieved of the outward pressure exerted by the vaulting above. The walls were reduced in thickness, and thus could be pierced by much larger openings for windows. The result was a transformation of the interior. The Gothic cathedral was flooded with light. Also, and just as important for the general effect of the

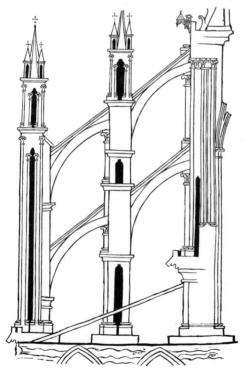

Flying Buttresses. From the *Notebooks* of Villard de Honnecourt (first half of thirteenth century). NEW YORK PUBLIC LIBRARY.

Notre Dame, Paris (left), and Reims: Gothic naves (late twelfth and early thirteenth centuries). PHOTOS: MARBURG—ART REFERENCE BUREAU, AND EUROPEAN.

interior, the flying buttresses made possible a change from massive piers along the nave to a series of thinner columns bearing an arcade.

In the Romanesque interior, massiveness and horizontal lines emphasize the solidity of the structure. In the Gothic interior, almost all the lines are vertical and weight has been eliminated wherever possible. The proportion of space to mass is exaggerated in the later Gothic cathedrals to the point where the structure appears to be unstable and insecure, conveying an illusion of soaring upward. This illusion of movement is increased by the use of stained-glass windows which flood the interior with multicolored, shimmering light. The central feature of the façade of a Gothic cathedral, viewed from the interior, is the rose window, a circular space that is filled with tracery holding stained glass arranged in a complicated pattern. The northern and southern transept walls are almost wholly cut away, in the developed Gothic style, so that the area before the altar is provided with a maximum of light to correspond with the focus of liturgical interest. Often, as in the cathedral of Notre Dame in Paris, the stained glass of the north window of the transept will be predominantly blue, while the south window catching the sun has been given an extravagant amount of red, yellow, and orange hues.

The early Gothic period, c.1150–1250, witnessed the building or the

Cathedral of Reims: façade (thirteenth century).

beginning of most of the best examples of Gothic architecture. Northern France led in the development of the style, and by general consent the cathedrals at Paris, Chartres, Reims, and Amiens represent the Gothic style in its most nearly perfect form. Gothic architecture is sometimes referred to as being "functional" in the sense that each weight-bearing element of the structure reveals its function clearly and also is proportioned so that it appears to be neither too bulky nor too slim to bear its assigned weight. The early Gothic, which still suggests some of the rugged simplicity of the Romanesque, gave way to the elaborate articulation and profuse decoration that characterizes the later Gothic style.

In England the names Decorated and Perpendicular are accurate descriptive terms for the Gothic building of the fourteenth and fifteenth centuries. Ornamentation and the use of vertical lines are so exaggerated that the total effect is that of architectural ingenuity, a *tour de force* displaying the builders' skill, rather than an esthetically satisfying structure. Later Gothic churches exhibit complicated variations of ribbed vaulting, flying buttresses more abundant than strictly necessary for bearing the weight, and a superfluity of decorative patterns in the masonry. In France the goal of the later builders was to build higher and more daringly.

Between towns there was often great rivalry to build the biggest cathedral. The cathedral at Amiens, begun in 1220 and largely completed by 1269, was enormous. Its nave was 141 feet high. The citizens of the neighboring Beauvais resolved not to be outdone, and began to build their new cathedral in 1247 on an even larger scale. Beginning, as usual, with the choir and apse, they built their vaulting thirteen feet higher than at Amiens, but it came tumbling down almost immediately. In 1272 they began rebuilding the choir but in 1284 the vaulting collapsed again. Again

Salisbury Cathedral. Begun in 1220, consecrated in 1258; spire added in fourteenth century. PHOTO: BRITISH TRAVEL ASSOC.

Gothic Sculpture: portals, cathedral of Reims (left), and statues of Ekkehard and Uta, cathedral of Naumburg (second half of thirteenth century). PHOTOS: RAPHO GUILIU-METTE, AND MARBURG—ART REFERENCE BUREAU.

they rebuilt, introducing additional supporting columns and doubling the number of arches so that the vertical lines were especially pronounced. Although a transept was added, much later, the church as a whole was never finished. The final triumph of the citizens of Beauvais was a choir rising to 157 feet, the height of a modern fifteen-story building and higher than any Gothic vaulting achieved elsewhere. But the limit had been reached: the choir at Beauvais had to be reinforced with iron rods to hold the structure together.

Gothic sculpture, like Romanesque, was integrated with and sub-ordinated to the cathedral, and it continued to be primarily didactic in purpose. The sculptured scenes that adorned the walls and portals were "sermons in stone." According to Suger, abbot of St. Denis, "Our poor spirit is so feeble that it is only through sensible realities that it raises itself to the truth." The subject matter remained much the same as in the Romanesque period, ranging from stories and figures from the Old and New Testaments to the details of daily life and common experience.

Philosophers and theologians taught that everything in the physical universe, when interpreted allegorically, suggested a truth of the higher or supernatural order. Consequently Romanesque and Gothic sculptors and other artists were free to range far beyond what would generally be considered today as appropriate for religious art. In the Gothic period, however, there seems to be a greater interest in the subject matter for its own sake rather than for the allegorical content. The earlier abstract and transcendental quality gives way to a new interest in naturalistic representation. The portrayal of human, animal, and plant forms in Gothic sculpture often reveals an accurate knowledge and skillful reproduction of nature that could only be based on observation. Romanesque sculpture often tended to be flat; Gothic sculpture is three dimensional and more plastic. The surface treatment of drapery about the human figure reveals the form and posture of the body underneath, in contrast with the earlier monumental and abstract conventions of the Romanesque style.

Painting in the thirteenth century did not change so much as sculpture, possibly because artists were less interested in purely stylistic considerations than in perfecting the new technique of pictorial representation through stained glass set in windows. In stained glass the dye is actually in the glass; except for the lead in which the glass was set and except for the occasional use of black paint to bring out lines and shadows, the artist used nothing but small pieces of brightly colored glass in making his mosaic-like picture. Most authorities on the subject agree that the stained glass picture windows of the early Gothic period are, both esthetically and technologically, the best work done in this medium, including the modern efforts to revive the art.

The use of stained glass was the great pictorial innovation of the high Middle Ages, but even more important for future developments was the beginning of life-size or monumental painting in the thirteenth century. The Gothic cathedral did not have much wall space, sometimes none at all. But when it happened that a building was begun in one style and finished in a later style, as at the great abbey church of St. Albans in England, the combination of Romanesque wall surfaces and Gothic lighting made possible the decoration of the interior with wall paintings. In Italy the Gothic style of architecture was never developed fully because in that sunny climate there was no great need for large windows to admit more light into the interior, so Italian churches continued to have large wall surfaces for decoration. By the end of the thirteenth century Italian painters had developed the new technique of fresco painting, in which paint is applied to new plaster while the surface is still wet. Gothic wall painting in Italy was little different in style from that of the north, until the fourteenth century when both painting and sculpture in Italy were given a radically different development under the influence of classical models.

Latin and Vernacular Literature

Before the end of the thirteenth century most medieval writing was in Latin. For the modern student of the early and high Middle Ages, a knowledge of Latin will give access to about ninety-five percent of the sources of general history in the original language. Latin was the language of religion, learning, government, law, and business. It was also the language in which a large proportion of the literature for enjoyment or entertainment was written.

One obvious difficulty stands in the way of surveying and evaluating medieval Latin literature, a difficulty that does not confront the student of classical Latin. Any diligent reader can read through the whole of the surviving Latin writings of classical antiquity; it would be no greater task to read through all the books written in Latin since the end of the Middle Ages. But the bulk of medieval Latin literature is so great, including both published and still unpublished works, that in a single lifetime no one could read more than a small part of it. This statement remains true even if literature is construed, in a fairly narrow sense, to mean poetry and what is meant today by the terms "fiction" and "nonfiction"—excluding technical or specialized works in science, philosophy, theology, law, and official or unofficial documents and records.

The student who is interested in medieval literature rather than general history, for the period before 1300, would definitely be handicapped without a knowledge of the vernacular languages if he wished to read the sources in the original. The use of vernacular increased rapidly during the high and later Middle Ages in all fields in which Latin had hitherto been exclusively or predominantly employed. We have already considered the earliest extensive body of vernacular literature, the feudal epic, the lyric poetry of the troubadours, and the northern romance—all three constituting the courtly literature of feudal society. Later vernacular literature developed the themes and the verse and prose styles of these earlier genres, and also expanded to include a wider range of reader interest. The only kinds of medieval literature in which vernacular language was seldom employed were the liturgy of the Church, scientific treatises, and theological and philosophical works.

59   MEDIEVAL LATIN LITERATURE

Latin composition was taught in the schools, at an elementary level according to the rules of Donatus and other grammarians, and at the university level as part of the liberal arts of grammar and rhetoric. Learning to write was essentially a process of committing to memory the rules of grammar and then observing the rules in practice. Practice, however, tended in fact to outrun principles. The rules of Donatus and Priscian were more concerned with the cases and tenses, the number and gender of words, than they were with word order or what medieval grammarians called "construction" of sentences. Classical grammarians had never developed an adequate Latin syntax—the principles underlying sentence structure, according to which word forms are arranged to show properly their mutual relations within the sentence.

The medieval teachers of grammar took up the problems of syntax in an effort to apply dialectic to their subject and thus make it a science. At the textbook level the best known work was Alexander of Villa Dei's *Doctrinale* (1199). In his more elaborate treatment of syntax he was the first to use extensive excerpts from the Vulgate and from patristic writings as illustrative examples of his rules. The success of the *Doctrinale* was thus partly due to Alexander's effort to bring grammar into conformity with the best Latin usage of his own day. He decried the subservience of contemporary humanists who imitated classical Latinity. Another reason for the popularity of the *Doctrinale* was that it was written in rhymed verse, so that it could easily be memorized by students. It became the standard textbook of grammar until the humanistic reaction in favor of classical Latin pushed it into the background in the sixteenth century.

In the northern universities some teachers treated grammar and rhetoric in typically scholastic fashion, as disciplines to be investigated scientifically for their own sake. In addition, the two disciplines had a practical value that was appreciated even more by students; this practical

interest was most highly developed in the Italian universities. Italian grammarians taught the *ars dictaminis,* the art of composing letters and drawing
up business and legal documents. One branch of rhetoric in the Italian
universities was the *ars notaria,* devoted to legal training and the execution
of legal instruments. These more specialized studies were the extreme examples of the medieval attitude toward all Latin composition: that it
should conform with definite rules from which deviation was considered
inappropriate. Writing was a craft; poets were not born but made. There
was little premium, under these conditions, on originality or inspiration.
The spell of the classics and the authority of the Bible helped to narrow
the limits within which individuality was conventionally acceptable.

The largest single class of Latin writings in the high Middle Ages
was that of religious works—devotional, didactic, and dogmatic. Many
active churchmen, who were not primarily authors, made a contribution to
this body of literature that was not, strictly speaking, theological. For example, the canonist Lothaire de Segni wrote a devotional tract on the
contemplative life entitled *De Contemptu Mundi* ("On Contempt of the
World") before he became pope as Innocent III. In the same class must
be included a great number of sermons that were written down. Collections
of sermons began to be made in the thirteenth century for the use of parish
priests. For the edification of the faithful, the most popular literary works
continued to be the Lives of the Saints. With a few exceptions the high
Middle Ages was not so fruitful a period for this kind of writing as the
preceding age. But the number of Lives did not abate. The several Lives of
St. Thomas Becket contain the greatest number of miracle stories connected with the name of any medieval saint. And yet these Lives of St.
Thomas and of other twelfth- and thirteenth-century saints often lack the
simplicity, charm, and imaginative quality of earlier saints' Lives or of the
contemporary stories about the miracles of the Virgin. More notable than
the original Lives being written in the thirteenth century were the compilations of condensed or paraphrased older Lives. The best of these was the
Golden Legend, by James of Voragine (d.1298), who collected and retold
over two hundred Lives.

To the modern historian one of the most impressive achievements
of the high Middle Ages was the revival of the writing of history. Compared
with the meager Carolingian and post-Carolingian annals, the chronicles
written in the period c.1050–1250 are fuller, more accurate, and composed
with greater consideration for style. The best chroniclers of the twelfth century departed from a rigidly chronological organization, at least when dealing with the history of their own times. It was conventional to begin a
chronicle with the Creation, the Flood, the Incarnation, or some other great
event in sacred history, and then to present a summary of events derived
from earlier chronicles down to the author's own day. At this point the
chronicler relied upon his own knowledge of events as he observed them

or as they were accessible through oral reports or through documents and other contemporary written evidence. The most important and reliable part of a medieval chronicle was thus the author's own times, for which he is today considered a source of history in contrast with the earlier period for which he gives a secondary account. Perhaps the most remarkable thing about medieval history writing is that it improved so much despite the fact that—in contrast with philosophy, theology, law, and the physical sciences —it never became a formal discipline in itself, a subject in the curriculum of the schools and universities. History was simply one small part of grammar, although grammar, as it was taught in the schools, included both grammar as it is understood today and what would now be considered to be general literature.

Since history was part of general literature, the writing of history tended to be literary rather than analytical and critical. But the best writers were not content to give a superficial narrative. They inquired into motive and causation, they were aware of the complexity of human affairs and the interrelationships between historical events, and some of them even attempted to relate historical knowledge to the total framework of human knowledge and divine revelation. The German historian Otto of Freising (d.1158) not only wrote a detailed and accurate narrative of events but also attempted to show how these events exemplified the Christian philosophy of history as expounded in Augustine's *City of God*. Otto's two most important works were *The Two Cities* and *The Deeds of the Emperor Frederick I*, which together cover the period from Adam down to the year 1156. The best history written in France was the *Ecclesiastical History* of Ordericus Vitalis (d.1143), whose work began with the Incarnation and is especially valuable for the history of Normandy and for the relations between the kings of England and France after the Norman Conquest of England in 1066. In England there were more historians of the first rank than in any other country. Ordericus' contemporary William of Malmesbury (d.1142) and William of Newburgh (fl.1198) were both monks who wrote general accounts of English history in which they not only recorded but tried to explain historical events. Because he rejected the legends about King Arthur and the Round Table, popularized by Geoffrey of Monmouth's pseudo-historical *History of the Kings of Britain* (1147), Newburgh has been called "the father of historical criticism."

The twelfth century was the golden age of the monastic chronicle. From then until the end of the Middle Ages there was a steady decline in the value of historical works produced by monks. In England the only important exception to this general rule was Matthew Paris (d.1259), a monk of St. Albans, a monastery located just north of London which had intimate connections with the royal court. Matthew's four main works, and particularly his *Greater Chronicle*, have earned him the reputation of being the best of all medieval historians.

Meanwhile history began to be written more often by members of the secular clergy (like Otto of Freising, who was a bishop), and particularly by clerks who had entered the service of secular rulers and who frequently witnessed or even participated in the events they described. Such a writer was Roger of Howden, author of the *Deeds of Henry II and Richard* and a *Chronicle* of English history down to 1201. Roger was active in the government as a clerk, judge, and adviser of the great men who shaped royal policy. One of the chief values of the work of writers like Howden is that these clerks included verbatim copies of documents in their narratives, thus preserving important records that otherwise would not have survived.

The Crusades aroused great interest, and most chroniclers included long chapters on the subject. William of Malmesbury, for example, in his *Deeds of the Kings of the English* gives a long derivative account of the First Crusade, with digressions on the Council of Clermont and the topography of the city of Rome. The best-written history of the First Crusade was the *Deeds of God Through the Franks*, by Guibert of Nogent (d. 1124), based on an account by an anonymous eyewitness. Of equal importance was the *Historia Hierosolymitana* by Fulcher of Chartres, who brought his chronicle down to the year 1127. On the Second Crusade and its aftermath an excellent account was written by William, archbishop of Tyre (d.1185), entitled *History of Deeds Done Across the Sea*. The best histories of the later Crusades were written in the vernacular rather than in Latin.

Closely related to historical writing were biography and autobiography. The Lives of the Saints do not quite fall under the first heading, their purpose being edification, and little was written that was strictly biographical in the modern sense. The *Life of Louis VI* by Suger (d.1151) is by far the best medieval biography in Latin, but it is almost unique. The first works since Augustine's *Confessions* that were truly autobiographical (rather than primarily devotional) were written by Guibert of Nogent in France and Salimbene (d.1290) in Italy. Each gives a lively account of his times and reveals his own personality. It is altogether exceptional for a medieval author to convey to the reader so full and so individualized a self-portrayal.

In medieval Latin poetry, the greatest change from the Carolingian period to the high Middle Ages was the abandonment of classical meter based on quantity (long and short syllables) in favor of accentual meter and rhymed versification. As in prose, the greatest amount of poetry was written on religious themes, and most of it was rather mediocre. The finest religious poetry was written for liturgical use—the sequence or hymn. The greatest of these were the *Sequences* of Adam of Saint-Victor (d. 1192), as perfect a literary expression of the new emotional piety of the twelfth century, especially of that centered on the Virgin, as the Romanesque cathedral was in architecture. The sequence was sung during the service of the Mass, and was composed with special reference to a particular festival. The two most familiar sequences were written by Franciscans in the thirteenth century, the *Stabat Mater Dolorosa* and the *Dies Irae*. The latter is generally considered to be the greatest hymn, and by some the greatest poem, in the Latin language. The opening stanza is a truly majestic introduction to its mighty theme, the Day of Judgment:

> *Dies irae, dies illa*
> *Solvet saeclum in favilla*
> *Teste David cum Sybilla.*

> [The day of wrath, that dreadful day,
> Shall all the world in ashes lay,
> As David and the Sybils say.][1]

The *Dies Irae* is a supreme example of a poem that cannot be translated without vitiating the beauty and power of the original. No English version exists that has satisfied either the translator or the reader who understands Latin.

Another literary form, the drama, grew out of the liturgy of the medieval Church. The ultimate origin of modern drama is in the trope, a dialogue sung antiphonally by the choir, inserted into the Mass for one of the great festivals, such as Easter or Christmas. This dialogue took place between characters who were appropriate for the festival—for example, between the three Magi for Christmas. When the primitive trope was elaborated with the addition of more "parts" in the dialogue, and with a more extensive dialogue involving some representative action, the result was a religious drama for the instruction and edification of the faithful. To give the "actors" more room and to accommodate a larger audience the play was moved outside the church, thus separating it from the liturgy. To increase the appeal, in the later Middle Ages the dialogue was changed from Latin to the vernacular, and by that time laymen had taken the place of clergy in acting the roles.

The earliest and simplest medieval drama was the mystery play, a simple dramatization of some story from the Old or New Testament. In the twelfth century the miracle play became popular; this presented an incident in the life of a saint or of the Virgin, the climax of which was the miraculous intervention by the saint in the daily affairs of human beings. In the later Middle Ages the so-called morality play was developed. In this kind of drama the author was free to deal with themes that might be far removed from religion. Most of the morality plays were allegorical dramatizations, very moral and didactic, but some included comic scenes and real-

---

[1] F. B. Artz, *The Mind of the Middle Ages* (2nd ed.; New York, 1954), p. 333, reprinted by permission of the publisher, Alfred A. Knopf, Inc.

istic characterization. The best of the morality plays, and the one that is most familiar to modern audiences, is *Everyman*, a drama that exists in several versions and several languages.

The most novel Latin literature of the whole Middle Ages was the new secular lyric poetry of the twelfth and thirteenth centuries. This was the Goliardic verse written by students who called themselves disciples of Golias—that is, Goliath the Philistine, who in medieval allegory signified the devil. Most of this poetry was satirical and humorous, and it dealt at great length with the pleasures of wine, women, and song. The authors, many of whom later became honored and respected officials in the Church, have been characterized as "lewd fellows of the baser sort," or so they appeared to be in some of their lyrics. It was all in good fun. One of the best Goliardic poems was by the anonymous clerk known as the Archpoet, *The Confessions of Golias* (c.1165), from which the following stanza is taken:

> In the public-house to die
> Is my resolution;
> Let wine to my lips be nigh
> At life's dissolution:
> That will make the angels cry,
> With glad elocution,
> "Grant this toper, God on high,
> Grace and absolution!"[2]

The Goliards were experts at parody, and they turned their talents occasionally to sharply critical and anticlerical satire. A favorite device of theirs was the acrostic. For example, everyone knows that the root of all evils is avarice, and in Latin the Goliards gave this a clever antipapal twist in the acrostic (reading the first letters downward):

> Radix
> Omnium
> Malorum
> Avaricia

Finally, the same group of authors, most of them anonymous, were responsible for a considerable body of satire and parody in prose, directed against peasants, women, monks, and higher clergy,—and even the Bible. Among the more popular anticlerical prose satires was the *Gospel According to St. Mark(s of Silver)*, and of course there were animadversions on the Gospel attributed by the satirists to the "evangelist" St. Lucre. Historians who have called the Goliardic poetry and prose "pagan" or "irre-

---

[2] J. A. Symonds, tr., *Wine, Women and Song* (London, 1925), p. 69, reprinted by permission of the publisher, Chatto and Windus.

ligious" have really missed the main point of this literature. People who are seriously pagan or irreligious do not poke fun at their religion or themselves. Medieval satire, humor, and parody were not directed against religion, but against the discrepancy between the ideal and the actual, between what people ought to do and be and what they are and do in everyday life. This literature shows that medieval writers had a sense of humor, even if according to modern taste this humor is a little naïve.

60 MEDIEVAL VERNACULAR LITERATURE: DANTE

Latin literature and vernacular literature were not separate and mutually exclusive categories. We have already noticed that vernacular and secular drama grew out of the original liturgical Latin of church services. The themes, styles, versification, and even the grammar of Latin literature influenced the growth of vernacular prose and poetry, and the reciprocal influence of vernacular upon Latin literature was just as great. Latin changed more slowly, it was bound by more rigid rules of grammar and syntax, and it remained the language of the learned. Latin was written for readers; vernacular literature was originally written for oral recitation, to be heard by an illiterate audience. The main purpose of the great bulk of vernacular literature was the entertainment or edification of the laity, at first the feudal nobility and later the upper middle class or bourgeoisie as well. There was a great diversity of dialects within the main vernacular languages —Romance, Germanic, Celtic, and Slavic—and it was only by a very slow process that one or another dialect became the language of today. The reader of modern French, for example, can understand medieval French as it was written in the Île-de-France but he is hopelessly lost in Provençal.

The courtly literature of feudal society dominated vernacular writing in the twelfth century, as we have already noted in discussing epic and lyric poetry and the later chivalric romance in northern and southern France. Except for the fragmentary *Hildebrandslied* (c.800), the earliest surviving German epic is the *Nibelungenlied* (c.1200), which preserves legendary tales connected with the historical kingdom of Burgundy and its destruction by the Huns in the fifth century. It is, however, strongly influenced by Christian values and by the *courtoisie* of contemporary French romance. German lyric poets or minnesingers owed even more to French sources, both the versification of the troubadours and the Celtic themes so popular in French romance. The German versions of some of the Arthurian stories, notably Gottfried von Strassburg's *Tristan* (c.1210) and Wolfram von Eschenbach's *Parzival* (c.1220), are considered superior to the French and Latin originals of Chrétien of Troyes and Geoffrey of Monmouth. The greatest of the German lyric poets was Walther von der Volgelweide (d.1228), whose love poetry and satirical verse are comparable to the best

Chivalric Romance: Banquet and Duel. Manuscript illustration showing scenes from Wolfram von Eschenbach's *Parzival* (thirteenth century). BAYRISCHE STAATSBIBLIOTEK, MUNICH.

work of the troubadours. In Italy and Spain the vernacular epic and lyric developed much more slowly than they developed north of the Alps and Pyrenees, and the quality of the poetry was much less distinguished. The one exception was the epic poem *The Cid*, a collection of legends and stories about the eleventh-century hero of the Christian reconquest of Spain, which has become the greatest monument of Spanish medieval literature.

The vernacular literature of the Scandinavian north and of Celtic Ireland developed almost independently of French or other continental influence. The surviving written examples are epic in style and are nominally Christian, but the religious influence is merely formal. Although compiled in Iceland during the twelfth century, the *Poetic Edda* dates back to a much earlier age, some of its legends being based on oral traditions antedating the conversion to Christianity. The social values and conventions revealed in the early Scandinavian literature are those of the prefeudal and tribal society of the Teutonic world. The *Prose Edda*, put together by Snorri Sturluson (d.1241), is the last great collection of Scandinavian mythology. The later sagas or prose tales often deal with historical personages and events, and even some of the earliest stories have a historical kernel.

The distinguishing characteristic of medieval Irish literature is its imaginative and exuberant quality. The Irish bards used exaggeration as the standard means of expressing emotion or giving emphasis in their lyric poetry and prose narratives. For example, the hero Cu Chulainn is so described:

> A beautiful boy indeed was he: seven toes to each foot he had, and to either hand as many fingers; his eyes were bright with seven pupils apiece . . . on either cheek he had four moles, a blue, a crimson, a green, and a yellow one.

The earliest Irish poetry dates from the ninth century, although the surviving manuscripts come from the eleventh and twelfth centuries.

In France during the thirteenth century the vernacular romance continued to be popular, but the genre had become fairly stereotyped and little was produced that could rival the best of the twelfth century. The most important work, the *Romance of the Rose*, was more impressive for its quantity than its quality. The first part, four thousand lines, was left unfinished by William of Lorris (c.1237) and was completed thirty years later by Jean de Meun in an incredibly long-winded conclusion of almost eighteen thousand lines. The poem is an allegory of love, an exhaustive recitation of everything that the two authors could think of to say about their subject. The narrative portions are slow-moving, and the allegorical presentation substitutes abstract types for characterization. The main interest of the poem lies in the contrast between William of Lorris' part, a conventional allegory of courtly love designed to please a noble audience, and the part by Jean de Meun, who was an educated layman of bourgeois origin. In the latter section Jean presents what amounts to an encyclopedia of bourgeois satire and criticism of the clergy, the nobility, women, rulers, and villeins, together with miscellaneous information and misinformation on dozens of topics. Into the allegory, fantasy, and artificial *courtoisie* of romance, Jean injects a note of realism.

This element of realism had already appeared in a type of literature that was alien to the chivalric romance, the *fabliaux* or brief tales written in rhymed verse for a bourgeois audience. Some of these may originally have been folk tales handed down in oral tradition; others derived from stories preserved from Greco-Roman antiquity in such prose collections as the Latin *Gesta Romanorum*. The *fabliaux* were in some ways the vernacular equivalent of the Goliardic verse, in that each subjects to biting satire the interests and values of the feudal nobility, the clergy, and the peasantry. One of the main purposes of the *fabliaux* was to amuse, and the humor is crude and broad. Stock characters appear, as in the romance, but they are characters of a wholly different world. Monks and priests are hypocritical and unscrupulous; the innkeeper usually has a beautiful daughter and a deficiency of common sense; the wealthy merchant is sharp in trade and stupid in all else; and women are usually portrayed as either amoral or simply immoral. In this literature there are no ideals of conduct, as in courtly romance, other than the tricks and maneuvers by which the clever rogue outwits "respectable" or conventional people. The hero is often a wandering scholar or a poor but quick-witted commoner.

The Crow and the Fox. From the Bayeux Tapestry (late eleventh century). THE BAYEUX
TAPESTRY, ED., SIR FRANK STENTON, PHAIDON PRESS, LONDON.

Sometimes these *fabliaux* point a moral, and this didactic element
links them to another popular form of vernacular literature, the fable. The
fable or animal story derives both from classical antiquity, which produced
the fables attributed to Aesop, and from Germanic folklore. As in later
forms of romance, the allegorical element is prominent: each animal represents a type of human being. The most popular of medieval fables were
those collectively known as the *Romance of Reynard*, in which Reynard the
Fox plays approximately the same role as the heroes of the *fabliaux*.

France, particularly in the northern towns, was the center of the
new bourgeois vernacular literature of the thirteenth century, as it had been
the center of chivalric romance in the twelfth. Although the bourgeois literature of all other countries was influenced by that of France, in Italy short
stories in prose were especially popular. These were the *novelle*, a kind of
up-to-date and vernacular version of the *Gesta Romanorum* in which there
was greater diversity of subject matter and thus greater freedom on the part
of the author to create original plots and characters. The earliest collection,
Il Novellino, dates from the end of the thirteenth century.

The growing amount of vernacular religious literature in the high
Middle Ages probably indicates an increasing bourgeois interest in literature as well as an increasing bourgeois piety. In the twelfth century parts
of the New Testament were translated into French by the Waldensians,
and the earliest Lives of Saints were translated or paraphrased in the vernacular. The *Life of St. Dominic* and the *Life of St. Francis*, both in
French, were derivative from earlier Latin Lives. St. Francis and the later
Franciscan, Jacopone da Todi (d.1307) were among the earliest to write
poetry in Italian instead of in the literary language of their country, which
was still French. Francis' *Canticle of the Sun* is one of the finest expressions of the devotion that inspired the founder of the Order of Friars
Minor. In England the French of the nobility and the Latin of the clergy

almost drove the native tongue out of written literature, but the *Ancren Riwle* (c.1210) in Middle English prose compares favorably with any of the contemporary devotional works written in the vernacular on the continent. It was popular enough to be translated into both French and Latin.

The twelfth century was a turning point for vernacular history, biography, and travel literature. The termination of the Anglo-Saxon Chronicle in England, in 1154, marks the close of the Old English period. Henceforth until the end of the fourteenth century vernacular history in England was written in French, beginning with the mediocre verse of Wace's *Roman de Rou* (c.1170), a tedious history glorifying the dukes of Normandy commissioned by Henry II. At about the same time the *Kaiserchronik* was composed, in seventeen thousand verses, relating the history of the medieval Empire in German. None of these works was so important as the first great history in French prose, *The Conquest of Constantinople* by Villehardouin (d.c.1213), a layman and a participant in the Fourth Crusade.

The best biographies of the thirteenth century were also written in French and by laymen, the first at the beginning of the century in verse and the second at the end in prose. These were the anonymous *History of William the Marshall*, recounting the deeds of a simple knight who rose to be regent of England, and the *History of Saint Louis* by Jean de Joinville (d.1317). These works, especially the latter, are full accounts of both the life and times of their subjects. No better guides exist to the realities, the values, and the ideals of the feudal nobility of the high Middle Ages. Just as popular as the vernacular histories and biographies were the autobiographical works written by travelers, the most familiar of which is Marco Polo's account (c.1298) of his travels through the Orient and his residence for seventeen years in China. Although Marco Polo was a Venetian, his work was written in French.

Italian vernacular literature developed late, but in it was written the greatest of medieval creative works, the *Divine Comedy* of Dante (d.1321). Like so many other writers of his times, Dante was an educated layman and townsman, but his ideals and interests were not typically bourgeois. They embraced so much that was characteristic of every phase of medieval life that his works as a whole, and especially the *Comedy*, represent a synthesis of medieval culture. Active in the politics of his native Florence, he was exiled during an uprising supported by the pope. He became bitterly antipapal and pro-imperial in his political views, and in his social views favored a return to the good old days of the nobility when virtue (as he thought) rather than wealth led to honor. Because the supreme end of civil society was peace, Dante advocated the reassertion of imperial authority throughout Italy. Only a strong emperor could restore order in the peninsula. In none of his political views was Dante a profound or original thinker, and the same must be said of his mastery of theology, philosophy,

Dante. Fresco, cathedral of Florence, showing Florence on the poet's left and representation of *The Divine Comedy* on his right (mid-fifteenth century). PHOTO: ALINARI.

and the liberal arts. But he was intelligent and industrious, and he possessed
true genius as a poet.

Dante began as a writer of lyrics, for which he deliberately chose the
vernacular of his native Tuscany rather than the French of the Provençal
troubadours which had until then dominated Italian verse. He next wrote
a popular exposition of philosophy, *The Banquet* (c.1308), partly in prose
and partly in poetry; this was the first work of learning to be written in
Italian. Next came a treatise on *Writing in the Vulgar Tongue*, written in
Latin for the learned in defense of his preference for the vernacular. Then,
moved by the hope of effective intervention in Italy by the new emperor,
Henry VII (1308–1313), Dante wrote a Latin tract *On Monarchy* in which
he expounded his political theory. Finally, the mature work of his later
years (c.1314–1321) was the *Divine Comedy*, from whose language modern
Italian is directly descended.

The *Comedy* is a truly monumental work, a combination of the
author's personal experience, scholastic learning in its full development, and
the teaching of the medieval Church. It is a Christian allegory of the end
and purpose of mankind, taking both God and the created universe into
account as well. Dante's use of allegory, while not original, differed from
the usual allegory of medieval romance. In the latter the allegorical figure
is usually a purely imaginative, personified abstraction. For example, the
good knight Courage rides out to do battle with the knave Fear who is

supported by his companions Shame and Timidity. In the *Comedy*, Dante uses real persons who are familiar to his readers as symbolic figures. Thus, Dante's guide through Inferno is not a personified abstraction called Wisdom or Reason or Knowledge but rather the poet Virgil who symbolizes or stands for these abstractions. Since the characterizations are all convincing, there is both a literal sense and an allegorical meaning to all the action. This combination of realism with symbolism is superbly effective. It allows Dante to present a running commentary on history and contemporary events while at the same time discussing the most fundamental and universal questions of mortal and eternal life.

PART FIVE

THE RISE OF THE WESTERN MONARCHIES AND THE DECLINE OF THE MEDIEVAL PAPACY AND EMPIRE

PART FIVE. illustration:
Edward I in Parliament, with Alexander, king of Scotland, and Llywelyn, Prince of Wales, lords spiritual on left and in foreground, and lords temporal on right. Manuscript illustration (late thirteenth century). PHOTO: RADIO TIMES HULTON, LONDON.

The Growth of Secular Culture

During the thirteenth century the papacy achieved its final and complete victory over the Empire. The popes who succeeded Innocent III (1198–1216) were, on the whole, abler and better trained for their responsibilities than the popes of any other century. And yet by the end of the period the prestige and power of the papacy had sunk to a lower level than before the investiture struggle.

The medieval papacy and Empire claimed universal authority. In Latin Christendom the claims of the papacy came very near to being realized because the papacy was the recognized head of a universal institution, the Church. Until the end of the thirteenth century the political and cultural life of Europe was dominated, and the economic and social institutions were largely influenced, by the teachings of the Church. Gradually, the competing claims of other authorities grew stronger until the papacy and Empire no longer held the primary allegiance of most people. In western Europe the balance of power shifted to the kings of England, France, and Spain. In central Europe power shifted to the greater ecclesiastical and lay lords in Germany and to the communes in Italy.

Beneath the surface of political events, changing conditions made it more difficult for the Church to maintain its leadership. The institutions and the values of feudal Europe were slowly transformed. The rise of the western monarchies and of the Italian communes was thus achieved at the expense not only of a moribund Empire and a declining papacy, but of a disintegrating feudal society as well. The bonds which held together the local geographical communities remained strong, but the political units of society that were essentially feudal—counties, baronies, lesser lordships—grew weaker or were absorbed by the administrative machinery of the new monarchies and the burgeoning communes. To this generalization Germany was the major exception, but not so much of an exception as might at first appear. The territorial lordships of the princes of the Empire represent a triumph over the lesser feudal nobility just as significant for Germany as the rise of the monarchies at the expense of the feudal lords was for France and England. This chapter is concerned with developments which underlay, and to a large extent made possible, these major political changes.

61   THE TRANSFORMATION OF FEUDAL SOCIETY

Although they continued to be the predominant social class, the feudal nobles in most of Europe declined in power and influence during the thirteenth century. There were many reaons for this decline. The essential function of the feudal nobility had always been to fight. But outside of Italy there was little large-scale warfare in Europe between the opening and closing years of the thirteenth century. When kings and greater lords no longer needed the ready support of their feudal host, the interests and desires of the feudal nobles no longer bulked so large in governmental policy. For police power, garrisoning castles, and defense of frontiers, feudal rulers turned increasingly to mercenary troops. Paid soldiers were more reliable and their service was not dependent on feudal custom, which usually limited military service to forty days. Rulers found it advantageous to commute such service into money payments. When a fief was held by a vassal unable to fight personally, the payment of money in lieu of service was the obvious solution. For example, the vassal might be a minor, or too old to fight, or an heiress holding the fief in her own right. When military service grew less important as the preeminent obligation of vassalage, the bonds uniting lord and vassal were less intimate and personal, in contrast with older days when the trust between lord and vassal had been nurtured by service together in the field.

The heavy cavalry of mounted knights—the feudal nobility-in-arms—continued to be the core of the medieval army, but two developments in the art of warfare diminished the relative importance of the ordinary knight. One was the change from wooden to stone castles. Only the greater lords could afford these more expensive structures, a fact that made the feudal nobility less homogeneous. The second development was the great improvement in the art of siege warfare, which made the ordinary knight less valuable than the engineer and the sapper in the all-important job of taking or defending castles.

The political influence of the nobility declined also. In a very general way the political and military influence were connected, but more specifically the rise of competing jurisdictions circumscribed the political activity of the nobles. The most powerful of these were the western monarchies which, during the thirteenth century, were rapidly building up professional and bureaucratic governments. Royal courts provided a better and cheaper justice, thus draining business from feudal courts. The judgments of royal courts were enforced by a growing machinery of law enforcement that preserved peace better than the less powerful lords could. Since peace and justice were the essence of medieval government, the governmental influence of feudal lords waned as that of the royal bureaucracies waxed. In Germany and Italy the same pattern emerged with important variations. In each country the central authority was weak. North of the Alps the peace and justice provided by the princes of the Empire grew at the expense of both the imperial government and the local feudal jurisdiction of lesser lords; in Italy the communes generally won out at the expense of the Empire and the rural nobility.

The net result of these developments can be described as the emergence of territorial states with definite boundaries, states that were still not unified or sovereign like the modern national state but which were definite geographical areas within which the central power of king or duke or arch-

Castle of the Counts of Flanders, Ghent. Begun c.1180, with later additions. PHOTO: EWING GALLOWAY.

bishop or commune was recognized and enforced. Some areas, like England, had already reached this stage early in the thirteenth century; in other areas the competing feudal jurisdictions continued to be a serious handicap to such centralizing tendencies until late in the Middle Ages.

The generalizations can best be illustrated by the attitude of feudal lords of the middle rank, those barons who were not counts or dukes or kings but who were possessed of baronies that numbered from a dozen to several dozen fiefs held by about the same number of vassals. Such a baron in the year of grace 1100 thought of his barony as being his "honor." The honor consisted not only of his own demesne manors and all the fiefs held by his vassals; it also included all his rights of jurisdiction and his rights as feudal lord of his vassals. These rights the baron exercised effectively over all his vassals and their scattered fiefs from the center of his barony, his feudal or honorial court. The essence of the honor or barony was the set of personal and individual relationships between lord and vassals, symbolized by the act of homage performed by each vassal when he received his fief. The court often acted as a unit, and the vassals thought of themselves as "peers" or equal participants in the affairs of the honor, but the honorial court never became a corporate body with rights or functions of its own. It was the baron's court, not the peers'. The ties uniting the baron as lord to each vassal individually were stronger than the interests which might on occasion bring vassals together in opposition to their lord. Thus the strongest bonds of feudal society may be described as both individualistic and "vertical," that is, between lord and vassal, superior and inferior, as individuals.

By the year 1300 the baron who was possessed of a barony of similar size had quite a different attitude, because of changed conditions. His barony would probably consist of many more fiefs of much smaller size, so that his vassals were not so important, individually, to his own interests. His feudal court no longer met so often nor did it do so much business because his vassals had discovered that a better brand of justice, less encumbered by feudal custom, was available in royal courts. Since the baron's right of private warfare had been restricted by the peace enforced by kings or Church or higher lords, the old relationship between baron and vassals as comrades in arms had all but disappeared. The relationship was no longer really feudal: the lord looked upon his vassals as tenants of fiefs from which he derived revenues. The lord had become, to use the modern term, a landlord.

With the "vertical" ties between lord and vassal thus attenuated, and with the decline of feudal jurisdiction, lords who had once devoted most of their energy to governing their baronies were ready to recognize and act upon their mutual interests against the rising power of central authorities. In the same way, the lesser nobility were less concerned with their immediate lords but were more involved with the governments of kings or of great lords and communes. Gradually the feudal world was becoming more stratified into classes whose "horizontal" ties, the interests which bound together groups of the same social status and economic condition, superseded the older "vertical" ties. In central Europe, and to a lesser degree in France, where the central authority of king or prince was slow in developing, such tendencies toward "horizontal" social organizations led to the formation of estates. An estate was a class defined in terms of similar social status, economic interests, and political ambitions. Most historians would agree today that wherever these estates were able to organize and to counterbalance the authority of the central government of a territorial state, feudalism had ceased to exist even though many relics of the feudal organization of society survived until the French Revolution or even beyond.

These military and political changes could not have taken place without profound economic and social changes. The economic revival after the middle of the eleventh century increased the importance of money, as compared with land, as a source of wealth. During the twelfth and thirteenth centuries prices gradually rose—the prices of goods, and consequently the price or wages of labor. This inflationary trend worked against the economic position of most of the feudal nobles, based on their landed wealth. The revival of trade led to a rising standard of living which in turn led to greater consumer demands from the nobility. But the nobility could afford the higher standard of living only by getting more money to spend. This they often did by commuting the customary labor services and payments in kind, collected from the peasants of their manors, into cash rents. Because the old services and payments had been fixed by custom, the new cash payments into which they were commuted also tended to be customary or fixed. Hence, the nobles were caught between fairly fixed incomes and slowly rising prices, which resulted in a gradual decline in their relative standard of living. In other words, the standard of living of the nobles rose less rapidly than that of other classes. Pressed for money to maintain their more expensive standard of living, or to pay off indebtedness, the nobles often found their only financial solution in selling land, a solution which undercut further the kind of wealth on which the nobility was based. Finally, some rulers paid more attention to the interests of the bourgeoisie than formerly because the latter were more easily taxed for revenue. They had money but not the privileges, the power, and the exemptions which so many nobles enjoyed. Hence, the rise of central governments was often dependent on the growing economic importance of the bourgeoisie.

Meanwhile there were other, built-in causes working toward the breakdown of feudalism. These were the feudal customs governing subinfeudation and the inheritance of fiefs. Subinfeudation was the act by which a lord's vassal granted part of his fief to another noble, so that the lord's vassal became the lord of a new vassal, who thus became the original lord's subvassal. This was the process by which the so-called feudal "hierarchy" was built. In the thirteenth century there were instances of as many as a dozen or even twenty nobles intervening between the highest lord and the lowest vassal of a given fief, each intervening noble being the vassal of the noble immediately above him in the hierarchy and the lord of the noble immediately below him. This may appear at first glance to be complicated or incomprehensible, but actually it was quite simple. All that is necessary to understand the process is to visualize a given lord possessing a given fief, and then granting half of it as a fief to a vassal who then in turn grants half of *his* fief to be held as a fief by another man as vassal, and so on. This process could in theory be continued indefinitely.

Originally the chief motive for subinfeudation was to supply the lord with the military service due to him. For example, if your lord granted you a fief in return for the service of five knights in the feudal host, then you either had to find four knights who would fight for you in return for room, board, and keep in your household, or else you could grant to each of the four a fief carved out of your own fief by subinfeudation. In the latter case the four knights would be your vassals and your lord's subvassals. You would find several advantages in subinfeudation. Not only were the four knights no longer cluttering up your life, but the subinfeudated part of your fief was now no longer a burden on your own time, either for administration or economic exploitation. Finally your status or prestige would be enhanced in the feudal world because you had four vassals. If you could enlarge your own fief and enfeoff a few more vassals, people would begin to call you a baron.

In the thirteenth century, and even earlier in some areas, another motive for subinfeudation became important: the desire for cash income, already discussed. It should be noted, however, that there was an additional important reason for the nobility's need of money: the growing practice of kings and other rulers of increasing their revenues by collecting taxes from their immediate vassals. This was most commonly done by commuting military service to cash payments or by obtaining an extraordinary feudal aid. When we hear of a fief held for the twentieth part of a knight's service, we are not dealing with a vassal who comes to the feudal host for two days (one twentieth of forty days) and then goes home. Rather the vassal has been enfeoffed in return for a cash rent equal to a twentieth of the military tax or commutation of military service, called scutage, levied on his lord in lieu of the service of one knight. Lords were also granting fiefs with increasing frequency in return for stipulated rents which bore no relation to the scutage they owed, such as a fief to be held in return for twenty shillings with no military service required. With the appearance of this kind of fief, feudalism was rapidly dying. Under the forms of feudal tenure, a new relationship had emerged—an impersonal cash nexus had become more important than the older and personal binding ties of homage.

The tendency toward more fiefs, smaller fiefs, and the replacement of personal service by money payments, which is best illustrated by subinfeudation and its consequences, was also promoted by the feudal laws of inheritance. Primogeniture (inheritance of the whole fief by the oldest surviving son) tended to preserve the integrity of the fief, but what if no son were born or survived? In most regions feudal custom provided that on the failure of male heirs the fief descended to the surviving daughters equally as co-heiresses. Feudal families were large, so this did not happen frequently; but when it did happen there were often many co-heiresses among whom the fief was partitioned. A great fief could suddenly become a collection of rather insignificant fiefs. Other feudal customs provided that the surviving widow should retain part of her late husband's fief as her dower to possess during her lifetime, or that a younger son could be enfeoffed of part of the father's fief during the father's life, or even permanently if the oldest son consented, or that a daughter should be enfeoffed with a "marriage portion" of her father's fief which meant that she and her heirs would deprive the oldest son of that portion of the inheritance. These and many other customs tended to reduce the size of fiefs, either temporarily or permanently, although occasionally they might work to increase the size. But despite the bewildering complexity of feudal law the main generalization is clear: historically the tendency was in the direction of more fiefs, smaller fiefs, and the conversion of services into money payments.

The net result was that, below the level of the kingdoms and greater principalities, the old feudal lordships—fiefs, honors, baronies—became less important as political units. The old personal relationships and the jurisdictional powers of lords over vassals were giving way to new and impersonal relationships which were proprietary and economic. These relationships might lead to endless disputes as to rights and duties between the parties involved, thus providing an opportunity for the greater rulers with their more effective governments—the king of England, the count of Flanders, the archbishop of Cologne—to intervene and control the feudal society within the area of their jurisdiction. This transformation of feudal society was gradual, and to the modern historian its course is almost imperceptible. But when the feudal world of the twelfth century is contrasted with the structure of society and the concentration of political authority evident in the fourteenth century, it is clear that the intervening period was one of profound change.

62 TOWN AND COUNTRY: ECONOMIC CONDITIONS IN THE HIGH MIDDLE AGES

Commerce continued to prosper and expand during the thirteenth century, though at a slower rate of expansion. Medieval towns, in contrast, continued to develop with no decline in their rate of growth. The reason is simple. In the eleventh and twelfth centuries towns meant trade and trade meant towns. But by the thirteenth century, and even earlier in Italy and Flanders, a new activity in economic life had become important: the manufacture of goods. Medieval industry was, by modern standards, very small-scale; it was almost wholly domestic—scattered about in the homes or backyard workshops of artisans, whether they were villagers in the country or urban craftsmen. In the thirteenth century manufacturing increased in the towns, and this accounts for the continuing growth of urban population and urban economic activity, an increase that exceeded the rate of growth of commerce alone.

Manufacture in the simplest sense—the making of goods by hand and with hand tools—exists in any society no matter how primitive. In the early Middle Ages most peasants of necessity followed the modern practice of "do-it-yourself," for skills were simple and tools rudimentary. Industry grew out of specialization. In the earliest stage the buyer brought his own raw material (e.g., grain) to the producer who sold the use of his equipment (a mill) and of his skill (operating the mill) in making the product (flour). For other products, by their nature (e.g., a castle or church) the producers (carpenters or masons) had to bring their equipment and skill to the raw material supplied by the buyer.

A second stage of industry was reached when the producer worked on raw material which he owned. He made as many goods as he hoped to sell, either immediately or in the future. Production was more efficient because it did not have to start and stop in response to demand but could be adapted to the conditions of manufacture. The producer devoted all his time to manufacturing and sold directly to the consumer, either at his own workshop or by peddling his wares. This stage was that of retail handicraft, since the manufacturer was also his own salesman in a retail market. Retail handicraft continued until long after the Middle Ages to be the most common type of industrial activity. The volume of manufacture for each shop was small and the market was local.

Large-scale industrial enterprise was not possible until after the commercial revolution was well under way. In this third stage, merchants rather than craftsmen were the organizers. They had access to raw materials not obtainable locally, they could buy them in larger quantities at lower prices, and they could secure raw materials of better quality in distant markets. Just as important, the great merchant could sell in large quantities in foreign markets at prices which might be higher because of greater demand. Both in buying raw material and in selling finished goods the great merchant could take advantage of market conditions, of improving credit facilities, and of the efficiency of transactions of greater volume. So far as manufacture was concerned, he used what is called a "putting-out system." He would secure raw material from the market, which might be remote (e.g., wool from northern England), transport it to his warehouse (e.g., in Flanders or Florence), put out the material to craftsmen who sold the merchants their skilled labor and the use of their equipment (e.g., spinning, weaving, and dyeing), after which the merchant would take the finished product (woolen cloth) and sell it in the most favorable market (e.g., northern Germany). Between the sheep raiser and the ultimate retail consumer there were many operations, all controlled by a merchant, as in this example, or by several merchants each specializing in one particular operation, such as exporting the wool or dealing in finished cloth. The craftsmen at no stage owned either raw material or product; the manufacture was for a wholesale transaction or what has been called wholesale handicraft.

Craftsmen who were engaged in large-scale manufacture were essentially wage earners with little control over their own economic welfare. To protect themselves from exploitation by the merchants they had to organize —just as the merchants had earlier organized to protect themselves in a hostile feudal world. Many of these artisans were never able to organize effectively, but others adopted a form of organization that had grown up with the older retail handicraft. This was the craft gild, an association of men engaged in the same handicraft or trade for their mutual benefit. The earliest craft gilds go back to the eleventh century, and in their origin were probably voluntary associations for social and religious as well as economic purposes. In the earliest craft gild records we hear as much about worship in common, provision for burial, care of the sick, and drinking wassail as we do of economic rules and regulations. The religious and social elements were never lost, but by the end of the thirteenth century the primary business of the craft gild was business.

The main objective of the craft gild was to protect its members from each other, from outsiders, from consumers and from merchant suppliers of raw materials. To this end gild regulations minutely controlled almost all activities. Fair trade (or minimum) prices were set, as well as the wages of hired labor. The quality and quantity of goods produced, the standards of workmanship, the hours of work, the training of apprentices, the requirements for entrance into the gild as a master, and other matters were all regulated. One main purpose of the gild was to provide and enforce equal opportunity for all members and to prevent any one member from gaining an unfair competitive advantage. The notion of free private enterprise was anathema. In the small and relatively stable local market the rapid rise of one member's trade could be achieved only at the expense of other members. The craftsmen's goal was monopoly for the gild. Stringent penalties were laid on members and economic sanctions were invoked against outsiders who endangered the gild's control of the market. This control was often enhanced by privileges granted by rulers or town governments.

During the twelfth and thirteenth centuries, it was fairly easy for a youthful apprentice to enter a craft and work his way up to the status of a master or full member of a gild. He did so by learning his trade at the expense of a master (in return for his labor) for a period which was often as long as seven years. After apprenticeship he might in some cases, especially if related by marriage or blood to a master, become a master himself at once. Entrance to the mastership depended on having the requisite skill as a craftsman, possessing citizenship in the town, owning or having the use of an adequately equipped shop, and being able to post bond against claims from customers or breach of gild rules. Not everyone could satisfy these requirements immediately after apprenticeship. Most workers became journeymen for a period of years, traveling about and hiring themselves out, until they had gained enough capital and experience to become a master.

Of the three most significant developments in commerce during the high Middle Ages, one has already been noted, the entrance of merchants into the industrial field in connection with their large-scale and long-distance trade. Another development was the fair. Beginning in a few localities as early as the eleventh century, their number and importance grew until the thirteenth century, the golden age of the medieval fair. What the weekly village market or the daily town market were for local and retail trade, the annual or semiannual fair was for wholesale and long-distance trade. Every region with a substantial population had its fair and many a countryside had its smaller fair—like the modern state and county fairs. A few of the greatest fairs were truly international institutions. Their success depended upon a favorable geographical location, where two or more important trade routes crossed or converged. The most famous were those held east of Paris in the county of Champagne, a region from which navigable streams and land routes spread out in all directions. The fairs of Champagne were held at six different times at one or another of four different towns, from early spring to late autumn of each year. The counts of Champagne, like other enlightened feudal rulers, encouraged and protected the fairs because tolls and taxes collected there were a considerable source of revenue.

This revenue included the fees and fines collected in a special court held during the fair. Since the fair usually lasted no more than several days —even the largest ended after a fortnight or three weeks—merchants needed speedy justice in the settlement of their disputes. This was provided by the informal procedure of a court administering the law merchant, in England called the Court of Piepowder because merchants could come into court with the dust of the fair still on their feet (*pieds poudrés*, dusty feet). Here also merchants could have their contracts, bills of exchange, agreements, and other documents authenticated by the seal of the clerk of the fair.

The third important commercial development in the thirteenth century involved more complex financial methods. The origins of modern credit operations lie in the transactions of the great merchants, especially the buying and selling of large quantities of goods at the fairs. Rather than take the risk of carrying with them the huge sums of money necessary to purchase goods, merchants preferred to take the smaller risk of trusting each other. The seller would accept from the buyer a written and sealed promise to pay in the future. Since most merchants were both buyers and sellers of goods, they were both creditors and debtors to other merchants. Many of these debts and credits canceled out, or nearly so. It was found expedient therefore to settle accounts by the exchange of actual money at infrequent intervals, after the net sums due or owed were determined during the last day of an annual fair. Money changers supplied the currency for these clearing houses at the fairs. The money changers also developed methods for safekeeping the money of others held on deposit, from which they would pay out, on order of the depositor, sums owed to a third party. This was one origin of the modern check.

The bill of exchange was a convenient device by which credit did the work of money. It was a promise to pay, a negotiable piece of "commercial paper" allowing merchants to settle accounts and transfer payments without going through clearing houses or money changers. In its simplest form, supposing merchant A owes B 100 shillings and C owes D 100 shillings: A sends B a promise to pay 100 shillings which B sells to C for that amount; C then sends the promise (i.e., to pay off his debt) to D, and D recovers the 100 shillings from A who originally promised to pay it. The real convenience of this kind of credit is obvious if, in this example, A and D are merchants of one town and B and C are merchants of another town. No money needs to be shipped from either town, but both A and C have paid off their debts in the same amount.

Despite the importance of industrial and commercial developments, the total economy of Europe in the thirteenth century remained predominantly rural and agricultural. Traditional ways of working and living on the manor, and the techniques of agricultural exploitation, did not greatly change. Impressed by these facts, historians have often emphasized the static nature of medieval European society as a whole. But a closer investigation of rural economic conditions has revealed several changes or developments, two of which were highly significant. The first consisted of divergent tendencies away from traditional manorial management. In some parts of Europe, notably England, manorial lords turned their energies to farming for market and for profit. They enlarged their manorial demesnes and exacted full labor services from their peasants, or even increased these services. The earlier trend toward leasing the demesne to peasants and commuting services into cash rents, a practice which caught lords between rising prices and fixed money income, was reversed. The period c.1200–1340 in England was the great age of "demesne farming" to increase production and improve farming methods in order to take advantage of rising prices. When the manorial economy of subsistence gave way to high farming for the market the peasants suffered greater exploitation, but they were in no position to offer effective resistance. When leases expired lords canceled them; lords won most of the disputes concerning the amount of labor services owed by the peasants; and lords were usually able to encroach upon the peasants' customary rights of common in meadows, woods, waste, and pasture. Finally, it should be added that the actual situation varied from manor to manor and that no general rule applied everywhere. Not all lords were willing to commute services in the twelfth century, and by no means did every lord require services in the thirteenth. Many lords reserved the right to require either services or cash rent, from year to year, as they saw fit. A sure sign of the interest of English lords in the various means by which manorial income might be increased was the appearance, toward the end of the thirteenth century, of the earliest treatises concerning estate management. Such was the little work *On Husbandry* by Walter of Henley.

If demesne farming was the growing practice in some areas, the reverse tendency characterized the rural economy in other areas, notably many parts of France, the Low Countries, and on the eastern frontier. French lords were willing to lease their demesnes and to commute services. It has been conjectured that the reason was the relatively greater importance to French lords of their political activities. The seigniory in France was primarily a unit of local government. In England royal officials in shire and hundred had come to predominate in local government, so that the English manor was increasingly an economic rather than a jurisdictional unit. In any case the French nobility did not develop the economic interests that characterized their English counterparts. French lords gradually relinquished the various services and payments in kind in return for annual rents from the peasantry. The predominance of peasant rentals in the Low Countries and on the eastern frontier was probably a consequence of the premium on labor in those parts. Great efforts were expended in draining the low country in Flanders and clearing forests in the east, and this labor could be attracted only by offering favorable terms and conditions.

The other most important rural development of the thirteenth century was the extension of the eastern frontier beyond central Germany. In the north it reached the Vistula by about 1200 and was extended all the way around the Baltic shores and into Latvia and Estonia by the end of the century. The resistance put up by the Slavic Pomeranians, the Baltic Prussians and Letts, and the Finnish Livs and Esths was broken during the middle years of the thirteenth century by the Knights of the Teutonic Order, a military crusading order which abandoned the Holy Land in favor of converting the heathen peoples of the north when the king of Poland invited it to conquer the Baltic area. In the wake of the Teutonic Knights came immigrants from the Low Countries and Germany to settle towns and villages under the lordship of the Knights and of a small number of the German nobility. By the end of the century this area had begun to flourish as a center of production and trade. Food was exported westward, and German merchants began to replace Scandinavians in the trade of the Baltic and farther east with Russia. This thrust into northeastern Europe constituted the final medieval expansion of Latin Christendom.

63 THE SECULARIZATION OF MEDIEVAL INSTITUTIONS AND VALUES

The influence of both the Church and, to a lesser degree, Christianity began to decline in the high Middle Ages. With a gradual and uneven progress, secular institutions and values have become increasingly important ever since. The secularization of medieval society can be illustrated by almost every aspect of life in the thirteenth century. It should, however, be kept in mind that "secularization" is a relative term. At no time was medieval civilization as secular as the modern world.

The causes of so complex a development were numerous, and it is impossible to assess the weight or exact role of any one of them. Here it will have to suffice merely to illustrate what was happening in several fields. A more complex economic life helped undermine the teachings of the Church on economic matters. The Church taught that people engaged in trade should avoid the sin of avarice. They should charge a "just price" for their goods, this being defined as the cost of the material plus the value of the labor expended on it. Any higher price was uncharitable to one's neighbor (the buyer), and the good Christian was expected to give to charity the difference between the just price and any higher price at which he sold. In a totally stable, local, and small-scale market such counsels of perfection might provide a healthy ideal for the exchange of goods, but by the end of the thirteenth century the teaching was obsolete. Merchants who stood ready to suffer occasional losses of large sums, in order to transact their far-flung business, felt justified in rejecting the formula of the just price. They not only increased the price to cover their risks, but, since risks are difficult to calculate, they erred on the side of raising the price as high as the market would bear—just in case their next transaction were a total loss through piracy or shipwreck. Canon lawyers recognized the impossibility of the just price in a complex economy, and they were willing to modify the formula by recognizing the element of risk, the effect of varying supply and demand, and what today would be called overhead costs. Meanwhile gilds were regulating prices and individual merchants were charging what they could, and neither paid much attention to the moral consequences of their decisions.

The teaching of the Church on usury was also based on the concept of avarice as a sin. Anyone who could lend money was assumed to have more than he needed for his own livelihood; anyone who borrowed was assumed to be too poor to sustain himself—else why should he want to borrow? Under these circumstances, to lend freely was a charitable act, but to charge interest on the loan was to take advantage of another's poverty. Today usury means exorbitant interest; in the early Middle Ages any interest at all was called usury, and even the lowest interest rate was considered morally exorbitant. But the facts were rapidly outstripping the moral teaching of the Church. Most of the men who sought loans were not charity-fed paupers but businessmen and manorial lords who needed capital for commercial or agricultural enterprise, or nobles who were living beyond their normal means to keep up the proper appearances. The most important borrowers of all were governments. When political policy or military exigencies required castle building along frontiers or the fortification of towns, such projects could not be paid for out of ordinary revenues. The only recourse was to borrow money against future income, and this could be done only by paying interest. Even the papal government, while deploring usury, found it necessary to borrow heavily and pay interest. The simple teaching of the Church on usury broke down before the elaborate and sometimes devious exceptions developed by the canonists to allow interest under certain conditions. For example, if the lender were risking the loss of his money a moderate interest charge was not to be considered usury. Like the history of the just price, the history of usury illustrates the gradual triumph of secular over religious values.

In even more dramatic fashion political developments illustrate the growing secularization of society in the thirteenth century. As we have seen, the Church took the lead in trying to establish orderly and peaceful conditions during the turbulent early days of feudalism. Dramatic struggles, like those between Gregory VII and the emperor Henry IV or between Archbishop Thomas Beckett and Henry II of England, should not obscure the fact that in general the Church supported strong rulers who could keep their vassals under control. The Church not only taught the virtue of obedience to secular rulers; most secular governments were largely staffed by churchmen—clerks in lower positions and prelates in the higher offices. In the coronation service kings were consecrated with holy oil, a symbol of divine sanction for just rule. Partly because of Church support, royal governments grew more powerful. The king's peace supplanted the Peace of God.

About the year 1200, most Europeans would have been hard put to decide where their primary loyalty or allegiance was placed. Was it to the local political unit, the barony or the town; or was it to the greater unit, the kingdom or feudal principality; or was it to the totality of Latin Christendom? Opinion would certainly have been divided, but most people would have felt their greatest emotional attachment directed toward the universal Christian commonwealth and their greatest material interests bound up with the locality in which they lived. The intermediate unit of kingdom or duchy (or even the county in some regions) would have been last in the division of loyalties. By the end of the thirteenth century this situation was largely altered. The sense of belonging to a local community or of being a member of Christendom persisted, but the balance of men's allegiance had shifted to the kings and greater lords who governed territorial principalities.

This shift took place at different times and in different ways in different regions. In England and France the monarchies won out, but in northern Italy the struggle for power was most often won by the communes as they expanded into territorial city-states. The main goal of the governments of the thirteenth century was to eliminate divided loyalties within the territories under their jurisdiction. This did not mean the destruction of competing jurisdictions, such as the seignioral rights and privileges of the lay nobles or of the Church, but rather the definition and limitation of those jurisdictions so that the central government was recognized as supreme over all subordinate authority. The characteristic expression of this supremacy was the power of the government to determine and settle all jurisdictional disputes within its territory. The central government did not directly take over the functions of feudal or ecclesiastical courts, nor did it abolish local seigniorial administration. But it did insist upon drawing the line between its own jurisdiction and that of lords and prelates. In doing so, the government usually resolved disputes in its own favor and always claimed that subordinate jurisdiction was exercised as a delegated power subject to supervision and correction by the central authority.

This growth of lay governments in the high Middle Ages undermined the influence of the Church in many ways. As their powers grew their activities increased. This meant that governments had to recruit increasing numbers of officials and "civil servants" to assess and collect taxes, preside over and staff courts, maintain peace, keep jails, guard prisoners, investigate complaints, and eliminate abuses of local jurisdiction. Government service became a new career open to the talents, as joining the clergy always had been. By the end of the thirteenth century government "clerks" were no longer always clerics. Laymen trained in the legal profession found easy access to important posts, and the minor officialdom of government attracted increasing numbers of ambitious but uneducated laity.

Contemporaries objected—then even as today—to the evils of bureaucracy. By bureaucracy they meant not only the number of officials but also the way they operated. Older and more casual methods were replaced by the impersonal and ruthless efficiency of royal agents whose own profit lay in promoting the power of their masters. Specialization of function marked the expansion of administrative and judicial work. Different departments or bureaus of the central government were responsible for different activities; orders to local officials were sent out and reports received. Government by discussion gave way to government by writing. Records were kept carefully, and the official memory of the government was preserved in those duplicates and triplicates of communications and correspondence that are the characteristic feature of every bureaucracy.

The size and power of medieval "big government" should not be exaggerated, especially as compared with the governments of modern times, but it is a basic political fact of the high Middle Ages that the thirteenth century witnessed the origins of modern governmental bureaucracy, as it also witnessed the still small beginnings of modern "big business." For the first time the well-organized Church was confronted with an equally well-organized lay authority aggressively competing for power and influence. The Church as a whole responded by improving its organization and making its ecclesiastical administration more efficient. This was a great age of provincial and diocesan synods, of episcopal visitation of monasteries and other ecclesiastical foundations, and of the enforcement of clerical reform at the parish level. The reform of the discipline and the morals of the clergy was vigorously carried forward by both bishops and papal legates. In its spiritual and ecclesiastical functions the Church in the thirteenth century came nearer to realizing the religious ideals of her own teaching than in any earlier age. But in activities where ecclesiastical and secular authority overlapped or collided, the Church (and especially the papacy) more and more frequently seemed guided by the same secular values that dominated lay governments.

In this sense the Church may be said to have become more secularized. The Church had formerly possessed a far greater proportion of the total wealth of Europe; she had often been despoiled and her offices invaded by greedy lay lords who, quite literally, secularized the Church. But these were not the important causes of secularization in the thirteenth century. The general complaint of critics like Dante was that the Church and, specifically, the papacy were too much embroiled in politics and competed all too well in worldly matters that should have been left to secular rulers. The papal *curia* was more advanced than most lay governments in bureaucratic specialization. What impressed contemporaries even more was the willingness of the papacy to impose frequent and heavy taxes on the clergy to support the essentially political or secular goals of papal policy in Italy and elsewhere. Also, the effectiveness of such religious sanctions as excommunication and the interdict was declining, together with papal prestige, because popes used these spiritual penalties as political weapons against emperors, kings, and others.

As the power and influence of the Church declined, the arguments and claims of papal apologists grew. Political theory did not keep pace with changing political realities. Supporters of the papacy made more and more extreme statements; but most of their arguments were couched in the well-worn terms of competing jurisdictions within Christendom as a whole, the *respublica Christiana*, at a time when that unity was being fractured by the rise of the national monarchies of the West. Lawyers in the service of the French monarchy, for example, spelled out the notion of royal supremacy within the territorial limits of the French realm, best summarized by the formula, "The king is emperor within his kingdom." Another popular idea was expressed, toward the end of the thirteenth century, by French and English lawyers who adapted the canonical doctrine of necessity to serve the interests of their secular rulers. According to this doctrine, the king might exercise what are today called "emergency powers" in the defense of national welfare. Thus, the king might legitimately tax the clergy in time of war, and the vested rights or privileges of both the nobility and the Church had to give way to the higher demands of the community as a whole. The community was, of course, defined as the national community under royal jurisdiction. Against these views favoring the temporal authority theorists on the other side were no less eager to promote the universal claims of papal jurisdiction. Perhaps the most popular of all the treatises advocating the supreme temporal as well as spiritual power of the pope was the *Summa de Potestate Ecclesiastica* (c.1325) by Augustinus Triumphus. In this work Augustinus assembled and systematically presented all the arguments of his predecessors. In typically scholastic fashion he argued from first principles logically to the conclusion that the pope holds his power immediately of God and therefore is the supreme judge of, and on earth the source of, all law and secular (as well as spiritual) authority. There is nothing really new in these arguments except the extreme lengths to which they are pushed.

These ideas, as presented by royal legists and papal apologists alike, may be considered typically medieval in the sense that they were concerned primarily with the nature of authority: rights, duties, and the delimitation of conflicting jurisdictions. A radically new note was struck in a contemporary treatise, the *Defensor Pacis* (1324), whose joint authors, John of Jandun and Marsiglio of Padua, added to the usual legalistic arguments about authority a sociological analysis of the structure of society and of the role of government in society. According to John and Marsiglio the maintenance of peace required that there should be no conflict of jurisdictions. The only way to prevent conflict between the secular and spiritual authorities was to abolish the jurisdiction of the latter. The civil government, they argued, should be supreme and the Church ought not to have any coercive authority whatever, whether temporal or spiritual. The Church, in this view, was to be simply a department of the state. In the *Defensor Pacis* the new secularism of the high Middle Ages was finally made explicit in political theory.

England in the High Middle Ages

Henry II died in 1189, an embittered old man. His grandiose plans for the Angevin empire had come to naught. But so far as England was concerned, his rule was the strongest of any feudal monarch of his times; his reforms and innovations provided a solid foundation for the constitutional development of England during several centuries. The system of government which he bequeathed his successors continued to grow stronger even under unfavorable circumstances. Richard was for all practical purposes an absentee ruler. John was the most unpopular monarch ever to rule England. And Henry III, succeeding to the crown as a boy of nine, gave England her first regency; later, he tried ineffectually to impose his own weak and vacillating will upon his realm. And yet when Edward I became king in 1272 the English monarchy was flourishing as never before, despite major political crises in each of the three preceding reigns. French kings might have more officials and greater resources in both wealth and manpower, but France was too large and the French nobility too strong to be controlled as effectively as the English kings governed their tight little island realm.

The main interest of English history in the Middle Ages lies in the constitutional development of a country whose political institutions matured earlier and have endured longer than those of any other nation. The foremost of these was Parliament. Perhaps the most striking fact about this venerable institution was that contemporaries paid so little attention to it. Chronicles and governmental records ignore its beginning, quite properly, for there was no one meeting that can be said to have been the "first parliament," and thus no date can be assigned to its beginning. Parliament just grew. Although it grew out of the feudal monarch's *curia regis*, Parliament in the later Middle Ages also contained elements unknown to the earlier *curia regis*. The most important of these were the representatives of local communities, the knights of the shires and the burgesses of the boroughs.

What made the English Parliament unique was not how it began but how it survived and grew in the later Middle Ages and in early modern times. Not only in England, but all over Europe medieval rulers summoned assemblies of great lords (ecclesiastical or lay or both together) and of representatives of local communities (meeting by themselves or together with the great lords). The difference was that in England representative institutions continued to flourish, while elsewhere they withered.

64   THE LOSS OF NORMANDY, MAGNA CARTA, AND THE BARONS' WAR

Richard I (1189–1199) had already taken the cross when he became king. Before departing for the Holy Land he visited England for four months, to receive his crown and arrange for the government in his absence. After he returned from the Third Crusade he was in England two more months; he spent the rest of his reign on the continent. Richard had grown up in France, had made his mark as duke of Aquitaine, and was the least English of all medieval kings of England. He cared little for the art of government, and even less for England. His consuming interest was warfare; for recreation he dabbled with poetry and music, and he was a patron of troubadours. He was a popular king because he was an able leader in war. His barons respected him on the battlefield and he was indefatigable in defending his dominions against his greatest enemy, who was also his feudal lord, the French king.

In his initial arrangement for the government in his absence, Richard made the mistake of dividing authority between two justiciars and his brother John, a situation that invited a struggle for power. One justiciar was a representative aristocrat; the other was a civil servant who had risen from humble origins in the service of Richard of Aquitaine. The latter was William Longchamp, who combined his office of justiciar with that of chancellor and (after he was made bishop of Ely) papal legate. In the three-cornered struggle that followed, Longchamp's unscrupulous methods won him a temporary supremacy, while John was cast in the anomalous role of leading the opposition against Longchamp's tyranny. In 1191 most of the bishops and barons, together with John and his personal supporters, deposed Longchamp by a formal judgment of the *curia regis* acting in the king's absence. Out of this crisis there emerged a rudimentary notion of the right of the baronage to act collectively in defense of their rights through the ordinary judicial machinery. In contrast with the great rebellion of 1173 against Henry II, the movement in 1191 was not against the government but against misgovernment. John, seeking only his own advantage, was in strange company. He continued to conspire for power and even plotted to replace his brother on the throne.

In 1193 the government was once more firmly in the hands of Richard's supporters under the lead of Hubert Walter, one of the most capable administrators to serve any medieval king. As archbishop of Canterbury, papal legate, and justiciar, Hubert Walter combined the supreme ecclesiastical and secular authority of the realm. Itinerant justices increased their activity, local officials were appointed to keep the peace, the power of the sheriffs was curbed, and the central government became more efficient. It is from the period of Hubert Walter's administration that the earliest official records survive of the judicial work of the central court. These were the plea rolls or *curia regis* rolls, which are by far the oldest court records of any European government.

The main task of Richard's government in England was to raise money to support his several ventures and to pay off the king's ransom. While returning from the crusade Richard was captured in Austria by his enemies who turned him over to the emperor (1192–1194). In spite of occasional and local resistance the money was raised. Almost every medieval form of taxation was employed: an extraordinary feudal aid (owed by any vassal to ransom his lord, but in this case collected from subvassals as well under the guise of scutage), an income tax, a tax on personal property, a land tax, and a variety of other methods, such as tallages, extortionate fines, and forced loans. After Richard's return (1194) tremendous sums of money were extracted from England to pay for castle building in Normandy and to defray the expenses of reconquering territories lost to Philip Augustus, the French king. The war went well, but in the midst of it Richard was mortally wounded in a minor skirmish.

John's reign (1199–1216) got off to a bad start. The succession was disputed by supporters of his nephew Arthur, son of his older brother Geoffrey, late count of Brittany. The unexplained death of this nephew while in John's custody gave rise to unpleasant rumors. Even more important, John became embroiled with several of his French vassals who appealed for justice to their overlord, the French king. In accordance with feudal custom, John was summoned to answer his vassals' charges in the royal court of his French lord. When John refused to appear, Philip Augustus secured judgment against him and sentenced him to the loss of his French fiefs. John tried to defend himself but in the ensuing warfare he betrayed a fatal lack of military capacity, and within two years Philip had conquered Normandy (1204).

The loss of Normandy was a severe blow to John's prestige and power. His futile efforts to reconquer the duchy became a continuing drain on his resources. Of his three great defeats, this one was the most damaging. However, the separation of Normandy from England did contribute to the growth of nationalism—a sense of national interest and self-consciousness—because the barons who held lands in both Normandy and England now had to choose between John and Philip. If they continued their allegiance to John, Philip confiscated their Norman lands, while John confiscated the English lands of all barons who transferred their allegiance to Philip.

The next great crisis of John's reign was his quarrel with Innocent III over the election of Stephen Langton as archbishop of Canterbury, in 1206. England was placed under an interdict (1208) and John was excommunicated (1209), but not until 1213 did he capitulate. That he could hold out for seven years under such circumstances was proof of the strength of the royal government. John was supported by most of the barons and bishops on this issue, and his final capitulation did not in fact weaken his position. By becoming the vassal of the pope John now gained a powerful ally who could restrain his greatest foreign enemy, Philip Augustus. But meanwhile enemies were gathering at home.

These were the growing number of barons who objected to the desperate means by which John tried to raise funds for his campaign to recover his lost French lands. They were bold enough to speak out against the often arbitrary methods John employed in governing England and in exploiting his position as feudal lord. Stephen Langton, as archbishop and papal legate, tried to mediate between king and barons. By his insistence that John should observe the laws and customs of the realm—and especially to refrain from punishing his enemies without giving them a trial by due process of feudal law—Stephen succeeded in introducing some broader principles into the essentially feudal demands of the dissident barons. Thus Stephen allowed himself to become the spokesman for the opposition to John. The signal for a general uprising was the conspicuous failure of John's campaign to defeat Philip Augustus in the summer of 1214. The plan had been to crush Philip between John's forces, invading from Aquitaine, and the army of the emperor, Otto IV, who drove westward across the Low Countries. Philip's victory over the emperor at Bouvines put an end to that plan, and John's dilatory indecisions kept him from making any gains even while the French were committed against his German allies. John returned to England to raise money for another campaign and found instead a rebellion.

After fruitless negotiations the barons formally renounced their homage, by *diffidatio*, and John was forced to submit. The king met the rebels at Runnymede in June, 1215, and peace was preserved temporarily when he set his seal to a document containing their demands. From this draft the chancery clerks drew up a better worded and slightly modified version that is known as Magna Carta—the Great Charter. This version was issued under the great seal in numerous copies, of which four survive today. (There is no single document which can be called the "original" copy.)

The core of Magna Carta is the set of feudal grievances of the dissident barons, and the charter is essentially a statement of feudal laws and customs which the king bound himself to observe. This statement was detailed and specific: the document is a bill of particulars, not a "constitution" of principles. The barons were particularly insistent on limiting the financial exactions of the king as feudal lord. By defining the amount to be paid for reliefs, by limiting the king's rights with respect to the feudal incidents of wardship and marriage, and by requiring that no scutages or extraordinary aids be imposed without the consent of all the barons and prelates properly assembled, the charter restricted the financial resources of the monarchy. But Magna Carta was more than a definition of the rights and obligations of feudal society, and it was more than a reactionary feudal attack upon the king. In one clause the liberties of the Church in England were guaranteed, in others the rights and privileges of the boroughs, especially those of the merchants, were set forth; and the clauses dealing with administrative and judicial matters benefited all free men of England. For example, almost all the judicial reforms of Henry II were recognized to be important elements in the government and in the laws and customs of the realm. These broader provisions of the charter were the result of wiser heads than could be found among the rebel barons. They were probably the work of Stephen Langton and the moderate group that supported the king. Most important of all the clauses was the thirty-ninth, which enshrined the principle of due process of law: no free man was to be proceeded against except by legal judgment of his peers or by the law of the land.

The essence of Magna Carta was thus a recognition of the principle that the king was under the law, that his rule was not arbitrary but limited. But it went too far: it also incorporated, in the final clause, a provision for enforcement by a committee of twenty-five barons who were given a right of resistance by force if John should transgress any of his promises. That John accepted this clause shows that he had no intention of keeping his word. Nor did the barons. The latter were already preparing for war when John appealed to Innocent III, who annulled the charter as an illegal and immoral invasion of royal governance. Civil war broke out, and the barons appealed to Louis, son of Philip Augustus, offering him the crown in return for military assistance. Hence as a peace treaty Magna Carta had little actual effect on the course of events under John. Its significance lay in the future and in the amended version of 1225, which was confirmed again and again in the next three centuries as a statement of the fundamental laws and customs of the realm.

John's death shortly after the outbreak of civil war saved the situation for the government. Already some of the barons had deserted to the royalist side; now most of them came over to the government. Since Henry III (1216–1272) was a minor, a regency was established under the influence of two of the older barons, William Marshal and Hubert de Burgh, and of the papal legate. Resistance broke down quickly when the regency, as an act of good faith, immediately reissued Magna Carta, omitting all controversial clauses with the promise to reconsider them when peace had been restored. This promise was kept (in 1217 and again in 1225). The goal of the regency was to restore the monarchy on the basis of consultation and cooperation with the baronage. This balance of power was maintained until Henry came of age and even afterwards until Hubert de Burgh was dismissed from his office of justiciar, in 1232. Then Henry III tried to assert his full control over royal administration and royal policy. He was not well qualified for this task. He lacked the leadership to carry an unpopular policy and the personal independence necessary for good judgment. Henry III was well educated, a connoisseur of the arts, a good husband and father, a loyal friend and a devout Christian—a good man but a weak king. His personal relations with the majority of his barons remained cordial for many years, but slowly his authority and prestige were undermined.

Among the baronial grievances three were especially important. First, the barons disliked Henry's reliance on his friends and relatives from France, in his royal council and in the administrative offices of state, asserting that the king's natural councillors and governmental officials should be his English barons. Second, the barons opposed Henry's ambitious but unsuccessful efforts to reconquer the French lands of the crown. This opposition was caused partly by opposition to the necessary taxes and partly by a slowly developing reaction to Henry's military incompetence. Barons who had, earlier, been glad to follow the king and help pay for the campaigns became disillusioned and reluctant to take the field or raise money for such a hopeless project. Third, the barons were disgusted with "the Sicilian business" which took so much of Henry's time and money. This was the prolonged negotiation (1254–1258) that obliged Henry to pay off the huge debts incurred by the papacy in its war against the Hohenstaufen in Italy, in return for the grant of the kingdom of Sicily to his son, Edmund.

Henry, hopelessly in debt, had to turn to his barons for help. His appeal was greeted with a demand for reforms and for greater baronial participation both in the administrative work of the government and in the formulation of royal policy. The barons' program, beginning with the Provisions of Oxford (1258), put the government under the joint direction of the king and a baronial council. Abuses of local government were investigated, most of the sheriffs were replaced by new men, and inquiries were made into alienations of royal rights that might deprive the king of revenues. In foreign policy, the barons pushed forward negotiations already begun by Henry with Louis IX of France. The result was a general settlement and the establishment of peace—technically, England and France had been at war since 1204—by the Treaty of Paris, 1259. The constructive work of the first few years of reform was impressive, and Henry grudgingly went along with most of the demands. The great difference between the baronial action of 1215 and that of 1258–1264 was that the essential goal of Magna Carta was to *limit* the government, while the essential goal of the Provisions of Oxford and the other enactments preceding the Barons' War was to *control* the government. The events of 1258 have been aptly summed up in the statement that the monarchy was "put into commission," and it was a baronial commission.

There was little, actually, that Henry could do except bide his time. There was no practicable way to re-establish his control over the government or bring back his friends and relatives into official positions. But time played on the king's side. Gradually the barons developed rifts in their ranks—sometimes by the clash of personalities, often by a clash of interests. From the beginning Henry enjoyed the support of a minority of the barons, and now the more moderate barons of the opposition began to join this group. It was only a small number of extremists, led by Simon de Montfort, who pressed for the full execution of the baronial program. After much acrimonious debate and a brief resort to arms, the leaders of the extremist faction and of Henry's party agreed to submit their differences to the arbitration of Louis IX, who was asked to pass judgment on the Provisions of Oxford and disputes growing out of them. It took Louis IX less than a week to decide and declare in his Mise of Amiens, 1264, that the Provisions were null and void, an illegal invasion of royal rights. Simon and his followers were shocked. All along they had been acting in the king's name and on every issue they had gained the king's acceptance, however grudgingly granted. This meant war.

The Barons' War was settled by two major battles. At Lewes, in 1264, Simon de Montfort was victorious. During the next fifteen months he was in fact the sole ruler of England, although he continued to rule in the king's name. Then the royalist forces were rallied under the lord Edward, son and heir of Henry III, and at the battle of Evesham, 1265, Simon was killed, his army defeated, and his cause destroyed. The outcome, however, was not simply a royalist reaction. It took more than a year of fighting before Edward could track down all the rebels. By that time passions had cooled and a papal legate, the cardinal Ottobuono, arrived to take the lead in re-establishing peace.

Ottobuono's influence is seen in the Dictum of Kenilworth, 1266. By this royalist proclamation the king was recognized to have full control over the royal government, former rebels were allowed to redeem their confiscated lands by paying the king up to one half their value, and the laws and customs of the realm were confirmed as they had existed "before the time of this disturbance." Then, in 1267, most of the constructive reforms of the preceding nine years were incorporated into the Statute of Marlborough, which also contained a clause confirming Magna Carta. The work of the barons in 1258 and later was thus not wholly in vain. Furthermore, these years provided an education in kingship for the lord Edward, who as king never forgot the lessons he had learned. Chief of these was the necessity for cooperation with the community of the realm—the barons and their followers of lesser status—if a king would be strong.

65   EDWARD I

Edward I (1272-1307) was perhaps medieval England's greatest king. Personally he was both a chivalrous leader and a ruler jealous of his rights and sometimes unscrupulous in maintaining them. His greatness did not lie in any unusual qualities but in the high degree to which he typified or realized the conventions of his age. He did everything that a king was expected to do. He was a crusader, he led his troops in battle, he made foreign conquests. And for most of his reign he ruled strongly and well, strengthening the laws, reforming the government, maintaining the peace, protecting the Church.

It is hazardous to reduce to a few generalizations a reign so important, so long, and so complex. With this caution in mind, three general conclusions may be stated concerning the significance of the reign of Edward I. First, the guiding principle of Edward's rule was the concept of the community of the realm, a concept midway between the feudal notion of individual rights as determining the relationship between ruler and subject, and the modern notion of the state. According to this concept the ruler is both obligated and empowered to act for the common welfare. To meet this great responsibility the ruler must possess and exercise the full range of royal authority, undiminished and unshared with anyone unless he is responsible to the ruler (e.g., a royal official appointed and dismissed at the king's pleasure). At the same time, according to this concept, subjects possess and exercise rights which are beyond the reach of royal governance except to maintain and protect. Hence subjects deserve to be consulted on all questions that concern their rights within the community. This was a highly legal concept, and Edward was a legal-minded ruler in a legalistic age. To him and his advisers the natural conclusion to draw from these premises was that the rights and obligations of all classes or groups must be subordinate to the common welfare of the whole community of the realm, and the king alone could be the ultimate judge of what would promote or be necessary for the common welfare. As we shall see in the next section of this chapter, these were some of the basic ideas underlying the rapid growth of parliament under Edward I.

Second, Edward's reign marks a stage in the growth of the common law equal in importance to the work of Henry II. Unlike the latter, Edward was not an innovator. The importance of Henry II's reforms lay in the area of procedure—the regular and frequent use of writs, juries, and itinerant justices as essential elements in the machinery of the law—while the importance of the statutes of Edward I lay in reconciling contradictions or eliminating inconsistencies in the laws. Edward I has been called the "English Justinian" because, like the Roman emperor, he was a great legislator. And like Justinian, Edward was less interested in creating new laws than in codifying and systematizing the old laws.

Third, the superficial brillance of Edward's reign—again like that of Justinian—obscured the fact that on his death the king left a government hopelessly in debt and committed to foreign wars that failed eventually, after huge costs in men and money.

The general pacification following the Barons' War proceeded so well that in 1270 Edward could depart on his long-planned Crusade. He was returning from this venture when he received the news of his father's death. In England the royal council proclaimed Edward king in his absence, took oaths of allegiance, and kept the administration running in orderly fashion. It was the first time that an English king was recognized to have succeeded from the day of his predecessor's death, rather than from the day of his own coronation. Edward did not get home until 1274, after attending to business in his French fiefs and enjoying a leisurely journey, often interrupted by hunting and jousting with friends.

On his arrival in England Edward launched a series of inquests into almost every aspect of local government. Searching questions were put to juries who were required to answer as to the state of royal manors and royal rights, the conduct of sheriffs and other officials, and the exercise of local jurisdiction (franchises) by feudal lords. Because the information was gathered hundred by hundred, within each county, the results were recorded and preserved on what are called the Hundred Rolls. These records were used by Edward to reform abuses and to regain illegally alienated or usurped royal lands and rights. The most important result of these inquests of 1274–1275 was a long series of judicial proceedings in which the lords of franchises were summoned to the royal courts by writs of *quo warranto*. These writs required each lord to prove "by what warrant" or authority he held his franchise. If the lord could produce a royal charter granting the franchise to him or one of his ancestors, he received a confirmation of his grant and was quit. However, most lords based their rights of jurisdiction on prescription, that is, long usage, and could not defend themselves with documentary evidence. To meet this situation, Edward directed his justices to confirm all franchises which had been continuously exercised since the accession of Richard (1189). Under these *quo warranto* proceedings some usurped franchises were recovered, but the primary motive was not an attack upon feudal jurisdiction. Edward wanted to establish the principle that all private jurisdiction was a delegation from the crown so that the royal government could supervise, intervene, and correct abuses within franchises just as it did in the local administration of county and hundred.

In the sphere of central government, Edward's goal was to secure efficiency, better organization, and a firmer personal control of the whole bureaucratic structure. The Exchequer and the Chancery were departments of state which by this time had already developed traditional and routine methods that sometimes had the force of law. They were unresponsive to the personal will of the ruler in the way that any cumbersome bureaucracy becomes an obstacle to efficient autocracy. Hence Edward relied increasingly on his own household officials as instruments of government directly under his control. The keeper of the Wardrobe used the privy seal, in his custody, to dispatch royal commands that required either the speed or secrecy no longer obtainable through the official channels of Exchequer or Chancery. The Wardrobe and other offices in the royal household did a great variety of business, from the purchase of wine for Christmas at court to the collection of taxes or the provisioning and financing of a major military campaign.

It was also during the reign of Edward I that the central courts emerged from the *curia regis*, after a century of development, as three separate and distinct tribunals, each with its own personnel, records, and jurisdiction. These were the Court of Common Pleas, where civil disputes were adjudicated; the Court of Exchequer, whose common law jurisdiction grew out of pleas involving debts to the crown; and the Court of King's Bench, which was concerned primarily with pleas of the crown or criminal cases and other cases in which the king was an interested party. The king remained the fount of justice. He exercised his residual and all-inclusive jurisdiction in his council. The royal council consisted of the greater officials, plus the judges and others (bishops, barons, servants or friends, clerk or lay) whom the king was pleased to appoint. Councillors might come and go on the king's business, but the council as a body was continual in the sense that it was always with the king. Its jurisdiction was undefined, its powers indefinite, its work unrestricted by the common law procedures followed by other courts. The council corrected errors on appeal from other courts and determined cases referred to it by judges because of their difficulty or importance or because they did not fall under the common law. As a contemporary writer put it, in the council "judicial doubts are determined and new remedies created for new wrongs, and . . . justice is done to every one according to his deserts." *Every* one, even the high and mighty: it was to the council that cases were often referred that involved malefactors of such rank and power as to overawe a local jury. The council also provided administrative supervision of the whole government and advised the king on royal policy. Its decisions, whether legal or administrative, were often promulgated by the king as one form of legislation. Its functions were undifferentiated, but in modern terminology the royal council was the executive, legislative, and judicial center and heart of the government.

In foreign affairs Edward had two main objectives, to extend his control over the British Isles and to protect his continental fiefs. Wales presented an immediate problem. Llywelyn ap Gruffyd, lord of the Welsh princes, refused to do homage. When Llywelyn ignored three successive summonses to appear before his lord's court, Edward launched an invasion. This was by no means the first effort to conquer Wales. English kings had claimed the overlordship of Wales since before the Norman Conquest, and this claim had been formalized during the twelfth century by the feudal bond of homage uniting the more important Welsh princes to the king, as vassals to lord. Endless disputes between the king, the Welsh princes, and aggressive Anglo-Norman lords only increased the natural turbulence of Wales and the Marches (frontier). Henry II tried and failed to bring order through conquest. John tried and failed, and a nationalistic reaction followed under Llywelyn the Great (1194–1240), whose supremacy in Wales was recognized when he did homage to Henry III (1218). His grandson was Llywelyn ap Gruffyd, who, taking advantage of Henry III's difficulties, reconquered most of the southern and eastern parts and, in 1258, created for himself the title of Prince of Wales.

Edward's invasion was carefully organized and ably supported by the Marcher lords. Llywelyn was forced to submit, renew his homage, and relinquish most of his power though not his title. By the treaty of Conway (1277) English rule was extended into many parts of Wales. Then in 1282 the Welsh suddenly rebelled against the new order, Llywelyn taking the lead. Edward had previously treated Llywelyn as a contumacious vassal who nonetheless deserved respect for his dignity and rights. Now, taken by surprise and furious, Edward threw all his resources into crushing the rebellion, dealing with Llywelyn and the Welsh simply as rebels whose aggression forfeited any consideration of rights. Llywelyn was killed (1283) and his brother David was captured; their heads were chopped off and exposed on lances on the Tower of London. By the Statute of Rhuddlan, 1284, Edward introduced an English type of administration throughout most of Wales. Welsh civil laws were preserved and administered in the old local districts by Welsh officials. English criminal law was introduced to preserve order under sheriffs who were the English administrators of the larger shires into which Wales was now divided.

The conquest of Wales was Edward's greatest glory, but it was also England's greatest burden. The campaigns of 1276–1277 and 1282–1284 required large armies not only of the feudal host but of even greater numbers of mercenary soldiers and as many more auxiliary scouts, woodsmen, road builders, carters, and, still more important, diggers, carpenters, and masons to construct field fortifications and castles. Edward conquered because he consolidated each gain by erecting a castle. War had become

Castles of Edward I in Wales. Harlech (above) and Caernarvon (late thirteenth century). PHOTOS: J. DIXON-SCOTT, AND BRITISH INFORMATION SERVICE.

very expensive. In twenty-five years of castle building after 1277 Edward spent £80,000, an unprecedented drain on the treasury. Raising taxes became the most prominent single feature of Edward's domestic policy in the later years of his reign—a policy that led to important constitutional results. Meanwhile, the title of Prince of Wales had lapsed with Llywelyn's death. Edward's queen, Eleanor of Castile, had accompanied her husband on the great campaign and in 1284 gave birth to a son in the new castle of Caernarvon. This son, Edward of Caernarvon, became heir apparent on the death of an older brother and—after two more rebellions in Wales had been suppressed at great expense—was created Prince of Wales in 1301. This gesture of conciliation was welcomed by the Welsh. Except for a few unimportant incidents, the problem of Wales was solved.

Ireland presented a quite different situation. Henry II had made his son John lord of Ireland in 1177. Although John failed as a youth to promote English interests in the half-conquered island, as king he was successful (his only success abroad) in expanding the area under English control and in strengthening the royal administration. After John, an endless round of petty wars of the Irish kinglets and English lords, both between each other and among themselves, characterized Irish history. The appointment of Edward as lord of Ireland in 1254 brought no great change. The English area, called the Pale, continued to grow slowly and the economic prosperity of the towns accentuated the difference between the more advanced occupied territory and the still primitive Gaelic lands, beyond the Pale, held by "the wild Irish," as the English called them. The natives found the peace and order brought by English domination not worth the high price of their loss of independence and of freedom to fight out their differences. During the reign of Edward I the most significant development was the introduction by the king's justiciars of English political institutions, notably an Irish parliament modeled closely on the English assembly.

Relations with Scotland were of a different order from those with Wales and Ireland. Scotland was a kingdom over which the king of England claimed rights of overlordship that had been acknowledged on several occasions. The king of Scots held lands in England for which he did homage as a matter of course. Under Alexander III (1249–1286) a united and prosperous Scotland finally wrested the western islands (the Hebrides and the Isle of Man) from the waning power of Norway. Alexander III's sons predeceased him and died childless; his daughter (married to the king of Norway) died giving birth to Margaret, "the Maid of Norway," who thus became heiress of Scotland. Unfortunately, Margaret died on the voyage taking her to her kingdom, in 1290. The question of the succession to the Scottish crown awakened old rivalries. More than a dozen claimants appeared, and they all appealed to Edward I to decide among them. This Edward was glad to do, since he could now claim that it was a recognition of his position as superior lord and since it gave him an opportunity to define his rights over Scotland, especially the right to hear appeals from vassals of the Scottish king.

The "great cause" of 1291–1292 turned out to be a prolonged debate about rules of succession and about the nature of a medieval kingdom. Going back for three generations, the male line of the royal family was extinct. Of the claimants the nearest of kin were John Baliol, grandson of the older daughter, and Robert Bruce, son of the younger daughter, of the brother of a Scottish king. Baliol's claim was the better by the feudal rule of primogeniture (i.e., a male of the older female line), but Bruce's claim was better by proximity, being one generation nearer to a crowned king. When Edward's legal advisers unanimously favored Baliol's claim, Bruce supported the argument put forward by other claimants that

England and France
in the High Middle Ages

Scotland was held of the English king like any English barony, and therefore it was partible between the descendants of the daughters as co-
heiresses. Edward's legal advisers ruled once more in favor of Baliol on the
ground that a realm was different from an honor: a kingdom was impartible
while a barony could be divided between co-heiresses or their heirs.

Baliol did not last long as king. His royal council was dominated by
anti-English magnates who entered into an alliance with the king of France
—an alliance that lasted until the union of England and Scotland in 1603.
Edward retaliated by invading Scotland (1296), deposing Baliol, and an-
nexing Scotland to England, but this action was followed by a widespread
rebellion led by William Wallace. Edward returned north and defeated
Wallace but was unable to subdue the rebels until 1304. In the following
year Wallace was captured and executed as a traitor. A form of government was drawn up to provide a joint Scottish-English administration
under Edward's control. Then Robert Bruce (grandson of the claimant in
1291–1292), who had already changed sides twice, murdered the only other
strong claimant to the throne and had himself crowned king of Scotland
in 1306. Edward organized a merciless suppression of Bruce's supporters,
but before the aging king could complete the task he died. Edward II had
no stomach for the grinding effort that had taxed his father's strength.
Bruce, a fugitive with only a small coterie of friends, returned to lead a
successful movement for Scottish independence.

In contrast with his generally aggressive policy toward Wales, Ireland, and Scotland, Edward I was on the defensive in his relations with
the king of France. The main problem was to enforce English rule in the
great southwestern fief of Gascony, held by Edward of the French crown,
against the French king's efforts to bring the lords of that area under more
effective control. As overlord, King Philip claimed the right to adjudicate
disputes and redress the grievances of Edward I's vassals, a claim that
Edward himself asserted over the vassals of the king of Scotland. In this
desultory struggle for power Edward found his most uesful allies in
Flanders, where the count and a faction of the townsmen aspired to independence against the king of France (the count's lord). When Anglo-
French relations deteriorated to the point of armed conflict, Edward chose
to fight in Flanders rather than in Gascony. But the French war never
developed into full-scale hostilities. Edward's policy was unwelcome to his
subjects, because expensive, and it was vigorously opposed by a faction of
his nobles. The latter took advantage of the king's desperate need for
money and his absence in Flanders to force Edward in 1297 to agree to a
solemn Confirmation of the Charters (Magna Carta and the Charter of
the Forest), and to agree that he would not impose unaccustomed levies or
collect taxes without the consent of his magnates. Baronial opposition to
his continental policy, in contrast with the general support he received for
his wars in Wales and Scotland, kept Edward from achieving any success

in his quarrels with the king of France, though he did retain possession of Gascony.

66 THE GROWTH OF PARLIAMENT IN ENGLAND AND THE ORIGINS OF MODERN REPRESENTATIVE INSTITUTIONS IN WESTERN EUROPE

The word "parliament" originally did not refer to any such institution as the British Parliament of today. It was simply a literary and descriptive term referring to any meeting and more especially to a meeting in which some conversation, or "parley," took place. When the king of England met the king of Scotland on the border between their realms to discuss matters of mutual concern, chroniclers could refer to their "parliament" on the northern English frontier; and when the queen of France met her husband, Louis IX, on the backstairs of the palace to exchange sweet nothings out of earshot of her mother-in-law, chroniclers could call that a "parliament" too. In this general sense any meeting of a feudal court, such as the *curia regis* or court of the lord king, could be called a parliament for much parleying might well go on at such a meeting, like the pleas and counterpleas of litigants in a legal dispute heard before the king and his *curia*. Contemporaries recognized the institution as the *curia regis*; the occasion of its meeting they might call a parliament or a *colloquium* (literally, a "talking together") or a great council.

Thus parliament in its origins was not an institution but an occasion, when the king met not only with his councillors who were always with him but also with his immediate vassals and other officials, servants, or important people whom he had summoned to attend upon him. The core and center of such a meeting was the king and his council. Hence the business which a parliament was preeminently equipped to handle was judicial business, and the medieval parliament not only began as but continued to be the king's High Court of Parliament. As a matter of convenience (the king's convenience, that is) parliament might serve other purposes as well. With the great men of his realm, the important tenants-in-chief, gathered about him the king might wish to discuss political questions and bind his prelates and barons to the support of royal policy, or he might wish to hear complaints and avail himself of advice for the better governance of his realm, or he might take the opportunity to receive the fealty and homage of vassals who recently had succeeded to baronies and estates held directly of the crown. Parliament was thus a High Court but like any medieval *curia* it was more. It was ultimately and essentially a meeting of those whom the king had summoned to his presence on a particular occasion.

Where kings were strong, as in England, such meetings took place frequently, and during the thirteenth century the character of such meetings began to change. In England the change was more profound and more rapid, and by the end of the Middle Ages the English Parliament was the strongest representative institution in Europe. The change was twofold. About the time that chroniclers were beginning to refer to certain meetings of the *curia regis* as parliaments, the magnates who attended such meetings were beginning to think of themselves not as a collection of individuals doing court service to their lord but as a group who spoke for and represented the nation as a whole. The king encouraged this development. There are instances where the prelates and barons granted taxes for themselves and also for all others in the kingdom—something that no king would object to and which could only enhance royal power on the theory that the whole kingdom was one "commune" or corporate society of which the magnates were leaders among the king's subjects. By the end of the thirteenth century the ecclesiastical and lay lords, as a group, not only spoke for or represented but even referred to themselves as if they *were* the "community of the realm." The origins of the later House of Lords can be traced back to this sense of corporate interest among the lords of the thirteenth century.

The other change that was to produce the Parliament of the later Middle Ages was the addition of representative elements to meetings of the *curia regis*. Representation as a method of government is far older than Parliament; in its origins Parliament was not representative—and in no way democratic. During the thirteenth century the English government employed the device of representation more frequently and effectively, but it was in no way radical or revolutionary. From an early day the priest, reeve, and four villeins of a township had represented the whole township for some purposes of local government. Juries in the courts of itinerant justices in the twelfth century spoke for and thus represented the countryside in law cases. And when a case was transferred from the county court to be heard by royal justices of the Bench at Westminster four knights "bore the record," or reported formally and orally to the justices the facts of the case as it had proceeded in the county court. The four knights thus represented the county court; the county and its court were bound by their statements.

Under John and again under Henry III knights elected by and representing their counties had on a few occasions been called together at a central meeting-place to give the government information. This was an alternative to the more usual method of sending itinerant justices out to the county courts to obtain the information. Then in 1254 representative knights were summoned to meet together with the prelates and barons during a parliament, and in 1265 burgesses elected by the boroughs were summoned to meet with the prelates, barons, and knights at a parliament.

During the reign of Edward I knights and burgesses attended parliaments more frequently although they were not yet an essential part of parliament. Often Edward did not summon them; and occasionally he summoned representatives of the cathedral and parochial clergy as well. During the next reign these latter had ceased to attend parliament, and the two knights of each shire and two burgesses of each borough had come to be recognized as an integral part of parliament. It was much later, toward the end of the fourteenth century, that the knights and burgesses in Parliament coalesced to form a single group, the parliamentary Commons, with one Speaker to preside over their sessions.

The primary purpose for summoning representatives was fiscal, to spread the burden of taxation more effectively over the whole nation by gaining the consent of the knights and burgesses to extraordinary aids granted by the prelates and barons (the king's vassals) in parliament. From the surviving records of the parliaments of Edward I, there is little to suggest that the knights and burgesses did much more than grant taxes. The beginning of parliamentary representation reflects the growing expense of government and the drain on royal revenues resulting from Edward's costly foreign policy.

The main business of Edward I's parliaments was the judicial business conducted by the royal council. This included hearing cases and receiving petitions concerning disputes or grievances which the courts of common law could not settle. In this way the gaps, defects, and inconsistencies in the law came to the attention of the council. In addition to judgments in particular cases and the redress of particular grievances the council drew up official statements by which this or that point in the law was settled or "established" (*statutum*). These were the statutes enacted in parliament. The reign of Edward I was the great age of parliamentary statutes in the Middle Ages, rivaled in historical importance only by the parliamentary enactments of Henry VIII in the sixteenth century and the legislation of the nineteenth century.

Medieval statutes were not thought of by contemporaries as making new law (in accordance with the will of a legislative organ of government) so much as declaring, clarifying, and improving what the old laws and customs really were, or should be, in accordance with principles of justice which were beyond the authority of any ruler to alter in any fundamental way. Changes in the law did in fact take place, but these changes were recognized as necessary because of changing conditions which produced a conflict of rights. It was the duty of a king to maintain the rights of his subjects by administering the laws and customs of the realm in the royal courts. Statutory changes in the laws and customs, to clarify the law or adjust a conflict of rights, could be accomplished only by a public act of the king under this duty and by the counsel and assent of the community of the realm—or the prelates and barons as spokesmen for the community

—whose rights were affected. Under Edward I, then, statutes were not "passed by" Parliament, as today. They were enacted by the king with the consent of the lords spiritual and temporal, and it was most convenient to obtain this consent when the lords were assembled before the king in his parliament.

Most of the statutes of Edward I concerned the incidents of feudal tenure and the relations between lords and vassals. For example, in 1279 the Statute of Mortmain prohibited grants of land to religious houses by which superior lords lost their rights of wardship, marriage, relief, and escheat. A church or monastery as a tenant of land obviously could not be a minor heir or an eligible bride or an heir or a deceased vassal lacking hiers. In legal terminology it was "dead" before the civil law and held its land with a "dead hand" (*mort main*). But this prohibition should not mislead the reader. What was forbidden in general by statute was allowed by royal permission in a particular case—for a fee, of course. Royal license to alienate land in mortmain was granted freely, and the main result of the statute was pecuniary profit to the king. The Church lost little, and lay lords continued to complain about grants in mortmain which diminished their revenues. Another great statute of Edward I was the second Statute of Westminster (1285), a code of miscellaneous provisions largely concerned with procedure. Its most important chapter, *De Donis*, was the legal basis of the common law doctrine of entailed estates (i.e., property that was inalienable by the owner because its descent was regulated by the original charter granting the property). One final example of the parliamentary legislation of Edward I was the important Statute of *Quia Emptores* (1290) which the king enacted in response to complaints from lay lords who were losing escheats, marriages, and wardships because of subinfeudation of lands by their vassals to subvassals. The statute prohibited all further subinfeudation by making the donee the direct vassal of the donor's lord. This rather drastic solution of the problem ended any further extension of the feudal hierarchy. These three statutes (Mortmain, *De Donis*, and *Quia Emptores*) were each designed to amend or clarify feudal custom on particular points. The fact that changing conditions made them necessary serves to remind us that feudal custom as a whole, not enacted law such as statutes, was the main ingredient of the common law of England, as it is still the ultimate basis of much of the law of property today in the English-speaking world.

One final word must be said about medieval representative institutions in general, in order to evaluate properly the significance of the rise of parliament in England. Throughout western Europe any ruler might on occasion hold especially large meetings of his *curia*, attended by the greater clergy and nobles among his vassals. In the thirteenth century some rulers were also summoning to special assemblies the representatives of their cities and towns, and sometimes such assemblies coincided with meetings of the *curia* or royal court. The earliest instances may be found in Italy where Innocent III summoned such a meeting in 1207 and where Frederick II held a representative assembly as early as 1232. In Spain the rulers of Catalonia, Leon, Aragon, and Castile had begun to hold similar meetings of their *curia* or Cortes in the thirteenth century, and the same was true of Germany and the Low Countries. Everywhere it was the ruler's convenience or need (and the vassals' or others' obligation or burden to attend) that determined the composition and function of such assemblies.

Generically these continental assemblies were the same as the English parliament, but there were important differences. The role of the knights of the counties in England was unique. The knights combined with the burgesses to form one "estate," while on the continent the lesser nobility of the country were included in the "second estate" of the nobles, and their function in assemblies was never so important as that of the higher nobility or of the townsmen who formed the "third estate." In France, for example, when the Estates General began to be summoned after 1302 there was no representation of the lesser nobility as a distinct class. The reason for this difference lies in the greater strength of the English monarchy after the Norman Conquest. English kings were able to preserve the county courts as effective parts of the royal administration, and to require the services of the knights and free men of the counties in the local government centered in the county court. It is not an exaggeration to say that the Commons in parliament presuppose the county court, from which they are partly derived. In the English Commons the county courts, as well as the borough courts, are concentrated through representation into an agency of the central government.

Another major difference was the essentially judicial character of the English High Court of Parliament, in contrast with the continental assemblies of estates. Because the English royal council, with its judicial and legislative activities, was the heart of the medieval parliament, the Lords and Commons participated in some if not all of that work. In France on the other hand, to cite one example, the "parliament" or *Parlement de Paris* remained distinct from the Estates General, the former being the highest royal court and the latter being used primarily for consultation with the estates. It should also be noted that while the English parliament actually *granted* taxes, French kings usually employed the early meetings of the Estates General merely to gain consent to the general principle that taxes were necessary to support an approved royal policy. The actual granting of taxes then followed on the basis of local negotiations with each of the several estates in the various provinces of the kingdom. Again the essential difference between England and France lay in the stronger English monarchy whose royal administration relied upon an advanced system of local government. Representatives of the county courts were accustomed to binding the court and the county, through long experience in judicial and administrative work supervised by the central government. Now that these representatives were summoned to parliament their consent to taxes bound the counties to parliamentary grants.

In France this situation did not exist. Because representatives of the third estate could not effectively bind their constituents, they could not be used effectively in securing taxes for the government. Because they were not very useful in raising government revenue they were not frequently called to meet in the Estates General, and the judicial and legislative functions of the central government developed without any effective participation by representatives of the third estate or by the lesser nobility who were not represented at all. In other words, because English kings were strong enough to make parliament an effective tool of their government, parliament later grew into an institution strong enough to limit and then control the English monarchy. In France the kings were too weak to build the Estates General into an effective organ of the central government, and thus the Estates General of a later age were an ineffective obstacle to the growth of royal power toward absolutism.

The Growth of Royal Power in France

When Louis VII of France died in 1180 it appeared that after a period of consolidation the French monarchy had been marking time while the greater royal vassals were growing stronger. With the accession of Philip II Augustus the situation changed rapidly. By the end of his reign the crown had become the greatest single power in France, a position gained at the expense of the most powerful lords. For his achievements against great odds, in war and in statecraft, Philip Augustus may properly be called the founder of the greatest monarchy in all of medieval Europe.

This does not mean that the French king possessed as much direct control over all his subjects as, for example, the king of England. But he did command greater resources. There were two aspects of the growth of royal power: the enlargement of the royal domain, or the territory directly under the rule of the king, and the development of a larger and more effective government at both the central and local levels. In both the territorial and the governmental sense, before the reign of Philip Augustus the king was *primus inter pares*, first in dignity but not in power among the lords of France, his peers. After Philip Augustus the French king was not only first in prestige but in power as well, and his power was based on the solid realities of more territory, more officials and more subjects, and more wealth under his control than any other French lord could claim.

Philip Augustus made the monarchy feared and respected. Louis IX made it loved. One of the few Capetians not to be dubbed with a sobriquet, Louis made up for it by achieving canonization. No ruler came nearer to fulfilling the ideals of medieval kingship than St. Louis. Outwardly gentle, merciful, and mild, he could be firm, just, and strong to a degree unmatched by any contemporary ruler. He had an intuitive grasp of the role of Christian ethics in the relationship between king and subjects and between the several rulers of Christendom. It is an error to think of St. Louis as being in any way a weak ruler. He was the antithesis of his aggressive grandfather, Philip II, but by an irony of historical development it was the long reign of St. Louis that consolidated the gains of his predecessors and won the support of the great majority of Frenchmen for a strong monarchy.

At the turn of the fourteenth century, the strength of the Capetian monarchy was put to its greatest test under Philip IV the Fair. This was a dramatic struggle between the king and the papacy which will be discussed more fully in the next chapter. Here we shall be concerned primarily with events in France and with the royal policy, often unscrupulous and opportunistic, by which Philip the Fair exploited these events. Philip personally directed the acts of his government, but he usually kept out of the public view. Contemporaries associated the ruthless and sometimes brutal methods by which the monarchy reached the height of its power with his royal officials rather than attributing them to him personally. Needless to add, his sobriquet "the Fair" referred to his handsome face and figure (or, possibly, his complexion or hair)—the term was not intended as a synonym of "just." Philip may have been fair of visage, but toward none of his enemies and few of his subjects could he be described as fair-minded or exhibiting a sense of fair play.

67 *PHILIP AUGUSTUS AND THE NEW MONARCHY*

It would be difficult to imagine less promising beginnings than those of the reign of Philip II (1180–1223). Philip succeeded to the throne as a youth of fifteen, unhealthy and unimpressive physically, and lacking in most of the conventional virtues of knight or lord. He was neither bold nor dashing; instead, he was patient and avoided mistakes, while quick to turn to his own advantage the mistakes of others. His personality repelled the sort of men who would gladly do and die for Richard the Lion Heart. But if his personal characteristics did not conform with the values of his age, he possessed a keen practical intelligence and a capacity both to formulate and to execute long-range plans. He was superbly endowed with the cunning, tenacity, and unscrupulous opportunism that enabled him to wring the last advantage out of every situation confronting him. By the end of his reign he had even acquired some measure of popularity among his subjects.

Philip's dominating ambition was to enlarge his royal domain and increase his power. When his reign began the domain hardly extended beyond the country immediately surrounding Paris and Orléans, while the paramount influence at his court was exercised by his mother's relatives of the house of Champagne and Blois. Philip's first important step toward independence was his marriage with an heiress connected with the house of Flanders, whose dowry was the county of Artois on the Channel coast. This marriage was opposed by Philip's relatives, and in the ensuing quarrel Philip was able to involve both Champagne and Flanders in a losing fight which he ended only when his relatives and in-laws agreed to his annexation in 1185 of the county of Vermandois. This was a valuable addition to the royal domain because it connected the older Capetian lands with Artois on the coast.

During these years Henry II of England, Philip's greatest vassal and long-time foe of his father, refrained from intervening—perhaps with the hope that Philip would exercise similar restraint when the time came to divide the great Angevin inheritance among Henry's sons. Any such hope was dispelled by the greed and ambition of the younger Plantagenets, who were already conspiring against their father. Philip played upon their jealousies and when the final revolt of Richard and John came, in 1189, Philip actively promoted the downfall of the old king. Friction between Richard and Philip grew into open hostility while both kings participated in the Third Crusade. Many factors entered in: a clash of personalities, conflict over strategy and leadership of the campaign, Richard's refusal to marry Philip's sister Alice in accordance with a previous agreement, and some other minor issues. But underlying their relationship was a mutual suspicion, in each case equally well-founded, that the one coveted the lands and lordships of the other.

Philip's heart was not in the Crusade, and on the plea of ill health he returned to France in 1191 convinced that Richard would be as great a danger to him as ever Henry II had been to his father. To weaken him wherever he could, Philip seized some territory on the border of Normandy, stirred up dissension among Richard's vassals in Aquitaine, and intrigued with Richard's brother John. When news came that Richard was held prisoner by the emperor, Philip did all he could to prevent his release and encouraged John to seize the English crown. Richard's return from Germany, of course, meant war. From 1194 until 1199 the fighting slowly went against Philip, and it was a lucky stroke for him when Richard was killed by a crossbowman's bolt during a minor siege operation.

In the contest between John and the supporters of Arthur of Brittany for the succession to the English crown Philip favored Arthur but refrained from active intervention. He did not have long to wait, however. John provided the occasion for Philip's next move by suddenly marrying the daughter of the count of Angoulême, whose hand was already pledged to John's vassal, the count of La Marche. When the latter appealed for justice to Philip, his lord's lord, John was summoned to Paris to answer charges. As we have already seen, John refused to appear and his French fiefs were declared forfeited.

In the war that followed Philip reduced Normandy without much difficulty and incorporated it into the royal domain in 1204. By the end of the following year all of John's other lands north of the Loire—Maine, Anjou, Brittany, and Touraine—were under Philip's control and many of the barons of Poitou had submitted. All these territories, except Brittany, were added to the royal domain. John's lordship over Brittany was extinguished and the count now held directly under Philip. South of the Loire the only part of Aquitaine that John could rely on was Gascony in the southwest. The Gascons were not particularly pro-English but they did not want to jeopardize their lucrative wine trade with England, and they preferred a weak king far removed to a strong king near at home. John used Gascony as his base for an attempted reconquest of his French lands, but after reoccupying part of Poitou in 1206 he could do no more because of his struggle with Innocent III and the opposition of many of his barons.

Meanwhile, the aggrandizement of the French monarchy had begun to alarm the lords of the Low Countries, including the count of Flanders, and Philip's support of the Hohenstaufen candidate for the imperial crown antagonized the Geulph party in Germany. Otto IV, the Guelph emperor and John's nephew, revived the traditional alliance between his house and that of the Plantagenets. After several years of negotiations, during which Otto and John won over most of the lords of the Rhineland and the Low Countries, western Europe was divided into two great international coalitions. One was based on the alliance between the Plantagenets and the Guelphs, and the other included the supporters of the Capetians and the Hohenstaufens.

The forces of John and Otto were ready to move in the summer of 1214. The English army coordinated its attack from Gascony in the southwest with an invasion of German, English, and Flemish troops from the northeast, with the intention of crushing Philip's forces between two arms of a great pincers movement. This strategy was well conceived but the execution left something to be desired. John failed to press home his initial advantage in Poitou and Anjou, and this gave Philip his opportunity. Whether it was by a brilliant stroke of well-planned strategy or merely by a desperate gamble forced on him by circumstances, Philip correctly gauged the situation in leaving the defense of the southwest to his son Louis with only 800 knights. Philip then hastened north with the bulk of his army. At Bouvines in Flanders the French feudal levy, backed up by footmen supplied by the towns of the royal domain, met and defeated Otto's Anglo-Flemish-German army. It was the kind of battle in which the chivalry of France excelled—a confused melee during which discipline

Battle of Bouvines, 1214. Philip II, unhorsed, saved by his bodyguard. Manuscript illustration (mid-thirteenth century). CORPUS CHRISTI COLLEGE, CAMBRIDGE.

broke down and tactics were soon obscured by the clouds of dust raised by charging cavalry. The battle of Bouvines was the French king's greatest hour. Unhorsed in the fight, and saved only by the stout defense of his personal bodyguard, Philip Augustus emerged from the ordeal a national hero. The battle ended Otto's rule as emperor, it rendered hopeless John's effort to regain his French lands, and it established the French monarchy as the greatest European power of the thirteenth century.

On his return from the great victory, Philip Augustus was greeted with wild rejoicing—the students at the University of Paris feasted and reveled for a week. Philip did not object to any of this, but after Bouvines he abstained from any further battlefield heroics and entrusted military operations to his son, Louis. By temperament wholly unsuited to the hardships and skills of fighting, Philip had gained more by war in ten years than all of his more bellicose contemporaries put together. The royal domain had been tripled in size, and in revenues his conquests increased the wealth of the crown by four times.

It was not alone by military conquest that Philip Augustus enlarged the domain and his royal revenues. We have already noted the acquisitions of Artois by marriage and Vermandois (to which Philip had put forward a doubtful claim as heir) by treaty. Philip and his successors annexed fiefs on a small scale whenever occasion might allow. There were many methods by which this was done. If a vassal had revolted, his fief was forfeited for treason and added to the domain; where there was a failure of heirs the fief escheated to the domain; sometimes fiefs were wholly or partially annexed simply by purchase, sometimes under more complicated agreements by which lands were shared between vassal and king. All these and other methods used by Philip were quite legal; they represented the legitimate and normal exercise of the king's rights as feudal overlord. Because ultimately the rise of the monarchy meant the relative decline of the political power of the feudal nobility, it has sometimes been alleged that the growth of royal power in France was "antifeudal." Such an allegation would have astonished Philip II and his successors. So far from being antifeudal, their policy was basically nothing more than a shrewd exploitation of their rights as highest feudal lord of the realm.

It should be added, however, that in addition to these rights the king was under certain obligations, as anointed king, which were not connected with his feudal position. And these obligations implied duties which the ruler could exploit to his own advantage. For example, the king was in a special sense obligated to defend the Church, maintain peace, protect the poor and the weak, and do justice to all and sundry. These duties and the rights they implied were not clearly defined but they were universally recognized. In terms of practical politics this meant that the king could intervene to provide royal protection or to extend to favored subjects the right to use royal courts of justice. The result was often an extension of royal jurisdiction beyond the normal limits of feudal relations. Such an extension of royal authority was not itself necessarily antifeudal because any lord who enforced his local authority in the interests of peace and justice did not need to fear royal intervention. What it did mean was that wherever local government under feudal lords broke down, or failed to fulfill its purpose, the king could send his royal officials to redress grievances and correct abuses. Where such action was necessary the local area affected was often, for all practical purposes, assimilated to the royal domain.

Under Philip Augustus such use of royal officials outside the royal domain was infrequent because Philip's main problem was to govern effectively the vastly enlarged territories now under his direct rule. The royal domain which he had inherited was divided into small districts under the administration of *prévôts* who farmed the royal revenues. This meant that each *prévôt* paid in to the central government a fixed sum of money each year and then recouped himself and tried to make a profit by collecting the royal taxes, tolls, profits of justice, feudal dues, and other revenues owing to the king from his district. As the middleman in this scheme the *prévôt* often as not cheated both the king and his subjects, and each *prévôt* aspired to make his office hereditary. This system was not efficient, nor did it serve the king very well because the interests of the *prévôts* were more like those of a local lord than of a royal official.

Throughout the newly conquered territories and wherever feasible in the older royal domain Philip established new and larger bailiwicks for local government, each under the administration of a new official called a *bailli*. Farming the revenues was replaced by fixed salaries, and local interests or connections were circumvented by the rule that no *bailli* should remain in one district more than a few years. Like the *bailli* himself, subordinate officials were appointed by the king and held their office at the king's pleasure. This put an end to the threat that a hereditary officialdom might encroach on royal authority. Most of the new officials were recruited from the ranks of the lesser nobility or the bourgeoisie. Their loyalty was thus assured by the fact that their status and income were dependent on serving the king well. When large acquisitions to the royal domain were made later, in the south of France, much the same system was extended to that area also. The main differences were that the local governor was called a seneschal, rather than *bailli*, and that the seneschals were usually nobles of some rank and power who were entrusted with more important military commands than their northern counterparts. This modification in the scheme was necessary because the greater distance from the central government required a more powerful royal official on the spot, and because in the more turbulent south the military aspect of local government was more prominent.

By the end of the reign of Philip Augustus it was clearly apparent to all who had lived through the period that their king had given France a new monarchy. In its prestige, influence, and power the Capetian dynasty had never stood so high, nor had its realm been so well governed.

68   ST. LOUIS

Louis VIII (1223–1226) was the first Capetian to succeed to the throne without having already been crowned during his father's lifetime. The royal house was secure enough not to have to safeguard the hereditary succession against possible competitors. Louis had been active in the government for several years before his accession, and his reign was little more than a continuation of Philip II's policy. He completed the conquest of Poitou and intervened successfully in the south of France against the Albigensian heretics. The final success of his southern policy was the annexation of the greater part of Languedoc to the royal domain. This was accomplished by the marriage of Louis' third son with the heiress of the count of Toulouse, and their subsequent deaths without heirs so that their lands escheated to the crown, in 1271. The royal domain now extended from the Channel to the Mediterranean.

Louis VIII is best known in history as the alleged creator of the Capetian system of appanages. Actually he did not originate the granting of lands from the royal domain to younger sons, but when he resumed the practice the domain had grown so large that any substantial fief, or appanage, granted from it was almost certain to have important political consequences. On his death Louis VIII left a will to be executed by his oldest son, St. Louis, directing that when his sons came of age his second son should be given Artois, his third son, Alphonse, who married the heiress of

Toulouse, should have Poitou, and his youngest son, Charles, whom we shall meet later as king of the Two Sicilies and founder of the Angevin royal house of Naples, was to have Anjou. This royal policy of appanages has been criticized by historians who can look back on the difficulties it later created for the monarchy, but this was something Louis VIII could scarcely have foreseen. For the thirteenth century this system worked well, providing strong and friendly rulers for large areas in France which were still beyond the strength of the royal government to rule directly. For example, Alphonse of Poitou was not only completely loyal to his brother, but he extended to his two great counties many of the methods of administration employed by the royal government. When he died the absorption of Poitou and Toulouse into the royal domain was simplified by the transitional period of his rule. It was only after appanages had remained in the hands of a collateral branch of the royal house for several generations that these great fiefs became a menace to the crown. By that time ties of family loyalty had weakened and the political situation in France had deteriorated from the relative stability of the thirteenth century.

When Louis VIII died at an early age, he left the throne to a boy of twelve. He also left a redoubtable widow, Blanche, daughter of Alphonso the Noble of Castile and granddaughter of Henry II of England. Blanche of Castile headed a stormy regency until her son, Louis IX (1226–1270), came of age in 1234. During this regency Blanche had to meet and quell the only serious reaction against the growing powers of the government during the whole century. The royal officials stood by her, she had the support of most of the towns, and the papacy was a helpful ally. But even more decisive was the fact that the greater royal vassals who participated in the confused and at times half-hearted revolt had no program and were unable to unite in an enduring alliance. Each lord was jealous of his own rights as against the central government but uninterested in the plight of his fellows in other regions. France was a large kingdom, and it was difficult to find common interests on which all the nobles could unite. The royal administration was as yet too weak outside of the royal domain to have imposed any real unity on the country. Henry III of England intervened in 1230 to support the rebellion and to reconquer his lost fiefs. When the English campaign only demonstrated Henry's ineffectiveness, Blanche was able to stifle the ambitions of the rebellious lords, some by force and others by conciliation.

When Louis attained his majority the monarchy was as strong as ever. As a personality among medieval rulers St. Louis was unique, but he was neither individualistic nor an innovator. He was thoroughly conventional—without being dull. His reign and his personality formed a living commentary on the medieval ideal of kingship. In both private and public life he not only accepted the basic ideas and values of the Middle Ages, he embraced them with passionate conviction and put them into action. What made him a saint was the strength of character with which he put into practice the ideals to which others did lip service. There was nothing weak or effeminate in his gentleness or saintliness. And if he was very pious, even to the extent of personal austerity and mortification of the flesh, he was also very human. Because he had so strong-willed a mother, his wife Margaret of Provence had, of course, her share of in-law troubles; but Margaret was, if anything, even more forceful and domineering than Blanche of Castile. The remarkable fact is that St. Louis could show not only a heartfelt filial devotion to Blanche, an ardent and faithful love for his wife, and a full measure of paternal affection for his six children, but as king of France was never dominated by mother, wife, or private family considerations. St. Louis also embraced the ideals of chivalry which, together with his high respect for both his own rights and for those of others, made him a good leader as king and crusader—though it must be added that he was a better knight than he was a soldier.

For St. Louis the ideals of kingship can be summed up in the two words, justice and peace. His concept of justice was essentially conservative; justice involves the maintenance of rights and the enforcement of obligations or duties. In a very general sense, every individual (or group) in society has a certain status which he holds as his right—just as a vassal holds his fief. Rights and duties correspond with status and tenure; they are determined by custom and are beyond the reach of human will. It is the king's supreme duty not to create or change but to protect and preserve these rights and duties. Essentially, justice implies the maintenance of the *status quo*. Under St. Louis, obviously, the French monarchy was not on the offensive. The aggressive days of Philip Augustus and his son were over. If the government continued to grow stronger it was not because the king was greedy for power. Such was St. Louis' reputation for justice that Henry III of England and his barons were willing to submit their dispute to his arbitration in 1264, as we have already noticed in the preceding chapter. His decision, in the Mise of Amiens, was entirely on the side of the traditional and conservative view of medieval monarchy.

St. Louis' concept of justice was conservative, but it was not blind or reactionary, and it did allow for change. He accepted the existing political and social order only so far as it corresponded with what he believed were the underlying principles of justice. Justice, not custom, was the final sanction. Hence it was during the reign of St. Louis that the customary judicial method of trial by battle was abolished in courts throughout the royal domain. Furthermore, as the royal fount of justice for his realm St. Louis insisted on the right of the rear-vassals, or vassals of his own vassals, to appeal to royal courts when their lords' courts failed to do justice. He insisted on the maintenance of his own royal rights of jurisdiction in areas where, as in the south of France especially, these rights had for a long time been accepted in theory only because they were never enforced in practice. St. Louis' conservatism, as it turned out, could be a potent weapon in the hands of zealous officials eager to enhance royal authority.

The duty of the Christian ruler to maintain peace was the other central concept of St. Louis' understanding of the nature of kingship. His attitude was almost the converse of the theory of Pope Innocent III, already discussed, by which the great pope had justified his intervention in the relations between feudal rulers where the threat of war created an imminent danger of commission of sin by Christians. To St. Louis the duty of repressing violence and war within his realm, and of preserving the peace between himself and other rulers, was justified ultimately by the Christian king's responsibility for the welfare of his subjects. Although directly responsible only for their temporal welfare, he recognized his "indirect power" over their spiritual or eternal welfare. By maintaining a peaceful and stable society he was contributing to the care of souls which was the immediate task of the clergy.

Under St. Louis the time-honored feudal right of private warfare was severely curbed, much to the resentment of the lords of France. In this repression of feudal warfare most of the lesser nobility, the townsmen, and the clergy supported the king. Even more striking was Louis' policy of peace in the "international" sphere. There was no more faithful son of the Church than St. Louis, but again and again he refused the pope's request to aid in the struggle against the Hohenstaufen emperor, thus passing over several opportunities to enlarge his realm at the expense of the Empire.

In his relations with other monarchs Louis showed similar forbearance in the interests of peace. Often provoked by the efforts of Henry III to regain the lost English fiefs, Louis could easily have converted his victories on the battlefields into conquests of territory. Instead he chose to negotiate the Treaty of Paris in 1259. By this settlement Louis gave up several disputed districts on the borders of Gascony, and confirmed Henry in his possession of the duchy of Aquitaine, for which he received Henry's homage. In return, Henry renounced all claims to the former Angevin provinces lost by John: Normandy, Maine, Anjou, and Poitou. Although criticized for this generosity, Louis was pleased with the outcome. His suzerainty over Aquitaine was acknowledged; his direct lordship over the four northern provinces recognized; and a former enemy had become his vassal. But above all, in Louis' view, the treaty was justified because it ended hostilities. The previous year Louis had settled his inherited dispute with Aragon, in the Treaty of Corbeil, 1258. French claims to lands south of the Pyrenees (descending from the Carolingian Spanish March) were extinguished, and in return the king of Aragon gave up all claims to Languedoc except the city of Montpellier, for which he did homage.

Louis was no pacifist, however. He felt that one great purpose of maintaining peace among Christian rulers was to free the resources of Christendom to make war on the infidel. He was more enthusiastic for the

Holy War than any ruler of his age, leading one ill-fated expedition to Egypt and the Holy Land in 1248–1254 and another to Tunis where he died as a crusader in 1270.

The royal government continued to grow stronger during Louis' reign, partly on the momentum provided by the aggressive policy of Philip Augustus and partly because of reforms and administrative developments introduced by Louis and his officials. The *baillis* and seneschals needed no urging from the central government to extend royal authority in their regions. In fact these officials were so eager to expand their jurisdiction and increase the number of their local agents that complaints began to reach the ear of the king. To reform abuses of local government, Louis sent out new officials from the *curia regis*, called *enquêteurs*, whose functions were similar to some of the duties of the itinerant justices in England. The *enquêteurs'* main job was to tour the bailiwicks and *sénéchaussées* and, by holding inquests among the local population, search out evidence of corruption or oppression by the *baillis* and seneschals. On the basis of these inquests the local officials were punished or transferred to another region or dismissed, as the case might warrant. The *enquêteurs* were effective enough to add to Louis' reputation for justice and good government. In later reigns they became simply one more set of royal officials working for the aggrandizement of the monarchy, so that a system initiated to curb abuses ended as a new agency for the expansion of royal power.

At the center of government, the *curia regis* under Louis was more efficient and better organized than before. The beginning of specialization is indicated by the earliest surviving judicial records, the *Olim*. The members of the *curia* who devoted most of their time to litigation eventually formed the permanent staff of the *Parlement* or high court at Paris. The *Parlement* of Paris was restricted to judicial business; its functions were never merged with the consultative and representative assemblies of estates that were called later. Royal revenues had grown so large that the receipts from *baillis* and seneschals were scrutinized by a group of clerks and members of the *curia* before they were finally accepted by the government. This group of financial experts kept records—only a few have survived—and they were responsible for the occasional inquests into feudal services and dues owed by vassals of the crown, the earliest examples of which survive from the reign of Philip Augustus. A separate financial department of the *curia regis* did not yet exist. Under St. Louis, as under his grandfather, the Knights Templars at Paris safeguarded royal revenues on deposit and acted as an unofficial royal treasury for the receipt and disbursement of funds.

The prestige of the medieval French monarchy reached its zenith under St. Louis. By the end of the reign royal power stood higher than ever before. The monarchy was not only respected, it was popular. Louis seemed to have accomplished all this without even trying. No charge of grasping power, nor of courting popular approval, can be brought against him. All he stood for was peace and justice, as every other feudal ruler should have—and often did. How to explain his remarkable success? St. Louis' personal popularity cannot be left out of account, but the most important reason for the continued growth of royal power under the crowned saint was that the aggressive new monarchy built by Philip Augustus had been put on a leash. Without permitting his officials to invade the rights of others, Louis insisted on exercising his own rights as king. Since these rights were often difficult to define in practice, though admitted by all in theory, the royal government was able to resolve most conflicts over rights in favor of the king. At the same time Louis' subjects had confidence that the king would protect them against violence and oppression either from the feudal lords or from the officials of his government. In later years opposition to the crown was almost always accompanied by a demand for a return to conditions as they were in the days of St. Louis.

69   PHILIP THE FAIR AND HIS SONS

The reign of Philip III (1270–1285) demonstrated that the power of the monarchy did not as yet extend very effectively beyond the borders of France. Under the influence of his uncle Charles of Anjou, Philip allowed himself to be a candidate for the imperial throne in 1272. Unsuccessful in that venture, Philip next intervened in favor of his nephews during the disputed succession to the throne of Castile, again in vain. Later, his uncle Charles involved Philip more deeply in Spanish affairs. As we shall see in the next chapter, Charles of Anjou had become king of Sicily in 1265. At first successful, his regime collapsed suddenly when the Sicilians revolted in 1282 and proclaimed King Peter of Aragon as their king. Since Peter was married to the heiress of the last Hohenstaufen king of Sicily, the papacy vehemently denounced the Sicilian rebels and their allies. Peter was excommunicated and his throne declared vacant. Philip was invited by the pope and urged by his uncle to conquer the vacated throne for one of his sons. But the "crusade" against Aragon, in 1285, was a dismal failure despite elaborate preparations and the large number of troops raised for the expedition. Philip's army had penetrated halfway to Barcelona when an Aragonese naval victory cut off French supplies, and the king was forced to turn back. Philip died shortly after recrossing the Pyrenees.

Besides foreign policy the only important events of the reign of Philip III concerned the further growth of the royal domain. Poitou and Toulouse were added by escheat, as already mentioned. An even more important addition was prepared by the marriage of Philip III's son with the heiress of the county of Champagne and the kingdom of Navarre. When Philip IV became king he ruled these areas as lord in right of his wife, from whom his son Louis inherited both the county and the kingdom. On

Philip IV the Fair of France and royal family. His son and heir, the future Louis X, on Philip's left; Louis' first wife, Margaret of Burgundy, on Philip's right. Manuscript illustration (early fourteenth century). BIBLIOTHEQUE NATIONALE, PARIS.

becoming king of France in 1314, Louis X incorporated them into the royal domain. The county of Champagne, second in value only to the duchy of Normandy, remained permanently in the hands of the crown.

Philip IV (1285–1314) surrounded himself with a group of able but unscrupulous professional civil servants, many of them well trained in Roman law. To contemporaries Philip the Fair was a handsome and self-effacing, but fearsome, enigma. Was he, as an enemy put it, "the handsomest man in the world, who could do nothing but stare speechless at people," or was he, according to a friend and supporter, a king of such majesty as to be a worthy successor to St. Louis? More simply, some of his southern subjects dubbed him "King Owl."

Regardless of his personal qualities, there is no question that under Philip the monarchy ruthlessly exploited all opportunities to increase its power. He was determined to become in fact what the propaganda of his officials proclaimed in theory: "the king of France is emperor within his kingdom." Philip the Fair became the strongest ruler in all of Europe. There are three main aspects of this striking increase of royal power. First there was a rapid institutional development of the central government; second, an aggressive assertion of royal authority over all competing powers within the realm; and third, there was conflict with Philip's major opponents outside of France—castles in Spain were ignored in favor of an all-out struggle against the count of Flanders, Edward I of England, and the pope.

Between France and England there is an instructive contrast in the development of the central government. In England, where the king's juris-

diction over the whole realm was unquestioned after 1066, the earliest specialization of function within the general *curia regis* was for the collection
and auditing of royal revenues. In France almost all the ordinary revenues
came from the royal domain alone; as for the realm as a whole, the most
important problems of the government concerned jurisdiction, not revenue.
The earliest specialization of function in the *curia regis* was the development of the *Parlement* of Paris by the end of the thirteenth century.

Under Philip the Fair the *Parlement* usually met once a year for a
term lasting three or four months. In addition to the professional judges,
clerks, notaries and other permanent members of its staff, for important or
extraordinary cases the king might appoint other royal officials, or great
nobles and prelates, to afforce the court. The volume of business had grown
so large that specialization within the *Parlement* was necessary. The main
tribunal was called the *Chambre des Plaids*. In it alone were pleadings
heard and judgment in suits pronounced. For cases involving the written
(i.e., Roman) law of the south of France, it was assisted by a special bureau
called the *Auditoire du Droit Écrit*. Two other offices of the *Parlement* relieved the main tribunal of part of the judicial work. These were the
Chambre des Requêtes which received petitions and exercised what would
later be called the gracious or equitable jurisdiction of the crown; and the
Chambre des Enquêtes which was responsible for judicial inquests preliminary to the initiation of suits and for supervision of the local administration of royal justice in the bailiwicks and *sénéchaussées*.

Other special departments of the central government emerge clearly
in the reign of Philip the Fair, for it is from that time that most of the
earliest records of their activities have survived. When the king wanted
advice on problems of royal policy, he summoned the more important
officials of the government, plus whichever nobles, prelates, and others he
desired. Such a meeting was called a great council. For day-to-day business
of the government Philip relied on a smaller and permanent body, the
secret council or *conseil étroit*, consisting of the officials of the royal household who were always with the king wherever he traveled. These were the
professional civil servants, like Guillaume de Nogaret and Pierre Flote, who
might also hold high offices in the government in addition to being members of the household.

Royal finances under Philip the Fair were transferred from the control of the Templars to royal officials who were organized into a *Chambre
des Comptes* for the receipt, auditing, and disbursement of funds. The
secretariat of the central government was burdened with far more work
than ever before. Of this work the Chancery was responsible for most of the
formal or public documents and correspondence, while the Chamber was
the household secretariat in charge of business and correspondence within
the government or intimately connected with the king's private business.

A meeting of the Estates General could hardly be considered part of the central government. It was rather a great public occasion when the king summoned prelates (the first estate), nobles (the second estate), and representatives of the towns (the third estate) in order to win support for royal policy. Such meetings usually took place during a crisis of foreign or domestic policy, but they did not result in any significant institutional growth.

The first serious crisis of the reign grew out of Philip's relations with his royal vassal Edward I, duke of Aquitaine and king of England. As overlord of Scotland Edward had always insisted on his right to hear and adjudicate appeals from the Scottish king's vassals, but he resented the French government's encouragement of his own French vassals to appeal their disputes to the *Parlement* of Paris. Relations were also embittered by jurisdictional disputes between Philip and Edward in areas along the Gascon border. Matters were brought to a head when some Gascon and English ships routed a Norman fleet off Brittany and went on to the coast of Poitou where they sacked the town of La Rochelle. Each side accused the other of piracy. Although this was but the latest of a long series of such incidents between sailors, Philip chose to make an issue out of it. A French army occupied parts of Gascony to ensure compensation for damages suffered by Philip's subjects. Edward was cited to appear before the *Parlement*. When he refused, the duchy of Aquitaine was declared to be forfeited. France and England were at war from 1294 until 1303, though hostilities were interrupted by frequent and lengthy truces during which negotiations were continued.

Before peace was restored, both Scotland and Flanders had been drawn into the conflict, the former in alliance with France and the count of Flanders as Edward's ally. The Flemish situation was further complicated by a revolt against the count and an appeal to Philip, the count's lord. The French invaded Flanders in 1297, and the county was subjected to French control until a rising in favor of the count drove out the garrisons occupying several towns. Philip then assembled a large army which was met and routed by the Flemings at Courtrai, in 1302. Although Philip recovered from this defeat, and even annexed a few towns, after the battle of Courtrai Flemish resistance was strong enough to forestall the future efforts of French kings to subjugate the county.

The foreign policy of Philip the Fair was far too expensive for the ordinary revenues of the government to support. Various expedients were employed to raise more money. Frenchmen were taxed as never before. Feudal aids were collected from the nobility; towns were regularly tallaged; vassals who did not fight in person paid scutage at a high rate; a sales tax was imposed on certain commodities like salt and wine; and extraordinary aids or grants were demanded because of the national emergency. Most of these latter taxes were negotiated locally with regional meetings of one or more of the three estates. Only one meeting of the Estates General was asked specifically to approve or grant a tax, and even on that occasion local negotiations followed approval. The monarchy thus did not permit the Estates General to consent to or refuse a tax, but employed it only to gain general approval of the principle of taxation, in order to pave the way for successful local negotiation with taxpaying groups.

Another and more dangerous expedient for raising money was tampering with the currency, a practice that netted the government an immediate gain but had a damaging effect on trade. Opposition to the government's first experiment led to a restoration of the coinage. That was followed by later debasement, further opposition, and another restoration. Later kings were tempted into the same practice, and fluctuation in the value of money was an important cause of the growing economic difficulties of France in the first half of the fourteenth century.

Philip's need for money led to even more desperate measures. Taxation of the clergy was not new, but it had always been infrequent and for some special purpose such as the support of a crusade, with the approval of the pope. Now Philip asserted the right to tax the clergy whenever it was necessary for the defense of the realm. Edward, his enemy, also asserted this "doctrine of necessity" to tax the English clergy in defense of the realm. Neither king claimed a general right to tax the clergy for a war of aggression. Confronted with two kings each taxing their clergy for "defense," Pope Boniface VIII precipitated the struggle, discussed in the following chapter, from which Edward and Philip emerged triumphant. Still sorely pressed for money, Philip confiscated the property of the Jews in 1306 and collected their debts for the crown.

Next Philip attacked the wealthy Knights Templars. With the decline of crusading this military order had become little more than a banking organization. The Templars had been financial agents of the French monarchy for most of the thirteenth century, and Philip was heavily in their debt. The temptation was too great. Charges of heresy and iniquitous crimes were trumped up and the leading Templars brought to trial. Confessions were extorted and the royal persecution was justified by a flood of propaganda. An Estates General was called in 1308 to gain support. By 1312 the pope had been won over, partly by blackmail, and the Order was suppressed as a matter of expediency, not because the charges had been proved. Royal debts to the Templars were canceled, and money on deposit with them was seized for the crown. The Hospitallers, to whom the Templars' extensive lands were transferred, paid Philip heavily for the privilege of entering their new fiefs. It was a sordid business, from beginning to end. Guillaume de Nogaret, who directed the proceedings, led Philip to expect a huge windfall but in fact the ruin of the Templars provided only a temporary alleviation of royal finances. It was almost an anticlimax when Philip expelled the Lombard bankers from his realm, in 1311. Their greatest offense was to have lent large sums to Philip; these debts were canceled, and debts owed to them were collected for the crown. Many people besides French subjects had reason to regret the good old days of St. Louis.

Philip IV was succeeded by his eldest son, Louis X (1314–1316). A reaction among the nobility against the growing centralization of the monarchy had been brewing during the last years of the reign of Philip the Fair. Now it broke out in a series of "leagues" against the crown in which some of the towns and lesser nobles joined the greater lords. But this opposition was never consolidated. The "leaguers" could not unite on a common program. Louis was able to appease each regional group by granting a series of charters under which various grievances were redressed or alleviated. In all other respects the short reign of Louis X was merely a continuation of the policies of his father: further development of the central government, and conflict with Flanders. When Louis died the succession was in doubt. He left no son, but the queen was expecting the birth of a child in a few months. A boy was born and was proclaimed King John I (1316) immediately, but died in a few days. The throne then passed to Louis X's brother: for the first time in over three centuries the direct succession of father to son in the Capetian line was broken.

Philip V (1316–1322) was an able ruler, but the events of his reign were not so important as the fact that only his daughters survived him. The succession was again given to a brother, Philip the Fair's third son, Charles IV (1322–1328). Charles dabbled in the politics of the Empire, even aspiring to the imperial throne, but to no avail. When he died, incredible as it may seem, for the third time in the same generation no son survived the king, although he had been married three times. Charles was the last male survivor of the direct line of Hugh Capet.

The Papacy and the Empire

The thirteenth century is often considered to be the culmination of medieval civilization, as if everything preceding that period somehow leads up to a climax, and then all subsequent events are measured by their decline from this "height" of medieval development. Like every generalization about periods of history, this view is necessarily a simplification that cannot embrace all the relevant evidence. There is enough truth in the view to make it helpful in understanding the significance of the medieval contribution to Western culture, but the arts, literature, and thought of Europe fit the pattern much better than do the political and institutional developments.

From another viewpoint, the thirteenth century (like any century, for that matter) can be considered an age of transition. In different parts of Europe the transition led to different results. In France and England the strong feudal monarchies of the close of the twelfth century had by the beginning of the fourteenth century become far stronger national monarchies. In each country the lord king (*dominus rex*) had begun in 1200 more as "lord" and ended in 1300 more as "king" of his realm. In the intervening years the loyalties of his subjects had definitely shifted from Church or local region to the secular ruler and the kingdom.

In Germany and Italy the transition in the fortunes of both papacy and Empire was far more dramatic and in the opposite direction. The power of the Hohenstaufen emperors collapsed in the middle of the century, and the papacy suffered a catastrophe at the end of the century. Frederick II was the last great medieval emperor; Boniface VIII was the last great medieval pope. More significant, the character of both papacy and Empire was radically transformed, and the claims of each to universal authority were seriously undermined. The most important cause of this transformation was the savage struggle between the popes and Frederick II, a struggle in which the papacy triumphed only by employing secular methods and by subverting spiritual weapons to secular ends.

Another development partly resulting from the struggle between the popes and the Hohenstaufen was the concentration of power on the local or regional level rather than in the larger unit of the Empire or the kingdom of Italy or the kingdom of Germany. North of the Alps the greater ecclesiastical and lay princes built effective governments which did not lag far behind the institutional development of the western monarchies. In Italy the political unit was more often the town, especially in Lombardy, whether the town were a self-governing commune or ruled by a local despot. Local autonomy was in some instances almost complete although the theoretical superiority of the emperor continued to be recognized.

70 FREDERICK II

The reign of Frederick II (1215–1250) was filled with dramatic events and colorful personalities. And the most fascinating personality was the emperor himself. His reign was a crucial turning point in the history of both Germany and Italy. Some historians believe that if Henry VI had not died prematurely, in 1197, he might well have succeeded in carrying out the basic Hohenstaufen policy. This policy may be summarized under four headings: (1) a strong German monarchy as the basis of imperial power, this monarchy being served by a large corps of royal officials, or *ministeriales*, who exploited and enlarged the crown lands and who preserved and administered the regalian rights of the crown; (2) maintenance of imperial authority in Burgundy; (3) the enforcement of imperial authority in northern Italy in accordance with the Peace of Constance (1183); and (4) the union of Sicily with the Empire as a counter against papal opposition. The cardinal feature of this Hohenstaufen policy was a strong German monarchy.

When Frederick came to the throne the political situation throughout the Empire had deteriorated seriously as the result of a struggle for power in Sicily during his own minority and the struggle between Philip of Swabia and Otto IV of Brunswick for the imperial crown. In Germany both Philip and Otto had made grants of crown lands and regalian rights in their futile efforts to win supporters. After Philip's death the Hohenstaufen *ministeriales* refused to recognize Otto IV and treated their offices and lands as their own feudal possessions. For eighteen years no effective royal jurisdiction had been exercised in Germany. Although the nobles accepted Frederick after Otto's defeat at Bouvines, in 1214, the balance of power was already shifting from the monarchy to the greater territorial princes. In Italy this period (1197–1215) witnessed the growth of autonomy beyond the terms of the Peace of Constance among the Lombard communes, and the collapse of the Norman monarchy in Sicily.

Young Frederick and his advisers now had to decide where to concentrate their efforts to restore the Empire. The situation was complicated by the fact that Frederick had won papal support for the imperial throne at a high price: a promise that he would abdicate the Sicilian throne in favor of his son, Henry, so that the kingdom of Sicily and the Empire would never be united. Innocent III died before Frederick could have been expected to complete arrangements to this end. The next pope, Honorius III (1216–1227), was agreeable to a postponement of the Sicilian question if Frederick would fulfill his crusader's vow taken when he was crowned king of the Romans and recognized as emperor-elect in 1215.

By the year 1220, Frederick's policy had become clear. It was almost a reversal of the traditional Hohenstaufen policy. Sicily and Italy were given priority of attention, the German monarchy was subordinated to his Italian policy, and Burgundy was almost ignored. Frederick had no intention of carrying out his promise to separate Sicily from the Empire. His son Henry, already crowned king of Sicily, was elected and crowned king of the Romans in 1220. Nevertheless, in the same year Honorius III willingly officiated at Frederick's formal coronation as emperor. Papal-imperial relations were strained, but the pope wanted, above all else, to sponsor a crusade led by the highest power in Latin Christendom, and no conflict could break out so long as Frederick would fulfill this desire.

Frederick, however, was determined to secure his position at home before going off to the Holy Land. This took much longer than he could have foreseen. From Germany Frederick wanted only recognition of his own authority, recognition of the succession of his son, and support for his program of restoring his power in Italy. Beyond that, for the time being at least, he was willing to let Germany go her own way without any effort to increase his powers, or even to exercise them fully. On three occasions he conceded extensive privileges to the ecclesiastical and lay princes. To gain the support of the magnates for his own election, he issued the Golden Bull of Eger, 1213, which confirmed the *status quo* in Germany, including the powers acquired by the nobility since 1197. By his Confederation with the Ecclesiastical Princes, 1220, he won the support of the bishops for the election of his son by making ecclesiastical lands practically exempt from the royal administration. And later, his Constitution in Favor of the Princes, 1231, made the greater lay lords practically independent within their own territories. In return for these grants the German nobility put no obstacle in the way of Frederick's Italian policy and from time to time supplied troops for his armies.

After 1220 Frederick practically ignored Germany, and only once after that date did he personally intervene, briefly, in German affairs. Like Tacitus long before, Frederick's Mediterranean temperament was repelled by the gloomy forests, rude towns, and long winters of his lands beyond the Alps. He was born and brought up in the kingdom of Sicily, and he always thought of himself as first and foremost the heir of the Norman rulers of the south. The highest value he placed on his imperial title was that as ruler of Germany he could protect his Italian kingdoms against attack from the north.

Frederick's first task in Italy was to restore the Norman monarchy of Sicily. In complete contrast with his treatment of Germany, Frederick considered all the powers and privileges acquired by the Sicilian nobility since 1197 as illegal usurpations, and he set out to recover them for the crown. By 1224 this had been largely accomplished. Meanwhile Honorius III was patiently waiting for the emperor to proceed with the crusade. The break between Frederick and the pope was precipitated by the emperor's determination to restore imperial authority in northern Italy. Now the old papal fears of being crushed between a strong power to the north and one to the south were revived. Honorius sought to mediate the impending quarrel and to salvage the crusade by arranging for Frederick's marriage in 1225 to the heiress of the kingdom of Jerusalem. But to no avail.

Frederick's position at this juncture was not wholly unreasonable. The pope had accepted earlier delays in the crusade. Also, in contrast with Henry VI and Otto IV, both of whom had claimed the direct rule of the Papal States, Frederick restored central Italy to papal rule and was willing to respect the pope's temporal authority over that area. Before leaving the country, therefore, Frederick wanted to establish a strong imperial administration in the north. In Lombardy the communes had long since exceeded the limits of autonomy granted by the Peace of Constance, and Frederick seized this as the excuse for revoking the settlement of 1183 and declaring the whole of northern Italy to be directly subject to the emperor. This meant war. Under the leadership of Milan the Lombard League was revived, but hostilities had not yet begun when Honorius died. By this time the custom had developed that when the cardinals could not agree on whom they wanted as the new pope, they simply elected the oldest of their colleagues—so that the papacy should not remain vacant and also to provide an interim of several months, or perhaps a few years, during which the cardinals could reconcile their differences and be ready to elect a successor with the required two-thirds majority. Such a stalemate in the College of Cardinals seems to have been why Gregory IX (1227–1241), at the age of 80, was elected. He was very able and, as it turned out, very long-lived. He survived most of the cardinals who had elected him and, after Innocent III and before Boniface VIII, he was perhaps the most vigorous of all the thirteenth-century popes. We have already noticed his contribution in the development of canon law and in the establishment of the Inquisition.

With respect to Frederick's projected crusade, Gregory IX would brook no delay and presented the emperor with the simple alternatives of immediately fulfilling his crusader's vow or being excommunicated. Under this prodding Frederick sailed in 1227, on the date previously agreed upon with Honorius. But his fleet was ridden with sickness, and the emperor himself fell ill and returned to port. Gregory was furious at what appeared to be merely a stratagem to evade a solemn obligation: he excommunicated Frederick forthwith. Pope and emperor were divided not only by policy but by personality as well. It would be difficult to imagine two men less suited to understand each other. Each was equally imperious and uncompromising, each was equally aggressive and jealous of his own prerogatives. Their personal relations help to explain the bitterness of the rupture between papacy and Empire that followed.

Frederick, ignoring Gregory's excommunication, recouped his forces and sailed off to the Holy Land in 1228. Gregory took notice of this by excommunicating the emperor again for presuming to lead a crusade while excommunicated. Frederick replied by denouncing the pope for worldliness and political ambition. Then he proceeded to negotiate an advantageous treaty with the sultan which gave Frederick Jerusalem and other cities without a fight. Still excommunicated, he then had himself crowned king of Jerusalem. All these events, to Gregory, were a travesty of the crusading ideal. The pope launched an attack on the kingdom of Sicily, excommunicated the emperor a third time for his dealings with the infidel, and tried to stir up rebellion in Germany and Italy. Frederick returned from the Holy Land in a vengeful spirit. He easily routed the papal army and put an end to Gregory's meddling in southern Italy, but by the Peace of San Germano, 1230, he deliberately left the pope's rule of the Papal States unimpaired.

Frederick now turned to the task of strengthening his government in Sicily. He was no longer interested in simply restoring the Norman monarchy. His goal now was to create a centralized state, whose main outlines were revealed in 1231 by the Constitutions of Melfi, and then to extend this centralized system to northern Italy—and, possibly, to central Italy, Germany, and Burgundy, though we shall never know what were his ultimate plans. By the Constitutions of Melfi the privileges of both clergy and nobility were severely curtailed, and all rights of local jurisdiction were so circumscribed that the royal bureaucracy was given a monopoly of governmental power. The kingdom of Sicily under Frederick II was little less than a modern absolute monarchy. Legislation was by royal fiat, the royal courts had jurisdiction over almost all criminal and civil matters (even heresy was defined as a crime against the state), and the whole administrative system was controlled by the will of the king. The kingdom as a whole profited from this strong and arbitrary government. Unruly barons were kept in their place. Taxes were high but they fell on all classes in accordance with capacity to pay. Frederick carefully fostered the economic welfare of his realm. The production, export, and import of economically important commodities were controlled, internal customs were abolished, and duties on foreign trade were regulated to encourage commerce.

Frederick was now ready to impose this system on northern Italy, by force if necessary. Gregory IX was equally resolved to prevent any such thing. Unexpected help for Gregory came from Germany, where the emperor's son Henry revolted in 1234. The Lombard League threw its weight on the rebel's side. Frederick crushed this rebellion, deposed Henry in favor of another son, Conrad, and returned to Italy determined to destroy the Lombard League. Hostilities reached a climax in an imperial victory at the battle of Cortenuova, 1237. At first it seemed that Cortenuova meant a complete reversal of all that the battle of Legnano had won for the communes. The Lombard League fell apart, most of the towns submitted, and a strong imperial party was built up in the north. Many of the nobility saw their chance to gain power in the emperor's service and at the expense of the communes.

There were several reasons why Frederick's victory on the battlefield did not end the war. Instead of accepting terms the emperor insisted on unconditional surrender. This intransigence drove the remaining towns into a resistance born of desperation. Gregory IX intervened aggressively, asserting his right to re-establish peace as mediator between the two sides. When the emperor refused, Gregory sent agents into Lombardy to organize the anti-imperial forces, and Frederick was excommunicated again. In the field, Frederick's military operations against Brescia and Milan failed, and he finally turned to an attack on the Papal States. At this point Gregory died and it was two years before the new pope, Innocent IV (1243–1254), was elected.

Meanwhile, Frederick's conquest of the Papal States continued. The cost of war, however, was beginning to drain his resources, and he was eager to come to terms. Innocent IV renewed Gregory's demand to mediate the quarrel between Frederick and the communes; Frederick refused because he would not admit the pope's claim to define imperial rights in northern Italy. Then, in the midst of negotiations, Innocent IV fled from Rome to France where he called a general council at Lyons in 1245. The strife between the papacy and Empire had now reached the point where a negotiated peace was impossible. By the Council of Lyons the emperor was declared guilty of sacrilege and an enemy of the faith, while Innocent deposed and excommunicated him. The pope appealed to the public opinion and conscience of all Europe for support, but the crusade he preached against Frederick failed to interest more than a few adventurers.

The war dragged on for five more years without definite result. Savage fighting characterized hostilities in Lombardy, where the communes

Emperor Frederick II, with falcon (left), and Pope Innocent IV excommunicating Frederick at the Council of Lyons. Manuscript illustrations (thirteenth century). VATICAN LIBRARY, ROME AND CORPUS CHRISTI COLLEGE, CAMBRIDGE.

were irrevocably alienated from the Empire. Just as the tide seemed to be turning in the emperor's favor, Frederick died. Neither side won the war; indeed, both lost it. Frederick had failed to re-establish imperial control of northern Italy and had overtaxed the resources of his kingdom of Sicily in the effort. In Germany and Burgundy this failure resulted in the further development of "particularism"—the breakdown of central authority in favor of the territorial princes, who were from now on practically independent under the vague suzerainty of the emperor. As for the papacy, what it gained from the defeat of the Hohenstaufen was more than counterbalanced by what it lost in prestige. Pressed to the point where extreme measures seemed necessary for survival, both Gregory IX and Innocent IV employed every resource at their disposal, including an all-too-free use of excommunication and the crusade as instruments of an essentially political and secular policy. It is difficult for the modern historian to judge just what else these popes should have done, but there is no doubt that most contemporaries agreed with St. Louis, who turned a deaf ear to the popes' call for a crusade against a ruler who was at least nominally Christian and who had not been properly and convincingly convicted of heresy.

71   ITALY AND GERMANY
IN THE THIRTEENTH CENTURY

Frederick II's unsuccessful struggles brought disastrous consequences to both imperial and papal authority, but it would be a mistake to suppose that Italy and Germany as a whole were adversely affected to the same degree. Towns continued to grow in wealth and power, despite the temporary calamities which afflicted the Lombard communes. In Germany the rural society of nobility and peasantry was no less prosperous and peaceful than before the civil wars that followed Henry VI. It was during the thirteenth century that the first important literature was written in the vernacular, on both sides of the Alps, while in Italy the beginnings of Renaissance art may be traced back to Niccolo Pisano (d.1280) and Giotto (1266–1336). What did come to an end in Italy was the predominance of the kingdom of Sicily.

During the reign of Frederick II the leading cultural center in all of southern Europe was the court of the emperor at Palermo. By some historians Frederick has been considered the prototype of the Renaissance despots who patronized the arts in order to enhance their own glory. Frederick, however, was not only a patron but also a participant. His interests dominated the scholars and writers who were attracted to his court, and he himself produced the most important literary work of this group, a treatise on falconry entitled *The Art of Hunting with Birds*, which is still considered an excellent introduction to that sport as well as a good handbook of ornithology. Frederick reveals himself as a keen observer of nature. This interest is further illustrated by the zoo he collected, including such exotic animals as elephants, giraffes, lions, and other African and Asian specimens. The emperor's curiosity led him to make many experiments, especially with animals and human beings, experiments whose imaginative quality caught the fancy of contemporary chroniclers, and led them to embellish and exaggerate the marvels of nature which the emperor investigated. For example, he had some children brought up in isolation from human speech in an unsuccessful effort to learn what language Adam and Eve spoke. In another experiment he had several convicted criminals disemboweled in order to ascertain the functions of the internal organs of the body. Nothing came of these "experiments," and the main scientific achievements of the court of Palermo were the work of translators of Arabic and Greek texts or of scholars like the mathematician Leonard of Pisa. Frederick assembled several poets who wrote lyrics in the Italian vernacular after the manner of the Provençal troubadours. The cosmopolitan character of the court is illustrated by the presence of scholars from Moslem Africa and the Greek-speaking East, like Theodore of Antioch.

These intellectual interests of Frederick II and his political struggle with the papacy combined to make him notorious to his and later generations. He was *Stupor Mundi,* the "wonder of the world," a colossus of impertinence, curiosity, and skepticism in an age when such qualities were not appreciated. Although not overtly anti-Christian, his tolerance of Jews and Moslems and his seeming belief that Christianity did not monopolize the truth were attitudes that gave rise to the charge that he was an enemy of the faith. To his bitterest critics he was antichrist: he defied the pope, he consorted with infidels, and he behaved more like a sultan than a consecrated Christian ruler. To his subjects who were not offended by this side of his character, Frederick was unpopular because, more than any of his Hohenstaufen predecessors, he wanted to revive the absolute power of the Roman emperors of antiquity. To the trappings of absolutism he added such bizarre elements to his court as a troupe of Moslem dancing girls, an innocent innovation in view of the courtesans and hangers-on that cluttered up most medieval courts, but different enough so that the chroniclers accused Frederick of maintaining a harem. These and similar charges were so nearly true that most people agreed with Dante, who selected Frederick II as the only medieval emperor to be consigned to hell.

After the death of Frederick II, the imperial cause in Italy rapidly deteriorated and the papacy finally triumphed over the last of the Hohenstaufen. Conrad IV (1250–1254), who had been governing Germany for his father, hurried south to continue the struggle but died before he could achieve any notable results. Conrad's half-brother Manfred then assumed control of the imperial or Ghibelline forces in Italy as regent for Conrad's infant son, Conradin, who remained in Germany. For several years Manfred's effective authority was confined to the kingdom of Sicily, but after defeating a papal army in 1258 he turned to the task of reviving imperial power in northern Italy.

Meanwhile the popes were desperately seeking foreign aid. Innocent IV had excommunicated the whole Hohenstaufen family as a "viper brood" of oppressors of the Church and had begun negotiations with France and England. Innocent's successor had reached an agreement with Henry III of England by which Henry's son Edmund was to be granted the Sicilian throne in return for Henry's underwriting of papal debts incurred in the wars against the Hohenstaufen. As we have already seen, this plan failed and it was Henry's commitment to the pope that touched off the baronial rebellion of 1258 in England. Louis IX of France at first turned a deaf ear to papal appeals. Finally Clement IV (1265–1268), alarmed at the growth of Manfred's power in Italy and supported by the ambitions of Louis' brother, Charles of Anjou, was able to convince the French king that a friendly power in Sicily was necessary for the peace of Christendom and for a successful crusade. Accordingly, Charles of Anjou was granted the kingdom of Sicily, in 1265, to hold as a papal fief. In return, Charles agreed to keep the kingdom of Sicily independent of the Empire forever, to make a substantial payment against papal debts, and to render an annual tribute in recognition of papal overlordship.

Charles of Anjou led a French army into Italy and, after defeating and killing Manfred in the battle of Benevento, 1266, found the situation remarkably easy to control. The kingdom of Sicily submitted with little resistance, the Ghibellines throughout the peninsula were discredited, and the Guelph factions took over most of the Italian cities. In Tuscany and Lombardy Charles was hailed as a liberator. He even became the lord or *signore* of Florence for a few years. The only serious threat to the new

Angevin kingdom of Sicily lay in the supporters of the youthful Conradin, who was persuaded to invade Italy and assert his hereditary claims. The Ghibellines rose in Lombardy and in Sicily, but the issue was quickly decided in favor of the Angevins when Charles defeated and captured Conradin in 1268. Ghibelline resistance collapsed and savage reprisals against the imperial leaders culminated in the public execution of Conradin. Many Ghibelline nobles in the kingdom of Sicily suffered confiscation of their lands and were replaced by a new French nobility, who had already taken over most of the important government offices. A dangerous situation was brewing.

Oblivious to the resentment of his new subjects. Charles of Anjou now turned eagerly to his dreams of a Mediterranean empire. Already count of Provence in right of his wife, he was also the dominant influence in Italian politics. His kingdom of Sicily was strategically located as a base for the conquest of the southern Balkans, Constantinople, and the Holy Land. To prepare the way, Charles arranged several marriage alliances for his children and bought the claims of one of the pretenders to the kingdom of Jerusalem. For ten years Charles' plans were blocked by the popes, especially Gregory X (1271–1276), who had no use for an adventurer whose ambitions could only interfere with that pope's desire for a grand crusade by a united Christendom. Gregory undermined Charles' influence in northern Italy and entered into negotiations with the Byzantine emperor, Michael VIII Palaeologus (1261–1282). Michael promised the reunion of the Greek and Latin Churches under papal supremacy (though he also warned that such a reunion would be unpopular and difficult to achieve); Gregory forbade Charles of Anjou to attack Constantinople. Not entirely trusting the efficacy of this papal prohibition, Michael sent agents to contact enemies of Charles, especially the Ghibellines in Italy and supporters of the Hohenstaufen cause both in Sicily and in the kingdom of Aragon. These agents also tried to win over important lords or town officials by arguments which they backed up with an adroit distribution of Byzantine gold. But Charles of Anjou's fortunes took a turn for the better when he finally secured the election of his own nominee as pope, Martin IV (1281–1285). Martin obliged his patron by excommunicating all Greeks who opposed reunion of the Churches and by lifting the papal ban against attacking Constantinople.

At this point the Angevin cause suffered a complete reversal. The resentful Sicilians might well have revolted at any time during this period; but it just happened that in 1282 a certain minor French official (who had consumed too much wine) joined with more exuberance than discretion in the festivities observed locally each year on Easter Monday afternoon in the square before the little Church of the Holy Spirit, outside the walls of Palermo. The husband of the Sicilian woman on whom he pressed his convivial but unwelcome attentions stabbed him to death. Other

Frenchmen came up to avenge their countryman, and the Sicilians slew them all. Just as this was happening, church bells began to ring for Vespers. The news spread quickly and the streets of Palermo were soon filled with armed Sicilians crying "Death to the *Franchiski!*" as the church bells tolled throughout the city. By the following morning all the French who had not escaped from the city were dead. The revolt, the so-called Sicilian Vespers, spread throughout the island. The natives' resentment against excessive taxation and foreign rule was appeased by the slaughter of several thousand French. The throne was offered to Peter of Aragon, who was married to Constance, the daughter of Manfred. The war of the Sicilian Vespers dragged on for twenty years—Philip III's "crusade" against Aragon in 1285 was an incident in the struggle—but in the end Aragonese sea power was decisive. Charles of Anjou (1265–1285) withdrew to the mainland, where his descendants ruled the kingdom of Naples, while Peter of Aragon (1282–1285) and his descendants ruled a separate kingdom of Sicily. The two kingdoms were not reunited until 1435 when Alfonso the Magnanimous, already king of Sicily, succeeded to the throne of Naples and became king of the Two Sicilies.

In central and northern Italy, the waning influence of Charles of Anjou was the signal for a Ghibelline revival. Party strife provided opportunities for tyrants to seize power in many cities, and a few of these lords built up fairly extensive dominions, including several cities and stretching across many miles of the *contado* or countryside. Some towns, striving to preserve their freedom and autonomy, joined together in leagues. Neither such leagues nor the petty states of the tyrants were very stable. Guelphs and Ghibellines struggled for power, and these internal divisions led to appeals for outside help which embroiled most of the Italian cities in constantly shifting alliances and nearly endless, though usually inconsequential, warfare. Such instability threatened the economic security of the wealthy merchants. Tyranny was not a constitutional principle or system; it was the last resort of the merchant class to preserve order. The tyrant was usually an outsider called in by the merchants to put an end to factional struggle. Neither the tyrants nor their mercenary troops had any vested interest in the life of the town which they dominated or served. By the end of the thirteenth century central and northern Italy had already begun to develop the complex and confusing pattern of the Renaissance states system.

In Germany the years immediately following the death of Frederick II marked the transition from the age of the emperors to the age of the princes. The balance of power had been shifting for several generations. After 1250 it was irrevocably in the hands of the magnates. There was no longer any chance, for Germany, that the central theme of her history would be the history of her monarchy. Even if Frederick's policy had succeeded, this development was possible because of his concessions to the German nobles and prelates. Frederick's failure made it inevitable. Papal policy speeded the process. Perhaps the greatest single reason for Frederick's weakness in the last years of his reign was the growth in Germany of an anti-imperial party encouraged by the popes. In 1246, after Innocent IV had excommunicated and deposed Frederick at the Council of Lyons, the papal party elected an antiking in the person of Henry Raspe, "the clerics' king." German prelates were required to recognize Henry under pain of excommunication, and the popes did not hesitate to employ the full force of ecclesiastical discipline to crush the Hohenstaufen north of the Alps. On Henry Raspe's death, William of Holland was elected King of the Romans in 1247; he was little more than the puppet of the ecclesiastical princes.

On the unexpected death of William of Holland in 1256 the lay princes joined the prelates in asserting the right to elect their king, as against the hereditary claims of Conradin. The princes agreed that a foreigner was to be preferred to any German lord who might revive the strength of the central government, but they were divided on the question of whom to elect. One group chose Richard of Cornwall, brother of Henry III of England; another group elected Alfonso X of Castile. The result was highly gratifying to the German princes. Since neither could make good his claim to the throne, both Richard and Alfonso sought to gain supporters by granting rights and revenues to princes who were not yet committed or who could be won over. The Great Interregnum, as the period 1254–1273 is called, witnessed the virtual collapse of all central authority. The "government" of Richard was little more than a chancery office for the issuance of charters of privileges. Each local ruler looked to his own interests without regard for the kingdom as a whole.

The Great Interregnum was an anarchical period in the sense that disputes between the German states were as often settled by armed force as by arbitration, but the anarchy of these years should not be exaggerated. Peace was fairly well preserved and the functions of government were carried on within the several states. Regional agreements to keep the peace, the *Landfrieden*, effectively maintained order in some areas, while the autonomous and privileged Free Cities of the Empire formed leagues for the same purpose. Despite the confused political situation towns and trade continued to grow and the eastward expansion of Germany continued unabated. This expansion resulted in the growth of larger territorial states in the eastern parts—notably Austria, Bohemia, and Brandenburg. The shift in power from the emperor to the princes in the thirteenth century was thus paralleled by a shift in the balance from the older western principalities of the Rhineland to the newer principalities of the east.

It was Gregory X who took the initiative in bringing the Interregnum to a close following the death of Richard of Cornwall in 1272. As we have seen, Gregory had reason to fear the ambitions of Charles of Anjou and he was eager to launch a grand crusade. To counterbalance the threat from Charles and to unite Christendom, Gregory secured from Alfonso of Castile a renunciation of his claims to the Empire, defeated Charles' plan to have his nephew Philip III of France elected, and used papal influence in Germany to obtain the unanimous election of a new emperor: Count Rudolf of Habsburg. He was acceptable mainly because he did not appear powerful enough to enforce imperial authority. Rudolf of Habsburg (1273–1291) had a keen eye for realities; he ignored or even renounced imperial rights which were beyond his strength to maintain. Thus he confirmed the temporal rule of the popes in the Papal States, abandoned Italy entirely, and refused to protect the western border of the Empire against French encroachments. He did not interfere in the affairs of greater lords, either within their states or in their relations with each other, but he did suppress maraudings of petty knights and barons, thus gaining the support of the Free Cities.

Rudolf's one major venture in German politics turned out to be a resounding success, but it was a success for the Habsburg family, not for imperial power. This was his war against the king of Bohemia, a war in which Rudolf was supported by the magnates because Bohemia had grown into the largest territorial state in the Empire. From this war Rudolf acquired Austria and at one stroke became one of the most powerful princes of Germany. The Habsburg lands now stretched from scattered holdings in Alsace, southern Germany, and Switzerland into the Danube valley all the way to the eastern frontier. From having been a western German power of the second rank the Habsburgs became an eastern dynasty of the first rank.

Fear of Habsburg aggrandizement and of Rudolf's efforts to re-establish the hereditary principle of succession led the princes to pass over Rudolf's son, Albert of Austria, and elect another weak ruler, Adolf of Nassau (1292–1298). Adolf followed the example of his predecessor in using his office to enhance his family's territorial position, but with less notable success. Albert of Austria organized an opposition party which deposed Adolf, who had grown too strong, and elected Albert (1298–1308) in the hope that he would maintain the *status quo*. These events were complicated by the absence of a strong central authority in Germany, which made intervention from outside an irresistible temptation. Edward I of England tried to build up an alliance of German lords against France, led by Adolf of Nassau. Philip the Fair countered that move by supporting Albert of Austria and subsidizing enough princes to swing the election to Albert. After gaining office, however, Albert made peace with Philip's greatest enemy, the pope, and consequently French influence helped defeat Albert's effort to pass on the imperial title to his son. The premature attempt of the Habsburgs to replace the Hohenstaufen dynasty with a new hereditary dynasty thus failed. The course of German history in the later Middle Ages and well into modern times was fixed. Germany remained a congeries of territorial states lacking any effective central government. The Empire became a shadow, a dream, an ideal—but no longer a reality.

72 *BONIFACE VIII*

The closing year of the thirteenth century was the first year of jubilee. Thousands of pilgrims journeyed to Rome to celebrate the Holy Year of 1300 proclaimed by Boniface VIII. Those who, being truly penitent, made the pilgrimage and visited the ancient basilicas and holy shrines of the Eternal City were granted plenary indulgences. Nominally this was a religious event, an expression of the unity of Christendom under the spiritual leadership of the pope. In the light of earlier and subsequent events it may also be considered as a symbol of the triumph of the papacy, a fitting close to the century of greatest papal power. Equally symbolic of what was happening to the papacy, none of the rulers of western Europe was among the faithful who flocked to Rome and we are told by an eyewitness that "from the offerings made by the pilgrims much treasure was accumulated."

The essential foundation of papal power was its control of the hierarchy of the Church. The growing centralization of the Church in many ways paralleled the centralization of the western monarchies. Like the kings of France and England, the popes made no radical changes in their government and they introduced no revolutionary claims. Rather, in characteristically medieval fashion, the papacy increased its power by the development of institutions already existing and by the more frequent and regular use of rights that in earlier times had rarely been exercised. For example, it was a recognized principle that a disputed election to the office of bishop should be judged by the pope. But what constituted a disputed election? The cathedral chapter usually elected whomever the king, or other secular ruler, nominated. Opposition to the royal nominee was rarely beyond the power of the king to suppress. If the case were referred to the papal *curia* for settlement, the pope normally confirmed the royal nominee in recognition of the importance of bishops in secular governments. During the thirteenth century, however, the popes were more willing to accept any local dissatisfaction with the results of an episcopal election as evidence of a dispute that would justify papal intervention and judgment. Frequently this authority was exercised to prevent the election of a purely political candidate who was unworthy on moral or other grounds for episcopal office. On other occasions the popes used this right to build up a political party in support of papal policy, as in Germany during the struggle with the Hohenstaufen.

Associated with the right to judge disputed elections were other rights which, by more frequent use, the popes employed to increase their control of the hierarchy. The pope reserved the right of provision or appointment to long-vacant sees or to bishoprics directly under papal jurisdiction, and in the case of bishops who died in Rome. The deposition of an unfit bishop from episcopal office could be accomplished only by a papal judgment. By his power to dispense individuals from the penalties of the canon law the pope could permit prelates to hold more than one ecclesiastical benefice. Control of such pluralities gave the pope an additional weapon to use for or against friend or enemy. The translation of a bishop from one see to another required papal approval, and thus the pope in effect also controlled the promotion of bishops to the rank of archbishop. Each archbishop was required to come to Rome to receive his pallium, the white woolen band which archbishops wear as the sign of their office. Although the requirement to come to Rome was often relaxed it became the rule that no archbishop could exercise his authority until he had been given his pallium by the pope personally or by messenger. The pope thus possessed what amounted to a veto power over the election of archbishops even where no dispute was involved or where there was no translation from another see.

It would be a distortion to portray the papal administration of the Church in terms of power alone. In the first place, papal policy had goals other than merely increasing papal power. The popes spent much time and effort promoting the reform program inherited from their predecessors and reaffirmed by the Fourth Lateran Council in 1215. At the first and second councils of Lyons (in 1245 and 1274) Innocent IV and Gregory X carried forward the work of improving the morals and discipline of the clergy, eliminating abuses, and combating heresy. In the second place, the Church in the thirteenth century was a huge and unwieldy organization, the only organization that was coextensive with Latin Christendom itself. The mass of conflicting customs, rights, and privileges asserted and defended by both clergy and laity could be adjudicated effectively only if the Church possessed a strong central government. Papal centralization was a response to this need, a need felt as much by churchmen at every level of the hierarchy as by the members of the papal *curia*.

The growth of papal government necessitated an increase in papal revenues. In addition to the ordinary revenues of the papacy, already noticed as they existed in the time of Innocent III, the popes of the thirteenth century relied more and more on extraordinary taxes levied from the clergy. Such extraordinary taxes had been collected a few times in the twelfth century to help finance the Crusades. The main differences between these earlier taxes and those of the thirteenth century were that now they were collected with increasing frequency, at higher rates, and for the support of papal political interests as well as, nominally, for a renewal of the Crusade. It was not for the normal operation of the papal government that these taxes were raised, but rather for the war against the Hohenstaufen, then for the war against the Aragonese, and by the end of the century for other wars in Italy. Against their enemies the popes preached crusades, partly to gain popular support, but even more to enlist crusaders who were then allowed or encouraged to commute their vows for a money payment. Since crusaders were regularly granted indulgences, anyone who contributed to the expenses of these papal wars was granted an indulgence. This extension of the theory of crusading indulgences put the papacy in the position of selling spiritual benefits.

The net result of all these developments was that the success of the papacy against its enemies was too dearly bought. Opposition to taxation of the clergy mounted, not only among northern churchmen who cared little about what was happening in Italy but also among secular rulers. The latter resented this drain on the resources of their realms in support of the secular goals of the papacy, goals which sometimes opposed their own political interests. During the thirteenth century this latent antagonism had been compromised by the practice of assigning part of the revenues raised from the clergy to the use of the kings. In theory, these funds were to be used for crusading, following twelfth-century precedents such as the Saladin Tithe on clergy and laity alike. In fact, the kings of France and England came to view clerical taxation by papal consent as a regular source of income for ordinary expenses.

Relations between the papacy and the western monarchs reached a crisis on this issue of taxation during the pontificate of Boniface VIII (1294–1303). When the papal supremacy over the Church became involved with papal relations with the kings of England and France, a new and more dangerous struggle confronted Boniface VIII than any of his predecessors had been called on to meet. Philip the Fair and Edward I were the aggressors in this struggle. They claimed the right to tax the clergy of their realms without the consent of the pope, on the ground that the money was necessary for the protection of all their subjects, both clerical and lay. In time of war, all are threatened; therefore all should bear the expense of war.

Boniface was not the sort to allow such claims to go unchallenged. In the first place he needed the proceeds of clerical taxation for his own wars—one against the Colonna faction in central Italy and another against the Ghibellines of Florence. Far more crucial, he could not accept what seemed to him a denial of papal supremacy over the clergy: the principle on which papal taxation of the clergy was based and according to which the consent of the pope was required for the use of clerical revenues by secular rulers. Furthermore Boniface was by personality the least likely of all the popes of the thirteenth century to reach an amicable settlement of the issue. An irascible old man, he came to the papacy after long service as a cardinal and a distinguished career as a canon lawyer. Temperamentally incapable of compromise, Boniface held an extreme view of the exalted position of his office.

Unfortunately for him, Boniface had acceded to the pontificate

*Pope Boniface VIII
Proclaiming Jubilee of 1300.*
Fresco in St. John Lateran,
Rome, attributed to Giotto
(early fourteenth century).
PHOTO: ALINARI.

under circumstances that cast doubt on the legality of his title. For two
years the College of Cardinals was so evenly split that no pope could be
elected. Then, to end the prolonged vacancy, a compromise candidate was
agreed upon. This was Pietro di Morrone, a holy hermit who came down
from the cave where he lived to become pope as Celestine V in 1294. If his
election was unusual, his pontificate was sensational. Altogether unsuited
not only to the ways of the world but to the duties of office, he abdicated
after five unhappy months, expressing doubts as to his own salvation because of the experience. The whole transaction was a subtle but telling
blow at papal prestige. Opponents of Boniface VIII were quick to argue
that abdication from the papacy was impossible and illegal, and that therefore Boniface's election was invalid as were all the acts of his pontificate.
Critics of the papacy were equally quick to point out that Celestine's
"grand refusal," as Dante dubbed the act, proved that the papacy had become too worldly for a truly pious man. The brief pontificate of Celestine
seemed to confirm all the arguments of those who were already critical of
popes who would preach the crusade against Christian rulers, who would
use spiritual weapons against political enemies, who would levy taxes on the
clergy for secular purposes, and who would devote more time to the administrative tasks of papal government than to the spiritual leadership of the
faithful.

Boniface's acts as pope soon gave further credence to these views.
Against the claim of Philip the Fair and Edward I to levy clerical subsidies,

Boniface issued the bull *Clericis laicos* (1296) in which he carefully but forcefully restated the canon law on the subject. Because the clergy were especially privileged, both in their persons and in their property, secular rulers were prohibited from taxing the clergy without authorization from the papacy. To prevent all future unauthorized taxation, the bull provided that any ruler who presumed to levy such taxes was, by that act, to be automatically excommunicated. The reaction in France and England was equally forceful. Philip, with the support of the majority of the clergy, forbade the export of money from his realm: this effectively cut off all papal revenues from France. Edward I withdrew royal protection from all clergy who did not pay taxes: this in effect outlawed them and put them at the mercy of any marauding thief or covetous lord who would take their goods or seize their property. While Philip struck directly at the pope, Edward struck at the English clergy, whom he knew to be divided on the issue. Opposition was so strong that Boniface in 1297 declared that *Clericis laicos* did not apply to emergency taxation for defense of a kingdom and that the king could decide when such an emergency existed.

Boniface thus lost the first round of the struggle. The second round began when Philip the Fair arrested a French bishop who was accused of treason. When the bishop appealed to Rome for trial, the question of jurisdiction was raised. This brought forth from Boniface some of the most extreme statements ever made officially concerning the supremacy of the pope. In 1301 he reinstituted *Clericis laicos* in full force and issued the bull *Ausculta fili*. This bull asserted the superiority of the pope over kings and the right of the pope to intervene in temporal affairs when the ruler was impious and wicked. Then followed a long list of charges against Philip's government and the summons of a synod of bishops to consider these charges and other alleged abuses. Philip's officials stirred up public opinion in France by publishing falsified copies of *Ausculta fili*, in which Boniface was misrepresented as claiming direct temporal authority over France. The height of the propaganda war was reached at a meeting of all the estates of France in 1302, when Philip received almost unanimous support for his formal protest against Boniface's claims.

At this point the French suffered their defeat at Courtrai, which checked Philip's designs on Flanders. It was the signal for Boniface, presiding over his lately summoned council, to promulgate the most famous of all bulls, *Unam sanctam*, 1302. The circumstances, combined with the "magniloquent thunder" of its rolling phrases, have made the bull seem to claim more than it did. It ends with the resounding statement: "Furthermore we declare, state, define, and proclaim that it is altogether necessary to salvation for every human creature to be subject to the Roman pontiff." A careful reading of *Unam sanctam* leads to three important conclusions. First, it makes the highest claims to papal supremacy ever asserted officially. Second, it nevertheless contains no claim that had not been made earlier.

And third, there is no claim to direct temporal authority—only a vigorous reassertion of the right to intervene *ratione peccati*, the so-called indirect power of the papacy in temporal affairs. Boniface deliberately refrained from stating officially the doctrine held unofficially by the canonists, that the pope was equally supreme in the temporal as in the spiritual sphere. For this he had good reason. He had already seen the reaction of the clergy and laity to the falsified version of *Ausculta fili*, in which a claim to direct temporal authority had been interpolated.

The reaction in France was swift. Philip's advisers, led by the well-trained lawyer and clever ruffian Guillaume de Nogaret, drew up an indictment against Boniface ranging from the accusation that his election was illegal and that he had murdered Celestine to such charges as being guilty of heresy, simony, adultery, schism, and the keeping of a private demon as a pet and a sorcerer as an adviser. The extremes of invective and abuse hurled at the pope had never been equaled. Under this propaganda and royal pressure, Philip's great council called for a trial of the pope by a general council of the Church.

Nogaret set out with an armed band to arrest Boniface and bring him to France for trial. In Italy he was joined by several hundred retainers of the Colonna, Boniface's enemies. The "outrage of Anagni" followed. The pope was caught in a surprise attack on his palace in Anagni, where he was held under guard for several days. Nogaret found himself in a ridiculous position: he had to restrain his fellow conspirator, Colonna, from murdering the pope, which would have ruined the whole plan; but he dared not risk the journey back to France with only Colonna's troops for protection. The townsmen of Anagni ended the plot by expelling Colonna's troops after a few hours' street fighting. Boniface returned to Rome where he died a month later, a broken man after his humiliating experience.

Perhaps the most significant thing about the tawdry episode was the fact that public opinion was ready to accept the outrage as one of the risks the papacy must accept in an aggressive contest with secular rulers. People were shocked, but not shocked enough to hurt the French cause. No better index can be found for the decline of papal prestige than the sequel to this event. The cardinals, with no stomach to carry forward Boniface's truculent policy, elected a compromiser, Benedict XI (1303–1304), whose every effort was bent toward pacification. When Benedict absolved the king of France from complicity, while withholding pardon from Nogaret, Philip the Fair could be sure that the victory was his. Half a century after its triumph over the Empire, the papacy lost its struggle with the national monarchies. The character of the papacy had already changed; the defeat of Boniface marked a decisive stage in that change. Never again was the papacy to rise to the ideals of Gregory VII, Alexander III, and Innocent III.

Spain, the Mediterranean, and the East

In the high and later Middle Ages developments on the periphery of Latin Christendom were as portentous for the modern world as the course of events in western and central Europe. The Spanish and Portuguese kingdoms were consolidated under strong and adventurous rulers who played a major role in discovering the New World and in opening that older "new world" of the East to Europeans, both of which led to the expansion of European civilization around the globe. The initial momentum of Iberian expansion came from the *Reconquista*, the expulsion of the Moors. In the eastern Mediterranean the struggle between Cross and Crescent went the other way. After the fall of Jerusalem in 1187 Christendom was on the defensive. By the end of the Middle Ages the Moslems had destroyed the Latin states in Syria, and Islam was firmly planted in Europe.

It would be a mistake to emphasize the religious aspect of the eastern contests between the rising and declining powers of the Moslem world. Neither the Holy War nor the jihad aroused much enthusiasm on either side. The decline of the Seljuk Turks granted a reprieve to the Latin kingdom of Jerusalem. The rise of the Mameluks within Islam resulted from struggles that hardly affected the Christian principalities. Only after defeating new conquerors from farther Asia did the Mameluks end the life of the

Latin kingdom, and this was a mere mopping-up operation. The later expansion of the Ottoman Turks into Europe was not inspired by religious zeal against Christendom: the Byzantine Empire was easier to conquer than the Mameluk Sultanate.

Meanwhile the steppes of central Asia had, early in the thirteenth century, produced one more tribal wave of conquerors: the Mongols under Genghis Khan. In the Near East their coming brought few permanent results, but to the north and east they settled down to live on the tribute of the inhabitants of the Russian plains. The Mongol domination hastened the decline of Kiev and was the main reason for the rise of the principality of Moscow. By the end of the Middle Ages Moscow was the center of a new Russian nation whose life depended on successful resistance against invaders from both east and west. With the fall of Constantinople in 1453, Moscow also became the center of Orthodox Christianity, the heir of Byzantine civilization.

The Mongols struck terror everywhere, but they also raised the hopes of western Christians who nursed the illusion that Genghis Khan and his successors either were Christian or could be converted, and would form an alliance against the Moslems. Emissaries traveled between the court of the Great Kahn and the courts of Innocent IV and St. Louis. But these first efforts at diplomatic intercourse between the West and the farther East produced little beyond the fascinating accounts written by several of the ambassadors, notably those of John of Pian de Carpine and William of Rubruck. The character of the negotiations provides some light relief in an essentially dismal chapter of European history. For example, in 1246 Pian de Carpine brought to the Great Khan a letter from Innocent IV in which the pope stipulated acceptance of Christianity as a basis for further negotiation. The Khan sent back a letter ordering the pope forthwith to come in person to outer Mongolia, together with all the rulers of western Europe, so they could all do homage to the Khan—as the basis for further negotiation. It is not surprising that the hoped-for grand alliance against Islam never materialized.

73 MEDIEVAL SPAIN:
THE CHRISTIAN RECONQUEST

In 1469 Isabella, heiress of the kingdom of Castile, was married to Ferdinand the Catholic, heir of the kingdom of Aragon. Five years later the royal pair were proclaimed king and queen of Castile, each ruling jointly with the other. After five more years Ferdinand succeeded to the throne of Aragon. Thus after 1479 the two great monarchies of medieval Spain were united. Spanish history entered the age of "the Catholic Kings," and the modern reader can follow the main theme of a successful drive for power by the strong monarchy of Ferdinand and Isabella. In contrast, the events that led to this unification of Spain present the reader with a confusing and complicated picture of cross currents, false starts, endless intrigues, civil wars, and diplomatic maneuvers.

We have already discussed in Chapter 12 the establishment of the Moslem Caliphate of Cordova during the early Middle Ages, its flourishing and decline, and the rise of the Christian states in the Iberian peninsula. During the eleventh and early twelfth centuries these Christian kingdoms expanded, largely at the expense of the Moors. This expansion southward was the Christian reconquest, the *Reconquista,* which gave to medieval Spanish history and legend its martial and dramatic quality. The first phase of the *Reconquista* drew to a close with the failure of the Almoravides (c.1086–1146) to revive Moorish power and drive back the Christians. At the end of this period most of Christian Spain was divided between three kingdoms: Portugal, Castile (with Leon), and Aragon (united with Barcelona or Catalonia since 1140).

A new phase of the *Reconquista* began with the arrival in 1146 of a new Moslem power from Africa, the Almohades. The leading contestants in the wars that followed were the Almohades and the Castilians, but as in the earlier fighting there were frequent conflicts between Moor and Moor

Spain in the Later Middle Ages

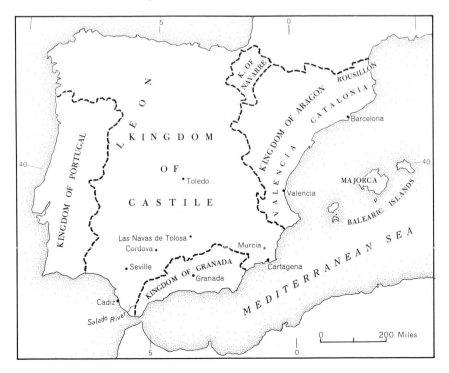

or Christian and Christian. The first task of the Almohades, for example, was to conquer the Moorish states of the Almoravides, and Christian rulers sometimes helped the latter in their defense. Castile's Christian neighbors were not above taking advantage of a turn in the fighting against the Almohades to seize some of her territory. During the second half of the twelfth century victories in the field were shared about equally by either side. Then, as the Almohades seemed to be gaining the upper hand after the turn of the century, Innocent III proclaimed a special crusade in Spain. Crusaders from north of the Pyrenees joined the combined Christian forces under Castilian leadership. The decisive battle was fought at Las Navas de Tolosa, 1212, a defeat from which the Almohades never fully recovered.

In the thirteenth century the reconquest was carried forward under Ferdinand III of Castile (1217–1252) and James I the Conqueror of Aragon (1213–1276). Their efforts were aided by the disintegration of the Almohade empire into a half-dozen warring states. Ferdinand III occupied Cordova in 1236 and Seville in 1248. Castile reached the southeastern coast at Murcia and Cartagena by 1243 and the southwestern coast at Cadiz in 1262. Between these areas lay the kingdom of Granada, and by 1270 only this kingdom remained in Moorish hands. Meanwhile, James the Conqueror extended Aragon southward along the coast. His most important acquisition was Valencia (1238) which became, with the original kingdom of Aragon and the principality of Catalonia, one of the three constituent parts of the kingdom of Aragon on the Spanish mainland.

Expansion southward by the kingdom of Portugal collided with the Castilian advance. The conquered Moorish territories were divided between the two kingdoms by treaty in 1267, by the terms of which Portugal acquired her present southern coastline. After 1270 the only real threat from the Moors lay in the possibility of reinforcements from Africa. In the fourteenth century this threat materialized, but the result was a decisive victory for the Castilian forces at the battle of the river Salado in 1340. For another century and a half the *Reconquista* accomplished little, until finally Ferdinand and Isabella completed the conquest of Granada in 1492.

The political history of Castile and Aragon from the middle of the twelfth to the end of the fifteenth century presents a few parallels and many contrasts, as between the two kingdoms. Except for the *Reconquista* it is no great exaggeration to say that Castile had no foreign policy beyond the arrangement of a few politic marriage alliances. The only notable exception to this generalization was the ill-conceived effort by Alfonso X the Wise (1252–1284) to become emperor. The German electors toyed with his candidacy long enough (1254–1273) to profit from whatever Spanish bribes came their way. Alfonso X was a man of many talents, notably in literature and jurisprudence, and his reign was important in the cultural development of Spain. His greatest achievement is acknowledged to be the production of a great legal code, the *Siete Partidas*, in which Castilian customs were set forth and adapted to the principles and maxims of Roman law and canon law.

As a ruler Alfonso was not successful. His reign was troubled by rebellion and on his death Castile was weakened by a struggle for the succession between his younger sons and the sons of his oldest son. Disputed successions were by no means new in Castile, but after the reign of Alfonso they became endemic. In six of the nine reigns separating Alfonso X from Isabella, Castile was troubled with civil wars and court intrigues over disputed successions to the crown. In the other three reigns the accepted heirs were minors, so the struggles revolved around control of the regency instead of the succession. The endless turmoil and strife between claimants to the throne and their noble factions during the fourteenth and fifteenth centuries have led historians to dismiss the history of Castile in that period as without political importance. It is perhaps instructive that in an age when torture, assassination, and routine duplicity were accepted instruments of policy a Castilian monarch was actually nicknamed "the Cruel." At least men could still draw distinctions between degrees of cruelty.

Aragon was beset with many of the same difficulties, but because of the ambitious foreign policy of the Aragonese rulers her political rivalries were played out on a much larger stage, involving the whole Mediterranean world. James the Conqueror launched Aragon on her expansion into the Mediterranean with his conquest of the Belearic Islands (c.1229–1235). That larger plans were already afoot is clear from the marriage alliance between James' son Peter and Constance, daughter of Manfred, the *de facto* ruler of the Hohenstaufen kingdom of Sicily. This was the Peter III of Aragon (1276–1285) who became ruler of the island kingdom after the Sicilian Vespers (1282) had expelled Charles of Anjou and the French.

One difficulty in establishing an Aragonese empire was the custom of the kings of Aragon of dividing their possessions among their sons. James the Conqueror divided the mainland kingdom and the Balearics, which came to be called the kingdom of Majorca, between two sons. Peter tried to keep Aragon and Sicily united, but his effort failed. A separate Aragonese dynasty ruled Sicily from 1296 until the fifteenth century. Majorca was reunited with Aragon in 1349, about the time when the island of Sardinia was conquered from Genoa after several campaigns. Sicily was not firmly reunited with Aragon until the reign of Alfonso V the Magnanimous (1416–1458), who added the kingdom of Naples to his empire in 1435. This was the height of Aragonese territorial expansion in the Mediterranean. After the death of Alfonso the Magnanimous, one son, John II, took over Aragon and Sicily, while his illegitimate son, Ferrante (1458–1494), became king of Naples.

Another difficulty confronting the Aragonese kings was the division of interests between the constituent parts of their Spanish kingdom. Old Aragon and Valencia were essentially land powers; their nobility could be interested in the *Reconquista* or in aggression against Castile, but not in maritime adventures eastward. Catalonia provided the men and ships for Aragonese expansion; the conquests of the Balearics, Sardinia, and Sicily were all essentially Catalan enterprises. What the Normans were for the eleventh century the Catalans were for the fourteenth. Catalan language, culture, and social institutions followed every Aragonese conquest. The farthest extension eastward of Catalan influence was a sequel to the war of the Sicilian Vespers, which ended in 1302. The Catalan mercenaries who had fought on the Sicilian side, now unemployed, took service with the Byzantine emperor. Organized as the Catalan Grand Company under their own captain, these mercenaries fought back the Turks in Asia Minor, but like all other westerners fighting in the East they tended to settle down on the conquered territory and establish their own states. Hence they were recalled in favor of Byzantine troops, and the emperor tried to get rid of them by the simple process of executing their leaders. The Grand Company then turned to raiding Thrace and Macedonia until the Frankish duke of Athens employed them to conquer part of Greece. Relations with their new employer were no better than with the emperor, however, and in 1311 the Catalans conquered Athens. For most of the fourteenth century Athens was a Catalan duchy, independent in fact although nominally under the suzerainty first of the kings of Sicily and later of the kings of Aragon.

Aragon was plagued by fewer struggles for succession than Castile, but her kings had difficulty controlling the nobles, especially those of Old Aragon and Valencia who were uninterested in Mediterranean expansion. Like the Hohenstaufen emperors, the Aragonese rulers paid for their aggressive foreign policy by the concession of privileges at home. Under Peter III and his successor the nobles leagued with the towns in Old Aragon and extorted the General Privilege of 1282, confirming the laws and customs of the realm, and the Privilege of the Union in 1288, granting more power to the Cortes. Fortunately for the kings, the nobles of Catalonia, Old Aragon, and Valencia had no political vision beyond their own frontiers. The monarchy never had to deal with a united opposition. In the fourteenth century the balance was redressed in favor of the king. In the fifteenth century separatist tendencies in Catalonia combined with the ineptitude of John II the Faithless (1458–1479) to produce a full-scale revolt for Catalan independence. John II's throne tottered, but he purchased French help by ceding his claims to Roussillon, and the Catalans were finally defeated in 1472. Meanwhile, John had negotiated the marriage of his son Ferdinand with Isabella of Castile, his greatest triumph.

The constant civil strife in Castile and the prolonged revolt of the Catalans form the background for the reign of Isabella of Castile (1474–1504) and Ferdinand of Aragon (1479–1516). The Catholic Kings, as they styled themselves, established the strong monarchy on which was based the predominance of Spain in Europe during the sixteenth century. The power they attained and the methods they used make their reign the turning point in Spain from medieval to early modern times. The territorial expansion of Spain in the Iberian peninsula was completed by the conquest of Granada (1481–1492); the retrocession of Roussillon from France in 1494; and the conquest of the part of Navarre lying south of the Pyrenees in 1512. Within the realm the Catholic Kings enforced a unity hitherto unknown in Spain. Catalan separatism was crushed, nobles were everywhere held in check, and Moors and Jews were given the choice of conversion or exile. The ensuing flight of the Sephardic Jews was a blow from which Spanish economic and cultural life suffered for two centuries. To enforce unity of faith as the basis of national unity Ferdinand and Isabella gained control of the Inquisition in Spain, making it little less than a department of state. Political opponents often found themselves convicted of heresy.

The degree of unification, or of "absolutism" as the reign is frequently characterized, should not be exaggerated. The force of local custom and the strength of regional institutions and privileges remained important factors in Spanish history. Centralization was almost wholly administrative. In contrast with England, where administrative institutions were employed by royal officials to enforce a common law for the whole realm, in Spain the royal governors presided over local tribunals which enforced local custom. Another obstacle to real unification was the fact that there was no single Cortes for the whole kingdom. The Cortes of each of the original kingdoms or principalities—Castile, Old Aragon, Valencia, and Catalonia—continued to legislate and to grant taxes for its region.

The diversity of Spanish political interests is illustrated by the projects which engaged the attention of the two Catholic Kings. Isabella, inheriting the Castilian interest in Moslem Africa and the Castilian competition with Portugal, patronized Columbus. Colonization of the New World owed much to the institutions and to the methods worked out in the Castilian settlement of the wasted areas taken over during the *Reconquista*. Ferdinand, meanwhile, devoted his energies to Europe. Inheriting Sicily along with Aragon, he opposed French designs on the kingdom of Naples and during the subsequent Italian wars ended by becoming its king. Ferdinand brought Spain even more directly into European politics by arranging the marriage alliance between his daughter Joanna and Philip, son of the emperor, a marriage which ultimately united Spain with the Habsburg dominions in the Empire and in the Low Countries.

74   FROM THE FALL OF JERUSALEM TO THE FALL OF CONSTANTINOPLE

On July 4, 1187, the greatest army ever assembled by the kingdom of Jerusalem was annihilated in the battle of Hattin. The whole history of the kingdom had been one of recurrent crises and catastrophes, but this was the greatest. As usual, the immediate cause of the defeat was the divided and jealous counsels of the crusaders, which led to a horrible miscalculation of when and where to fight. Given the distance that separated Saladin's forces from their base, the Christian army never should have fought a battle at all. Given the local disposition of the two armies, the crusaders should have forced upon Saladin the dilemma in which he was actually caught: either to attack or to retreat. The desert always fought on the side of the defender. Instead, the crusading army marched off from its local water supply and, half broken by thirst and heat, gave Saladin the priceless advantage of dictating the scene of battle. Thousands of Christians were slaughtered or captured, and the bottom dropped out of the Moslem slave markets in Syria. Three months later Jerusalem fell to the infidel; within the year all of the kingdom was in Saladin's hands except the port of Tyre, a few isolated castles, and the northern counties. A desperate appeal for succor went forth to the western rulers. It was not the first, nor the last, such appeal.

After the First Crusade and the foundation of the Latin kingdom of Jerusalem in 1100, many of the crusaders returned to their homes. Others stayed on to take service with one or another of the barons of the new kingdom, or to try their luck in carving out a barony for themselves. Still others did not arrive until later on in the century. The Latin kingdom which these adventurers established was a loose-knit collection of four major principalities under the feudal suzerainty of the king, whose power was based on his direct rule of the principality of Jerusalem. The other three were the counties of Tripoli and Antioch on the coast and, farther north, the inland county of Edessa stretching northeastward. Within the four principalities were many baronies and lesser fiefs held by vassals and subvassals. The laws and institutions of the kingdom faithfully reflected the structure of society and government of western and feudal Europe, whence the majority of crusaders had come.

Meanwhile the Moslems recovered from the first shock and began to organize a counterattack. If they had been able to coordinate their efforts the Latin kingdom probably would have been destroyed fairly soon. Fighting was almost continuous after 1100, but it was not all between the Crescent and the Cross. The most able Turkish leader, Zengi, spent most of his time gaining mastery over the other Syrian Moslem rulers and in this task he relied upon the neutrality, and sometimes even the military help, of certain of the Christian lords. The crusaders had their own domestic quarrels and they were sometimes not above employing Turkish allies against their Christian enemies. Power politics explains more than either the Holy War or the jehad in the relations of the Latin kingdom with Moslem states in the period from 1100 to 1144. In the latter year Zengi had grown powerful enough to conquer Edessa.

The fall of Edessa was correctly recognized as a great threat to the crusaders, since that county protected the northern flank of the kingdom. We have already noticed the reaction in Europe: the pope preached a new crusade, St. Bernard became its leading spirit, and both Louis VII of France and Conrad III of the Empire took the cross. The Second Crusade (1147–1149) was inconclusive, and in some ways the net result was even harmful. The armies of Louis and Conrad were each defeated before they reached the Holy Land; the recovery of Edessa was abandoned in favor of a foolish and fruitless siege of Damascus; and the Moslems learned once and for all that the "Franks" (as all western Europeans were called in the East) could be defeated in pitched battle. Even more significant for the future, it was now apparent that there was a split between the older crusaders and the new. The inhabitants of Outremer had settled down in the Levant, became accustomed to the ways of the East, and valued their higher standard of living. The newcomers were fired by zeal to crush the infidel. Most of the former were well skilled in military tactics but they were also prone to be tolerant of the Moslems, many of whom were their own subjects or occasional allies. The newly arrived crusaders excelled in valor but were usually deficient in the use of arms in the desert and in the niceties of Christian-Moslem relations. The inevitable consequence was further division and dissension among the Franks.

After the Second Crusade the Moslems grew stronger under Saladin, a new leader whose strength was based upon Egypt. He spent his early years in unifying Moslem Syria and then turned to the conquest of the kingdom of Jerusalem in 1187. The fall of Jerusalem was the occasion for the Third Crusade (1189–1192), which was a failure although led by Europe's three greatest monarchs. The emperor Frederick I Barbarossa died before he reached the Holy Land. Philip II Augustus of France reached the coast of Palestine where he took part in the first phase of operations, the siege of Acre. Falling ill, and with no heart for crusading anyway, Philip returned to France where he quickly recovered his health and turned to the task of increasing the royal domain. Richard I of England spent two years fighting against Saladin. The conquest of Acre and other coastal cities was made possible by naval power supplied mainly by Venice, Genoa, and Pisa —and it was the Italian merchants who gained most from the Crusade, through trading privileges in return for naval assistance. In the end, Richard was able to negotiate a treaty under which the coastal cities were returned to the kingdom, the Moslems retained the interior, and Christian pilgrims were allowed to visit Jerusalem. After the Third Crusade it was apparent to western rulers that a united Moslem Syria could not be defeated without a major effort.

After the death of Saladin in 1193 Moslem unity broke down rapidly in a struggle for power between Saladin's brothers and sons. Conditions were ideal for a new crusade. The emperor, Henry VI, took the cross and even sent troops on ahead to prepare the way, but he died before he could depart for the Holy Land. Crusading by emperors and kings, as in 1147 and 1189, had not been very successful. Innocent III was not displeased that Henry VI's plans had come to naught, for it was rumored that the emperor was less interested in redeeming the Holy Land than he was in conquering the Byzantine Empire and the kingdom of Jerusalem for his own rule. Innocent decided to sponsor a crusade by lesser men in the hope that higher politics could be kept from diverting the crusade from its real purpose. The original proposal for a new expedition came from some barons of northern France and the Low Countries, including Baldwin, count of Flanders. They asked for and immediately received papal blessings from Innocent, who then strove, but with little success, to control or at least influence the decisions of the leaders.

These barons were certainly motivated by a love of feudal adventure, and some of them by political ambition as well, but it is doubtful that many above the rank and file were moved by any pious desire to liberate the Holy Land. We have already discussed in Chapter 17 some of the main results of the Fourth "Crusade" (1202–1204): the agreement with Venice; the conquest of Zara; Innocent's excommunication of the whole army; and the conquest of Constantinople in 1204. The immediate instigator of this diversion of the Crusade to Constantinople was Alexius, whose father Isaac Angelus had been deposed in a palace revolution. The crusaders agreed to restore Alexius and his father in return for substantial payments toward their indebtedness to the Venetians for transport and in return for supplies and troops to use in the reconquest of Jerusalem. An additional feature of the agreement was the reunion of the Greek and Latin Churches under papal supremacy. Most of the rank and file of the crusaders welcomed the attack on Constantinople. Western Europeans generally believed that the Byzantines were faithless allies and probably heretics, and that Constantinople should be forced to do her share in the task of freeing the Holy Land. Innocent got wind of the plan and vainly prohibited the Venetians and crusaders from attacking any more Christians unless they were overtly opponents of the Crusade.

The combined sea and land attack on Constantinople was inconclusive, but it frightened the usurper into flight from the throne. The way was now open for the restoration of Isaac and his son Alexius. At this point the crusaders suddenly realized that Alexius was in no position to keep his side of the bargain until he had consolidated his power both in Constantinople and throughout the Byzantine Empire. As the crusaders impatiently waited for the promised money, supplies, and troops, friction developed not only between the Latins and the Greeks but between different Greek factions. Isaac and Alexius were again deposed, the one imprisoned and the other murdered. Now, whatever had been their earlier intentions, the crusaders and Venetians agreed to take Constantinople for themselves. The city was put to the sack. The crusaders elected Baldwin of Flanders as emperor, divided the spoils of the city, and proceeded to conquer the European provinces of the Empire. The Venetians, meanwhile, took over many of the islands and most of the trading ports as their share of the loot. This Latin Empire of Constantinople endured from 1204 until 1261, when the throne of a much diminished Byzantine Empire was regained by Michael VIII Palaeologus, a descendant of Alexius and ruler of the so-called empire of Nicaea—the unconquered part of the Empire which consisted mainly of the provinces of Asia Minor.

The Fifth Crusade (1217–1221) was the one which Innocent had proclaimed at the Fourth Lateran Council of 1215, and the one in which Frederick II was expected to participate, after taking the cross in the same year. As we have seen, the expectation was not fulfilled and that was one reason for the failure of this Crusade. For some time it had been the conviction of experienced crusaders that the key to victory in Palestine was Egypt. Egypt was both a source of reserve strength for the Moslems and a base for turning the southern flank of Moslem Syria. Hence the military effort of the Fifth Crusade was directed against Egypt's chief port of Damietta, which was taken, and then against Cairo. The Franks of Outremer were appalled by these plans, realizing the futility of any attempt to penetrate inland beyond the range of western seapower. As they fore-

The Later Crusades

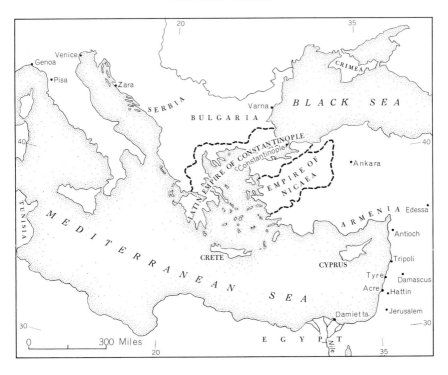

saw, the crusading army—whose leaders not only miscalculated the strength of their foe but also expected reinforcement from Frederick II at any moment—was caught between a Moslem army and a flooding Nile. Disaster was averted only by the fact that Damietta was securely in Christian hands and could thus be traded to the infidel in return for the safe retreat of the invading force. For the failure of the Fifth Crusade the papal legate in charge blamed Frederick II, and the Franks of Outremer blamed the fatuous strategy of the legate. Meanwhile the Moslems were vastly relieved to be able to resume normal trading relations with the Italian merchants who, like the Moslems, deplored any interference with their lucrative commerce.

Frederick II finally did fulfill his crusader's vow, although under somewhat bizarre circumstances. The emperor secured possession of Jerusalem in 1229 by treaty with the infidel, and then crowned himself king—since he was excommunicated no prelate would officiate at the coronation. Jerusalem was placed under an interdict for his impious act. Frederick's success by negotiation, where his predecessors had failed in warfare, was the measure of Moslem division and weakness after the death of Saladin. The Moslems were unable even to take advantage of the civil wars among the Christians, which began as a reaction against Frederick's attempt to curtail the privileges of the barons in the Latin kingdom and to impose, through imperial officials, a centralized state on the model of his kingdom of Sicily. The struggle against Frederick's absentee absolutism degenerated into a simple struggle for power among the lords of Outremer. Christian lords and Moslem potentates alike shifted their loyalties as circumstances of the moment dictated. A few crusaders from western Europe arrived at intervals, but they were simply absorbed into the local political turmoil. The surprising fact is that in this period, from Frederick's departure in 1229 until the arrival of St. Louis in 1248, the Latin states not only survived but were enlarged in territorial extent.

The major event of the years following Frederick's "Crusade" was the capture of Jerusalem once more by the Moslems in 1244. This called forth the last major Crusade, Louis' first expedition (1248–1254). It followed the same course as the Fifth Crusade: the easy capture of Damietta and an invasion of Egypt ending in disaster. The army extricated itself only by surrendering Damietta and paying a huge ransom. Louis stayed on in the kingdom of Jerusalem for four years, but his efforts did little to strengthen the Latin principalities or to end their petty struggles. Louis' second expedition was diverted to Tunisia; his death while there (in 1270) sealed the failure of the Crusade. St. Louis was the last of the real crusaders, although expeditions continued to go out to the Levant from time to time.

Christian Syria could no longer be protected by intervention from western Europe. The new Mameluk dynasty in Egypt, which took over the country during the invasion by St. Louis, gradually extended its power northward, conquering Moslem and Christian states alike. Acre was spared because its ruler possessed the foresight, or luck, to have formed an alliance with the Mameluks during the time when the whole Levant was threatened by a Mongal invasion. The Latin kingdom of Jerusalem finally came to an end when the alliance between Acre and the Mameluks was violated by some newly arrived westerners. The city was taken in 1291, along with a few other remaining Christian towns. The only surviving Latin outpost in the East was now the island of Cyprus.

The thirteenth century was also the crucial turning point in the history of the Byzantine Empire. The so-called Latin Empire of Constantinople (1204–1261) was actually nothing but a congeries of loosely knit feudal principalities incapable of united action. The restoration of the Palaeologi in 1261 did not restore Byzantine power. Many of the Frankish states held out against the Greeks, some of them until the end of the fourteenth century. The Byzantine state, for centuries the bulwark of Christendom against invasion from the East, had been irreparably weakened. Its Balkan provinces had largely been absorbed first by the kingdom of Bulgaria and later by the kingdom of Serbia, which reached its height of power under Stephen Dushan (1331–1355). Stephen's kingdom extended from the Danube to the Aegean. But an even greater threat to Byzantine existence rose in the East. For a decade or two it appeared that the Mongols would be that threat. However, the combination of Mameluk resistance and internal difficulties in their own sprawling empire kept the Mongols from more than temporary control of part of Asia Minor.

It was one of the tribes displaced from their homeland in central Asia during the Mongol expansion that finally destroyed the Byzantine Empire: the Ottoman Turks. Appearing first in Asia Minor as mercenary troops, by the opening years of the fourteenth century they had built their own independent state and had expanded at the expense of both the Greeks and the independent Moslem states. They entered Europe in 1354 as the allies of the Byzantine Empire, now threatened by the expanding kingdom of Serbia. The Ottomans ended the threat from Serbia and crushed the kingdom of Bulgaria as well. But then they settled down and held their conquests as an independent Ottoman state. By the end of the fourteenth century they had subjugated most of the Balkans and Greece and had resumed the conquest of the rest of Asia Minor.

At this point, with almost all her provinces lost except for an island or two, Constantinople was granted a stay of sentence from the Ottoman executioner. The Ottomans were proceeding methodically with the reduction of Asia Minor when there suddenly appeared a new invasion from central Asia, under Tamerlane. In 1401 Tamerlane overran Syria; the next year his army swept through Asia Minor, where it met the Ottoman Turks in the great battle of Ankara, in 1402. It took the Ottomans a generation to recover from the loss of manpower suffered in this crushing defeat. And yet the Ottoman empire did not collapse. Tamerlane's interests turned to

China, and when he died three years later his empire disintegrated. The emperor at Constantinople was too weak to take full advantage of this last opportunity to stop the Ottoman rise. A few provinces were reconquered, but they were soon lost again. Under Murad II (1421–1451) the Ottoman empire was pulled firmly together for a new phase of expansion. Murad's enemies included Venice, Albania, a much diminished Serbia, Hungary, and Poland. These states were reinforced by some western troops under papal sponsorship of a crusade against the Turk. The decisive battle was fought at Varna, 1444, in Bulgaria. Their victory now freed the Ottomans to complete their reconquest of most of Greece and the Balkans, and to turn finally to another attack on Constantinople.

If the so-called Crusade of Varna had come a generation earlier, when the Turks were weak, rather than as a response to growing Turkish strength, the whole course of eastern European history might have been different. As it was, the final siege and capture of Constantinople was a fairly easy task for Mohammed II the Conqueror (1451–1481), who justified his sobriquet by further conquests in Europe and in Asia. Serbia and Albania were subjugated; Venetian control of the Aegean islands was restricted; Armenia was overrun; and the Crimea came under Ottoman rule.

The fall of Constantinople was thus only an incident in the rise of the Ottoman empire, an incident which did not materially alter the balance of political power in the East. Nor did it have much effect on the economic life of the area, for the Italians—even the Venetians to some extent—were able to resume their normal trading relations with the markets and ports of the Levant. But as a symbol of the rise of Moslem power in the East, as a symbol of the threat to the Christian West, the fall of Constantinople created a sensation. For half a century after 1453 each pope proclaimed a crusade against the Turk, but the secular rulers were too much concerned with their own affairs to worry about the Turkish peril. In the centuries-long struggle between Christendom and Islam, the offensive had long since shifted to the Moslems and the fall of Constantinople did not change that fact. The fall of Jerusalem in 1187 and the battle of Varna in 1444 were more significant, as turning points in the general course of European expansion, than was the fall of Constantinople. The future of European expansion lay with the policy of the monarchs of Spain and Portugal. With the discovery of new worlds, not with the resumption of the Holy War against the infidel, Europe passed from the medieval into the modern era.

75   EASTERN EUROPE: THE GOLDEN HORDE AND THE RISE OF THE PRINCIPALITY OF MOSCOW

Historians, who are wise with the knowledge of later events, do not generally pay much attention to a development which in the thirteenth century struck contemporaries as a major threat to the very existence of Europe. This was the sudden and ominous rise of the Mongol empire of Genghis Khan (1167–1227). The Roman Empire of antiquity was but a province compared with the vast territories and the millions of subjects of Genghis Khan and his successors. The rise of the Mongol empire was by far the most dramatic and terrifying event on the eastern frontiers of Europe. It is difficult to explain, on other grounds than sheer good fortune, how Europe was spared the supreme ordeal of a Mongol invasion. The most enduring result of the Mongol peril was the rise of the principality of Moscow in Russia.

The Mongols of the twelfth century lived in the northern parts of east-central Asia. They were but one of a half-dozen nomad tribes, each consisting of several independent or semi-independent clans, that inhabited the steppes of central Asia. The earliest years of the rule of Genghis Khan are reminiscent of Clovis the Frank. By success in a local feud, by assassination or betrayal, by diplomatic agreement adhered to so long as it was profitable—in fact, by any means fair or foul—Genghis Khan clawed his way upward in the politics of the steppes until in 1206 he was recognized as supreme ruler of all the Mongol clans and several of the neighboring tribes. At this point in his career he defined the policies which were to remain basic in the Mongol empire as it grew. The clan and tribal organization of subject people was recognized and confirmed, thus preserving the semblance of local autonomy. The central government demanded little, but what it demanded was categorically required of all subjects: tribute as specified, military service from all adult males, and unqualified submission to the criminal, property, and commercial laws laid down by the will of the Khan. On the one hand Genghis Khan offered to his subject clans their fair share of the booty of conquered enemies. On the other hand, subjects who did not entirely submit to his will in all things were in danger of the utter destruction of their lives and property.

The system worked remarkably well—under a leader like Genghis Khan, that is. The hardened nomads of the central Asian plains needed a leader to fear and respect. They admired the Khan's brilliantly conceived and daring campaigns as much as they loved the booty of conquest. Their natural bent was brutality, they cared nothing for human life, and they found sheer pleasure in the act of destroying anything or inflicting pain on anyone. The Mongol camp after a victory in the field was a sadist's delight. Terror was their ally. They usually outnumbered their enemies in any given battle and they always struck swiftly, depending on the speed and endurance of their tough little horses to carry them far into enemy territory before adequate defense could be organized. We cannot know for sure, because of the unreliability of reports by contemporary chroniclers, but the rise of the Mongol empire probably cost as many lives as the total of military personnel killed and civilians exterminated during World War II.

After 1206 Mongol expansion followed every point in the compass. The Chin empire of northern China put up the best and longest resistance, and the Mongols did not completely control it until 1226, a year before Genghis' death. Meanwhile the Mongols conquered Korea, overran various tribal states in central and eastern Asia, such as that of the Tartars, and invaded the far-flung dominions of the Moslem Khwarismian Turks, the largest and most powerful kingdom in the Middle East. This Khwarismian campaign (1219–1222) was the Mongols' finest hour. At the city of Bokhara the Turkish garrison resisted stoutly; therefore all who survived were butchered. At Samarkand the Turks surrendered their city without a fight and offered to join the Mongols; therefore they were all put to death. As Genghis told them, they were obviously unreliable if they would desert their master and he had no use for treacherous soldiers. Some cities were spared, but not the city of Bamian, where the Turks put up a magnificent stand. The Khan's grandson was among those slain. For this unpardonable error of judgment, no living creature—two-legged or four-legged—was allowed to survive.

As the Mongols moved westward they began to compromise, allowing the four hundred best skilled artisans to survive in any town whose capture led to the death of a Mongol leader. These artisans were sent to outer Siberia. At Herat, in Afghanistan, a new situation had to be dealt with, for the city submitted at first and then revolted. Mongol jurisprudence decreed the slaughter of the entire population. But this was an extreme example, rarely repeated because the mass execution took a whole week and the Mongols hated to tarry so long when there were new lands to conquer. At about this time other signs of civilized values began to appear in Mongol policy. For example, from the population of a city not only were artisans spared but attractive young women, separated from the plain or ugly. Future generations of Mongols began to lose the characteristic bowlegs, ferocious stance, and misshapen features of the original Mongols.

An incident of the Khwarismian campaign led to the first appearance of the Mongols in Europe. With a Mongol army in hot pursuit, the Khwarismian ruler fled westward, only to die on a little island in the Caspian Sea in 1220. The frustrated Mongols decided to scout out the area before returning to central Asia. They sacked several towns south of the Caspian and then moved northward into Georgia, between the Caspian and the Black Sea. Here in 1221 they defeated the Georgians and moved farther northward into the plains of southern Russia, between the Volga and the Don. Pressing westward across the Don, the Mongols were met by a combined army of most of the Russian princes from as far as Kiev. At the battle of the Kalka river, 1223, north of the Black Sea, these Russians were routed. The Mongols, who were now about a thousand miles away from where they had planned to be, contented themselves with pillaging the Crimea before returning eastward to their Siberian steppes.

The return of the Mongols to Asia, and the death of Genghis Khan in 1227, gave eastern Europe a respite. After the death of each Khan a great assembly of the leading Mongols was held to select a new Great Khan and to divide the empire among the relatives of the succeeding ruler. All this took time, since the assembly was held in the original homeland of Mongols and it was a leisurely affair. In 1237 the Mongols reappeared in eastern Europe. Led by Batu, grandson of Genghis Khan, the Tartars (as Westerners called the Mongols) swarmed all over Russia. Most cities were sacked and laid waste, whether they resisted or submitted. At Kiev, the leading city and seat of Russia's strongest principality, the destruction of life and property was almost complete. From Kiev the Mongols raided far into Poland, Silesia, and Hungary, and in 1242 a Mongol reconnaissance even reached the shores of the Adriatic.

At this point, by a stroke of luck for the Europeans, the Great Khan died and Batu hurried eastward to attend the assembly where a successor would be chosen. Mongol garrisons were left behind at strategic points in Russia, but the threat to central Europe had passed. When Batu returned to Russia, he and his successors established the Khanate of the Golden Horde (from the Russian, *Zolotaya Orda*, the word *orda* or horde meaning a tribal group of Mongolian nomads), as one of the half-dozen khanates into which the Mongol empire was divided under the supreme rule of the Great Khan. The fact that Kublai Khan (1257–1294), the last truly great Mongol ruler, spent most of his reign in China meant that the western khanates were practically free to pursue an independent course. The Golden Horde continued to dominate most of central, southern, and eastern Russia until well into the fifteenth century.

Besides Kiev there were several other Russian states that had aspirations to become dominant in the twelfth and early thirteenth centuries, but the Golden Horde put an end to that sort of competition. Each state was required to produce its quota of tribute. Occasional marauding expeditions by the Mongols kept each principality in line and made sure that the tribute was paid on time. This practice also kept the Mongols in training for any possible rebellion or foreign war. The influence of the Mongol domination on the development of Russia is a question of great controversy among historians who lack the benefit of a Communist party line on the subject. Perhaps the safest conclusion is that the "Tartar yoke" did not fundamentally alter the nature of Russian religious, social, and even local political institutions, or culture. The Rusians were not "Mongolized," but any period of two centuries leaves its mark on a nation's development. The later rise of the principality of Moscow owed something to the Mongol methods of conquering and organizing subject peoples. Beyond that, the initial shock of the Mongol invasion disrupted the economic life of Russia for at least a generation, and the continuing payment of tribute to the Mongols was a nonproductive drain on the income and wealth of the Russian peoples.

A special position among Russian principalities was occupied by Novgorod in the northwest. Her terrain protected her from Mongol conquest; her extensive commerce made her wealthy; and her republican form of government guaranteed the control of policy by a mercantile oligarchy that elected the prince. The greatest of Novgorod's princes was Alexander Nevsky, who not only led the resistance against the Mongols but also defended Russia against encroachment from the West. In 1240 at the battle of the Neva River he defeated the Swedish effort to expand eastward. Two years later at the battle of Lake Peipus he defeated a similar effort by the Teutonic Knights. The expansion of the Knights was thus limited to Prussia and the Baltic lands west of Lake Peipus. His prestige high, Alexander then was appointed Grand Prince of Vladimir (1246–1263); in this position he became the chief spokesman for all the Russian princes in their relations with the Golden Horde. The Tartars, who were never expert in administrative or financial affairs, were satisfied to deal with their subjects through the Grand Prince as their deputy. The first Russian Grand Prince to use this authority effectively was Ivan I of Moscow (1328–1341).

The principality of Moscow had recovered from the Mongol inundation rather better than other areas, primarily because it was favorably situated to profit from the river trade in the heart of Great Russia. The princes of Moscow in the thirteenth century, among whom was a son of Alexander Nevsky, eschewed higher politics and contented themselves with building up their own local power until Ivan I felt strong enough to make the office of Grand Prince an instrument of further aggrandizement.

Eastern Europe
in the Later Middle Ages

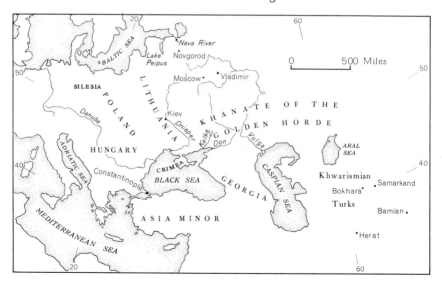

Ivan was granted permission by the Tartars to be the sole tribute-collector for all the Russian states, and he also secured the succession of his own son to the office of Grand Prince. The princes of Moscow built their power on this office and on the support of the Church, whose metropolitan held the see of Moscow, and whose teachings promoted the unity of Slavic Christendom. In disputes with other princes, the rulers of Moscow could count on the support of the Church, whose power was all the larger because the Tartars allowed the clergy and their property to be exempt from tribute. If a dispute among princes concerned the amount of tribute to be collected, the Grand Prince of Moscow could rely on the military assistance of the Tartars. Rather than suffer such a catastrophe the other princes gradually recognized the superior authority of the ruler of Moscow to adjudicate disputes among the Russian princes.

The first efforts by Russian princes to free themselves from the "Tartar yoke" began in the second half of the fourteenth century. Up to this time the princes of Moscow had been thoroughly subservient to the Golden Horde, for obvious reasons. But in 1380 Grand Prince Dimitri of the Don (1359–1389) put Moscow at the head of a grand coalition of princes and defeated the Tartars in a great battle on the Don river. Although the Golden Horde suppressed this revolt within three years the battle was memorable in the growth of Russian nationalism: it proved that Russians could defeat the Tartars, and it strongly implied that Muscovite leadership was necessary for ultimate victory. That the princes of Moscow retained the office of Grand Prince after 1380 was the happy result of a series of crises that weakened the Golden Horde. Civil wars were followed by subjection of the Horde to Tamerlane at the end of the century. In the fifteenth century, the history of the Tartars in Russia is a complicated story of intrigues for power, civil wars, and an inevitable decline. It was the weakness of the Tartars rather than Russian strength that led to the gradual reduction of tribute, and then to the final repudiation of all Tartar rule in 1480, exactly one century after the great battle of the Don.

The rise of Moscow after 1380 was by no means sure and certain. As the "Tartar yoke" grew lighter, civil strife among the boyars, or greater nobles, broke out. Even more ominous, a new power loomed in the west. The kingdom of Lithuania, dynastically united with the kingdom of Poland, expanded eastward and southward into Russia during the fifteenth century. Not until the reign of Ivan III the Great (1462–1505) was it clear that a strong Russian state could be built upon the principality of Moscow. Ivan III consolidated the piecemeal conquests of his predecessors, threw back the Lithuanians from large areas in Russia, and forced the other princes to recognize his superiority. To his title of Grand Prince he added the more resounding title of "Autocrat of all the Russias."

The rise of Moscow was steadily supported by the Church. The struggle against Lithuanian expansion was in part a struggle against Latin

Christianity and papal supremacy. After 1453, with the fall of Constantinople, the metropolitan of Moscow claimed to be head of the Greek Orthodox Church. Moscow became the "Third Rome," the true heir of the ecclesiastical supremacy which—according to Orthodox teaching—had passed from Rome to Constantinople and now to Moscow.

PART SIX

THE DECLINE OF
MEDIEVAL CIVILIZATION

England and France
in the Later Middle Ages

In the later Middle Ages Europe was confronted with difficulties and disorders more serious than those of any period since the disintegration of the Carolingian empire. The fourteenth and fifteenth centuries witnessed the decay and transformation of many institutions and values that were characteristically medieval, and the appearance of new conditions that mark the transition to modern times. It was not an especially happy or optimistic age.

The fundamental difficulty was economic. For many reasons that are complex and not fully understood, the increase in wealth and population that had been fairly steady since the eleventh century was not maintained after the generation of Dante, Boniface VIII, Philip the Fair, and Edward I. Some of the achievements of that age had to be paid for at a price which later generations found burdensome. For example, the growth of the national monarchies entailed expenses of government and of foreign policy that presupposed the ability and willingness of subjects to pay high taxes. The failures of the late thirteenth century had repercussions from which Europe suffered during the fourteenth and fifteenth centuries, notably the failure of the Church to maintain its moral and spiritual leadership of a united Christendom. These generalizations apply to the period as a whole and to Europe as a whole. There were, of course, important exceptions; in

Italy, for example, developments seemed to usher in the conditions of modern times more rapidly than elsewhere.

In western Europe the most dramatic event of the later Middle Ages was the conflict between France and England called the Hundred Years' War. The causes of this war were not new. Some of the issues dated back to the Norman Conquest, but none of them was beyond amicable settlement. The results of the Hundred Years' War permanently affected the future of Europe. These two nations, whose internal affairs had been complicated for centuries by the English position in southwestern France, were now free to develop independently. This "national disentanglement" ushered in a new phase of European nationalism. Another result was the recuperation of the French monarchy from a state of almost chronic crisis. By the end of the fifteenth century the kings of France possessed more power than any of their predecessors. In England failure in war produced an acute crisis from which the monarchy had to recover or else suffer eclipse. The result was the strong monarchy of the Tudors. In each country the monarchy not only survived the disorders of the later Middle Ages, but it became the center and basis of the national state in modern times.

76   THE HUNDRED YEARS' WAR:
THE FIRST PHASE

In France and England the predominant position of the monarchy under Philip the Fair and Edward I was achieved primarily at the expense of the papacy and the nobility. Against the papacy both monarchs were supported by their nobility and even by the majority of their clergy. In the fourteenth century the nobles of each country made strenuous efforts to redress the balance of power in their own favor. It became clear that under lesser kings than Philip the Fair and Edward I the triumph of the monarchy was by no means certain.

The fourteenth-century kings depended, in fact, as much on their nobility as they did on the ambitious bureaucracies of their government. The nobles controlled by far the largest share of the wealth, and thus any successful program of taxation depended on their cooperation. The nobles still formed the core of the royal army, which was no longer the feudal host of old, but an army of mercenary soldiers whom the nobles were commissioned to recruit, train, provision, and lead in the name of the king. Finally, although the political ambitions of the nobles may have been suppressed temporarily, they were ready at any propitious moment to try to regain their former influence. In the fourteenth and fifteenth centuries this aristocratic reaction against the monarchy was almost invariably opportunistic and irresponsible. In England the barons of 1215, 1258 and 1297 were motivated by some notion of constitutional principles, even if not very articulate and scarcely going beyond the belief that government should be limited by law. It is difficult to see in the aristocratic revolts after Edward I's reign anything more than a struggle for power and an effort by the nobles to seize control of the royal administration for their personal benefit.

The reaction against the growing power of the monarchy in England built up quickly under Edward II (1307–1327). The situation called for a forceful ruler: the government was burdened with huge debts, the Scots were far from subdued, and the nobles were restless and resentful. But Edward II cut a poor figure as king. He was weak-willed and frivolous, idle and incompetent. Instead of hunting, for diversion he even enjoyed digging ditches, thatching roofs, and other rustic pursuits and mechanic arts. It was a medieval king's business to govern, but here was a king who left the government to civil servants and personal favorites. A group of the barons, called the Lords Ordainers, forced Edward to accept the Ordinances of 1311, which severely curtailed the governmental powers of the royal household and which required the approval of the magnates in parliament for appointment of the greater officers of state and for important policy decisions. Edward hoped to regain some power by a successful campaign against the Scots, but the disastrous defeat of his army at Bannockburn in 1314 ensured Scottish independence and discredited both the king and the barons of England. Although the barons now dominated the government, their incompetence and selfishness were so obvious that a moderate royalist party was able to restore the king to power in 1322. At the parliament held at York that year Edward enacted a statute declaring null and void the Ordinances of 1311, and any similar future provisions, but also recognizing that important legislation should be enacted by the king in parliament with the consent of those summoned and present "as it hath been hitherto accustomed." After this royalist restoration, the king again fell under the influence of favorites, and the tragicomedy of his reign was climaxed when Queen Isabella ran off with her paramour, Mortimer, and then returned to lead a successful rebellion against her husband. For the first time since the days of the Anglo-Saxons, an anointed king was deposed.

Edward III (1327–1377) succeeded as a minor, while Isabella and Mortimer controlled the throne to their own advantage. Then in 1330 the young king was able to throw off their tutelage in a *coup d'état* which cost Mortimer his life and Isabella her freedom. The early years of Edward III were auspicious. He revived the royal household as the center of government and temporarily appeased the barons by yielding on minor issues; on major issues he made promises that he later failed to keep. Personally Edward III was popular with the nobles, whose interests and tastes he shared. He gave England the solace of a victory over the Scots, at Halidon Hill in 1333, although the battle led to no permanent results. Edward's greatest achievement was to recognize that foreign adventures could distract his nobles from domestic grievances that disrupted his father's futile reign.

Queen Isabella, holding the future Edward III, received by her brother, Charles IV of France. Manuscript illustration from Froissart's *Chronicles* (late fourteenth century). THE PIERPONT MORGAN LIBRARY, NEW YORK.

The basic conditions for war between France and England had existed ever since 1204, when Philip Augustus conquered Normandy. The Treaty of Paris, in 1259, had brought peace between monarchs who sincerely desired peace, but it had not removed the sources of conflict. War had broken out sporadically under both Edward I and Edward II, but neither they nor the French kings were in a position to carry through a major campaign. There were no special causes that explain why the Hundred Years' War began under Edward III rather than earlier. The main grievance of the English was the continuing pressure by French kings to assert their authority over Gascony—the greater part of the old duchy of Aquitaine—in much the same manner that the English kings asserted their rights over Scotland. Added to this were the French support of the Scots against England and the English support of the Flemings against France, plus the interminable squabbles of sailors on both sides of the Channel. These sailors were by nature little more than pirates whose misdeeds could be disowned by either monarch as occasion or convenience demanded. The only solid and undeniable difference of national interests lay in the English dependence on Flanders as the major market for English wool production and the necessity of protecting and preserving that market, as against the French determination to dominate if not absorb Flanders because of her lucrative trade and industry. But it would be a distortion to portray the Hundred Years' War as growing out of any real economic necessity on the part of either country. The problem of Gascony alone was sufficient reason for war, so soon as a king of either nation desired war.

As it turned out, both kings were eager and willing to go to war. The king of France was Philip VI of Valois (1328–1350), a man of about the same romantic and chivalrous mettle as Edward III. Each ruler looked to foreign adventure to distract his nobles from discontent at home. Philip precipitated hostilities in 1337 by declaring Gascony forfeit because of a defect in Edward's oath of homage. The role of Flanders was always vital to English military planning. In friendly hands it provided a secure flank that made it possible to attack from the north in combination with an invasion directed toward Paris from Gascony. The count of Flanders remained loyal to his lord, Philip VI, but the working classes and some of the merchants wanted to throw off French control. In 1339 their spokesman, Jacques van Artevelde, negotiated an alliance with Edward III by which Edward agreed to provide military aid and to guarantee a steady supply of English wool for Flemish looms. In return, the Flemings recognized Edward as lawful king of France. Thus an essentially old-fashioned feudal war over conflicting jurisdictions became a dynastic war of conquest.

Edward's claim to the French crown descended through his mother, Isabella, daughter of Philip the Fair. Philip VI was the son of Philip the Fair's younger brother. Hence Edward was a nephew of the last three kings of France, while Philip was their cousin; Edward was a grandson of Philip the Fair, while Philip was a grandson of Philip III, the father of Philip the Fair. No matter how the lawyers figured these relationships, Edward Plantagenet stood one degree nearer the throne of France than Philip of Valois. But there were two fatal flaws in Edward's claim. First, it descended through a female. The daughters of the last three kings had all been excluded from the succession, and the French lawyers argued that one who could not inherit a claim could not transmit that claim. Second, and more serious, Edward was the king of England and the French royal council would not accept the duke of Aquitaine and hereditary enemy of the Capetians as ruler of their own kingdom. Thus the house of Valois replaced the house of Capet.

The military side of the Hundred Years' War can be summarized in the statement that the English won most of the battles and the French won the war. The end result reflected the fact that the kings of England during the period had at their disposal approximately one third of the resources in manpower and wealth at the disposal of the French kings. During the first phase of the War (1337–1360) the English army applied brilliantly the new weapons and tactics which they had learned to use during the battles against Welshmen and Scots in the preceding half-century. Chief among the new weapons was the longbow, made wholly of wood and unencumbered with the mechanism that the crossbowman had to keep in repair. The longbow had a greater range, greater impact with a heavier missile, and a far greater rate of fire than the crossbow. The pike was not completely new but the English used it in ways which were new to the French.

The first great English victory illustrates the foregoing points. In the summer of 1346 the English were retreating after a fruitless expedition aimed at Paris, when they were overtaken by a superior French force at Crécy. Edward dismounted his knights and took up a defensive position on

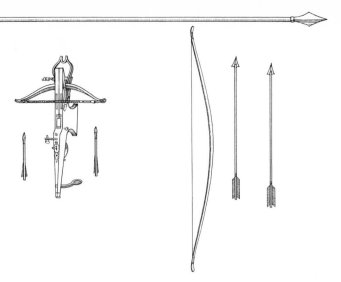

Pike, Crossbow, Longbow: Later Middle Ages

a slope protected on one flank by a stream and on the other by a rise of ground. His archers were ranged on the flanks of each of the three divisions of his army. The French army began arriving toward mid-afternoon, but rather than wait to organize his attack properly Philip threw his cavalry against the English in piecemeal fashion, as each major contingent arrived. The English archers slaughtered each succeeding wave of charging horsemen. The few French knights who got through the rain of arrows found their mounts gutted on the ends of anchored pikes or sharpened logs, making it impossible to escape being killed or captured by the English knights and men-at-arms. The French far outnumbered the English, but because the French cavalry was committed only one part at a time the numerical advantage at any given point in the battle was with the English.

Before the French had recovered from the defeat at Crécy, Edward was able to take the port of Calais (1347) and thus secure a base on the coast for future operations. However, the Black Death of 1348–1349 intervened, and it was several years before either side could put a large force in the field again. When hostilities were resumed France had a new king who was even less able than Philip VI. This was John the Good (1350–1364), whose sobriquet referred not to his merit or virtue but expressed the sense of our phrase "good fellow." In 1356 John caught an army led by the Black Prince, heir of the English crown, near Poitiers. The whole story of Crécy was repeated, except that most of the French knights dismounted and advanced over broken country for a mile before engaging the waiting English army. Some knights survived the hail of arrows, but they were so exhausted from marching in full armor that they were no match for the outnumbered English knights and pikemen. The battle of Poitiers was another resounding defeat for the French, climaxed by the capture of King John himself.

France suffered greatly during these years. The war was harder on noncombatants than on the soldiers. To the normal ravages of medieval war, in which armies lived off the countryside through which they passed, were added the terrors of the Black Death and the destruction wrought by systematic pillaging raids sent out by the English. The prestige of the French monarchy sank to a new low. The lower classes of both town and country were restive, and the nobles had difficulty collecting revenues from their war-weary tenants. In Paris a revolutionary communal movement led by Étienne Marcel extracted privileges from and forced reforms upon the government of the Dauphin in 1358. Marcel, who was both a wealthy cloth merchant and a rabble-rousing demagogue, certainly had political ambitions for himself, but his reforms were also designed to strengthen the inefficient and wasteful royal government. The Dauphin, thoroughly terrified, lived out the storm of unrest and finally suppressed the revolutionists, but he also adopted their program for a stronger government. Meanwhile, his father enjoyed his pleasant and honorable captivity in England.

At this low point in French fortunes the first phase of the Hundred Years' War was brought to an end by the treaty of Brétigny-Calais in 1360. A huge ransom was fixed for King John. John ceded to Edward all the Gascon lands in dispute. In addition Edward acquired Calais and Ponthieu, the county in which Crécy was situated. Furthermore, the two monarchs agreed that when these conditions had been fulfilled—the ransom paid and the territories actually transferred—they would make a simultaneous renunciation. Edward was to renounce his claim to the French crown; John was to renounce his suzerainty over all the lands Edward held in France. If carried out, the treaty of Brétigny-Calais would have effected a general pacification, and Edward would have traded a nebulous claim to the throne for full sovereignty over more than a third of France. Actually neither side was eager to fulfill the terms. Edward took advantage of the failure of the French to pay the ransom to try to negotiate a revision of terms that would be still more favorable to the English. The French welcomed this or any other delay as an excuse to postpone carrying out the original terms. When one of the French hostages held by the English escaped from custody, King John, chivalrous to the last, felt honor bound to return to captivity. He died in London in 1364, and the treaty of Brétigny-Calais became a dead letter.

77   ENGLAND TO THE ACCESSION OF HENRY TUDOR

Success in war made Edward III (1327–1377) a popular king. The nobles enjoyed fighting and they profited from the booty and ransoms of the French campaigns. For a time at least, the war was welcomed by the middle and lower classes. The Flemish wool market was preserved for the merchants; soldiering and pillaging in France had far greater appeal for many peasants than did the drudgery of field work at home. The cost of war was borne willingly as long as conquests in France held out prospects of ultimate victory. But after the treaty of Brétigny-Calais these prospects dimmed. War was resumed in 1369, and by the end of the reign of Edward III only Calais and the region around Bordeaux in the southwest remained under English control. Ever since the Black Death had struck in 1349, England had been suffering from economic dislocation, and to this was now added a veterans' problem. Soldiers returning from overseas were usually unskilled except in the use of arms. Most of them were former peasants who did not relish a return to their former status. Some veterans became outlaws, pillaging the English countryside in the fashion they had learned in France. Others hired themselves out to ambitious lords who needed armed retainers to advance their local power in the counties or to support their factional quarrels with other nobles.

Under these unsettled conditions, opposition to the monarchy increased during the last decades of the reign of Edward III. This opposition was focused in parliament, for a meeting of that body brought together most of the nobles, and it was only their opposition, or opposition which a faction of them led, that could be dangerous. Thus parliament, which Edward I had shaped as an agency of royal power, became under his successors a means of resisting royal power. The financial straits of the government forced Edward III to convoke parliament frequently in order to obtain money for his wars. He tried other means of raising taxes, but the parliamentary subsidy was the most profitable and encountered the least resistance. By the end of the reign the standard form of taxation had become the grant by parliament of a fifteenth of the value of the movable goods or personal property from the inhabitants of the counties and a tenth from those who lived in boroughs.

The increased political importance and frequent meetings led to an institutional development of parliament which transformed its nature. Under Edward I parliament was still more an occasion than an institution. It was a meeting of the king's council afforced by nobles summoned individually and, often but not always, representatives of the shires and boroughs. The only real organization was simply the organization already possessed by the king's council. By the middle of the fourteenth century, the knights of the shires and the burgesses of the boroughs habitually met together to discuss matters (such as taxation or proposed legislation) referred to them by the council, and to draw up petitions (which often became the basis of statutory legislation) for submission to the council. This practice of consultation between knights and burgesses may be considered the origin of the House of Commons, which by the end of the century regularly elected a speaker or presiding officer. Meanwhile the organization of the clergy in parliament was changed. Representatives of the lower clergy, who had occasionally been summoned at the beginning of the century, ceased to attend parliament in favor of meeting and granting taxes in a separate convocation of their own. The higher clergy or lords spiritual (bishops and abbots) then joined with the lords temporal to form the House of Lords. Although no particular event or date marks the transition, under the three Edwards Parliament as an occasion was slowly transformed into a definite institution, the Parliament consisting of a relatively stable membership organized into a House of Lords and a House of Commons.

During the reign of Edward III the Commons in Parliament gained certain powers and rights that became a real limitation on the king. Chief of these was the Commons' control of direct taxation. The king had other ways of raising taxes than by parliamentary grant, but the Commons resisted and remonstrated over every arbitrary levy or tax granted by a nonparliamentary group, and at the same time were liberal in consenting to taxes granted in Parliament, so that finally the king gave up trying to raise money in any other way than by the consent of the Commons and Lords in Parliament. From this effective, if not exclusive, control of taxation grew the Commons' later right to withhold taxes until the fulfillment of specified conditions. This right in turn led ultimately to the principles that redress of grievances must precede supply, and that money bills must originate in the Commons. The Commons also claimed, and sometimes made good, the right to appropriate taxes for specified uses and to audit public accounts to determine whether the money had been spent as directed. In the sphere of legislation, the right of the Commons to assent to all statutes grew out of the regular practice of initiating legislation by means of a single petition which included all petitions of a general nature presented by the knights and burgesses. The "common petition" would then be formally approved by all the Commons and sent to the Lords for their assent before being presented to the council for the king's acceptance or rejection.

The last major gain of the Commons was the right to impeach the king's ministers for misconduct. By the procedure of impeachment the Commons collectively brought charges against the minister before the Lords, who pronounced the minister innocent or guilty. This was a powerful weapon to use against the king—and also, as it turned out, a powerful weapon which the king did not hesitate to use against his opponents as well. This device of impeachment as a political weapon illustrates the nature of most of the gains made by Parliament and, particularly, those made by the Commons. The institutional development of Parliament resulted mainly from its value to the king and to the lords in their political struggles. Most of the knights and burgesses were under the patronage or influence of lords, and they followed the lead of their patrons. The Commons were the agents of a struggle for power. It was no love of democracy or desire for limited monarchy that sent the Commons before the bar of the House of Lords to impeach a minister. It was merely another episode in which a faction of the nobles had gained control of Parliament and felt strong enough to destroy its enemies.

The reign of Edward III ended on just such a note. The new king was the minor son of the Black Prince, who had predeceased his father. During his minority Richard II (1377–1399) was the center around whom revolved endless plots and maneuvers to gain power which engaged most of the time of the nobles. Government was neglected. The local administration fell under the control of the local aristocracy, and the courts were often corrupted by bribery and undue influence. In 1381 discontent, which had been mounting for several years, broke out in a full-scale rebellion called the Peasants' Revolt. The movement took on the character of a social revolution, aimed against all kinds of exploitation and motivated by vague aspirations toward social equality. The government was badly shaken. The archbishop of Canterbury, who was the chancellor, and the treasurer were both murdered, and the rioting and destruction of property brought all law and order to an end. The boy-king Richard played a heroic role in putting a temporary halt to the movement, and finally the aristocracy united with other propertied classes in brutally suppressing the rebels.

After these events Richard II can scarcely be blamed for deciding, once he came of age, that the country needed a strong monarch who could preserve order and curb the ambitions of the bungling magnates who had jockeyed for power during his minority. But he went too far. Perhaps he even aimed at creating an absolute monarchy. In any event, he alienated most of the nobles and lost the support of the middle classes. When Richard confiscated the duchy of Lancaster, thus disinheriting his cousin Henry, it was clear that no property was safe with a king on the throne who held himself above the law. Henry of Lancaster raised a baronial rebellion to reclaim his inheritance and to claim the crown for himself. Richard was no match for the arms of Lancaster. The king was captured and a Parliament was summoned in his name. Claiming to represent the estates of the realm, this assembly received Richard's abdication and approved his deposition. Then Henry of Lancaster claimed the crown by conquest, by inheritance, and by the acceptance of the estates of the realm. A new Parliament was summoned, consisting of the members of the old, and the "liberty royal" of Henry IV (1399–1413) was solemnly affirmed. This elaborate attempt to legalize a *coup d'état* was followed by parliamentary acts recognizing the right of Henry's heirs to succeed to the throne. But no amount of legal fiction and constitutional theory could remove "the nemesis of Lancaster," the fatal flaw in the usurper's title wrested by force.

The Lancastrian period, 1399–1461, has been called an age of "premature constitutional monarchy," but the realities of English politics were not radically altered. If Parliament seems more prominent, it is because

Parliament was useful in sanctioning the measures of whichever faction happened at the moment to be in control. The usefulness of Parliament guaranteed its survival in the fourteenth and fifteenth centuries. By making it their means of trying to control or limit the king, the English nobles made it an indispensable part of the machinery of government. Because of their need for parliamentary support, no Lancastrian king tried to enact laws or raise taxes without the approval of Parliament. Furthermore, all important political decisions, though arrived at earlier by king or nobles, were made public in and thus made formally by Parliament, as the best means of securing widespread support for royal policy or for an attack on royal power. The institutional development of Parliament continued in the fifteenth century along the lines already indicated, but the institution itself remained essentially the tool of contending groups: the king and his supporters, or one or another faction of magnates ambitious for more power. The real center of government was not Parliament but the royal council. Since the Lancastrians owed their crown to the support of the nobles, and needed their cooperation to stay on the throne, the nobles usually dominated the council rather than the professional civil servants who had done the will of the Plantagenet kings.

Henry IV hung on to his throne by suppressing several rebellions and by reducing governmental expenses to retain the support of the middle classes. This cautious policy was jettisoned by his son and successor, Henry V (1413–1422). Conditions in France, where strife among the nobility had degenerated into anarchy and civil war, were ideal for a renewal of the Hundred Years' War. Henry V seized the opportunity to divert his nobles from quarrels at home by leading them on a new foreign adventure. He revived Edward III's claim to the French throne and proclaimed to the French that he was coming to restore peace and prosperity to his realm of France.

The campaign of 1415 was climaxed by a brilliant victory at Agincourt, where the English won their third great battle of the Hundred Years' War using the same tactics as at Crécy and Poitiers. The reduction and occupation of Normandy followed in the next few years, and in 1420 Henry won his greatest triumph, the Treaty of Troyes. This treaty provided for the marriage of Henry V and Catherine, daughter of the insane French king Charles VI, together with the recognition of Henry as heir to the French crown and regent during the life of his father-in-law. Within two years most of France north of the Loire had fallen to the English, but the task of conquering and occupying all of France was beyond the resources of any fifteenth-century English king. Fortunately for his later reputation, Henry V died prematurely at the height of his power. Having spent most of his time in foreign ventures, Henry had done practically nothing toward re-establishing an effective central government in England firmly under royal control. The circumstances after his death made that less likely than ever.

Henry VI (1422–1461) was a nine-months-old baby when he inherited the throne. Because he later lapsed into several months of mental incompetence (1453–1455) from which he probably never fully recovered, he was also thought by some contemporaries to have inherited, through his mother Catherine, the insanity of his grandfather Charles VI. Considering the constant and mounting elements of pressure, uncertainty, danger, and sudden desertions from his cause that beset him all his life, it is not surprising that Henry should have experienced anxiety. He might well have suffered a nervous breakdown without any contribution from his French heredity. During his minority England was governed by a regency of the king's relatives, who were divided into two major factions. Both council and Parliament were dominated alternately by one or the other group of magnates. On the continent English expansion actually continued slowly until by 1428 the English regent for France, John, duke of Bedford, penetrated as far south as Orléans. This success was the measure of French weakness and Bedford's personal ability, rather than the result of a concerted English effort. Parliament was weary of the cost of war. The regents in England were jealous of Bedford and fearful lest he exploit military success to gain power in England. The French recovery began in 1429, under Joan of Arc, and proceeded rapidly after the death of Bedford in 1435. By 1453 only Calais was left to English rule.

The war abroad was followed by the Wars of the Roses at home, a civil conflict which lasted intermittently for thirty years (1455–1485). The contending sides were the Yorkists (whose emblem was a white rose) and the Lancastrians (whose emblem was a red rose). So far as it was a dynastic contest, the Lancastrian king, Henry VI, derived his claim to the throne through his father and grandfather from a younger son of Edward III, while the dukes of York based their claim to the throne on descent from an older son of Edward III through the female line. But aside from dynastic legalities, the war was actually nothing more than a struggle for power, involving no political principles or constitutional issues. The fighting did not seriously affect more than a small minority of Englishmen. There was little pillaging such as France had endured so long, and the daily life of the middle and lower classes was not seriously disturbed.

In one way England gained from the civil strife. The ranks of the factious nobility were depleted, and the nobles who fought and fell in the Wars of the Roses were no great loss. They were a far cry from the baronage of the thirteenth century. Between the great nobles and the gentry of the fifteenth century there was a much greater gap than in the age of Edward I. The number of great lords had diminished and their wealth had increased. Each lord retained armed servants, often veterans of the French wars, who wore the livery (distinctive colors or uniforms) of their lord. These armed retainers were useful in settling the private feuds and quarrels in which the magnates were constantly engaged. The normal course of law enforcement was perverted in favor of powerful lords by a system called maintenance, which usually consisted of bribery or intimidation of local officials, courts, and juries. Livery and maintenance were the great abuses of the age. Law-abiding gentry and merchants, whose voices could occasionally be heard through their representatives in Parliament, desired above all else "abundant governance," that is, the strong rule of a king who could restore order, repress the ambitions and quarrels of the nobles, and enforce the law.

The Wars of the Roses came to a temporary halt when Edward of York defeated Henry VI. As Edward IV (1461–1483) he gave England the "abundant governance" that the Lancastrians had failed to provide. But Lancastrian opposition was not extinguished. There were occasional uprisings in favor of Henry VI, who even regained the crown for a few months

England and France
in the Later Middle Ages

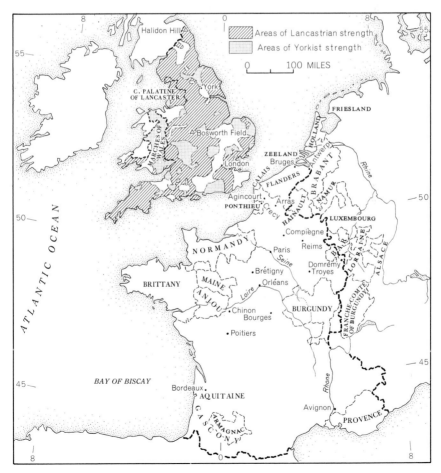

in 1471. That temporary success cost Henry his life, and in the following years judicial murders and acts of attainder eliminated other great nobles whose fate was sealed by their royal blood. On the death of Edward IV, the last grisly act of the times was played out. Edward's young son succeeded as Edward V (1483), but the duke of Gloucester (Edward IV's brother) usurped the throne as Richard III (1483–1485) and the boy-king with his younger brother disappeared into the Tower, where both were probably murdered. A dutiful Parliament recognized the succession of Richard III, just as it had sanctioned the titles and ratified the acts of Edward IV, Henry VI in 1471, Edward IV again in 1471, and Edward V.

The long tale of intrigue, treachery, and assassination was finally brought to an end at Bosworth Field in 1485 when Richard III was defeated and killed by Henry Tudor. Henry VII (1485–1509) was the grandson of Catherine, Henry V's widow, and a Welsh lord named Owen Tudor. On his mother's side he was descended from Edward III. Many others stood nearer the throne, but none had Henry Tudor's courage and ability. He strengthened his flimsy hereditary rights by marrying a daughter of Edward IV, uniting in his children both Yorkist and Lancastrian claims.

The accession of Henry VII established the Tudor dynasty which brought England over a century of relative peace and prosperity. But it took several years to convince contemporaries that Henry's success was not simply another violent episode in the civil wars. There was little that anyone could recognize as new. The foundations of Tudor policy had been laid by Edward IV: "abundant governance," the encouragement of commerce and industry, royal control of the council, and economy in government. Henry VII's task was lightened by the decimation of the nobility during the preceding thirty years and by the nearly universal desire for orderly government. The Wars of the Roses had discredited the nobility, and the Tudor strong monarchy was the beneficiary of the nobles' incompetence.

The fifteenth century in English history appears on the surface to be an age of confusion, violence, and failure: there were so many events that led to nothing permanent or constructive. But behind the dramatic scenes there were elements of strength in the English state, notably a sound economy which had begun to revive by mid-century and the institutions of local and central government which survived and even flourished throughout the disorders of the period. On the local level, for every Englishman who looked to the maintenance of a great lord there were a hundred who relied on the normal machinery of justice and administration provided by the county officials. For every mercenary who wore the livery of a great lord there were thousands of law-abiding subjects who cared nothing about the fate of either white or red rose. It was not one or another faction of lords but this great majority of Englishmen—the gentry, the freeholders of the counties, the burgesses—who welcomed the Tudor monarchy.

In the central government the influence of this majority was always present in Parliament, no matter how much one or another aristocratic faction might dominate the decisions of higher politics. Kings might come and go; each faction might have its day of power. But the dutiful Commons in Parliament, who sanctioned dynastic revolutions or reversals of policy, were necessary to the state no matter who was in power. Without their consent new laws could not be made and enforced, nor could taxes be raised. In the packed and dominated Parliaments of the fifteenth century this consent was easy to secure, but that very fact ensured the survival of Parliament, the most important single fact of that age. Not even the strongest of the Tudor monarchs could dispense with Parliament, if he would enact laws and raise taxes.

78   FRANCE: CHARLES V TO LOUIS XI

Charles V the Wise (1364–1380) served his apprenticeship in royal rule during the years following Poitiers, when his father was a prisoner of the English. As Dauphin he joined with the nobility in suppressing the great *Jacquerie* or peasants' uprising of 1358, while he accepted some of the reforms demanded by a revolutionary movement in Paris in the same year. These reforms later became the basis of a more efficient royal administration and system of collecting taxes. More difficult to control were the troopers, or *routiers*, who were released from service in the English and French armies after the treaty of Brétigny-Calais. These "free companies" of mercenary soldiers fought under a captain who hired out his services in time of war. When peace came the companies were without pay, so they swarmed all over France pillaging the countryside, putting villages to ransom or to flames, and capturing castles from which they could systematically loot the towns and highways of a region. Charles solved this problem by meddling in the disputed succession to the throne of Castile. Charles' general, Bertrand Du Guesclin, rounded up most of the *routiers* and led them south of the Pyrenees. This venture was inconclusive because the Black Prince immediately intervened to preserve English interests in Castile, but Charles' main object was accomplished: ridding France of the "free companies."

Du Guesclin was put in command of the army when the Hundred Years' War was renewed in 1369. Having noted that his general lost every major engagement in Spain but had distinguished himself in the hit-and-run tactics of which the *routiers* were masters, Charles forbade Du Guesclin to meet the enemy in force. Instead the French harried English supply lines, cut off small raiding or scouting parties, struck swiftly at vulnerable points, and always retreated before any major English army. These harassing tactics paid off splendidly. The English exhausted themselves sending large raiding parties to pillage the land. The French finally wore them down and forced the English to relinquish all of their occupied territories except Calais and the area around Bordeaux.

Charles V aided the French recovery by carrying through several reforms in the royal government. In military organization there was nothing really new, but the soldiers were paid more regularly and more emphasis was placed on the infantry, whose training and discipline were improved. Castles were repaired and properly garrisoned so that English raiding parties found it difficult to seize fortified bases for their operations. The collection of taxes was made more efficient by the institution of new tax districts under collectors who were responsible to the central government. Under Charles V the monarchy gained the consent of various regional meetings of estates to continue to collect the emergency taxes imposed originally for the ransom of King John. These included the hearth tax and several indirect taxes on merchandise, notably the salt tax. Theoretically these taxes were temporary and subject to consent by the taxpayers' representatives at meetings of the estates, but in practice the king won the right to impose taxes to meet a national emergency. This meant that the French monarchy could count on a permanent revenue far larger than could any other government in Europe.

Despite these reforms, the task of completing the expulsion of the English was beyond French resources. Discontent broke out into occasional rebellion during the last years of Charles' reign, and on his death the throne descended to a minor. Fortunately for France, England was equally exhausted and also confronted with a royal minority. The new French king was Charles VI the Mad (1380–1422), who earned his sobriquet by succumbing to an attack of madness in 1392 and, except for a few lucid intervals, remaining insane until his death. A struggle for power ensued. The constitutional results of this struggle in France were almost diametrically opposite to the results of the contemporary struggle in England under Richard II. In England Parliament was the main tool of contending factions. In France, there was no institution of the central government in which the struggle could be focused. The Estates General met very rarely, and the *Parlement* of Paris was wholly a law court whose judges did not play an influential role in higher politics. The French nobility had no intention of destroying or limiting the central government: their purpose was to seize control of the government in the name of Charles VI.

Within a few years the two leading contestants were Philip the Bold, duke of Burgundy, the king's uncle, and Louis, duke of Orléans, the king's brother. Like other royal princes, both held large appanages of the crown. This custom of endowing cadet branches of the royal house was not, in normal times and under a strong king, a danger to the crown. But during the reign of Charles VI the appanages were not only independent principalities, they were also, for all practical purposes, the bases of power from which the princes strove to gain control of the royal administration. Philip the Bold held the French duchy of Burgundy, Franche-Comté (a county within the Empire), and Flanders which he acquired by marriage. In addition to Orléans, Duke Louis held four counties in France. The quarrel remained fairly peaceful during the life of Philip the Bold, but his son John the Fearless lacked any scruples. To eliminate his rival he simply had Louis of Orléans murdered by thugs in 1407.

Leadership of the Orleanist faction now passed to the father-in-law of the late duke's son and heir. This was the count of Armagnac, from whom the Orleanist party derives its more familiar name. The quarrels between Armagnacs and Burgundians plunged France into civil war punctuated by frequent truces and false reconciliations. The highlight of the next few years was the assassination in 1419 of Duke John the Fearless by the Armagnacs—during a prearranged conference to restore peace. Meanwhile Henry V of England had invaded France and won the great victory at Agincourt in 1415. The Burgundians now threw in their forces with the English. John's successor, Duke Philip the Good, controlled both King Charles VI and his influential wife. It was in the Burgundian interest that the Treaty of Troyes, 1420, was negotiated. The spineless Dauphin (the future Charles VII) reigned but hardly ruled in southern France, while the duke of Bedford and Duke Philip divided the north. Bedford's troops laid siege to Orléans in 1428 and the fortunes of the French monarchy reached their nadir.

At this point Joan of Arc appeared. It is impossible to separate the legendary from the historical person, for the legend of Joan affected the course of events in the next twenty years as much as Joan herself did. During the brief period (March 1429 to May 1431) in which she played an active role her influence was decisive but it did not extend beyond the court of Charles VII and the troops with whom she participated in several battles. Only later did she become the symbol of national resistance and of the liberation of France from foreign domination. She herself was the result, rather than the cause, of French nationalism—though the legendary Joan certainly stimulated the further growth of nationalism.

Joan's birthplace, Domrémy, was a village situated near the border of France and Lorraine, a region that had suffered greatly from the civil war between Armagnacs and Burgundians. She and her family had experienced the plundering of Burgundian raids and the temporary exile these raids forced upon a defenseless peasantry. As she grew up she imbibed the inarticulate resentment of the common people against the disorders and misfortunes which were associated with the English occupation, the abasement of the monarchy, and the Burgundian ascendancy in northern France. In Joan's case, however, the resentment was not wholly inarticulate. As an adolescent, she began to hear voices and to have visions. She was convinced that they were the voices of angels; on one occasion she was visited by that militant archangel, St. Michael. From these voices she received instructions which overawed her, but she was finally convinced that she had been chosen as an instrument of divine will. All this we know from Joan's statements at her trial. Was she mentally deficient or emotionally unstable or even a paranoiac? Quite possibly. And yet few historians doubt that Joan honestly and sincerely believed what she said. Her contemporaries put it more simply. To them the question was, did the Maid come from God or from the devil? As one chronicler put it, "God only knows."

Whether divinely inspired or the product of a peasant's common sense, Joan's program was straightforward and politically realistic. The king must receive his crown, and to accomplish this and restore his kingdom to him the English must be driven out and their Burgundian allies must be reduced to obedience. Joan resolved to carry out this program shortly after news of the siege of Orléans reached her region. Morale in Armagnac-controlled France had hit a new low. It seemed to many that only by a miracle could the royalist cause be saved. Joan convinced the local military governor of her mission, and he gave her arms, armor, and an escort to the court of Charles VII at Chinon. After some hesitation Charles also was convinced that the Maid was sent by heaven to drive the English out of France. Although Charles and his advisers had some misgivings about this girl who cut her hair like a boy and wore the clothes of a man, she was allowed to ride off with troops that had been assembled for the relief of Orléans. The English forces were depleted and weary, and the presence of Joan sent a thrill through the French ranks. Although legend has it otherwise, Joan did not actually lead the troops. More important, she rallied their sagging morale and with a sure instinct she repeatedly made her dramatic appearance at just the critical juncture of a battle or skirmish to swing the victory to French arms. The siege of Orléans was raised ten days after Joan's arrival, and the Maid got the credit. Thus inspired, the French troops reduced all the other English outposts on the Loire, and the way was cleared for a drive northward toward Paris.

At this juncture Joan once more intervened to determine the course of events. She insisted, and the royal advisers finally agreed, that Charles should be crowned at Reims. From a military point of view the project seemed hazardous, for Reims was deep within enemy-occupied territory. Actually, however, Charles' army drove through to Reims without difficulty. Town after town shifted allegiance and opened its gates to the royalist forces. A simple coronation service took place in July, 1429, with only three peers of France—and Joan—in attendance. Now once more, after seven years of devastation and defeat, the kingdom had a solemnly anointed king and Frenchmen rallied to the support of their monarchy. Many towns deserted the English or Burgundian cause without a fight. But in the military sphere Joan's earlier successes did not continue. An assault on Paris failed and efforts to capture towns where adequate English garrisons were stationed were also unsuccessful. The Anglo-Burgundian forces even resumed the offensive. In the defense of the royalist town of Compiègne, during a sortie to break up the besieging forces, Joan was captured by the Burgundians, in May, 1430.

What happened next can be understood only in terms of contemporary ideas and values. The code of war at this time was a latter-day chivalry which allowed and expected "honorable" treatment of prisoners of war who were noble, but which also allowed the most brutal treatment of mercenary soldiers who fell into enemy hands and of peasants who dwelt in enemy territory. Charles VII has been severely criticized for not rescuing Joan of Arc from her Burgundian captors. It is possible that this could have been done, but all the values and attitudes of the age were against it. Joan was neither the squire nor the personal retainer nor the valet of the king. No compulsion of honor required Charles to come to her aid. She was a phenomenon unknown to contemporary standards of proper conduct. Even worse, for her personal welfare, she seemed at this point to have served her purpose. No success had come her way since the coronation at Reims, and Charles did not demean himself to come to the peasant girl's rescue. Joan was handed over to the English who in turn handed her over to the Inquisition for trial as a heretic and a witch. It was an easy matter to convict an illiterate girl with the mind of a child—she told the tribunal that she thought she was nineteen, but was not sure. When she faltered and seemed to recant, but then persisted in her earlier statements about her visions, she was convicted as a relapsed heretic so that she could be burned at the stake by the English.

Meanwhile, French recovery proceeded rapidly. All across northern France national resistance mounted, guerrilla fighting broke out in isolated regions, and the English were unable to collect taxes and maintain order. At court Charles VII's Armagnac advisers were replaced by more nationally minded officials who were ready to patch up the quarrel with Burgundy and who favored an energetic prosecution of the war. At the Congress of Arras, in 1435, Duke Philip the Good broke with his English allies, papal legates condemned the Treaty of Troyes as invalid, and the Burgundians recognized Charles VII as king. Negotiations for peace with the English now bogged down, and in the same year the duke of Bedford, England's best general and governor, died. In 1436 Paris fell. With the reoccupation of the capital all of France except Normandy, Maine, and part of Gascony was once more united under one king, Charles VII the Well Served (1422–1461).

These developments were the work of an able group of ministers whose efforts gave Charles VII his sobriquet. Weary of the ambitions and quarrels of the nobles, Burgundian and Armagnac alike, Charles replaced as many councillors and officials as he dared with new men whose bourgeois origins were some guarantee of dependence on royal favor. These

King Charles VII of France. Portrait (c.1460); at right, Charles presides over meeting of *Parlement* in 1458; both by Jean Fouquet. PHOTOS: GIRAUDON.

ministers now turned to the restoration of the royal administration and the strengthening of the central government. The task was not difficult, for the prestige of the monarchy stood high. Public opinion associated peace, order, and the expulsion of the foreigner with the monarchy. The king was the beneficiary of the successful conclusion of the Hundred Years' War in 1453, when only Calais remained in English hands. The war taxes were continued on a permanent basis, although occasionally the government found it expedient to gain the consent and approval of local or even national meetings of the estates. Conditions justified a permanent army, for in addition to war against the English the government had to wage unceasing campaigns against bands of unemployed mercenary soldiers who roamed the country. The desolation of France actually strengthened the monarchy. Although already burdened with heavy taxation, the people gladly paid extra taxes for a royal army to protect them from the pillaging of these lawless bands.

Charles VII was succeeded by the fascinating and unscrupulous Louis XI (1461–1483), who completed the reconstruction of the French monarchy. Louis' goal was to build what may be called, with some exaggeration, an absolute state. He had no taste for chivalry and he looked upon the feudal privileges of his nobles simply as obstacles. He shrank from warfare, preferring to use his consummate skill in diplomacy and bribery to achieve his ends. He filled the offices of government with low-born men and constantly traveled the length and breadth of his kingdom supervising the minutest affairs. Parsimonious and pious in the extreme, he dressed

Duke Philip the Good of Burgundy. Attributed to Rogier van der Weyden (c.1460). LOUVRE, PARIS. PHOTO: GIRAUDON.

shabbily and treated the Virgin and the saints like allies to be won by diplomatic maneuvers and timely offerings. Louis was the antithesis of the Valois ideal of kingship; he was bourgeois in sympathies and the bourgeoisie profited from his strong rule more than any other class.

One reason for Louis' attitude was the aristocratic reaction that took place in the opening years of his reign. The nobles leagued together in an effort to regain the powers in the central government from which Charles VII had systematically excluded them. The coalition of great nobles was led by Duke Philip the Good of Burgundy, whose ambition was to establish a completely independent "middle kingdom" between France and the Empire. To this end he had added to his original territories the duchies of Luxembourg and Brabant, and the counties of Holland, Zeeland, Friesland, Hainault, and Namur—most of them acquired by the marriage alliances of his relatives who had died without heirs. The dukes of Burgundy attempted, with some success, to unify this complex of territories under a central administration modeled on that of France and staffed largely with officials trained in the French royal administration. But local privileges were respected and regional governments continued to function under ducal supervision, while another obstacle to unification was the geographical fact that the duchy of Burgundy and Franche-Comté, in the south, were separated from the duke's other lands by Alsace and Lorraine.

Although Louis XI weathered the storm of aristocratic reaction, by promising much and parting with little, the danger from Burgundy remained. Philip's successor was the even more ambitious Duke Charles the Rash (1467–1477). Louis carefully avoided committing French troops to battle, but he stirred up Duke Charles' enemies in Alsace and Lorraine. The crowning achievement of his diplomacy was to bring the Swiss into conflict with Burgundy. Twice the Swiss pikemen met and defeated the Burgundian cavalry, and in the second battle Charles the Rash was killed. Rejoicing over the death of his cousin, Louis XI moved swiftly to declare the French fiefs of the duchy escheated to the crown, although this disinherited Charles' daughter Mary of Burgundy. Mary's later marriage to Maximilian of Habsburg brought to that dynasty her claims to these fiefs, which led to the great Habsburg-Valois struggles of the sixteenth century. Louis' good fortune persisted. Before the end of the reign the duchy of Anjou and the counties of Maine, Bar, and Provence also escheated to the crown. Only Flanders and Brittany remained outside the royal domain.

When Louis XI died, the foundations of the strong monarchy of early modern France had been established: a centralized royal administration, a judicial system which reflected provincial diversity but which was under royal control, a kingdom almost entirely under the direct rule of the king, and a system of government in which the nobility were subordinate and the bourgeoisie prominent. Even more than Henry Tudor of England, Louis XI typified the "new monarchy" based on medieval institutions, but relatively free from medieval limitations, that marked the close of the Middle Ages.

The Church
in the Later Middle Ages

The history of the Church in the two centuries before the Reformation may be divided into four chronological periods. This chapter will be concerned with the first three: the period of the Avignonese papacy (1305–1378), the Great Schism (1378–1409), and the Age of the Councils (1409–1447). The failure of the conciliar movement marked the end of the medieval Church as an effective international or universal force in Western society. The fourth period (after 1447) will be dealt with when we consider Italy in the fifteenth century, for the so-called "Renaissance papacy" can best be understood in terms of the politics and rivalries of the Italian city-states.

The clergy of the later Middle Ages were probably, on the whole, better disciplined and better educated than in any preceding period. Yet the vitality and leadership once provided by the Church steadily declined. Part of the reason for this decline was the vigor and growth of secular governments, especially those of the western monarchies. But the malady went deeper than competition from secular institutions. Within the clergy the capacity for reform was waning. No new religious order founded in the fourteenth and fifteenth centuries had anywhere near the importance or influence of the Cistercians in the twelfth century or of the Franciscans and Dominicans in the thirteenth. The last general reform legislation affecting the regular clergy in the Middle Ages was issued by Benedict XII (1334–1342). His monastic constitutions were, however, largely a re-enactment and confirmation of existing regulations, including the mitigations of the Benedictine Rule that had grown up by custom.

In the fourteenth century a new wave of anticlerical criticism assailed the Church. Some of this criticism developed into new heresies. Most of it was directed primarily against the worldliness, corruption, or uselessness of the secular and regular clergy. Europeans were no less religious than before; if anything, they were more so. But the clergy were no longer able to absorb or give direction to the new currents of piety and devotion, which appealed especially to the laity. The most conspicuous failure was that of the papacy, just as the popes were also the most conspicuous targets for anticlerical criticism. The decline and fall of the medieval papacy continued steadily amidst the wealth and splendor of Avignon, through the divided obedience and disillusioning quarrels of the Great Schism, and into the conciliar movement, which enlisted the ablest minds and the most sincere reformers of the period. The final triumph of the papacy over the councils was a hollow victory. The unity of Christendom was undermined, if still formally unbroken.

79   THE BABYLONIAN CAPTIVITY AND THE GREAT SCHISM

After the brief pontificate of Benedict XI (1303–1304), the cardinals chose an outsider, a man acceptable to Philip the Fair who was not committed to any of the factional struggles that divided the College of Cardinals. This was the archbishop of Bordeaux, who became Clement V (1305–1314). Clement intended to go to Rome, but he kept postponing his trip. The situation in Italy offered little to attract a French pope. Guelphs and Ghibellines had reduced most of central and northern Italy to anarchy. The Papal States were torn by the feuds of the Colonna, Orsini, and other noble families. With the appearance of the emperor Henry VII in Italy the city of Rome became a battlefield for the imperial and papal forces. Meanwhile, there was urgent business to detain Clement on the other side of the Alps: negotiations for peace between Edward I and Philip the Fair; the accusations against Boniface VIII which had never been terminated; Philip's attack on the Templars; and the council of Vienne in 1312.

In all these affairs, Clement displayed unwonted timidity and he sedulously avoided any conflict such as had brought Boniface VIII to his inglorious end. But it would be an exaggeration to portray Clement simply as a subservient tool of the French monarchy. Papal residence at Avignon actually resulted from Clement's desire to be free from Philip's pressure and at the same time to live in surroundings more congenial than strife-

Pope Clement V Consecrating an Archbishop at Avignon. Manuscript illustration (fourteenth century). PHOTO: MARBURG—ART REFERENCE BUREAU.

ridden Rome. The imperial city of Avignon was French in everything except political allegiance. Situated on the east bank of the Rhone, it lay within a county of Provence that belonged to the papacy. Clement filled vacancies in the College of Cardinals with French prelates, and by the end of his pontificate the majority were quite content to elect another French pope and remain in Avignon.

Continued residence at Avignon invited criticism. If absenteeism was a vice, it was all the more vicious for a pope. If earlier popes had been forced to flee from Rome, most of them did so in the heroic tradition of Gregory VII—because they "loved justice and hated iniquity"—and not for their own security and comfort. If St. Peter had faced the dangers of pagan Rome, even at the price of martyrdom, why should his successor shrink from the perils of Christian Rome? The Avignonese popes sensed their responsibility, but they could not bring themselves to live up to it. Three times, at the last minute, they called off plans to return to Italy, because the situation was too dangerous. The price of security came high. The popes at Avignon could no longer speak with the authority and prestige that for centuries had been associated with the Holy City.

Furthermore, the popes were criticized, unfairly, for being little more than "chaplains of the French king." This charge had a specious basis in the fact that all the Avignonese popes were French, as were most of their cardinals. In fact, however, the popes were remarkably independent, especially during the brief reigns of the sons of Philip the Fair (from 1314 to

1328) and during the reign of John the Good (1350–1364). On several occasions they intervened to re-establish peace between France and England when it was definitely against French interests to do so. Finally, when the situation in Italy was at last favorable for a return of the papacy, the strongest French king of the period, Charles V, was unable to prevent the pope from resuming his residence in Rome.

On the whole the Avignonese popes were able men if not outstanding religious leaders. Their talents lay in the fields of administration, law, and finance. The Avignonese papacy marked the culmination of the centralization of the medieval Church. The characteristic feature of this centralization, which critics then and now single out for special condemnation, was the system of financial extortion. The main author of this system was John XXII (1316–1334), who was almost constantly engaged in political or ecclesiastical struggles. It was his conviction that the Church could not be independent of temporal rulers unless the papacy were wealthy enough to meet them on equal terms. The other characteristic feature of papal centralization was the increasing control of all ecclesiastical business by the papal *curia*. Here too the justification, in John XXII's view, was the necessity of papal supremacy over the clergy if the Church were to be free from secular control. The net result was the rapid growth of offices and officials, a bureaucratic proliferation at Avignon that made the *curia* of Innocent III seem primitive.

At the center of the papal government, as of any other medieval government, was the household. The pope's household differed mainly in being larger and more elaborate than the others. There were members of the staff whose functions were essentially domestic and personal: porters and ushers, chaplains and chamberlains, knights and squires (the predecessors of the modern Swiss Guard), cooks and kitchen scullions, butlers and food buyers (including a *buticularius* who stocked the wine cellar and tasted the wine before it was poured into the pope's cup), marshals, grooms, stableboys, etc. Other members of the household combined domestic and governmental duties; e.g., couriers not only carried messages but acted as summoners for papal courts and exercised such police functions as finding, arresting, and bringing persons accused of crimes under papal jurisdiction back to Avignon for trial by the appropriate court. Counting such minor officials as the keeper of the papal plate, the keeper of the papal zoo, physicians and barbers, and all the others, there were more than three hundred, perhaps more than four hundred, members of the household.

The College of Cardinals was the Senate of Christendom, as some contemporaries (including most of the cardinals) thought. The pope always consulted the cardinals on major decisions and rarely acted on an important matter (such as appointing a new cardinal) without their collective advice and approval. Although their most important function as a college was to elect a new pope, the cardinals were more than a corporate body. Individually they were active in every phase of papal government, whether as legates representing the pope at courts of secular rulers or as officials in the several departments of the government at Avignon. Each cardinal, as a "prince of the Church," maintained a household on a princely scale. One fourteenth-century cardinal's household included a chamberlain, auditor, porter, attorney, physician, apothecary, groom, and several chaplains, not to mention a dozen or more lesser servants, clerks, and scribes. John XXII, in an effort to keep his cardinals from living too lavishly, forbade them to have more than ten squires in their retinue. Because of their status, influence, and interests, many cardinals also attracted protégés and hangers-on—poor scholars, artists, writers, entertainers, or ambitious but unbeneficed clerks in minor orders—to adorn their households or simply to exploit their patronage.

The papal government at Avignon was divided into four main branches: the chancery, the *camera apostolica*, the Datary, and a hierarchy of judicial tribunals. The papal *curia*, just as in the case of the *curia* of a king or emperor, originally transacted whatever business was at hand, without separate offices or specialized officials. The earliest department to be differentiated from the *curia* as a whole was the chancery. By the fourteenth century it consisted of seven offices whose main business was the dispatch of various kinds of routine administrative correspondence. The chancery also received petitions, examined the qualifications of candidates for benefices, and had official custody of the records of the *curia*.

The financial business of the *curia* was transacted in the *camera apostolica*, which emerged as a separate department in the thirteenth century. Its administrative head was the treasurer, and its policy-making head was the chamberlain. Finance and policy, or politics, were inseparable (e.g., negotiating with a secular ruler for a new collection of clerical taxes, or for the appointment of a bishop and the payment of fees in connection therewith). Hence the chamberlain became the equivalent of a papal prime minister, the most trusted councillor of the pope. Most instructions to papal legates and correspondence of a confidential nature went through the chamberlain. He had his own secretarial staff, and most of the officials in the papal *curia* were responsible to him. The papal mint was under his control, and legal disputes concerning papal revenues were determined in the court of an auditor under his jurisdiction.

The chamberlain also supervised the work of a host of tax collectors and other agents, and was responsible for the receipt and auditing of revenues. Some of the older papal revenues were declining, such as the taxes and rents collected from the Papal States. To make up for these losses and to increase the total income, collection of extraordinary taxes from the clergy was intensified and other revenues were collected more rigorously. Revenues paid by the clergy were of various kinds. For example, bishops and abbots appointed or provided by the pope paid annual income taxes, in addition to a multitude of fees and gratuities charged at the time of appointment, plus a tax called "common services" payable from the first year's revenues (i.e., "first fruits") of the see or abbey, a tax that corresponded with the annates paid by the lesser clergy from benefices reserved for papal appointment. In many dioceses (though not in France or England), on the death of a prelate provided by the pope, the papal *curia* exercised the right of *spolia* (i.e., confiscation of the personal property of the deceased), and then collected the revenues of the benefice so long as it was vacant. Because so many revenues were collectible from clergy who were provided by the pope, papal provisions were extended steadily until by the end of the fourteenth century all episcopal and most monastic benefices, and a multitude of lesser ones, were reserved for papal nomination. These reservations were also made to produce revenue by the practice of selling "expectancies" to hopeful candidates for the right to be considered for provision to benefices when they became vacant.

In the first half of the fourteenth century the Datary became a separate department of the papal *curia*, taking over several functions previously the responsibility of the chancery. Its main business consisted of the receipt of and action upon petitions that did not require judicial determination by one of the tribunals. Where no dispute between parties was involved, and in cases that did not concern matters of conscience, the Datary disposed of appointments to benefices, dispensations from provisions of the canon law (especially in routine cases of marriage irregularities), and the granting of papal approval to the disposition of ecclesiastical property or offices among the clergy.

In the judicial branch of the *curia* there were several tribunals, the highest being a full meeting of pope and cardinals in the Consistory. Cases were usually referred from the Consistory to local judges delegate or to some other court of the *curia* for preliminary investigation. Any number, or even all, of the cardinals could constitute a court for a particular case. Such special courts usually delegated their functions to auditors for most of the litigation, after which the case was normally referred back to the pope for judgment based on the recommendation of the lower tribunal. At each stage there were notaries, clerks, ushers, secretaries, and other minor officials whose duties were necessary for the advancement of litigation—at a fee, of course. The more routine side of papal jurisdiction was administered by the *Rota*, where the litigant could secure final judgment without reference of his case to the pope or cardinals. Cases were normally initiated through a petition submitted in the chancery, or else by reference from the Consistory. The judges of the *Rota* were a panel of auditors from whom several were appointed to hear each case, but judgment was pronounced by all the auditors (or a majority) after a review of the evidence and arguments. Finally, there was a special tribunal, or *Audientia,* for the determination of technical legal points and the investigation of documentary evidence, to which a case might be referred at any stage in the proceedings in some other court. Even from this brief description it is obvious that litigation at the papal *curia* could be complicated and lengthy. The judicial machinery was ideal for defendants who sought to delay the due process of law. Because of the many stages through which each case had to be taken there were numerous occasions for the plaintiff or defendant to be tapped for a notary's fee or a clerk's honorarium.

The Penitentiary was a quasi-judicial body that administered the canon law with respect to ecclesiastical penalties. Its jurisdiction ranged from the relaxation of excommunication or interdict to the granting of dispensations. A cardinal presided over the Penitentiary and delegated to his assistants the hearing of particular cases, such as the petition of a layman to be allowed marriage within the prohibited degrees of consanguinity, or of a bishop to hold more than one bishopric. Difficult cases or those involving the relations of the papacy with important persons were referred to the pope for judgment.

The operation of this vast machinery of papal government absorbed most of the time and energy of the popes. Critics who thought the clergy as a whole were too wealthy and worldly denounced the papacy for setting a bad example. How could bishops be expected to tend their flocks when the supreme shepherd fleeced them? Papal provisions were the main target for much of this criticism. When a benefice was reserved for papal provision, not only did the local patron lose his right (often lucrative) of nomination but frequently a nonresident was appointed to the benefice, with most of the revenues drained away to foreign parts, while an underpaid vicar attended to the duties of the parish or other benefice. Also encouraged by papal provisions was pluralism, the holding of more than one benefice by papal dispensation, a practice that often compounded all the abuses of absenteeism. The multiplication of fees for all the services offered by the papal *curia*, and payable at every stage of litigation in papal courts, led to the charge of simony at the see of St. Peter.

Criticism came from diverse quarters. The Avignonese regime suffered a desertion of the intellectuals, led by Petrarch (d.1374) who coined the phrase "Babylonian captivity" to castigate all the evils of the *curia* at Avignon. St. Catherine of Siena (d.1380) bombarded the popes and the rulers of Europe with indignant letters demanding the return of the papacy to Rome. Earlier, the disputes between John XXII and the emperor Lewis IV—which merely continued and refined old arguments about the superiority of spiritual or secular authority—brought forth bitter denunciations of the papacy as an institution subverted by political ambition and ill-gotten wealth. From within the ranks of the clergy the Franciscan Order produced acrimonious debates about the ownership of property by friars. One group of the Order, the Spiritual Franciscans, attacked the others, called Conventuals, for not adhering strictly to St. Francis' injunction against owning property. From a squabble within the Order the dispute took on wider significance when the Spirituals generalized their views into the theory of apostolic poverty applying to all the clergy. According to this theory, Christ and the Apostles possessed no property, and therefore the clergy and above all the pope as vicar of Christ should give up all earthly possessions. This conclusion stupified John XXII, who denounced the whole theory as heretical in 1323. Antipapal feeling was turned to the profit, in some cases, of the secular rulers. The most notable example comes from England, where Edward III was able to redress the balance of ecclesiastical control in favor of the crown. The Statute of Provisors (1351) formally prohibited papal provisions but left the king free to negotiate compromises on particular appointments, and the Statute of Praemunire (1353) prohibited appeals from English courts to the papal *curia* in cases where, by English interpretation, the jurisdiction of royal courts was competent.

There was mounting pressure on the Avignonese popes to return to Rome. The Romans, deprived of their profits of the tourist trade to the Holy City, and with injured pride, clamored for the return of the pontiff whose presence was necessary to restore the city to its place as the capital of Christendom. Meanwhile conditions in Rome were much improved during the pontificate of Innocent VI (1352–1362), who sent the cardinal Albornoz to re-establish authority and order in the Papal States. As France was ravaged by the Hundred Years' War, Avignon lost its appeal as a secure haven, especially after Innocent VI was held prisoner within the fortified papal palace by one of the free companies until he paid tribute. Urban V (1362–1370) actually brought the *curia* back to Rome, but after three years of vain efforts to re-establish papal authority he returned to Avignon. Gregory XI (1370–1378) tried it again, with the same result. But before he could actually depart from Rome he died.

The sixteen cardinals (eleven French, four Italian, and one Spanish) who were with Gregory XI in Rome met immediately in conclave to elect a new pope. After a brief stalemate because the French cardinals could not agree, a compromise candidate favored by the Italian cardinals was elected with the necessary two-thirds majority. This was the archbishop of Bari, who had served the papal *curia* and the cardinals successfully in various important administrative capacities, though he had not been elevated to the rank of cardinal himself. Since he was not then in Rome, messengers were sent to inform the archbishop before public announcement could be made. Meanwhile, unaware that the election had already taken place, a tumultuous mob gathered outside the conclave, shouting for a Roman, or at least an Italian, to be elected pope. When some of the demonstrators broke into the conclave, threatening physical violence, most of the cardinals fled in terror. Order was restored and on the next day the archbishop arrived. The remaining cardinals confirmed his election, he assumed the papal name of Urban VI, and ten days later he was crowned on Easter Sunday before an enthusiastic crowd.

Urban VI (1378–1389) had been an exemplary and efficient, if somewhat colorless, prelate; as an able servant of the cardinals for many years he was thoroughly familiar with the way of life and the inner politics of the *curia*. Now, much to everybody's surprise (especially the cardinals'), the new pope suddenly became an ardent and even ruthless reformer, determined to root out the worldliness of the clergy, and to begin at the top with the papal *curia* and the cardinals. The latter bitterly resisted Urban's efforts to reduce their personal revenues, eliminate corrupt practices, and put a bridle on their influence. Goaded by their resistance, Urban became arbitrary and violent, according to his enemies. (Even his supporters admitted he was tactless and unusually suspicious.) At this point the French cardinals fled to Anagni, where they declared Urban's election invalid because it was forced upon them by the Roman mob. Following the logic of this pronouncement they later elected a new pope, Clement VII (1378–1394), with whom they then returned to Avignon.

Thus began the Great Schism, during which Europe was divided in obedience between the Roman and the Avignonese line of popes. The abuses of "the Babylonian captivity" were multiplied by two. The additional scandal of schism was charged against both popes, while each hurled anathema at the other. Charles V of France supported the French cardinals and their pope, Clement VII of Avignon. In what was really nothing more than a political alignment, the French allies—Scotland, Navarre, Castile, Aragon, and various German princes under French influence—fell into line in support of the Avignonese papacy. The enemies of France recognized the Roman line: England (with Gascony), Flanders, Portugal, the emperor and most of the German princes, together with Bohemia and Hungary. Italy as usual was divided, and the Italian states were ready to change sides as expediency might suggest.

80   THE AGE OF THE COUNCILS

The immediate problem created by the Schism was: which of the rival popes was the true pope? With Europe so evenly divided, and with no clear legal theory by which one or the other pope could be preferred in this unprecedented situation, the conflict between Avignon and Rome did not rise above the level of personalities and power politics. Each pope excommunicated the other, together with their respective supporters. Each pope was willing to accept the other's abdication on lenient terms but refused to consider the judgment of any secular prince or ecclesiastical body. There was no provision in canon law or in the tradition of the Church for any higher jurisdiction than that of a true pope—and neither pope was prepared to admit that he was not canonically elected as the true pope. The result was a complete deadlock. The Church suffered because the overwhelming majority of people believed in the essential rightness and necessity of the unity of the Church and of Christendom under one supreme head, just as in the twentieth century the overwhelming majority of people believe in the essential rightness of the sovereign and independent national state.

Neither Urban VI of Rome nor Clement VII of Avignon was able to lead the way out of the difficulty. Nor were the cardinals. When Urban VI died the Roman cardinals elected Boniface IX (1389–1404), whose claims were undiminished, and when Clement VII died the Avignonese cardinals elected the redoubtable Benedict XIII (1394–1423). It was clear that the "way of fact" or the resort to power politics as a means of mobilizing support behind one pope had failed. Next was tried the "way of cession," or a policy (supported especially by the French king and clergy) of persuading each pope to abdicate so that both colleges of cardinals could combine to elect a new pope who would restore unity. The Roman college apparently accepted this solution, for in the elections of Innocent VII (1404–1406) and Gregory XII (1406–1415) each cardinal had, before the election, bound himself to resign if elected, if by that act the Schism might be ended. But the realities of politics made it impossible for the Roman popes to abandon their supporters unless Benedict XIII of Avignon was equally willing to abdicate. Benedict played a remarkable game. At every turn, he stubbornly resisted the final step of abdicating, while he was repeatedly able to maneuver his Roman opponents into seeming to be responsible for the breakdown of negotiations. Even when the French monarchy withdrew its support, from 1398 to 1403, so that Benedict XIII lost the papal revenues and papal control of the Church in France, the Avignonese pope weathered the storm because his Roman opponents (sensing victory) refused to compromise.

There was a third way out of the difficulty, the "way of the council." As the Schism continued, more and more theologians, lawyers, and administrators—both among the clergy and among the advisers of the secular rulers—were convinced that it was necessary to call a general council to restore unity. As the demand for a council grew, the professors at the University of Paris took the lead in propounding a justification of the authority of a general council to assume jurisdiction in the dispute. There were some neat problems involved. Who is authorized to summon a council? Who presides? Is the jurisdiction of a council superior or inferior to that of the head of the Church, and if not inferior is the pope head in any real sense? As these questions were raised and discussed, it became clear that what had begun as a dispute over which claimant was true pope had now become a constitutional debate over the distribution of authority within the Church. A weakness of conciliar thought was the diversity of views, the failure to unite on a single program. But one basic premise was accepted by all the conciliarists: the distinction between the universal Church and the papacy, and the superiority of the former over the latter. Many conciliarists became convinced that in addition to healing the Schism there should also be a reform of the Church "in head and members," by which they meant that papal authority should be limited.

Everybody wanted to end the Schism, but many shrank from the idea that a council was superior to a pope. The restoration of unity and the suppression of heresy were generally considered more urgent than reform. The fact that both the Spiritual Franciscans and the publicists of Lewis IV had appealed to a council against John XXII did not help the conciliarists' cause. But the latter were able to rely on the doctrine of the canon lawyers that a general council of the Church could not err in matters of faith, and that if a pope were guilty of heresy he could be judged by a general council. It was but a short step to insist that prolonging a schism was tantamount to heresy. This argument, plus the mounting public demand for an end of the Schism, finally convinced the cardinals of each college that only a general council could get results. In the midst of negotiations on behalf of Gregory XII and Benedict XIII, most of the Roman and Avignonese cardinals withdrew their obedience from either pontiff and joined in calling a general council to meet at Pisa in 1409.

Over five hundred prelates met in the Council of Pisa to end the Schism, suppress heresy, and reform the Church. Both popes were deposed as "schismatics and notorious heretics, guilty of perjury and the sources of open scandal to the Church." The cardinals present at Pisa were commissioned to elect a new pope: Alexander V (1409–1410). Gregory XII and Benedict XIII promptly denounced the council and excommunicated Alexander V. The result was a triple schism. The situation was unchanged when Alexander died and was succeeded by John XXIII (1410–1415).[1] John's character was reprehensible and his interests were almost wholly confined to defeating the reforms promulgated by the Council of Pisa and defending the Papal States against invasion by the king of Naples.

The failure of the Council of Pisa led to demands for a new council. In accordance with medieval precedent, John XXIII, as the pope recog-

[1] The canonical status of the elections of Alexander V and his successor John XXIII must be considered identical, given the circumstances of each; however, Alexander died in office while John was deposed by a council and then ratified (whether under duress or not is another question) his own deposition. Alexander VI (1492–1503), Alexander VII (1655–1667), and Alexander VIII (1689–1691), by the numeration they employed tacitly recognized the validity of their conciliar-sponsored predecessor's election and pontificate. The pope who was closely connected with the mid-twentieth century conciliar movement (including, it should be added, a firm papal leadership of the movement) took the papal name of John XXIII (1958–1963), thus rejecting the fifteenth-century John XXIII as having been a false pope. Modern lists of popes that omit the fifteenth-century John XXIII also take no notice of any Alexander between Alexander IV (1254–1261) and Alexander VI.

nized by the conciliar party, was the proper authority to summon the new council. When he procrastinated, the conciliarists appealed to the emperor Sigismund on the precedent of the general councils of antiquity which had been convened by the Roman emperors. At this time, John XXIII was in a difficult situation. Rome had fallen in 1413 to the king of Naples, who also occupied much of the Papal States. Any hope of recovering these losses depended on the support of Sigismund, whose troops were then in northern Italy. John XXIII therefore reluctantly approved the principle of calling a new council, and Sigismund forthwith issued an imperial summons to all prelates and princes to attend or send representatives to a new general council at Constance. There was nothing for John to do but issue his own summons to the same effect.

Sigismund's motives in calling the Council of Constance (1414–1418) were mixed. He probably approved of strengthening the Church by reform and by the suppression of heresy. Also, it enhanced imperial prestige to assume the initiative in business that affected all of Christendom, and to hold the council within the Empire. The summons to lay rulers as well as the clergy was well calculated to commit the former to support the acts of the council. The council itself was a leisurely, though magnificent, affair. The representatives of the rulers, the bishops and abbots or their representatives, and the representatives of the universities and other ecclesiastical corporations were not all assembled until months after the council opened. The organization of the council was novel. Instead of voting by head, the traditional method which would have favored John XXIII because of the numerous Italian clergy present, the council was organized into five nations after the pattern of medieval universities. Each nation—Italian, German, English, French, and Spanish—had one vote in the formal casting of ballots.

The main agenda were the same as at Pisa. The Schism was finally healed by the deposition of all three popes. After much futile maneuvering, including a brief flight from Constance disguised as a stableboy, John XXIII accepted and ratified the action of the council. With more grace and acumen Gregory XII anticipated the action by first formally summoning the council as true pope and then notifying it of his voluntary abdication—thus preserving the legal fiction of papal independence and supremacy over a general council. Benedict XIII, together with four faithful cardinals, obstinately held out and hurled anathemas at all and sundry from his castle in Spain until his death in 1423. Even then this Avignonese-Aragonese line was not ended. In a comic-opera denouement three of his cardinals elected an antipope who finally abdicated in 1429, while the fourth cardinal created a schism within the schismatic line by electing a rival antipope of whom little beyond his name is known. Meanwhile in 1417 at the Council of Constance the cardinals, afforced by representatives of each of the five nations, elected Martin V (1417–1431), and for all practical purposes the Great Schism was ended.

The suppression of heresy was more readily handled but with less enduring results. The main problem was John Huss, whose followers in Bohemia not only accepted his religious views but used them as a rallying point for anti-imperial Czech nationalism. Sigismund was hopeful that disturbances in Bohemia could be quelled by getting Huss to recant; Huss was delighted to appear at the council, convinced that he could persuade the fathers that his views were orthodox. Huss was all the more ready because he had received an imperial safe-conduct guaranteeing his journey to Constance, a hearing before the whole council, and a safe return to Bohemia. Shortly after his arrival, his enemies persuaded the council that for an accused heretic an imperial safe-conduct could not prevail against the due process of canon law. Accordingly, Huss was thrown into prison to await trial. He was accused of holding thirty-nine specific views which the fathers of the council already condemned as heretical. Huss denied holding some of these; he denied that the others were heretical, adding that he would be happy to retract any statement which could be proved false or heretical. Huss wanted to debate; the fathers of the council wanted only to hear from him "yes" or "no" as each charge was read to him, so that an opportunity to abjure was provided the accused before they gave judgment. Thus he was accused of denying transubstantiation, a doctrine on which his teaching was in fact orthodox. The charges were worded so that he could neither affirm the teaching attributed to him, nor could he "recant" the alleged teaching without admitting that he was unorthodox before he "recanted." Nor would the council allow him to explain his position. His view of the nature of the Church—a congregation of all the faithful under Christ, with no true authority vested in Peter or Peter's successors, the popes—he refused to recant unless it was proved false. The council pronounced him an obdurate heretic. This outcome had been inevitable from the beginning. Huss was consigned to the flames and his ashes were thrown into the Rhine. The burning of Huss, of course, did not extinguish his teaching. It took another three centuries for civilized men to learn that religious ideas cannot be destroyed by the execution of their author.

In the matter of reform, the conciliarists won two signal victories on paper but lost on almost all practical issues. In the decree *Sacrosancta* the Council of Constance roundly affirmed that a general council represented the whole Church, held its power directly from Christ, and must be obeyed by all men including the pope in matters pertaining to the faith, the abolition of schism, and reform. Having formally stated the doctrine of conciliar supremacy, the council promulgated the decree *Frequens* as a fundamental law of the Church. This decree required the convocation of another general council in five years, the meeting of future councils at regular intervals, and the automatic meeting of a council in the event of a future schism. On specific matters, however, it was a different story. The council spent two years working, in various committees, on the reform of abuses connected mainly with papal revenues and papal provisions. Everyone was ready to reform whatever did not affect his own selfish interests. For example, representatives of the University of Paris were eager to abolish annates or to reduce fees charged at the papal *curia*, but they supported papal provisions because the popes tended to favor graduates of their university. The net result was that Martin V was presented with a bill of particulars which he accepted in principle as reforms—but then did not bother to enforce.

As a cardinal, Martin had supported the conciliar movement, but as pope he worked without stint for papal supremacy and he resisted all reforms which derogated from papal power. His policy was moderate but tenacious. On the dissolution of the Council of Constance he pronounced that as pope he approved and ratified all the work of the council that had been accomplished in matters of faith *conciliariter* (a peculiar word meaning, literally, "in the manner of a council" and implying "as a council ought"). No one could really object to Martin's statement, for how else could a council act except *conciliariter?* But it left open to the papal party the arguments that conciliar action was not valid until ratified by the pope, and that no action even in matters of faith was valid if it exceeded the proper authority of a council. Martin summoned but would not preside over the council required by the decree *Frequens,* in 1423, at Pavia. It was ill-attended, and under the astute guidance of papal legates it accomplished little beyond reiterating the condemnations of the Council of Constance against heretics. Martin sidetracked proposals for reform but was unable to prevent the council from proclaiming the place of meeting of the next council, scheduled to be held in 1431. This was Basel. By that time the conciliar movement had so languished that Martin would have ignored the whole business except for the conviction among a growing number of German princes that a new council was necessary to deal with the Hussite movement in Bohemia. Reluctantly, Martin made arrangements on February 1 for a papal legate to convene the council; on February 20 he died of apoplexy.

The legate reached Basel at the appointed time, but nobody else had arrived. For three months the legate waited, and the "attendance" grew to one bishop, two abbots, and a few delegates from the University of Paris. Martin V would have dissolved the council immediately, but the new pope, Eugenius IV (1431–1447), was too distracted with politics in Italy to take prompt action. Then the Hussites scored some notable victories, and from its inauspicious beginnings the Council of Basel began to flourish. Alarmed at the spread of heresy, prelates from all of Europe swelled the attendance, and the Hussite leaders were invited to discuss the restoration of unity. Meanwhile, Eugenius IV, unaware of this resuscitation of the council, issued a bill dissolving the assembly. When he learned of the council's invitation to the Hussites, he indignantly repeated the dissolution and ordered the continuance of war against the Hussites. The council refused to obey, appealed to public opinion and the emperor, and issued a decree denying that anyone could dissolve, prorogue, or transfer a council but the council itself. In the ensuing quarrel Eugenius was forced to withdraw his bulls of dissolution and confirm the acts of the council.

The prestige of the Council of Basel now stood at its highest point. Negotiations with the Hussites had been rewarded by a serious split in Bohemia and the reconciliation of the moderate elements with the Church. From these victories the conciliarists turned to reform, and their power and effectiveness began to decline. They were divided by national jealousies, disagreement over the rightful authority of the pope, and divergent views about reform. In contrast, Eugenius had a clear-cut program and he had shown himself capable of some degree of compromise. The more timid and moderate members of the council began to waver when confronted with radical proposals that would have practically stripped the papacy of all authority.

An open breach between Eugenius and the council came in 1437. The council summoned Eugenius to answer for misconduct; the pope replied by transferring the council from Basel to Ferrara. Most of the moderate conciliarists obeyed Eugenius. His overt purpose, in transferring the council, was to meet with representatives of the Greek Orthodox Church, including the Byzantine emperor, John VIII Palaeologus, with a view toward reunion of the Eastern and Western Churches. The Council of Ferrara met in 1438 and was adjourned to Florence the next year. After much debate, prolonged by Eugenius' insistence that all doctrinal and liturgical differences be fully discussed, agreement was actually reached. Doctrinal disputes (including the famous *filioque* controversy) were compromised and papal supremacy was recognized by the Greek representatives. With great jubilation Eugenius and John VIII proclaimed at Florence, 1439, the reunion of the Latin and Greek Churches. But while everyone talked about reunion at great length, John VIII really wanted military aid against the Turks, for which he (like his predecessors Alexius I Comnenus in the eleventh and Michael VIII Palaeologus in the thirteenth century) was willing to pay the price of reunion under papal supremacy; for Eugenius this triumph for papal prestige was a double victory—achievement of the long-sought goal of reunion was a long step toward achieving his other goal of defeating the conciliar movement. However, when John VIII returned to Constantinople he was confronted with such vigorous opposition to the concessions made at Florence that the agreed upon reunion was never, in fact, put into effect. Fourteen years later the ideal of reunion had become a dead letter with the fall of Constantinople to the Turks.

With the desertion of the moderates to Ferrara-Florence, the Council of Basel fell under the control of extremists who rapidly lost much of the support and prestige formerly enjoyed by the council. Their deposition of Eugenius as a heretic struck most people as irresponsible and foolhardy. A more serious error was their election of an antipope, Felix V (1439–1449). The conciliar movement was discredited as leading to a new schism. Earlier reforms were now ignored by Eugenius with impunity. In a final and tragicomic display of futility, the rump Council of Basel proceeded to quarrel with Felix over *his* papal prerogatives. It was merely to clean up loose ends that after the death of Eugenius, Nicholas V condescended to negotiate a settlement with the council, now removed to Lausanne. Felix abdicated with some relief, the council voted its own dissolution in one expiring assertion of independence, and the conciliar movement was at an end.

To understand the failure of the conciliar movement one more factor must be noticed. This was the gradual alienation of secular rulers from the reform program. During the closing months of the Council of Constance, when it became clear that no general program of reform could be agreed upon by the whole council, Martin V had negotiated a series of treaties or concordats (1418) with the several nations. The interests of secular rulers were scrupulously observed. This policy was carried forward by Eugenius IV, who by making concessions to the rulers was able to win their support for papal supremacy. Without their support the conciliar movement was bound to fail. In 1438 Charles VII of France issued the Pragmatic Sanction of Bourges, under which many of the reforms of the Council of Basel were accepted as binding in France and many papal rights over revenues and appointments were declared to be vested in the French crown. Although these so-called "Gallican Liberties" were never fully enforced, the Pragmatic Sanction became the basis for negotiations with the papacy. The net result was that control over the French clergy and ecclesiastical revenues was divided between the king and the pope, in return for loyal recognition of papal supremacy over the Church. A similar division of control over the German church was effected by the legislation of the Diet of Mainz in 1439, modeled on the Pragmatic Sanction of Bourges, and by the later Concordat of Vienna, 1448. Other concordats were negotiated during the fifteenth century.

The popes, then, were not unqualified victors in the struggle. Defeat of the conciliar movement had been won at the price of sharing papal authority with secular rulers. The unity of the Church had been preserved, and constitutional reform of the Church had been curbed, but a long step had been taken toward the national churches created by the Protestant Reformation. More than that, the papacy suffered a less tangible or obvious loss in prestige. The problems of the Great Schism and the Age of the Councils were primarily political. Their solution crowded into the background the spiritual mission of the supreme pontiff. Control of the clergy north of the Alps, security in Rome, the Papal States, and Italy: these objectives seemed more pressing than the solution of problems that

were primarily religious in nature. The reformers of the conciliar movement and even the secular rulers had a better record than the popes in
dealing with heresy, the discipline and morals of the clergy, promotion of
learning in the universities, the support of charitable organizations, and
other nonpolitical matters which had always been the concern of the
medieval Church under the leadership of the popes.

Italy and Germany in the Later Middle Ages

On a hot afternoon in June 1312, Henry VII of Luxembourg was solemnly crowned emperor of the Holy Roman Empire. The ceremony took place in the Lateran palace because Henry's German troops had been unable to dislodge his Italian enemies from the half of Rome that included St. Peter's basilica, where an imperial coronation ought properly to have taken place. Papal legates officiated because the pope refused to leave the safety of Avignon. After the ceremony, the open-air coronation banquet was broken up by enemy archers shooting down on the guests from the heights of the Aventine. The whole incident was symbolic of the degradation of the medieval Empire and the hopeless involvement of imperial dreams with Italian partisan politics.

Henry VII, to whom Dante had appealed for the re-establishment of universal peace through a revival of the Empire, has been called "the last of the medieval emperors." The phrase is appropriate. He was the last German ruler to make a determined effort to control Italy and Burgundy, and although his successors as Kings of the Romans (the official title of the German king) are conventionally called "emperors," few of them bothered to receive that title officially through an imperial coronation. After the reign of Henry VII the connection between Italy and Germany, originally established by Otto I the Great in 962, was for all practical purposes at an end. Thus the history of Italy and Germany during the later Middle Ages follows the general pattern of "national disentanglement" that characterizes the later medieval history of France and England. There were few other parallels, however. The tendency toward "particularism," or the autonomy of local political units, continued unabated in central Europe. Already apparent in the thirteenth century, this tendency was in direct contrast with the growing centralization of the western monarchies.

The fourteenth century ushers in the "Age of the Despots" in Italy and the "Age of the Princes" in Germany. The actual situation was more complex than such labels can suggest. Both north and south of the Alps, the constitutional structure of the various territorial states and the political relations between these states were so diverse and complicated that few generalizations hold for all of them. The main difference between conditions in Germany and Italy was that the balance of political and economic power in the north was still held by the greater nobles, an essentially rural class based on agricultural wealth, while in Italy power was shifting rapidly to the urban bourgeoisie whose wealth lay in commercial, industrial, and financial enterprise rather than in land.

81 THE AGE OF THE DESPOTS: CITY-STATES IN ITALY AND THE RENAISSANCE PAPACY

In the early fourteenth century most of northern and central Italy consisted of independent and self-governing towns. In part this can be explained by the failure of Henry VII (1309–1313) to re-establish effective imperial authority and by the indifference of later emperors to Italian affairs. Also, the withdrawal of the papacy to Avignon, followed by the Great Schism, eliminated the only power capable of preserving some unity and order in central Italy. The Papal States disintegrated into a congeries of towns and petty principalities, each striving with varying degrees of success to throw off papal rule. Only in the south, where town life lagged behind, were larger territorial units preserved in the kingdom of Naples and the kingdom of Sicily. And there frequent civil wars stirred up by the feudal barons kept the central governments weak.

The internal organization of most of the towns of Tuscany and Lombardy was republican in form and oligarchical in fact. Participation in the government was restricted almost entirely to the upper classes. The most striking feature of political life was incessant party strife. Although the party tags, Ghibelline and Guelph, were still used, neither stood for any clear set of political principles or any definite program. The only real goals that all parties and factions recognized were independence of the town from outside authority and control of the town government. Even where a faction of the Ghibellines might make a token submission to the emperor, this was usually nothing more than a maneuver to oust the opposition. By the end of the thirteenth century imperial authority rarely amounted to more than the right to appoint an official, the *podesta*, who would collect a few taxes and be the nominal executive head of the government.

Two new factors entered Italian politics in the course of the fourteenth century. One was the *popolo minuto*, the lower economic classes. The other was the despot. The political ambitions of the lower classes found more violent expression, and led to a greater destruction of property and loss of life, than the plots and conspiracies of the nobles and the wealthy merchants and manufacturers. Political strife in towns where industry thrived often took the form of a revolutionary class struggle. Sometimes it was the frightened upper and middle classes, sometimes the lower classes in their moment of victory, who adopted some form of tyranny or despotism—the one to maintain order, the other to preserve newly won liberties. The despot was theoretically above faction. Hence he was often an outsider called in to impose peace impartially on all groups. Actually, of course, the despots were more concerned for their own power than for the welfare of the town, so they usually acted in the interests of the dominant group.

The origins of the various despots were diverse. Some were nobles of the surrounding *contado*, others were officials such as the *podesta* of a neighboring town, others were *condottieri*, captains of mercenary troops. Some were elected by constitutional methods and then seized dictatorial powers and established themselves as hereditary rulers. Others usurped their authority with the connivance of a faction in the town. Of all the despots those who began as *condottieri* were the most colorful and usually the most successful, for despotism rested ultimately on force. Very few of the despots had a completely legitimate right to all the governmental powers they exercised. Many of them adopted resounding titles with a specious ring of legitimacy, such as "Captain of the People" or "*Podesta* of the People," as if to compensate for their dubious origins. For the same reason some of the despots held splendid courts and patronized the arts and letters, while most of them sought to win support from their subjects and to increase their power by territorial conquests. The political methods of the despots ranged from the traditional wars and marriage alliances to such devices as assassination, betrayal, and calculated dissimulation—all unknown to the medieval and feudal code of honor among nobles. Methods that were once the exception to the rule became in the Renaissance the accepted means by which petty rulers clawed their way to the top and the greater rulers were unseated from power.

Not all the Italian city-states were ruled by the despots, nor were all of them petty and local in their political importance. By the end of the fourteenth century five states had become dominant: Venice and Milan in the north; Florence and the Papal States in central Italy; and the kingdom of Naples in the south. Of these only Milan conformed with the typical pattern of despotism. Here the Visconti dynasty was established early in the fourteenth century and continued in power until the middle of the fifteenth. The height of Milanese power and territorial expansion came under Gian Galeazzo Visconti (1385–1402), who married a daughter of the French

Central and Eastern Europe
in the Later Middle Ages, c.1490–1494

king, purchased the title of duke from the emperor, and aspired to become king of Italy by conquest. In an age of violence and treachery, the Visconti despots distinguished themselves by the enormities of gross brutality they perpetrated. Under Gian Galeazzo, Milan controlled most of Lombardy and pushed eastward toward Venice and southeastward into the Papal States and Tuscany.

Venice was the least typical of the Italian city-states. Her constitution was a model of oligarchy, her commerce stretched throughout the eastern Mediterranean and into the Black Sea, and her fleets regularly visited northern Europe. Until the fifteenth century Venice was more of a world power than an Italian city-state. The state was rigidly controlled by the greater merchants who, after 1297, alone had a hereditary right to membership in the Great Council. Executive authority was originally vested in an elected doge. After the failure of a conspiracy aimed at establishing a despotism, in 1310, the Great Council instituted the Council of Ten. Together with the doge and six councillors, the Council of Ten was the supreme authority. There was no real limitation on its powers, other than the provision for annual election of its members by the Great Council. As a sort of committee of public safety, the Council of Ten moved with speed and secrecy against suspected enemies of the state, whether domestic or foreign. The main object of governmental policy was the advancement of Venetian commerce. The government regulated trade minutely, built and owned all shipping, and organized the great fleets into convoys protected by swift naval vessels. Commercial rivalry with other Italian ports frequently led to armed reprisals and petty wars, but in 1376 an all-out war with Genoa began. It lasted until the Genoese forces besieging Venice were annihilated on the island of Chioggia in 1380, the first major military operation in which cannon and gunpowder played an important role. From this disaster the Genoese never fully recovered.

After defeating Genoa on the seas, Venice was confronted with the threat of Milanese expansion. Venice adopted her *terra firma* policy, that is, the conquest of lands to her west in order to safeguard trade routes north over the Alps and to ensure a food supply for her population. This territorial expansion for the first time committed Venice to participation in the politics of the Italian mainland. At the height of her expansion the Venetian empire included a large hinterland to the west and north of the city, plus areas on the eastern shores of the Adriatic, more than a dozen islands in the eastern Mediterranean, including Crete, and many trading stations in the cities of the Levant. But this territorial expansion of Venice coincided with the slow decline of her commerce, and of the importance of Mediterranean commerce in the total economy of Europe. By the middle of the sixteenth century Venice was no longer a world power.

Like Venice, Florence also resisted despotism in the fourteenth century, both within the republic and beyond her frontiers. But although

Venice, c.1400. Manuscript illustration (the scene depicts the departure of Marco Polo for the Orient, more than a century earlier). BODLEIAN LIBRARY, OXFORD.

Florentines made much of their republican institutions and championed the independence of smaller states from Milanese aggression, Florence was in many ways a typical Renaissance city-state, both in her internal development and in her foreign policy. In contrast with Venetian constitutional stability, Florence was torn with almost continual strife. Power shifted from party to party until the rise of the Medici in the fifteenth century. The main reason for these violent changes was the complexity of Florentine society, which reflected the highly developed and often divergent economic interests in the state. As we shall see in the next chapter, Florence was the leading industrial and financial power in Italy as well as a rival to Venice in commerce. Finally, there was a class of nobles who lived in Florence but whose wealth lay in the countryside beyond the city. Class conflict was endemic in Florentine politics. The gravest crisis came in 1378, when the *popolo minuto* revolted during the Ciompi rising. On several occasions the Florentines had invited a foreign despot to bring peace, but that plan never worked because the situation was too complex for an outsider to control, and Florence was too strong to be held down by force alone.

Political stability finally came to Florence with the rise of the Medici family, the most powerful bankers not only in Italy but in all of Europe. The Medici had been associated with the more popular elements in Florentine politics ever since the Ciompi rising, and they were acceptable to the wealthy merchants and bankers. Cosimo de' Medici was the real ruler of Florence from 1434 until his death in 1464, though he preserved republican institutions and rarely held office himself. He controlled the elected officials like a modern political "boss," and manipulated Florentine policy by exerting his influence behind the scenes. Carefully avoiding the name and the appearance of a despot, he lived a simple life but on state occasions held a magnificent "court." Success earned him the more extravagant title of *Pater Patriae* ("father of his country") toward the end of his long rule.

Cosimo de' Medici was just as successful in bringing peace to Italy as he was in maintaining order in Florence. The essential point in Florentine policy had always been resistance to the domination of the peninsula by any one power. The greatest threat had come from Gian Galeazzo Visconti of Milan, at the end of the fourteenth century, when Florence held out almost alone until Gian's fortunate death saved the situation in 1402. Gian's successors inherited his title but not his ability. The Visconti empire almost collapsed. Some towns recovered their independence; Venice conquered the eastern Milanese lands; and the popes worked hard to restore their authority in the Papal States, both against the Milanese domination in the north and against the petty independent despots of the central States. Florence, having conquered Pisa in 1410 and thus gained her outlet to the sea, now held out for the *status quo* and for peace, refusing to take advantage of the weakness of the Visconti. Then, in addition to the scramble for territory and power in central and northern Italy, a new threat of conquest arose from the south. Ladislas, king of Naples—flaunting his motto, *Aut Caesar aut nullus*—set out to conquer and found a united kingdom of all of Italy. Initially successful, he seized Rome and occupied part of the Papal States. Only Florence stood between him and conquest of the north when he died prematurely in 1414. "Death was the best friend of the Florentines," as Machiavelli later observed.

The threat from Naples was replaced by a new threat from Milan, and Florence once more took the lead in resisting aggression. When the last of the Visconti died in 1447, Cosimo de' Medici sponsored the rise of Francesco Sforza, who seized control of Milan. Sforza was formerly a *condottiere* in the hire of both the Visconti and their enemies. Because of the gratitude of the other states whose territories had been protected from Visconti aggression, Cosimo was the leading spirit behind the general pacification of Italy by the Peace of Lodi in 1455. By this settlement, Venice, Milan, Florence, the papacy, and the kingdom of Naples all guaranteed each other's territorial security and that of their allied city-states.

The peace of Italy was assured for another generation, and the balance of power became the guiding principle in relations between the city-states of Italy as it was later between the national states of Europe.

The Peace of Lodi was also a triumph for the papacy, since it guaranteed the integrity of the Papal States. After defeating the conciliar attack upon papal supremacy, the popes were free to turn to other problems. In calling the conference which led to the Peace of Lodi, Nicholas V (1447–1455) hoped that the restoration of peace in Italy would make possible a crusade against the Ottoman Turks, who had just completed the conquest of Constantinople. Papal sponsorship of a crusade became one of the goals of the Renaissance popes. But more characteristic were their other interests. Nicholas V, a humanist himself, adorned the papal court with scholars and men of letters, after the fashion of the Renaissance despots. An avid collector of manuscripts, Nicholas founded the Vatican Library, of which his personal collection of several thousand volumes became the nucleus. Calixtus III (1455–1458) had no use for humanism, but he filled the offices of the papal government with his own relatives. His name is thus associated with the characteristic (though by no means new) element of nepotism in the Renaissance papacy. Among others, he appointed his nephew Roderigo Borgia as cardinal. Aeneas Sylvius Piccolomini, as Pius II (1458–1464), united in his person all the characteristics of the Renaissance papacy. A leading humanist, his court attracted and rewarded other humanists as well as relatives from his native Siena. He died during his last vain effort to organize a crusade, having taken the cross himself. Paul II (1464–1471), a Venetian, actually launched a crusade to recapture some of the Aegean islands from the Turks, but the expedition was not well supported and ended in disaster. Otherwise Paul II is chiefly remembered for closing the Roman Academy, a center of humanistic studies, and for his patronage of the sport of horse racing.

Sixtus IV (1471–1484) was a man of very different mettle. He set out to enforce papal authority throughout the Papal States, and his methods were typical of Renaissance despotism. As usual, Florence stood in the way of any change in the *status quo*. Cosimo's son Piero had succeeded to his father's dominant position; on his death Piero passed on the control of Florence to his two sons, Lorenzo and Giuiliano. Sixtus IV lent his support to a group of conspirators, headed by the banking family and rivals of the Medici, the Pazzi. The so-called Pazzi conspiracy (1478) was designed to eliminate their competitors in Florence by the simple expedient of assassination—at High Mass on Easter Sunday and by the hand of a priest. No other incident was so damaging to the prestige of the papacy during the Renaissance, although it is impossible to determine the exact role, or degree of complicity, of the pope in the plot. Giuliano was killed, but Lorenzo survived to continue and strengthen the Medicean rule of Florence.

Sixtus IV had already attempted to upset the balance of power by forming an alliance with Naples against Florence. Moving swiftly to cement his relations with Milan and Venice, and making a dramatic personal appeal to the king of Naples, Lorenzo de' Medici prevented the outbreak of a major war in Italy and preserved the precarious Peace of Lodi. His success in this critical hour, his patronage of the arts and letters, and his rule of Florence in the interests of peace and prosperity for Florentines—and incidentally, also, for all Italians—earned him the title of Lorenzo the Magnificent (1469–1492).

After Lorenzo's death the balance of power in Italy broke down rapidly. Innocent VIII (1484–1492) was the least able of all the Renaissance popes, meddling ineffectively in the affairs of other Italian states but best known, perhaps, as the first pope to recognize the paternity of his own children and to dine publicly with lady friends. Cardinal Roderigo Borgia succeeded as Alexander VI (1492–1503). His great ambition was the creation of a central Italian state for his son, the notorious Caesar Borgia. This threat to Milan, together with an ill-timed claim by the king of Naples to the Milanese duchy (based on an earlier marriage alliance), frightened Ludovico Sforza of Milan to appeal to the French king for help. Charles VIII of France (1483–1498) responded by asserting the French Angevin claims to the kingdom of Naples and, later, the claims of France to the duchy of Milan as well. The French invasion of Italy in 1494 was a turning point in Italian history. After 1494 Italy was the cockpit of Europe, as the Habsburgs of Austria and the Valois of France fought out their respective claims to Italian lands: the Valois as heirs of the French claims to Milan and Naples, the Habsburgs as heirs of the Aragonese claims to Naples and of imperial claims to the overlordship of northern Italy.

82   THE AGE OF THE PRINCES: GERMANY UNDER THE LUXEMBOURGS AND HABSBURGS

For Germany the reign of Henry VII of Luxembourg was just as important a turning point as it was in Italian history. From the accession of Rudolf of Habsburg in 1273 until the death of Albert of Austria in 1308, each ruler had tried unsuccessfully to restore the rights of the German crown and to re-establish the hereditary principle of succession. To this end they had built up their own hereditary lands as the basis of a revived monarchy. The princes' opposition to this policy was climaxed by the deposition of Adolf of Nassau (1298) and the murder of Albert of Austria. Henry VII (1309–1313) abandoned the policy. Unable to oppose the princes, he tried—unsuccessfully, as we have seen—to revive the Hohenstaufen policy of basing his power on control of Italy. After Henry VII the king

*Henry VII Crossing Alps and
Crowned as Emperor in Rome.*
The absent pope sent three cardinals
as his legates to officiate at the
ceremony. Manuscript illustration
(fourteenth century).
STAATSARCHIV KOBLENZ.

no longer possessed effective authority, and the dignity of the crown provided little more than an opportunity for dynastic aggrandizement.

At his accession, Henry VII was head of a small western house of Luxembourg. Before the end of his reign he had established his son John on the throne of the kingdom of Bohemia, thus transforming the Luxembourgs into an eastern dynasty rivaling the Habsburgs. When Henry died prematurely, King John of Bohemia was only sixteen and the Luxembourg party of the German magnates swung their support in the electoral college to the strongest anti-Habsburg prince, Lewis, duke of Bavaria. The supporters of Lewis and of Frederick of Habsburg were about equally divided. A disputed election was followed by civil war from 1314 to 1322, when Lewis IV of Bavaria (1314–1347) won the throne by defeating Frederick in battle.

The reign of Lewis of Bavaria was little more than an ignoble scramble for territory and power among the magnates, in which Lewis himself took the lead. Without any regard for the unity of Germany or the regalian rights of his office, Lewis used the waning powers of the crown primarily as the means of promoting the dynastic interests of his family.

Meanwhile, John XXII (1316–1334) had become pope and refused to recognize either of the rival candidates. John asserted the right of the papacy to judge a disputed imperial election and denied that the fortunes of battle gave Lewis any superior right over Frederick. Summoned by the pope to renounce his prerogative until papal recognition of his title, Lewis utterly refused. The pope excommunicated Lewis, the final phase of the medieval contest between the pope and the emperor began. It was a war of words. All the old theories were trotted out and given more extreme expression. Although John of Jandun and Marsiglio of Padua found refuge and patronage at the court of Lewis, after being forced to flee Paris for having written their *Defensor Pacis* (1324), they made no further contribution to the polemics of Lewis' reign. Lewis obviously approved what little he could understand of the *Defensor Pacis*, which remained (as we have already noted) the most significant treatise on political theory in the later Middle Ages.

Most of the German magnates supported Lewis, but only because they could gain more substantial concessions from the emperor than from a pope who could grant no lands or regalian rights in return for support. The princes thought they saw in the struggle an opportunity to enhance their own electoral powers at the expense of the papacy. They issued the Declaration of Rense in 1338, in which they asserted that whomever they chose as King of the Romans was, by that election, qualified to assume the title of king and to exercise the imperial authority without confirmation by the pope. In the same year Lewis promulgated the imperial ordinance *Licet juris* at the Diet of Frankfort. This ordinance confirmed the Declaration and further stated that election by the German electors was sufficient authority for the ruler so chosen to assume the titles of both king and emperor, without papal approval. The ordinance further provided that those who resisted the imperial authority of Lewis should suffer confiscation of their imperial fiefs and of all privileges granted by Lewis and his predecessors.

In his hour of seeming triumph, Lewis revealed the degree of incapacity to which he could sink. Still hopeful of extracting papal confirmation of his imperial title, he entered into negotiations with the pope. This, of course, offended the princes. For the same purpose he allied with the English against France in the early years of the Hundred Years' War, hoping thereby to bring pressure on the papacy for recognition. This maneuver lost him the support of Bohemia, whose Luxembourg rulers were closely associated with the French court. Lewis' land-grabbing tactics alienated many of the German magnates, and a majority of them were ready to acquiesce in a scheme whose success reflected little credit on any of the participants. To rid themselves of Lewis in 1346 the princes acted on the papal theory that the office of emperor was vacant and proceeded to elect a more satisfactory ruler—without, of course, admitting that such behavior contradicted their earlier Declaration of Rense. The pope had already agreed secretly to recognize the new emperor-elect if he would request papal confirmation before exercising the authority of the King of Romans—without admitting that this agreement in any way limited papal authority as asserted by John XXII. And the candidate who made this agreement and who was in due course elected, Charles of Luxembourg, heir of King John of Bohemia, promised to wait for papal approval before being crowned king or emperor—without admitting that his coronation was in any way necessary for the valid exercise of royal authority in Germany. The whole business was a complicated series of subterfuges, a sort of political shadowboxing in which each party hoped for some material gains at the price of theoretical concessions.

Civil war broke out immediately after the election of 1346, but within a year both King John of Bohemia and Lewis of Bavaria were dead, and Charles IV (1347–1378) was accepted by the majority of the princes and towns as emperor. Charles IV devoted most of his time and effort to strengthening his rule in Bohemia and expanding the kingdom. But he did not wholly neglect the German monarchy and the imperial dignity. He pacified the greater princes, including the Habsburgs and the successors and supporters of Lewis of Bavaria, by confirming them in the possession of all their lands and privileges. By tacit agreement each prince had a free hand to pursue his own dynastic ambitions. Beyond that Charles used his prestige and influence (there being nothing else to use, for lack of a royal administration or army) to preserve the peace. These efforts usually resulted in *Landfrieden,* or regional agreements among the magnates to keep the peace, which had begun to be an important part of German public law during the Great Interregnum. Pacification of Germany was important to Charles. He was determined to receive the imperial crown and could not risk disturbance or rebellion at home while he journeyed to Rome for his coronation. Charles scrupulously adhered to his agreement with the pope before his election in 1346, to refrain from exercising any authority in Italy without papal authorization, and to enter and leave Rome within the same day of his coronation. This was Easter Sunday, 1355. Aside from gaining the imperial crown, to fortify his position in Germany, Charles had no interest in Italy beyond selling imperial titles to ambitious Ghibellines and gathering whatever taxes he could extract from the northern towns.

Back in Germany Charles turned to the task of excluding the papacy from German affairs as he had accepted exclusion from Italian affairs. After discussion in the diet, he promulgated the Golden Bull of 1356. This act confirmed the ordinance *Licet juris,* but instead of denying papal authority in imperial elections the Golden Bull simply ignored the pope. Otherwise, the document regularized and legalized the *status quo.* Because of divided successions in several princely houses, disputes over electoral rights had become a source of conflict among the greater nobles. Therefore, the Bull provided that henceforth only seven princes were to be electors: the archbishops of Mainz, Trier, and Cologne, the count Palatine of the Rhine, the duke of Saxony, the margrave of Brandenburg, and the king of Bohemia. These great ecclesiastical and lay princes were confirmed in their regalian rights, so that each was practically independent of the emperor. In the electoral college a majority vote was defined as being legally a unanimous vote; royal and imperial authority were stated to be effective immediately upon election; the count Palatine and the duke of Saxony were named regents during a vacancy in the throne; and provisions for a speedy election after the death of an emperor were set forth—including rations of bread and water for the electors if they took more than thirty days to reach a vote. Although the pope was not mentioned, these provisions nullified papal claims to adjudicate a disputed (i.e., not unanimous) election, to confirm an election before the exercise of royal authority, and to govern the Empire during a vacancy.

The Golden Bull was the last important public act of any medieval emperor, and it was one of the most effective. The oft-quoted pronouncement of Bryce, that Charles IV "legalized anarchy and called it a constitution," is misleading. The Golden Bull did not increase but merely recognized the existing independence of the electoral princes, and it was in fact the only important deterrent to the general process of German decentralization or particularism. The electoral principalities were declared indivisible, and henceforth succession to the lay electorates was by primogeniture alone. The other principalities, not covered by the act, continued to be subdivided. Thus between the electoral states and the others the difference in size and power grew steadily. As the magnates of the middle and lesser ranks declined in power, the relative strength of the class of knights (or lowest nobles) and of the towns increased. Also, the towns holding privileges granted by the emperors, the Free Cities of the Empire, often leagued together for mutual protection against the ambitions and avarice of the nobles.

The history of Germany in the later Middle Ages is the history of more than a hundred principalities. The emperors are no longer important, after Charles IV, and even he paid more attention to his kingdom of Bohemia than to Germany. Charles was succeeded by his son Wenceslas (1378–1400), whom the electors finally deposed after he lapsed into a prolonged drunken stupor. The next emperor was Rupert, count Palatine of the Rhine (1400–1410), whose ineffective reign was brought to a close by an early death. The second son of Charles IV, Sigismund (1410–1437), was more able but he dissipated his energies in attempting too much with too little, both in resources and in personal capacity. At one point in the conciliar movement it appeared that Sigismund might reassert imperial leadership in a disunited Christendom, but, as we have seen, he failed to play any significant role in the struggle between the popes and the councils. One reason for this failure was the rebellion confronting him in the kingdom of Bohemia, which he inherited after his brother Wenceslas' death in 1419. Here the Hussites stirred up a national resistance against German domination until internal divisions among them weakened the movement.

Anticipating his own death without an heir, Sigismund arranged a settlement whereby the marriage of his daughter with Albert of Austria brought to the Habsburg dynasty the Luxembourg lands, including the kingdoms of Hungary and Bohemia, together with the strongest claim on the imperial title. Albert II (1438–1439) was duly elected, and the Habsburgs continued on the throne of the Holy Roman Empire for three more centuries. The change of dynasty, however, brought no change in imperial policy or power. Actually, it was during the reign of Frederick III (1440–1493) that the nadir was reached. Political conditions in Germany made the chances of any revival of imperial authority slim, but the lethargy and incapacity of Frederick reduced those chances to zero. Bohemia and Hungary were lost to the Habsburgs after 1457, and Frederick was unable even to preserve the duchy of Austria intact. In western Germany he could not prevent the absorption of imperial fiefs into the burgeoning duchy of Burgundy. And yet by a niggardly persistence this shadow-emperor effected the most important single dynastic triumph of the whole later Middle Ages. Having resisted mounting pressure to concede the title of king to Duke Charles the Rash of Burgundy, Frederick III negotiated the marriage of Charles' heiress, Mary of Burgundy, with his son Maximilian. Thus Maximilian (1493–1519) acquired the Burgundian inheritance and laid the basis for the predominance of the Habsburgs in Europe during the sixteenth century.

Germany more than any other part of Europe suffered, under the Luxembourgs and Habsburgs, that "lack of governance" which afflicted England during the fifteenth century. Besides the seven electors there were less than two dozen princes of the Empire who ruled territorial states of any substantial size. Only a few of these states were compact blocks of land under an effective central administration. The rest of Germany was a confusing conglomeration of tiny principalities, Free Cities, and fiefs held by knights who admitted no superior authority under the emperor. Constant subdivision of territories, wars and rebellions, and the transfer of lands through marriage or sale contributed to the general instability. Each petty prince sought only the aggrandizement of his own family possessions and power, without much regard for the legal rights of others or for the welfare of his subjects. The age of the princes was also the age of the robber-barons. Private warfare between these petty princes and imperial knights could not be suppressed. The burghers of the towns found some protection in their leagues, but the mass of peasantry—who ultimately footed the bill for this lack of system—could only suffer exploitation or contribute to the general confusion by their sporadic and futile revolts.

83   CENTRAL EUROPE AND SCANDINAVIA IN THE LATER MIDDLE AGES

In all of European history, the most striking political success achieved by peasants belongs to the hardy inhabitants of the three Forest Cantons of Uri, Schweiz, and Unterwalden on the northern slopes of the Alps. From their struggle to wrest independence from their Habsburg overlords grew the modern state of Switzerland. The Swiss valleys offered little to the farmers and shepherds who eked out a subsistence living, but their strategic location made them important in the control of trade and communications between Italy and Germany. The St. Gothard pass was opened in 1231 and at that time the emperor, Frederick II, granted privileges to the peasants of the Cantons because the other passes were controlled by his enemies. The Forest Cantons relied upon their imperial privileges against the Habsburgs until, when Rudolf of Habsburg was emperor, they formed a confederation in 1291 for the maintenance of peace and mutual assistance against foreign intervention. Later Swiss legends depict the Habsburgs as cruel tyrants intent on crushing the freedom and draining the wealth of the liberty-loving mountaineers. Actually, the Habsburgs' main interest in the Forest Cantons was the encouragement of trade so that heavy taxes could be levied on the goods of German and Italian merchants using the St. Gothard pass.

For a while the Habsburgs were able to reassert their direct rule of the area, but under Henry VII of Luxembourg the Cantons were once more freed from all external authority except that of the imperial government. On Henry's death the Habsburgs decided to recover their rights by force. In 1315 the invading Austrian army was met in the mountain pass at Morgarten and decisively beaten. This was the first great victory of the Swiss infantry over the feudal cavalry of Europe. Following this victory the emperor Lewis of Bavaria was delighted to confirm the Cantons in their privileges, and the Habsburg duke could do no more than conclude a truce which, in effect, recognized the independence of the Forest Cantons.

After Morgarten, other cantons and Swiss towns scented freedom from Habsburg rule. The original confederation grew with the addition of neighboring districts, beginning with Lucerne in 1332. Each canton or town retained its own institutions and local self-government, while agreeing to maintain the peace and assist other cantons against enemies outside the confederation. Relations between the cantons and towns were complicated by the fact that new members frequently had to make exceptions to their adherence to the confederation or else risk open rebellion. When the city of Berne joined, for example, its terms of alliance reserved the right of neutrality in any war against the Habsburgs, unless the Habsburgs attacked Berne. Meanwhile the confederation had grown aggressive. Incessant conflict marked the relations of the cantons with their neighbors, some of whom were forced to submit and join the confederation on dictated terms. The Habsburgs and other south German lords whose territorial rights were infringed by these developments now determined to crush the Swiss. In 1386 and again two years later full-scale war led to decisive victories by the burghers and peasants over the knightly armies of their feudal lords. In these campaigns the Swiss infantry, armed with crossbows and long pikes, proved their effectiveness in attack as well as in the defense of prepared positions. The threat of Austrian conquest led to a greater consolidation of the Swiss cantons. Military obligations of the several members were defined more precisely, and the jurisdiction of ecclesiastical courts was limited by common agreement; but the confederation continued to exist without any central or federal government.

Another truce with the Habsburgs was concluded in 1394, but real security did not come until the Perpetual Peace of 1474, negotiated between the Swiss and the Habsburgs with French help. This treaty drew the Swiss into the conflict between Louis XI of France and Charles the Rash, duke of Burgundy. As we have seen in Chapter 28, it was by defeat at the hands of the Swiss that the Burgundian threat to both France and the Empire was ended and Duke Charles himself was killed in battle. The Perpetual Peace lasted until 1499, when Maximillian once more tried but failed to subdue the Swiss. The confederation continued to grow throughout the period: by the end of the fifteenth century it consisted of thirteen confederate cantons, a dozen allied cantons, towns, and smaller districts, and about two dozen subject territories and bailiwicks. The local institutions of the allied and subject territories were respected, but participation in policy and control of revenues were restricted to the thirteen member cantons.

The strongest aspect of the confederation was its military organization. The fame of the Swiss infantry spread far. The most important Swiss export was her mercenary soldiery, which could be found in the armies of all the major European rulers, including the papacy. The Swiss Guard which today protects the Vatican descends with unbroken continuity from the pikemen who came down from the Alps to fight in the Habsburg-Valois wars of the sixteenth century.

The Swiss demonstrated that under special circumstances a larger territorial unit could be built up by the confederation of small and contiguous areas. In the north of Germany the Hanseatic League was the most successful of several efforts by towns to form similar confederations. The Hanseatic towns were not able to achieve a permanent union. They were allied primarily for economic purposes, and they were spread out over northern Europe. In the next chapter we shall consider their rise and decline, which affected economic developments more than the political history of the north. Here it is sufficient to notice that their treatment of Scandinavia as a backward area for economic exploitation was an important factor in the tardy development of the kingdoms of Denmark, Norway, and Sweden in the later Middle Ages.

In Scandinavia the nobles were the preponderant class at the opening of the fourteenth century. They controlled the Church, whose prelates were recruited from their ranks, and they effectively limited their kings by continual opposition and occasional rebellion. The royal houses of the three kingdoms were closely related by intermarriage, as were many of the noble families. There was little sense of national tradition or of loyalty to the monarchy in any of the kingdoms. German princes dabbled in Scandinavian politics, and in the endless northern wars the Hanseatic League threw its weight on whichever side would protect its monopoly of trade.

Toward the end of the fourteenth century a determined effort to unite the three kingdoms was made by Margaret, daughter of the King of Denmark and the wife of the king of Norway. When her father died in 1375 she secured recognition of her infant son as king in Denmark, and on the death of her husband this son inherited Norway. For both kingdoms Margaret acted as regent. She had plans underway for her son to succeed to the throne of Sweden when the youth died in 1387. Nothing daunted, Margaret had herself elected regent for life in Denmark and Norway at the expense of the nearest collateral heirs, the unpopular king of Sweden and a German duke. At the same time the nobles of Sweden rebelled once more against their king and called on Margaret to rule their kingdom and nominate her own successor. In the war that followed Margaret triumphed and united all of Scandinavia under her rule. As heir she chose her infant grandnephew, the duke of Pomerania, whose right of succession to all three kingdoms was recognized by the nobles. To legalize this succession, Margaret assembled the nobles at Kalmar in Sweden and obtained their consent to a document which provided for the union of all three kingdoms under a common law of succession. However, the Union of Kalmar (1397) was never ratified by the separate assemblies of the three realms. When Margaret died in 1412 new struggles for power broke out, and by 1435 Sweden was independent of Norway and Denmark, which remained united for four centuries.

Margaret's efforts for union and a strong monarchy under essentially Danish predominance thus failed. The three northern kingdoms continued to be troubled by frequent political upheavals. The nobility were the predominant power, but peasants' uprisings and the ambitions of a slowly rising mercantile class in the towns contributed to the general instability. Nowhere in Europe were the medieval foundations of modern national states less impressive. Sporadic efforts in the fifteenth century to reunite Sweden with Denmark and Norway failed. The only beneficiaries of these efforts were the nobles. No one in the year 1500 could have predicted that Sweden was to become an important European power in early modern Europe, or that Norway would lapse even further into the somnolence that characterized her existence under the tutelage of Denmark until the nineteenth century.

To the east of Germany there were four states whose fortunes influenced the general course of European history. In the north were the territories won by the Teutonic Knights; south of these were the kingdom of Poland with the principality of Lithuania to its east; then the kingdom of Hungary with its Slavic vassal-states; and finally the kingdom of Serbia in the Balkans at the far south. During the later Middle Ages the eastward expansion of Germany in these areas was checked and in some cases thrown back by Slavic resistance. By the occupation of Estonia in 1326 the Teutonic Knights ruled the whole Baltic coast with its hinterland from the Oder river in eastern Germany all the way to Lake Peipus, on the confines of Russian territory ruled by the Grand Prince of Moscow. As each area was subdued German merchants and nobles moved in to monopolize the trade and the landed wealth of the territory. Only in Prussia did a substantial German population follow the Knights; elsewhere the German occupation brought only an upper class to exploit the native population. But the eastward movement of German merchants was not confined to following the sword and the cross (the Baltic peoples were heathen and had to be converted and organized into a German-dominated church). By peaceful penetration the Germans settled in large numbers in Polish towns as well, where they formed the bulk of a small middle class of tradesmen.

The German expansion cut off both Poland and Lithuania from access to the Baltic and threatened further territorial losses to each state. Under her native heathen princes Lithuania in the fourteenth century expanded rapidly toward the southeast, stretching all the way to the Black Sea. The height of Lithuanian power was attained under Jagiello (1377–1434), to whom the Polish nobles looked for protection against the aggressive Teutonic Knights. Poland during this period was suffering a series of dynastic crises and wars from which only the nobility profited by extracting more and more privileges from the king. Poland then had no strong central power to resist the encroachments of her neighbors, and the nobles promoted a dynastic revolution in 1386, offering Jagiello the Polish crown and the hand of the princess Jadwiga, in return for the conversion of himself and his people to Latin Christianity. It was also expected that Jagiello would repel the Teutonic Knights. While it lasted, this dynastic union made the kingdom of Poland and Lithuania the largest state in Europe, in area if not in strength. But there was no organic union. Lithuania almost always, even under Jagiello, had her own Grand Prince. So far from there being any single central government, it can hardly be said that either Poland or Lithuania possessed what a western ruler would recognize as a central government. The king of Poland and the Grand Prince of Lithuania exercised over their privileged nobles even less authority than was wielded by the emperor over his German princes and nobles.

On the battlefield Jagiello acquitted himself well on behalf of his Polish supporters, though he was in no hurry to do so. It was only after further acquisitions of Polish territory by the Teutonic Knights that he finally raised a huge and motley army of Poles, Lithuanians, Russians, Tartars, Czechs, and still-heathen Balts and invaded Prussia. At Tannenberg in 1410 Jagiello's horde overran the German army and then occupied most of Prussia. Only the great headquarters fortress of Marienburg on the lower Vistula held out. But neither Jagiello's army nor his government were capable of a sustained military effort. Troubles at home diverted the king's attention, and by the Peace of Thorn (1411) the Teutonic Knights were left in possession of their lands except Samogitia which was restored to give Lithuania access to the Baltic.

The power of the Knights was broken, but their oppressive rule continued to alienate both the native and the German population of Prussia. After Jagiello's successor in Lithuania, Casimir IV (1434–1492), became king of Poland (1447–1492) as well, a coalition of nobles and towns known as the Prussian League appealed to Casimir for help in their revolt against the Knights. Hostilities dragged out for years until by the second Peace of Thorn (1466) West Prussia was restored to Poland. East Prussia was thus severed from territorial connection with Germany, and it was to be held by the Grand Master of the Teutonic Knights as a fief of the Polish crown. By the end of the Middle Ages, German expansion eastward had been brought to a halt and thrown back.

The kingdom of Hungary in the fourteenth and fifteenth centuries was, like all her neighbors, torn by dynastic struggles for the throne. These conflicts involved claims by the kings or princes of Lithuania, Poland, Bohemia, Luxembourg, Naples, and even Anjou in France. One reason the emperor Sigismund was so ineffective in Germany was his constant embroilment as king of Hungary (1387–1437) in the politics of Italy and the Balkans. Against the Turks Sigismund led a disastrous expedition, the so-called "crusade" of Nicopolis (1396), from which the badly mauled knights straggled back to their homes throughout western and central Europe. Meanwhile the Turks had destroyed the kingdom of Serbia (1389). For the rest of the Middle Ages, Hungary replaced the Byzantine Empire as the eastern bastion of Europe. Under Matthias Corvinus (1458–1490) the Magyars firmly blocked the Danube valley against Ottoman expansion.

The Decay of Medieval Economic and Social Institutions

The fourteenth and fifteenth centuries witnessed a general economic recession. The full effects were not felt in some areas until c.1350, and other areas were well on the way to recovery c.1450, but stagnation set in earlier and lasted later in many places. Not all economic activities suffered, but medieval agriculture, trade, and industry as a whole were contracting. Enterprise was no longer so rewarding as in the high Middle Ages, a period of expanding economy. For this general condition there were many interacting causes which were also in turn the results of other causes. Perhaps the basic factor was a slow decline in total population, a decline that diminished both the supply of labor and the market for goods produced. Other factors contributing to economic instability were the international and civil wars of the later Middle Ages and a resulting strain on governmental finances, which often led to a policy of devaluing the coinage, which in turn upset prices. Sometimes the strain on governmental resources was so great that repudiation of debts was the only way out. When this happened bankers, merchants, and others who had advanced credit were dragged into bankruptcy, further disrupting both industry and commerce.

The nobles, bourgeoisie, and peasants were all confronted with straitened circumstances, declining incomes, and an uncertain future. Between the thirteenth and the fifteenth century there was a general shift from confidence in change for the better to caution against change for the worse. Along with economic difficulties went social discontent. Every class was on the defensive. Lords secured legislation favorable to the landowning class, the bourgeoisie protected their monopolies with charters from rulers or with gild rules and regulations, and the peasants tried to sell their services for higher wages or else to flee from exploitation. These conditions were aggravated by an unexpected and almost catastrophic ordeal, the Black Death, which was followed by continuing local outbreaks of the plague in various localities.

In most of Europe people found their social and economic conditions less favorable than their ancestors had found them. It is evident to the modern historian that the old social order based on status was going through a transition to a new order based on a money economy. Contemporaries were only vaguely aware of what was happening, and to them the best solution of their difficulties seemed to be the preservation of what was old and familiar. Hence the last two centuries of the Middle Ages present the anomaly of relentless social and economic change coupled with a determined effort to preserve the decaying feudal society and to reaffirm medieval values in a world that was no longer really medieval.

84   AGRARIAN AND URBAN UNREST

The economic position of the nobility was based on control of land, and land continued to be the most important form of wealth. We have already seen in Chapter 23 how the nobility, enjoying a rising standard of living in the twelfth and thirteenth centuries, exploited their landed wealth for the money income it would provide. The two ways of extracting profits from the land were by renting part or all of the manor to peasants, and by exploiting the manor directly by employing peasant labor on the demesne, that part of the manor reserved for the lord's own occupation. In an age of rising prices the latter method was generally more successful. Then in the fourteenth century prices of agricultural products began to decline. This situation was aggravated by the fact that prices of nonagricultural commodities tended to hold firm or even to increase. Thus the landholding class was caught between lower prices for what was sold and steady or higher prices for what was bought.

Except in especially favorable circumstances for direct exploitation— as when a manor was very productive and located near a good market —many lords were willing to convert their manorial rights into a money income. The demesnes were let out to the peasants, whose services were commuted for money payments to the lords. From the lords' point of view this system was satisfactory if rents held up, but the peasants were now squeezed between high rents and declining prices. The old bonds that held

Peasants Harvesting on Lord's Demesne. Manuscript illustration (fourteenth century).

the manorial population together were being dissolved by the new cash nexus between landlord and tenant, the result being a relatively greater freedom of movement for the peasants. Hence lords found it difficult to hold their tenants to their contractual obligations. Some peasants moved to more prosperous regions where they found opportunity to work for wages, others went to the towns to hire out their labor. Manorial lords were therefore under increasing pressure to lower rents. In some cases the manorial population declined to the point where tenements were actually deserted. To keep their land in production some lords turned to hiring labor for wages. This system had the advantage of flexibility. Instead of adapting the operations of a manor to the labor supply on hand, lords could hire as much labor as was needed at a particular time, for example during spring plowing or for harvesting. These generalizations apply to many regions north of the Pyrenees and the Alps, but the economic picture of rural Europe in the fourteenth century was extremely complex and exceptional conditions were found everywhere: exceptionally prosperous and exceptionally depressed localities, depending mainly on fluctuations in local production and prices.

Then in 1348 the Black Death struck Europe. It moved slowly westward from the Far East, carried along the trade routes. This was by far the worst "invasion" from Asia since Attila the Hun. All the wars of the Middle Ages did not cause such loss of life as the first onslaught and the successive waves of bubonic plague during the second half of the fourteenth century. The disease was spread by fleas infected by plague-stricken rats. In an age wholly ignorant of sanitation there was no defense against what seemed to be the wrath of God: to the destruction of life was added the horror and uncertainty in which men lived. The economic results must therefore be measured not only by the loss of population but also by the disruption of normal existence. Men fled from stricken areas, deserting their jobs and spreading the plague to new regions. Some people squandered their money

Procession Supplicating for Cessation of the Plague. Manuscript illustration (c.1400). PHOTO: GIRAUDON.

in one last fling; others abandoned their wealth and worldly goods in a last desperate effort to earn salvation by a life of asceticism and penance before death overtook them. The mortality has been variously estimated, ranging from a fifth to a third of the total population. More important was the incidence of mortality: death struck most heavily in the centers of greatest urban and rural population, that is, where economic life was most advanced. Some backward and isolated regions escaped the plague altogether. It was not a matter of the survival of the fittest, but of the least fit.

The immediate results of the Black Death were deceptive. The mortality produced a labor shortage and a sudden increase in the amount of money per capita. Employers, both urban and rural, could therefore pay higher wages, while producers could demand higher prices. The result was an apparent prosperity. Peasants migrated to the towns to replace urban workers who had died, and the shortage of rural labor made possible not only higher wages for peasants but also the purchase of freedom from the manorial obligations of serfdom. For a few years everyone had more money and prices increased sharply. Then the reaction set in. Prosperity had been based on inflation, not on an expanding market. Production of agricultural and industrial commodities was soon able to meet the now diminished demand, and employers sought to cut their costs by rolling back wages to the level of 1348. Where the power of the state was strong enough to be effective, this effort took the form of maximum wage laws. In England the Statute of Laborers (1351) and later statutes required laborers to accept customary wages (those prevailing before the plague) and also fixed the prices of food and other basic necessities at the 1348 level. Such legislation could not be enforced completely, but the peasants were prevented from taking full advantage of the labor shortage resulting from the Black Death.

Despite such legislation, rural wages tended to rise. Under these circumstances manorial lords clung tenaciously to the customary labor services of the peasants, since it was too costly to hire workers to exploit the manorial demesne. However, the process of commutation and leasing the demesne for rent was not arrested entirely. Lords who had already commuted services for a money rent found it no longer profitable to exploit the demesne with hired labor: these lords leased their demesnes and collected rents from their whole manors. In either case—whether it was to the lord's advantage to enforce customary services or to convert his whole manor into rent-paying tenancies—the interests of the peasants and their lords clashed. Peasants agitated for the commutation of services into cash rents, since they could make more money as wage-earning laborers. This agitation grew into a general demand for the abolition of all manorial obligations, as lords tried to make up for their declining incomes by enforcing their rights over the manorial commons such as the meadows, fisheries, pastures, and woods, and to enforce the customary payments for use of mills, ovens, and other "appurtenances."

The lot of the urban working class was no better than that of the peasantry. Individual employers, the craft gilds, and town governments all tightened up on regulations and laws designed to keep wages low and to protect the static or declining market from outside competition. The Black Death struck impartially at both employer and worker, but after the plague had passed it was more difficult than ever for artisans to gain admittance into the craft gilds. The economic and social gulf between masters and workers widened as economic conditions deteriorated. Europe as a whole was confronted with the problem of overproduction. New opportunities to acquire fortunes by taking risks in an expanding market were extremely rare. Under these conditions the efforts of merchants and manufacturers to cut the costs of production (including wages) actually depressed the urban working class below the level of subsistence enjoyed by the peasants of the country.

The workers and peasants had no legal means for improving their lot. Many peasants were still unfree and subject to the jurisdiction of their lord's manorial court. Those who were free from the customary services were restive under legislation which favored the propertied classes by fixing wages and prices. In the towns discontent was even greater because urban workers were not protected by the customary rules which regulated the services and obligations of the manorial population. The result of these economic grievances was a series of revolts and uprisings during the second half of the fourteenth century. We have already noticed the Peasants' Revolt in England in 1381, the sporadic risings of the *Jacquerie* in France, and the Ciompi rising in Florence in 1378. These movements were by no means confined to the exploited urban and rural proletariat. Free peasants and some of the lesser nobles often participated in and sometimes led the uprisings, while the independent artisans and small shopkeepers of the towns, who resented the restrictions imposed by gild regulations, gave their support to revolutionary movements. The great merchants and the masters of the craft gilds controlled the urban governments in the interests of their gild organizations, just as the nobility dominated the lawmaking and the law-enforcing authorities in the country as a whole. The common cause that united all dissident groups was the absence of economic opportunity. The movements of the later fourteenth century were symptoms of a contracting economy in both town and country. The Peasants' Revolt was widely supported by townsmen in depressed areas in eastern and southern England, and the *Jacquerie* united with a radical movement in Paris led by Étienne Marcel, who was by no means a proletarian—actually, he was an influential member of the merchants' gild of the city.

The violent uprisings were aimed blindly at the existing order. Not only serfdom and the regulations restricting manufacture and trade, but the dominant classes were themselves attacked without much purpose though often with brutal and destructive results. Manor houses were burned down, shops and town residences were wrecked, and sometimes there was loss of life. Most of the movements were also strongly anticlerical, because the Church was the greatest landlord, the most powerful single vested interest in maintaining the economic and social *status quo*. Peace and order, in almost every instance, were restored with even more violence and brutality, often with great loss of life among the lower classes. Few peasants or urban workers were better off as the result of revolt.

Rural economic conditions slowly improved during the middle years of the fifteenth century in western Europe. In France and England, by the end of the Middle Ages the great majority of peasants held their land in return for rents and subject to the payment of the customary heriot or fee recognizing the lord's superior rights when the tenancy changed hands or passed to the heir. In France especially, and elsewhere in smaller degree, the nobles clung to certain seignorial rights which were fixed in terms of cash payments—such as tallage, tolls, fees for use of the lord's share of meadows or commons. On the whole, the peasants were not so well off as their ancestors of the twelfth and thirteenth centuries, but they were more secure and a little more prosperous than their parents and grandparents who lived during the ravages of plague, famine, and the Hundred Years' War.

In central Europe economic recovery in the country lagged behind that of the towns. Declining incomes for both lords and peasants led to sporadic outbursts of violence from the latter during the fifteenth century, repressed with equal violence by the lords. In western Germany conditions generally resembled those of France, but in central and eastern Germany the earlier tendency toward emancipation of peasants was reversed. Lords exacted labor services and enforced manorial obligations to the full. The eastward movement began to slow down during the fourteenth century, and the defeat of the Teutonic Knights in the early fifteenth century closed the Baltic area to any further expansion. Peasants ceased to benefit from the competition for labor on the frontier. However, the situation in central Europe was extremely complex, varying from region to region even more than in western Europe. The main general difference between western and central Europe, so far as the urban and rural lower classes were concerned, was the relatively depressed condition of the majority of German peasants at a time when German towns were in a relatively thriving condition. This is illustrated by the fact that few class conflicts in the towns actually broke out into violence.

85   COMMERCE, FINANCE, AND INDUSTRY: THE ORIGINS OF CAPITALISM

One of the most striking features of the economic history of the later Middle Ages was the amassing of huge private fortunes by a few enterprising individuals or families. In the expanding economy of the twelfth and thirteenth centuries income and wealth were far more evenly distributed among members of the same social class than they were during the later period of diminishing opportunity and contracting markets. Not only was the gulf between rich and poor growing wider but within the merchant and industrial class inequalities were increasing. In Venice, for example, during the last quarter of the fourteenth century about two-thirds of the merchant oligarchy possessed from 1,200 to 12,000 ducats, one-third had more than 12,000, and seven great merchants possessed fortunes of over 140,000 ducats. In Basel one-fourth of the citizens possessed less than 10 florins of taxable wealth in 1424, and by 1453 the number had grown to one-third of the citizens. In contrast, one-twentieth of the citizens owned half of the city's wealth.

While the majority of merchants suffered from the economic decline, a small number were able to pile up amazing profits. Those who did so either diversified their interests or entered the field of "public" finance or did both. With their wealth of experience as well as of money, the Italians were most conspicuously successful. Francesco Datini (1335–1410) lived through the worst part of the later medieval depression. Left an orphan by the plague, he had no inherited wealth. Setting out in a small way, he began to sell arms to the French during the Hundred Years' War, using capital partly saved by himself and partly supplied by others. He branched out into other commodities: cloth, spices, objects of art, and other goods that commanded high prices. Then he put some of his capital into the manufacturing and dyeing of woolens and silk cloth. Part of the profits of these commercial and manufacturing activities he put into banking. Datini's operations soon extended throughout the Mediterranean and southern Europe, and even to the markets of London and the Low Countries. For each activity he organized a separate company, only partly financed by himself. Datini's success was based on a combination of excellent management, good judgment, and above all a meticulous attention to current market prices. His accounts survive to illustrate the beginning and development of double-entry bookkeeping. Among his records are more than 300,000 letters, most of them dealing with the purchase and sale of goods. Datini's agents kept him constantly informed of changes in the prices, demand, and supply of all types of commodities. Generally, Datini never bought anything for which there was not an assured market and never transported to the market more than the demand. By this careful balancing of trade and by taking advantage of declining prices to buy and of rising or firm prices to sell, he became one of the wealthiest businessmen of his age.

Datini's methods were typical of the later medieval merchant, though his success was exceptional. Other remarkably prosperous businessmen were the Medici family of Florence and Jacques Cœur of France. The Medici got their start in the wool trade and soon branched out into cloth, silks, spices, furs, and other high-priced goods. They had branches and agents scattered all over Europe, who bought and sold at their direction. At the very time that the Florentine population was declining and the textile industry was stagnant the Medici were rapidly becoming the wealthiest family in Europe. They avoided politics almost entirely until they had outstripped their rivals in business. Then they were able to dominate Florence for three generations. Meanwhile the Medici diverted capital into the field of banking. Their extensive trading involved many separate credit operations, and their profits gave them funds to lend at interest to others. The success of the Medici bank attracted deposits from merchants with surplus capital, and by the time of Cosimo de' Medici (1434–1464) the Medici bank was the largest in Europe. The Medici acted as fiscal agents for the papacy, advancing loans and collecting ecclesiastical taxes. They also lent to secular governments, a risky enterprise that had involved earlier Florentine banking houses in failure when Edward III of England repudiated his debts (1345). On a smaller scale merchant-bankers in Italy and elsewhere supplied princes all over Europe with credit to pay for the wars of the later Middle Ages—wars that cost more than ordinary revenues could support.

Jacques Cœur of Bourges (1395–1456) got his start by supplying luxury articles to the court of the French king, Charles VII. This contact led to his appointment as director of the mint, a position from which he advanced in the service of the government until he finally had control of all finances and fiscal policy. His enterprises included extensive trade with the Levant, and he invested in factories, mills, and mines. Aided by privileges and financial support from the government, he built a fleet of ships and dreamed of replacing the Italians and Aragonese in the control of Mediterranean trade. In his rapid rise, and—having incurred the king's displeasure as well as the enmity of his many noble debtors—in his spectacular fall from favor, the career of Jacques Cœur illustrates the possibilities and the dangers of public finance in the fifteenth century. More typical of the successful French bourgeoisie of the period were the merchants who made their fortunes out of the miseries of war. Through illicit speculation, disposal of war booty, and the sale of food at inflated prices in famine-struck areas, many tradesmen of modest means made huge profits. But the risks of commerce were so great that this activity did not lead to a real commercial revival. After taking their profits most of these ancestors of the modern blackmarket profiteers withdrew from business and invested their money in land. Within another generation many of them had entered the ranks of the nobility.

Commerce in northern Europe had a different character. There was less emphasis on luxury trade, and few great fortunes were suddenly made. Banking played a role, but there were no great banking houses such as the Italians developed. Hence there were practically no great merchant princes like the Medici or Jacques Cœur. Rigid regulation of local trade by the merchant gilds left little room for individual initiative. The rising importance of craft gilds introduced a new factor, and in the fourteenth century German and Flemish towns were often disturbed by class conflict. But in Germany the greater merchants re-established themselves in control, at the expense of the masters of the craft gilds, and the net result was an even more stringent control by the merchant gilds. Since this was also the period when the imperial Free Cities were gaining independence from all lords, except for token allegiance to the emperor, the greater merchant families ruled in political as well as in economic matters. By this time the gilds were practically closed to outsiders. The families that ruled were a self-perpetuating oligarchy or patriciate. Earlier tendencies toward wider participation in the political and economic life of the towns were arrested, as the patricians made determined efforts to exclude competitors from their dwindling markets. The cause of the reactionary policy of the urban patriciate was thus the general decline in trade and industry that affected all of Europe.

Before this decline set in, however, northern commerce had enjoyed a vigorous growth. The Champagne fairs decayed at the end of the thirteenth century, and the growing use of the sea route from Italy to Flanders made Bruges the new emporium for international exchange of goods between northern and southern Europe. The trade routes over the Alps into southern Germany carried a steadily increasing traffic that brought prosperity to many towns. The backward regions of Scandinavia were opened to exploitation. And the eastward expansion of the Teutonic Knights led to a flourishing Baltic trade. Cheap Baltic grains in the later Middle Ages helped keep grain prices depressed throughout northern Europe.

From an early time the German merchants had found that cooperation in foreign parts served their mutual interests better than competition. In England, for example, the Germans had a trading station in London and had secured common privileges from the crown by the end of the twelfth century. By the end of the thirteenth century similar stations were scattered from Lisbon in Portugal all the way to Novgorod in Russia. Merchants from a score of German towns participated in their business and shared their privileges. The association of these merchants in foreign parts was the origin of the later association of the towns from which they came, the Hanseatic League.

The Hanseatic League grew up originally for economic reasons alone, primarily to increase and protect the Hansards' commerce and to secure a monopoly of trade where possible. The towns of the League combined their military and naval power to sweep pirates from the North and Baltic seas and to protect their merchants traveling inland by river or road. These purposes did not at first involve the merchants or their towns in any very systematic organization. During the fourteenth century the earlier occasional cooperation of several towns to meet various exigencies was transformed into a permanent and united federation of towns with a central diet or assembly capable of formulating a common policy. At the same time the League grew until at its height about seventy towns belonged. These included towns in the Baltic region, Scandinavia, and the Low Countries as well as in Germany. Each town was assessed for its share of taxes, ships, and manpower in support of the League's policies. The basic reason for this stronger federation of the fourteenth century was the decline in trade, which made firm action necessary to protect the Hanseatic commercial interests from foreign competition. Hence the League was largest and most powerful after the main German commercial expansion came to an end.

In order to protect their trade the Hansards used both diplomacy and force. The critical struggle came in 1367–1370, when the League fought its first war. The king of Denmark was trying to restore royal authority and to extend his power into Sweden. The Danish conquest of Scania, in southern Sweden, was a direct blow at the League because the Hanseatic merchants enjoyed exclusive control of the great herring fisheries, the most important single economic asset of northern Europe at that time, so long as they were under Swedish control. Beyond that, the Danish king attacked the Hanseatic town of Wisby, on the island of Gotland, the key town in all the Baltic trade, and he raised and enforced the collection of tolls on shipping through the straits between the Baltic and the North seas. In its first effective united action, the Hanseatic League defeated Denmark and imposed the Treaty of Stralsund (1370) which granted the League extensive privileges and helped maintain the supremacy of Hanseatic merchants throughout Scandinavia.

The Hanseatic League declined slowly, yet inevitably. There was no method, short of economic reprisals or war, to force towns to remain in the

League or even to abide by League policies. Divergent regional interests tended to separate the eastern, central, and western towns. Danzig and the Baltic towns desired unrestrained access to the markets of England and the Low Countries through the straits, while the central group wanted to preserve the older routes which brought trade overland through northern Germany. The western towns were not interested in the special difficulties of the Baltic and were reluctant to contribute ships and money for the suppression of piracy in eastern waters. Even more serious was the rise of English and Dutch trade in northern waters. The English threat was staved off until after the Middle Ages, but the Dutch slowly increased their trade in Scandinavia and the Baltic area until the Hanseatic predominance was broken and Antwerp in Brabant replaced Bruges in Flanders as the most important western terminus of the northern and northeastern trade.

In the generally declining European economy of the later Middle Ages there were a few signs of strength or growth, most of them connected with technological improvements in industry. In the manufacture of woolen cloth, the invention and introduction of the spinning wheel and the fulling mill (to clean and shrink cloth) reduced the amount of labor required while increasing production. The water-driven fulling mill, appearing in the twelfth century and widely adopted by the fourteenth, was the first substitution of mechanical power for human effort in the textile industry. By its use, triphammers replaced human feet in the fulling process. The results were far-reaching. To take advantage of the fulling mill the industry had to be at least partially dispersed into hitherto backward areas where the fall of streams provided power. In the older urban textile centers this resulted in unemployment and unrest among the working classes, but regions where water power was abundant, especially in England and Italy, benefited from the greater efficiency of the mill.

The infant woolen industry in England also possessed the advantage of cheaper raw material. The Flemish merchant paid not only the cost of transporting the wool from England to Flanders but also the export duties levied by the English government. In contrast, his English competitor had low transportation costs and a great tax advantage. There was no tax on English wool consumed in English looms, the duty on exported cloth was low, and the duty on cloth imported from abroad was high. Thus encouraged by fiscal policy, the infant industry slowly grew and by the middle of the fourteenth century English textiles had captured the home market, while by the middle of the fifteenth England exported more woolen cloth than raw wool. The growth of English textiles was by no means even or easy, but by the end of the Middle Ages English woolens in European markets had outdistanced those of both Flanders and Italy. The Yorkist and Tudor kings reaped the profits of their predecessors' policy of fostering the woolen industry, for customs duties on exported cloth were an important revenue for the new strong monarchy.

Another strong sector of the later medieval economy of Europe was the mining and metallurgical industry. Here again technological improvements played an important role. New methods of extracting metals and the application of water power—for pumping out mines, operating bellows in blast furnaces, and crushing the ore—reduced costs and increased production, including the production of metal from low-grade ores hitherto unusable. Central and southern Germany led the way in iron, copper, and silver mining and extraction. The growth of mining and metallurgy was accelerated after c.1450, to become one of the important industries of the sixteenth century as well as the basis of new fortunes made by enterprising investors.

A final word is necessary concerning the medieval economy as a whole. If attention is shifted from particular persons, events, or developments to the general nature of business methods, it is clear that much of medieval industry and commerce—and the financial operations that supported them—was capitalistic both in spirit and in method. The question of when capitalism began is largely a quibble, since the answer will depend on the definition of the term. Characteristic features of modern capitalism were certainly present and in some regions conspicuous. These include the accumulation of capital in the form of money or goods, the extensive use of credit in both manufacturing and commercial transactions, and the separation of management from ownership. Such typically capitalistic attitudes and practices as large-scale and long-range planning, the assumption of calculated risks, the subordination of other considerations to the profit motive, and the treatment of labor merely as a factor in the production and distribution of goods for market—all these were present if not prevalent in the fourteenth and fifteenth centuries, and had appeared even earlier. Medieval capitalism had not yet achieved the refinements of modern techniques of industrial organization. Mass markets, joint stock companies, exchanges for the sale of stocks and bonds, and other features or agencies of modern capitalism had not yet appeared. But on a small scale, and within the limits of a society whose population and purchasing power were no longer expanding, it is clear that the capitalistic economy of modern times was already beginning to develop long before the close of the fifteenth century.

86   THE DECAY OF FEUDALISM:
THE "NEW CHIVALRY"

A popular chronicler, writing in the fifteenth century, paused in his task of narrating chivalrous deeds to describe briefly the orders or estates of society. His account is conventionally hierarchical. God, he wrote, created the common people to labor in the fields and to supply the goods of life through trade, the clergy for worship and the works of religion, and the nobles to cultivate virtue and maintain justice. The nobility, according to this account, protect the Church, defend the faith, shelter the people from oppression, oppose tyranny and violence, maintain the peace, and support the common weal. The virtues of the nobility are honor, truth, courage, largesse, and integrity. This is a typical view: it is also a beautiful illustration of that triumph of fiction over fact which especially characterizes the ideas and values of the period. Contemporary chroniclers do not provide the historian with very reliable evidence about the classes of society and the changes in their condition.

The character of the dominant class, the aristocracy, was transformed during the later Middle Ages. Some of the developments that were undermining the "classical" feudal institutions of the twelfth and thirteenth centuries have already been discussed in Chapter 23. These forces continued to have their effect, and by the end of the fourteenth century it is no longer strictly accurate to speak of a feudal society in most of Europe.

Later medieval society still contained feudal elements. Some particular elements or aspects of feudalism survived well beyond the Middle Ages. For example, the modern law of real property in English-speaking countries derives partly from feudal custom. But these survivals obviously do not explain the nature of modern society. Less obviously, the continuity of feudal institutions in the later Middle Ages does not reveal the real nature of the society of that period. There were still lords and vassals, but their relations had changed. There were still fiefs and feudal incidents, feudal jurisdictions and feudal privileges, but their nature had changed and their effectiveness had been circumscribed. In two ways feudal institutions were no longer the real framework of later medieval society. First, the obligations of the noble to the lord from whom he held his fief were no longer so important as his obligations to the territorial ruler. Within the aristocracy the vassal-lord relationship was less immediate and binding than the subject-ruler relationship. Second, the economic position of the aristocracy was no longer assured merely by the possession of landed wealth. Nobles who could not make their manors pay a profit in an age of uncertain markets, declining agricultural prices, and depreciated currency were no longer able to maintain their status. Many of the lesser nobles sank into an economic and social condition hardly superior to that of their peasants. Their manor houses were dubbed *châteaux de la misère*, and their noble status was little more than a legal fiction.

Other nobles held their own or even advanced in economic status or political power. This section is primarily concerned with them. For convenience, the several developments affecting the status of nobles in the later Middle Ages may be classified as military, economic, and political. For reasons that are complex and not fully understood, the feudal levy of vassals in many regions gradually disappeared as an effective military arm of the territorial rulers. Some reasons are clear enough. We have noticed the rise of the infantry as the dominant arm in the English forces of the Hundred Years' War and in the Swiss forces that conquered Duke Charles the Rash of Burgundy. But even the French armies, which continued to be predominantly cavalry until well into the fifteenth century, no longer consisted primarily of the feudal levy of vassals acquitting their fiefs of forty days' knights' service. The cavalrymen were often royal vassals, or vassals of royal vassals fighting for their immediate lords in the service of the king—but they fought when needed, as long as needed, and for pay. What had actually happened, whether rulers wanted infantry or cavalry troops, was that warfare had become part of the money economy. Poorer vassals could not equip themselves properly for cavalry fighting, and rulers did not want their service. It was more efficient to commute their military obligations into money payments with which to hire the services of well-equipped and trained mercenaries. Often as not, such cavalrymen fighting for pay were in fact nobles. But now their service was performed as the result of an indenture between the ruler and themselves, without regard to the tenure of a fief or the general obligations of vassalage.

The indenture of the later Middle Ages was not essentially new. It grew out of a practice, going back at least to the early twelfth century, by which lords occasionally granted their vassals annual sums of money in lieu of fiefs consisting of one or more manors. Originally these money-fiefs often carried the same obligations of vassal to lord as ordinary fiefs. But it was a simple matter to change the terms of the charters creating such money-fiefs into written contracts for specific military service in return for a stipulated salary. Such a contract was an indenture. It often included, or took the form of, a commission authorizing the noble to recruit a company of troops. As their captain, the noble would train, provision, and lead them in battle at a stipulated rate of pay to be supplied by the ruler. An important feature of such indentures was the agreement between the two parties concerning the division of the spoils of war. It was usual to reserve a third, or some other fraction, of the captain's ransoms and booty for the ruler, while the captain was granted the right to collect a third of the spoils garnered by his soldiers—with the ruler collecting his third of this third, as well.

The net result was that often military service and feudal institutions no longer had any significant connection. Lords both great and petty entered into agreements to raise and lead troops for pay, and the size of such contingents of mercenaries bore no relation to the fiefs held by these nobles. In the Hundred Years' War some very minor lords accumulated fortunes from the booty and ransoms they and their men collected. Also, it was possible to rise to a higher position in the government by successful leadership of mercenary companies—from commander of a minor garrison stationed in a village to the custody of a key castle to the command of an important city and its region with administrative as well as military duties. The aristocracy continued to play a leading role in warfare, but no longer as the feudal host of an earlier age.

The political role of the aristocracy also declined during the thirteenth century, when the western monarchies were building governments that employed professional civil servants and no longer needed to depend so much on the cooperation of the nobles. In central Europe no central government was strong enough to subordinate the nobility, but the tendency toward disintegration or particularism resulted in the multiplication of petty principalities. The power of the nobles as a whole, as an estate, increased; but the power of individual nobles declined as the territories and populations which the majority of nobles ruled grew smaller. Two different tendencies are therefore apparent. In the western monarchies the aristocracy struggled to regain its lost political power; in central Europe the aristocracy was jealous to preserve its rights of local political autonomy against any assertion of authority by the emperor or by the greater princes of the Empire or, in Italy, by the pope. Despite these divergent tendencies and the special conditions that prevailed in Italy, the basic fact for all of Europe is that in the later Middle Ages the political activity of the aristocracy can no longer be described adequately by the feudal phrase "aid and counsel," according to which the vassal owes his lord advice and material assistance in the formulation and execution of political policies.

In England, France, and Spain the nobles took advantage of frequent periods of weakness or defeat to try to capture control of the central government. They turned to their own use the system of indentured retinues, retaining for their private employment the mercenary soldiery hired originally for service to the crown. By these means and by bribery or threats of violence the nobles attempted to gain control of the administrative and judicial machinery of the government in their localities. In the west, generally, the monarchies withstood such ambitions during the fourteenth century, but in the fifteenth century the nobles were able to diminish the powers of the crown to the point where their struggles took the form of civil wars among themselves rather than conflict between the crown and the baronage. In England the Wars of the Roses and in France the strife between Armagnacs and Burgundians were both essentially struggles for power between baronial parties. The prize was control of the central government. Specifically, the nobles sought appointment to the offices of the royal council which directed policy and administration.

The main constitutional significance of these later medieval struggles among factions of the aristocracy lies in the fact that they were simply struggles for power. There was no thought of political theories or principles. All the nobles contended for was control of the government, in contrast with earlier baronial opposition to the crown that appealed to the medieval principle that all government should be limited by law. The political ambitions of the nobility achieved few constructive results, but they did teach contemporaries an important lesson. A nearly universal complaint through-out western Europe was that overmighty subjects must be forced to obey the laws and keep the peace. Therefore the strong monarchies in France and England, under Louis XI and Edward IV, enjoyed the support of a large majority of the people. The obvious cure for disorder and faction seemed to be the establishment of a central government so powerful that no group of nobles dared to defy it. Hence the tendencies toward absolute monarchy which characterize the transition from medieval to early modern Europe were successful because they were popular.

In the political sphere, as in the military, the aristocracy of the later Middle Ages was no longer feudal in the same sense in which the barons of the twelfth and thirteenth centuries pursued essentially feudal goals and acted in accordance with feudal custom governing the relations between vassals and lords. For all the crudity and violence of the earlier age, the rules of the game according to feudal values were still observed well enough so that a breach of accepted standards of conduct was scandalous. In the later period it would be difficult to find any standards by which nobles vied with each other and with rulers to increase their power. Partly this can be explained by the fact that the political stakes were far higher. The twelfth-century lord generally fought only for his fief—either to defend it against attack or to enlarge it at the expense of his immediate neighbors. In the fifteenth century the English and French nobles were struggling for con-trol of a whole nation. In the difference may be seen the decline of feudalism.

In the economic sphere the confusion of ideals and realities in the decadent feudal society of the later Middle Ages is a striking feature. Just as the noble was ideally supposed to maintain the peace and repress tyr-anny, but often spent his time fighting civil wars or oppressing the weak and defenseless, he was also supposed to promote the general welfare of the people, but actually devoted his energies to exploiting or simply robbing whatever poor peasants or wealthy merchants came within his reach. The "robber-barons" of Germany are appropriately so called. In western Europe simple lawlessness was not quite so easy, but exploitation was at least as great as the law would allow, and usually a little more so. We have seen that the economic tendencies of the later Middle Ages generally worked against the interests of the landowning aristocracy and to the benefit of the peas-antry. The more aggressive nobles recouped themselves with the spoils of war or the spoils of political office, but there were some who found more peaceful ways of preserving or even improving their economic status.

Deep-rooted prejudice against the occupations of the lower-classes prevented all but a tiny minority of the aristocracy from diverting their re-sources into commercial enterprise. Of the few who did, most were Italians of the lesser nobility. The trend was actually the other way around. Pros-pering commoners who were engaged in trade or industry bought their way by marriage into the ranks of the aristocracy. More typical were nobles who followed the lead of the greater ecclesiastical landowning corporations and turned to large-scale or commercial agriculture. Rather than extract services from unwilling peasants or collect rents that tended to decline with every change in tenancy, these lords expelled their peasants and consolidated their manorial fields in favor of production for market, using hired labor. This system worked best where little labor was required, or where conditions were well suited for a single crop which could be produced more economically in a particular region. Thus in northern England some lords converted their manors into sheep farms for growing wool exclusively, while in eastern Germany lords often found it profitable to eliminate all but the production of a single grain crop for market. This sort of specialization was the rural counterpart of the commercial and financial enterprise of such people as Datini or the Medici. Nobles who were so engaged made their profits by careful management of hired labor and equally careful attention to current prices in various markets. They were essentially rural businessmen, no longer in any real sense members of the feudal nobility holding fiefs merely to support their service to their lords.

As the realities of feudal society gave way to a new social order, in its military, political, and economic aspects, the ideals and values of feudalism were asserted even more strongly. People seemed unwilling to recognize the changes that were shaping a new Europe. The age that witnessed the triumph of the foot soldier over the mounted knight, the relative rise of both peasants and townsmen to a greater share in the total wealth of Europe, and the advent of strong monarchies in the west and power politics in all regions, was also the age in which the ideals of chivalry were expressed most extravagantly. The vogue of the "new chivalry" reached its climax in the foundation of several new knightly orders. Edward III, for example, founded the Order of the Garter; John the Good of France established his Order of the Star; and Duke Philip the Good instituted the Order of the Golden Fleece. The overt aims of these orders may be indicated by a contemporary explanation of the high purpose of the Order of the Golden Fleece:

> Not at all for play or pastime,
> But to the end that praise be given
> First to God above all,
> And also glory and high renown to good men.[1]

Actually, these orders were sponsored by the courts almost exclusively for courtiers, noble politicians, and foreign nobles whose political support was

[1] J. Huizinga, *The Waning of the Middle Ages* (London, 1948), p. 75, translation slightly paraphrased and reprinted by permission of the publisher, Edward Arnold and Co., Ltd.

coveted. They had an elaborate and artificial ceremonial, complete with special offices, titles, and chivalrous vows, and they were very popular with the aristocracy, or at least with those who had social and political ambitions. In contrast with the Knights Templars, Hospitallers, and Teutonic Knights of earlier times, these latter-day orders of chivalry performed no military, social, or economic function of immediate practical value. They provided a kind of organized social dream world for the nobles who made good in the later Middle Ages.

Cultural Developments
in the Later Middle Ages

Medieval culture came to a double end. In Italy it ended in the blaze of humanism and classical revival that characterized the Renaissance. North of the Alps there was greater continuity of medieval interests, and very little that was spectacular in literary and artistic achievement. The great differences between the Gothic North and Renaissance Italy have been variously explained. Perhaps no period in history has been more difficult to define and evaluate than the one called the Renaissance. Interpretations have ranged all the way from a denial that there was, in any meaningful sense, a "renaissance" to an affirmation of the Renaissance in Italy as a unique and distinctive period that sharply separates the Middle Ages from modern times. The first interpretation minimizes the importance of the achievements of the period; the latter interpretation distorts and exaggerates the changes and achievements while minimizing the element of continuity.

The cultural differences between Renaissance Italy and the high Middle Ages, and between Italy and the North, are important enough to warrant our use of a special term to designate the period, if it be kept in mind that the historical realities are still particular events and particular people, not the labels used to refer to people and events. If we take the term strictly and literally, meaning a true "rebirth," then only a cursory survey of Italian cultural developments in the fourteenth and fifteenth centuries reveals that much of the so-called rebirth was being reborn before the period begins; that much of the rebirth was abortive; that many of the characteristic interests and activities of the period were not part of any rebirth at all—no matter how the term is defined; and that much of the culture of classical antiquity was by no means revived. For example, one of the chief glories of antique pagan thought was philosophy, a field in which Italian humanists were weak and imitative; or, if one shifts to the revival of Christian antiquity, one of the great triumphs of the Age of the Fathers was the development of theology, another field in which the humanists of the Renaissance were neither interested nor productive.

The nature of the Renaissance in Italy can be explained in the same way that medieval culture in its final phase north of the Alps can be explained: by cultural tendencies already apparent in the high Middle Ages, by characteristic attitudes toward the past, and above all by the needs and interests of the dominant social and economic classes. Art, literature, and thought are always influenced by political and social conditions, even if a generous allowance is made for the role of individual genius.

87   *HUMANISM: THE RENAISSANCE IN ITALY*

The most prominent feature of the Renaissance was humanism, which for that period may be defined as an enthusiastic interest in classical Latin letters, both pagan and Christian. Humanism was not absent from the culture of the high Middle Ages. Most of the classical Latin authors were read and appreciated in the twelfth century, and all the manuscripts in which the works of these classical authors were preserved were medieval copies. What distinguishes Renaissance from medieval humanism is a different attitude toward the classics. In the high Middle Ages priority was given to the philosophical, scientific, and theological writings of antiquity. The humanists of the Renaissance preferred classical belles-lettres, that is, poetry, drama, essays, and general literature as opposed to useful or informational literature. Interest shifted from the utilitarian value to the esthetic value of classical letters. Cicero replaced Aristotle. For that matter, in the early Renaissance the Greeks as a whole were neglected, compared with the medieval scholastic interest in Greek philosophy and science.

Another difference of attitude was that humanists of the Renaissance were more sophisticated than their medieval predecessors in their appreciation of the classical authors. The humanists drew a sharp distinction between ancient and medieval literature and thought, in contrast with the typically medieval attitude, which appreciated the classics without drawing invidious distinctions between ancient and more recent authors. The distinction drawn by the humanists of the Renaissance was based mainly on style rather than content. The "barbarism" of medieval Latin was repugnant to humanists who were firmly convinced that the beautiful, the good, and the true were one.

A third difference between the culture of the high Middle Ages and that of the Renaissance was that the former was cosmopolitan or "international," although the most important centers of learning and art were in France. The Renaissance in Italy was an Italian movement—by comparison, it was a provincial culture. It was not until the second half of the fifteenth century that humanism began to exert any significant influence north of the Alps.

Humanism in the Renaissance, then, was a special development of tendencies already present in the high Middle Ages, a development that led to new attitudes and interests that were especially characteristic of Italy, in contrast with northern Europe where the earlier humanistic movement withered during the later Middle Ages. How to explain the divergence? The problem is very complex, but at the risk of oversimplification two basic facts may be emphasized as explaining much though not all of the nature of humanism in the fourteenth century. These are first the rise of nationalism and, second, the predominance of a class of *nouveaux riches* in Italy, the merchant princes who could support a culture in harmony with their values.

Nationalism in the later Middle Ages was not the aggressive force that it became after the French Revolution and the Napoleonic wars. Perhaps the phrase "national self-consciousness" would be more descriptive. Later medieval nationalism took the form of hatred of foreign interference or oppression, as with Joan of Arc and the French in the second quarter of the fifteenth century. In Italy the same spirit is well expressed in the poem by Petrarch (d.1374) entitled *Italia Mia*:

> My Italy . . . in whose hands Fortune put the rein
> Of places beautiful . . . and for what?
> To let your verdant plain
> Be painted by barbaric blood and art?
> Nature did well provide for our weak state
> When she raised that mountain screen,
> The Alps, to guard us from the German rage.
> O gentle Latin blood, throw down this burthen,
> Rise up from this shame, do not worship a name
> Empty of all subject. To let a Nordic fury,
> A savage race, conquer our minds and souls
> Is our own sin—and that no natural disgrace.[1]

Here the foreign oppressor is the German, the barbarian *par excellence*,

---

[1] *Petrarch Sonnets & Songs*, tr. A. M. Armi (New York, 1946), pp. 203–07, reprinted by permission of the publisher, Pantheon Books Inc.

from whom Italians had suffered for centuries. This appeal of humanism to patriotic sentiments was aimed directly at those who stood to profit from the decline of the medieval Empire.

Petrarch first popularized the notion that the period of European history following the death of Constantine (337) was a "dark age," and it was Petrarch who first stigmatized the artistic and literary achievements of the Middle Ages as "Gothic," by which he meant not only esthetically unworthy but "barbarian" and "non-Latin." Behind these value judgments lay the same spirit of nationalism that inspired *Italia Mia*. Nationalism always appeals to the past for a justification of the present and the hoped-for future. Nationalism is nourished by a heroic tradition. But what, in the history of medieval Italy, could provide that need? With the exception of the battle of Legnano (1176) the annals of medieval Italy consist of an inglorious series of invasions from beyond the Alps or struggles between Italians. Nationalism could not focus on the papacy, far less on the medieval Empire, for each was by its nature an ecumenical institution. As Petrarch and the humanists realized, it was necessary to go all the way back to ancient Rome to find the historical model or inspiration for Italian nationalism. The cult of classical letters served the cause of national revival. Although the ideal was never realized, it did stimulate interest in the classical pagan authors.

The humanistic works of the humanists were not very impressive. Both Petrarch and his most devoted admirer, Boccaccio (d.1375), intended their fame to rest upon their Latin writings on classical themes. However, few people today have ever read or even heard of Petrarch's long and tiresome Latin epic, *Africa*, or Boccaccio's learned and more interesting Latin treatise *On the Genealogy of the Gods*. Petrarch was so much under the spell of the classics that his Latin works tended to be simply imitative. His *Letters*, for example, are interesting today not for their style (as he intended) but for the information they contain. His greatest work was a collection of sonnets written in the Italian vernacular; Petrarch said he considered these mere trifles of which he was really ashamed—though he spent years in revising and polishing them. Boccaccio's greatest work was also written in Italian and reflects none of his humanistic interest. This was the immortal *Decameron*, in form a collection of short stories on varied themes like the medieval *fabliaux*, but far more entertaining, better written, and psychologically more profound than any previous work of fiction.

Although none of the Latin works on which the humanists prided themselves has taken its place as an important or enduring contribution to European literature, it would be a mistake to condemn humanism as being only sterile and imitative. Among their positive contributions, the humanists awakened a new enthusiasm for literature that led to extensive manuscript hunting. The discovery of long-neglected and sometimes superior texts of ancient authors led, in turn, to the collation of manuscripts and the improvement of texts. Humanistic scholarship also encouraged first-hand knowledge of literature, in contrast with the tendency of medieval scholars to rely on *florilegia,* or compilations of extracts. Enthusiasm for classical letters also led the humanists to a new interest in Greek literature. As for Petrarch and Boccaccio, their enthusiasm far exceeded their knowledge— Petrarch's prized copy of Homer was a closed book because he could not read Greek. In the fifteenth century the study of Greek advanced slowly in Italy. The fall of Constantinople had little to do with this—the movement was under way long before 1453. In the next century the great achievement of the northern humanists was their mastery of Greek literature.

Another positive achievement of the humanists was the introduction of a new concept of education. The humanists, with their emphasis on belles-lettres, had little use for the rigorous study of logic and the formal training required in the universities as the basis for higher specialized studies in law, medicine, philosophy, and theology. Instead, they emphasized the intellectual, moral, and physical development of the whole man. The foundation of this Renaissance ideal of "liberal education" was the study of the classics, together with suitable attention to such things as physical exercise, social manners, and the development of good personal habits and traits of character. The schools of Vittorino da Feltre (d.1446) at Mantua and of Guarino da Verona (d.1460) at Ferrara were leading centers of the new education. Out of these schools emerged the ideal of the "gentleman and scholar"—an ideal that has pervaded academic and educated circles down to the time of mass education in the twentieth century. The finest expression of this ideal was the early sixteenth-century treatise by Castiglione, *The Book of the Courtier,* which describes the perfect gentleman as being preferably of noble birth, at ease in the best society, trained in arms, practiced in sports, and acquainted with the arts, music, and literature. Such a gentleman was well fitted to be a courtier, but it comes as no surprise that none of the graduates of these schools made a significant contribution to the political or cultural history of Europe.

In higher education the humanists founded no new schools of medicine, law, or theology, but there were efforts to establish "academies" for the study of philosophy. The most notable were the short-lived group in Rome devoted mainly to the resurrection of Epicurean ideas, and the more important Platonic Academy in Florence under the patronage of the Medici. The members of the latter group were distinguished more by ambition than achievement. Their goal was to synthesize the philosophy of Plato with Christianity, but they never really distinguished Plato's thought from the vast and nebulous body of pseudo-philosophy which goes under the name of Neo-Platonism. The leading intellects of the Platonic Academy were Marsilio Ficino (d.1491), whose most valuable contribution was a translation of the *Dialogues* of Plato, and Pico della Mirandola (d.1494), who was the most eminent philosopher among the Italian Renaissance humanists. Pico's philosophy has been called eclectic; it was a potpourri whose ingredients included not only Christianity and Plato but selected bits from the secret lore of the Jewish *Cabala*, Arabic commentators on Aristotle, Zoroastrianism, the medieval scholastics, and other sources both ancient and medieval. Pico believed that some truth could be found in every religious or philosophical system, for each shares some part of the ultimate Truth that lies beyond them all, and he was chary of discarding anything he found as being in error. Instead of considering contradictory statements to be mutually exclusive, he considered it the philosopher's task to seek the hidden truth that would reconcile them. This search led him to the occult and magical "sciences"—a more congenial intellectual environment than that of systematic scholastic philosophy. Pico's enthusiasm and his ambitious intellectual program attracted the support of such patrons as Lorenzo de' Medici, but nothing substantial or influential resulted from his display of youthful exuberance. He died at the age of thirty-one.

The schools and academies were essentially adornments of Renaissance society, but the humanists were more than mere hangers-on at the courts. They were employed as ambassadors and as writers of diplomatic correspondence. Their prestige was so great that the service of an outstanding humanist was sometimes considered more valuable than that of an army. Even more obviously and effectively the art of the Renaissance was an adornment of society and a measure of the great wealth accumulated by the businessmen who supported the courts of the rulers or who themselves patronized the arts.

Between humanism and Renaissance art there were some obvious similarities. Each had medieval roots. The tendency toward realism in sculpture and painting, for example, can be found in Gothic work of the thirteenth century, just as Renaissance humanism has roots in medieval humanism. Also, Renaissance art was largely a classical revival in its developed form, although the architects, sculptors, and painters were more independent and original than the great majority of literary humanists. Another parallel was the growing tendency in the fifteenth century toward more secular, and even pagan, themes for artistic portrayal. However, the great majority of artists who painted mythological subjects or portrayed biblical figures as Greek gods were no less Christian for that, just as the great majority of the humanist devotees of Plato thought of themselves as devout Christians putting philosophy to the service of their religion.

On the other hand, humanism and art were not very closely related. The textual and literary criticism of the humanists represented a technical advance in their field, but it bore no relation to the even more impressive technical advance in the arts, such as better composition, mastery of perspective, use of light and shade to produce three-dimensional effects, better knowledge of anatomy, better oil paints, the casting of alloyed metals, and the solution of engineering problems involved in the construction of huge

St. Peter and the Tribute Money. Fresco by Masaccio, Brancacci Chapel, Church of the Carmine, Florence (c.1427). PHOTO: ALINARI.

domes. The artists of the Renaissance were essentially artisans. They learned from the ruins of antiquity in their midst. Sculptors and even painters took some interest in classical models, but it was to further their goal of realistic representation rather than to bring about any general revival of the ancient world. To an even greater degree architects studied the ruins of ancient structures, but they adapted the knowledge thus gained to their own ends. A Renaissance church is not simply a Roman temple, despite the use of classical columns, arches, and domes.

The ideal of the *uomo universale* ("universal man"), the man whose versatility was proved by excellence and creative achievement in many fields, was widely accepted but rarely realized in the Renaissance. There were many who dabbled in several fields, but a man like Leon Battista Alberti (d.1472) was exceptional. He was a leading classical scholar and a working architect of the first rank; he wrote treatises on the arts, education, and politics; he composed music and wrote a comedy that was mistaken for the work of Terence; and he was also an athlete and dancer of some renown. His essay *On the Family* is the most interesting vernacular work of the fifteenth century. In it Alberti reflects the optimism and self-reliance of his age: "Men are themselves the source of their own fortune; fame and wealth should be attributed not to fortune, but to ability." The ideal family exemplifies the bourgeois virtues of thrift and enterprise, while the greatest virtue of the good wife is submissiveness (an interesting reminder that Renaissance women had gained little beyond the status of the twelfth-century feudal lady). Alberti's most important work was *On Architecture,* the first modern treatise on that subject. Combining his reading of Vitruvius with his own observations and theories, he discusses at length the problems of design that must be solved to achieve architectural beauty. His interest is

San Francesco, Rimini: façade (c.1450), by Leon Battista Alberti. PHOTO: ALINARI.

in esthetics rather than in engineering; the perfect building is the one from which nothing may be taken and to which nothing may be added, nor any of its parts altered, except for the worse. This concept of beauty strictly subordinates architecture to the classical principles of unity and harmonious proportion—principles of which the Romanesque and Gothic builders were unaware.

A final estimate of the culture of Renaissance Italy must stress the very narrow social base on which it rested. Humanism and Renaissance art were produced for and supported by the urban aristocracy of princes and merchants. The common people as a whole neither participated in the culture of the period nor did they value it greatly. Far more people heard the old-time revivalist preaching of Savonarola (d.1498) in Florence then went to see the paintings or sculpture of Leonardo da Vinci, Michelangelo, and Raphael. These considerations must be kept in mind in assessing the contemporary importance of the Renaissance, which was a break away from traditional and religious values. It was worldly in the sense that the writers, scholars, artists, and their patrons were worldly in their interests. The new urban wealth needed a cultural expression different from medieval culture, which was primarily the expression of the teachings of the Church and the social predominance of the rural aristocracy. But this new bourgeoisie of Italy and the culture it promoted represent just as great a schism in Italian society as a break from medieval culture. The superficial brilliance of the Renaissance in Italy should not obscure the fact that the country was divided culturally between an aristocracy of wealth and talent and the mass of the people who continued in older ways, just as the country was hopelessly disunited politically.

88 INTELLECTUAL AND RELIGIOUS TENDENCIES IN THE FOURTEENTH AND FIFTEENTH CENTURIES

Cultural developments in Europe north of the Alps were more varied than in Italy during the later Middle Ages. There were a few significant similarities and there were a number of important differences. If the Renaissance in Italy can be given the label, the Age of Enthusiasm, the fourteenth and fifteenth centuries in the rest of Europe might well be called the Age of Pessimism. In England, France, the Low Countries, and Germany there are few signs of the optimism, self-confidence, and buoyancy of spirit that characterize the work of writers and artists in Italy, and there is an almost complete absence of the slavish reverence for antiquity that is the hallmark of Italian humanism. On the other hand, northern developments showed in different ways a growing doubt or even a rejection of some of the intellectual and religious interests and values that were typically medieval.

Theology, queen of the sciences, and her handmaiden philosophy, continued to attract many of the best minds. A sure evidence of continuing vitality in these fields was the development among the scholastics of two different schools of thought. By the end of the Middle Ages, when such men as Martin Luther, Desiderius Erasmus, and John Calvin were going to school, teachers were referred to as "ancients" or "moderns," while the curricula under these masters were distinguished as the *via antiqua* and the *via moderna*. The so-called "ancients" of the northern universities were not humanists: they were the teachers of the theology and philosophy of the high Middle Ages, specifically that of St. Thomas and the other Dominican rationalists. Nor were the "moderns" in any way connected with a revival of classical studies: they were the later medieval critics of Thomistic theology and philosophy.

The attack on the optimistic rationalism of St. Thomas began almost immediately after his death. His earliest important critic was Duns Scotus (d.1308), an Oxford Franciscan, whose main contribution was an exhaustive analysis of Thomistic epistemology, that is, the premises of the then accepted scholastic theory of knowledge. There were, in Aquinas' account of how knowledge is attained, certain technical ambiguities arising from the Aristotelian account of man's knowledge. With a wealth of distinctions between finite and infinite being, between categories recognized and categories created by human reason, and between knowledge ascertained by reason and knowledge perceived by reason but only perfected by divine grace, Duns Scotus earned his sobriquet of "the Subtle Doctor."

Duns Scotus accepted, while desiring to improve, the basically rationalistic metaphysics of medieval scholasticism. His most important successor, William of Ockham (d.1349), another English Franciscan, went beyond constructive criticism to a position that was basically antirationalistic. The two spheres of reason and revelation, which Aquinas sought to join, Ockham now rent asunder. Christian dogma, he insisted, must be accepted on faith only, because it could not be demonstrated by reason. This position implied the converse: that the sphere of natural truth should be open to rational investigation unimpeded by metaphysical or theological considerations. In the same spirit, Ockham argued that as between two hypotheses or principles the simpler should always be preferred in offering an explanation of natural phenomena. It followed that all discussion of universals was simply irrelevant because knowledge thereof added nothing to knowledge of particulars or individual things, of which unaided reason can attain a direct apprehension. Ockham's nominalism—in this attack on universals called "Ockham's razor"—condemned the metaphysical speculation so popular among the earlier realists as useless and misleading. It also consigned the data of revelation to a doubtful, if not needless, category so far as human knowledge of the natural world is concerned. It is in this sense that Ockham has been called one of the founders of modern science. In his own and the next generation at the University of Paris some important contributions were made by Ockham's followers, such as Jean Buridan (d.1358) and Nicholas Oresme (d.1382), who advanced beyond Aristotle's theory of motion and groped toward conclusions achieved later by Copernicus and Galileo in the field of celestial mechanics. These and similar efforts, however, did not lead to any general development of scientific enquiry in the fifteenth century, although the later work of Nicholas of Cusa (d.1464) and others kept the University of Paris in the forefront of later medieval science.

The trend of Ockham's philosophical and theological thought, at the highest level, was reflected in religious movements on a lower intellectual level: mysticism and lay piety. The connection between Ockham and these movements was not direct, however, and the transition to later medieval mysticism is already apparent in the life and work of the German Dominican teacher, Meister Eckhart (d.1327). The decline of the Church in the later Middle Ages was an important factor. In a time when the papacy was at Avignon and under attack, when Europe was divided by the Great

Schism, and when the conciliar movement threatened the traditional hierarchical structure of the clergy, conditions were ideal for a flourishing of religious experience outside of the formal organization of the Church. The mystic stresses the individual relationship with God. The externals of worship are subordinated to an inner devotion: the surrender of personality to the divine will, an emphasis on the "yearning of love" in seeking God, and a conviction that the culmination of religious experience is reached only after the intellect or human reason has been left behind and the soul has risen in its quest to a union with the deity.

Mysticism is not uniquely Christian, nor is mysticism unique to any age of Christianity. In each age it has exhibited certain distinctive characteristics. The mystics of the high Middle Ages and those of the later period were in agreement on the basic points just mentioned, but there were also significant differences. Many of the earlier mystics were minds of the first rank, important leaders in society, and members of the clergy. So far as their writings were concerned, they appealed to other individuals and not to any communal or organized movement of mystics. Obvious examples would be Bernard in the twelfth century and Bonaventura in the thirteenth. Also, while mysticism was important in religious life, it was not a predominant element. In contrast, later medieval mysticism was a large-scale movement that attracted many people who were neither well educated nor leaders nor clerics. It was primarily an expression of lay piety, a vocation open to all men, and it tended to be channeled into communal movements. Of all the later medieval mystics, only Nicholas of Cusa could possibly be put in the same rank with Bernard or Bonaventura.

The wider appeal of later mysticism gave rise to a voluminous and popular devotional literature. The *Imitation of Christ,* attributed to Thomas à Kempis (d.1471), was the outstanding work, and there were a score of important treatises and a hundred mediocre ones of a similar nature. All these works, in greater or lesser degree, appeal to the emotion rather than to the intellect. They provide a program of salvation emphasizing inner spirituality, faith, and love above reason and good works. They were not, with a few exceptions, unorthodox. But by minimizing the role of the clergy and of the sacramental system they helped create a climate of religious experience that was favorable to the Protestant reformers of the sixteenth century. Martin Luther was profoundly moved by the anonymous fifteenth-century *German Theology,* a typical tract of the times.

Most of the new religious organizations of the later Middle Ages found their inspiration in mysticism, especially those whose work or teaching tended toward extreme expressions of piety. Best known and most influential were the Brethren of the Common Life, founded by Gerard Groot (d.1384), a popular lay preacher in the Low Countries and a follower of Jan van Ruysbroek, who in turn was a disciple of Eckhart. The teachings of Groot and the Brethren, at first suspected for heretical tendencies, soon became the finest example of the "new devotion" or *devotio moderna*. Like the mendicant friars, they were dedicated to preaching and charitable work among the poor and the downtrodden, but they were not mendicants. The majority of Brethren were laymen, and although they lived in common they took no monastic vows. Their most lasting contribution was in the field of education. If the humanist educators of Italy were proud of their "rounded" or "progressive" education, the Brethren did a far more effective job without benefit of publicity or of any new pedagogical theory. Among the intellectual leaders of northern Europe who went to their schools or attended classes in schools where Brethren taught were Nicholas of Cusa, Thomas à Kempis, Rudolf Agricola (d.1485), who was the first important German humanist, Erasmus of Rotterdam, and Martin Luther.

Closely related to popular mysticism were many other communal movements, more or less organized, such as the lay brotherhood of the Beghards and the sisterhood of the Beguines, the Brethren of the Free Spirit, the Friends of God, the Humiliati, and the Flagellants. The last two were especially strong in Italy and Spain. Some of these groups were extreme to the point of a perversion of asceticism and of exaggerated piety, and lapsed into heretical beliefs or practices. None of their leaders made a significant contribution to European thought or literature, but as movements they were important symptoms of unrest and dissatisfaction with the established order and with the teachings of the Church.

On a higher intellectual level, but expressing the same dissatisfaction, were the heretical movements led by John Wycliffe (d. 1384) in England and John Huss (d.1415) in Bohemia. Both Wycliffe and Huss criticized contemporary ecclesiastical abuses, of which there were many; they leveled their attack primarily at the papacy. In theology Wycliffe was influenced strongly by Ockham in emphasizing the priority of faith over reason. He also stressed the priority of the Scriptures over *Traditio*, the traditional customs and teachings of the Church. Many of Wycliffe's views verged on heresy without quite being heretical, but his stand on apostolic poverty and his denial of transubstantiation definitely placed him outside the orthodox fold. Even after he was condemned for heresy, however, Wycliffe was secure in his person and died peacefully. For this good fortune he had to thank his supporters at the English court of Richard II and the fact that his attack on the papacy and upon ecclesiastical wealth and privilege was popular with the English aristocracy. His was one of the early voices of English nationalism. Wycliffe's ideas were developed further and spread throughout England by his followers, or by those who claimed to speak in his name and called themselves Lollards. Because Lollardy emphasized a program of economic and social reform together with an attack on ecclesiastical abuses, and associated itself with the Peasants' Revolt of 1381, the movement was ruthlessly suppressed.

Wycliffe's teachings were preserved, by a curious circumstance, not in England but in far-off Bohemia. The courts of the two countries were in close communication because of the marriage of Richard II with Anne of Bohemia, who was the half-sister of Wenceslas and the sister of Sigismund, both kings of Bohemia and emperors. Czech students who went to England in the entourage of Queen Anne brought the works of Wycliffe back to the University of Prague. Here Wycliffe's ideas fanned the first flames of Czech nationalism when the rector of the University, John Huss, adopted them as part of his program of Church reform and of independence from German political and cultural predominance in Bohemia. We have already seen that Huss' fate was different from that of Wycliffe. To most Czechs the death of Huss at the stake was the martyrdom of a national hero, not the burning of a heretic. The resulting Hussite movement in Bohemia was the most important instance of the growth of nationalism in central Europe.

After the middle of the fourteenth century, Wycliffe and Huss were the only outstanding intellectual leaders convicted of heresy. The only other historically important individual convicted as a heretic in the period was Joan of Arc, who was canonized as a saint in the year 1920. Each of these three was a symbol, in different ways, of nationalism. Other heretics there were, but they were either followers of these leaders or else people of only local importance. However, later medieval heterodoxy produced a large number of ordinary people who were collectively important and at least as interesting, whether on modern standards or on the standards of their own age. These people were witches, the majority of whom were beautiful young women or ugly old women. Belief in witches goes back far beyond the later Middle Ages, but in the fifteenth century the threat, as contemporaries believed, was particularly great. The period which historians have denominated the birth of modern times was also the age of the great witchcraft delusion. The difficulties—political, social, and economic—were general to all of Europe, but the common people were aware of these difficulties only as particular misfortunes within the range of their immediate and local experience. The easiest explanation was to blame a witch. If all of western Europe suffered drought, in scores of villages there were resident witches to blame for preventing the rain from falling in each village.

The essence of witchcraft was "congress with the devil." This gave the witch supernatural powers to wield against God-fearing folk. Harm could be inflicted in a number of ways. By the use of wax or graven images, or by charms of various sorts, witches destroyed crops and killed off and prevented the reproduction of cattle and fowl. In an age of high infant mortality it is not surprising, to the modern reader, that a large number of witches were elderly women who performed the services of a midwife. The most interesting witches were those who transformed themselves into wolves or other animals and attacked men, or who rode broomsticks into the moonlit night, or who possessed the bodies of otherwise good men and forced their attentions on good women. This fascinating shadow-world of the later Middle Ages was officially recognized by Pope Innocent VIII in 1484, when he issued a bull defining witchcraft as a form of heresy and authorized the Inquisition in Germany to extirpate the menace. This bull was followed by a manual of theory and procedure written by two inquisitors engaged in that work, entitled *Malleus Maleficarum* ("Hammer of Witches"). The witchcraft delusion was another symptom of the decline of confidence and the failure of the Church to keep superstition within bounds during the later Middle Ages. The advent of modern times did not eradicate this mass psychosis. The Protestant reformers were just as zealous in rooting out witchcraft as their predecessors, and the last witch was not executed until the seventeenth century. Who knows? There may still be witches lurking in odd corners of the world today.

89 THE REASSERTION OF TRADITION AND AUTHORITY IN THE NORTH

The literature and art of northern Europe in the fourteenth and fifteenth centuries were conservative. Compared with contemporary Italy, writers and artists showed respect for medieval precedents rather than interest in innovation or classical revival. Compared with the art and literature of the high Middle Ages, there was little of the creative and daring quality that produced new literary forms and themes or such radical changes as ribvaulting and flying buttresses in architecture. In general, the weight of tradition north of the Alps brought a decline in the quality without decreasing the quantity of literary and artistic works.

To this generalization there are exceptions. An important new vernacular literature began to appear in England during the later fourteenth century. Beginning with the mystic Richard Rolle (d.1349), there was a considerable body of religious or devotional writing to which contributions were made by the anonymous author of *The Cloud of Unknowing* (c.1360); Walter Hilton (d.1396), whose *Scale of Perfection* was more widely read in England than the *Imitation of Christ*; Dame Julian of Norwich (d.1420); and the redoubtable and incomparable Margery Kempe (d.1438), who wrote a fascinating autobiographical account of her spiritual experiences. Wycliffe's most important purely literary achievement consisted of translations of Scriptures into English which he initiated and which his followers largely carried through. *The Vision of Piers Plowman* by William Langland (d.1395) was an allegorical poem of the most conventional form, but it combined deep religious feeling with a sturdy critical view of the clerical and lay society of the author's day, together with an intense desire to edify the reader. It may be characterized as a rude, country equivalent of the greatest of all medieval symbolic works, Dante's *Divine Comedy.*

Geoffrey Chaucer (d.1400) was in a different category from the other English writers. He accepted all the medieval ideals and values, as did they, but his work was in the medieval tradition of the *fabliaux.* The foibles and failures of contemporaries did not scandalize him, though his satire could be as biting as ever Langland's criticism was righteous. Chaucer's narrative poems, notably the *Canterbury Tales,* are often compared with Boccaccio's prose *Decameron.* They are all good tales, delightfully realistic, full of sharply delineated individual personalities who are, at the same time, often typical of their rank or station in life. Chaucer portrays the society of his age without idealizing it or distorting it to fit any preconceptions of what society ought to be. He was admirably equipped to do so. His experience included business, service in the government, travel in foreign parts, membership in Parliament, and a wide acquaintance with the learning and literature of his day. He made translations, and the themes of some of his tales are borrowed from contemporary Latin, French, and Italian stories. In the development of the English language Chaucer also occupies an important place. His language is not the rustic English of Langland and earlier religious writers, but that of London and the home counties where the influence of the French-speaking upper classes was greatest.

Continental Europe, outside of Italy, produced almost nothing in literature during the fourteenth and fifteenth centuries comparable with the works of the English writers of the age of Chaucer, either in Latin or in the vernacular languages, before the advent of humanism at the end of the period. Of lyric poetry there was a great outpouring by the German Meistersinger and the French versifiers. Of chivalric romance in prose there were many works concerning which the most charitable comment is silence. The *Morte d'Arthur* by the Englishman Sir Thomas Malory (d.1471) is wholly exceptional on artistic grounds, but like all the other romances it is thoroughly conventional in subject matter and in the values of a decadent chivalry.

A better mirror of the new chivalry was the work of the historian Jean Froissart (d.1410). His French chronicle of the Hundred Years' War down to 1399 is almost totally oblivious of political issues, economic conditions, considerations of strategy, or the impact of war on society. Froissart portrays the whole history of western Europe in the fourteenth century as essentially one long series of chivalrous adventures. Noble deeds, state occasions, particular battles, tournaments, royal weddings, the knightings of noble youths, and other chivalrous ceremonies are zestfully described in one anecdote after another. It made for good entertainment—it still does —but it was rather superficial history whether on modern standards or on the standards of the better chroniclers of the twelfth century. Froissart's chronicle was continued in the fifteenth century by other writers who shared his predilection for presenting history in the guise of a chivalric romance. Medieval French historiography was then brought to a close on a note of realism by Philippe de Commines (d.1509), whose *Memoirs* penetrate beneath the panoply of colorful events and present a shrewd account of the motives of individual statesmen such as Louis XI and Charles the Rash of Burgundy.

The same note of realism is even better illustrated by the poetry of François Villon (d.1463), the only poet of the fifteenth century whose genius was equal to that of Petrarch or Chaucer in the fourteenth. In his poetry, as in his life, may be discerned the spirit of the medieval wandering scholar—like the Goliardi he was a "lewd fellow of the baser sort." Several times a convicted thief, guilty at least of manslaughter in a street brawl, and an associate of the riffraff of Paris, Villon divided his allegiance between the tavern and whoever might bail him out of jail. At the university he was a student of theology. Villon expressed better than anyone else of his generation the pessimism and poignancy, the cynical realism, and the feeling of insecurity that characterize the waning of the Middle Ages north of the Alps. Conscious that he was a gross sinner, he clung to the hope of salvation. Like so many of his contemporaries he was fascinated by the gruesome theme of death and its consequences. Formal religion meant as little to him as it did to the mystics, and his appeal is equally emotional and anti-intellectual. All this comes out in his poetry with a humorous self-pity and a contemptuous lampooning of others that deprive him and everyone else of heroic stature.

Later medieval architecture in the north may be characterized as an almost endless elaboration of the Gothic style. Nothing esthetically new was achieved. The Gothic cathedral at its best—in the thirteenth century— is beautiful because the structure is relatively simple and each part of the structure reveals its function clearly. The nature of later Gothic is suggested by the terms "flamboyant," "decorated," and "perpendicular," by which some of the regional styles are known. The common features are an exaggeration of vertical lines, the multiplication of ribs and buttresses far beyond structural requirements, and the use of so much decorative detail all over the building that ornamentation takes the place of structural beauty. Some of the fan-vaulting, with its delicate stone tracery and intricate geometrical patterns, is impressive evidence of the skill of the masons, but so far as the Gothic style as a whole is concerned technique far outdistanced art. Sculpture continued to be primarily subordinated to an architectural background, but the trend was toward works that were independent of their setting, notably the tombs of rulers and nobles. This gave the artist more freedom. The earlier tendency toward naturalism in Gothic sculpture was developed by the sculptors of northern France and

Cathedral of Cologne. Begun c.1300, largely completed by c.1521. PHOTO: GERMAN TOURIST INFORMATION SERVICE.

the Low Countries into a degree of realism that paralleled the literary realism of such writers as Villon, Commines, and Chaucer.

In painting also the tendency was away from subordination to architecture, and toward more realistic portrayal. Here the Flemish masters of the fifteenth century were clearly the leaders. Their technique consisted of a meticulous reproduction on canvas of everything visible, as if the artist looked at his subject through a window and painted everything he saw, omitting no detail whether it were a blemish on a lady's cheek or a dog romping in a field a mile away. The work of Hubert van Eyck (d.1426) and his more able brother Jan van Eyck (d.1440) combined remarkable skill in drawing with a mastery of the use of light and shade to suggest a tridimensional effect. Many of the northern painters had visited Italy, but except in some elements of technique their painting exhibits little to parallel the revival of art in Italy. It was an essentially different kind of realism that grew gradually out of earlier tendencies of Gothic naturalism in manuscript painting. The developed realism of the van Eycks and their successor Rogier van der Weyden (d.1464)[2] emphasized detail, while the contemporary Italians were working toward a realistic style in which detail was subordinated and the goal was idealized beauty rather than the accurate reproduction of nature. Also, there were significant differences in subject matter. Northern artists were almost wholly uninterested in classical themes. In religious painting the northern artists, like contemporary sculptors and writers, concentrated on the themes of death, the Last Judgment, and the life and passion of Christ. Italian artists and writers were not interested in death and its consequences, but rather in life and its pleasures, and so far as religious subjects were concerned their work emphasized the importance not of Christ but of God the Father. These divergent tendencies in art and thought can largely be explained by the continuity of medieval ideas and values in the north in contrast with the rising vogue of classical revival, with its pagan and Neo-Platonic elements, in Italy.

Finally, two technical advances in the north are worth noting for the effect they had on the development of European culture. One was the invention of oil pigments, for which the Flemish painters were responsible. Without oil, the only suitable media had been tempera on small surfaces and fresco on walls. The one was not a permanent pigment, the other subordinated painting to architecture. Modern easel painting was made possible by the successful development of oil paints. Only then did the painter achieve complete freedom of choice in design and arrangement. By removing pictures from church walls it was possible to depict subjects of purely secular interest.

The second technical advance was the invention of printing with separate types that could be reused. This is usually associated with the name of Johann Gutenberg (d.1468), who was undeniably one of the earli-

[2] See p. 551.

est printers. The invention would have come in any case, however, for printing with full-page blocks was becoming common and the development of movable type was a rather obvious refinement. The ultimate effects of the printing press have been incalculable, but its immediate results are often exaggerated. The number and kinds of books available, the size of the reading public, and even the cost of books were not materially changed before the end of the fifteenth century. In Italy there was even an initial antipathy toward printed books as representing a cheap imitation suitable only for poor scholars or for those who did not appreciate beautiful hand-written books.

A final word must be said about the influence of later medieval cultural developments on the growth of nationalism. Distinctive regional styles in architecture and the arts had little effect, but the religious and literary movements of the period were in some instances important expressions of national feeling which, in turn, caused a further development of national self-consciousness. Wycliffe in England, Huss in Bohemia, and Joan of Arc in France are obvious examples, and in the lives of each, religion and politics were intimately connected. In a less obvious way the mystics made a contribution. By minimizing the importance of the organized Church they encouraged the already widely held view that the Church was too wealthy and that the papacy was a foreign power living unjustly on the revenues of other lands. Martin Luther in the next century was initially supported by many people who were not so much interested in his new theology as they were in a way to escape papal taxation and eliminate Italian influence in the German church. Luther did not create this national sentiment; it was already there and it had been developing slowly ever since the thirteenth century. German nationalism, like Italian, did not lead to a national state because no single political authority was strong enough to exploit national feeling for its own profit. In both countries nationalism remained primarily a cultural phenomenon.

In Spain, France, and England the situation differed because each country possessed a medieval monarchy which survived the troubles of the fourteenth and early fifteenth centuries. The institution of monarchy was at once the focus and the beneficiary of nationalism. Culturally, the western countries persistently held to older ways, and an essential part of this emphasis on tradition was the acceptance of the authority of the national monarchy. The achievements of Charles VII and Louis XI in France, of Edward IV and Henry VII in England, and of Ferdinand and Isabella in Spain provided ample justification of this confidence. The civil wars, the economic difficulties, and the ambitions of the local aristocracy in each country were curbed and suppressed. The rulers accomplished these results by strengthening existing political institutions. Royal councils and representative assemblies became instruments of monarchical power, no longer the means of aristocratic revolt.

The reassertion of authority and re-establishment of order were popular with all classes of people except the now-discredited aristocracy, and even the aristocrats found it advantageous to serve the government rather than strike out again along the uncertain path of rebellion. Loyalty to the monarchy was all the more secure because in each country the crown was held by inherited right and sanctioned by the religious ceremony of anointment and coronation. Central authority was thus buttressed by two of the most enduring values in the medieval tradition: the legitimacy of inheritance and the divine sanction of the temporal power. The secret of the "new monarchies" that ushered in the early modern period was that to their subjects they were not new but old. They were based on right, while the upstart despotisms of Italy were based on might. The dominant forces of early modern Europe were thus a medieval legacy and not the result of any rebirth of ancient institutions or ideas as sponsored by the dominant minority of Renaissance Italy.

Conclusion

90 THE LEGACY OF THE MIDDLE AGES

There are two different ways to consider the legacy of the Middle Ages. There is the immediate legacy: the influence of medieval events, institutions, and ideas on the early modern period. There is the permanent legacy: the medieval contribution that has endured as part of our twentieth-century Western civilization. In part, the distinction is a difference between tangible and intangible survivals. The sixteenth century was still medieval in most of the material conditions of life, and the great majority of the people of Europe were unaware that they were living in an age called the "Renaissance" or the "Reformation." The medieval peasant of the fourteenth century would have found more that was familiar to him two or three or even four centuries later than the "common man" of the twentieth century would find familiar in the eighteenth century. Except for the cathedrals and castles that have survived—the former weathered and faded from their medieval brilliance, the latter in ruins or restored—the physical appearance of medieval Europe is suggested today only by an occasional landscape or by the older streets and a few buildings of a few dozen towns. But when the intangibles are taken into account—the institutions, ideas, values, and attitudes that date from the Middle Ages—there is a far more impressive medieval legacy that not only influenced the succeeding age but has survived as part of our world today.

The year 1500 is conventionally assigned as the approximate end of the Middle Ages and the beginning of the early modern period of European history. Several important events cluster around that uneventful year. Between 1488 and 1522 Diaz sailed around the Cape of Good Hope, Columbus discovered America, and Magellan's expedition circumnavigated the globe. In 1494 Charles VIII's invasion of Italy set the stage for a new series of international struggles that was dominated by the Habsburg-Valois wars beginning in 1521. Erasmus published the first Greek edition of the New Testament in 1516, two years after Machiavelli's *The Prince* appeared and a year before Martin Luther nailed his Ninety-Five Theses to the door of his church in Wittenberg. Without minimizing the importance of any of these events, we should not allow their dramatic character to suggest that the close of the fifteenth century and the opening of the sixteenth witnessed the beginning of a radically new or different age. Every major development in the early modern period had medieval origins or a medieval background that must be taken into consideration for a complete and correct understanding of the new age.

Politically, the salient fact is that the Middle Ages produced the early modern national state. The central governments of Spain and Portugal, France and England, the Scandinavian countries, the Holy Roman Empire and the states of Italy, Germany, and the Low Countries within the Empire—all had medieval origins. The strongest of these governments were built by the feudal monarchies of the west, especially by France and England. The problems they encountered and the obstacles to absolute power that confronted them were also part of the political legacy of the later Middle Ages. Like their medieval predecessors, the would-be "absolute" monarchs of the sixteenth century relied on their professional bureaucracies and the middle classes for support against the political privileges and pretensions of the nobility and the churches within their kingdoms. The sixteenth-century monarchies had greater power and more ambitious goals than their predecessors, but the means at their disposal were primarily the political institutions created in the Middle Ages: the royal councils, the parlements and parliaments, the royal courts, and local royal officials.

The policies pursued by the rulers of Europe during the early modern period are often described as "dynastic," because of the identification of dynastic aggrandizement with national welfare and the occasional sacrifice of national interests to dynastic ambitions. But however prominent dynasticism may have been in the politics of the early modern period, it was not an invention of the "age of absolutism." We have seen how policies that were essentially dynastic in nature motivated the English kings during the Hundred Years' War and the Burgundian dukes in the fifteenth century; initiated the rise of the Habsburgs and shaped the roles played by the electors of the Empire in the later Middle Ages; and stimulated the rivalry between the Angevin and the Aragonese claimants to the kingdom of the Two Sicilies—to mention only the most familiar examples of later medieval dynasticism. Actually, the policy of every feudal ruler of the high Middle Ages was essentially dynastic, in the sense that the interests of the ruling family were rarely if ever distinguished from the welfare of the principality or kingdom.

The transition from medieval to early modern times was accompanied by no sudden or fundamental changes in European society. The nobility remained the dominant class, while the relative importance of the bourgeoisie, both economically and politically, continued to grow. The ranks of the nobility continued to be replenished by merchants or bankers or manufacturers whose success gave them the wealth to purchase land and arrange marriages with the sons or daughters of impecunious nobles. Among the peasantry, medieval serfdom was nearly extinct by the end of the sixteenth century in western Europe, although it was not until the French Revolution that the last manorial rights of the nobility were swept away. In central and eastern Europe labor services and payments in kind, together with manorial obligations and personal unfreedom, continued until the eighteenth and nineteenth centuries.

Some of the most striking features of the economic life of the early modern period developed from medieval undertakings. The great voyages of discovery had medieval precedents dating from the twelfth and thirteenth centuries, and by the fourteenth century mariners were familiar with Iceland, the Azores, and part of the Atlantic coast of Africa. The most important post-medieval expeditions were undertaken by the western European powers—Spain, Portugal, France, and England—who had enjoyed an economic recovery in the second half of the fifteenth century but were not in a position to expand their commerce into the eastern waters of the Mediterranean or the North and Baltic seas. In Portugal, the voyages sponsored by Prince Henry the Navigator (1394–1460) were motivated as much by a desire to expand Christendom and renew the Crusades against Islam as they were by economic considerations. The commercial revival of the early modern period had its beginnings soon after 1450, led by a revival of the cloth industry and supported by the later medieval growth of the mining and metallurgical industries. The increasingly complex and efficient credit operations characteristic of early modern Europe were rapidly developing before the end of the fifteenth century. By that time Antwerp had already emerged as the dominant financial and commercial center—a position she was to occupy through most of the sixteenth century.

The relationship between the medieval legacy and the most important development of the early modern period—the Protestant Reformation —is more difficult to assess. Historians have disagreed as to whether, or to what degree, there was any significant connection between the medieval heresies and the Lutheran, Calvinist, and other Protestant movements of the sixteenth century. The answer depends largely on what is meant by the term "Reformation." If the essential aspect of the Reformation is considered to be doctrinal divergence and rejection of the papacy and the medieval Church, then there is no direct connection between Protestant leaders and the medieval heretics. Theologically, Luther and Calvin were far less indebted to any medieval heretic than they were to St. Augustine; in their attitude toward individual devotion and toward the role of the clergy they were more congenial with the later medieval orthodox mystics than they were with such organized movements as the Albigensians of the thirteenth century.

It is not in any direct, cause-and-effect relationship but rather in the general conditions of the later Middle Ages that the Reformation may be considered as part of the medieval legacy: anticlerical criticism, lay piety and popular mysticism, growing nationalism, and (especially in the case of Calvin) a scholastic enthusiasm for logical and systematic theological debate formed the social and cultural background favorable to the success of Protestantism. For example, many of Luther's earliest supporters hardly understood what he meant by "justification by faith alone." But they were critical of the clergy and the social teachings of the medieval Church, they welcomed his emphasis on piety, they resented the intervention of Italians in German ecclesiastical affairs, and they looked upon Luther as a national hero. These attitudes were forming in the later Middle Ages, and they can be traced back into the twelfth and thirteenth centuries.

The Reformation may also be defined in much broader terms, to include the social, economic, and political as well as the religious and ecclesiastical developments of the sixteenth century. In this broader sense, the legacy of medieval conditions and medieval problems contributed to the course of events, but again without any necessary cause-and-effect relationship between the medieval past and the early modern future. For example, the conflict between the spiritual and secular authorities was already being resolved in favor of the secular authority in the period following the pontificate of Boniface VIII. It was a natural if not inevitable result of the Reformation that rulers in Protestant countries generally dominated national churches and that Catholic rulers also increased their ecclesiastical powers beyond those of medieval kings. Another example, of a quite different sort, of the influence of the medieval legacy upon the Reformation in this broader sense was the fate in Protestant countries of hospitals, charitable institutions, and schools. These were the responsibility of the Church in the Middle Ages. With the suppression of ecclesiastical foundations and the confiscation of Church wealth that attended the Protestant Reformation, the social services and the education supported by the Church were undermined or destroyed. This loss was not quickly repaired; in some countries several generations elapsed before state-supported or privately endowed organizations began to provide adequately for the sick and poor or to offer the educational opportunities that the medieval Church had provided for several centuries.

The intellectual and cultural legacy of the Middle Ages to early modern Europe was so great and so diverse that space allows mention of only a few salient features. Historians have stressed the changes and new developments of the beginning of modern times more often than they have taken note of the continuity of medieval interests and activities after the fifteenth century. For example, the rapid progress of scientific thought in the seventeenth century stands in contrast with the efforts of medieval scholars to assimilate the scientific tradition of the Greeks and the Arabs. And yet it was only because the older materials had been thoroughly mastered by medieval scholars that later investigators were able to make their remarkable discoveries. A medieval invention, the printing press, promoted the spread of knowledge; Latin, the language of learning in the Middle Ages, continued to be a universal medium of communication, promoting the circulation of ideas across the barriers of different vernacular languages. Literature in the vernacular continued to grow from its medieval origins, until by the end of the seventeenth century it was the vehicle for scientific, philosophical, and scholarly subjects as well as for belles-lettres. The humanists' attack on scholasticism during the Renaissance should not obscure the fact that such "modern" philosophers as Descartes, Spinoza, and Leibniz owed much to scholastic method and accepted many of the premises of scholastic philosophy. Finally, the increasingly secular atmosphere of European culture, especially characteristic of modern times, is a development that has been continuous not merely from the sixteenth or the seventeenth century but from the high Middle Ages.

When attention is shifted from the immediate to the permanent legacy of the Middle Ages, an equally impressive number of medieval contributions to Western civilization readily come to mind. Among modern institutions that have medieval origins perhaps the university or liberal arts college is the most obvious. If the reader of this book attends, or has been graduated from, such an institution, he is the beneficiary of that part of the medieval legacy—though it must be added that institutions of higher learning also afford an excellent illustration of historical change as well as of continuity. For example, the seven liberal arts of medieval education have been quite transformed to produce the modern curriculum of the liberal arts college. It is easy to imagine what John of Salisbury, that vigorous twelfth-century critic of vocationalism and "snap" courses in the schools of his day, would have to say about some of the subjects that lead to a bachelor of arts degree today. We may be sure that he would be fascinated with the tremendous increase in the kinds and the range of courses in scientific subjects, and he would probably approve the studies offered in foreign languages and literature, in English literature, and in many of the other humanities and social "sciences" that were unknown to medieval students. But there is also little doubt that not only John but even such educational reformers as Vittorino da Feltre would be at a loss to understand or appreciate how a mastery of such subjects as home economics, accounting and bookkeeping, or physical education could possibly contribute to a student's qualifications for a university degree. And yet the teachers in modern colleges and universities who profess these subjects are the institutional, if not exactly the intellectual, descendants of such medieval teachers as Irnerius of Bologna, Bernard of Chartres, Abelard, Thomas Aquinas, and Bonaventura.

The Roman Catholic Church is a significant illustration of the continuity of medieval institutions into modern times. Although, unlike the university, it descended originally from antiquity, much of its organization, liturgy, teachings, and dogma were developed in the Middle Ages. The British Parliament is a better example of a distinctively medieval institution that has survived—again with changes which have profoundly altered its nature—into modern times. The legal institution of the jury, an integral part of Anglo-American jurisprudence and one of the foundations of modern liberty, has survived essentially unaltered from its medieval origins. The twelfth-century jury of presentment has developed into our grand jury; service on the trial or petty jury continues to be one of the obligations of all "free men" of England and citizens of other countries whose legal systems derive from that of England.

In addition to these and a few other institutional survivals of the Middle Ages, another important part of the permanent medieval legacy consists of values or principles that are fundamental to political life in the Western world today. Representative government, the creation of the high Middle Ages, has become the foundation of modern Western democracy —without some representative form of government great nations could not possibly be in any real sense democratic. No less important is the principle expressed in the phrase, "the rule of law, not of men." This concept is the essence of medieval political thought. Nations that have preserved this legacy of the Middle Ages have resisted "statism" and dictatorship. The obvious example of a modern expression of the principle is the Constitution of the United States. Closely related to this concept is the proposition that there is a basic contractual relationship between the ruler and those who are ruled, between government and citizen. In the Middle Ages this relationship was implicit in the feudal bond between lord and vassal; today it survives as a fundamental right of revolution against tyranny, a right that has motivated many great events in modern history since the signing of the American Declaration of Independence.

Finally, modern literature, thought, and life have preserved, and in preserving have changed, a variety of other medieval ideals and interests.

Our popular and romantic literature, the idealization of womanhood, and many of the fashions or conventions of modern etiquette derive ultimately from the courtly life of the feudal nobility. Standards of conduct, such as the concept of *noblesse oblige* or the basic notion of honor, have roots in the feudal values of the high Middle Ages. Medieval art has inspired the latter-day monuments of Gothic and Romanesque architecture that are as numerous among churches and campus college buildings today as are public buildings in neo-classical style. The Gothic revival in architecture is paralleled by the intellectual revival of the rationalistic thought of St. Thomas, first in theology late in the nineteenth century and later by the neo-Thomistic philosophy of our own times.

These examples illustrate but by no means exhaust the medieval survivals in modern times that constitute the legacy of the Middle Ages, a legacy of which many people are only vaguely aware. For the student of history there is another medieval "legacy." The Middle Ages present us with a civilization that was unique: history records no other civilization of such long duration with so much detail about its beginning, its culmination, and its decline. Because it is directly related to our own world a study of the Middle Ages can give us a better understanding of the nature of modern Western civilization.

The Medieval Popes[1]

Sylvester I, 314–335
Mark, 336
Julius I, 337–352
Liberius, 352–366
(Felix II, 355–365)
Damasus I, 366–384
Siricius, 384–399
Anastasius I, 399–401
Innocent I, 401–417
Zosimus, 417–418
Boniface I, 418–422
Celestine I, 422–432
Sixtus III, 432–440
Leo I the Great, 440–461
Hilary, 461–468
Simplicius, 468–483
Felix III, 483–492
Gelasius I, 492–496
Anastasius II, 496–498

Symmachus, 498–514
Hormisdas, 514–523
John I, 523–526
Felix IV, 526–530
Boniface II, 530–532
John II, 533–535
Agapitus I, 535–536
Silverius, 536–537
Vigilius, 537–555
Pelagius I, 555–561
John III, 561–574
Benedict I, 575–579
Pelagius II, 579–590
Gregory I the Great, 590–604
Sabinianus, 604–606
Boniface III, 607
Boniface IV, 608–615
Deusdedit, 615–618[2]
Boniface V, 619–625

[1] This list is based on Angelo Mercati, "The New List of the Popes," *Medieval Studies*, IX (1947), 71–80, which reprints with corrections the list in the *Annuario Pontificio* for 1947. Names and dates in parentheses are those of antipopes.
[2] Also known as Adeodatus I.

Honorius I, 625–638
Severinus, 640
John IV, 640–642
Theodore I, 642–649
Martin I, 649–655
Eugenius I, 654–657[3]
Vitalian, 657–672
Adeodatus II, 672–676
Donus, 676–678
Agatho, 678–681
Leo II, 682–683
Benedict II, 684–685
John V, 685–686
Conon, 686–687
Sergius I, 687–701
John VI, 701–705
John VII, 705–707
Sisinnius, 708
Constantine, 708–715
Gregory II, 715–731
Gregory III, 731–741
Zacharias, 741–752
Stephen II, 752–757[4]
Paul I, 757–767
Stephen III, 768–772
Adrian I, 772–795
Leo III, 795–816
Stephen IV, 816–817
Paschal I, 817–824
Eugenius II, 824–827
Valentine, 827
Gregory IV, 827–844
Sergius II, 844–847
Leo IV, 847–855
Benedict III, 855–858

Nicholas I the Great, 858–867
Adrian II, 867–872
John VIII, 872–882
Marinus I, 882–884
Adrian III, 884–885
Stephen V, 885–891
Formosus, 891–896
Boniface VI, 896
Stephen VI, 896–897
Romanus, 897
Theodore II, 897
John IX, 898–900
Benedict IV, 900–903
Leo V, 903
(Christopher, 903–904)
Sergius III, 904–911
Anastasius III, 911–913
Lando, 913–914
John X, 914–928
Leo VI, 928
Stephen VII, 928–931
John XI, 931–935
Leo VII, 936–939
Stephen VIII, 939–942
Marinus II, 942–946
Agapitus II, 946–955
John XII, 955–964[5]
Leo VIII, 963–965
Benedict V, 964–966
John XIII, 965–972
Benedict VI, 973–974
(Boniface VII, 974 and 984–985)
Benedict VII, 974–983
John XIV, 983–984
John XV, 985–996

[3] Martin I was exiled, and Eugenius I was crowned pope before Martin's death.
[4] On later lists known as Stephen III because a priest by the name of Stephen was elected to succeed Zacharias, but died three days after election and without being consecrated. The numeration of all Stephen's on this list follows the medieval usage, which omits the unconsecrated "successor" of Zacharias.
[5] John XII was deposed at a Roman council in 963 where Leo VIII was elected, under the influence of Otto I, the emperor. On the death of John XII, Benedict V was elected by John's supporters and was promptly deposed at another council held by Leo VIII and Otto I. Under these circumstances either Leo VIII or Benedict V may be considered an antipope.

Gregory V, 996–999
(John XVI, 997–998)
Sylvester II, 999–1003
John XVII, 1003
John XVIII, 1004–1009
Sergius IV, 1009–1012
Benedict VIII, 1012–1024
John XIX, 1024–1032
Benedict IX, 1032–1044
Sylvester III, 1045
Benedict IX, 1045
    [for the second time]
Gregory VI, 1045–1046
Clement II, 1046–1047
Benedict IX, 1047–1048
    [for the third time]
Damasus II, 1048
Leo IX, 1049–1054
Victor II, 1055–1057
Stephen IX, 1057–1058
(Benedict X, 1058–1059)
Nicholas II, 1059–1061
Alexander II, 1061–1073
Gregory VII, 1073–1085
(Clement III, 1080 and 1084–1100)
Victor III, 1086–1087
Urban II, 1088–1099
Paschal II, 1099–1118
(Theodoric, 1100)
(Albert, 1102)
(Sylvester IV, 1105–1111)
Gelasius II, 1118–1119
(Gregory VIII, 1118–1121)
Calixtus II, 1119–1124
Honorius II, 1124–1130
Innocent II, 1130–1143
(Anacletus II, 1130–1138)
Celestine II, 1143–1144
Lucius II, 1144–1145
Eugenius III, 1145–1153

Anastasius IV, 1153–1154
Adrian IV, 1154–1159
Alexander III, 1159–1181
(Victor IV, 1159–1164)
(Paschal III, 1164–1168)
(Calixtus III, 1168–1178)
(Innocent III, 1179–1180)
Lucius III, 1181–1185
Urban III, 1185–1187
Gregory VIII, 1187
Clement III, 1187–1191
Celestine III, 1191–1198
Innocent III, 1198–1216
Honorius III, 1216–1227
Gregory IX, 1227–1241
Celestine IV, 1241
Innocent IV, 1243–1254
Alexander IV, 1254–1261
Urban IV, 1261–1264
Clement IV, 1265–1268
Gregory X, 1271–1276
Innocent V, 1276
Adrian V, 1276
John XXI, 1276–1277[6]
Nicholas III, 1277–1280
Martin IV, 1281–1285[7]
Honorius IV, 1285–1287
Nicholas IV, 1288–1292
Celestine V, 1294
Boniface VIII, 1294–1303
Benedict XI, 1303–1304
Clement V, 1305–1314
John XXII, 1316–1334
Benedict XII, 1334–1342
Clement VI, 1342–1352
Innocent VI, 1352–1362
Urban V, 1362–1370
Gregory XI, 1370–1378
Urban VI, 1378–1389
   [8] Clement VII, 1378–1394

[6] Although he was the twentieth pope of this name (or the nineteenth if John XVI be excluded), by an error of enumeration this pope has always been called John XXI.
[7] Numbered "IV" because Marinus I and Marinus II were also considered as "Martin."
[8] Of the Avignonese line.

Boniface IX, 1389–1404
  [8] Benedict XIII, 1394–1423
Innocent VII, 1404–1406
Gregory XII, 1406–1415
  [9] (Alexander V, 1409–1410)
  [9] (John XXIII, 1410–1415)
Martin V, 1417–1431
  [8] (Clement VIII, 1423–1429)
  [8] (Benedict XIV, 1425–?1430)

Eugenius IV, 1431–1447
(Felix V, 1439–1449)
Nicholas V, 1447–1455
Calixtus III, 1455–1458
Pius II, 1458–1464
Paul II, 1464–1471
Sixtus IV, 1471–1484
Innocent VIII, 1484–1492
Alexander VI, 1492–1503

[8] Of the Avignonese line.
[9] Elected at the Council of Pisa.

Genealogical Tables

I THE CAROLINGIANS

Pepin of Heristal (Mayor 680-714)

Charles Martel (Mayor 714-41)

PEPIN THE SHORT (Mayor 741-51, K. 751-68)

- Carloman (Mayor 741-47, abd.)
- CHARLEMAGNE (K. 768-814, Emp. 800-14)
- CARLOMAN (K. 768-71)

LOUIS THE PIOUS (Emp. 814-40)

- LOTHAIR (Emp. 840-55)
  - LOUIS II = Engelberga (Emp. 855-75)
  - LOTHAIR II (K. of Lotharingia 855-69)
  - CHARLES (K. of Provence 855-63)
  - Ermengarde = Boso (K. of Provence 879-87)
    - LOUIS THE BLIND (K. of Provence 887, K. of Italy 900, Emp. 901, d. 928)
- LOUIS THE GERMAN (K. of East Franks 840-76)
  - Carloman (K. of Bavaria 876-80)
    - ARNULF (K. of East Franks 887-99, Emp. 896-99)
      - LOUIS THE CHILD (K. of East Franks 899-911)
  - Louis (K. of Saxony 876-82, K. of Bavaria 880-82)
  - CHARLES THE FAT (K. of Swabia 876-84, sole K. and Emp. 884-87, dep.)
- CHARLES THE BALD (K. of West Franks 840-77, Emp. 875-77)
  - LOUIS THE STAMMERER (K. of West Franks 877-79)
    - LOUIS III (K. of West Franks 879-82)
    - CARLOMAN (K. of West Franks 879-84)
    - CHARLES THE SIMPLE (K. of West Franks 898-922)
      - LOUIS IV D'OUTREMER (K. of West Franks 936-54)
        - LOTHAIR (K. of West Franks 954-86)
          - LOUIS V (K. of West Franks 986-87)

II THE SAXON, SALIAN, AND HOHENSTAUFEN DYNASTIES

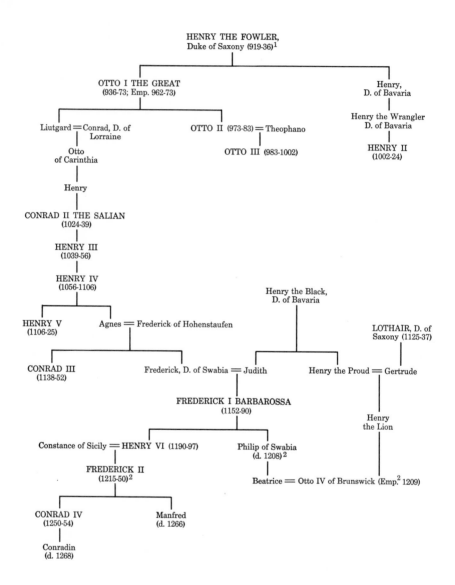

[1] Dates are regnal dates as King of Germany or Emperor, or both, unless otherwise indicated.
[2] For the claims of Philip of Swabia, Otto IV of Brunswick, and Frederick during the period 1198–1215, see pp. 350–51 and 358.

III THE CAPETIAN DYNASTY

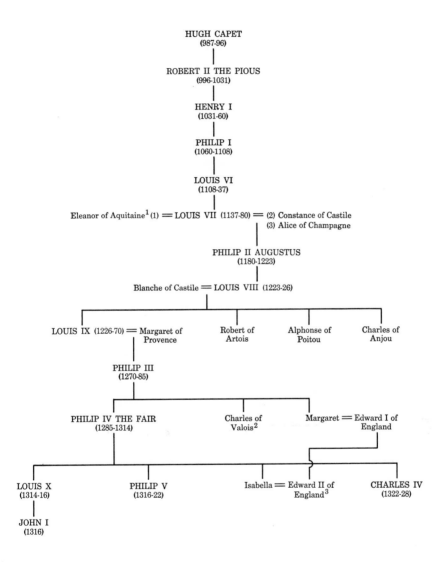

---

[1] Eleanor of Aquitaine later married Henry of Anjou who became Henry II of England (1154–89); see Table IV.
[2] Philip VI of Valois (1328–50) was the son of Charles of Valois; see Table VI.
[3] Edward III of England (1327–77) was the son of Isabella and Edward II; see Table IV.

IV NORMAN AND PLANTAGENET RULERS
OF ENGLAND

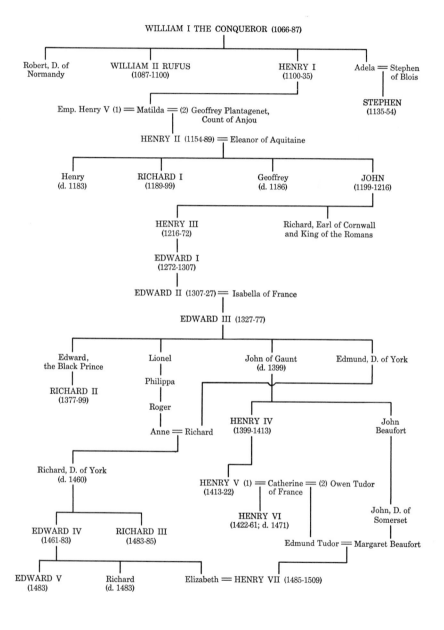

V GERMANY UNDER THE LUXEMBOURGS AND HABSBURGS

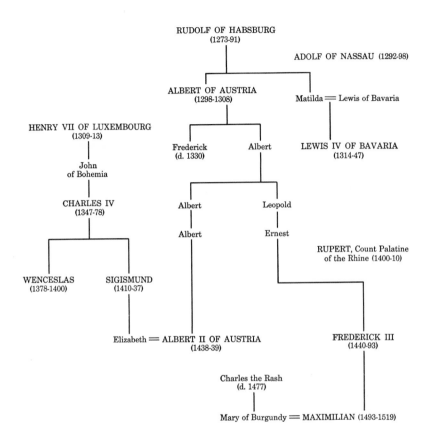

VI   THE VALOIS KINGS OF FRANCE

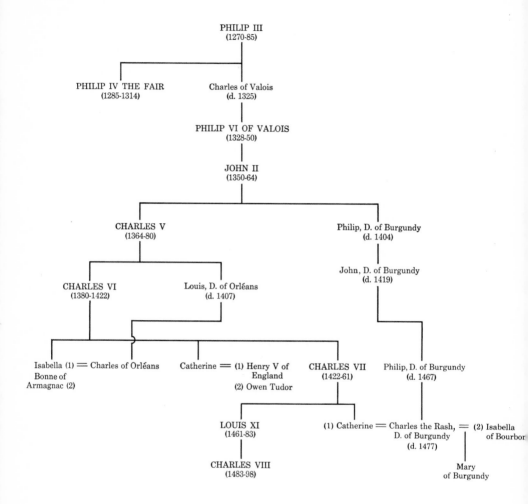

A Guide to Further Reading

The works listed below have been selected for their value, interest, and bibliographical data for the nonspecialist who desires to read further in some of the best modern literature and sources of the subject. This literature is enormous: secondary works in all modern European languages; critical editions of practically all the literary sources; editions and calendars of most of the record sources for the early and high Middle Ages and of the most important records of the later Middle Ages; and translations of these sources into English and other modern languages. No selection from this vast number of general works, monographs, and editions—not to mention the extensive literature to be found in learned journals—could possibly satisfy every reader's interests or needs, nor would two historians ever quite agree on which works deserve selection. The following list is arbitrarily limited to books (with the exception of two outstanding articles) and to works in English (with three exceptions, where adequate accounts in English are unavailable), and when there is a choice between books of equal value, preference is given to those with more extensive bibliographies.

Many of the following titles are paperback volumes or have been, and many more will undoubtedly be, reprinted in paperback editions (often with different places and later dates of publication than listed here). Publication dates below refer to the earliest date of the latest current edition, ignoring dates of later reprints. For paperback originals and reprints currently available, reference should be made to the annual brochure entitled *Paperbound Book Guide for Colleges*.

GENERAL WORKS

1. BIBLIOGRAPHIES.   L. J. Paetow, *Guide to the Study of Medieval History* (rev. ed., New York, 1931) and C. Gross, *The Sources and Literature of English History* (rev. ed., New York, 1915) are the standard bibliographies for Continental and English medieval history. For English history before 1485 the bibliographical sections in the first six volumes of *The Oxford History of England*, ed. G. N. Clark (Oxford, 1937–1961), should be consulted. For translations of sources published before 1942, see C. P. Farrar and A. P. Evans, *Bibliography of English Translations from Medieval Sources* (New York, 1946) and, for English history prior to 1189, *English Historical Documents*, Vols. I and II, ed. D. C. Douglas (New York, 1953–1955).

2. HISTORICAL ATLASES.   W. R. Shepherd, *Historical Atlas* (8th ed., rev., New York, 1956) is standard. Two other good atlases are Colin McEvedy, *The Penguin Atlas of Medieval History* (Baltimore, 1961), and the medieval section of R. R. Palmer, *Atlas of World History* (Chicago, 1957).

3. GENERAL MEDIEVAL HISTORY.   The most nearly exhaustive history of the Middle Ages is *The Cambridge Medieval History* (8 vols., Cambridge, 1911–1936), of which C. W. Previté-Orton, *The Shorter Cambridge Medieval History* (2 vols., Cambridge, 1952) is both a concise and revised version. A good four-volume work (which, however, excludes most of English history) is M. Deanesly, *A History of Early Medieval Europe, 476–911* (London, 1956); Z. N. Brooke, *A History of Europe from 911 to 1198* (3rd ed., London, 1951); C. W. Previté-Orton, *A History of Europe from 1198–1378* (2nd ed., London, 1948); and W. T. Waugh, *A History of Europe from 1378 to 1494* (London, 1932). The first medieval volume to be published in a new general history of Europe is C. N. L. Brooke, *Europe in the Central Middle Ages, 962–1154* (London, 1964). Of the many one-volume general histories, J. W. Thompson and E. M. Johnson, *An Introduction to Medieval Europe* (New York, 1937) is the most extensive and detailed.

4. INTELLECTUAL AND CULTURAL HISTORY.   Still unsurpassed is H. O. Taylor, *The Medieval Mind* (2 vols., 4th ed., New York, 1925), which is now supplemented by F. B. Artz, *The Mind of the Middle Ages* (2nd ed., New York, 1954). For medieval philosophy the standard full-length work is M. de Wulf, *History of Medieval Philosophy* (3 vols., New York, 1925–1953); a recent textbook is A. A. Maurer, *Medieval Philosophy* (New York, 1962); in one volume the two best works are Étienne Gilson, *History of Christian Philosophy in the Middle Ages* (London, 1955), and David Knowles, *The Evolution of Medieval Thought* (London, 1962); introductory essays in brief compass are Gordon Leff, *Medieval Thought from Saint Augustine to Ockham* (Baltimore, 1958), and F. C. Copleston, *Medieval Philosophy* (London, 1952). The basic work in its field is R. W. and A. J. Carlyle, *A History of Medieval Political Theory in the*

West (6 vols., London, 1903–1936), while the best treatment in one volume is C. H. McIlwain, *The Growth of Political Thought in the West* (New York, 1932). For literature and science good general introductions are E. R. Curtius, *European Literature and the Latin Middle Ages* (New York, 1953) and A. C. Crombie, *Augustine to Galileo*, A.D. 400–1650 (London, 1952). C. R. Morey, *Medieval Art* (New York, 1942) and Nikolaus Pevsner, *An Outline of European Architecture* (5th ed., Baltimore, 1957) provide a general introduction to art. A brilliant essay on aspects of monastic culture is Jean Leclercq, *The Love of Learning and the Desire for God* (New York, 1961).

5. ECONOMIC HISTORY. The standard work is now *The Cambridge Economic History*, Vols. I–III, eds. J. H. Clapham *et al.* (Cambridge, 1941–1961); the best short survey will be found in Herbert Heaton, *Economic History of Europe* (rev. ed., New York, 1948). The other two most valuable general works are H. Pirenne, *Economic and Social History of Medieval Europe* (New York, 1937) and P. Boissonade, *Life and Work in Medieval Europe* (New York, 1927).

6. THE MEDIEVAL CHURCH. M. Deanesly, *A History of the Medieval Church, 590–1500* (8th ed., London, 1954) and W. R. Cannon, *History of Christianity in the Middle Ages* (Nashville, 1960) are useful surveys. Longer accounts may be founded in Philip Hughes, *A History of the Church*, Vols. II and III (New York, 1935–1947) and K. S. Latourette, *A History of Christianity* (New York, 1953). Of the many books dealing with the medieval papacy, the best narrative history is now a volume written by several authors, *The Popes A Concise Biographical History*, ed. Eric John (London, 1964).

7. ENGLAND AND FRANCE. The first six volumes of *The Oxford History of England* cover the medieval period: R. G. Collingwood and J. N. L. Myres, *Roman Britain and the English Settlements* (2nd ed., Oxford, 1937); F. M. Stenton, *Anglo-Saxon England* (2nd ed., Oxford, 1947); A. L. Poole, *From Domesday Book to Magna Carta 1087–1216* (2nd ed., Oxford, 1955); F. M. Powicke, *The Thirteenth Century 1216–1307* (2nd ed., Oxford, 1962); May McKisack, *The Fourteenth Century 1307–1399* (Oxford, 1959); and E. F. Jacob, *The Fifteenth Century 1399–1485* (Oxford, 1961). There are three excellent medieval volumes in the much briefer Pelican History of England: Dorothy Whitelock, *The Beginnings of English Society* (Harmondsworth, 1952); D. M. Stenton, *English Society in the Early Middle Ages 1066–1307* (Harmondsworth, 1951); and A. R. Myers, *England in the Late Middle Ages 1307–1536* (Harmondsworth, 1952). The medieval volumes of the most recent general history of England are: P. H. Blair, *Roman Britain and Early England 55 B.C.–A.D. 871* (Edinburgh, 1963); Christopher Brooke, *From Alfred to Henry III 871–1272* (Edinburgh, 1961); and George Holmes, *The Later Middle Ages 1272–1485* (Edinburgh, 1962). For the period from the tenth to the thirteenth century, both France and England are dealt with in Ch. Petit-Dutaillis, *The*

Feudal Monarchy in France and England (London, 1936). For France there is nothing in English of sufficient value to replace the monumental cooperative work edited by E. Lavisse: *Histoire de France* (Vols. II–IV, Paris, 1901–1903). There is more general history, for the period it covers, than is implied by the title of the excellent work by Robert Fawtier, *The Capetian Kings of France Monarchy & Nation* (987–1328), tr. Lionel Butler and R. J. Adam (London, 1960).

8. ITALY AND GERMANY.   L. Salvatorelli, *A Concise History of Italy* (New York, 1939) gives a general survey, while G. Barraclough, *The Origins of Modern Germany* (2nd ed., Oxford, 1947) is a stimulating essay of interpretation. J. Bryce, *The Holy Roman Empire* (rev. ed., New York, 1904) is a classic.

9. THE BYZANTINE EMPIRE AND THE EAST.   A work of great merit, sound scholarship, and provocative style is A. A. Vasiliev, *History of the Byzantine Empire, 324–1453* (2nd ed., Madison, Wisc., 1952). Another excellent one-volume general work is G. Ostrogorsky, *History of the Byzantine State* (Oxford, 1956). Equally valuable and more interesting is C. Diehl, *Byzantium: Greatness and Decline* (New Brunswick, 1957). On Islam in the Middle Ages, the best brief account is B. Lewis, *The Arabs in History* (4th ed., London, 1958), and Arab history in greater detail will be found in P. K. Hitti, *History of the Arabs* (6th ed., London, 1958) and G. E. von Grunebaum, *Medieval Islam* (2nd ed., Chicago, 1954). On eastern Europe see Francis Dvornik: *The Slavs: Their Early History and Civilization* (Boston, 1956) and *The Making of Central and Eastern Europe* (London, 1949). For Russia the best general account is by G. Vernadsky: *Ancient Russia* (New Haven, 1943), *Kievan Russia* (New Haven, 1948), and *The Mongols and Russia* (New Haven, 1953), and in briefer compass, *The Origins of Russia* (Oxford, 1959).

10. GENERAL COLLECTIONS OF TRANSLATED SOURCES.   There are many useful volumes. An old and still valuable one is E. F. Henderson, *Select Historical Documents of the Middle Ages* (London, 1896); recent collections of translations are *The Medieval Pageant*, ed. Norton Downs (New York, 1964); and (for the period down to 1300) *The Early Middle Ages 500–1000*, ed. Robert Brentano, and *The High Middle Ages 1000–1300*, ed. Bryce Lyon (New York, 1964), *Medieval History   A Source Book*, ed. D. A. White (Homewood, 1965), and *The Medieval World*, ed. N. F. Cantor (New York, 1963); while the later medieval sources are emphasized in *The Portable Medieval Reader*, eds. J. B. Ross and M. M. McLaughlin (New York, 1949). More specialized collections are the excellent *Medieval Literature in Translation*, ed. C. W. Jones (New York, 1950); *Documents of the Christian Church*, ed. H. Bettenson (New York, 1947), and *Readings in Church History*, Vol. I, *From Pentecost to the Protestant Revolt*, ed. C. J. Barry (Westminister, Md., 1960); *Medieval Philosophy: Selected Readings from Augustine to Buridan*, ed. Herman Shapiro

(New York, 1964); and *Medieval Commerce*, ed. H. L. Adelson (New York, 1962). The *Compass History of Art* includes several volumes of reproductions of medieval painting, notably *Medieval Manuscript Painting*, ed. Sabrina Mitchell (New York, 1965).

I.   THE TRANSITION FROM ANCIENT TO MEDIEVAL CIVILIZATION, c.400–750

11. SECONDARY WORKS. One of the great works of historical scholarship published in the twentieth century is M. Rostovtzeff, *Social and Economic History of the Roman Empire* (Oxford, 1926). A recent and excellent survey is A. H. M. Jones, *The Later Roman Empire, 284–602 A Social, Economic, and Administrative Survey* (2 vols., Norman, 1964). More specifically and briefly concerned with the transition to the Middle Ages are W. C. Bark, *Origins of the Medieval World* (Stanford, 1958), Solomon Katz, *The Decline of Rome and the Rise of Mediaeval Europe* (Ithaca, 1955), and Mortimer Chambers, ed., *The Fall of Rome Can It Be Explained?* (New York, 1963). The standard work in greater detail is Ferdinand Lot, *The End of the Ancient World and the Beginnings of the Middle Ages* (New York, 1931). A monumental narrative of great interest is Thomas Hodgkin, *Italy and Her Invaders* (8 vols., Oxford, 1892–1916). An introduction to controversial views concerning the period may be gained from H. Pirenne's stimulating *Mohammed and Charlemagne* (New York, 1939), A. Dopsch, *The Economic and Social Foundations of European Civilization* (New York, 1937), and *The Pirenne Thesis Analysis, Criticism, and Revision*, ed. A. F. Havighurst (Boston, 1958). For economic developments see the first two parts of Robert Latouche, *The Birth of Western Economy*, tr. E. Wilkinson (London, 1961). C. Dawson, *The Making of Europe* (New York, 1934); H. St. L. B. Moss, *The Birth of the Middle Ages* (Oxford, 1935); and J. M. Wallace-Hadrill, *The Barbarian West, 400–1000* (London, 1952) are excellent one-volume surveys, while the older works by S. Dill, *Roman Society in the Last Century of the Empire* (London, 1910) and *Roman Society in Gaul in the Merovingian Age* (London, 1926), are still useful. For the early Church, E. R. Goodenough, *The Church in the Roman Empire* (New York, 1931) is an introductory sketch, and L. Duchesne, *The Early History of the Christian Church* (3 vols., London, 1914–1922), is a classic. Two interesting biographies are Hugh Pope, *St. Augustine of Hippo* (rep. New York, 1961) and A. J. McCann, *Saint Benedict* (rev. ed., New York, 1958). Outstanding works on cultural developments are C. N. Cochrane, *Christianity and Classical Culture* (2nd ed., New York, 1944); E. K. Rand, *Founders of the Middle Ages* (Cambridge, Mass., 1928); M. L. W. Laistner, *Thought and Letters in Western Europe, a.d. 500–900* (London, 1931); and C. Dawson, *Religion and the Rise of Western Culture* (London, 1950). Two quite different

but equally interesting volumes on their subject are Hippolyte Delehaye, *The Legends of the Saints*, tr. D. Attwater (New York, 1962), and Eleanor Duckett, *The Wandering Saints of the Early Middle Ages* (New York, 1959). A recent introductory essay, both concise and provocative, is P. N. Ure, *Justinian and His Age* (Harmondsworth, 1951). Older and standard shorter works are C. Diehl, *History of the Byzantine Empire* (Princeton, 1925) and N. H. Baynes, *The Byzantine Empire* (London, 1925). On Islam see H. A. R. Gibb, *Mohammedanism* (2nd ed., London, 1953). R. E. Sullivan, *Heirs of the Roman Empire* (Ithaca, 1961) is a brief survey of developments in the Latin West, Byzantium, and Islam.

12. SOURCES. A convenient translation of Tacitus is H. Mattingly, *Tacitus On Britain and Germany* (West Drayton, Middlesex, 1948); the only complete translation of Gregory of Tours' *History of the Franks* is by O. M. Dalton (2 vols., Oxford, 1927); and an excellent work is K. Fischer's translation of *The Burgundian Code* (Philadelphia, 1949). Two new collections of patristic writings in English translations are now in progress: *Ancient Christian Writers*, eds. J. Quasten and J. C. Plumpe (Westminster, Md., 1946 ff.) and *The Fathers of the Church*, eds. R. J. Deferrari *et al.* (New York, 1947 ff.). Good translations of Augustine's *City of God* and *Confessions* are by Marcus Dods and by E. B. Pusey, respectively, in several editions. The Benedictine Rule will be found in Henderson (§ 10 above); two excellent and early Lives of the Saints are *The Life of Bishop Wilfrid by Eddius Stephanus*, tr. B. Colgrave (Cambridge, 1927) and *The Life of Saint Columba*, tr. W. Huyshe (London, 1908). *The Letters of Cassiodorus*, tr. T. Hodgkin (London, 1886) are a monument of their times, far more interesting for general history than *Cassiodorus' Introduction to Divine and Human Readings* (New York, 1946), edited with a valuable introduction by L. W. Jones, and Boethius' *The Consolation of Philosophy*, tr. W. V. Cooper (New York, 1943). Two fascinating contemporary accounts by the same author are Procopius' *The History of the Wars*, tr. H. B. Dewing (5 vols., London, 1914–1928), and his *Secret History*, tr. R. Atwater (Ann Arbor, 1961). For early Anglo-Saxon England the outstanding historical work is Bede, *A History of the English Church and People*, tr. L. Sherley-Price (Harmondsworth, 1955).

II.   THE EMERGENCE OF FEUDAL EUROPE, 750–1050

13. POLITICAL AND NARRATIVE HISTORY. The most important works in English are Heinrich Fichtenau, *The Carolingian Empire*, tr. Peter Munz (Oxford, 1957), Stenton (§ 7 above), and Barraclough (§ 8 above). The best account of the Vikings is Peter Sawyer, *The Age of the Vikings* (London, 1962); see also Johannes Brøndsted, *The Vikings* (Harmondsworth, 1960), and, especially

good on Scandinavian art and archeology, Holger Arbman, *The Vikings* (New York, 1961). The works of Dopsch, Dawson, Moss, Wallace-Hadrill, and Laistner (cited in § 11 above) are equally useful for this period. An excellent introduction to a fascinating historical problem is R. E. Sullivan, ed., *The Coronation of Charlemagne What Did It Signify?* (Boston, 1959). Interesting portraits of Carolingian personalities may be found in E. S. Duckett, *Alcuin, Friend of Charlemagne* (New York, 1951), and *Carolingian Portraits A Study in the Ninth Century* (Ann Arbor, 1962).

14. FEUDALISM AND MANORIALISM. The best succinct introduction is F. S. Ganshof, *Feudalism* (London, 1952); on a more elementary level is C. Stephenson, *Mediaeval Feudalism* (Ithaca, N.Y., 1942). The standard full-length treatment is Marc Bloch, *Feudal Society*, tr. L. A. Manyon (London, 1961). In addition to the economic histories list above (§ 5), see Lynn White, Jr., *Medieval Technology and Social Change* (Oxford, 1962), Latouche (§ 11 above), and, for an excellent introduction, N. Neilson, *Medieval Agrarian Economy* (New York, 1936).

15. SOURCES. For Carolingian letters see Paul the Deacon's *History of the Langobards*, tr. W. D. Foulke (Philadelphia, 1907); *The Letters of Saint Boniface*, tr. E. Emerton (New York, 1940); *The Life of Saint Boniface by Willibald*, tr. G. W. Robinson (Cambridge, Mass., 1916); and *Early Lives of Charlemagne*, tr. A. J. Grant (London, 1922). A more comprehensive collection of documents is in S. C. Easton and Helene Wieruszowski, *The Era of Charlemagne Frankish State and Society* (Princeton, 1961). A general view of the tenth century from the sources is provided by R. S. Lopez, *The Tenth Century* (New York, 1959), *St. Odo of Cluny*, tr. and ed. G. Sitwell (London, 1958), and *The Letters of Gerbert*, tr. H. P. Lattin (New York, 1961). The anarchical state of tenth-century Italy is portrayed in a fascinating volume which also includes a westerner's view of Byzantium: *The Works of Liudprand of Cremona*, tr. F. A. Wright (London, 1930). For England see *English Historical Documents, c.500–1042*, ed. D. Whitelock (New York, 1955), which contains the Anglo-Saxon Chronicle complete for the period and a generous selection from other sources, together with valuable introductions and notes. For feudal documents with commentary, see R. S. Hoyt, *Feudal Institutions* (New York, 1961), and, for this period, the earlier part of J. R. Strayer, *Feudalism* (Princeton, 1965).

III. POLITICAL, ECONOMIC, AND CULTURAL REVIVAL OF THE TWELFTH CENTURY

16. POLITICAL AND NARRATIVE HISTORY. In addition to the general works listed above, for special aspects of the period see G. Barraclough, *Medieval Germany* (2 vols., Oxford, 1938); G. Tellenbach, *Church, State, and*

Christian Society at the Time of the Investiture Contest (Oxford, 1940); Schafer Williams, ed., *The Gregorian Epoch Reformation, Revolution, Reaction?* (Boston, 1964); C. H. Haskins, *The Normans in European History* (Boston, 1915)—this is a minor classic—and F. Barlow, *The Feudal Kingdom of England, 1042–1216* (London, 1955). An older work of interest is J. W. Thompson, *Feudal Germany* (Chicago, 1928), and G. O. Sayles, *The Medieval Foundations of England* (London, 1948) is an excellent introduction. More controversial (and zestfully revisionist) is H. G. Richardson and G. O. Sayles, *The Governance of Mediaeval England from the Conquest to Magna Carta* (Edinburgh, 1963). Of the many important personalities of the eleventh century, the best (and very detailed) biography is D. C. Douglas, *William the Conqueror The Norman Impact upon England* (Berkeley, 1964). For Spain the standard work is R. B. Merriman, *The Rise of the Spanish Empire*, Vol. I (New York, 1918).

17. THE FIRST CRUSADE. R. A. Newhall, *The Crusades* (rev. ed., New York, 1963) is a brief sketch. The best general history by one author is S. Runciman, *A History of the Crusades* (3 vols., Cambridge, 1951–1954). A five-volume *History of the Crusades*, ed. K. M. Setton, is now being prepared by a group of historians, and Vol. I, *The First Hundred Years*, ed. M. W. Baldwin (Philadelphia, 1955), and Vol. II, *The Later Crusades, 1189–1311*, eds. R. L. Wolff and H. W. Hazard (Philadelphia, 1962) have appeared. For a sampling of the more important literature of the Crusades, see J. A. Brundage, ed., *The Crusades Motives and Achievements* (Boston, 1964). More specialized works of interest are R. C. Smail, *Crusading Warfare* (Cambridge, 1956); D. C. Munro, *The Kingdom of the Crusaders* (New York, 1935); and J. L. LaMonte, *Feudal Monarchy in the Latin Kingdom of Jerusalem* (Cambridge, Mass., 1932).

18. ECONOMIC REVIVAL. To the general works listed above (§ 5) may be added Reginald Lennard, *Rural England 1086–1135* (Oxford, 1959), and Henri Pirenne, *Medieval Cities* (Princeton, N.J., 1925). Two more specialized studies should read in conjunction: C. Stephenson, *Borough and Town* (Cambridge, Mass., 1933) and J. Tait, *The Medieval English Borough* (Manchester, 1936).

19. FEUDAL EUROPE. There are three quite different but equally excellent books that portray daily life in feudal Europe: W. S. Davis, *Life on a Medieval Barony* (New York, 1923); A. Luchaire, *Social France in the Age of Philip Augustus* (New York, 1912); and U. T. Holmes, *Daily Living in the Twelfth Century* (Madison, Wisc., 1952). A work that defies classification but that deals largely with feudal institutions and ideas is the brilliant essay by R. W. Southern, *The Making of the Middle Ages* (London, 1952), a book that will amply repay close study. Another, more specialized, work of the highest merit is F. M. Stenton, *The First Century of English Feudalism* (2nd ed., Oxford,

1961), while F. Kern, *Kingship and Law* (Oxford, 1939) is useful for feudal political thought. A good introduction to the courtly literature of feudal society is S. Painter, *French Chivalry* (Baltimore, Md., 1940), and a standard account in greater detail is W. P. Ker, *Epic and Romance* (London, 1908).

20. THE RENAISSANCE OF THE TWELFTH CENTURY. The outstanding work is C. H. Haskins, *The Renaissance of the Twelfth Century* (Cambridge, Mass., 1927). E. Gilson, in his *The Spirit of Mediaeval Philosophy* (New York, 1936), *Heloise and Abelard* (Chicago, 1951), and *The Mystical Theology of St. Bernard* (London, 1940), covers many of the intellectual interests of the period. H. Rashdall, *The Universities of Europe in the Middle Ages*, eds. F. M. Powicke and A. B. Emden (3 vols., rev. ed., Oxford, 1936) is the standard work; an excellent introduction is Haskins' *The Rise of the Universities* (New York, 1923). A more recent introduction is L. J. Daly, *The Medieval University 1200–1400* (New York, 1961). A specialized work of interest is M. H. Carré, *Realists and Nominalists* (Oxford, 1946). C. C. J. Webb, *John of Salisbury* (London, 1932) and H. Liebeschutz, *Mediaeval Humanism in the Life and Writings of John of Salisbury* (London, 1950) deal with the most important philosopher and humanist of the period.

21. SOURCES. *The Correspondence of Gregory VII*, tr. E. Emerton (New York, 1932), and *Imperial Lives and Letters of the Eleventh Century*, tr. T. E. Mommsen and K. F. Morrison (New York, 1962) are fascinating collections; a near-contemporary account of the investiture struggle and events in Germany may be found in Otto of Freising's *The Two Cities*, tr. C. C. Mierow (New York, 1928). Many of the 115 documents (with commentary) in Brian Tierney, *The Crisis of Church & State 1050–1300* (Englewood Cliffs, 1964) concern the investiture struggle. A. C. Krey, *The First Crusade* (Princeton, 1921) is the best introduction to the sources, of which there are copious extracts in Régine Pernoud, *The Crusades*, tr. E. McLeod (New York, 1963). A complete account of the First Crusade from one of the three most important sources may be read in *Fulcher of Chartres: Chronicle of the First Crusade*, tr. M. E. McGinty (Philadelphia, 1941), while the Second Crusade is described in Odo of Deuil, *The Journey of Louis VII to the East*, tr. V. Berry (New York, 1948). J. A. Brundage, *The Crusades: a Documentary Survey* (Milwaukee, 1962) includes a generous selection of extracts, which are given ample commentary. For the economic revival, see J. H. Mundy and Peter Riesenberg, *The Medieval Town* (Princeton, 1958); R. C. Cave and H. H. Coulson, *A Source Book for Medieval Economic History* (Milwaukee, 1936; and *Medieval Trade in the Mediterranean World*, tr. R. S. Lopez and I. W. Raymond (New York, 1955). For English sources *English Historical Documents, 1042–1189*, eds. D. C. Douglas and G. W. Greenaway (New York, 1953) is a remarkable and monumental volume, including valuable introductions and bibliographies and a complete reproduction, with commentary, of the Bayeux Tapestry. For France and Germany there is nothing comparable. For feudalism in this period see

Strayer (§ 15 above). For the literature of this period there are many transla-
tions of *Beowulf*, the *Song of Roland*, and the vernacular lyrics and romances.
See *The Song of Roland*, tr. D. L. Sayers (Harmondsworth, 1957), and *Ruod-
lieb The Earliest Courtly Novel*, ed. and tr. E. H. Zeydel (Chapel Hill, 1959).
A work in Latin of special interest for its influence on courtly literature is *The
Art of Courtly Love of Andreas Capellanus*, tr. J. J. Parry (New York, 1941).
For universities see *University Records and Life*, tr. L. Thorndike (New York,
1944). *The Letters of Abelard and Heloise*, tr. C. K. Scott-Moncrief (New
York, 1926); *St. Anslem*, tr. S. N. Deane (Chicago, 1903, reprinted La Salle,
Ill., 1948); *Hugh of St. Victor On the Sacraments of the Christian Faith*, tr.
R. J. Deferrari (Cambridge, Mass., 1951); and John of Salisbury's works will
introduce the reader to many of the intellectual interests of the period. For John
see *The Statesman's Book of John of Salisbury*, tr. J. Dickinson (New York,
1927); *Frivolities of Courtiers and Footprints of Philosophers*, tr. J. B. Pike
(Minneapolis, 1938); *The Metalogicon of John of Salisbury*, tr. D. D. McGarry
(Berkeley, 1955); *The Letters of John of Salisbury*, eds. W. J. Millor
and H. E. Butler (2 vols., Edinburgh, vol. 1, 1955; vol. 2 in preparation); and
John of Salisbury's Memoirs of the Papal Court, tr. M. Chibnall (Edinburgh,
1956). In these works there is also much of interest for the general political
history of western Europe in the period.

IV. THE HIGH MIDDLE AGES:
MEDIEVAL CULTURE

22. THE MEDIEVAL CHURCH AND MEDIEVAL CHRISTENDOM. M. W.
Baldwin, *The Mediaeval Church* (Ithaca, 1953), and S. R. Packard, *Europe
and the Church Under Innocent III* (New York, 1927), provide a good introduction; the views of several modern historians are presented in J. M. Powell,
Innocent III Vicar of Christ or Lord of the World? (Boston, 1963). A specialized work of great value for the student of general history is C. R. Cheney,
From Becket to Langton (Manchester, 1956). There is no outstanding single
volume in English on the monastic reform movement as a whole; see W. Williams, *St. Bernard of Clairvaux* (2nd ed., Manchester, 1953); P. Sabatier, *The
Life of St. Francis of Assisi* (London, 1894); P. Mandonnet, *St. Dominic and
His Work* (London, 1944); and R. F. Bennett, *The Early Dominicans* (Cambridge, 1937). F. M. Powicke, "The Christian Life," in *The Legacy of the
Middle Ages*, eds. C. G. Crump and E. F. Jacob (Oxford, 1932), is a brilliant
essay, and the other contributions in this volume are valuable for the art, literature, and thought of the high Middle Ages. On anticlericalism, heresy, and the
Inquisition the monumental work is H. C. Lea, *A History of the Inquisition of
the Middle Ages* (3 vols., New York, 1888), written from a Protestant viewpoint; the best one-volume work on the subject is E. Vacandard, *The Inquisition*

(New York, 1908), written by a Catholic historian. A more specialized and recent work on heresy is S. Runciman, *The Medieval Manichee* (Cambridge, 1947).

23. THEOLOGY AND PHILOSOPHY. B. Smalley, *The Study of the Bible in the Middle Ages* (2nd ed., Oxford, 1952) is standard for its subject. On scholasticism in general see E. Gilson, *Reason and Revelation in the Middle Ages* (New York, 1938). His *The Philosophy of St. Thomas Aquinas*, tr. E. Bullough (2nd ed., rev., London, 1937) and F. C. Copleston, *Aquinas* (Baltimore, Md., 1955) are the best one-volume works; M. Grabmann, *Thomas Aquinas* (New York, 1928) is useful. On Bonaventura see Gilson's *The Philosophy of St. Bonaventure* (New York, 1938). For medieval science the basic work is L. Thorndike, *A History of Magic and Experimental Science* (6 vols., New York, 1923–1941); more specifically for this period see A. C. Crombie, *Grosseteste and the Origins of Experimental Science* (Oxford, 1953) and D. A. Callus, ed., *Robert Grosseteste* (Oxford, 1955).

24. LAW AND POLITICAL THOUGHT. P. Vinogradoff, *Roman Law in Medieval Europe* (2nd ed., Oxford, 1929) is an excellent introduction; for canon law see R. C. Mortimer, *Western Canon Law* (London, 1953), and S. G. Kuttner, *Harmony from Dissonance An Interpretation of Medieval Canon Law* (Latrobe, Pa., 1960); on feudal law and custom see the discussion of feudalism in McIlwain's *Growth of Political Thought* (§ 4 above). Some recent books worth consulting are W. Ullmann, *The Growth of Papal Government* (London, 1955); F. Schulz, *History of Roman Legal Science* (Oxford, 1953); and A. P. d'Entrèves, *Natural Law* (London, 1950). F. Pollock and F. W. Maitland, *The History of English Law before the Time of Edward I* (2 vols., 2nd ed., Cambridge, 1898) is a classic of modern scholarship with which every student of the Middle Ages should be acquainted; in the same field the medieval chapters of T. F. T. Plucknett, *A Concise History of the Common Law* (4th ed., London, 1948) provide a well-written, brief treatment that takes account of more recent scholarship. On political thought d'Entrèves' *The Medieval Contribution to Political Thought* (Oxford, 1939); C. H. McIlwain, *Constitutionalism Ancient and Modern* (rev. ed., Ithaca, 1947); W. Ullmann, *Medieval Papalism: The Political Theories of the Canonists* (London, 1949); M. P. Gilmore, *Argument from Roman Law in Political Thought 1200–1600* (Cambridge, Mass., 1941); and P. N. Riesenberg, *Inalienability of Sovereignty in Medieval Thought* (New York, 1956), deal with various aspects of the subject. E. H. Kantorowicz, *The King's Two Bodies* (Princeton, 1957), and Gaines Post, *Studies in Medieval Legal Thought Public Law and the State, 1100–1322* (Princeton, 1964), are especially important for the influence of "the two laws" on political ideas.

25. ROMANESQUE AND GOTHIC ART. On architecture see K. J. Conant, *Early Medieval Church Architecture* (Baltimore, 1942); T. G. Jackson, *Gothic*

Architecture (2 vols., Cambridge, 1915); and E. Panofsky, *Gothic Architecture and Scholasticism* (Latrobe, Pa., 1951). E. Mâle, *Religious Art in France in the Thirteenth Century* (London, 1913) is a classic; for an impressionistic survey of medieval art and culture, see Henry Adams, *Mont-Saint-Michel and Chartres* (Boston, 1922), also a classic. There is much interesting detail in Jean Gimpel, *The Cathedral Builders*, tr. C. F. Barnes, Jr. (New York, 1961). A useful introductory manual is D. M. Robb and J. J. Garrison, *Art in the Western World* (New York, 1935), and the most recent work is Otto von Simpson, *The Gothic Cathedral* (New York, 1956).

26. LATIN AND VERNACULAR LITERATURE.   The best guides will be found in the general works by Taylor and Artz listed above (§ 4). The basic works on medieval Latin poetry are by F. J. E. Raby: *A History of Christian Latin Poetry from the Beginnings to the Close of the Middle Ages* (2nd ed., Oxford, 1953) and *A History of Secular Latin Poetry in the Middle Ages* (2 vols., Oxford, 1934). J. W. Thompson, *The History of Historical Writing* (2 vols., New York, 1942) is a general work that treats the Middle Ages in detail. R. E. Messenger, *The Medieval Latin Hymn* (Washington, D.C., 1953) is a recent work on that subject. A good introduction to the environment and the people who produced Goliardic verse is H. Waddell, *The Wandering Scholars* (7th ed., London, 1934). An introduction to the vernacular literature of the Middle Ages may be gained through such standard works as U. T. Holmes, *A History of Old French Literature* (2nd ed., New York, 1948); *The Cambridge History of English Literature*, Vol. I, eds. A. W. Ward and A. R. Waller (Cambridge, 1907); R. S. Loomis, *The Development of Arthurian Romance* (London, 1963); J. G. Robertson, *A History of German Literature* (2nd ed., London, 1947); and E. H. Wilkins, *A History of Italian Literature* (Cambridge, Mass., 1954). Of the enormous and varied literature that is concerned with Dante, the basic work in English is K. Vossler, *Medieval Culture: An Introduction to Dante and His Times* (2 vols., New York, 1929); shorter and more recent works of value are E. Gilson, *Dante the Philosopher* (New York, 1949), A. P. d'Entrèves, *Dante as a Political Thinker* (London, 1952), and T. G. Bergin, *Dante* (New York, 1965); the older work, P. Wicksteed, *Dante and Aquinas* (London, 1913), is useful.

27. SOURCES.   Some useful works pertaining to religious life and the reform movement of the twelfth century are: *The Autobiography of Guibert, Abbot of Nogent-sous-Coucy*, tr. C. C. S. Bland (New York, 1926); *The Life of Ailred of Rievaulx by Walter Daniel*, tr. F. M. Powicke (Edinburgh, 1951); *The Chronicle of Jocelin of Brakelond*, tr. H. E. Butler (Edinburgh, 1949); and *The Life and Works of Saint Bernard*, tr. S. J. Eales (4 vols., London, 1889–1896). On the friars see *The Writings of Saint Francis of Assisi*, tr. P. Robinson (Philadelphia, 1906); *Saint Francis and His Friends*, tr. H. Grimley (Cambridge, 1908); *The Coming of the Friars Minor to England & Germany*, tr. E. G. Salter (London, 1926); and *From St. Francis to Dante*, tr. G. G. Coulton (2nd

ed., London, 1907). The varied business of a busy pope and his *curia* are illustrated by *Selected Letters of Pope Innocent III Concerning England*, eds. C. R. Cheney and W. H. Semple (Edinburgh, 1953). *The Basic Writings of Thomas Aquinas*, ed. A. C. Pegis (2 vols., New York, 1945) is a convenient collection; see also *Saint Bonaventure's De Reductione Artium ad Theologiam*, tr. E. T. Healy (Saint Bonaventure, N.Y., 1939). A basic source is *The Treatise on the Laws and Customs of the realm of England commonly called Glanvill*, ed. and tr. G. D. G. Hall (London, 1965). E. Lewis, *Medieval Political Ideas* (2 vols., London, 1954) is an extensive collection of extracts with commentary. *Aquinas: Political Writings*, tr. A. d'Entrèves (Oxford, 1948) is an excellent selection. For John of Salisbury see above (§ 21). Most of the medieval historians mentioned in the text may be found in English translations, notably in the older series, Bohn's Antiquarian Library and The Church Historians of England. For Latin poetry two standard collections are J. A. Symonds, *Wine, Women, and Song* (London, 1884), and H. Waddell, *Medieval Latin Lyrics* (London, 1929). There are numerous easily accessible translations of vernacular poetry, romance, and *fabliaux*, notably in Everyman's Library, where also will be found the best translation of Villehardouin, and in the Modern Library volume edited by R. S. Loomis and L. H. Loomis, *Medieval Romances* (New York, 1957). For Joinville see *The History of St. Louis by Jean Sire de Joinville*, tr. Joan Evans (Oxford, 1938). All of Dante's works may be found in translation, in many editions. Two excellent translations are Dorothy Sayers and Barbara Reynolds, *The Comedy of Dante Alighieri* (Harmondsworth, 1949–1962), and T. G. Bergin, *The Divine Comedy* (New York, 1965), both of which have good introductions and notes.

V.   THE RISE OF THE WESTERN MONARCHIES AND THE DECLINE OF THE MEDIEVAL PAPACY AND EMPIRE

28. THE GROWTH OF SECULAR CULTURE.   There is no book that deals specifically with the transformation of feudal society, although one aspect of change is well treated in Bryce Lyon, *From Fief to Indenture: The Transition from Feudal to Non-Feudal Contract in Western Europe* (Cambridge, Mass., 1957); for the military aspects see C. W. C. Oman, *The Art of War in the Middle Ages*, ed. J. H. Beeler (2nd ed., rev., Ithaca, N.Y., 1953) and R. A. Brown, *English Medieval Castles* (London, 1954), a good introduction. For economic developments in the high Middle Ages the general works listed above (§ 5) are the best introduction. H. S. Bennett, *Life on the English Manor* (Cambridge, 1937) and G. C. Homans, *English Villagers of the Thirteenth Century* (Cambridge, Mass., 1940) are good descriptive accounts, and E. A. Kosminsky, *Studies in the Agrarian History of England in the Thirteenth Cen-*

tury (Oxford, 1956) is a more specialized work of value; nothing comparable exists for the nobility or the bourgeoisie. In E. Power: *Medieval People* (New York, 1924) and *The Wool Trade in English Medieval History* (Oxford, 1941) will be found much interesting material. An older work that is still useful is J. W. Thompson, *Economic and Social History of Europe in the Middle Ages* (New York, 1928). For the teaching of the Church, and for difficulties encountered, see B. N. Nelson, *The Idea of Usury* (Princeton, N.J., 1949). On the secularization of medieval institutions and values there is no general work in English; see the essay by J. R. Strayer, "The Laicization of French and English Society in the Thirteenth Century," in *Speculum*, XV (1940), 76–86, a brief but important contribution.

29. ENGLAND AND FRANCE.   See the works by Poole, Powicke, and Fawtier cited above (§ 7), which contain ample bibliographies. More recent, J. C. Holt, *Magna Carta* (Cambridge, 1965); W. L. Warren, *King John* (London, 1961); and D. W. Sutherland, *Quo Warranto Proceedings in the Reign of Edward I, 1278–1294* (Oxford, 1963), are valuable. For France, T. N. Bisson, *Assemblies and Representation in Languedoc in the Thirteenth Century* (Princeton, 1964); and F. J. Pegues, *The Lawyers of the Last Capetians* (Princeton, 1962), are important recent studies. The best brief survey of the origins and early development of Parliament is G. L. Haskins, *The Growth of English Representative Government* (Philadelphia, 1948). For France a specialized work of interest to the student of general history is J. R. Strayer and C. H. Taylor, *Studies in Early French Taxation* (Cambridge, Mass., 1939).

30. THE PAPACY AND THE EMPIRE.   E. Kantorowicz, *Frederick II* (London, 1931) is the best work. A good recent book is D. P. Waley, *The Papal State in the Thirteenth Century* (London, 1961), while older works of value include W. F. Butler, *The Lombard Communes* (New York, 1906); H. D. Sedgwick, *Italy in the Thirteenth Century* (New York, 1928); and T. S. R. Boase, *Boniface VIII* (London, 1933). For Germany in this period see the works of Barraclough (above, § § 8 and 16); also, C. C. Bayley, *The Formation of the German College of Electors* (Toronto, 1949).

31. SPAIN, THE MEDITERRANEAN, AND THE EAST.   In addition to works listed above (§ § 3, 9, 16, and 17), the following are useful: R. Altamira, *A History of Spain*, tr. M. Lee (New York, 1949); H. J. Chaytor, *A History of Aragon and Catalonia* (London, 1933); D. J. Geanakoplos, *Emperor Michael Palaeologus and the West 1258–1282* (Cambridge, 1959); S. Runciman, *The Sicilian Vespers* (Cambridge, 1958), and *The Fall of Constantinople, 1453* (Cambridge, 1965); A. S. Atiya, *The Crusades in the Later Middle Ages* (London, 1938), and the same author's *Crusade, Commerce and Culture* and *The Crusade: Historiography and Bibliography* (both Bloomington, 1962); S. Runciman, *A History of the First Bulgarian Empire* (London, 1930); K. M. Setton, *Catalan Domination of Athens 1311–1388* (Cambridge, Mass., 1948); F.

Nowak, *Medieval Slavdom and the Rise of Russia* (New York, 1930); and, for a more extensive general treatment, Vernadsky's works listed above (§ 9).

32. SOURCES. Techniques of manorial exploitation are illustrated by *Walter of Henley's Husbandry*, tr. E. Lamond (London, 1890). A translation of Marsiglio's *Defensor Pacis*, together with commentary, will be found in A. Gewirth, *Marsilius of Padua* (2 vols., New York, 1951–1956). The most important documents, with commentary, on relations between the papacy and temporal rulers from Innocent III to Boniface VIII are given in Tierney (see § 21 above). For Magna Carta and other English documents see C. Stephenson and F. G. Marcham, *Sources of English Constitutional History* (New York, 1937). For Joinville see § 27. *The Art of Falconry, Being the De Arte Venandi cum Avibus of Frederick II*, tr. C. Wood and F. M. Fyfe (Stanford, Calif., 1943) is an important and interesting treatise. An excellent translation is *The Travels of Marco Polo*, tr. and ed. R. E. Latham (Harmondsworth, 1958). The accounts of Pian de Carpine and William of Rubruck are easily accessible in *Contemporaries of Marco Polo*, ed. M. Komroff (New York, 1928). *The Chronicle of James I, King of Aragon*, tr. J. Forster (2 vols., London, 1883) is the Conqueror's own account of the *Reconquista* during the thirteenth century. For Villehardouin see § 27.

VI. THE DECLINE OF MEDIEVAL CIVILIZATION

33. ENGLAND AND FRANCE IN THE LATER MIDDLE AGES. The most recent works on England covering the whole period are listed above (§ 7). G. M. Trevelyan, *England in the Age of Wycliff* (4th ed., London, 1909) is a classic. K. H. Vickers, *England in the Later Middle Ages* (2nd ed., London, 1919) and C. W. C. Oman, *The History of England from the Accession of Richard II to the Death of Richard III* (London, 1918) are standard works. Two more-specialized works of great interest and value are F. Thompson, *A Short History of Parliament, 1295–1642* (Minneapolis, 1953) and S. B. Chrimes, *English Constitutional Ideas in the Fifteenth Century* (Cambridge, 1936). For the Hundred Years' War and for later medieval France the best work in English in one volume is E. Perroy, *The Hundred Years' War* (London, 1951). A more specialized study of value is Richard Vaughan, *Philip the Bold The Formation of the Burgundian State* (London, 1962). P. Champion, *Louis XI* (New York, 1929) is useful.

34. THE CHURCH IN THE LATER MIDDLE AGES. A. C. Flick, *The Decline of the Medieval Church* (2 vols., New York, 1930) and L. E. Binns, *The Decline and Fall of the Medieval Papacy* (London, 1934) are standard works. More recent works of especial value are G. Mollat, *The Popes at Avignon 1305–1378* (Edinburgh, 1963); W. A. Pantin, *The English Church in the Fourteenth Century* (Cambridge, 1955); W. Ullmann, *Origins of the Great*

Schism (London, 1948); Brian Tierney, *Foundations of the Conciliar Theory* (Cambridge, 1955); E. F. Jacob, *Essays in the Conciliar Epoch* (2nd ed., Manchester, 1953); and Joseph Gill, *Eugenius IV Pope of Christian Union* (London, 1961).

35. ITALY AND GERMANY IN THE LATER MIDDLE AGES.   For Italy, J. A. Symonds, *The Renaissance in Italy:* Vol. I, *The Age of the Despots* (London, 1926); E. Emerton, *Humanism and Tyranny* (Cambridge, Mass., 1925); and F. Schevill, *A History of Florence* (New York, 1936) are useful. More recent and more specialized are two valuable works by H. Baron: *The Crisis of the Early Italian Renaissance* (2 vols., Princeton, N.J., 1955) and a more detailed study, *Humanistic and Political Literature in Florence and Venice at the Beginning of the Quattrocento* (Cambridge, Mass., 1955). The politics of this period of great political tension are well set forth in two important studies: W. M. Bowsky, *Henry VII in Italy The Conflict of Empire and City-State* (Lincoln, 1960), and G. A. Brucker, *Florentine Politics and Society, 1343–1378* (Princeton, 1962). For Germany there is very little in English beyond general works (§ § 3 and 8 above), although important aspects of central European history are well treated in F. J. Heymann, *John Zizka and the Hussite Revolution* (Princeton, 1955), and F. L. Carsten, *The Origin of Prussia* (Oxford, 1954). For the Swiss Confederation see E. Bonjour, H. S. Offler, and G. R. Potter, *A Short History of Switzerland* (Oxford, 1952), and for Scandanavia, K. Larsen, *A History of Norway* (Princeton, 1948); J. H. S. Birch, *Denmark in History* (London, 1938); and A. S. Stomberg, *Sweden* (New York, 1931).

36. THE DECAY OF MEDIEVAL ECONOMIC AND SOCIAL INSTITUTIONS.   For later medieval economic developments the best guides are listed above, § 5. See also J. W. Thompson, *Economic and Social History of the Later Middle Ages* (New York, 1931) and E. E. Power and M. M. Postan, eds., *Studies in English Trade in the Fifteenth Century* (London, 1933). For the Hanseatic League see H. Zimmern, *The Hansa Towns* (New York, 1889). Some chapters of J. Huizinga, *The Waning of the Middle Ages* (London, 1924), and A. Cartellieri, *The Court of Burgundy* (New York, 1929) are excellent for social developments and the "new chivalry." Among more recent works of smaller scope but great value are: David Herlihy, *Pisa in the Early Renaissance: A Study of Urban Growth* (New Haven, 1958); S. L. Thrupp, *The Merchant Class of Medieval London, 1300–1500* (Chicago, 1948); Iris Origo, *The Merchant of Prato* (New York, 1957); Raymond de Roover, *Money Banking and Credit in Medieval Bruges* (Cambridge, Mass., 1948) and *The Rise and Decline of the Medici Bank, 1397–1494* (Cambridge, Mass., 1963); A. R. Bridbury, *England and the Salt Trade in the Later Middle Ages* (Oxford, 1955); and A. B. Kerr, *Jacques Coeur* (New York, 1928).

37. THE RENAISSANCE IN ITALY.   J. Burckhardt, *The Civilization of the Renaissance in Italy* (New York, 1954) is a classic. W. F. Ferguson, *The Renais-*

sance (New York, 1940) is a brief introduction. Some recent works of great value are Ferguson, *The Renaissance in Historical Thought* (Boston, 1948); G. C. Sellery, *The Renaissance* (Madison, 1950); P. O. Kristeller, *The Classics and Renaissance Thought* (Cambridge, Mass., 1955); E. H. Wilkins, *Studies in the Life and Works of Petrarch* (Cambridge, Mass., 1955); and Denys Hay, *The Italian Renaissance in Its Historical Background* (Cambridge, 1961). Basic works on Italian art are B. Berenson, *The Italian Painters of the Renaissance* (rev. ed., Oxford, 1930); Erwin Panofsky, *Studies in Iconology: Humanistic Themes in the Art of the Renaissance* (Oxford, 1939); and R. Wittkower, *Architectural Principles in the Age of Humanism* (London, 1949), while A. C. Krey, *Florence, A City that Art Built* (Minneapolis, 1936) is an interesting introduction to several aspects of art and life in the period.

38. INTELLECTUAL AND RELIGIOUS TENDENCIES. For philosophy and science in the later Middle Ages, the following are useful: E. A. Moody, *The Logic of William of Ockham* (New York, 1935); S. C. Tornay, *Ockham: Studies and Selections* (La Salle, Ill., 1938); L. Thorndike, *Science and Thought in the Fifteenth Century* (New York, 1929); and G. Sarton, *The Appreciation of Ancient and Medieval Science during the Renaissance* (Philadelphia, 1955). For later medieval mysticism J. M. Clark, *The Great German Mystics: Eckhart, Tauler, and Suso* (Oxford, 1949) and A. Hyma, *The Youth of Erasmus* (Ann Arbor, Mich., 1930) contain good accounts. H. B. Workman, *John Wyclif* (2 vols., Oxford, 1926) is the basic modern work, while K. B. McFarlane, *John Wycliffe and the Beginnings of English Nonconformity* (London, 1952) is an interesting essay. Of equal interest is Montague Summers, *The History of Witchcraft and Demonology* (2nd ed., New York, 1956).

39. TRADITION AND AUTHORITY IN THE NORTH. On later medieval vernacular literature the general works (§ § 4 and 26 above) may be supplemented by E. K. Chambers, *English Literature at the Close of the Middle Ages* (London, 1951); E. F. Chaney, *François Villon in His Environment* (Oxford, 1946); and H. S. Bennett, *Chaucer and the Fifteenth Century* (Oxford, 1947). The works of Huizinga and Cartellieri (§ 36 above) are the basic surveys of later medieval culture. On later medieval art in the North see J. Evans, *English Art, 1307–1461* (Oxford, 1949) and E. Panofsky, *Early Netherlandish Painting: Its Origins and Character* (Cambridge, Mass., 1953). On the origins of printing G. P. Winship, *Printing in the Fifteenth Century* (Philadelphia, 1940) and P. Butler, *The Origin of Printing in Europe* (Chicago, 1940) cover most of the problems involved.

40. SOURCES. Useful general collections are F. Schevill, ed., *The First Century of Italian Humanism* (New York, 1928); J. B. Ross and M. M. McLaughlin, *The Portable Renaissance Reader* (New York, 1953); and E. Cassirer et al., eds., *The Renaissance Philosophy of Man* (Chicago, 1948). The following works are a selection of the more interesting of the translated sources for the

later Middle Ages: J. H. Robinson and H. W. Rolfe, *Petrarch* (2nd ed., New York, 1914); *Petrarch: Sonnets & Songs*, tr. A. M. Armi (New York, 1946); *The Decameron of Boccaccio*, tr. John Payne (Modern Library and other editions); *The Imitation of Christ* (many editions); *Theologia Germanica*, tr. T. S. Kepler (Cleveland, 1952); *The Revelations of . . . Julian of Norwich*, ed. R. Hudleston (London, 1952); *The Book of Margery Kempe*, tr. W. Butler-Bowden (London, 1936); T. Morrison, *The Portable Chaucer* (New York, 1949); Froissart and Commines (both in several editions); an abridged edition of the *Memoirs of a Renaissance Pope: The Commentaries of Pius II*, tr. and ed., F. A. Gragg and L. C. Gabel (New York, 1959); and *I Laugh Through Tears: The Ballades of François Villon*, tr. G. P. Cuttino (New York, 1955), the most recent effort to convey the thought and feeling of Villon to modern readers.

Index

Italicized page numbers refer to illustrations.

Free Cities of the Empire, 501, 582–583, 597
Free companies, 545, 560
Freiburg, 260
Friars: *see* Dominican Order; Franciscan Order
Frisians, 63
Friuli, march of, 134, 144, 165
Froissart, Jean, 621
Fulbert of Chartres, 323, 328
Fulcher of Chartres, 422
Fulda, monastery of, 83, 160

Gaeta, 257
Gaiseric, 58, 60–61, 66
Galen, 330, 389
Galerius, 14
Galileo, 616
Galla Placidia, 57–58, 60
Gallican Liberties, 568
Garigliano river, 183, 198, 237
Garter, Order of the, 605
Gascony, 466, 476, 482, 487, 534, 537, 549: *see also* Aquitaine
Gaul, prefecture of, in later Roman Empire, 14–15, 23, 56–61; Merovingian, 45, 63–66, 70–72, 95–97, 100, 119–121, 124, 185
Gelasius I, 42; his theory, in political thought, 42–43, 139, 400
Gelasius II, 232
Genghis Khan, 510, 523–525
Genoa, 244, 257, 513, 517, 574
Geoffrey, count of Anjou, 274, 276, 297
Geoffrey, son of Henry II of England, 278–279, 285, 454
Geoffrey of Monmouth, 421, 425
Gerard of Cremona, 329
Gerbert (Sylvester II), 177, 314–316, 323
Germania of Tacitus, 48–51
Germanic kingdoms, 16, 22, 47, 55, 57–74
Germans, and decline of Roman Empire, 6, 9–10, 12, 14, 16–17, 22, and Chapter 3 *passim*; early tribes, 31, 48–51; invasions by, 42–43, 45, 55–65; conversion of, 71, 83, 123–124, 133, 146, 153; early village community of, 209; early literature of, 307, 425

Germany, in antiquity, 11; Frankish expansion into, 64, 66, 130, 134, 143; Avars in, 134, 172; in ninth and tenth centuries, 167–169, 172–178, 191, 258; feudalism in, 185, 190, 300; manorialism in, 208, 594–595; economic conditions in later Middle Ages, 594–598, 604–605; towns in, 597–598; nationalism in, 625: *see also* Empire, the medieval
Ghibellines, 286, 498–500, 505, 554, 571, 581
Gibraltar, 118
Gilbert de la Porrée, 367
Gildas, 98
Gilds, merchant, 258–260, 443, 594, 597; craft, 443–444, 447, 593–594, 597
Giotto, 497, 506
Glanvill, 299, 395
Glossators, 330–331, 391–393, 400
Godfrey of Bouillon, 250–252
Godwin, 268–269
Golden Bull, of 1356, 581–582; of Eger, 492
Golden Fleece, Order of the, 605
Golden Horde, Khanate of the, 525–527
Goliardic verse, 424–425, 427, 622
"Gothic," a humanist epithet, 4, 610
Gothic art and architecture, 410–417, *411–416*, 612, 614, 622–624, *623*
Gothic wars in Italy, 43, 67–68
Goths, 53, 105: *see also* Ostrogoths, Visigoths
Gottfried von Strassburg, 425
Gottschalk, 160
Grammar, 33–34, 328, 419–420
Granada, 512, 515
Gratian, emperor, 16, 53
Gratian, canonist, 332, 392–394
Greco-Roman religion, 25–26
Greece, ancient, 2, 6; in later Roman Empire, 54–56; in Byzantine Empire, 109–110, 244, 514
Greek learning, preservation and recovery of ancient, 23, 104, 247–248, 323, 329–330, 387–389, 608, 611–612
Gregory I the Great, 34, 43–46, 77, 83, 94–96, 122–124, 159, 227
Gregory II, 123

Visconti, Gian Galeazzo, 574–576
Visigoths, 45, 53–60, 63–65, 97, 118
Visitation, 340–342
Vittorino da Feltre, 611, 631
Vladimir, Alexander Nevsky, Grand Prince of, 526
Vladimir, prince of Kiev, 238
Vouillé, battle of, 64
Vulgate Bible, 36–37, 42, 419

Wace, 429
Walafrid Strabo, 160
Waldensians, 366, 428
Wales, 98, 148, 462, 463, 464
Walid I, 119
Wallace, William, 466
Wallia, 58
Walter of Henley, 446
Walther von der Vogelweide, 425
Water mills, 18, 266
Wearmouth, monastery of, 100, 102
Welfs, 286: *see* Guelphs
Wenceslas, 582–583, 619
Weyden, Rogier van der, 551, 624
Whitby, synod of, 83, 146
William I the Conqueror, duke of Normandy and king of England, 267–273, 270, 283
William II Rufus, 273
William of Holland, king of the Romans, 501
William I the Bad, king of Sicily, 289

William II, 293
William, count of Poitou and duke of Aquitaine, 309–310
William, archbishop of Tyre, 422
William of Champeaux, 325
William of Lorris, 427
William of Malmesbury, 421–422
William of Moerbeke, 378
William of Newburgh, 421
William of Rubruck, 510
William Longchamp, 453
William Marshal, 457
Winchester school of painting, 403–404
Windmill, 266
Witchcraft, 99, 619–620
Witigis, 67
Wolfram von Eschenbach, 425
Worms, synod of, 230; Concordat of, 233, 267, 351
Writs, royal, in England, 281–282
Wycliffe, John, 618–620, 625

York, archbishopric of, 146, 341; kingdom of, 191
Yorkists, 542–544, 599

Zacharias, 124–125, 130
Zara, 353, 517
Zengi, 516
Zeno, 61, 105–106

NOR

NORTH

SEA

SCOTLAND

Edinburgh

IRELAND

THE
PALE
Dublin

WALES

ENGLAND

Oxford
Thames
London

Amsterdam

Bruges
Ghent
Antwerp

FLANDERS

Rhine

Cologne

Meuse

Mainz

ENGLISH CHANNEL

Rouen

Seine

Reims

Paris

Troyes

HOLY

Loire

Orléans

Tours

Poitiers

FRANCE

Basel

Rhône

Besançon

Consta

E

AQUITAINE

Limoges

Bordeaux

Garonne

Albi

Toulouse

Lyons

Avignon

PROVENCE

Marseilles

Milan

Aug

Bolo

Genoa

Pisa

Flore

A T L A N T I C   O C E A N

León

Duero

PORTUGAL

PYRENEES

NAVARRE

Saragossa

Ebro

ARAGON

CASTILE

Tagus

Madrid

Lisbon

Toledo

Guadiana

Barcelona

CORSICA

Valencia

Guadalquivir

Cordova

BALEARIC ISLANDS

SARDINIA

GRANADA

Granada

M E D I T E R R A N E A N

GIBRALTAR

TUNISIA

A F R I C A

J. P. TREMBLAY